Civic Education in the Twenty-first Century

Civic Education in the Twenty-first Century

A Multidimensional Inquiry

Edited by Michael T. Rogers
and Donald M. Gooch

LEXINGTON BOOKS
Lanham • Boulder • New York • London

Published by Lexington Books
An imprint of The Rowman & Littlefield Publishing Group, Inc.
4501 Forbes Boulevard, Suite 200, Lanham, Maryland 20706
www.rowman.com

Unit A, Whitacre Mews, 26-34 Stannary Street, London SE11 4AB

British Library Cataloguing in Publication Information Available

Library of Congress Cataloging-in-Publication Data

Civic education in the twenty-first century : a multidimensional inquiry / edited by
Michael T. Rogers and Donald Gooch.
    pages cm
Includes bibliographical references and index.
ISBN 978-0-7391-9349-5 (cloth : alk. paper) — ISBN 978-0-7391-9350-1 (electronic)
1. Civics—Study and teaching—United States. 2. Citizenship—Study and teaching—
United States. 3. United States—Politics and government—Study and teaching.
I. Rogers, Michael T.
LC1091.C528775 2015
370.11'50973—dc23
                                                                      2015026980

♾™ The paper used in this publication meets the minimum requirements of
American National Standard for Information Sciences—Permanence of Paper
for Printed Library Materials, ANSI/NISO Z39.48-1992.

Printed in the United States of America

Contents

Civic Education in the Twenty-first Century

Civic Education in the Twenty-first Century

A Multidimensional Inquiry

Edited by Michael T. Rogers
and Donald M. Gooch

LEXINGTON BOOKS
Lanham • Boulder • New York • London

Published by Lexington Books
An imprint of The Rowman & Littlefield Publishing Group, Inc.
4501 Forbes Boulevard, Suite 200, Lanham, Maryland 20706
www.rowman.com

Unit A, Whitacre Mews, 26-34 Stannary Street, London SE11 4AB

British Library Cataloguing in Publication Information Available

Library of Congress Cataloging-in-Publication Data
Civic education in the twenty-first century : a multidimensional inquiry / edited by
Michael T. Rogers and Donald Gooch.
     pages cm
  Includes bibliographical references and index.
  ISBN 978-0-7391-9349-5 (cloth : alk. paper) — ISBN 978-0-7391-9350-1 (electronic)
1. Civics—Study and teaching—United States. 2. Citizenship—Study and teaching—
United States. 3. United States—Politics and government—Study and teaching.
I. Rogers, Michael T.
  LC1091.C528775 2015
  370.11'50973—dc23
                                                                 2015026980

♾️TM The paper used in this publication meets the minimum requirements of
American National Standard for Information Sciences—Permanence of Paper
for Printed Library Materials, ANSI/NISO Z39.48-1992.

Printed in the United States of America

Contents

Introduction

A Tocqueville-inspired Assessment of America's Twenty-First-Century Civic Ecology

Michael T. Rogers

I was especially struck by their collective illumination of schools' positioning within a larger *civic ecology*.

—Meira Levinson, "The Third C" in *Making Civics Count*

It is essential to study political socialization in context. . . . Political, economic, and social contexts are also essential for tracing out how institutional and systemic conditions shape the formation of a sense of citizenship. Often, the focus of political socialization research is on microlevel explanations, but these micro explanations must be embedded in cultural, political, economic, and social macrolevel explanatory contexts in order to establish their political and philosophical relevance.

—Pamela Johnston Conover & Donald D. Searing
"A Political Socialization Perspective"
in *Rediscovering the Democratic
Purposes of Education*

In the early 1800s, Alexis de Tocqueville produced a most renowned investigation of American democratic life with the two-volume work, *Democracy in America*. His analysis is the handbook for early nineteenth-century American civic education. Tocqueville's tomes inspire this edited volume, as almost two centuries before Conover and Searing's call for a synthesis of micro-level examinations with macrolevel context he achieved it. *Democracy in America* is more than just an analysis of America's democratic way of life; it is the gold standard for the type of comprehensive, multilevel analysis needed for America's "civic ecology" today.

Disappointingly, scholars rarely undertake such ecological investigations.[1] The beauty of Tocqueville's analysis is his ability to show how civic education occurs through a set of mechanisms like jury duty, town hall meetings, and the laws, while simultaneously demonstrating such instruction is complimented and reinforced through mechanisms like political parties, public and private associations, and mass media.[2] Before political scientists began empirically studying political socialization, Tocqueville laid the philosophical foundation for such inquiries. His work lays out the civic ecology of America in the 1800s, suggesting how civic identity formation and a democratic way of life were realized at that time.

An equivalent understanding of America's twenty-first-century civic ecology is rather lacking. In an attempt to replicate Tocqueville's analytic achievement, *Civic Education in the Twenty-first Century: A Multidimensional Approach* cheats. We bring together an eclectic group of scholars, some who provide microlevel analyses and others who provide macrolevel explanations. The idea is for the reader (with the help of the editors) to take each individual contribution on civic education and engagement as a puzzle piece. The challenge is to use each piece to assemble today's American civic ecology landscape. The terrain in the United States has certainly changed since Tocqueville wrote. Given developments like widespread access to formal education; the advent of new technologies like the computer, Internet, and smart phone; a vastly more developed federal, state, and local governmental structure and welfare state; and the twenty-first-century opulence of America, we need to once again piece together microlevel analyses of civic education processes for a better understanding of our twenty-first century civic ecology.

Luckily, the task is easier by the fact that some pieces are already well known. For one, Tocqueville and other scholars have established the traditional factors of this puzzle. In particular, the political socialization literature has established the importance of family; schools and peers within schools; social, political and religious groups; media; and government among others.[3] All play important roles in civic identity formation and the realization of a democratic way of life. Still, a number of scholars—most notably Robert Putnam—have documented disturbing patterns suggesting a marked decline in America's civic political socialization. Whether the argument focuses on declining social capital, checkbook membership, or simply less group engagement, dealignment within political parties, a decline in public trust after Vietnam and Watergate, or transformations in print media, scholars increasingly have painted a bleak picture of America's twenty-first-century civic ecology.[4]

Also, there are numerous excellent inquiries into various microlevel aspects of civic education by scholars, practitioners, politicians, the media, think tanks, and the public that can be drawn on to speculate about the civic ecology of America.[5] Yet, that speculation has not been optimistic; most believe civic education has been in a state of decline in the United States, some even lamenting a "civic crisis" or "recession."[6]

THREE FACTORS UNDERLYING
THE PERCEIVED CIVICS CRISIS

While numerous factors contribute to the concern Americans have for civic education today, three in particular stand out. Foremost is American civic illiteracy.[7] Dudley and Gitelson's observation that research on America's poor civic literacy has become a race to discover the most appalling lack of knowledge" seems well founded.[8] Today, the more appalling the finding the more likely mass media is to share the study. For example, in 2006 most major media outlets—*USA Today*, the *Boston Globe*, and Foxnews.com among others—seized on survey findings showing Americans knew more Simpsons cartoon family members than first amendment rights.[9] Similarly, Busch and White note the popularity of shows like Jeff Foxworthy's *Are You Smarter than a Fifth Grader* or segments like Jay Leno's "Jaywalking" to illustrate American educational ignorance.[10] To put it simply, the case against Americans for low civic literacy is pretty damning.

Hand in hand with this first civic fault line comes a second, the sense there has been a substantial decline in civic education, both informal and formal. At the epicenter of the research on the decline of informal civic education is the research of Robert Putnam on the decline of social capital.[11] Family, friends, and groups seem to be socializing fewer Americans into active civic lives. Additionally, various political figures like Sandra Day O'Connor and Robert Graham espouse a third fault line—the decline in America's formal civic education curriculum. In particular, O'Connor and Graham lament the decline in the civics curriculum at the secondary education level from the mid-nineteenth century norm of three semesters of civics to one semester today.[12] Similarly, as president of the American Political Science Association (APSA) in the mid-1990s, Elinor Ostrom likewise expressed unease over the decline in the civics curriculum at the collegiate level.[13] Federal and state initiatives over the last decade suggest our government shares this concern. Most notably, the Civic Mission of Schools movement in the 2000s led California and Oregon to scrutinize their formal civic education programs at the primary and secondary levels.[14] At the federal level, there have been civic education and engagement initiatives launched by both the Bush and Obama administrations.[15] Concern over formal civic education is widespread today.

Concomitant with these concerns, there is a similar groundswell over the pronounced decline in youth civic and political engagement. Poor civic participation rates of youth is not new, but the decline in its most basic form—voting—with the dawn of the twenty-first century raised concern to new levels. The problem of youth disengagement, as well as whether it is a lifecycle or generational issue, is initially raised by Putnam in his seminal work *Bowling Alone*.[16] Much of the ensuing research has coalesced around the idea that the problem is a generational phenomenon.[17] Some of the best scholarly research on youth civic literacy and engagement is from the Center for Information & Research on Civic Learning and Engagement, better known as CIRCLE.[18] Although there is no agreement in the literature on the cause of this fault line, all in all, research on youth civic engagement has found that there is something distinct about our young today that makes them less politically inclined than past generations.

A BROAD CONCEPTION OF CIVIC
EDUCATION AND ENGAGEMENT

In the face of these tripartite concerns over civic crisis, *Civic Education in the Twenty-first Century: A Multidimensional Inquiry* offers a new, more optimistic look at civic education. In recent years, too much energy and resources have been expended on only one side of the story of America's civic ecology. America has been consumed with identifying the decline of and threats to civic education. Where is scholarship on new developments in civic education, on the novel ways people are civically socialized and engaged today? Both emergent technologies and increased academic knowledge of what works (see the discussion of the scholarship of teaching and learning [SoTL] in chapter 1 and Strachan and Bennion's chapter 14) are creating new opportunities to revitalize America's civic ecology. Jonathan Yonan puts it best when he argues there are good reasons for concern about civic education today but "The sky is not falling."[19]

Simply put, we need a fresh perspective on what civic education is and can be today. We need not romanticize past methods of civic improvement, especially outdated ones. They will only blind us to new, alternative civic education processes. Yonan rightly recommends "we must consider ourselves and our world with all of the disciplinary resources that have always been at our disposal."[20] Taking this recommendation to heart, *Civic Education in the Twenty-first Century* brings together a diverse group of scholars who provide original research that contributes to a number of current debates on civic education and its perceived decline. Through groundbreaking, original inquiries—particularly those exploring the civic implications of the routine operations of governmental institutions and political actors—this volume encourages other scholars to use their disciplinary tools to investigate and uncover similar undocumented civic education mechanisms. Americans need to continue to explore the new innovations *in* and possibilities *for* civic education given technological advances; a more expansive, service-oriented political apparatus at all levels of government; and new scientific research into effective teaching. What possibilities do these and other changes create for a revolution in civic political socialization today?

To enhance the likelihood of discovering these new processes, this work necessarily utilizes a broad conception of civic education and engagement. Fundamentally, we need to avoid seeing civic education as simply a curricular issue in formal schooling. Tocqueville showed in the 1800s civic education was accomplished as much through informal mechanisms, particularly private associations. Civic education is not just a product of formal schooling or participation in government. Thus, while contributors to this edited volume often offer their own definitions of civic education, the work collectively is motivated by the belief—as espoused by Margaret Stimmann Branson from the Center for Civic Education—that "civic education in a democracy is education in self government (sic)," that means all the forms that education in self-government takes.[21] As the *Stanford Encyclopedia of Philosophy* explains:

> In its broadest definition, 'civic education' means all the processes that affect people's beliefs, commitments, capabilities, and actions as members or prospective members of communities. Civic education need not be intentional or deliberate; institutions and communities transmit values and norms without meaning to. It may not be beneficial: sometimes people are civically educated in ways that disempower them or impart harmful values and goals. It is certainly not limited to schooling and the education of children and youth. Families, governments, religions, and mass media are just some of the institutions involved in civic education, understood as a lifelong process.[22]

Similarly, the volume takes an expansive view of civic engagement. Rather than split hairs about differences between civic and political engagement, this volume accepts Levine's operational definition of civic engagement that sees its typical activities as community participation, political engagement, and political voice.[23] He adds these typically occur through means like "deliberation, persuasion, collaboration, participation in legal politics, civil disobedience, and the giving of money," etc.[24] Levine acknowledges there are a variety of ways people can contribute to the commons and this volume is motivated by the belief we need to better understand all that variety of ways.[25] Then, Ehrlich helps explain the bridge between civic engagement and civic education, writing "civic engagement means working

to make a difference in the civic life of our communities and developing
the combination of knowledge, skills, values, and motivations to make the
difference. It means promoting the quality of life in a community, through
both political and nonpolitical processes."[26] When he discusses making a
difference in the community, whether through political or nonpolitical action, Ehrlich emphasizes civic engagement; when he discusses the knowledge, skills, values, and motivations learned through political and nonpolitical processes, he has shifted to a discussion of civic education, a discussion
that is promoted and enhanced by civic engagement.

Just as Ehrlich suggests discussions of civic engagement slide quickly into
discussions of civic education and vice versa, Colby et al. present a capacious
understanding of community and what constitutes activity oriented toward it.
They complement Ehrlich's broad sketch of civic engagement with a multilayered conceptualization of community. They point out that, when we talk
about civic engagement in the community, that community can be "local,
state, national, or international."[27] The broadening of these categories beyond
conventional definitions invites controversy and presents conceptual challenges for scholars of civic education. Yet, it is necessary to ensure scholars
overcome their tendency toward specialization, narrow perspectives, and the
preference for primarily microlevel investigations. It is essential that students
of civic education and engagement broaden their perspectives. Our investigations of civic education and engagement must be open to new arenas and new
mechanisms; we must look for these political phenomena in a multiplicity of
places in our rapidly evolving, twenty-first-century landscape.

Put simply, this edited volume provides ample evidence the processes by
which civic education and engagement occur have evolved significantly. The
political socialization literature has noted the declining influence of mechanisms like the family; the question is: What, if anything, has or can fill the
void? Has and/or can formal education through schools or civic education
by a service-oriented government counteract this decline? What about public
and private groups, particularly philanthropic ones, do they make up some of
the difference? S. Raia inspires some hope that these mechanisms can serve
such ends. He recognizes the important contributions made to civic education
through formal initiatives like the Mikva Challenge in the Chicago school
system. S. Raia tempers this praise by simultaneously recognizing new informal civic socialization through nonprofit group programs like that of the Center for Civic Education and the Freedoms Foundation at Valley Forge.[28] We
need similar bimodal or, better yet, multimodal understandings like his today.

As scholars, we know—as Friedman and Aubin emphasize in chapter 5—
that people are more likely to engage when given opportunities and asked
to do so.[29] A thorough evaluation of today's civic ecology needs to uncover

where all civic education occurs, i.e. where all citizens are challenged to enhance their civic knowledge, develop their political skills and asked to engage in their communities. How often are Americans given opportunities to become more civically educated and/or engaged? What contexts challenge people to enhance their knowledge? Which contexts are most conducive to getting them to actually follow through and become involved? While not a definitive portrayal of our twenty-first-century civic ecology, this edited volume begins to answer such questions. Our intent is to counteract the excessive pessimism that America faces a civics crisis. We give voice and greater weight to an underrepresented side in the civics debate today, the side defending what is new and positive in the civic education of America today. We suggest the new possibilities for civic education and engagement by exploring some traditional and some novel, evolving mediums and methods of civic education and engagement to show advances in civics today. The theme of this volume is that civics remains vibrant today; numerous political actors and institutions are promoting civic education and engagement in ways we have often not noticed.

OVERVIEW

Civic Education in the Twenty-first Century is written by social scientists on the front lines in the campaign for enhanced civic education and engagement. Many chapters suggest new avenues for inquiry at the microlevel, offering case studies of political actors and institutions, states, schools, and/or various types of interest groups. It is through such multidimensional, microlevel investigations that the macrolevel, multifaceted civic ecology in America can be pieced together. No other works or edited volumes on civic education offer such a rich combination of original scholarship exploring today's civic education and engagement processes.[30]

In Section I: The Case for Civic Education, the edited volume contains four chapters exploring the history of and debates about civic education. In chapter 1, I explore the episodic nature of America's interest in civic education. Arguments for enhanced democratic education in the United States recur throughout our history, but are not persistent. I show efforts to improve civic education in America peaked early in the nineteenth, twentieth, and now again in the twenty-first century. The past shows these revitalizations in civics tend to be short-lived even as civic education has become more institutionalized. I ponder if the story of civic education in the twenty-first century will be any different.

Following this chapter are two works offering polar opposite perspectives on civic education. First, Robert Maranto makes a Hirschian argument for a uniform civic education curriculum. Maranto claims that, given the strong consensus on what civics should entail among Americans in general and social studies teachers in particular, such a program is realizable. He then speculates on how we might use this underlying consensus to overcome the stalemate among competing interests plaguing the civic education debate today.

In contrast, in chapter 3 Jeffrey Hilmer rejects such Hirschian arguments. He argues civic education through schools is to be avoided as a medium for civic socialization. In Hilmer's view, formal educational institutions and civic instruction are oil and water; the state cannot properly instruct citizens on methods of citizenship when an essential element of civic engagement is participation that challenges state power. Given the state is a conservative institution interested in promoting stability and protecting its own power, formal education inevitably becomes a tool for it to promote loyalty, even indoctrination. He says there is a paradox of civic education today, and that our civic crisis of passive citizens should not be surprising given it. Passive citizens are exactly what a formal civic education through state-run schools produces. Hilmer gives good reason for why civic education must occur outside of the purview of formal state education. The rest of his chapter is a blueprint of what an anti-statist civic education might look like.

In the last chapter of Section I, Gary Bugh provides an examination of civic education pedagogies. Interestingly, Bugh suggests the arguments of Maranto and Hilmer represent opposite ends of a continuum of approaches to civic education. Bugh examines this spectrum from an education perspective, arguing it contains at least four distinguishable pedagogies (formal pedagogy, political participation, minority dissent, and civic engagement). Practically, these range from traditional lecturing on the political system to more radical training and developing of behaviors that challenge it in order to make it better, more responsive or inclusive. Bugh's work raises the possibility that the pedagogy used for instruction is likely to affect the type of citizenship practiced. Thus, we need to carefully choose our pedagogy based on our specific civic education goals. If our goals are loyal, passive citizens, then traditional lecture may be good enough, but if we want a more active citizen, we may need to explore and complement traditional instruction with less conventional pedagogies.

Then, in Section II: Twenty-First-Century Innovations in Civic Education a number of original, groundbreaking investigations of civic education are provided. The first three chapters make up Part A: National Government. They look at how political actors at the federal level of government can and do promote civic education and engagement. Until now, these activities have largely gone on but not been recognized by scholars or Americans as civic education. In chapter 5 Friedman and Aubin open these inquiries by encouraging a new direction for research on Congress. They explore how the websites of legislators can be tools for civic education and engagement. They claim scholars have not adequately examined how the routine behavior of politicians can provide civic instruction and encourage civic engagement, even when they appear as self-serving actions reflecting Mayhew's observation of legislators as "single-minded seekers of reelection."[31] Actions serving a legislator's reelection motives can also result in civic education and engagement in the community. To substantiate this observation, Friedman and Aubin show civic engagement and education—while not a predominant feature—are identifiable components of congressional webpages. While a webpage is primarily a way for legislators to advertise themselves to their constituents, they are also a mechanism by which some members of Congress some of the times civically inform their constituents and encourage them to get involved in the community and/or political system.

In chapter 6, Evans builds on Friedman and Aubin's work. She sees if this same behavior is identifiable in congressional tweets. Like Friedman and Aubin, she finds some congressional twittering by legislators that has civic implications. While the findings suggests these activities make up a limited portion of the use of these mediums, both find discernible levels of such civic activities showing congressional scholars need to further explore the civic activities of members of Congress. More importantly, chapters 5 and 6 highlight the potential politicians have for enhancing America's civic ecology by expanding on the civic activities that at least some members engage in already.

In chapter 7, Drury and Drury provide just as groundbreaking a study for the United States presidency. They examine the potential of presidents to be "civic educators" in chief. Their analysis of presidential leadership on mental health shows that a president's choice of how to handle and frame an issue can affect the political literacy and civic engagement of Americans. In particular, they argue Obama broke with the tendency of past presidents to be a "communicator in chief" or teacher on the issue of mental health. Instead, Obama chose to play a different role, civic educator in chief by encouraging, facilitating, and empowering local communities to develop their own solutions to mental health issues. Like Friedman and Aubin in the congressional literature, Drury and Drury challenge future presidential scholarship to consider the civic implications of presidential leadership. Presidential scholars need to investigate what other presidents have chosen to be civic educators in chief, as well as if presidents take such an approach over similar types of policies.

For Part B: State and Local Government, groundbreaking explorations of civic education and engagement continue with three chapters exploring how state and local political actors and institutions promote such activities. First, to complete this volume's study of civic education across the three branches, Brendan Toner investigates in chapter 8 the judiciary's civic education activities. Toner finds many state courts have active civic education agendas. Through an analysis of the descriptive statistics of all fifty states and case studies of two state courts (Arkansas and Michigan courts of last resort) and one city court (New York City Civil Courts), Toner is able to show how courts may be the most active institution with respect to enhancing the civic education of Americans.

Then, in chapter 9 Armato and Friedman look at arguably the most important local political figure, mayors. They conduct a content analysis of mayoral press releases to assess the extent to which mayors routinely promote political or community engagement. While they find great variation across cities, in their sample all mayors except one encouraged civic education activities through press releases.

In chapter 10, Warner looks at a level of regional government often neglected by scholars, county government. Through a comprehensive study of Arkansas counties, she evaluates the potential of county governments to promote political literacy and civic engagement through e-government. While she does not find statistical evidence that the presence of county e-government increases voting, she does map out a standard of what e-government for localities should look like. She suggests that most counties have just scratched the surface in their ability to promote political literacy and civic engagement through their webpages. Given Warner's analysis, we are left to ponder how the development of e-government at all levels of government (municipal, regional, state, and federal) could enrich the civic ecology of the United States.

Section II concludes with Part C: Private Institutions. The one chapter of this section explores how twitter is transforming the ways interest groups promote civic education. Through chapter 11 Gelbman explores how interest groups use Twitter to promote political knowledge and encourage civic engagement. Through a content analysis of the Twitter usage of eight interest groups, she shows how such civic activities are an identifiable component of interest group mobilization efforts. Like Evans's analysis of the use of Twitter by members of Congress, Gelbman finds interest groups are using Twitter as a medium for some civic education, but notes it is not an extensive allocation of their time. Her findings reinforce the idea that political actors and groups have only begun to explore how new technologies are transforming the civic ecology of the United States.

Section III: Civic Education in Institutions of Higher Education contains six chapters that add to the scholarship on teaching and learning (known as SoTL), as well as provide some best practices in civic education. Part A:

Classroom-based Studies opens with research by Gooch and myself on how a course in American government affects the civic knowledge and political behavior of students at three different regional universities in two Southern states. In chapter 12 we continue to challenge the conventional view that a civics course does not per se enhance civic literacy. We find a one-semester course on American government does improve student knowledge of politics. While we find the traditional lecture pedagogy can enhance civic literacy, it has mixed and weak effects on the political efficacy and civic engagement tendencies of students. We conclude more research is needed in this area to explore if a) different pedagogies similarly affect civic literacy and civic engagement and b) whether more than one course on government matters. In chapter 13, Galatas and Pressley provide a similar examination of civic literacy, although it is more narrowly focused on how a module over American fiscal policy can enhance student understanding of the government's budget, deficit and finances. Like our findings in chapter 12, they find significant but modest gains in literacy and affective behavior. Collectively, the two chapters strengthen the argument that a civics curriculum matters if the goal is enhanced political literacy.

With chapter 14, Strachan and Bennion discuss the importance of the scholarship of teaching and learning (SoTL) movement and advertise a new research resource in the discipline of political science. To further the explanatory power of studies like those in chapters 12 and 13, Strachan and Bennion have created a consortium for replicating such studies throughout colleges and universities across the country. By expanding microlevel studies beyond one or two institutions of higher education, the Consortium for Inter-campus SoTL Research holds great potential to enhance our scientific understanding of civic education in institutions of higher education.

In Part B of Section III, there are three chapters that suggest what some scholars are doing outside the college classroom to enhance civic education. In chapter 15, Rackaway and Campbell explain what a robust, technology-driven, multilayered, civic ecology on a twenty-first-century campus looks like. They explain how modern technology, particularly Web 2.0 tools, are aggressively used at Fort Hays State University (FHSU) to create multiple and overlapping opportunities for civic education and engagement. FHSU really is a great blueprint for what a civic-oriented institution of higher education can do to promote virtual democracy, especially when a substantial number of the students are never physically on campus.

Next, with chapter 16 Mike Yawn explains how universities can partner with local government to enhance civic education. He explains how the Academy can be a vehicle for providing "citizens academies." Yawn explains how Sam Houston State University collaborates with the local county government to bring students, local citizens, and government officials together to learn and explore how local government works. As the ranks of those getting involved in local politics thins in this country, citizen academies may just be the answer for recruiting and training the next generation of engaged citizens. In fact, one cannot help but wonder if people would be talking about a civics crisis today if more local communities had similar citizen academies. If colleges and universities throughout the country routinely collaborated with their local governments through citizen academies, we just might see a revival of local politics reminiscent of the New England town hall meetings Tocqueville described in the early 1800s.

With chapter 17, Elizabeth Bennion challenges college professors to use their expertise to benefit not just their students, but their community. She uses her expertise as a service for her region by moderating a political talk show, while encouraging her students to be more civically engaged and knowledgeable as they run the program. By partnering with her local PBS station, Bennion gives her students an invaluable hands-on experience in television production, watches them enhance their civic knowledge and research skills as they prepare for guests, and brings them into face-to-face contact with political figures. In addition, she enhances her school's civic reputation while promoting the civic literacy and engagement of people in the region that consume her program. She gives new meaning to how institutions of higher education can serve their civic missions and enhance the civic ecology of the country.

To close, Gooch draws on formal theory to speculate on how all these (often disparate) elements, if combined, could transform the civic ecology of the United States today. One must remain concerned that—as disparate actions—such civic education and engagement practices operate largely in isolation of or sometimes in conflict with one another and fail to produce significant civic gains for the country. Yet, preserving the more optimistic tone of this volume I want to paint a different picture. Imagine an America where politicians, governmental institutions, schools, new technologies, and interest groups all work together to promote informed, engaged citizens. The contributions in this volume suggest how politicians, government institutions, schools, and interest groups are engaging in promising activities and programs in the struggle to educate and engage Americans in democracy. New technologies and new innovations in civic education have laid the foundation for a revitalized American civic ecology. Since each educational process within this volume exists in the same civic ecology and contains some potential to enhance political knowledge and promote civic engagement, they can potentially complement, even reinforce each other.

While those interested in civic education and engagement must remain concerned about the poor political knowledge of Americans, perceived declines in formal and informal civic education, and the disturbing generational effect of youth political apathy, this may simply represent a time of great opportunity. Rather than dwell excessively on the factors scholars and politicians have identified as driving a civics decline, we should shift some energy to identifying new (as well as tried-and-true) techniques for civic education and engagement. The civics solution is an ecology of overlapping and reinforcing environments where citizens are asked and challenged to be informed and get involved.

NOTES

1. Ecological scholarship on a subject like civic education is uncommon today. One example is Robert N. Bellah et al., *Habits of the Heart: Individualism and Commitment in American Life*, Second ed. (Berkley: Univeristy of California Press, 1996). Still, *Habits of the Heart* lacks the engagement of the plethora of subjects that Tocqueville covers and, therefore, is more limited in the generalizability of its findings. More recently, Putnam's *Bowling Alone* is worth mentioning, although substantial scholarship continues to challenge his thesis. Simply put, today's scholars are conditioned and rewarded for specialization; there are few incentives to produce macrolevel works capable of discussing the larger ecology. Sure, if one successfully produces such an analysis, it can make your career as it did for Putnam. However, scholars discourage works like Tocqueville's. They attack such works for neglecting consideration of the details in order to produce a comprehensive ecological picture. Put differently, such works impose too integrated a depiction of the whole on all the diverse microlevel parts. While this criticism has merit, scholars are too quick to pursue and dismiss such grand works given such limitations. Scholarship suffers as a result. We lack the valuable insights and healthy debates produced by such works. Comprehensive ecological works are rare and usually occur only after microlevel studies are rampant. It is then that a scholar who is well-read in the field synthesizes all these works in his/her own field to produce an explanation of the larger ecology

2. Alexis de Tocqueville, *Democracy in America*, ed. Phillips Bradley, 2 vols., vol. 1 & 2 (Vintage Books, 1990). Also, for further explanation of the distinction between formal versus informal civic education processes, see Michael T. Rogers, "A Civic Education Crisis," *Midsouth Political Science Review* 13, no. 1 (2012).

3. While the importance of these factors has been well established since the 1960s scholarship of David Eaton and Jack Dennis (among others), more recent scholarship continues to find these factors matter. See Hugh McIntosh, Danil Hart, and James Youniss, "The Influence of Family Political Discussion on Youth Civic Development: Which Parent Qualities Matter?," *PS: Political Science & Politics* XL, no. 3 (2007); Hugh McIntosh and James Youniss, "Toward a Political Theory of Political Socialization of Youth," in *Handbook of Research on Civic Engagement in Youth*, ed. Lonnie R. Sherrod, Judith Torney-Purta, and Constance Flanagan (Hoboken: Jon Wiley & Sons, Inc., 2010); Molly W. Andolina et al., "Habits from Home, Lessons

from School: Influences on Youth Civic Engagement," *PS: Political Science & Politics* 36, no. 2 (2003); Pamela Johnson Conover and Donald D. Searing, "A Political Socialization Perpesctive," in *Rediscovering the Democratic Purposes of Education*, ed. Lorraine M. McDonnell, P. Michael Timpane, and Roger Benjamin (Lawrence: University of Kansas Press, 2000); David E. Campbell, *Why We Vote: How Schools and Communities Shape Our Civic Life* (Princeton: Princeton University Press, 2006). The latter work by Campbell also provides a succinct overview of the political socialization of the 1960s and 1970s literature, see ibid., 96.

4. See, for example, Robert Putnam, *Bowling Alone: The Collapse and Revival of American Community* (New York: Simon and Schuster, 2000); Robert Putnam, "Bowling Alone: America's Declining Social Capital," *Journal of Democracy* 6, no. 1 (June 1995); Robert Putnam, "Tuning in, Tuning Out: The Strange Disappearance of Social Capital in America," *PS: Political Science and Politics* 28, no. 4 (Dec. 1995); Theda Skocpol, *Diminished Democracy: From Membership to Management in American Civic Life* (Norman: University of Oklahoma Press, 2003); Kenneth Stroupe Jr. and Larry Sabato, "Politics: The Missing Link of Responsible Civic Eduation," (2004), http://www.civicyouth.org/PopUps/civicengagement-stroupe-final.pdf; Vincent Ostrom, *The Meaning of Democracy and the Vulnerabilities of Democracy: A Response to Tocqueville's Challenge* (Ann Harbor: The University of Michigan Press, 1997); Martin Wattenberg, *The Decline of American Political Parties: 1952–1994* (Cambridge: Harvard University Press, 1996). For additional discussion of this literature, see Rogers, "A Civic Education Crisis."

5. For a good scholarly example of an assessment of America's civic ecology, see Stephen Macedo et al., *Democracy at Risk: How Political Choices Undermine Citizen Participation, and What We Can Do about It* (Washington, DC: Brookings Institute Press, 2005). Conversely, for a work containing the thoughts of politicians, journalists, and bureaucrats on the subject, see David Feith, ed. *Teaching America: The Case for Civic Education* (Lanham: Rowman & Littlefield, Inc., 2011). To see the negative evaluations of civic education by a think tank, there are the various reports by ISI (Intercollegiate Studies Institute), see ISI, "The Coming Crisis in Citizenship" (Wilmington, DE: Intercollegiate Studies Institute's National Civic Literacy Board, 2006); "Failing Our Students, Failing America: Holding Colleges Accountable for Teaching America's History and Institutions" (Willmington, DE: Intercollegiate Studies Institute's National Civic Literacy Board, 2007); "Our Fading Heritage: Americans Fail a Basic Test on Their History and Institutions," in *Intercollegiate Studies Institute's American Civic Literacy Program* (Intercollegiate Studies Institute, 2008–2009). For more balanced inquiries suggesting both the strengths and weaknesses in the civic education of youth, there is the scholarship published by CIRCLE (The Center for Information & Research on Civic Learning and Engagement). See CIRCLE, The Center for Information & Research on Civic Learning and Engagement, http://www.civicyouth.org/.

6. See Bob Graham and Chris Hand, *America, the Owner's Manual: Making Government Work for You* (Washington, DC: CQ Press, 2009), xv; Bob Graham and Chris Hand, "A Failure of Leadership: The Duty of Politicians and Universities to Salvage Citizenship," in *Teaching America: The Case for Civic Education*,

ed. David Feith (Lanham: Rowman & Littlefield Education, 2011); Sam Dillon, "Failing Grades on Civics Exam Called a 'Crisis,'" *The New York Times* 2011; Michael C. Johanek, "Preparing Pluribus for Unum: Historicial Perspectives on Civic Education," in *Making Civics Count: Citizenship for a New Generation*, ed. David E. Campbell, Meira Levinson, and Frederick M. Hess (Cambridge: Harvard Education Press, 2012); Richard M. Battistoni, "Should Political Scientists Care about Civic Education?," *Perspective on Politics* 11, no. 4 (2013): 1135. Similarly, Heather Malin argues the crisis is an identity crisis, particularly for minorities. See Heather Malin, "America as a Philosophy: Implications for the Development of American Identity among Today's Youth," *Applied Development Science* 15, no. 2 (2011): 57–59. Of course, such concerns are highly linked to the perceived decline in social capital and civic engagement. See Putnam, *Bowling Alone*; "Bowling Alone: America's Declining Social Capital"; "Tuning in, Tuning Out;" *Making Democracy Work: Civic Traditions in Modern Italy* (Princeton, NJ: Princeton University Press, 1993).

7. For an introduction to such inquiries, see the studies by the Intercollegiate Studies Institute (ISI). For example, ISI, "The Coming Crisis in Citizenship"; "Failing Our Students, Failing America: Holding Colleges Accountable for Teaching America's History and Institutions"; "Our Fading Heritage: Americans Fail a Basic Test on Their History and Institutions." Alternatively, see Ilya Somin, *Democracy and Political Ignorance: Why Smaller Government Is Smarter* (Stanford: Stanford University Press, 2013); Richard G. Niemi, "What Students Know about Civics and Government," in *Making Civics Count: Citizenship Education for a New Generation*, ed. David E. Campbell, Meira Levinson, and Frederick M. Hess (Cambridge: Harvard Education Press, 2012); Henry Milner, *Civic Literacy: How Informed Citizens Make Democracy Work* (London: University Press of New England, 2002); Richard G. Niemi and Jane Junn, *Civic Education: What Makes Students Learn* (New Haven: Yale University Press, 1998); and Michael Delli Carpini and Scott Keeter, *What Americans Know about Politics and Why It Matters* (New Haven: Yale University Press, 1996). For a study of the civic illiteracy of college students, see Donald M. Gooch and Michael T. Rogers, "A Natural Disaster of Civic Proportions: College Students in the Natural State Falls Short of the Naturalization Benchmark," *Midsouth Political Science Review* 13, no. 1 (2012).

8. Robert L. Dudley and Alan R. Gitelson, "Political Literacy, Civic Education, and Civic Engagement: A Return to Political Socialization?," *Applied Development Science* 6, no. 4 (2002): 176.

9. For the details of the survey, see "Characters from 'The Simpsons' More Well Known to Americans Than Their First Amendment Rights, Survey Finds," (2006), http://www.mccormickfoundation.org/news/2006/pr030106.aspx. For a sample of the major media frenzy, see "Study: More Know 'The Simpsons' Than First Amendment Rights," *USA Today*, 3/1/2006; "Study: More Know 'Simpsons' Than Constitution,' FoxNews.com, http://www.foxnews.com/story/2006/03/01/study-more-know-simpsons-than-constitution/; Anna Johnson, "Tuned to America: 'Simpsons' Trumps Civics in Study, Many Know Sitcom but Not Their Rights," *The Boston Globe*, March 1, 2006.

10. Elizabeth Kaufer Busch and Jonathan W. White, "Introduction," in *Civic Education and the Future of American Citizenship*, ed. Elizabeth Kaufer Busch and Jonathan W. White (Lanham: Lexington Books, 2012), 7. Along these same lines, see the youtube videos from Olympia High School at "Lunch Scholars," (2/2/2012), https://www.youtube.com/watch?v=MHtDF-z77wk.

11. See Putnam, "Bowling Alone"; "Tuning in, Tuning Out"; *Bowling Alone*; Ilya Somin, *Democracy and Political Ignorance: Why Smaller Government Is Smarter*. See also, Skocpol, *Diminished Democracy: From Membership to Management in American Civic Life*; Theda Skocpol and Morris P. Fiorina, eds., *Civic Engagement in American Democracy* (Washington, DC: Brookings Institution Press,1999); Macedo et al., *Democracy at Risk*.

12. Sandra Day O'Connor, "The Democratic Purpose of Education: From the Founders to Horace Mann to Today," in *Teaching America: The Case for Civic Education*, ed. David Feith (Lanham: Rowman & Littlefield Education, 2011), 6; Graham and Hand, "A Failure of Leadership: The Duty of Politicians and Universities to Salvage Citizenship," 64; Graham and Hand, *America, the Owner's Manual: Making Government Work for You*, 22.

13. Elinor Ostrom, "Civic Education for the Next Century: A Task Force to Initiate Professional Activity," *PS: Political Science and Politics* 29, no. 4 (1996). See also, Harry Boyte and Elizabeth Hollander, "Wingspread Declaration on Renewing the Civic Mission of the American Research University," (1999), http://www.compact.org/wp-content/uploads/2009/04/wingspread_declaration.pdf; Barry Checkoway, "Renewing the Civic Mission of the American Research University," *The Journal of Higher Education* 72, no. 1 (2001).

14. See Cynthia Gibdon et al., "The Civic Mission of Schools" (The Center for Information & Research on Civic Learning and Engagement with Carnegie Corporation of New York, 2003); "The Civic Mission of Schools," (2006), http://www.class roomlaw.org/files/posts-pages/about/2006_or_civics_survey.pdf. For the response of a couple states, see "The California Survey of Civic Education," *Educating for Democracy: California Campaign for the Civic Mission of Schools* (2005), http://www.cms-ca.org/civic_survey_final.pdf; "Oregon Civics Survey 2006," *Educating for Democracy: Oregon Coalition for the Civics Mission of Schools* (2006), http://www.classroomlaw.org/files/posts-pages/about/2006_or_civics_survey.pdf.

15. For the response of the Bush administration after 9/11, see John M. Bridgeland, "Civic Nation: My White House Mission after September 11," in *Teaching America: The Case for Civic Education*, ed. David Feith (Lanham: Rowman & Littlefield Education, 2011). Then, for the Obama administration there is the "Civic Learning and Engagement in Democracy" initiative that followed its publication of "A Crucible Moment: College Learning & Democracy's Future" (Washington, DC: National Task Force on Civic Learning and Democratic Engagement, 2012). See also the Department of Education's "Advancing Civic Learning and Engagement in Democracy: A Road Map and Call to Action" (Washington, DC: U.S. Department of Education, 2012).

16. Putnam, *Bowling Alone*, 247–48.

17. For further discussion of this generational argument, see Niemi, "What Students Know about Civics and Government," 25–28; Macedo et al., *Democracy at Risk*; Campbell, *Why We Vote*, 184–85, 92; William Galston, "Political Knowledge, Political Engagement, and Civic Education," *Annual Review of Political Science* 4, no. 1 (2001). It is also worth noting there is now a *Handbook of Research on Civic Engagement in Youth*. In it, Sherrod et al. explain how the turn of the twenty-first century saw "the coming of age of the field of youth civic engagement"; see Lonnie R. Sherrod, Judith Torney-Purta, and Constance Flanagan, "Research on the Development of Citizenship: A Field Comes to Age," in *Handbook of Research on Civic Engagement in Youth*, ed. Lonnie R. Sherrod, Judith Torney-Purta, and Constance Flanagan (Hoboken: Jon Wiley & Sons, Inc., 2010), 2.

18. To sample their extensive research on the subject, visit their webpage: CIR-CLE, http://www.civicyouth.org/ (accessed 11/3/2014).

19. Jonathan Yonan, "Majoring in Servitude: Liberal Arts and the Formation of Citizen," in *Civic Education and the Future of American Citizenship*, ed. Elizabeth Kaufer Busch and Jonathan W. White (Lanham: Lexington Books, 2012), 122.

20. Ibid.

21. The Center for Civic Education, "The Role of Civic Education: An Education Policy Task Force Position Paper with Political Recommendations," September 1998, http://new.civiced.org/promote-rationale/position-paper-with-policy-recommend ations (accessed 11/3/2014).

22. http://plato.stanford.edu/entries/civic-education/ (accessed 11/3/2014).

23. Peter Levine, *The Future of Democracy: Developing the Next General of American Citizens* (Tufts, 2007), 1–2.

24. Ibid., 8.

25. Ibid., 5–7.

26. Thomas Ehrlich, "Preface," in *Civic Responsibility and Higher Education, Series on Higher Education* (Phoenix, AZ: American Council on Education and Oryx Press, 2000), vi.

27. Anne Colby et al., *Educating Citizens: Preparing America's Undergraduates for Lives of Moral and Civic Responsibility* (San Francisco: The Carnegie Foundation for the Advancement of Teaching, 2003), 18.

28. Jason L. S. Raia, "Citizens for the 21st Century: Civics Education Today," *Judges Journal* 51, no. 3 (2012).

29. For example, see Donald P. Green and Alan S. Gerber, *Get Out the Vote: How to Increase Voter Turnout* (Washington, DC: Brookings Institute Press, 2004); Steven J. Rosenstone and John Mark Hansen, *Mobilization, Participation and Democracy in America* (New York: Pearson Education, Inc., 1993).

30. There are a number of edited volumes and books, some proscriptive and many critical, of civic education today. For example, see Elizabeth Kaufer Busch and Jonathan W. White, eds., *Civic Education and the Future of American Citizenship* (Lexington Books, 2012); David E. Campbell, Meira Levinson, and Frederick M. Hess, eds., *Making Civics Count: Citizenship Education for a New Generation* (Harvard Education Press, 2012); David Feith, in *Teaching America: The Case for Civic Education*, ed. David Feith (Lanham: Rowman & Littlefield Education, 2011); Robert E. Calvert,

ed. *To Restore American Democracy: Political Education and the Modern University* (Rowman and Littlefield Publishers, 2005); Diane Ravitch and Joseph P. Viteritti, eds., *Making Good Citizens: Education and Civil Society* (New Haven: Yale University Press, 2001); Thomas Ehrlich, ed. *Civic Responsibility and Higher Education*, Series on Higher Education (Phoenix: The Oryx Press, 2000); Lorraine M. McDonnell, Roger Benjamin, and P. Michael Timpane, eds., *Rediscovering the Democratic Purposes of Education* (Lawrence: University Press of Kansas, 2000). See also Alison Rios Millett McCartney, Elizabeth A. Bennion, and Dick Simpson, eds., *Teaching Civic Engagement: From Student to Active Citizen*, State of the Profession Series (Washington, DC: The American Political Science Association, 2013); Meira Levinson, *No Citizen Left Behind* (Harvard University Press, 2012); Levine, *The Future of Democracy: Developing the Next General of American Citizens;* Macedo et al., *Democracy at Risk*; James G. Gimpel, J. Celeste Lay, and Jason E. Schuknecht, *Cultivating Democracy: Civic Environments and Political Socialization in America* (Washington, DC: Brookings Institution Press, 2003); Colby et al., *Educating Citizens*.

31. David Mayhew, *Congress: The Electoral Connection*, Second ed. (New Haven: Yale University Press, 2004 [1974]), 5.

BIBLIOGRAPHY

"Advancing Civic Learning and Engagement in Democracy: A Road Map and Call to Action." 28. Washington, DC: U.S. Department of Education, 2012.

Andolina, Molly W., Krista Jenkins, Cliff Zukin, and Scott Keeter. "Habits from Home, Lessons from School: Influences on Youth Civic Engagement." *PS: Political Science & Politics* 36, no. 2 (2003): 275–80.

Battistoni, Richard M. "Should Political Scientists Care about Civic Education?" *Perspective on Politics* 11, no. 4 (2013): 1135–38.

Bellah, Robert N., Richard Madsen, William M. Sullivan, Ann Swindler, and Steven Tipton. *Habits of the Heart: Individualism and Commitment in American Life.* Second ed. Berkley: Univeristy of California Press, 1996.

Boyte, Harry, and Elizabeth Hollander. "Wingspread Declaration on Renewing the Civic Mission of the American Research University." (1999), http://www.compact.org/wp-content/uploads/2009/04/wingspread_declaration.pdf.

Bridgeland, John M. "Civic Nation: My White House Mission after September 11." In *Teaching America: The Case for Civic Education*, edited by David Feith, 41–49. Lanham: Rowman & Littlefield Education, 2011.

Busch, Elizabeth Kaufer, and Jonathan W. White, eds. *Civic Education and the Future of American Citizenship*: Lexington Books, 2012.

Busch, Elizabeth Kaufer, and Jonathan W. White. "Introduction." In *Civic Education and the Future of American Citizenship*, edited by Elizabeth Kaufer Busch and Jonathan W. White, 1–12. Lanham: Lexington Books, 2012.

"The California Survey of Civic Education." *Educating for Democracy: California Campaign for the Civic Mission of Schools* (2005), http://www.cms-ca.org/civic_survey_final.pdf.

Calvert, Robert E., ed. *To Restore American Democracy: Political Education and the Modern University*: Rowman and Littlefield Publishers, 2005.

Campbell, David E. *Why We Vote: How Schools and Communities Shape Our Civic Life*. Princeton: Princeton University Press, 2006.

Campbell, David E., Meira Levinson, and Frederick M. Hess, eds. *Making Civics Count: Citizenship Education for a New Generation*: Harvard Education Press, 2012.

"Characters from 'The Simpsons' More Well Known to Americans Than Their First Amendment Rights, Survey Finds." (2006), http://www.mccormickfoundation.org/news/2006/pr030106.aspx).

Checkoway, Barry. "Renewing the Civic Mission of the American Research University." *The Journal of Higher Education* 72, no. 1 (2001): 125–47.

CIRCLE. The Center for Information & Research on Civic Learning and Engagement, http://www.civicyouth.org/.

"The Civic Mission of Schools." (2006), http://www.classroomlaw.org/files/posts-pages/about/2006_or_civics_survey.pdf.

Colby, Anne, Thomas Ehrlich, Elizabeth Beaumont, and Jason Stephens. *Educating Citizens: Preparing America's Undergraduates for Lives of Moral and Civic Responsibility*. San Francisco: The Carnegie Foundation for the Advancement of Teaching, 2003.

Conover, Pamela Johnson, and Donald D. Searing. "A Political Socialization Perpesctive." In *Rediscovering the Democratic Purposes of Education*, edited by Lorraine M. McDonnell, P. Michael Timpane, and Roger Benjamin, 91–124. Lawrence: University of Kansas Press, 2000.

"A Crucible Moment: College Learning & Democracy's Future." Washington, DC: National Task Force on Civic Learning and Democratic Engagement, 2012.

de Tocqueville, Alexis. *Democracy in America*. Edited by Phillips Bradley. 2 vols. Vol. 1 & 2: Vintage Books, 1990.

Delli Carpini, Michael, and Scott Keeter. *What Americans Know about Politics and Why It Matters*. New Haven: Yale University Press, 1996.

Dillon, Sam. "Failing Grades on Civics Exam Called a 'Crisis.'" *The New York Times*, 2011.

Dudley, Robert L., and Alan R. Gitelson. "Political Literacy, Civic Education, and Civic Engagement: A Return to Political Socialization?" *Applied Development Science* 6, no. 4 (2002): 175–82.

Ehrlich, Thomas, ed. *Civic Responsibility and Higher Education*. Edited by American Council on Education, Series on Higher Education. Phoenix: The Oryx Press, 2000.

Ehrlich, Thomas. "Preface." In *Civic Responsibility and Higher Education*. Phoenix, AZ: American Council on Education and Oryx Press, 2000.

Feith, David. In *Teaching America: The Case for Civic Education*, edited by David Feith, xvii-xx. Lanham: Rowman & Littlefield Education, 2011.

Feith, David, ed. *Teaching America: The Case for Civic Education*. Lanham: Rowman & Littlefield, Inc., 2011.

Galston, William. "Political Knowledge, Political Engagement, and Civic Education." *Annual Review of Political Science* 4, no. 1 (2001): 217–41.

Gibdon, Cynthia, Peter Levine, Richard Battistoni, and Sheldon Berman. "The Civic Mission of Schools." The Center for Information & Research on Civic Learning and Engagement with Carnegie Corporation of New York, 2003.

Gimpel, James G., J. Celeste Lay, and Jason E. Schuknecht. *Cultivating Democracy: Civic Environments and Political Socialization in America*. Washington, DC: Brookings Institution Press, 2003.

Gooch, Donald M., and Michael T. Rogers. "A Natural Disaster of Civic Proportions: College Students in the Natural State Falls Short of the Naturalization Benchmark." *Midsouth Political Science Review* 13, no. 1 (2012): 53–82.

Graham, Bob, and Chris Hand. *America, the Owner's Manual: Making Government Work for You*. Washington, DC: CQ Press, 2009.

Graham, Bob, and Chris Hand. "A Failure of Leadership: The Duty of Politicians and Universities to Salvage Citizenship." In *Teaching America: The Case for Civic Education*, edited by David Feith, 61–68. Lanham: Rowman & Littlefield Education, 2011.

Green, Donald P., and Alan S. Gerber. *Get Out the Vote: How to Increase Voter Turnout*. Washington, DC: Brookings Institute Press, 2004.

ISI. "The Coming Crisis in Citizenship." Wilmington, DE: Intercollegiate Studies Institute's National Civic Literacy Board, 2006.

———. "Failing Our Students, Failing America: Holding Colleges Accountable for Teaching America's History and Institutions." Willmington, DE: Intercollegiate Studies Institute's National Civic Literacy Board, 2007.

———. "Our Fading Heritage: Americans Fail a Basic Test on Their History and Institutions." In *Intercollegiate Studies Institute's American Civic Literacy Program*: Intercollegiate Studies Institute, 2008–2009.

Johanek, Michael C. "Preparing Pluribus for Unum: Historicial Perspectives on Civic Education." In *Making Civics Count: Citizenship for a New Generation*, edited by David E. Campbell, Meira Levinson, and Frederick M. Hess, 57–87. Cambridge: Harvard Education Press, 2012.

Johnson, Anna. "Tuned to America: 'Simpsons' Trumps Civics in Study, Many Know Sitcom but Not Their Rights." *The Boston Globe*, March 1, 2006.

Levine, Peter. *The Future of Democracy: Developing the Next General of American Citizens*. Tufts, 2007.

Levinson, Meira. *No Citizen Left Behind*: Harvard University Press, 2012.

"Lunch Scholars." 2/2/2012.

Macedo, Stephen, Yvette Alex-Assensch, Jeffrey M. Berry, Michael Brintnall, David E. Campbell, Luis Ricardo Fraga, Archon Fung, William A. Galston, Christopher F. Karpowitz, Margaret Levi, Meira Levinson, Keena Lipsitz, Richard G. Niemi, Robert D. Putnam, Wendy M. Rahn, Robert Reich, Todd Swanstrom, and Katherine Cramer Walsh. *Democracy at Risk: How Political Choices Undermine Citizen Participation, and What We Can Do about It*. Washington, DC: Brookings Institute Press, 2005.

Malin, Heather. "America as a Philosophy: Implications for the Development of American Identity among Today's Youth." *Applied Development Science* 15, no. 2 (2011): 54–60.

Mayhew, David. *Congress: The Electoral Connection*. Second ed. New Haven: Yale University Press, 2004 [1974].

McCartney, Alison Rios Millett, Elizabeth A. Bennion, and Dick Simpson, eds. *Teaching Civic Engagement: From Student to Active Citizen*. Edited by American Political Science Association, State of the Profession Series. Washington, DC: The American Political Science Association, 2013.

McDonnell, Lorraine M., Roger Benjamin, and P. Michael Timpane, eds. *Rediscovering the Democratic Purposes of Education*. Lawrence: University Press of Kansas, 2000.

McIntosh, Hugh, Danil Hart, and James Youniss. "The Influence of Family Political Discussion on Youth Civic Development: Which Parent Qualities Matter?" *PS: Political Science & Politics* XL, no. 3 (2007): 495–99.

McIntosh, Hugh, and James Youniss. "Toward a Political Theory of Political Socialization of Youth." In *Handbook of Research on Civic Engagement in Youth*, edited by Lonnie R. Sherrod, Judith Torney-Purta, and Constance Flanagan. Hoboken: Jon Wiley & Sons, Inc., 2010.

Milner, Henry. *Civic Literacy: How Informed Citizens Make Democracy Work*. London: University Press of New England, 2002.

Niemi, Richard G. "What Students Know about Civics and Government." In *Making Civics Count: Citizenship Education for a New Generation*, edited by David E. Campbell, Meira Levinson, and Frederick M. Hess, 15–35. Cambridge: Harvard Education Press, 2012.

Niemi, Richard G., and Jane Junn. *Civic Education: What Makes Students Learn*. New Haven: Yale University Press, 1998.

O'Connor, Sandra Day. "The Democratic Purpose of Education: From the Founders to Horace Mann to Today." In *Teaching America: The Case for Civic Education*, edited by David Feith, 3–14. Lanham: Rowman & Littlefield Education, 2011.

"Oregon Civics Survey 2006." *Educating for Democracy: Oregon Coalition for the Civics Mission of Schools* (2006), http://www.classroomlaw.org/files/posts-pages/about/2006_or_civics_survey.pdf.

Ostrom, Elinor. "Civic Education for the Next Century: A Task Force to Initiate Professional Activity." *PS: Political Science and Politics* 29, no. 4 (1996): 755–58.

Ostrom, Vincent. *The Meaning of Democracy and the Vulnerabilities of Democracy: A Response to Tocqueville's Challenge*. Ann Harbor: The University of Michigan Press, 1997.

Putnam, Robert. "Bowling Alone: America's Declining Social Capital." *Journal of Democracy* 6, no. 1 (June 1995): 65–78.

———. *Bowling Alone: The Collapse and Revival of American Community*. New York: Simon and Schuster, 2000.

———. *Making Democracy Work: Civic Traditions in Modern Italy*. Princeton, NJ: Princeton University Press, 1993.

———. "Tuning in, Tuning Out: The Strange Disappearance of Social Capital in America." *PS: Political Science and Politics* 28, no. 4 (Dec. 1995): 664–83.

Raia, S., Jason L. "Citizens for the 21st Century: Civics Education Today." *Judges Journal* 51, no. 3 (2012): 10–17.

Ravitch, Diane, and Joseph P. Viteritti, eds. *Making Good Citizens: Education and Civil Society*. New Haven: Yale University Press, 2001.

Rogers, Michael T. "A Civic Education Crisis." *Midsouth Political Science Review* 13, no. 1 (2012): 1–36.

Rosenstone, Steven J., and John Mark Hansen. *Mobilization, Participation and Democracy in America*. New York: Pearson Education, Inc., 1993.

Sherrod, Lonnie R., Judith Torney-Purta, and Constance Flanagan. "Research on the Development of Citizenship: A Field Comes to Age." In *Handbook of Research on Civic Engagement in Youth*, edited by Lonnie R. Sherrod, Judith Torney-Purta, and Constance Flanagan. Hoboken: Jon Wiley & Sons, Inc., 2010.

Skocpol, Theda. *Diminished Democracy: From Membership to Management in American Civic Life*. Norman: University of Oklahoma Press, 2003.

Skocpol, Theda, and Morris P. Fiorina, eds. *Civic Engagement in American Democracy*. Washington, DC: Brookings Institution Press, 1999.

Somin, Ilya. *Democracy and Political Ignorance: Why Smaller Government Is Smarter*. Stanford: Stanford University Press, 2013.

Stroupe, Kenneth, Jr., and Larry Sabato. "Politics: The Missing Link of Responsible Civic Eduation." (2004), http://www.civicyouth.org/PopUps/civicengagement-stroupe-final.pdf.

"Study: More Know 'The Simpsons' Than First Amendment Rights." *USA Today*, 3/1/2006.

"Study: More Know 'Simpsons' Than Constitution." FoxNews.com, http://www.foxnews.com/story/2006/03/01/study-more-know-simpsons-than-constitution/.

Wattenberg, Martin. *The Decline of American Political Parties: 1952–1994*. Cambridge: Harvard University Press, 1996.

Yonan, Jonathan. "Majoring in Servitude: Liberal Arts and the Formation of Citizen." In *Civic Education and the Future of American Citizenship*, edited by Elizabeth Kaufer Busch and Jonathan W. White, 111–23. Lanham: Lexington Books, 2013.

Section I

THE CASE FOR CIVIC EDUCATION

Chapter One

A Meta-history of Formal Civic Education

An Episodic History to Be Repeated?

Michael T. Rogers

Public concern about "education for democracy" is not new. . . . It always
has currency in a democratic society but emerges with special enthusiasm
on an episodic basis under historical conditions that affect its consideration
and its institutional results.

—Barry Checkoway
"Renewing the Civic Mission of the American Research University"
in *The Journal of Higher Education*

At the turn of the twenty-first century, a revival, even a national movement,
for civic education has materialized in the United States. Participants in this
revival include the federal and state governments and the political leaders in
them; primary, secondary, and higher education institutions; interest groups
and nonprofits; and academics. Yet, before we become too optimistic about
the future of civics, we should heed Checkoway's observation such civic out-
bursts recur episodically throughout American history and just as assuredly
recede. How long will today's concern for civic education remain salient?
Can scholars, politicians, and other interested entities come together to produce a civic education program more durable than past generations?

To begin to answer these questions, as Checkoway's quote above indicates
it is worthwhile to investigate the "historical conditions" and "the considerations" that gave rise to past civic revivals, as well as note the "institutional
results" of such movements.[1] It appears necessary to look backward to move
forward. Therefore, this chapter explores the peaks and valleys in the history
of America's formal civic education programs.

Methodological Notes

For a framework, this analysis draws on Samuel Huntington's macrolevel language of "waves of democracy." Huntington's analysis of the democratization of the world suggests outbreaks of democratic government occur in waves through a domino-like effect as one country encourages others in the area to make a similar transition. His theory also notes how initial periods of democratization are followed by eras where democracy recedes and retracts, as some countries slip back into more authoritarian forms.[2] Arguably, the history of civic education in the United States follows a similar, wavelike pattern with some fundamental differences. First, the catalysts are not countries but federal and state governments, political actors, political parties, interest groups, and nonprofits. Civic education initiatives by one of these entities often influences others to follow suit. More importantly, Huntington's waves of democracy theory is a theory of people seizing governmental power and instilling greater popular control through free and fair elections. However, the story of American civic education is a reactionary one, a response to a perceived crisis in democracy within the United States. In some ways, the dynamic of American civic education has more in common with Sheldon Wolin's "fugitive democracy" theory than Huntington's waves of democracy. Just as the periods where true democracy materializes are rare or fugitive for Wolin, the decades of meaningful and enhanced civic education are rare in the overall history of America. The norm is static or declining civic education practices with occasional outbreaks of enhanced civics.[3] Thus, I offer the "perceived crisis theory" of civic education as a more accurate depiction of its historical dynamic than Huntington's waves of democracy. It will be shown that periodically America has seen the increased saliency of education for democracy, but these decades are followed by civic stagnation and/or decline. As Checkoway suggests, the history of civic education in the United States is an episodic one. America has long struggled to institutionalize a durable formal civic education program.

To present these waves of civic education, the history provided here breaks American formal civic education into eight eras: the late 1700s, the early 1800s, the mid-1800s, the late 1800s, the early 1900s, the mid-1900s, the late 1900s, and the early 2000s. For each period, the rhetoric and motivations for civic education are explored. Then, the institutional practice of it is assessed.[4]

Like Busch and White, this analysis finds calls for a liberal (arts) education as inclusive of calls for civic education.[5] The conflation of arguments for civic education in ones for liberal education is pervasive in the late 1700s into the 1800s, but becomes less common as that widespread, liberal education is fully institutionalized by the 1900s. Then, the educational debate shifts to one over subject coverage in the curriculum (e.g., science and math versus reading and English versus social sciences, etc.). In this context, one finds more direct calls for civic education; today liberal education serves less as a proxy.

As for the mode of inquiry, this march through the history of American civic education is made possible by a series of preexisting mini-histories on the subject. Scholarly investigations into the history of civic education are increasingly common. In fact, for a comprehensive global perspective there are the various works of Derek Heater, most notably the *History of Education for Citizenship*.[6] However, there is no such comprehensive narrative on education for citizenship in the United States. Most scholarship narrowly focuses on either a specific time period or a specific issue over time. In contrast, my analysis constructs a meta-history by synthesizing these mini-histories.[7] For example, my discussion of the late 1700s draws heavily on the seminal mini-history of the Founders provided by Pangle and Pangle through *The Learning of Liberty: The Educational Ideas of the American Founders* and "What the Founders Have to Teach Us about Schooling for Democratic Citizenship."[8] Similarly, the 1800s uses the mini-history in Bob Taylor's *Horace Mann's Troubling Legacy*.[9] Then, my meta-history also draws on a number of articles examining specific issues of civic education over time. For example, I draw on R. Claire Snyder's historical overview of the civic education mission of higher education and Carl Kaestle's various works on the common school.[10]

By combining these and other mini-histories into one historical narrative, this work takes the much needed step toward a comprehensive understanding of the subject in America. Yet, this work remains an incomplete history of civic education in the United States. Foremost, this history is focused primarily on formal civic education processes (e.g., civic instruction through schools), as opposed to informal civic education which occurs through families, friends, political parties, interest groups, etc. That said, my meta-history offers a more comprehensive explanation of American civic education than previously available.

Educational Relativism

Before examining the history of American civic education, it is important to note the rhetorical tradition advocating such education in Western political thought. Checkoway notes such arguments are at least as old as Plato and Aristotle.[11] The Western tradition is rife with normative claims that a regime needs to provide its citizens with a civic education that cultivates political skills, abilities, norms, and behaviors essential to the regime. Gutmann dubs this theory "educational relativism." She traces such arguments through Aristotle, Montesquieu, and Durkheim, arguing they shared the belief that the education of the people should support "the deepest shared moral commitments of a society—its 'constitution' in Aristotelian terms or 'political principles' in Montesquieu's more modern terms."[12] Gutmann acknowledges educational relativism can be a conservative force in society but emphasizes this does not necessitate a mindless ideological conservation of the status quo. On the contrary, this represents a conscientious reproduction and socialization that maintains a society's social and political values. She writes, "Education must be guided by the *principles*, not the practices, of a regime."[13] Whatever the given regime form—republic, democracy, etc.—educational relativism endorses a political socialization that provides citizens instruction on their society's fundamental principles and ideals, training citizens in the skills and aptitudes necessary to regime maintenance.

In the American context, educational relativism holds government and/ or society responsible for providing a civic education in democratic republicanism. Gutmann "conclude[s] that 'political education'—the cultivation of the virtues, knowledge, and skills necessary for political participation—has moral primacy over other purposes of public education in a democratic society."[14] A review of the history of formal civic education demonstrates the pervasive acceptance of educational relativism in America.

PART I: THE FOUNDING AND EDUCATION FOR REPUBLICAN GOVERNMENT

The instruction of the people, in every kind of knowledge that can be of use to them in the practice of their moral duties, as men, citizens, and Christians, and of their political and civil duties, as members of society and freemen, ought to be the care of the public, and of all who have any share in the conduct of its affairs, in a manner that never yet has been practiced in any age or nation. The education here intended is not merely that of the children of the rich and noble, but of every rank and class of people, down to the lowest and the poorest. It is not too much to say, that schools for the education of all should be placed at convenient distances, and maintained at the public expense. The revenues of the state would be applied infinitely better, more charitably, wisely, usefully, and therefore politically, in this way, than even in maintaining the poor.

—John Adams, *A Defense of the Constitution of the United States of America*

In this quote, Adams epitomizes the belief in the logic of educational relativism. He, like many Founders, sees education in republican government (if not democracy) as essential to preserving their newly minted republic. Below, it becomes clear the motivations of the Founders may vary, but this overall belief was persistent. A civic education would be essential to the maintenance of the American experiment in democratic republicanism.

Late 1700s: The Founders' Pervasive Calls for a Moral, Republican Education

In his Farewell Address, George Washington imparts what wisdom he can on how to maintain the fragile republican government created by the Constitution. Central to his advice is the education of the people.[15] Former Supreme Court Justice Sandra Day O'Connor notes Washington is one among many Founders who believed such. She claims Thomas Jefferson, James Madison, John Adams, Noah Webster, and Benjamin Rush shared Washington's views about education.[16] Yet, her list is not exhaustive. Pangle and Pangle add to it Benjamin Franklin, Samuel Harrison Smith, Samuel Knox, Robert Coram, and Jefferson's friend Joel Barlow.[17] No wonder Griswold concludes the Founders "saw in education not merely the corollary to democracy but the key, the *sine qua non*" of it.[18]

Motivations of the Founders

Put simply, the Founders' advocacy of a widespread liberal arts education reflects their acceptance of the logic of educational relativism. They did so as they thought was essential to providing the training necessary to maintaining republican government. In *Civic Education and the Future of American Citizenship* Busch and White reinforce this point, writing "America was founded with the understanding that its citizens would perpetually have to be educated in the nation's first principles in order for the republic to survive and its citizens to flourish."[19] The Founders had learned the vices of excessive democracy under the Articles of Confederation. The crisis of regime instability led them to produce the U.S. Constitution as an immediate solution. However, they coalesced around a long-term one as well—a widespread, democratic, liberal arts education. As Pangle and Pangle explain, after ratification the Founders turned to "continued meditation on the older and more problematic or perplexing republican theme: the question of how to create and encourage a specific moral character and tone in the citizenry and its leaders."[20] The solution for many Founders was education in the principles of a democratic republic.

As Pangle and Pangle explain, "The overarching aim of the education the Founders promote is moral: the formation of character."[21] Elsewhere, they clarify the point by noting the Founders envisioned "a new sort of moral education," one promoting "a sense of common 'humanity.'"[22] They even summarize the curricular recommendations of the Founders. Generally, this included the study of English, history (political not social), and (auto-)biography (for models of inspiration and reflection).[23] Pangle and Pangle find "the strongest message from the Founders is that organization must follow and support curriculum and that curriculum must be unified around a specific and substantial notion of the sorts of character traits that need to be nurtured in young future citizens."[24] Essentially, the Founders' hopes for long-term regime stability rested in a widespread liberal arts education.

Yet, beneath this common hope that education would provide stability were a number of supplemental motivations. For example, many Founders, most notably Jefferson, valued direct participation in local government, particularly through citizen-juries as such activities trained citizens in the "safeguard of [their] personal security . . . a key component of human dignity."[25] Simply put, Jefferson's endorsement of civic education reflected his belief that it helped citizens guard their individual rights and liberties.[26] Alternatively, Founders like Franklin believed a liberal arts education served the material interests of individuals. Thus, his civics curriculum included the study of economic history along with training in prose, public oratory, and debate.[27] Robert Coram pushed the argument farthest. He shared Franklin's belief that such an education served an individual's material "subsistence."[28] However, Coram goes so far as to argue the government has some obligation to promote these economic rights. Sounding rather contemporary, he believed that "educational goals" should be "vocational or economic," not just "moral and civic." For Coram "the young were to be trained as citizens who understood their rights and were prepared to meet their civic responsibility; but they were to meet those responsibilities as persons chiefly devoted to work and business rather than leisure."[29]

Of course, this economic motive is not incommensurate with a democratic one. Webster, Knox, and Adams understood this, as all three believed educating the poor was essential to the success of the new republic. In true democratic spirit, they feared too great an old-world class division would lead to strife typical of monarchies and oligarchies. They feared such divisions would undermine the American experiment in democratic republican government.[30] Other Founders (including Washington) valued this widespread moral education because such civic training was highly compatible with a Christian one. For example, Benjamin Rush echoes Adams emphasizing a widespread liberal arts education is less about promoting academia and more about making Americans "men, citizens, and Christians."[31]

While not all Founders (particularly Jefferson) had the religiosity of Washington, Adams, and Rush, the emphasis on men of character who were capable republican citizens was pervasive. Summarizing the diverse motivations of our Founders, Pangle and Pangle write that some:

> ... added a strong emphasis on educating all individuals in their 'natural rights' as well as duties. Others pointed out the collective interest that all should take in protecting children from the negligence of those parents who might leave them too unenlightened to be capable of contributing to the intelligent mass vigilance required for defending everyone's rights. A few went so far as to interpret the social contract as implying that civic education was indeed a fundamental duty of government and even a basic right of individuals.[32]

The point is, the Founders did not let their supplemental hopes of such an education prevent them from coming together to endorse a widespread liberal arts education. For the Founders, the perceived crisis due to regime instability after the Revolutionary War necessitated overlooking the visionary differences they had for what a civic education would do. Thus, while Founders like Jefferson likely had reservations about the religious intentions of Founders like Rush, they still came together collectively to endorse a moral education for republican government as it promised to produce better citizens and, by extension, regime stability.

Minimal Institutionalized Formal Civic Education

For all the "education for a republic" rhetoric at the founding, the story of the late 1700s is one of minimal formal civic education. Given the highly sporadic and decentralized nature of education then, most political socialization occurred through informal processes at that time. Family, friends, or public and private associations were the primary civic educators with more limited formal socialization through higher education and participation in government. In fact, the bulk of the short story on formalized civic education comes from higher education.

While analyzing civic education in colleges and universities, Colby et al. note that early religious colleges were designed to provide the moral education of ministers.[33] These religious colleges influenced the Founders' calls for a liberal arts education. Snyder uncovers this connection in her analysis of the civic mission of higher education. She suggests the Founders believed in the importance of moral education because it was part of their own instruction in colonial "congregational colleges."[34] She explains how congregational colleges served three civic functions: producing future community leaders, giving these future leaders the knowledge and skills requisite for public life, and promoting normative thinking through a hybrid curriculum of civic humanism and Christian theology. The latter was essential to facilitating their ability to participate in the decision-making for public affairs at the local level.[35]

Clearly, the Founders' own educational experiences shaped their advocacy of a widespread liberal education. The "Christian humanism" curriculum, to borrow the term from Snyder, is widely reflected in many Founders' desires for a widespread liberal arts education. The hope was this would produce a common democratic humanity.[36] Yet, these were private, religious colleges and civic education was, at best, a by-product of their religious goals. It was Jefferson who was central in transforming higher education, making civic education a more institutionalized feature of it. Kaestle describes Jefferson as "the fountainhead of ideas about civic education" at the turn of the nineteenth century.[37] Jefferson is well-known for advocating primary education through local wards. However, of import here is his work founding the University of Virginia as a "proto-type" of a new "civic university."[38] Snyder argues the Revolutionary era was a more secular time; this changed the congregational colleges. They began teaching "political philosophy, current political controversies, and Enlightenment ideas" largely separate from Christian theology. She adds they taught students to exercise "personal judgments rather than simply to absorb accepted 'truths.'" It was the Founders, particularly Jefferson, who took the next evolutionary step in higher education. He offered "a new secularized model of higher education" with "the civic university."[39] Jefferson's University of Virginia became *the* model of the secular civic university for the land-grant colleges that sprung up over the next century throughout the United States.

Of course, Tyack and James note the important role the federal government had in promoting this civic-oriented education. While "the first century of the American nation was an era when public schools were entirely a grassroots affair," they claim the federal government's role on public education at the time was "more complex" and "more profound" than typically realized. In 1785 and 1787, two important federal ordinances facilitating this role were passed. They required the setting aside of land in every township for public schools. Also, the federal government used the sale of public lands to help fund public education, and they subsidized public education through grants. Then, the federal government made public education "a condition for admission to the union" for many new states.[40] This all fueled the creation by states of a number of "land-grant people's colleges." Thus, the federal government was pivotal in displacing congregational colleges with Jefferson's civic-oriented, land-grant colleges. Snyder shows the import of this, as she claims land-grant colleges enhanced formalized civic education in two important ways: they made higher education accessible to more than just elites and made institutions of higher education integral participants in the solving of society's problems.[41]

Alternatively, one of the most significant acts at the state level was in Massachusetts. Writing the state constitution, Adams inserted a requirement that the state government provide a civic education for its citizens.[42] Yet, such direct actions were rare at that time. Additionally, the late 1790s saw the first textbooks dealing with civics published.[43] These early textbooks reflected the civic motivations of the Founders. For example, Webster (and later in the mid-1800s William McGuffey) sought "to achieve commonality of language and knowledge and a shared loyalty to the public good" through textbooks.[44]

All in all, Kaestle puts it best when he says appeals by Founders for a widespread liberal arts education in "the early national period fell mostly on deaf ears." State legislatures lacked funds, had an electorate opposed to new taxes, and faced a tradition where education was not a federal issue but a local one.[45] Pangle and Pangle reinforce Kaestle's observation, claiming the Founders readily accepted federalism in education, deferring to states and localities for organized formal schooling.[46] Thus, while other Founders, like Benjamin Rush, shared Jefferson's desire for a public school system or a common elementary curriculum, it would be another half century before such desires bore fruit.[47]

PART II: VICISSITUDES IN FORMAL CIVIC EDUCATION IN THE 1800s

Early 1800s: Civic Stagnation

In the early 1800s, the story of formalized civic education remains short. Tyack and James observe that most state constitutions had provisions for public education (e.g., the 1802 Ohio Constitution). However, few states had taken much of a direct roll, leaving the details to localities.[48] This slowly begins to change. For example, Hirsch cites New York as a leader on this front. First, in 1812 New York passed the Common School Act creating a public elementary school system.[49] Then, in 1825 its legislature established a fund for common textbooks for schools.[50] Tyack and James, along with Hirsch, also note such early initiatives were guided by the Founders' desire to provide a moral education that produced competent citizens for the fledgling republic. Additionally, the early 1800s brought to the fore a new motivational factor: a desire that public education socialize the large immigrant population into the American way of life. Tyack and James claim public education rhetoric at this time developed an ideological quality. Public education became a common good; it was to be a unifying force cutting across party or sect lines, as well as a mechanism for bringing immigrants into the American fold.[51] Or, as Hirsch puts it, "[t]he conviction that our schools need to make Americans out of all children, native and immigrant, was a sentiment that grew in strength in the nineteenth-century."[52]

At the higher education level, congregational and land-grant universities and land regulation by the federal government remained the primary formal mechanisms promoting a public, liberal arts education into the early 1800s. Still, the bulk of civic education continued to occur through informal processes like the participatory, local, New England-style politics described by Tocqueville.[53] Although rhetoric for civic education was pervasive among Americans, it was not until the mid-1800s that a more formalized public education spread throughout the country.

Mid-1800s: The First Wave—The Common School Movement

Beyond a few federal programs, some state initiatives, and the civic mission of land-grant colleges, a liberal arts education went largely unrealized until Horace Mann and the Common School movement. As O'Connor explains, Mann gave the Founders' sentiments teeth during the Antebellum era.[54] As education was largely a state and local issue in the 1800s, it is not surprising a state politician emerged as the "Father of the American Public School." In 1837, Mann became the first secretary for the newly minted Massachusetts State Board of Education. He used this position over the next dozen years as a soap box, advocating for state governments to provide the democratic education of the common citizen through public schools.[55] Taylor argues Mann "was the defining voice in the American understanding of the relationship between public schooling and civic education in the nineteenth century— that is, when these ideas were first systematically formulated and advocated in a form that would become the standard model in the American political experience." He adds, "Mann set the historic agenda for civic education in American society."[56] This conclusion is well-made given Mann's work to institutionalize the common school in Massachusetts produced a model of public education which would spread to most other states by the end of the nineteenth century. Mann is *the* central figure in the institutionalization of a formal civic education program in public schools. Because he chose public schools increasingly open to all citizens as the mechanism for civic education, Mann ensured America's civics program would reach more and more American citizens over time.

Horace Mann's Civic Motivations for a Common School

Given Taylor's observations about the significance of Mann, it seems reasonable to use Mann's motivations as a proxy for the general motivations for civic education in the mid-1800s. Taylor explains Mann saw "himself as engaged in completing the unfinished work of the American founding."[57] Thus, Mann's advocacy of a common school correlates strongly with the Founders' calls for a widespread liberal arts education. First, Mann echoes Jefferson in arguing the common school will help free individuals understand their democratic obligations and give them the skills and moral training necessary for a democratic republic. Also, like many Founders, Mann sees the common school as a way to produce "harmony" in and among free individuals.[58] In fact, Hirsch praises Mann for claiming education needs to produce a common knowledge and civic identity to overcome the various, largely class, divisions that threaten the republic.[59] As a third commonality, Mann like Adams, Webster, and Knox shares the belief that social inequalities will undermine American government. The difference is context. Mann's argument is fueled by his concerns over nineteenth-century industrialization and commercial capitalism, not fear of eighteenth-century old-world class divisions between an aristocracy and the masses. He expected education to counteract the "economic domination of the rich over the poor."[60] Finally, Mann echoes other Founders' sentiments when claiming formal education was necessary to counteract the neglect of some parents for their children's enlightenment.[61]

That said, not all of Mann's motivations are similar to those of the Founders. Taylor notes Mann had a "prudish disgust with popular culture" that left him with a distaste for fictional literature. Mann believed literature allowed emotions to run rampant, which undermines our self-control and "ability to understand our obligations as free individuals."[62] Mann's distaste of fictional literature specifically and American culture generally was so severe, he believed "civic education of children" was essential if democracy was to overcome the "profound crisis" it faced.[63] He saw American society as giving life to Tocqueville's worst democratic fear—excessive selfish passions. For Mann, this was the natural product of democratic liberty and industrial capitalism.[64] Witnessing the effects of industrial capitalism in the mid-1800s, Mann had come to despise greedy companies that refused to allow children to leave work for school. Likewise, he was disgusted with selfish citizens who refused to pay the additional taxes necessary for common schools. Thus, the new feature of the mid-1800s Mann (and the Whigs) are reacting to is a perceived crisis from industrial capitalism. A common school education was the antidote for the anti-democratic tendencies of industrial capitalism.

More importantly, Mann was not alone in his view that public education was the key to fixing society's problems. Hirsch notes Governor Silas Wright warned in his 1845 address to the New York legislature that the only way to preserve our republic was through our schools.[65] Similarly, Busch and White find Abraham Lincoln also believed public education served such purposes.

They relate how Lincoln believed education "taught people to appreciate their nation and their history; it taught them how to be citizens of a free nation; and it would give them satisfaction and pleasure when they exercised the freedom to read and understand and appreciate the life of the mind."[66] Whether it is Mann, Wright, or Lincoln, the consensus in the Antebellum period was "[o]nly here, in the common school, do we find the means to break the degenerative cycles endemic to republican government."[67]

Unprecedented Growth in Institutionalized Civic Education

As a politician inhabiting state and federal offices from the 1830s to the 1850s, Mann was pivotal in institutionalizing common schooling geared toward citizenship training.[68] In the 1800s, Kaestle writes, civic education involved a training of citizens which combined a general moral and economic training and synthesized three core American values (republicanism, Protestantism, and capitalism).[69] He adds how the success of the Common School movement in states was intertwined with the success of the Whig Party. In fact, prior to the Civil War states routinely intervened in support of local schools when Whigs controlled office. They were the party that believed state governments needed to play a strong role in education. In contrast, where Democrats dominated, the Common School movement stalled. Democrats saw schooling as a local issue and had more of a noninterventionist approach.[70]

Still, at the macrolevel the gains across the United States in formal education through the Common School movement were substantial. This period represents unprecedented growth in public education generally and formal civic education specifically. Fueled by Mann's Whiggish concerns over the democratic crisis produced by industrial capitalism, the Common School movement swept through the states. More and more Americans gained access to education. By the Civil War, most Northern and Midwestern states had compulsory schooling. By the end of the century, much of the South followed suit.[71] The story, however, is not just about expanded availability of public education; it is also about compulsory public education. Massachusetts again lead the way. They made education of youth compulsory in 1852, and many others states did likewise through the remainder of the century.[72]

Late 1800s: A Lull in Civic Education

The nineteenth century opened with a lull in civic education and closed with one, as well. Most of the educational gains of the Common School movement were accomplished by the Civil War. In the South, where the Common School movement had yet to fully take root, progress was slower. The outbreak of the Civil War did not help. Federal and state governments had little time, energy, and resources left for advancing the Common School movement. More importantly, the Civil War transformed the political terrain. The Whigs, the partisan ally of the Common School movement, fell rapidly from power. By the close of the Civil War, Kaestle explains how partisanship and education were more complicated. The newly instituted Republican Party and the Progressives emerged and moved to centralize control of schooling. They sought to secure a more professionalized school free of politics, while Democrats remained active proponents of education as a local issue.

In this environment, schools continued to grow more accessible, yet a common curriculum remained unrealized. On the positive side, this is the era where local citizens became highly active in education. In addition to providing youth civic instruction, at this time public education saw the development of a forum for adult civic training as parents became highly involved in local school administration. On the negative side, this is when the moral education advocated by the Founders is challenged and knocked from its perch as the fundamental feature of our widespread liberal arts education. Over the next half century, the Progressive movement would promote an increasingly sterilized, nonpartisan education.[73] The full implications of this transformation would not materialize until the twentieth century.

Still, the overall story of civic education in the nineteenth century is one of substantial growth. Although the century opened with civic education occurring primarily through informal processes, it closed by complementing those informal processes with formal education through common schools. In the early 1800s, the typical formal civic socialization was rather limited, realized mostly by a select few active in local politics or attending congregational colleges. The bulk of civic socialization was through informal mechanisms like the family or public and private groups. By the end of the century, more and more Americans experienced some formalized education through compulsory common schools or civic-oriented, land-grant universities. Informal civic education was now reinforced by a formal program. As a result, more citizens were likely challenged to develop their basic knowledge of and skills for democratic republican government.

PART III: FURTHER VICISSITUDES IN THE 1900s

If the story of the 1800s is unprecedented growth, the 1900s is one of growth then decline. Ironically, the Progressive's attempts to free education from partisanship may have done more to politicize and undermine the whole enterprise. While the early 1900s continue the growth in formal civic education, by midcentury these gains level off and then experience a decline in the late 1900s.

Early 1900s: The Second Wave—The Progressive Movement

Much like the mid-1800s, a second wave for civic education materializes with the dawn of the 1900s. The perceived crisis causing this was two-fold. The first was the challenge of immigration; the second is governmental corruption via party machines. Jeffrey Mirel explains the former, arguing Americans showed great anxiety over immigration and desired a mechanism for integrating migrants into the American way of life. He labels the period of 1900 to 1925 as the "High Tide of Assimilation" in the American civic education program.[74] In response to high immigration, community and political leaders became concerned about the threat to American language, politics, and culture. Thus, the civic education program emphasized "the melting pot," which was not a mixing of all these cultures but rather a melting away of foreign elements to refashion immigrants in the White, Anglo-American, Protestant mold. Mirel adds, "The primary institution for achieving this assimilation would be public schools." He writes, "[t]he process of civic education was simple and straightforward. Immigrants had to learn English; learn to think of themselves as Americans rather than a member of distinct ethnic groups; had to proclaim that individualism was one of America's greatest character traits; espouse American political values; and learn patriotism through an interpretation of history that stressed America's triumphs and ignored its faults."[75] Mirel goes so far as to label the public school civics curriculum for this time as "American civil religion."[76]

So, what did this civil religion look like? Kaestle argues the synthesis of republicanism, Protestantism, and capitalism typical of the Common School movement materialized again at the turn of the twentieth century. However, the civic education program that ensued reflected the ideals of a new group: the Progressives. Advocating a "new civic education," Progressives produced a shift in the emphasis of civic education to more than simply participation in elections. Elections had been corrupted by party machines. To rise above the perceived crisis in government due to parties, the Progressives stressed civic education have a community service component. As Kaestle explains, "The Progressive era was strongly hierarchical, and the new civics was consistent with that central belief. It emphasized responsibility and community over rights and participation."[77] The iconic figure in this reform of education was John Dewey. Taylor writes, "Dewey's democratic concerns led him to become the foremost educational theorist of his era, and it would be no exaggeration to describe his democratic theory as being, at its base, a theory of civic education (and his theory of education as being fundamentally civic in character)."[78] The Deweyian vision of education as pragmatic, experiential learning transformed schooling in the early 1900s (and it continues to influence education today through initiatives like the service-learning movement).[79]

The practical implications of this Deweyian-inspired, Progressive education can be seen in Johanek's micro-history of the early 1900s. One key feature was the creation of social studies, the new curricular home for citizenship training. Johanek explains, "Educators developed the social studies as a central curricular remedy" to "the challenges of industrialization, urbanization, and immigration," as these are what "impressed themselves upon rapidly growing public schools."[80] This hybrid subject area combined traditional subjects (e.g., history, geography, and government) with new social science subjects (e.g., economics and sociology). Although in the late 1900s social studies will become a cause of the decline in civic education as it forces civics to compete with these other subjects for coverage in the increasingly limited curricular space for social studies, at this time it resulted in an expansion of the number of civics courses. In a Deweyian vein, two new civics courses (Problems of Democracy in high school and Community Civics in elementary school) became commonplace.[81] Over the next few decades a new norm emerged: students took civics typically in eighth or ninth grade and government in twelfth.[82] Thus, the American social studies curriculum became institutionalized in public schools.

Beyond these curricular innovations, Progressive reforms encouraged schools to become civic agents in the community. Johanek claims Dewey envisioned "The School as Social Center." Schools were to advance the community's democratic development. Johanek offers three case studies to illustrate what this meant: 1) the Rochester schools as social centers under Edward J. Ward, 2) the reproduction of the Hesperia movement of Michigan in West Virginia by M. P. Shawkey, and 3) the use of the local public school as an agent for community development in East Harlem by Leonard Covello.[83] All three show public schools can do more than simply provide formal civic education. Schools can also be political actors and potential sources of civic leadership; they are capable of taking and/or facilitating civic action at the local level.

Progressive reforms were not felt solely at the primary and secondary levels, as Thelin explains how universities in the early 1900s integrated their ideals. He claims "civic education was not central to the collegiate culture of the early twentieth century," but acknowledges Progressives like Woodrow Wilson saw universities as "tools for serving the national interest."[84] As president, Wilson argued universities should prepare students to be national leaders who "reined in science and technology to appropriate ends." With the onset of WWI, Wilson and Congress expanded the civic role of higher education. They felt "[s]tudents could serve the national interest by staying enrolled and preparing to be national leaders." Also, organizations like the Student Army Training Corps were formed. Still, Thelin explains "what had begun as a proud exercise in national service came to be tolerated by academics only as a necessary nuisance." In other words, college administrators where initially happy with the federal government policy as it permitted students to stay in school. However, they increasingly saw such government service and training programs as intrusions on regular college studies, as administrators feared it discouraged universities and students from being critical of the government.[85]

Overall, Progressives pushed schools to be more than just civic educators. Schools also acted as civic agents capable of facilitating civic engagement. More importantly, operating in these ways schools became an integral tool of Progressive politics. Schools were essential to countering the corrupt practices of party machines while also combatting the immigration issue. By a partisan-free education that emphasized facts and nationalism (and not the more "barbaric" side of politics), Progressives tried to kill two birds with one stone.[86] First, before party socialization could corrupt citizens, a rigorous civic socialization was used to train youth in proper, nonpartisan civic roles. Then, by emphasizing nationalism and an American identity, the un-American elements of immigrants were melted away by our new civil religion—the result, a three semester sequence of courses for primary and secondary education, which remains the single-most rigorous formal civics education program in our history.[87]

Of course, that civics program was also highly susceptible to criticisms of indoctrination. Multiculturalists like Mirel came to realize this formal civic education was unnecessarily destructive of "other" cultures and too often produced a society of conformists. Also, it is this type of sterilized civics that leads Sandel to lament how society has lost its "misfits," citizens "who do not take their society's established roles and practice as given but who regard these practices as open to criticism, contest, argument, dispute and revision."[88] Essentially, such concerns about political indoctrination, as well as debates over the content and effectiveness of a civics curriculum, amplify in the ensuing decades. The story of the next era is how schools embraced these sterilized curriculums, preferring to limit instruction to facts thus shielding themselves from their newly politicized civic missions.

Mid-1900s: The Not-So-Golden Age

On the surface, growth in formal civic education due to the perceived threat immigration posed to the American identity and the perceived crisis in government from corrupt party politics inspired innovation in and enhancement of America's formal civic education process. Some romanticize the next couple generations of Americans—the products of this formalized civics program of the Progressives, as representing America's civics golden age. While scholars continue to debate if it was Progressive educational reforms, the Great Depression, the New Deal, WWII, or other events that produced these patriotic and engaged citizens, there is no mistaking their tendency to gravitate to the people of this time. For example, there is Tom Brokaw's depiction of them as *The Greatest Generation*.[89] Likewise, it is the citizens of the 1950s and 1960s that produced unprecedented levels of social capital. In his various works, particularly *Bowling Alone*, Putnam documents America's steady decline in social capital from the highs of this generation.[90] Yet, it was also this era that gave rise to the Civil Rights movement, advances in Women's rights, and the Vietnam War protests. On the one hand, such movements call into question this period as a golden age, given that these movements were a reaction to the deprivation of minority and gender rights, as well as the prosecution of a foreign war through forced transcription. On the other hand, the activism and political unrest of the 1950s and 1960s is archetypical of the active and engaged citizen that one expects of a golden age. So, even such disruptive movements can be incorporated as titular examples of the midcentury golden age of civics.

Examining the facts of the formal civic education program of the time, O'Connor and Graham romanticize the rigorous civics curriculum that persisted in public schools at the time. Again, never have the formal course load requirements been greater than the three-course sequence of those decades. Also, if the Commission on Higher Education's 1940s report entitled *Higher Education for American Democracy* is any indicator, universities still embraced their civic mission and orientation.[91] Drawing on my introduction to this volume, this era does arguably represent the most robust civic ecology in our American history. It saw informal civic education processes producing substantial social capital, while formal programs reinforced and supplemented them. No wonder academics romanticize this time, a time when the nuclear family was largely intact and families still sat around the table together talking politics and were glued to their televisions for political events like party conventions. Likewise, one can see why civics scholars envy this formalized civics curriculum in schools.

However, characterizing this period as a golden age of civics goes too far. For one, it is not clear this was the most robust, informal civic education process in American history. For example, the informal socialization through parties was certainly stronger in the 1800s. Second, a number of scholars identify midcentury trends in civic education that highlight the hollowness of this "golden age" of civics. For example, Hirsch claims the student-centered pedagogy of the Progressive movement (with its emphasis on child-centered as opposed to subject-centered education) resulted in a formal civic education process less likely to realize a common American identity. Racial divisions only further undermined such a realization. Thus, the Progressive pedagogy and social tensions of the era combined to decrease the likelihood America's public schools produced a common civics curriculum and, by extension, a common American identity. Instead, it encouraged divisions (most notably racial). Thus, Hirsch argues America's shared knowledge declined dramatically during this era.[92] He writes:

> In the twentieth century a new set of ideas began to guide our schools, causing them by the 1930s to start losing their sense of urgent civic purposes. By the 1950s they no longer conceived their chief mission to create educated citizens who shared a sense of public commitment and community. Their main emphasis shifted to the individual student's personal development.[93]

To understand the implications of Hirsch's criticism, there is Mirel's explanation of how America transitioned from an assimilationist approach to civic education to a cultural pluralist and/or post-ethnicity one. He argues by midcentury America increasingly realized its civic nationalism by moving away from an ethnic nationalism of "White, Anglo-American Protestants."[94] Mirel draws on George Counts's *The Education of Free Men in American Democracy* to construct the logic of America's new "'intercultural education' programmes." The new democratic principle to be stressed was that "racial, cultural, and political minorities should be tolerated, respected, and valued."[95] There is much to value in respecting the unique cultural identity of each race and ethnicity in America, yet the Hirschians' concern that this American pluralism undermines a formal civics program that realizes a common American civic identity has import as well.[96] Still, this represents only one difference of opinion plaguing civic education today. Alternatively, while most accept American materialism and the expectation schools primarily provide vocational training (i.e., practical training for profit) today, some scholars argue this has lead schools, particularly universities, to neglect their civic missions.[97] Still others point to a combination of these arguments—individualism, on the one hand, and materialism and careerism, on the other—as what has displaced the civic mission of schools and weakened the formal civic education program of America.[98]

Regardless of where one falls in these civic debates, the fracturing of scholarly opinion as to the "golden age" status of the 1960s weighs against the thesis. The absence of consensus suggests there is good reason to doubt this was truly a golden age of civics. Progressive efforts to depoliticize civic education have backfired. Unlike at the founding, conflicting supplemental motivations for civic education now undermine the general realization of it formally. Not following the example of the Founders, Americans failed by the late twentieth century to rise above their particular conflicting motivations (common American identity versus multiculturalism and/or pluralism) for civic education to rally around the need for such a program. Worse, they began avoiding the debate. As civic education became increasingly plagued by this politicization, school administrators tended to abandon their civic missions.[99] This was particularly pronounced in colleges and universities, as Jefferson's model of the civic university gave way to the German model of the scientific research institution. Producing objective scientific information for society displaced citizenship training in higher education.[100] The moral development of citizens as advocated by the Founders grew increasingly incompatible with the goals of the modern scientific research institute. The civic missions and liberal arts curriculums of higher education eroded in the face of new demands for practical job training.

Late 1900s: Civic Recession

By the 1970s, the civic ecology that shaped America over the first half of the twentieth century had receded. Niemi and Smith document the decline in coverage of civics in public schools post-1960, most notably because of "reductions in the number of social studies courses required for high school graduation and an increase in the availability of local exceptions to state requirements"[101] They also find a rise in social studies electives (e.g., economics and psychology). As more subjects are brought into the fold of social studies, civics faces additional competition for coverage of civics within its limited curricular space.[102] Niemi and Smith conclude that by 1980 a "bleak picture" emerged as only about six in ten high school students experienced an American government course. This improved in the 1990s, but then still only about three-quarters of graduating high school seniors had an American government course. The net effect—less social studies and civic coverage in the later twentieth century as "rarely more" than one course in government was taken.[103]

On the positive side, there is some safeguard against the disappearance of civics from public education. Most states now have some educational requirement of civics. However, Niemi and Smith note only a few states had specified a course requirement as of the late 1900s. Advanced work or multiple courses like O'Connor and Graham romanticize remained rare. This explains why only about 2 percent of high school graduates took an AP exam in civics at the end of the century. Likewise, the diluted social studies curriculum meant only one in seven took an AP exam in any social studies area.[104] Niemi and Smith add "nearly 30 percent of graduating seniors in 1994 had less than a full year of *any* social studies" and emphasize the need for civics in the senior year.[105] Finally, they find a demographic inconsistency in who is likely to take American Government, as African Americans and Hispanics are more likely than Caucasians to take American government in high school. Also, students attending public schools are more likely to study American Government, as are students outside big cities and in the West. Students at private schools, big-city schools, and schools in the Northeast are least likely to have American government.[106]

By the end of the twentieth century, formal civic education in high schools did not guarantee every American exposure to adequate education about their government. Likewise, there was no common curriculum across states. If the task of formal civic education is to promote a common American identity, it was not likely to do so at the end of the 1900s. Not surprisingly, it was exactly at this time scholars, most notably Putnam, began to question the health of America's civic ecology.[107] Yet, indications of a problem materialized much earlier. The National Commission on Excellence in Education, at the behest of the Reagan administration, produced "A Nation at Risk" in 1983.[108] Although Kaestle notes it "barely mentioned citizenship" because "its central theme was economics," this report coincides with the decline in formal civic education as identified by Niemi and Smith.[109] Also, Hirsch argues this publication was important to bringing the poor educational performance of the United States to light. He sees this report as pivotal in producing the state-standards movement in education today.[110] Certainly, there has been a series of federal and state education initiatives since, including Goal 2000 in the 1990s, No Child Left Behind in the 2000s, and Common Core today. Such concerns over education have been fuel for the Civic Mission of Schools movement today, as well. While the late 1900s was a period of recession in formal civics, it did foreshadow a change.

PART IV: AN EPISODIC HISTORY TO BE REPEATED?

As with the nineteenth and twentieth centuries, the dawn of the twenty-first century has produced a rise in the tide of formalized civic education. While many of the past stimulants of civic educational (e.g., concern over a large influx of immigrants, promoting and/or preserving a common American culture and identity) are motivating factors in this most recent wave, a unique feature is its strong academic element. Driving today's wave is a perceived crisis in civics. It is partially conditioned by a continued concern that our American identity is threated by immigration, but it is more fundamentally driven by a concern over the withdrawal of Americans from democratic politics. Academics have been central in giving light to this threat, and their research remains integral in movements seeking to combat it. Below is a brief sketch of three educational movements—the Service Learning, the Scholarship of Teaching and Learning (SoTL), and the Civic Mission of Schools movements—which have culminated in a twenty-first-century attempt to revive and enhance formal civic education.

Early 2000s: The Third Wave

Today, Americans of all stripes are lamenting a "civic crisis" or "recession."[111] In the introduction, I claimed three trends are fueling this perceived crisis: poor civic literacy, declining civics coverage in schools, and youth civic disengagement. Here, I want to focus on the largely academic response to this perceived crisis. A widespread civic education movement has materialized in the United States, and academics are pivotal in this revival. In particular, pivotal to this current revival are three intertwined educational movements in academia: the Service Learning, the SoTL, and the Civic Mission of Schools movements. One leg of this growth in civics—the Service Learning movement—is in many ways a revival of nineteenth-century Deweyian experiential learning through community service and involvement. This movement materialized in the 1980s and 1990s and persists today as a central feature of the civic revival today.[112] Schools once again are being civic agents and not simply civic instructors.

As for the second leg, there is the SoTL movement of the 1990s. It has produced a paradigm shift in education, particularly for colleges and universities.[113] Teachers are no longer just thinking about pedagogy individually and prospectively; we are also retrospectively and systematically assessing the effectiveness of our pedagogies and sharing that information through scholarly publications. SoTL is transforming classrooms, helping teachers identify strengths and weaknesses in their instruction, and encouraging innovations that improve learning. As Strachan and Bennion (chapter 14) explain, SoTL research is increasingly accepted as a scholarly endeavor. Through initiatives like their consortium, today's teacher-scholars can conduct research that meets the expectations of rigorous, research-oriented higher education facilities. Important strides have been made already, as academics are realizing lecture is not necessarily the most effective civic instruction approach. If the goal is more than informed citizens, SoTL research has shown deliberation and service learning are pedagogical best practices.[114] As teacher-scholars, we are better informed and learning more every day about what works pedagogically.

For the last leg of this tripartite academic revival, there is the "Civic Mission of Schools" movement. At primary and secondary levels, CIRCLE (The Center for Information & Research on Civic Learning and Engagement), the Carnegie Foundation, the Leonore Annenberg Institution for Civics, and the ABA (American Bar Association) are all groups that have come together to promote civics in schools. They have presented a series of "Civic Mission of Schools" reports and have seen their initiatives acted upon by some states (California and Oregon).[115] Yet, the Civic Mission of Schools movement is not exclusive to primary and secondary education, as presidents and chancellors at colleges and universities throughout the United States have come together to revive the civic mission of higher education, as well.[116]

So, what are the practical outcomes of these movements on America's civic ecology? Actually, renewed interest in service learning, community involvement, and civic engagement has produced significant innovations in formal civic education. For example, for primary and secondary education in Chicago there is the Mikva Challenge, and in online education there is O'Connor's Icivics.[117] In this volume, there are other collegiate initiatives like the Fort Hays State virtual civic university (chapter 15) or citizens academies (chapter 16). Then, while curricular changes are difficult to track across higher education and we know most states rarely mandate any civics requirements for higher education, it is possible to gauge the impact of the Service Learning, SoTL, and Civic Mission of Schools movements by the popularity of Campus Compact.[118] Today, Campus Compact has grown to "a national coalition of more than 1,100 colleges and universities who are committed to fulfilling the public purpose of higher education," that is, it's civic mission.[119] State, regional, and national Campus Compact conferences discussing best practices in civic education and engagement now occur annually throughout the country. Also, colleges and universities increasingly seek recognition of their civic activities by coveting the prestigious Carnegie Community Engagement Classification.[120]

As a second gauge, there is the American Democracy Project (ADP) sponsored by the American Association of State Colleges and Universities (AASCU).[121] The positive impact the ADP is having on higher education is demonstrated by two chapters in this volume. Galatas and Pressley's creation of a federal budget module for the American Government classroom (chapter 13) and Rackaway and Campbell's use of Web 2.0 tools to promote a virtual civic democracy (chapter 15) are both ADP-sponsored initiatives. Combined, Campus Compact and the ADP are transforming civic education at the microlevel of individual colleges and universities. Faculty from a diverse set of disciplines are integrating more experiential, active learning opportunities into the curriculum. On a daily basis, such faculty innovations are enhancing the civic ecology of higher education, but the challenge remains seeing these activities expanded to more than just the few colleges and universities implementing them.

As a final point, in this century the federal government continues to play an integral role in encouraging civic education and engagement. The national government has long recognized the importance of civic education. It has assessed civics routinely at the fourth, eighth, and twelfth grades through the National Assessment of Educational Progress (NAEP) exam for some time. Unfortunately, there has been some backtracking, as 2014 saw the NAEP cut fourth and twelfth grade assessment of civis due to a lack of funding.[122] However, in the face of a dearth of resources for such activities at the national level, the Obama administration continues to encourage civic education and engagement. President Obama raised concerns for civics early in his campaign, noting "[t]he loss of quality civic education from so many of our classrooms." He added, "[i]t is up to us, then, to teach them," and has made promoting civics a focus of his administration.[123] First, he formed The Civic Learning and Democratic Engagement National Task Force which produced "A Crucible Moment" in 2012.[124] This was followed by the U.S. Department of Education launching the "Civic Learning and Engagement in Democracy" initiative, as well as producing its own report, "Advancing Civic Learning and Engagement in Democracy."[125] It is too early to say what impact these government actions are having. Regardless, the more promising route to new civic initiatives throughout the country remains the academic movements discussed above, especially since the Obama initiatives do not come with financial incentives or assistance.

CONCLUDING REMARKS

With this history of America's civic education, it is apparent the previous two centuries have laid a strong foundation for formal civic education in American. CIRCLE reinforces this point, noting that "[t]he establishment of American public schools during the nineteenth century was the manifestation of this vision, which assumed that all education had civic purposes and every teacher was a civics teacher. That vision is now embedded in 40 state constitutions that mention the importance of civic literacy among citizens; 13 of these constitutions state that the central purpose of their educational system is to promote good citizenship, democracy, and free government."[126] Updating the findings of Niemi and Smith, as of 2012 I found most states require at least a semester of American government. Also, a few have actually expanded their social studies and/or civics requirements in the last few years. The number of states making such changes is still small, but the decline in civics education coverage Niemi and Smith documented seems to have ceased. Such state mandates, however, remain rare for higher education.[127]

From this overview of formal civic education in America, the ebb and flow of civic education is apparent. While the trend is wavelike, the amplitude of the waves varies considerably over time, thus contributing to the episodic nature of civic education in America. Each wave was driven by some perceived crisis in the country, although the source and particulars of the crisis differ for each period. The founding crisis was regime stability, Mann's was the existential threat to democracy of industrial capitalism and immigration, the Progressive's was the governmental crisis due to immigration and corrupt party machines, and today's is political ignorance and apathy. The common denominator in these latter perceived crises is immigration as a threat to the American identity. However, the commonalities between crises end there. The first two waves had a pronounced political element, but it was the Whigs who spurred the first and the Progressives the second. The third is not clearly party-driven, as both a Republican (George W. Bush) and a Democratic (Barack Obama) administration have contributed to the revival. The heart of the current revival is academic, not political. However, the real issue is, if the pattern in past civic eras holds, the revival will be short-lived. For both the first two waves, the decades of revival were minimal. For each wave, there resulted some growth in formal civic education for two to three decades, while the bulk of the century saw stagnation and/or decline.

Given the historical pattern of civic education in America, it is vital to explore safeguards against a future stagnation and/or decline. It remains too early to fully assess if the Service Learning, SoTL, and Civic Mission of Schools movements or the Obama (and Bush) administration initiatives will produce a substantial macrolevel increase in American civic literacy and engagement. The question is: will the microlevel adjustments in some public schools and institutions of higher education produce an enhanced American civic ecology? Certainly, what makes the dawn of this century particularly interesting and unique is the immense scholarly energy invested in promoting effective civic education. Civic education has never received an adequate empirical focus by scholars. That said, academic knowledge of effective civic education processes is stronger today and growing stronger every day. Yet, much of our innovations in civic education are still isolated practices. The challenge is how to share these best practices to the widest audience possible, to promote their adoption across the country. The goal is to link and spread successful changes in a way that transforms American civic ecology throughout the country. Only through expanding the good microlevel work does it become possible that a macrolevel improvement will materialize.

One possible way to make civic education less susceptible to volatility over time is to follow Adams's example in Massachusetts. Today, some civic education is mandated by many state constitutions but not all fifty. Many states allow for ballot initiatives or referendums where the people or state legislatures could put the issue of civic education to public vote. Still, such actions tend to be symbolic; the resulting mandates often lack much substantive content. These actions are best thought of as states setting a base standard. Put succinctly, federal and state governments have never adequately endorsed or developed a comprehensive plan for the civic education of Americans or realized a common civics curriculum (see chapter 2 by Maranto) and—to the extent Hilmer's argument (chapter 3) represents a kernel of truth—we may not want governments to do so, at least not solely. In other words, I prefer to emphasize that formal civic education is only half the question. Civic education needs to always be a combination of formal and informal mechanisms. The informal promotes a guard against simple state indoctrination, while formal institutionalization encourages stability and longevity in a civics program. More importantly, this increases the likelihood people are asked and challenged on multiple fronts to be informed and engaged citizens.

Possibly, the most promising development is state and federal governments encouraging schools and academics to continue to study and develop innovations in civic education. It must be acknowledged that schools cannot solve the problem of civic education alone.[128] That said, it is still essential to appreciate that "[s]chools are the only institutions with the capacity and mandate to reach virtually every young person in the country. Of all institutions, schools are the most systematically and directly responsible for imparting citizen norms."[129] In other words, given their reach, schools are a good place—arguably, the best place—to pursue a civic education people can access throughout the country. In addition, schools are social institutions. Once effective formal civic education programs are institutionalized in schools, these institutions have a longevity that helps guard against recession and stagnation due to neglect. As Hirsch explains, "[o]ur educational thinkers in the eighteenth and nineteenth centuries saw the schools as the central and main hope for the preservation of democratic ideals and the endurance of the nation as a republic."[130]

If the civic past is indicative of our future, then Galston's "gloomy hypothesis" will likely be confirmed. He writes:

> Like citizenship itself, civic education may be a "public good" that self-interested individuals, groups, and institutions are not adequately motivated to supply. The result is likely to be a chronic shortage of civic-mindedness, relieved

only occasionally and temporarily when events conspire to heighten national unity and reinforce the efforts of the beleaguered band of civic educators.[131]

However, if the unique academic nature of our current revival is as positive a development as I suggest, then maybe we can break with the pattern of the past. Put simply, scientific study of what works combined with institutionalization of those practices through schools and other organizations may just be the way to develop a stable twenty-first-century formal civic education able to resist stagnation and decline. Through a healthy civic ecology that combines a formal civic education program that routinely promotes and assesses civic innovation with a robust informal one, America can produce an environment that encourages civic literacy and engagement. Such an environment will not undersupply this public good.

NOTES

1. Barry Checkoway, "Renewing the Civic Mission of the American Research University," *The Journal of Higher Education* 72, no. 1 (2001): 140.

2. Samuel Huntington, *The Third Wave: Democratization in the Late Twentieth Century* (Norman: University of Oklahoma Press, 1991).

3. See Sheldon Wolin, "Fugitive Democracy," *Constellations* 1, no. 1 (1994).

4. For explanation of the difference between informal and formal civic education, see Michael T. Rogers, "A Civic Education Crisis," *Midsouth Political Science Review* 13, no. 1 (2012): 2–6.

5. Elizabeth Kaufer Busch and Jonathan W. White, "Introduction," in *Civic Education and the Future of American Citizenship*, ed. Elizabeth Kaufer Busch and Jonathan W. White (Lanham: Lexington Books, 2013), 8.

6. Derek Heater, *History of Education for Citizenship* (New York, NY: RoutledgeFalmer, 2004).

7. My inspiration for describing this general history of formal civic education which is constructed from other historical narratives as a meta-history comes from Campbell's depiction of Wolf's review of fifty-nine studies of civic education as a "meta-analysis." See David E. Campbell, "Civic Education in Traditional Public, Charter and Private Schools: Moving from Comparison to Explanation," in *Making Civics Count: Citizenship Education for a New Generation*, ed. David E. Campbell, Meira Levinson, and Frederick M. Hess (Cambridge: Harvard Education Press, 2012), 235.

8. Lorraine Smith Pangle and Thomas L. Pangle, *The Learning of Liberty: The Educational Ideas of the American Founders* (Lawrence: University of Kansas Press, 1993); Lorraine Smith Pangle and Thomas L. Pangle, "What the American Founders Have to Teach Us about Schooling for Democratic Citizenship," in *Rediscovering the Democratic Purposes of Education*, ed. Lorraine M. McDonnell, P. Michael Timpane, and Roger Benjamin (Lawrence: University of Kansas Press, 2000).

9. Bob Pepperman Taylor, *Horace Mann's Troubling Legacy: The Education of Democratic Citizens* (University Press of Kansas, 2010).

10. See Claire Snyder, "Should Political Scientists Have a Civic Mission? An Overview of the Historical Evidence," *PS: Political Science and Politics* 34, no. 2 (2001); Carl F. Kaestle, *Pillars of the Republic: Common Schools and American Society, 1780–1860* (New York: Hill and Wang, 1983); Carl F. Kaestle, "Toward a Political Economy of Citizenship: Historical Perspectives on the Purpose of Common Schools," in *Rediscovering the Democratic Purposes of Education*, ed. Lorraine M. McDonnell, P. Michael Timpane, and Roger Benjamin (Lawrence: University of Kansas Press, 2000).

11. Checkoway, "Renewing the Civic Mission of the American Research University," 140.

12. Amy Gutmann, *Democratic Education*, Second ed. (Princeton: Princeton University Press, 1999), 19.

13. Ibid., 19.

14. Ibid., 287.

15. Washington advises, "Promote, then, as an object of primary importance, institutions for the general diffusion of knowledge. In proportion as the structure of a government gives force to public opinion, it is essential that public opinion should be enlightened." See George Washington, "George Washington's Farewell Address," *The Independent Chronicle* (1796), http://www.earlyamerica.com/earlyamerica/mile stones/farewell/text.html.

16. Sandra Day O'Connor, "The Democratic Purpose of Education: From the Founders to Horace Mann to Today," in *Teaching America: The Case for Civic Education*, ed. David Feith (Lanham: Rowman & Littlefield Education, 2011), 3–4. Other scholars provide similar lists, see for example E. D. Hirsch Jr., "The Inspiring Idea of the Common School," in *Civic Education and the Future of American Citizenship*, ed. Elizabeth Kaufer Busch and Jonathan W. White (Lanham: Lexington Books, 2013); Anne Colby et al., *Educating Citizens: Preparing America's Undergraduates for Lives of Moral and Civic Responsibility* (San Francisco: The Carnegie Foundation for the Advancement of Teaching, 2003).

17. Pangle and Pangle, "What the American Founders Have to Teach Us about Schooling for Democratic Citizenship"; Pangle and Pangle, *The Learning of Liberty*.

18. A. Whitney Griswold, *Liberal Education and the Democratic Ideal and Other Essays* (New Haven: Yale University Press, 1959), 2–3.

19. Busch and White, "Introduction," 1.

20. Pangle and Pangle, *The Learning of Liberty*, 4.

21. Pangle and Pangle, "What the American Founders Have to Teach Us about Schooling for Democratic Citizenship," 24.

22. Pangle and Pangle, *The Learning of Liberty*, 5.

23. Pangle and Pangle, "What the American Founders Have to Teach Us about Schooling for Democratic Citizenship," 31.

24. Ibid., 41.

25. Pangle and Pangle, *The Learning of Liberty*, 27.

26. Ibid., 28.

27. Pangle and Pangle, "What the American Founders Have to Teach Us about Schooling for Democratic Citizenship," 34–35.

28. Pangle and Pangle, *The Learning of Liberty*, 100–101.

29. Ibid.

30. Ibid., 96–97. For Adams, see the quote that opens this section.

31. Ibid., 93. Again, for Adams see the quote to open this section.

32. Ibid., 99.

33. Colby et al., *Educating Citizens*, 26–28.

34. Snyder, "Should Political Scientists Have a Civic Mission?," 302.

35. Ibid., 301–2.

36. Ibid.

37. Kaestle, "Toward a Political Economy of Citizenship," 48.

38. Snyder, "Should Political Scientists Have a Civic Mission?," 302. See also Hirsch, "The Inspiring Idea of the Common School," 16.

39. Snyder, "Should Political Scientists Have a Civic Mission?," 302.

40. David Tyack and Thomas James, "Education for a Republic: Federal Influence on Public Schooling in the Nation's First Century," in *This Constitution: A Bicentennial Chronicle* (American Political Science Association American Historical Association, 1985). www.apsanet.org/imgtest/PublicSchooling.pdf (accessed June 6, 2014).

41. Snyder, "Should Political Scientists Have a Civic Mission?," 302.

42. Antonin Scalia, "Constitutional Government and Civic Education," *Ultraque Unum* 1, no. 19–15 (2007): 13. Of course, emphasis of civic education in the Declaration of Rights in the Massachusetts Constitution was borrowed heavily from what George Mason did with the Virginia Declaration of Rights. See Busch and White, "Introduction," 1.

43. K. Langton and M. K. Jennings, "Political Socialization and the High School Civics Curriculum in the United States," *American Political Science Review* 62 (1968): 852.

44. Hirsch, "The Inspiring Idea of the Common School," 16.

45. Kaestle, "Toward a Political Economy of Citizenship," 48.

46. Pangle and Pangle, *The Learning of Liberty*, 37.

47. Hirsch, "The Inspiring Idea of the Common School," 16.

48. Tyack and James, "Education for a Republic."

49. Hirsch, "The Inspiring Idea of the Common School," 17.

50. Ibid., 18.

51. Tyack and James, "Education for a Republic."

52. Hirsch, "The Inspiring Idea of the Common School," 26.

53. For Tocqueville's depiction of America's civic education program in the early 1800s, see volume I (chapters V, VI, IX–XII, XVI–XVII) and volume II the first book (chapter V), the second book (chapters IV–VII), and the third book (Chapters IX–XI) in Alexis de Tocqueville, *Democracy in America*, ed. Phillips Bradley, 2 vols., vol. 1 & 2 (Vintage Books, 1990).

54. O'Connor, "The Democratic Purpose of Education," 4–5.

55. Taylor, *Horace Mann's Troubling Legacy*, 8–9.

56. Ibid., 13.

57. Ibid., 7.

58. Ibid., 21.

59. Hirsch, "The Inspiring Idea of the Common School," 24.

60. Mann went so far as to suggest a capitalist feudalism threatened American democracy. See Taylor, *Horace Mann's Troubling Legacy*, 18.

61. Ibid., 32–33.

62. Ibid., 19–20.

63. Ibid., 30.

64. Ibid., 25.

65. Hirsch, "The Inspiring Idea of the Common School," 18.

66. Busch and White, "Introduction," 4.

67. Taylor, *Horace Mann's Troubling Legacy*, 34.

68. Kaestle, "Toward a Political Economy of Citizenship," 53.

69. Ibid., 54. For the definitive history on the Common School movement see Carl Kaestle, *Pillars of the Republic: Commmon Schools and American Society, 1780–1860*, American Century (New York: Hill and Wang, 1983).

70. Kaestle, *Pillars of the Republic*.

71. Ibid.

72. Hirsch, "The Inspiring Idea of the Common School," 17.

73. Kaestle, "Toward a Political Economy of Citizenship," 63–64; Kaestle, *Pillars of the Republic*. Also, for a thorough treatment of this history and the failure to realize a uniform curriculum through the common school, Kaestle recommends Ira Katznelson and Margaret Weir's *Schooling for All: Class, Race, and the Decline of the Democratic Ideal* (Oakland: University of California Press, 1988).

74. Jeffrey Mirel, "Civic Education and Changing Definitions of American Identity, 1900–1950," *Educational Review* 54, no. 2 (2002): 144.

75. Ibid., 145.

76. Mirel's article where he makes this observation is cited in O'Connor, "The Democratic Purpose of Education," 5.

77. Kaestle, "Toward a Political Economy of Citizenship," 56–57.

78. Taylor, *Horace Mann's Troubling Legacy*, 6.

79. For an introduction to his educational ideals, see John Dewey, *Democracy and Education: An Introduction to the Philosophy of Education* (Free Press, 1997). See also John Dewey, *The Public & Its Problems* (Athens: Swallow Press/Ohio Univeristy Press, 1954 [1927]).

80. Michael C. Johanek, "Preparing Pluribus for Unum: Historicial Perspectives on Civic Education," in *Making Civics Count: Citizenship for a New Generation*, ed. David E. Campbell, Meira Levinson, and Frederick M. Hess (Cambridge: Harvard Education Press, 2012), 60–61.

81. Ibid., 61 & 64.

82. These courses materialized after the 1916 Social Studies Committee of the Commission on the Reorganization of Secondary Education recommended that there be courses in "civics, government and problems of democracy." See Richard G. Niemi and Julia Smith, "Enrollments in High School Government Classes: Are We Short-Changing Both Citizenship and Political Science Training?," *PS: Political Science and Politics* 34, no. 2 (2001): 281.

83. Johanek, "Preparing Pluribus for Unum," 65.

84. John R. Thelin, "Talk Is Cheap: The University and the National Project—a History," in *Teaching America: The Case for Civic Education*, ed. David Feith (Lanham: Rowman & Littlefield Education, 2011), 152–53.

85. Ibid., 154–55.

86. John R. Hibbing and Elizabeth Theiss-Morse, "Civics Is Not Enough: Teaching Barbarics in K–12," *PS: Political Science & Politics* 29, no. 1 (1996).

87. O'Connor, "The Democratic Purpose of Education," 6; Bob Graham and Chris Hand, *America, the Owner's Manual: Making Government Work for You* (Washington, DC: CQ Press, 2009), 22. For the empirical study verifying O'Connor's and Graham's claims, see Niemi and Smith, "Enrollments in High School Government Classes?." This is as close as America has come to realizing Hirsch's expectation of a common civics education program that promotes a common American identity. The one glaring defect, this three-course norm never quite gave life to a standard civics content throughout the country.

88. Michael J. Sandel, "Liberal Education and the Civic Project," in *To Restore American Democracy*, ed. Robert E. Calvert (Lanham, MD: Rowman and Littlefield Publishers, Inc., 2006), 47. For a similar argument, see Hilmer's chapter 3 of this edited volume.

89. Tom Brokaw, *The Greatest Generation* (New York: Random House, 2000).

90. Robert Putnam, *Bowling Alone: The Collapse and Revival of American Community* (New York: Simon and Schuster, 2000); Robert Putnam, "Bowling Alone: America's Declining Social Capital," *Journal of Democracy* 6, no. 1 (June 1995); Robert Putnam, "Tuning in, Tuning Out: The Strange Disappearance of Social Capital in America," *PS: Political Science and Politics* 28, no. 4 (Dec. 1995).

91. Harry Boyte and Elizabeth Hollander, "Wingspread Declaration on Renewing the Civic Mission of the American Research University," (1999), http://www.compact.org/wp-content/uploads/2009/04/wingspread_declaration.pdf.

92. Hirsch, "The Inspiring Idea of the Common School," 28–29.

93. Ibid., 31. See also Lorraine M. McDonnell, "Defining Democratic Purposes," in *Rediscovering the Democratic Purposes of Education*, ed. Lorraine M. McDonnell, P. Michael Timpane, and Roger Benjamin (Lawrence: University of Kansas Press, 2000); Tobi Walker, "Service as a Pathway to Political Participation: What Research Tells Us," *Applied Development Science* 6, no. 4 (2002).

94. Mirel, "Civic Education and Changing Definitions of American Identity, 1900–1950," 143–44.

95. Ibid., 149.

96. O'Connor, "The Democratic Purpose of Education," 6–7; Colby et al., *Educating Citizens*, 6–7.

97. For examples, see, Jonathan Yonan, "Majoring in Servitude: Liberal Arts and the Formation of Citizen," in *Civic Education and the Future of American Citizenship*, ed. Elizabeth Kaufer Busch and Jonathan W. White (Lanham: Lexington Books, 2013); John Agresto, "'Reflection and Choice': The Problem and the Promise of the Liberal Arts in America," in *Civic Education and the Future of American Citizenship*, ed. Elizabeth Kaufer Busch and Jonathan W. White (Lanham: Lexington Books, 2013); Kaestle, "Toward a Political Economy of Citizenship," 47; Frederick M. Hess,

in *Teaching America: The Case for Civic Education*, ed. David Feith (Lanham: Rowman and Littlefield Education, 2011), xiii; D. Sunshine Hillygus, "The Missing Link: Exploring the Relationship between Higher Education and Political Engagement," *Political Behavior* 27, no. 1 (2005); Thelin, "Talk Is Cheap."

98. Colby et al., *Educating Citizens*.

99. For an introduction to the politics of civic education, see the series of articles on the subject in *PS: Political Science & Politics* 37, no. 2 (April 2004): 231–266. For the social studies text all these articles are responding to, see James S. Leming, Lucien Ellington, and Kathleen Porter, *Where Did Scoial Studies Go Wrong?* (Washington, DC: Thomas B. Fordham Foundation, 2003). Also, see Barbara Finkelstein, "Rescuing Civic Learning: Some Prescriptions for the 1990s," *Theory into Practice* 27, no. 4 (1988).

100. For studies discussing this transformation in higher education to the German research model in the 1900s, see Snyder, "Should Political Scientists Have a Civic Mission?"; Colby et al., *Educating Citizens*; Stephen T. Leonard, "'Pure Futility and Waste': Academic Political Science and Civic Education," *PS: Political Science and Politics* 32, no. 4 (Dec. 1999).

101. Niemi and Smith, "Enrollments in High School Government Classes," 282.

102. Ibid., 284.

103. Ibid., 281–82.

104. Ibid., 283. For a more recent analysis that finds the norm largely the same after the first decade of the twenty-first century, see Rogers, "A Civic Education Crisis." For an additional article advocating enhancing the American civics curriculum through state mandates, see Jacques Benninga and Brandy Quinn, "Enhancing American Identity and Citizenship in Schools," *Applied Development Science* 15, no. 2 (2011).

105. Niemi and Smith, "Enrollments in High School Government Classes." Italics in original text.

106. Ibid., 284.

107. I have summarized this scholarship elsewhere; see Rogers, "A Civic Education Crisis."

108. The National Commission on Excellence in Education, "A Nation at Risk: The Imperative for Education Research," (1983). http://datacenter.spps.org/uploads/sotw_a_nation_at_risk_1983.pdf (accessed June 6, 2014).

109. Kaestle, "Toward a Political Economy of Citizenship," 57.

110. Hirsch, "The Inspiring Idea of the Common School," 30.

111. For an introduction to the diverse entities (politicians, government bureaucrats, journalists, etc.) concerned about American civic education, see David Feith, ed. *Teaching America: The Case for Civic Education* (Lanham: Rowman and Littlefield Education, 2011). Feith's edited volume gives one a sense of the concern about civic education during the George W. Bush administration. The Obama administration has been just as concerned. It has produced "A Crucible Moment: College Learning & Democracy's Future" (Washington, DC: National Task Force on Civic Learning and Democratic Engagement, 2012) and "Advancing Civic Learning and Engagement in Democracy: A Road Map and Call to Action" (Washington, DC: U.S. Department of Education, 2012).

In addition, for an exemplar of the scholarly take on the issue there is Stephen Macedo et al., *Democracy at Risk: How Political Choices Undermine Citizen Participation, and What We Can Do about It* (Washington, DC: Brookings Institute Press, 2005); Kenneth Stroupe Jr. and Larry Sabato, "Politics: The Missing Link of Responsible Civic Eduation" (2004), http://www.civicyouth.org/PopUps/civicengagement -stroupe-final.pdf.

Also, two think tanks in particular have done extensive research on the civics crisis: ISI (Intercollegiate Studies Institute) and CIRCLE (The Center for Information and Research on Civic Learning and Engagement). For the former see ISI, "The Coming Crisis in Citizenship," ed. Intercollegiate Studies Institute's National Civic Literacy Board (Intercollegiate Studies Institute, 2006); "Failing Our Students, Failing America: Holding Colleges Accountable for Teaching America's History and Institutions," ed. Intercollegiate Studies Institute's National Civic Literacy Board (Intercollegiate Studies Institute, 2007–2008); "Our Fading Heritage: Americans Fail a Basic Test on Their History and Institutions," in *Intecollegiate Studies Institute's American Civic Literacy Program* (Intercollegiate Studies Institute, 2008–2009). For the latter, see the numerous reports available through their website: CIRCLE, The Center for Information & Research on Civic Learning and Engagement, http://www .civicyouth.org/.

The civics crisis has even been known to make the headlines of mainstream newspapers. For example, see Sam Dillon, "Failing Grades on Civics Exam Called a 'Crisis,'" *The New York Times* 2011; "Study: More Know 'The Simpsons' Than First Amendment Rights," *USA Today*, 3/1/2006; "Study: More Know 'Simpsons' Than Constitution," FoxNews.com, http://www.foxnews.com/story/2006/03/01/ study-more-know-simpsons-than-constitution/; Anna Johnson, "Tuned to America: 'Simpsons' Trumps Civics in Study, Many Know Sitcom but Not Their Rights," *The Boston Globe*, March 1, 2006.

112. For an introduction to the history of service-learning, see the National Service-Learning Clearinghouse, "History of Service-Learning in Higher Education," (Learn and Serve America, January 2008); Timothy K. Stanton, Jr., Dwight E. Giles, and Nadinne I. Cruz, *Service-Learning: A Movement's Pioneers Reflect on Its Origins, Practice and Future* (San Francisco: Jossey-Bass, 1999).

113. For an introduction to the SoTL movement, see Ernest L. Boyer, *Scholarship Reconsidered: Priorities of the Professoriate* (New York: The Carnegie Foundation for the Advancement of Teaching, 1990); Charles E. Glassick, Mary Taylor Huber, and Gene I. Maeroff, *Scholarship Assessed: Evaluation of the Professoriate* (San Francisco: Jossey-Bass & The Carnegie Foundation fo the Advancement of Teaching, 1997); Kathleen McKinney and K. Patricia Cross, *Enhancing Learning through the Scholarship of Teaching and Learning: The Challenges and Joys of Juggling* (San Francisco: Anker Publishing, 2007); Pat Hutchings, Mary Taylor Huber, and Anthony Ciccone, *The Scholarship of Teaching and Learning Reconsidered: Institutional Integration and Impact* (Stanford: The Carnegie Foundation for the Advancement of Teaching & Jossey-Bass, 2011).

114. For a summary of known best practices, see James Youniss, "Civic Education: What Schools Can Do to Encourage Civic Identity and Action," *Applied Development*

Science 15, no. 2 (2011); James Youniss, "How to Enrich Civic Education and Sustain Democracy," in *Making Civics Count: Citizenship Education for a New Generation*, ed. David E. Campbell, Meira Levinson, and Frederick M. Hess (Cambridge: Harvard Education Press, 2012). The primary mechanism for sharing best teaching practices in political science is *The Journal of Political Science Education*.

115. For the two most influential reports, see Cynthia Gibdon et al., "The Civic Mission of Schools" (The Center for Information & Research on Civic Learning and Engagement with Carnegie Corporation of New York, 2003); "Guardian of Democarcy: The Civic Mission of Schools," ed. Jonathan Gould (2011). For state initiatives, see "The California Survey of Civic Education," *Educating for Democracy: California Campaign for the Civic Mission of Schools* (2005), http://www.cms-ca.org/civic_survey_final.pdf; "Oregon Civics Survey 2006," *Educating for Democracy: Oregon Coalition for the Civic Mission of Schools* (2006), http://www.classroomlaw.org/files/posts-pages/about/2006_or_civics_survey.pdf. For information on the Civic Mission of Schools campaign today, see the "Campaign for the Civic Mission of Schools: Education for Demcoracy," Leonore Annenberg Institution for Civics, http://www.civicmissionofschools.org/the-campaign/educating-for-democracy?gclid=Cj0KEQiAq_SkBRC3jLvJ1IPt2eIBEiQASUZy18brq8PFswjMk47TubpQkDNnPBIWIxo5KGChpSnJFnIaAvSl8P8HAQ.

116. See Boyte and Hollander, "Wingspread Declaration on Renewing the Civic Mission of the American Research University"; Checkoway, "Renewing the Civic Mission of the American Research University."

117. Ann Rosefsky Saavedra, "Dry to Dynamic Civic Education Curricula," in *Making Civics Count: Citizenship Education for a New Generation*, ed. David E. Campbell, Meira Levinson, and Frederick M. Hess (Cambridge: Harvard Education Press, 2012); "What Is Icivics?," Filament Games, http://www.icivics.org/About. For some other school initiatives, see Seth Andrew, "Fighting Civic Malpractice: How a Harlem Charter School Closes the Civic Achievement Gap," in *Teaching America: The Case for Civic Education*, ed. David Feith (Lanham: Rowman & Littlefield Education, 2011); Mike Feinberg, "The Kipp Approach: Be the Change You Wish to See in the World," in *Teaching America: The Case for Civic Education*, ed. David Feith (Lanham: Rowman & Littlefield Education, 2011). For additional digital opportunities, see Joseph Kahne, Jacqueline Ullman, and Ellen Middaugh, "Digital Opportunities for Civic Education," in *Making Civics Count: Citizenship Education for a New Generation*, ed. David E. Campbell, Meira Levinson, and Frederick M. Hess (Cambridge: Harvard University Press, 2012).

118. Rogers, "A Civic Education Crisis"; Karen Kedrowski, "Civic Education by Mandate: A State-by-State Analysis," *PS: Political Science and Politics* 36, no. 2 (2003).

119. "Campus Compact," http://www.compact.org/about/history-mission-vision/.

120. Campus Compact, "Carnegie Community Engagement Classification," http://www.compact.org/initiatives/carnegie-community-engagement-classification/.

121. American Association of State Colleges and Universities, "About ADP," American Association of State Colleges and Universities, http://www.aascu.org/programs/ADP/.

122. "Civics Framework for the 2014 National Assessment of Education Progress," National Assessment Governing Board, http://www.nagb.org/publications/frameworks/civics/2014-civics-framework.html.

123. "Barack Obama's Speech in Independence, Mo.," *The New York Times* June 30, 2008.

124. "A Crucible Moment."

125. "Advancing Civic Learning and Engagement in Democracy."

126. Gibdon et al., "The Civic Mission of Schools," 11.

127. Rogers, "A Civic Education Crisis."

128. See Stroupe and Sabato, "Politics."

129. "The Civic Mission of Schools," (2006), http://www.classroomlaw.org/files/posts-pages/about/2006_or_civics_survey.pdf.

130. Hirsch, "The Inspiring Idea of the Common School," 15.

131. William A. Galston, "Between Resignation and Utopia," in *To Restore American Democracy*, ed. Robert E. Calvert (Lanham, MD: Rowman & Littlefield Publishers, Inc., 2006), 35.

BIBLIOGRAPHY

"Advancing Civic Learning and Engagement in Democracy: A Road Map and Call to Action." 28. Washington, DC: U.S. Department of Education, 2012.

Agresto, John. "'Reflection and Choice': The Problem and the Promise of the Liberal Arts in America." In *Civic Education and the Future of American Citizenship*, edited by Elizabeth Kaufer Busch and Jonathan W. White, 139–50. Lanham: Lexington Books, 2013.

American Association of State Colleges and Universities. "About ADP." American Association of State Colleges and Universities, http://www.aascu.org/programs/ADP/.

Andrew, Seth. "Fighting Civic Malpractice: How a Harlem Charter School Closes the Civic Achievement Gap." In *Teaching America: The Case for Civic Education*, edited by David Feith, 99–109. Lanham: Rowman & Littlefield Education, 2011.

"Barack Obama's Speech in Independence, Mo." *The New York Times*, June 30, 2008.

Benninga, Jacques, and Brandy Quinn. "Enhancing American Identity and Citizenship in Schools." *Applied Development Science* 15, no. 2 (2011): 104–10.

Boyer, Ernest L. *Scholarship Reconsidered: Priorities of the Professoriate.* New York: The Carnegie Foundation for the Advancement of Teaching, 1990.

Boyte, Harry, and Elizabeth Hollander. "Wingspread Declaration on Renewing the Civic Mission of the American Research University." (1999). http://www.compact.org/wp-content/uploads/2009/04/wingspread_declaration.pdf.

Brokaw, Tom. *The Greatest Generation.* New York: Random House, 2000.

Busch, Elizabeth Kaufer, and Jonathan W. White. "Introduction." In *Civic Education and the Future of American Citizenship*, edited by Elizabeth Kaufer Busch and Jonathan W. White, 1–12. Lanham: Lexington Books, 2013.

"The California Survey of Civic Education." *Educating for Democracy: California Campaign for the Civic Mission of Schools* (2005), http://www.cms-ca.org/civic_survey_final.pdf.

"Campaign for the Civic Mission of Schools: Education for Demcoracy." Leonore Annenberg Institution for Civics, http://www.civicmissionofschools.org/the-campaign/educating-for-democracy?gclid=Cj0KEQiAq_SkBRC3jLvJ1IPt2eIBEiQA SUZy18brq8PFswjMk47TubpQkDNnPBIWIxo5KGChpSnJFnIaAvSl8P8HAQ.

Campbell, David E. "Civic Education in Traditional Public, Charter and Private Schools: Moving from Comparison to Explanation." In *Making Civics Count: Citizenship Education for a New Generation*, edited by David E. Campbell, Meira Levinson, and Frederick M. Hess, 229–46. Cambridge: Harvard Education Press, 2012.

"Campus Compact." http://www.compact.org/about/history-mission-vision/.

Checkoway, Barry. "Renewing the Civic Mission of the American Research University." *The Journal of Higher Education* 72, no. 1 (2001): 125–47.

CIRCLE. The Center for Information & Research on Civic Learning and Engagement, http://www.civicyouth.org/.

"The Civic Mission of Schools." (2006), http://www.classroomlaw.org/files/posts -pages/about/2006_or_civics_survey.pdf.

"Civics Framework for the 2014 National Assessment of Education Progress." National Assessment Governing Board, http://www.nagb.org/publications/frame works/civics/2014-civics-framework.html.

Colby, Anne, Thomas Ehrlich, Elizabeth Beaumont, and Jason Stephens. *Educating Citizens: Preparing America's Undergraduates for Lives of Moral and Civic Responsibility*. San Francisco: The Carnegie Foundation for the Advancement of Teaching, 2003.

Campus Compact. "Carnegie Community Engagement Classification." http://www .compact.org/initiatives/carnegie-community-engagement-classification/.

"A Crucible Moment: College Learning & Democracy's Future." Washington, DC: National Task Force on Civic Learning and Democratic Engagement, 2012.

de Tocqueville, Alexis. *Democracy in America*. Edited by Phillips Bradley. 2 vols. Vol. 1 & 2: Vintage Books, 1990.

Dewey, John. *Democracy and Education: An Introduction to the Philosophy of Education*: Free Press, 1997.

———. *The Public & Its Problems*. Athens: Swallow Press/Ohio Univeristy Press, 1954 [1927].

Dillon, Sam. "Failing Grades on Civics Exam Called a 'Crisis.'" *The New York Times*, 2011.

Feinberg, Mike. "The Kipp Approach: Be the Change You Wish to See in the World." In *Teaching America: The Case for Civic Education*, edited by David Feith. Lanham: Rowman & Littlefield Education, 2011.

Feith, David, ed. *Teaching America: The Case for Civic Education*. Lanham: Rowman and Littlefield Education, 2011.

Finkelstein, Barbara. "Rescuing Civic Learning: Some Prescriptions for the 1990s." *Theory into Practice* 27, no. 4 (1988): 250–55.

Galston, William A. "Between Resignation and Utopia." In *To Restore American Democracy*, edited by Robert E. Calvert, 29–43. Lanham, MD: Rowman & Littlefield Publishers, Inc., 2006.

Gibdon, Cynthia, Peter Levine, Richard Battistoni, and Sheldon Berman. "The Civic Mission of Schools." The Center for Information & Research on Civic Learning and Engagement with Carnegie Corporation of New York, 2003.

Glassick, Charles E., Mary Taylor Huber, and Gene I. Maeroff. *Scholarship Assessed: Evaluation of the Professoriate*. San Francisco: Jossey-Bass & The Carnegie Foundation for the Advancement of Teaching, 1997.

Graham, Bob, and Chris Hand. *America, the Owner's Manual: Making Government Work for You*. Washington, DC: CQ Press, 2009.

———. "A Failure of Leadership: The Duty of Politicians and Universities to Salvage Citizenship." In *Teaching America: The Case for Civic Education*, edited by David Feith, 61–68. Lanham: Rowman & Littlefield Education, 2011.

Griswold, A. Whitney. *Liberal Education and the Democratic Ideal and Other Essays*. New Haven: Yale University Press, 1959.

"Guardian of Democarcy: The Civic Mission of Schools." Edited by Jonathan Gould, 56, 2011.

Gutmann, Amy. *Democratic Education*. Second ed. Princeton: Princeton University Press, 1999.

Heater, Derek. *History of Education for Citizenship*. New York, NY: Routledge-Falmer, 2004.

Hess, Frederick M. In *Teaching America: The Case for Civic Education*, edited by David Feith, xi–xv. Lanham: Rowman and Littlefield Education, 2011.

Hibbing, John R., and Elizabeth Theiss-Morse. "Civics Is Not Enough: Teaching Barbarics in K–12." *PS: Political Science & Politics* 29, no. 1 (1996): 57–62.

Hillygus, D. Sunshine. "The Missing Link: Exploring the Relationship between Higher Education and Political Engagement." *Political Behavior* 27, no. 1 (2005): 25–47.

Hirsch, E. D., Jr. "The Inspiring Idea of the Common School." In *Civic Education and the Future of American Citizenship*, edited by Elizabeth Kaufer Busch and Jonathan W. White, 15–35. Lanham: Lexington Books, 2013.

Huntington, Samuel. *The Third Wave: Democratization in the Late Twentieth Century*. Norman: University of Oklahoma Press, 1991.

Hutchings, Pat, Mary Taylor Huber, and Anthony Ciccone. *The Scholarship of Teaching and Learning Reconsidered: Institutional Integration and Impact*. Stanford: The Carnegie Foundation for the Advancement of Teaching & Jossey-Bass, 2011.

ISI. "The Coming Crisis in Citizenship." Edited by Intercollegiate Studies Institute's National Civic Literacy Board: Intercollegiate Studies Institute, 2006.

———. "Failing Our Students, Failing America: Holding Colleges Accountable for Teaching America's History and Institutions." Edited by Intercollegiate Studies Institute's National Civic Literacy Board: Intercollegiate Studies Institute, 2007–2008.

———. "Our Fading Heritage: Americans Fail a Basic Test on Their History and Institutions." In *Intecollegiate Studies Institute's American Civic Literacy Program*: Intercollegiate Studies Institute, 2008–2009.

Johanek, Michael C. "Preparing Pluribus for Unum: Historicial Perspectives on Civic Education." In *Making Civics Count: Citizenship for a New Generation*, edited by David E. Campbell, Meira Levinson and Frederick M. Hess, 57–87. Cambridge: Harvard Education Press, 2012.

Johnson, Anna. "Tuned to America: 'Simpsons' Trumps Civics in Study, Many Know Sitcom but Not Their Rights." *The Boston Globe*, March 1, 2006.

Kaestle, Carl F. *Pillars of the Republic: Common Schools and American Society, 1780–1860*. New York: Hill and Wang, 1983.

———. "Toward a Political Economy of Citizenship: Historical Perspectives on the Purpose of Common Schools." In *Rediscovering the Democratic Purposes of Education*, edited by Lorraine M. McDonnell, P. Michael Timpane, and Roger Benjamin, 47–72. Lawrence: University of Kansas Press, 2000.

Kahne, Joseph, Jacqueline Ullman, and Ellen Middaugh. "Digital Opportunities for Civic Education." In *Making Civics Count: Citizenship Education for a New Generation*, edited by David E. Campbell, Meira Levinson, and Frederick M. Hess, 207–28. Cambridge: Harvard University Press, 2012.

Katznelson, Ira and Margaret Weir. *Schooling for All: Class, Race, and the Decline of the Democratic Ideal*. Oakland: The University of California Press, 1988.

Kedrowski, Karen. "Civic Education by Mandate: A State-by-State Analysis." *PS: Political Science and Politics* 36, no. 2 (2003): 225–27.

Langton, K., and M. K. Jennings. "Political Socialization and the High School Civics Curriculum in the United States." *American Political Science Review* 62 (1968): 862–67.

Leming, James S., Lucien Ellington, and Kathleen Porter. *Where Did Scoial Studies Go Wrong?* Washington, DC: Thomas B. Fordham Foundation, 2003.

Leonard, Stephen T. "'Pure Futility and Waste': Academic Political Science and Civic Education." *PS: Political Science and Politics* 32, no. 4 (Dec. 1999): 749–54.

Macedo, Stephen, Yvette Alex-Assensch, Jeffrey M. Berry, Michael Brintnall, David E. Campbell, Luis Ricardo Fraga, Archon Fung, William A. Galston, Christopher F. Karpowitz, Margaret Levi, Meira Levinson, Keena Lipsitz, Richard G. Niemi, Robert D. Putnam, Wendy M. Rahn, Robert Reich, Todd Swanstrom, and Katherine Cramer Walsh. *Democracy at Risk: How Political Choices Undermine Citizen Participation, and What We Can Do about It*. Washington, DC: Brookings Institute Press, 2005.

McDonnell, Lorraine M. "Defining Democratic Purposes." In *Rediscovering the Democratic Purposes of Education*, edited by Lorraine M. McDonnell, P. Michael Timpane, and Roger Benjamin, 1–18. Lawrence: University of Kansas Press, 2000.

McKinney, Kathleen, and K. Patricia Cross. *Enhancing Learning through the Scholarship of Teaching and Learning: The Challenges and Joys of Juggling*. San Francisco: Anker Publishing, 2007.

Mirel, Jeffrey. "Civic Education and Changing Definitions of American Identity, 1900–1950." *Educational Review* 54, no. 2 (2002): 143–52.

The National Commission on Excellence in Education. "A Nation at Risk: The Imperative for Education Research." 1983.

National Service-Learning Clearinghouse. "History of Service-Learning in Higher Education." Learn and Serve America, January 2008.

Niemi, Richard G., and Julia Smith. "Enrollments in High School Government Classes: Are We Short-Changing Both Citizenship and Political Science Training?" *PS: Political Science and Politics* 34, no. 2 (2001): 281–87.

O'Connor, Sandra Day. "The Democratic Purpose of Education: From the Founders to Horace Mann to Today." In *Teaching America: The Case for Civic Education*, edited by David Feith, 3–14. Lanham: Rowman & Littlefield Education, 2011.

"Oregon Civics Survey 2006." *Educating for Democracy: Oregon Coalition for the Civic Mission of Schools* (2006), http://www.classroomlaw.org/files/posts-pages/about/2006_or_civics_survey.pdf.

Pangle, Lorraine Smith, and Thomas L. Pange. "What the American Founders Have to Teach Us about Schooling for Democratic Citizenship." In *Rediscovering the Democratic Purposes of Education*, edited by Lorraine M. McDonnell, P. Michael Timpane, and Roger Benjamin, 21–46. Lawrence: University of Kansas Press, 2000.

———. *The Learning of Liberty: The Educational Ideas of the American Founders*. Lawrence: University of Kansas Press, 1993.

Putnam, Robert. "Bowling Alone: America's Declining Social Capital." *Journal of Democracy* 6, no. 1 (June 1995): 65–78.

———. *Bowling Alone: The Collapse and Revival of American Community*. New York: Simon and Schuster, 2000.

———. "Tuning in, Tuning Out: The Strange Disappearance of Social Capital in America." *PS: Political Science and Politics* 28, no. 4 (Dec. 1995): 664–83.

Rogers, Michael T. "A Civic Education Crisis." *Midsouth Political Science Review* 13, no. 1 (2012): 1–36.

Saavedra, Ann Rosefsky. "Dry to Dynamic Civic Education Curricula." In *Making Civics Count: Citizenship Education for a New Generation*, edited by David E. Campbell, Meira Levinson, and Frederick M. Hess, 135–59. Cambridge: Harvard Education Press, 2012.

Sandel, Michael J. "Liberal Education and the Civic Project." In *To Restore American Democracy*, edited by Robert E. Calvert, 45–54. Lanham, MD: Rowman and Littlefield Publishers, Inc., 2006.

Scalia, Antonin. "Constitutional Government and Civic Education." *Ultraque Unum* 1, no. 19–15 (2007).

Schacter, Hindy Lauer. "Civic Education: Three Early American Political Science Association Committees and Their Relevance for Our Times." *PS: Political Science and Politics* 31, no. 3 (1998): 631–35.

Snyder, Claire. "Should Political Scientists Have a Civic Mission? An Overview of the Historical Evidence." *PS: Political Science and Politics* 34, no. 2 (2001): 301–305.

Stanton, Timothy K., Jr., Dwight E. Giles, and Nadinne I. Cruz. *Service-Learning: A Movement's Pioneers Reflect on Its Origins, Practice and Future*. San Francisco: Jossey-Bass, 1999.

Stroupe, Kenneth, Jr., and Larry Sabato. "Politics: The Missing Link of Responsible Civic Eduation." (2004), http://www.civicyouth.org/PopUps/civicengagement -stroupe-final.pdf.

"Study: More Know 'The Simpsons' Than First Amendment Rights." *USA Today*, 3/1/2006.

"Study: More Know 'Simpsons' Than Constitution." FoxNews.com, http://www .foxnews.com/story/2006/03/01/study-more-know-simpsons-than-constitution/.

Taylor, Bob Pepperman. *Horace Mann's Troubling Legacy: The Education of Democratic Citizens*: University Press of Kansas, 2010.

Thelin, John R. "Talk Is Cheap: The University and the National Project—a History." In *Teaching America: The Case for Civic Education*, edited by David Feith, 151–59. Lanham: Rowman & Littlefield Education, 2011.

Tyack, David, and Thomas James. "Education for a Republic: Federal Influence on Public Schooling in the Nation's First Century." In *This Constitution: A Bicentennial Chronicle*: American Political Science Association American Historical Association, 1985.

Walker, Tobi. "Service as a Pathway to Political Participation: What Research Tells Us." *Applied Development Science* 6, no. 4 (2002): 183–88.

Washington, George. "George Washington's Farewell Address." *The Independent Chronicle* (1796), http://www.earlyamerica.com/earlyamerica/milestones/fare well/text.html.

"What Is Icivics?" Filament Games, http://www.icivics.org/About.

Wolin, Sheldon. "Fugitive Democracy." *Constellations* 1, no. 1 (1994): 11–25.

Yonan, Jonathan. "Majoring in Servitude: Liberal Arts and the Formation of Citizen." In *Civic Education and the Future of American Citizenship*, edited by Elizabeth Kaufer Busch and Jonathan W. White, 111–23. Lanham: Lexington Books, 2013.

Youniss, James. "Civic Education: What Schools Can Do to Encourage Civic Identity and Action." *Applied Development Science* 15, no. 2 (2011): 98–103.

———. "How to Enrich Civic Education and Sustain Democracy." In *Making Civics Count: Citizenship Education for a New Generation*, edited by David E. Campbell, Meira Levinson, and Frederick M. Hess, 115–33. Cambridge: Harvard Education Press, 2012.

Chapter Two

It Can Work

*The Surprisingly Positive Prospects for Effective Civic Education**

Robert Maranto

Some argue that contemporary divisions among American elites and the public make a public school emphasis on civic education problematic. After all, Democrats and Republicans have significant disagreements on the role of government and often have different interpretations of American history, based on nontrivial value differences as detailed by Jonathan Haidt, among others.[1] Further, in the era of the Common Core standards elites have chosen to focus on the workforce preparation role of schools rather than their citizenship preparation role, as David Feith and others lament.[2]

This essay will summarize the views of civic education pessimists, but go on to make a case that several empirical considerations offer cause for optimism. First, significant political divisions are nothing new in our vibrant democracy, and current disputes are no more intractable than those of days past; indeed they are likely less so. Second, as the development and adoption of Common Core standards demonstrate, standard-setting has always been the province of elites and technocrats; thus widespread consensus about what civic education schools should teach is a desirable but not essential precondition for reemphasizing citizenship education. It is essential, particularly in the age of Internet, that such standards be sufficiently "mainstream" as to survive some level of popular scrutiny. This leads to a third point. Evidence suggests that to a surprising degree a consensus regarding what civic values to teach already exists in the public, among social studies teachers of both major political parties, and likely among political (though not ivory tower) elites. I will summarize those key areas of agreement, while also noting issues dividing

*I wish to thank Don Hirsch, Mike Rogers, and Don Gooch for their assistance. The usual caveats apply. I also wish to thank Rick Hess and American Enterprise Institute's Program on American Citizenship, which shared data and also funded fieldwork related to this project.

Democrats and Republicans. I will conclude with policy recommendations. First, echoing E. D. Hirsch Jr.'s fine work, particularly *The Schools We Need: And Why We Don't Have Them* and more recently *The Making of Americans,* too much of the burden of civic education now rests on secondary educators. American schools need better prepared *elementary* educators.[3] Second, in the absence of transparency, academic content of all kinds including that related to civic education suffers; America thus needs clear and transparent civic education standards with specific content, unlike the Common Core. Third, the academic discipline of political science is uniquely suited to play the leading role in developing those standards. Finally, the experiences of model charter schools and private schools suggests that teacher qualifications, but not conventional certifications, are key to success in civic education, as indeed in many other things.

THE CIVIC EDUCATION PESSIMISTS

A common script of recent decades is that American consensus has broken down. Not so long ago, goes the story, American elites and masses believed in God and in American exceptionalism, the view that our nation is heaven-blessed and will steadily improve. Americans also believed in a key set of values including limited government (and a concordant separation of powers), property rights, representative government, the power and objectivity of science, and individual responsibility.[4] These classical liberal beliefs were reinforced by pop culture. As Powers, Rothman, and Rothman show in their extensive coding of scripts, before the 1960s American movies portrayed American business, religious, and government institutions including the presidency and the military positively; after the mid-1960s these portrayals, particularly of white males, were increasingly mixed to negative.[5] On the other hand, portrayals of women and minorities, limited in nature and often number in earlier times, were overwhelmingly positive, particularly when story lines had them challenging traditional (white male) institutions. Similarly, Lerner, Nagai, and Rothman report that early-twentieth-century texts typically portrayed very positive views of American history generally, though with limited representation of women and minorities. Starting in the Progressive Era, historians and education professors at elite universities began to embrace far darker views of traditional American institutions, particularly business. The limited government ideology of the U.S. Constitution was increasingly left out of our history texts, as were the religious motivations of abolitionists and the Civil Rights Movement.[6] By the late twentieth century Progressives dominated textbook writing, to the point that today's textbooks "downplay individual achievement in favor of group membership, and, above all, they are hostile to capitalism for its inequality and ugliness."[7] Of course, such portrayals were and are often contested by local boards of education, as well as by state and national policy-makers. This is particularly apt to happen when textbook and curricular decisions are transparent. An often noted example occurred when the Clinton administration proposed national history standards, which were written by respected historians. These standards mentioned McCarthyism nineteen times and the Ku Klux Klan seventeen times, while noting George Washington once and leaving out Paul Revere, Thomas Edison, Robert E. Lee, and Albert Einstein entirely. Not surprisingly, the public and elites alike counterattacked once the standards were brought to light. Critics acknowledged that American history has its dark side, but saw it as both inaccurate and un-American to portray *only* the dark side. The Clinton administration immediately stopped the standards writing effort, which in any event was almost unanimously condemned by the U.S. Senate. Elites and the mass public of both major political parties agreed that the "politically correct" approaches to American history taken by many historians were incomplete, if not actually offensive.[8] This episode does not necessarily indicate that standards cannot be written by technocrats, but does remind us that to work politically and in the classroom such standards must be acceptable to a range of elites and the mass public, and to teachers. That is in fact how policy in our pluralistic polity works generally.

In the pessimistic view of American politics and education, intellectual and cultural elites lost faith in the traditionally dominant American values. These elites now see values such as limited and constitutional government and property rights as thwarting elite-led efforts to improve society through central planning to impose both (economic) equality and general order. As NYU educational historian Jonathan Zimmerman argues, the sort of intellectuals who penned school social studies textbooks often saw social problems as reflecting "cultural lags," irrational popular attachments to constitutional (and often conservative) values that thwart corrective action led by the intellectual class.[9] For example, prominent Teachers College (Columbia) Professor George Counts in 1932 published a manifesto, *Dare the Schools Build a New Social Order?* For Counts and other prominent educational intellectuals of the day, the clear answer was yes they should, and indeed would if not saddled by limited and divided government.[10] In the pessimistic view, held by those on the center and the right like Lerner et al. and Powers et. al., though also to a degree by some leftists like Eric Uslaner, intellectuals lost faith in traditional American values (Uslaner emphasizes science and optimism rather than limited government).[11] Intellectual elites were soon followed by Hollywood and other cultural elites, followed by media and political elites, and finally the masses. Without agreement on what cultural values American schools must reproduce, and indeed whether America itself is worth continuing, civic education becomes impossible. Pessimists believe that such agreement does not exist.

Somewhat more complex interpretations are offered by University of Virginia sociologist James D. Hunter, and to a lesser degree Jonathan Zimmerman and Harvard law professor Noah Feldman.[12] In their views, aggression runs both ways in the cultural conflicts over what America was, is, and should be. Secular elites try to impose their values on the traditionally religious, but the traditionally religious do the same, at least when they make up local majorities. The ever-nuanced Zimmerman is optimistic about the ability of Americans to fold new immigrant groups into a grand national narrative of gradual inclusion while less so about the ability for religious groups to reach like compromises.[13] Hunter is notably less optimistic.

To a considerable degree what unites the various pessimists is concern that we lack consensus on proper *American* values, and thus on what to teach in school to prepare citizens. Accordingly, schools should focus on teaching what is economically valuable and socially adjusting (life skills courses, for example), which indeed seems to be the focus of the Common Core standards funded by the Gates Foundation. The Common Core seems to fall neatly in line with the Progressive Education notion of how secondary education should work, most clearly expressed in 1918 through the National Education Association's *Cardinal Principles of Secondary Education*, which even today shapes American secondary education. Just one of the seven principles, the unartfully named "command of fundamental processes," encompasses *all* traditional academic disciplines such as English, Math, History, foreign languages, and the sciences.[14] For better or worse, and most professors outside of schools of education would say worse, this uniquely anti-intellectual focus for schooling is an example of exceptionalism which accords with certain American capitalist traditions.[15] Notably, the *Cardinal Principles* predate our current culture wars by a good half century, suggesting that they reflect undercurrents even more potent than a desire to avoid political controversy. While "civic education" was one of the seven listed principles, in practice it referred to cooperation and "group problem solving" in the classroom and a shallow acceptance of the Progressive use of state power rather than a broader and deeper understanding of American history and values. Indeed as the *Cardinal Principles* gained importance through the twentieth century, required courses in civics and "problems of democracy," which had been common before World War II, became increasingly rare, as Peter Levine notes.[16]

THE CASE AGAINST PESSIMISM

The pessimistic case seems powerful, but ultimately fails to persuade. First, significant political divisions are nothing new in our vibrant democracy, and today's disputes seem intense only by the standards of the recent past, not in the sweep of American history. Indeed many of the founders, Federalists and Anti-Federalists alike, embraced common approaches to civic education, and indeed saw nation building as the prime role of education despite disputes over the nature of the American republic that were more heated than those of today.[17] Recall, for example, battles over the Alien and Sedition Acts. It is true that the *McGuffey's Readers* and after 1890 the common admissions requirements of elite colleges had something of a homogenizing impact on American public schools. Yet we must remember the extraordinary struggles over such matters as whether to teach Catholic or Protestant versions of the Bible and how to teach them, struggles which led to considerable bloodshed in Philadelphia and elsewhere.[18] This is to say nothing of disputes about whether to privilege an Anglo or more "American" Irish and German view of European politics and even the British lineage of the American Constitution. These were significant controversies in the period before and after World War I. Of course, the deepest disagreements were over the causes and nature of the Civil War (or the "late unpleasantness"), which led history textbook publishers to produce "mint julep" editions for white Southern markets. As Zimmerman details, each of these disputes played a role in local and even national elections featuring charges and countercharges as to which side was really American.[19] In short, the fact that there never was and never will be complete agreement as to how to teach American history and civics does not mean that the effort is not worth making. Indeed the history of textbook publishing and curricula suggests that national norms and standards are entirely possible, albeit with some variation in accord with local sensibilities. For example, Berkman and Plutzer show that across the nation biology teachers present evolution as central to our understanding of their field. Still, human evolution is taught with different degrees of emphasis and not always as uncontested. They find that teaching professionals make reasonable compromises between the competing values of professional expertise and local representation in a diverse nation.[20]

Second, no public policy requires absolute consensus: something approaching an elite consensus with mass acquiescence can suffice. Such an elite consensus may take years to develop, but when it does develop, it tends to institutionalize policy into what political scientists refer to as a *regime*. To take a recent education policy example, testing and standards, it was never clear that the mass public supported standards. The education establishment generally opposed standards, though at times mainstream educators and even teachers unions worked with policy-makers to make sure that any standards which did exist were as feeble as possible. Yet by the 1990s policy-makers on the center, the right, and the moderate left had *learned* from four decades of increased spending with little to show for it, along with examples from Europe and Asia. Policy-makers concluded that standards and testing were necessary for school improvement, and forced a very reluctant educational establishment to go along with numerous state laws culminating in the passage of George W. Bush's *No Child Left Behind*. NCLB was itself essentially identical to the original Clinton proposal to reauthorize Title I, before it was watered down by Congress. For its part, the Clinton plan resembled proposals going back to the Nixon administration. The chief Obama educational innovation, the Common Core national standards, was imposed quietly as a matter of elite politics with the full support of chief state school officers. In part, state education authorities were bribed by stimulus funding and Gates Foundation grants, though in this case the money served to give most state education authorities (SEAs) political cover to do what they had long wanted to do, impose national standards to "modernize" American education in the manner of European and Asian examples.[21]

Now that de facto national standards exist, albeit vague ones, it will not take much political courage to make civics education a part of those standards. Indeed the elite conversation justifying such moves is well underway, for the most part opposed by the establishment educational industrial complex (schools of education, administrators' associations, state and local education bureaucracies, and the National Education Association). Yet standards generally, and to a lesser degree civic standards, are increasingly supported by members of the political class, by the American Federation of Teachers (to distinguish itself from NEA), by renegade educators at places like the center right National Association of Scholars and the American Council of Trustees and Alumni and the center left Core Knowledge Foundation, and by at least two prominent think tanks, the Thomas B. Fordham Foundation and the American Enterprise Institute.[22] The elite conversation about national civics standards in some respects had its genesis with public opinion studies showing that young people in particular did not know enough about American government to make rational decisions about voting. Of course political scientists had found since the 1950s that voters at best, practice "low information rationality," a nice way of saying that voters act with less civic knowledge than democratic theorists wish.[23] Yet it took some time for education intellectuals, using surveys of young people, to connect the dots with the weaknesses of civic education and what this meant for our democracy. The paradigmatic example is Diane Ravitch and Checker Finn's 1987 *What Do Our 17-Year-Olds Know?*[24] For more recent summaries see anything by the influential E. D. Hirsch, Jr., as well as Bauerlein, Cole, and the works within Leming, Ellington, and Porter, particularly Rochester's provocatively titled "The Training of Idiots: Civic Education in America's Schools."[25] Certainly by the 1990s politicians of both parties lamented that public ignorance, particularly among young people, damaged democracy. Increasingly they and other Washington insiders began to put two and two together, realizing that public schools would have to change to produce a more civically knowledgeable and aware electorate. After all, as Hirsch Jr., Frederick Hess, and others stress, training for citizenship was the original *raison d'etre* for public schools.[26] Interestingly, considerable quantitative evidence indicates that Catholic schools do better at civic education. This may reflect a greater focus on content, and on the moral obligations to one's community. Even controlling for all observable student characteristics, Catholic schools do a better job than public schools producing citizens who are tolerant, public-spirited, and likely to vote and otherwise take part in our democracy. Indeed Catholic school graduates are more tolerant of gays and lesbians than are their public school counterparts, as extensive and methodologically sound research summarized by David Campbell and Patrick J. Wolf demonstrates.[27]

The concern elites show regarding an ill-informed electorate and the need for schools to do more to prepare that electorate is a frequent theme in what I consider the leading newspaper of the political class, the *Washington Post*. These elite concerns also appear in numerous recent books about civic education by scholars, educators, and political figures including senators and U.S. Supreme Court justices with titles like *Making Civics Count: Citizenship Education for a New Generation; Teaching America: The Case for Civic Education*; and *Civic Education and the Future of American Citizenship*.[28]

Of course, civic education pessimists might argue that a consensus on the need to teach civic knowledge and civic values generally is very different from specific agreement on what to teach and how to teach it; thus a third point. Fortunately, we now have some data to help resolve the issue of whether there is a consensus on what to teach. Among the institutions pressing for a renewed emphasis on civic education is the American Enterprise Institute's Program on American Citizenship, part of the education policy shop led by the peripatetic Frederick M. "Rick" Hess.[29] AEI has sponsored very useful national surveys of public and private high school social studies teachers, as well as of the general public, to ascertain what each group values in civic education. This enables us to divine whether there is in fact a hidden consensus among teachers and the mass public regarding what students should learn, and perhaps even on how they should learn it. As suggested in the prior paragraph, there is at least some evidence of such a consensus among political elites.

I should mention here that it is too much to expect consensus in the ivory tower. After all, a great many university professors believe that the only desirable outcome of civic education would be to overthrow rather than take part in American democracy. As James Ceaser puts it:

Many who invoke the lofty rhetoric of higher education, however, do so in bad faith. Their real aim is not open education, but a different form of political education that promotes a different kind of political order. They are opposed to civic education because it seeks to preserve the existing regime.[30]

Accordingly a civic education consensus among university professors is unlikely.[31] On the other hand, those who have worked with political appointees in both Democratic and Republican administrations see such a consensus among elite politicians. As we shall see, a similar consensus exists among teachers and the mass public.[32]

A Civics Education Street-Level Consensus?

In spring 2010 AEI commissioned a national survey of high school social studies teachers, receiving surveys from 866 public school teachers and 245 private school teachers, with the results published that fall as *High Schools, Civics, and Citizenship: What Social Studies Teachers Think and Do.*[33] Results must be interpreted with caution given low response rates, as typifies mail and e-mail surveys. This work is suggestive rather than definitive. Still, results resemble those from a small-scale replication survey I conducted which had a 54 percent response rate, offering some confidence in external validity.[34] The AEI survey finds Republicans are slightly more likely than Democrats to think that too many teachers use their classes as a soapbox for their personal views, with 44 percent agreeing compared to 29 percent of Democrats. On the other hand, on seven of twelve items listed in Table 2.1, social studies teachers of each party are in full agreement.

By identical or nearly identical margins, Republican and Democratic teachers agree that it is "absolutely essential" (1 on a 1–5 scale) that students learn about the protections in the Bill of Rights, develop good work habits, embrace civic responsibilities like voting, understand such concepts as federalism, and gain knowledge about historical periods like the Founding. By large majorities those of both parties prioritize tolerance of others and respect for authority, though predictably Democrats are more supportive of the former and Republicans of the latter. Each group is far less supportive of teaching economic principles, and of community service. Similarly, neither group wants to turn children into activists challenging the status quo, though Democrats are predictably more supportive than Republicans. Republicans and Democrats do disagree about the degree to which schools should prioritize teaching students to think of themselves as global citizens. Unfortunately, given what modern learning theory tells us, neither group is very supportive of teaching facts, though Republicans are more supportive than Democrats. This is important since without knowledge of facts, perhaps taught through

Table 2.1. Comparing Priorities of Republican and Democratic Teachers Regarding Civic Education.

	Absolutely Essential	
	Republicans	Democrats
To identify the protections guaranteed by the Bill of Rights	81	83
To have good work habits such as being timely, persistent, and hardworking	82	78
To embrace the responsibilities of citizenship such as voting and jury duty	78	78
To be tolerant of people and groups who are different from themselves	63	86
To understand concepts such as federalism, separation of powers, and checks and balances	63	64
To be knowledgeable about periods such as the American Founding, the Civil War, and the Cold War	68	72
To follow rules and be respectful of authority	70	55
To see themselves as global citizens living in an interconnected world	41	67
To understand economic principles such as supply and demand and the role of market incentives	53	48
To develop habits of community service such as volunteering and raising money for causes	38	45
To be activists who challenge the status quo of our political system and seek to remedy injustices	23	43
To know facts (e.g., the location of the fifty states) and dates (e.g., Pearl Harbor)	43	32

Percentages of teachers surveyed agreeing it is "absolutely essential" to learn a topic, marking 1 on a 1–5 scale. Results are modified from Steve Farkas and Ann M. Duffett, *High Schools, Civics, and Citizenship: What Social Studies Teachers Think and Do* (Washington, DC: American Enterprise Institute, Fall 2010, 51), who surveyed 866 public school teachers and 245 private school teachers.

stories, students lack cognitive frames within which to place new information, as Dan Willingham and Hirsch Jr. respectively detail.[35] Further, without some understanding of history students cannot understand modern debates. For example, students are ill equipped to argue about whether American involvement in Afghanistan resembles Vietnam or World War II unless they have some knowledge of history.

To return to the main theme, as Table 2.1 shows, there is consensus among social studies teachers on the role of patriotism in civics education: 83% of teachers agree that "the U.S. is a unique country that stands for something special in the world," while only 11% agree that "the U.S. is just another country whose system is no better or worse than other countries." Similarly 82% of teachers agree it is vital to teach students to "respect and appreciate their country but know its shortcomings," while only 11% simply want students to "love their country." A mere 6% want their students to "think of the

U.S. analytically, without sentiment," and just 1% want students to "know that the U.S. is a fundamentally flawed country."

A later AEI national survey conducted by Daniel Lautzenheiser and his colleagues compares views of public and private school social studies teachers with those of Americans generally on civic education, again finding considerable agreement.[36] There are of course predictable differences, with citizens more likely than teachers to stress knowing facts and understanding economic principles and less apt to stress tolerance. Regarding facts at least, as noted above, modern learning theory shows that the public is right. The public is also more likely to want students to love their country uncritically rather than to respect America but know its flaws. Just as with the teacher survey discussed above, Republicans are less apt to stress tolerance and more apt to stress following the rules than are Democrats. Generally, however, this survey research again suggests far more agreement than disagreement.

In short, quantitative evidence suggests that social studies teachers generally agree on what social studies needs to prioritize in civics education—the constitutional structure of government, freedoms in the Bill of Rights, property rights, tolerance, participation, and knowledge of the founding period. Like the public, those teachers are patriotic, certainly far more so than college professors; given current discussions of culture wars, this is not a trivial matter. America is not Lebanon, or even Ireland. This indicates the possibility that those charged with implementing a serious program of civic education would be capable of doing so in ways acceptable to the public and to the political class, though perhaps not to ivory tower intellectuals. There may well be an American culture war, but it seems to have skipped both Democrats and Republicans who teach social studies. This accords with fieldwork in schools, which suggests a consensus among social studies teachers.[37] Indeed where culture wars in social studies do break out, they may be sufficiently rare as to merit books or at least book chapters, as in the case of Richard Bernstein's notable (and hilarious) "Battle of Brookline."[38]

SO WHAT IS TO BE DONE?

In short, there is more than a little evidence that prominent elites, social studies teachers, and the mass public support a greater emphasis on civic education, and broadly agree on the knowledge and values such education should impart. The civic education cause is now supported by certain influential institutions, though as yet no Bill Gates–style financier has enlisted in the cause. Further, the development of national standards in the form of the new Common Core offers a possible means of imposing civic education standards nationally. Unfortunately, as Web Hutchins writes, "The core is barren of civics—the word does not appear in the 66-page standards document for English/language arts."[39] Further, survey research finds that 70 percent of social studies teachers feel that in the current era of testing their subject area is a lower priority than math or reading.[40] This cannot stand, given that no less than U.S. Education Secretary Arne Duncan has railed that:

> Nearly two-thirds of Americans cannot name all three branches of government. Yet three in four people can name all of the Three Stooges. Less than half of the public can name a single Supreme Court justice. And more than a quarter do not know who America fought in the Revolutionary War.[41]

So what is to be done? I would like to conclude with four recommendations which, if implemented, could over the long term remake civics education in America, bringing back what has been lost over the prior decades.

First, echoing Hirsch Jr., too much of the burden of civic education now rests on secondary educators. Learning theory shows that students must have basic background knowledge to understand more complex concepts; thus American schools need better prepared *elementary* educators. Quite simply, by middle school it may be too late to do civic education well. To get students to think about the causes, consequences, and different sides of the events that shape American history and institutions, they must know the basic facts and stories of that history and those institutions. One can hardly discuss baseball without knowing balls and strikes. Similarly, one cannot take part in a reasoned discussion of whether a president has too much or too little power without knowing something about the divided powers in the U.S. Constitution, and why the Founders selected this particular highly unusual governmental structure. These things must be taught, albeit in simple form, in the elementary grades. Fortunately, as Hirsch Jr. shows in his own series of books, *What Your First Grader Needs to Know, What Your Second Grader Needs to Know*, and so on through sixth grade, it is quite easy to teach the basic facts of American history and institutions through stories rather than merely rote memorization.[42] Such story-filled teaching, emphasizing the greatness rather than the seamy side of the American project, is the job of elementary teachers, who can set the stage for inevitably more complex and nuanced treatments in later grades. As Hirsch shows, this requires well-prepared elementary teachers who like to read, enjoy a wide range of subjects, can make connections across those subjects, and who model love of learning. Indeed one can argue that it is more important to have intellectual elementary than secondary teachers, since the former must know (and show enthusiasm for) many things, while the latter need know only one big thing. A biology teacher must know biology, while an elementary teacher should be a generalist.

Second, in the absence of transparency, academic content of all kinds suffers, including that related to civic education. America thus needs clear and transparent civic education standards with specific content, unlike the Common Core. Naturally, those standards must be backed by testing, with the results reported. As Mike McShane and I have argued elsewhere, transparency will over the long term erode silly and turgid standards, tending to replace them with standards likely to stand the test of time. If Americans, and for that matter journalists and the political class, can look up on the Internet to see the civic education children learn, this will foster more rigorous and better standards over the long run.[43] The fate of the national history standards, noted above, offers an example. Similarly, Diane Ravitch has shown that political correctness (usually of the left but occasionally of the right) can dominate in textbook writing and test making, but tends to recede when journalists and the public find out.[44] In this as in so many things, sunlight is the best disinfectant. Further, strong standards in civics and history will promote rather than detract from learning in other areas.[45]

Third, the academic discipline of political science is uniquely suited to play the leading role in developing national civic education standards. As James Ceaser argues, whether one traces the origins of political science to the Greeks or to the Founders, the very field was designed in part to develop stable governance. The American Political Science Association is the only academic professional organization which includes among its strategic goals the cultivation of representative democracy, in part through an informed public. Since the mid-1990s political scientists have increased their research and teaching in this area.[46] Further, as Matthew Woessner and I have argued, political science shares three other characteristics that make it uniquely able to contribute in this area.[47] First, it is relatively moderate ideologically. While most political scientists lean left, about a sixth typically vote Republican, far more than in other fields in the social sciences and humanities, save for economics. This makes political scientists better able than historians or education professors to develop standards that a wide range of citizens and politicians can support. Second, political science is relatively pragmatic and includes large numbers of practitioners, which indeed partly explains the field's relative moderation. Third, the dominant theoretical approach of American political science is pluralism as developed at Yale after World War II. Pluralism is uniquely suited to the continuation and propagation of our constitutional democracy; indeed our field's patron saint is James Madison; our founding documents the *Federalist Papers*. Despite this, the American Political Science Association has not involved itself in the development of K–12 education standards and curricula or in social studies teacher certification, preferring to complain about the product the high schools send us rather than work to improve it. It is time for our noninvolvement to end.

Finally, civics must be taught by smart, civically interested teachers. As private schools and outstanding charter schools like YES Prep and Democracy Prep show, it takes great secondary teachers to promote complex thinking about the difficult trade-offs within our American constitutional system, and the history of that system.[48] The broader literature on certification, and the experiences of these outstanding schools, suggests that currently, teachers with majors outside of education, particularly those coming from alternative certification programs ("Altcert") are more apt to have what it takes to guide students through what can be difficult intellectual terrain.[49]

Without such guidance, we will lose much. To quote from Web Hutchins's recent *Education Week* essay:

> As the 18-year-old [Martin Luther] King wrote while attending Morehouse College: "Intelligence is not enough. Intelligence plus character—that is the goal of true education." Civics captures this—it offers thoughtful analysis of democracy's timeless tensions, which often unearths students' higher character as they learn to value integrity, compassion, and their unique conception of patriotism and the common good.[50]

If we forget this, we will forget everything.

NOTES

1. Jonathan Haidt, *The Righteous Mind: Why Good People Are Divided by Politics and Religion* (New York: Pantheon Books, 2012).
2. David Feith, ed. *Teaching America: The Case for Civic Education* (Lanham: Rowman and Littlefield Education, 2011). For a detailed treatment of the Common Core generally, see Robert Maranto and Michael Q. McShane, *President Obama and Education Reform* (New York: Palgrave/Macmillan, 2012), chapter 6.
3. E. D. Hirsch, *The Schools We Need: And Why We Don't Have Them* (New York: Doubleday, 1996); *The Making of Americans* (New Haven: Yale University Press, 2009).
4. Donald J. Devine, *The Political Culture of the United States: The Mass Influence on Regime Maintenance* (Boston: Little, Brown and Company, 1972).
5. Powers, Stephen, David J. Rothman, and Stanley Rothman, *Hollywood's America: Social and Political Themes in Motion Pictures* (Boulder: Westview, 1996).
6. Lerner, Robert, Althea K. Nagai, and Stanley Rothman, *Molding the Good Citizen: The Politics of High School History Texts* (Westport: Praeger Publishers, 1995).
7. Ibid., 155.
8. Lerner et al., *Molding the Good Citizen*, 6; Chester E. Finn Jr. *Troublemaker* (Princeton: Princeton University Press, 2008); Jonathan Zimmerman, *Whose America? Culture Wars in the Public Schools* (Cambridge: Harvard University Press, 2002). On the political correctness of university faculty see Robert Maranto, Richard

Redding, and Frederick M. Hess, eds., *The Politically Correct University* (Washington, DC: AEI Press, 2009).

9. Zimmerman, *Whose America?*, 63.

10. Lerner et al., *Molding the Good Citizen*, 26–27.

11. Eric M. Uslaner, *The Decline of Comity in Congress* (Ann Arbor: University of Michigan Press, 1996).

12. James Hunter, *Culture Wars: The Struggle to Define America* (New York: Basic Books, 1991); Noah Feldman, *Divided by God* (New York: Farrar, Strauss, and Giroux, 2006).

13. Zimmerman, *Whose America?*, 6–7.

14. Maranto and McShane, *President Obama and Education Reform*, 9–11.

15. John Agresto, "Reflection and Choice: The Problem and the Promise of the Liberal Arts in America," 139–49 in Elizabeth Kaufer Busch and Jonathan W. White, eds., *Civic Education and the Future of American Citizenship* (Lanham: Lexington Books, 2012).

16. Peter Levine, "Letter to President Obama," 209–17 in David Feith, ed., *Teaching America: The Case for Civic Education* (Lanham: Rowman and Littlefield Education, 2011), 210–11.

17. Frederick M. Hess, *The Same Thing Over and Over* (Cambridge: Harvard University Press, 2010).

18. Feldman, *Divided by God*; Maranto and McShane, *President Obama and Education Reform*.

19. Zimmerman, *Whose America?*

20. Michael Berkman and Eric Plutzer, *Evolution, Creationism, and the Battle to Control America's Classrooms* (New York: Cambridge University Press, 2010).

21. See Maranto and McShane, *President Obama and Education Reform*, and Finn, *Troublemaker*. A similar example of a gradually forming elite consensus, at least in large cities, arguably occurred by the early 2000s when policymakers, including most mayors, had concluded that only school choice could serve disadvantaged children effectively, leading to considerable support for charter schools—though not necessarily vouchers—despite bitter and often well-funded opposition from teachers unions and the education establishment.

22. For an extensive discussion of the educational industrial complex and its opponents, see Maranto and McShane, *President Obama and Education Reform*.

23. Samuel L. Popkin, *The Reasoning Voter* (University of Chicago Press, 1991).

24. Diane Ravitch and Checker Finn, *What Do Our 17-Year-Olds Know?* (New York: Harper and Row, 1987).

25. Mark Baverlein, "Don't Believe the Hype: Young Voters Are Still Disengaged, and Universities Have Few Incentives to Fix It," in David Feith, ed., *Teaching America: The Case for Civic Education*, 161–70; Bruce Cole, "Revolutionary Ignorance: What Do Americans Know of the Original Tea Party," in David Feith, ed., *Teaching America: The Case for Civic Education*, 81–88; Martin J. Rochester, "The Training of Idiots: Civic Education in America's Schools," in James Leming, Lucien Ellington, and Kathleen Porter, eds., *Where Did Social Studies Go Wrong?* (Washington, DC: Thomas B. Fordham Foundation, 2003), 6–39.

26. Frederick M. Hess, *The Same Thing Over and Over*; E. D. Hirsch, *The Schools We Need: And Why We Don't Have Them*; *The Making of Americans*.

27. David E. Campbell, "Making Democratic Education Work," in Paul E. Peterson and David E. Campbell, eds., *Charters, Vouchers, and Public Education* (Washington, DC: Brookings Institution Press, 2001), 241–67; Patrick J. Wolf, "School Choice and Civic Values," in Julian Betts and Tom Loveless, ed., *Getting Choice Right: Ensuring Equity and Efficiency in Education Policy* (Washington, DC: Brookings, 2005), 210–44; and Patrick J. Wolf, "Civics Exam," *Education Next* 7, no. 3 (Summer 2007, 66–72).

28. David E. Campbell, Meira Levinson, and Frederick M. Hess, eds., *Making Civics Count: Citizenship Education for a New Generation* (Cambridge: Harvard Education Press, 2012); David Feith, ed., *Teaching America: The Case for Civic Education*; Elizabeth Kaufer Busch and Jonathan W. White, eds., *Civic Education and the Future of American Citizenship*.

29. In the interest of disclosure, I received a grant from the center, which enabled me to produce the 2013 report *In Service of Citizenship: YES Prep Schools and Civic Education*, AEI Program on American Citizenship Policy Brief 7 (Washington, DC: AEI), http://www.citizenship-aei.org/2013/01/teaching-citizenship-in-charter-schools/. Working on that project helped me on this one as well.

30. James W. Ceaser, *The Role of Political Science and Political Scientists in Civics Education* (Washington, DC: AEI, 2013), 7–8, http://www.aei.org/files/2013/08/07/-the -role-of-political-science-and-political-scientists-in-civic-education_161230853228.pdf.

31. Maranto, Redding, and Hess, eds., *The Politically Correct University*.

32. Robert Maranto, *Beyond a Government of Strangers* (Lanham: Lexington, 2005).

33. Steve Farkas and Ann M. Duffett, *High Schools, Civics, and Citizenship: What Social Studies Teachers Think and Do* (Washington, DC: American Enterprise Institute, fall 2010), http://www.aei.org/papers/society-and-culture/citizenship/high-schools-civics-and-citizenship/. Most data referred to here is taken from p. 51.

34. See Robert Maranto, *In Service of Citizenship*.

35. Daniel Willingham, *Why Don't Students Like School?* (San Francisco: Jossey-Bass, 2009); Hirsch, *The Schools We Need: And Why We Don't Have Them*; *The Making of Americans*.

36. Daniel K. Lautzenheiser, Andrew P. Kelly, and Cheryl Miller, *Contested Curriculum: How Teachers and Citizens View Civic Education* (Washington, DC: American Enterprise Institute, June 2011), http://www.citizenship-aei.org/wp-content/uploads/Contested-Curriculum.pdf. This work again suffers from low response rates, and thus must be seen as suggestive rather than definitive.

37. Maranto, *In Service of Citizenship*."

38. Richard Bernstein, *Dictatorship of Virtue* (New York: Alfred A. Knopf, 1994).

39. Web Hutchins, "Civics in the Common Core," *Education Week* 32, no. 37 (August 6, 2013): 33, 36, http://www.edweek.org/ew/articles/2013/08/07/37hutchins_ep.h32.html.

40. Daniel K. Lautzenheiser et al., *Contested Curriculum*, 2.

41. Ibid., 1.

42. For a good example suitable for use in secondary education or college and as a guide for teachers at all grades, see Terry Newell's *Statesmanship, Character, and*

Leadership in America (New York: Palgrave/Macmillan, 2013). Newell uses key speeches in American history to explain the history of particular events and the uses of rhetoric in shaping ideas. See also the *National Standards for Civics and Government* produced by the Center for Civic Education, at http://new.civiced.org/standards (I thank Don Hirsch for this recommendation.)

43. Maranto and McShane, *President Obama and Education Reform*, chapter 6.

44. Diane Ravitch, *The Language Police: How Pressure Groups Restrict What Students Learn* (New York: Knopf, 2003). On a similar theme regarding curricula, see Richard Bernstein, *Dictatorship of Virtue*, particularly on "the battle of Brookline," in which a politically correct school system attempted to end the teaching of Western Civilization.

45. This argument is perhaps best developed by Andrew Rotherham, "Core Curriculum: How to Tackle General Illiteracy and Civic Illiteracy at the Same Time," in David Feith, ed., *Teaching America*, 89–96.

46. Ceasar, *The Role of Political Science and Political Scientists in Civics Education*.

47. Robert Maranto and Matthew Woessner, "Seeking Relevance: American Political Science and America," *Academic Questions*, 25 (Fall 2012): 403–417; see also Robert Maranto and Matthew Woessner, "Diversifying the Academy: How Conservative Academics Can Thrive in Liberal Academia," *PS: Political Science and Politics*, 45, no. 3 (July 2012): 469–74. The rest of this paragraph summarizes arguments from these two articles.

48. Maranto, *In Service of Citizenship*; Seth Andrew, "Fighting Civic Malpractice: How a Harlem Charter School Closes the Civic Achievement Gap," in David Feith, ed., *Teaching America: The Case for Civic Education*, 99–110.

49. Maranto and McShane, *President Obama and Education Reform*, 61. On a personal note as someone who does considerable fieldwork in schools, altcert teachers generally seem more likely to understand that allowing free speech to say, Communists, does not mean endorsing their views. In contrast, I recall many conversations with traditional teachers who could not make this very important distinction, with one particularly dogmatic reading specialist responding "So I suppose you like the KKK."

50. Hutchins, "Civics in the Common Core," 33.

BIBLIOGRAPHY

Agresto, John. "Reflection and Choice: The Problem and the Promise of the Liberal Arts in America." In *Civic Education and the Future of American Citizenship*, edited by Elizabeth Kaufer Busch and Jonathan W. White, 139–49. Lanham: Lexington Books, 2012.

Agresto, John, Mark Bauerlein, Peter A. Benoliel, Jeff Bergner, Bruce Cole, Dana Gioia, E. D. Hirsch et al. *Civic Education and the Future of American Citizenship*. Edited by Elizabeth Kaufer Busch, and Jonathan W. White. Lanham, Lexington Books, 2012.

Andrew, S. "Fighting Civic Malpractice: How a Harlem Charter School Closes the Civic Achievement Gap." In *Teaching America: The Case for Civic Education*. Edited by David Feith, 99–109. Lanham, MD: Rowman & Littlefield Education, 2011.

Bauerlein, Mark. "Don't Believe the Hype: Young Voters Are Still Disengaged, and Universities Have Few Incentives to Fix It," In *Teaching America: The Case for*

Civic Education. Edited by David Feith, 161–70. Lanham, MD: Rowman & Littlefield Education, 2011.

Berkman, Michael, and Eric Plutzer. *Evolution, Creationism, and the Battle to Control America's Classrooms.* New York: Cambridge University Press, 2010.

Bernstein, Richard. *Dictatorship of Virtue: Multiculturalism and the Battle for America's Future.* New York, NY: Alfred A. Knopf, Inc., 1994.

Campbell, David. E. "Making Democratic Education Work." In *Charters, Vouchers, and Public Education.* Edited by Paul E. Peterson and David E. Campbell, 241–67. Washington, DC: Brookings Institution Press, 2001.

Campbell, David E., Meira Levinson, and Frederick M. Hess, eds. *Making Civics Count: Citizenship Education for a New Generation.* Cambridge: Harvard Education Press, 2012.

Ceaser, James W. *The Role of Political Science and Political Scientists in Civic Education"* AEI Program on American Citizenship, 2013. http://www.aei.org/files/2013/08/07/-the-role-of-political-science-and-political-scientists-in-civic-education_161230853228.pdf.

Cole, Bruce. "Revolutionary Ignorance: What Do Americans Know of the Original Tea Party," In *Teaching America: The Case for Civic Education.* Edited by David Feith, 81–88. Lanham, MD: Rowman & Littlefield Education, 2011.

Devine, Donald John. *The Political Culture of the United States: The Mass Influence on Regime Maintenance.* Boston: Little, Brown, 1972.

Farkas, Steve, and Ann M. Duffett. *High Schools, Civics, and Citizenship: What Social Studies Teachers Think and Do.* Washington, DC: American Enterprise Institute for Public Policy Research (2010). http://www.aei.org/papers/society-and-culture/citizenship/high-schools-civics-and-citizenship/.

Feith, David J. *Teaching America: The Case for Civic Education.* Lanham, MD: Rowman & Littlefield Education, 2011.

Feldman, Noah. *Divided by God: America's Church-State Problem—and What We Should Do about It.* New York: Farrar, Strauss, and Giroux, 2006.

Finn, Chester E., Jr., *Troublemaker: A Personal History of School Reform since Sputnik.* Princeton University Press, 2008.

Haidt, Jonathan. *The Righteous Mind: Why Good People Are Divided by Politics and Religion.* Random House LLC, 2013.

Hess, Frederick M. *The Same Thing Over and Over.* Harvard University Press, 2010.

Hirsch Eric D. *The Schools We Need: And Why We Don't Have Them.* Random House LLC, 2010.

———. *The Making of Americans: Democracy and Our Schools.* Yale University Press, 2009.

Hutchins, Web. "Civics in the Common Core," *Education Week* 32, no. 37 (2013). http://www.edweek.org/ew/articles/2013/08/07/37hutchins_ep.h32.html.

Hunter, James Davison. *Culture Wars: The Struggle to Define America.* New York, NY: Basic Books, 1991.

Lautzenheiser, Daniel K., Andrew P. Kelly, & Cheryl Miller. *Contested Curriculum: How Teachers and Citizens View Civic Education.* Washington, DC: American Enterprise Institute, 2011. http://www.citizenship-aei.org/wp-content/uploads/Contested-Curriculum.pdf.

Lerner, Robert, Althea K. Nagai, and Stanley Rothman. *Molding the Good Citizen: The Politics of High School History Texts*. Westport, CT: Praeger Publishers, 1995.

Levine, P. "Letter to President Obama." In *Teaching America: The Case for Civic Education*. Edited by David Feith, 209–17. Lanham, MD: Rowman & Littlefield Education, 2011.

Maranto, Robert. *In Service of Citizenship: YES Prep Schools and Civic Education*. Policy Brief 7. AEI Program on American Citizenship, 2013. http://www.citizen ship-aei.org/wp-content/uploads/Maranto_In-Service-of-Citizenship.pdf.

Maranto, Robert, and Michael Q. McShane. *President Obama and Education Reform: The Personal and the Political*. New York: Palgrave Macmillan, 2012.

Maranto, Robert, Richard E. Redding, and Frederick M. Hess, eds. *The Politically Correct University: Problems, Scope, and Reforms*. Washington, DC: AEI Press, 2009.

Maranto, Robert, and Matthew Woessner. "Diversifying the Academy: How Conservative Academics Can Thrive in Liberal Academia." *PS: Political Science & Politics* 45, no. 3 (2012): 469–474.

Maranto, Robert, and Matthew C. Woessner. "Seeking Relevance: American Political Science and America." *Academic Questions* 25, no. 3 (2012): 403–417.

Newell, Terry. *Statesmanship, Character, and Leadership in America*. New York: Palgrave Macmillan, 2012.

Powers, Stephen, David J. Rothman, and Stanley Rothman. *Hollywood's America: Social and Political Themes in Motion Pictures*. Boulder: Westview Press, Inc., 1996.

Ravitch, Diane. *The Language Police: How Pressure Groups Restrict What Students Learn*. New York: Alfred Knopf, 2003.

Ravitch, Diane, and Chester Finn. *What Do Our 17-Year-Olds Know?: A Report on the First National Assessment of History and Literature*. New York: Harper and Row, 1987.

Rochester, J. Martin. "The Training of Idiots: Civic Education in America's Schools." In *Where Did Social Studies Go Wrong?* Edited by James Leming, Lucien Ellington, and Kathleen Porter, 6–39. Washington, DC: Thomas B. Fordham Foundation, 2003.

Rotherham, Andrew, J. "Core Curriculum: How to Tackle General Illiteracy and Civic Illiteracy at the Same Time," In *Teaching America: The Case for Civic Education*. Edited by David Feith, 89–96. Lanham, MD: Rowman & Littlefield Education, 2011.

Uslaner, Eric M. *The Decline of Comity in Congress*. Ann Arbor: University of Michigan Press, 1996.

Willingham, Daniel. *Why Don't Students Like School?* San Francisco: Jossey-Bass, 2009.

Wolf, Patrick J. "Civics Exam: Schools of Choice Boost Civic Values." *Education Next* 7, no. 3 (2007): 66.

Wolf, Patrick. J. "School Choice and Civic Values." In *Getting Choice Right: Ensuring Equity and Efficiency in Education Policy*. Edited by Julian Betts and Tom Loveless, 210–44. Washington, DC: Brookings, 2005.

Zimmerman, Jonathan. *Whose America? Culture Wars in the Public Schools*. Cambridge: Harvard University Press, 2002.

Chapter Three

The Irony of Civic Education in the United States

Jeffrey D. Hilmer

Is it possible for an educational system to be conducted by a national state and yet the full social ends of the educative process not be restricted, constrained, and corrupted?

—John Dewey, *Democracy and Education*

Civic education is central to American democratic thought and practice, and remains a preoccupation of political scientists and central to the mission of the American Political Science Association. Political scientists today are vigorously proposing solutions to the "crisis of civic education" in American political life. This crisis involves the political ignorance and apathy of American citizens. The most commonly proposed cure for these ills is *more* civic education. The problem: citizens are uninterested in politics and their civic duties are neglected, and the political regime increasingly appears unresponsive and illegitimate. The solution: rigorous civic education in the public and private schools and colleges and universities. Yet despite the determined efforts of generations of political scientists the crisis of civic education persists.

This chapter argues that the solution to the crisis of civic education is not merely a *practical* matter of increasing the amount of civic education nor is it discovering and implementing novel methods of teaching citizenship. Rather, the problem is *conceptual*. The American crisis of civic education is at its root the ironic product of a state-centric American civic education that teaches citizens to celebrate the radically democratic citizen-centric politics of the American Revolution while simultaneously conducting an effective program of state-centric civic education. By "citizen-centric citizenship" I mean an anarchistic form of life that has as its core values consensus decision-making, horizontality, equality, and freedom. By "state-centric citizenship" I mean a statist politics that has as its core values elite decision-making, hierarchy, inequality, and discipline. This schizophrenic pedagogy creates a conceptual disconnect between the ideal of democracy and the reality of the American state that renders most citizens either passively state-centric or rationally ignorant and apathetic. Either way, the result serves the state and the elites who benefit from its hegemony.

This critique highlights the necessity of a conceptual shift away from the state-centric model of civic education and toward a citizen-centric alternative with practical implications. Again, by a citizen-centric civic education I mean a genuinely radical program of civics that is driven by the logic of democracy rather that the logic of the state. The chief prerequisite for a program of citizen-centric civic education is that it must be realized *outside* of the state. By outside I do not mean that it must necessarily *physically* occur outside of state boundaries, but rather, the mindset of the facilitator and student must *think* outside of the state. Or, as James Scott has suggested, citizens must learn how to avoid seeing and thinking like a state and, moreover, practice state evasion.[1] If the structure of a state involves state-centric features including hierarchy, territorial boundaries, monopolization and frequent use of violence, and minimalist democracy, on the contrary a citizen-centric civic education must teach citizens to *evade* the state by practicing horizontality. Borrowing from the "de-schooling" movement, this process might be referred, somewhat inelegantly, as "de-stating." By de-stating I mean an educational experience that will provide citizens with an alternative conceptual framework which is citizen-centric rather than state-centric and equip them with practical techniques of state evasion.

The chapter is organized as follows: Part 1 describes and critiques the "crisis of civic education" in the Unites States as characterized by various political elites and public intellectuals; Part 2 draws on recent anarchist political thought in order to describe and evaluate recent scholarship that anticipates citizen-centric civic education; Part 3 identifies various principles of citizen-centric civic education and tactics of state evasion (e.g., resisting a centralized program for civic education; civic education as *phronēsis;* practicing anarchist calisthenics; minding one's own business; and the acknowledgment of no absolute principles) in order to begin to describe a citizen-centric approach to civic education.

THE TWO CRISES IN CIVIC EDUCATION: HOW STATE-CENTRIC THINKING UNDERMINES DEMOCRACY

The danger of the "crisis in civic education" is stressed by various public officials and academics, including political scientists.[2] They argue that the

United States is in dire straits due to the poor civic habits of citizens. Various political elites and public intellectuals have proposed a myriad of solutions. Most of these proposals focus on civic education of one form or another. No doubt these critics have legitimate concerns and suggest reasonable tactical solutions, some of which have been implemented. Nevertheless, the crisis persists. Why? I argue that critics overlook a significant *conceptual* distinction that engenders intellectual confusion and *practical* problems. Critics of the system of civic-education generally ignore the power of the state to subordinate all action to its logic. All civic education is framed conceptually from in a state-centric perspective, thus placing the health and protection of the state and *not* the citizen at the forefront of the goal of civic education in the United States. I aim to remedy this ignorance by the juxtaposition of two concepts: state-centric thinking and citizen-centric thinking. This conceptual difference helps us to understand why state-centric thinking dominates civic education in the United States and, ironically, perpetuates the poor civic habits that critics of the crisis in civic education lament. This is what might be referred to as the "other crisis in civic education."

The Crisis in Civic Education

Scholars focusing on improving civic education in higher education suggest integrative and interdisciplinary learning, capstone experiences, intercultural educative experiences, service learning, and the like.[3] But seldom if ever do these critics address the pervasive problem of the logic of the state. In fact, civic education in the United States is state-centric civic education. The goal of state-centric civic education is to motivate citizens to be informed and politically active, but informed and politically active citizens of a *statist* association, and not necessarily of a *democratic* association. This is despite the frequent conjunction of statist and democratic associations, two very different forms of political association. For the most part this entails passively viewing formal political actors via the mass media and voting in elections. Some state-centric civic education goes further in which citizens are encouraged to participate in more robust ways: protesting, boycotts, and sundry forms of "civil disobedience." But this is the exception rather than the rule.[4] Thus, in the tradition of Martin Luther King Jr. unjust laws are broken and the consequences accepted. But as any student of politics knows, the distinction between "civil disobedience" and mere law-breaking is that the civilly disobedient person accepts the punishment for his or her "crime." There is a recognition that the political system at its core is just, but in a particular instance that justice has been denied. State-centric civic education teaches citizens to participate in conventional ways that affirm the dominant statist political system, and discourages unconventional political participation in all but the direst circumstances. Americans, of course, have always been schizophrenic in that regard. The American Revolution is celebrated, but few would advocate for revolution today. Martin Luther King Jr. is celebrated and he has been honored alongside the likes of Washington and Lincoln with a national holiday, yet the public often frowns upon civil disobedience.

The Other Crisis in Civic Education

The other crisis in civic education is largely a *conceptual* crisis. Nevertheless, it is a conceptual crisis with very real practical implications. The standard concept of the state deployed by political scientists originates with sociologist Max Weber. In his celebrated essay *Politik ALS Beruf* or *Politics as a Vocation* Weber conceptualizes the state as a human community within a given territory in which the legitimate use of physical force—that is, violence—is monopolized. Weber further explains how the practice of democratic politics—at least in the Germany of Weber's day—had become bureaucratized and monopolized by professional politicians who live *off* of politics rather than vocational politicians who live *for* politics.[5] Both of Weber's observations are well known to political scientists. Yet, when it comes to proposals for civic education, the significance of Weber's observations about politicians is lost on the civic education reformers. Instead, proposals for civic education ignore the power of the state and the ineffectuality of democratic politics. Instead, the state-centric ideal of politics is taken to be operative and is therefore quite evident in proposals for civic education. The proposals for civic education prescribe solutions for the crisis of civic education as if those prescriptions could affect and/or effect political change. In the face of state power, most if not all democratic solutions are either hopelessly ineffective or so diluted that they serve not to challenge the state but rather affirm and perpetuate state power.

This is evident in contemporary democratic theory. Political scientists who subscribe to the minimalist theory of democracy are understandably less inclined to see political apathy and ignorance and the lack of civic participation it engenders as a crisis, and therefore see no concomitant crisis in civic education.[6] If they bother to teach civic education at all, it will be consistent with state-centric politics. Citizens exposed to this approach will likely be of the sort that the second group of political scientists decries. This second group subscribes to some form of radical, direct, or participatory democratic theory. These political scientists are likely to view citizens' apathy and ignorance as a serious threat to the health of a democracy and therefore seek remedy in civic education.[7] The problem here is that both of these groups of political scientists are often guilty of underestimating, not understanding, or ignoring the logic of the state in which they seek to train and let loose citizens eager to practice real democracy. The irony of civic education in American education is political scientists seem unable or unwilling to recognize that their attempt at solving the crisis of civic education by providing more state-centric civic indoctrination is, in actuality, discouraging citizens from democratic participation. The more political scientists teach citizens about ideal democratic practices, the less likely citizens are to take those lessons seriously given the obvious contrary political realities.

Of course most citizens subjected to such training will likely be incredulous from the start. Democratic theory is one thing, democratic practice is quite another. This has, perhaps, the unintended consequence of reminding citizens of that which they already know: legitimate avenues for "democratic" participation in a state-centric political system are few, and those that do exist are likely to be either wholly ineffective or engender state repression. Again, civic education which has at its center the ideal of democratic participation is either co-opted by state-centric minimalist democratic thinking or presented in near utopian form by radical democrats. The result is the same: apathetic and ignorant citizens. It is ironic then that political scientists call for more civic education that will—as long as it is taught within the context of a state-centric political system—likely produce a less, not more, civically active population. For instance, citizen apathy is often cited as evidence of the product—at least in part—of poor or no civic education. Yet, political scientists are missing the point. In fact, because civic education is state-centric, it makes perfect sense that citizens refrain from political activity which they know to be irrelevant. More than just "rational ignorance," citizens learn that political action is rigorously circumscribed by the logic of the state. And where genuine democratic practices including civil disobedience do breakout, the consequences are inevitably repressive. A good example of this is the recent Occupy Wall Street direct action, which was met with state repression and was largely panned by the American mainstream mass media and subsequent public opinion.[8]

The first step toward solving the crisis of civic education must be the recognition of the power of the state and, more importantly, the recognition that state power rests on a state-centric conception that is directly at odds with the citizen-centric conception. What is required is, first, an alternative conception of the state that will serve not to replace one concept of the state with another, but rather undermine the seemingly all-powerful state by first challenging it conceptually. This conceptual shift is a prerequisite to the practical shift from state-centric to citizen-centric civic education. There is an alternative conception of state proposed by the anarchist thinker Gustav Landauer. Landauer argues in *Aufruf zum Sozialismus* or *For Socialism* for a conception of the state as a particular form of human relations.[9] The significance of this distinction is Landauer's alternative to Weber's far more influential conceptualization demonstrates that while the Weberian state manifests in tangible objects (e.g., police, military, borders, etc.) these are the result of a human choice to relate to other humans, and the world generally, in a specific state-centric way. The power of the state is the result of human beings *thinking* that the state has power and therefore legitimacy. The state has no independent existence; it is a human creation, an idea, a concept, that has meaning and power only because we believe it does. The significance of Landauer's conceptual shift is to remind us of the human artificiality of the state and, moreover, that the state is not a historical inevitability borne of some evolutionary process. Rather, the state is the product of human choice—albeit not always a consensual choice—that could be substituted with other forms of human relation. Therefore, the shift away from state-centric citizenship and civic education requires first and foremost a conceptual shift away from the Weberian idea of the state and toward an ideal of human association that is consistent with democratic ideals.

Political scientists who seek to encourage democratic participation through civic education must fully acknowledge that they work within a state-centric political system that by its organizational nature is *passively* opposed to minimalist democratic participation and *actively* opposed to radical democratic participation. They must also acknowledge that as long as they ignore the profound power of the state to influence their political action their efforts at civic education will inevitably be constrained and coopted by the logic of state power manifest in state-centric thinking. And as long as that remains the case, the "other crisis of civic education," namely the undemocratic character of the state and its pervasive power, will remain *the* crisis of civic education. Any sincere and effective attempt at education for real democracy must begin with a two-fold strategy of state-evasion that aims to de-state citizens, that is, to (1) encourage them to not think like a state—that is, to think in terms of nonhierarchy and direct democracy—and (2) to develop deep democratic thought and translate that into deep democratic practice within their communities.[10] To reiterate, the "crisis of civic education" in the twenty-first century is not merely one of citizen apathy and ignorance, but rather the pervasive power of an undemocratic and therefore illegitimate state.

Toward Citizen-centric Civic Education Or: Learning How *Not* to Think Like a State

Citizen-centric civic education encourages citizens to think like citizens of a democratic political association rather than like and for the state. According to this model, citizens are prompted to adopt democratic values including consensus decision-making, horizontality, equality, and freedom. Prefiguring these practices entails a *conceptual* shift away from state-centric thinking. Moreover, citizens are prompted to create social, political, and economic practices that prefigure these democratic values. Practices including mutual aid societies, consensus decision-making collectives, and *autogestión*—or workplace democracy and worker self-management—are just a few practical examples of these practices. This is a *practical* shift away from state-centric thinking. As noted in the previous section, the concept of state-centric thinking continues to dominate civic education and political practice. There is, however, a tradition of citizen-centric thinking evident in education theory and practice. These critics offer a starting point from which a primer of civic-centered civic education may be begun and a tactical plan for State evasion envisioned.

De-schooling, De-Stating, and Democracy

Public—and private—education in the United States has no shortage of critics. Authors including John Taylor Gatto, Paul Goodman, John Holt, Ivan Illich, Herbert R. Kohl, Diane Ravitch, and Charles E. Silberman, among many others, have criticized schools and colleges on a number of fronts.[11] These critics often discuss issues that relate implicitly to civic education. For instance, they often cite the problematic conflict between encouraging young people to be "free-thinkers" wary of authority, while just about every aspect of their formal educational experience is authority driven and demands unquestioning obedience. Yet, their criticisms tend to be broader in scope.

A more narrow focus can be found in the work of Amy Gutmann. Gutmann is perhaps one of the most well-known of the political scientists who have highlighted the symbiotic relationship between democracy and education.[12] Yet her argument is firmly state-centric in that her proposals for educational reform pay little attention to the corrosive and coercive logic of the state. Even seemingly unconventional arguments like Hibbing and Theiss-Morses' call for less "civics" and more "barbarics" remain clearly within the state-centric framework by underestimating the logic of the state imparted via civic education in influencing political action.[13] Some critics speak more directly to the role of state power in subverting democracy and democratic citizenship. For instance, Paulo Freire has long been recognized as an authority on the "pedagogy of the oppressed."[14] And Henry Giroux is a founder of "critical pedagogy" and continues to be an influential critic of state-centric educational practices.[15] The work of Bowles and Gintis has critiqued education in the United States from a Marxist perspective arguing that economic inequality undermines education.[16] The recent work of Sarah M. Stitzlein (discussed below) highlights the difficulties of teaching civil disobedience in schools that are, for the most part, designed to inculcate civic habits that will maintain the State.[17] The argument herein endeavors to go beyond these critiques, though there are obvious points of contact.

Resisting the State: Dissent and *Political* Disobedience

Of the recent critics of civic education that focus specifically on civic education's tendency to reproduce state-centric thinking, the best example is Sarah M. Stitzlein's *Teaching for Dissent: Citizenship Education and Political Activism*.[18] Stitzlein's argument points away from state-centric civic education and toward a citizen-centric alternative. She writes: "A close look at educational practice and policy today reveals a mismatch between the goal of education for active civic and political participation and the actual practice of schooling, which is largely one geared toward consensus and complacency. . . . I claim that schools should teach children how to dissent."[19]

Stitzlein's argument for the teaching of dissent is consistent with the idea of a citizen-centric civic education. Her typology of "good dissent" includes four modes of civil disobedience: active, passive, symbolic, and direct action.[20] Each of these can easily be incorporated into a citizens-centric civic education, with the direct action mode perhaps most consistent. Yet, Stitzlein stops short of the sort of state-evasive tactics at the core of the citizens-centric ideal. At one point she writes:

> There is a delicate balance between the state's need to be able to smoothly function with a populace that it can be relatively certain will be compliant with its rules and systems and also needing a populace that will question and challenge the decisions of government so that those decisions are kept in line with the experiences and the needs of the people. Good dissent arises at the fulcrum, wisely knowing when to shift tone side or the other.[21]

Moreover, she argues that the state has an "obligation to cultivate the skills of dissent in its young citizens."[22] But in a revealing and contradictory reversal, she notes that dissent is not taught in schools and, moreover "explicitly and implicitly worked against."[23] This, of course, is perfectly consistent with state-centric civic education. Teaching students to dissent is largely contradictory to state interests because the logic of the state is one of monopolization of power and authority, and dissent will inevitably threaten this monopolization. And while civil disobedience is often celebrated, it is done so from the safe perspective of hindsight wherein those who were at the time of their transgressions viewed as subversive—Rosa Parks, for example—are now viewed as model citizens.

Teachers, understandably, are reluctant to encourage students to consider the important role dissent plays in a democracy. Yet Stitzlein argues that this has more to do with student distrust of teachers, anti-intellectualism, and pressure for apolitical instruction and the like. While this is all true, the power of the state to discourage dissent and any ideas that challenge state authority is both a more obvious and persuasive explanation.[24] Furthermore, Stitzlein's proposal for a "humanities-based curriculum," which she argues "prepares students for political dissent by developing skills of critique and argument, supported by a keen understanding of language, morality, justice, and concern for others, which can be used to put forward alternative visions of change," while practical, omits any serious analysis of state power that would actively resist such a program.[25] Dissent is certainly an important aspect of any democracy, but dissent and its most visible manifestation, civil disobedience, are simply not enough to counter state power. And more to the point, it is hardly likely to be taught in any meaningful ways in schools controlled by the state.

While these critics of civic education in the United States share a common concern that young citizens are not being "schooled" in the practices of democracy, they approach this problem form various angles and often come to divergent conclusions. Yet, very few—if any—of them are willing to address the elephant in the room: most if not all civic education takes place within the context of a state and is understandably "state-centric."

The principles of state-centric civic education vary with the type of political regime associated with a particular state. The United States has a liberal-democratic political regime, whereas the Italian state under Mussolini had a fascist state. Each political regime seeks to inculcate within its young people the values and practices of their particular political regime. This is often conducted quite overtly and requires little examination to determine what sort of political regime a person is living in. Thus Aristotle's well-known observation still holds up, in that citizens' political views reflect the sort of regime in which they were raised. What is less obvious, however, and perhaps more significant, are the similarities between different political regimes. These similarities are evident in any political organization that is understood to be statist—thus, Max Weber's famous description of a state as "[T]he monopoly of legitimate physical force within a particular territory."[26] What is important to note for the purposes of this argument is that regardless of political regime type, the logic and institutions of the state are often at work below the surface. So, when a student is taught the liberal democratic value of political equality and socialized into the liberal democratic practice of voting for political representatives, she is certainly being taught to be a good liberal democratic citizen. Yet, she is also likely taught of historical events where voting was not enough; voting was not effective in removing unjust laws, and thus civil disobedience was used. But at this point the student is also taught that civil disobedience is "civil" in that the actor recognizes the legitimacy of the political regime—if not a particular law—and thus in a demonstration of obedience accepts the punishment. The act is largely a symbolic one. It may or may not affect political reality. The lesson in civics often ends here.

While not making a pedagogical argument per se, Bernard E. Harcourt nevertheless contributes to the argument for citizen-centric civic education by conceiving a novel concept of disobedience that is not civil, but rather, *political*.[27] According to Harcourt, recent political movements and direct actions—specifically, Occupy Wall Street—herald a new era in American politics. This new era is characterized by the popular rejection of extant political and economic institutions and practices. This rejection is captured by the distinction Harcourt draws between "civil disobedience" and "political disobedience." *Civil* disobedience "does not aim to displace the law-making institutions or the structure of legal governance but rather to challenge the governing laws by demonstrating their injustice."[28] In the tradition of Martin Luther King Jr., a law that is perceived to be unjust is transgressed and the punishment symbolically accepted. *Political* disobedience, on the contrary:

> resists the very way in which we are governed. It rejects the idea of honoring or expressing 'the highest respect for law.' It refuses to willingly accept the sanctions meted out by the legal and political system. It challenges the conventional way that political governance takes place, that laws are enforced. It turns its back on the political institutions and actors who govern us all. It resists the structure of partisan politics, the traditional demand for policy reforms, the call for party identification, and, beyond that, the very ideologies that have dominated the postwar period.[29]

As a mode of political action, political disobedience directly challenges state authority and power. Political disobedience shares with its civil cousin a recognition that there are appropriate and inappropriate contexts in which to disobey. Yet, when deemed appropriate, the political mode is profoundly democratic, perhaps anarchist, and serves not merely to challenge an unjust law, but challenges an unjust form of political organization. Thus, if teaching dissent in state-centric schools is unlikely, the teaching of political disobedience approaches absurdity. A state-centric program of civic education that prepares students to "turn [their] back[s] on the political actors and institutions that govern us" would be so irrational and contrary to the logic of the state as an institution, the very idea becomes inconceivable. Nevertheless, this is precisely the kind of thinking that a citizen-centric civic education would foster.

While we are made to think that low voter turnout, ignorance of political events, and the like are evidence of the civic sickness in need of cure, what we may be seeing is not so much a failure of civic education, but rather the success of state-centric civic education. In other words, all aspects of civic education in statist regimes are subtly constrained by the logic of the state—including civil disobedience. What ultimately is required is a paradigmatic shift in our angle of vision from a state-centric civic education and practice and toward a civic-centered civic education and practice. In affecting such a shift, the "problem" of voter apathy is not "solved" but rather "dissolved." The argument that civic-education must address the political illness of voter apathy is seen to be what it is: a misidentification of a problem for a potential solution. Until civic educators understand that all state-centric civic education is ironic, they will continue to perpetuate the very uncivic and undemocratic institutions and practices that they work so valiantly to overcome.

An Anarchist Alternative: The Modern School Movement

There is an alternative tradition of education in the United States that takes citizen-centric civic education as its philosophical and organizational principle. The "Modern School Movement" has its origins in the educational thought of Spanish educator, freethinker, and anarchist Francisco Ferrer y Guardia.[30] Ferrer envisioned a Modern School (Escuela Moderna) in which students are active participants in guiding their own educational development. As an anarchist, he understandably viewed state-sanctioned schools as an instrument deployed by the ruling class to perpetuate its domination. In other words, Ferrer understood well that state control of the schools would lead to state-centric thinking via state-centric civic education. Unlike most other alternative schools, teachers in the Modern School were drawn from the same working class as were the students. The objective was not merely the dissemination of information nor the inculcation of skills, nor harsh ideological indoctrination, but rather the cultivation of an anti-authoritarian disposition that would inspire individuals to prefigure alternative forms of association in which the practices of freedom, cooperation, and mutual aid were commonplace.

During the early twentieth century at least twenty modern schools were founded in the United States from coast to coast.[31] The pedagogic methods were diverse, but they shared commonalities in that they deemphasized rote memorization and emphasized teaching by experience and example. Moreover, the traditional formalities and discipline of the conventional classroom were dispensed with and replaced by participatory activities that encouraged individual development. Physical as well as mental growth was stressed, and work as well as play considered essential. As Avrich writes regarding the

Modern School approach, "Anticoercive and antiauthoritarian, it stressed
the dignity and rights of children, encouraging warmth, love, and affection
in place of conformity and regimentation. Among the key words of its vo-
cabulary were 'freedom,' 'spontaneity,' creativity,' 'individuality,' and 'self-
realization.'"[32] It is worth remarking that the entire curriculum of the Modern
School Movement is a paradigmatic example of citizen-centric civic education. Unlike state-centric civic education, the Modern School Movement was
consistent in both the values it professed and the methods it employed to
teach those values and practices. If these ideals were translated into practice,
supporters reckoned, the result would be a new society—or societies. And
while that goal has yet to be achieved, the Modern School Movement endures as an example of what a citizen-centric civic education might look like.
Whereas today political scientists have difficulty incorporating pedagogies
of dissent into contemporary state-centric curricula, it is not at all difficult
to envision a neo-Modern School fostering the values and practices of both
dissent and outright political disobedience.

Assuming that civic educators are receptive to this line of argument—and
some evidently are[33]—the question becomes: How might political scientists
help implement a citizen-centric civic education? As we have seen, this
would require two distinct steps: the first conceptual; the second practical.
The conceptual shift in the minds of political scientists from state-centric
to citizen-centric would probably find many partisans, given the hyper-
democratic rhetoric common to most civic education literature found in
political science publications. And given that academics are trained to think
conceptually, one would *hope* that such a shift would not be too difficult
to induce. However, the practical implementation would likely present the
most significant problems.

The Pedagogy of the Stateless: A Twenty-first-Century Primer of Citizen-centric Civic Education

The final section of this chapter presents a "primer of citizen-centered civic
education" or what might be described as "the pedagogy of the State*less*."
Consistent with most anarchists' thinking, any attempt to create a blueprint
for a future society is anathema. The characteristics of a future society, especially its educational practices, cannot be described in any specificity lest
the intentions of those participating in the association be ignored. The best
we can do is sketch a fragmentary list of principles that the pedagogy of the
stateless may reasonably be expected to exhibit. The following "principles"
speak to both the conceptual and practical shift in thinking discussed in this
chapter. They are by no means intended to be exhaustive.

Principle 1: No Centralized Program for Civic Education

The urge to instill virtues of civic-mindedness is strong, particularly among political scientists. The American Political Science Association publishes a guidebook for civic education and encourages political scientists to participate in "Constitution Day," during which members of the profession descend upon local schools to instruct students about the virtues of that document. But what, precisely, is the outcome of these efforts? According to one recent observer, political scientists have done little to alter civic education policies or practices.[34] More to the point, the argument of this chapter is that such efforts are largely counterproductive in that they seek to inculcate values and encourage practices that are state-centric rather than citizen-centric.

If one identifies the great exemplars of citizenship that political scientists often cite, it is immediately obvious that they are the product not of civic education programs, but rather the voluntary mutual aid of citizens who are spontaneously organizing and working to affect political change. The American Revolution had its Committees of Correspondence; the American Civil War had its Underground Railroad; the American Civil Rights Movement had its Freedom Schools; the Feminist Movement had it consciousness raising groups; the Alterglobalization Movement has its affinity groups; the Occupy Wall Street Movement has it spokes councils, and so on. *None of these were the discernible product of programmatic civic education in American schools.* In fact, these exemplars of citizenship represent a kind of political action that is discouraged by standard state-centric civic education. All of these were hostile to the state and were, in one way or another, condemned as disruptive, dangerous, un-American, and treasonous.

The sort of participatory politics that the ideal of citizen-centric education represents is most likely to manifest itself in contexts where citizens have not been schooled in state-centric civic education programs. The solution to the problem of political apathy is not, then, more state-centric civic education, but rather more citizen-centric civic education. Practices of citizen-centric education are first and foremost measured not by the usual metrics political scientists deploy to measure civic participation. Instead, political scientists ought to facilitate direct democratic practice including political disobedience aimed at any and all statist or otherwise centralized hierarchical power structures, and encourage direct democratic practices including consensus decision-making. The indicator of a healthy democratic community ought not to be measured by voter turnout, knowledge about political elites and the like, but rather by the frequency and quality of citizen disobedience to illegitimate structures of power and the creativity they exhibit in creating democratic or horizontalist practices. This would no doubt be difficult to measure, given the variety of practices a community may choose to employ.

Therefore, the concomitant question of what sort of standardized test should be used to measure how well students are learning to "be good citizens" also dissolves. With no general civics curriculum there can be no standardized test. This is not to say that communities would not or should not develop their own unique citizen-centric curriculum and assessments. But those would necessarily be local and the product of consensus. One would guess that these curricula would reflect the values of mutual aid, autonomy, egalitarianism, and freedom that animate the political practices.

Principle 2: Civic Education as Phronēsis

Consistent with the logic of the state, state-centric civic education measures the effectiveness of civic education by evaluating how obedient and docile its citizens are to state authority and power. Do citizens vote, thus legitimating the political process and therefore the state? Do citizens obey the laws and concede to punishment if they violate those laws? Do citizens pay their taxes? Do citizens fight and die for the maintenance of the state? These are the common metrics that political scientists use to determine the health of a democracy. By this point it should be clear that this is a problematic approach, given that what is often taken to be an indicator of a healthy democracy is, in fact, an indicator of not necessarily a democratic community but rather a healthy state. Therefore, the common metrics used for assessing the health of a democracy need to be rethought. The question thus becomes: What are the various learning objectives of a citizen-centric civic education and how are they measured?

What are the indicators of a healthy democracy or horizontal community? There are many. But one in particular stands out: political judgment. Sound political judgment or *phronēsis* as Aristotle explained, would inevitabily be at the core of citizen-centric civic education. *Phronēsis* is a singularly valuable component of civic-centric education because of its tendency to encourage what the English political thinker and proto-anarchist William Godwin (1793) deemed "private judgment." *Phronēsis* should be cultivated by any democratic or horizontal community because it is the essential capacity of each autonomous and free citizen to judge for him- or herself the proper course of action for the individual and community. Unlike voting turnout, knowledge about elites, and other similar metrics of civic competency, *phronēsis* is not merely the reflection of what may or may not be good information; rather it is the essential process by which a citizen *qua* citizen makes decisions about action. The question of did a citizen vote, or even did a citizen vote prudently, is nowhere near as significant as how did a citizen decide to vote for one rather than the other candidate or policy, or perhaps not to vote at all. Moreover, the *phronēsis* is a process of exercising one's practical judgment, practical wisdom, or prudence. As Bent Flyvbjerg has argued, the cultivation of *phronēsis* in citizens ought to be the objective of social scientists.[35] The argument advanced here builds on Aristotle, Godwin, and Flyvbjerg in that any program for civic education spearheaded by political scientists should similarly be guided by the goal of cultivating a phronetic citizenry.

Principle 3: Practice Anarchist Calisthenics

Citizen-centric civic education involves encouraging citizens to not merely "question authority" but to actively challenge illegitimate power, including that of the state. This requires more than book learning. As Aristotle argued long ago, while some knowledge (e.g., *episteme*) can be learned in the classroom, other forms of knowledge (e.g., *techne* and *phronēsis*), can only be learned in practice through practical trial and error.[36] Along these lines John Dewey argued that democracy was not merely a form of government, not merely the Constitution nor the institutions, but a practice, a "form of social life."[37] Therefore citizen-centric education must balance book learning with real-world practice. Of course this is the rationale behind internships and service learning popular at many if not most colleges and universities.[38] But citizen-centric civic education as we have seen involves much more than any internship or service learning experience will require. Indeed internships and service learning jobs are often related to, if not directly sponsored by, the state. One would not expect a White House intern to come away from his or her experience ready to resist the state. Quite the contrary is likely the reality. It is difficult then to envision an internship or service learning program that would offer a citizen the opportunity to practice political disobedience.

Instead, citizens will likely only find such opportunities in a context that is outside of the state—again, recall that this does not mean outside of state territorial boundaries, but rather outside of state-sanctioned "legitimate" activities. The examples of exemplary citizens listed in principle 1 suggest that genuine experience in citizen-centric education must likely occur in the context of direct action or—and this distinction is perhaps less distinct than it may seem—within the context of a self-governing horizontal community. But what about the majority of people that lack the opportunity or the courage to participate in these communities of resistance? This is where James Scott's idea of "anarchist calisthenics" is instructional. Something as seemingly innocuous as jaywalking is Scott's example.[39] To that we might add ingesting an illegal substance, transforming a privately owned yet vacant lot into an urban garden, and distributing food to the hungry without a permit are all examples of everyday acts of state transgression, of anarchist calisthenics. What Scott has in mind is an idea that must be part of any citizen-centric civic education, namely, average citizens must regularly, if somewhat subtly, resist the power of the state in small ways, thus keeping their mind limber and ready to act against the state if it becomes intolerably oppressive, and to act in their community in ways that keep alive civic-centric practices including mutual aid, consensus decision-making, and general resistance to illegitimate authority. To keep from thinking like a state, one must frequently think *and* act as a citizen.

It might by now be clear that whatever role political scientists and professional civic educators play in citizens-centric education, it is secondary to political practice and largely informational and perhaps somewhat inspirational. This, of course, is not a problem if one retains the state-centric model of civic education in which book learning is predominant and occasionally supplemented with similarly statist internships of service learning. But perhaps the most insidious facet of state-centric civic education—and state-centric education generally—is the implementation of standardized testing increasingly common at any educational levels, and to this we might add general curricula and testing. While critics of standardized teaching abound, they often neglect the most disturbing, and for our present purposes the most apt aspect, namely that these tests direct teachers' and professors' attention to what the state deems valuable, not merely in terms of educational outcomes, but in terms of political outcomes. That is to say, students must be—to borrow Foucault's terms—"disciplined" and rendered "docile" to state power.[40] Instead of exercising students' minds and bodies in creative and citizen-centric activities, educators are subtly coerced into "teaching" students not merely content, but practices that will further state power. A counter to this might be deemed "de-standardized testing," by which educators of whatever stripe determine what students need/want to know—ideally in conjunction with the students themselves—and then design civic education learning and assessment exercises. Yet the caveat remains that no civic learning is possible or complete without recourse to the real world of practice. This may take the form of overt political disobedience or jaywalking, but it is in action that *phronēsis* is activated and citizen-centric civic education occurs.

Principle 4: Mind Your Own Business!

The tradition of individuality is strong in the American cultural imagination. Yet the emphasis on the community is at least as old as Aristotle and as new as the Tocqueville-inspired "communitarian" arguments popular in contemporary political science.[41] And for every observer who cites Thoreau's individualism there will be another who cites the New England town meeting as evidence of the centrality of the community in American political life. The individual versus the community trope is mostly just that, a device for framing a certain argument. And one would be hard pressed to find a political ideology that fails to make room for both the individual and the community. Even the venerable tradition of anarchist thought and practice venerates both the individual and the community.[42] There can be no community without individuals, and it would be difficult—if not impossible—to envision an individual without some form of community, however tenuous the relationship may be.

That said, the role of education of any kind has always been to re-create social values and practices across time and space. It would be difficult to think of an educational system or set of practices that did not involve a community. And in the modern world the community and its educational values and practices are increasingly dominated by the state. Through the various technics of control we have already discussed, the state seeks to replicate its values and practices through the system of state-sanctioned educational practices. Perhaps it is more effective to think of this along Gramscian lines of counter-hegemonies vying for influence, or perhaps from Machiavelli's perspective of the two "humors" evident in humankind: the desire on the part of the few to dominate and the desire on the part of the many not to be dominated—that is, to be free. Either way, there are those who desire to be left alone to the fullest extent possible. Perhaps they want to live in solitude, or perhaps they seek to construct and live in a community which is horizontalist in design. In a phrase, they want to mind their own business. This is, of course, a vexing issue for statists who see any challenge to state power and authority as potentially destructive to the state. Education policy is obviously one—perhaps the most significant—area in which this tension between the state and the citizen is most apparent. Although the intelligent observer would likely agree that "civic-education" is but one facet of general education that, while not overtly, surely seeks to inculcate citizens with statist and other ideas. Thus the argument in support of citizen-centric civic education necessarily dovetails with the more general de-schooling movement that seeks to free the young from educational coercion. The general criticisms of the de-schooling movement is that it will endanger the lives and futures of children by not assuring they have the proper tools needed for success in life. Of course the counterargument made by the de-schoolers is that such schooling is not necessarily effective in that way, but it is often quite effective in teaching students via the "hidden-curriculum" values and practices that many citizens abhor (e.g., elitism, classism, racism, etc.). To that list must be added the state-centric thinking criticized in this chapter. Citizens want to mind their own business and therefore do not want the State telling them what to do, specifically how to raise their children. That must be left up to the parents and the community to decide for themselves. Thus a civic-centric civic education must always respect the autonomy of the individual and desist from any uninvited intrusion into that community lest it violate the principle of minding one's own business.

Principle 5: There Are No Absolute Principles

As noted above, a "blueprint" for a citizen-centric civic education is inherently problematic in that it suggests that an absolute plan may be devised that is applicable regardless of context. The idea of such a plan is entirely consistent with the sort of state-centric thinking a citizen-centric civic education aims to undermine. Thus, the final principle emphasizes this point. In the end, there are no trans-contextual principles beyond questioning. At best these principles may serve as a guide to aid in the resistance of state power and the inspiration for creative practices that enable people to live a life of autonomy and freedom.

CONCLUSION

The future of democracy in the United States depends upon the re-imagining of civic education as citizen-centric. This is paradoxical, however, given that such a mode of civic education may well lead to the dissolution of the United States. The overt rhetoric of civic educators has always been the sort of democratic vigilance associated with political thinkers including Thomas Paine, Thomas Jefferson, Henry David Thoreau, Emma Goldman, John Dewey, and Noam Chomsky, among many others. Yet in practice civic education has always fallen short of practicing what it preaches. The slogans "a little revolution now and again is a good thing" and "the government is best that governs least" stir the radical in each of us, but civic educators stop short of advocating such direct action. Instead, they fall back into the state-centric mode; voting, party membership, contributing to interest groups, and other "conventional" modes of political participation are encouraged. And when those methods fail, and the topic of disobedience arises, they are careful to note that *civil* disobedience is, after all, the breaking of a law with the willingness to accept the punishment—even if that law is understood to be unjust. Civil disobedience is first and foremost recognition of the legitimacy of a regime that is, at least in part, already understood to be illegitimate. Perhaps, as Bernard E. Harcourt argues, we need a new conception of disobedience, *political* disobedience, which both refuses to obey an unjust law *and* refuses to recognize the state's claim to legitimacy by actively evading punishment. What civic education in the United States must be re-imagined to do is encourage citizens young and old to think *not* like a State, but rather, for themselves as citizens of an autonomous voluntary community, horizontally organized, conducted via the consensus decision-making process, and federated with other similarly organized communities.

Some—perhaps most—readers may view the proposal for a citizen-centric civic education argued for in this chapter incredulously and presume it to be wildly unrealistic. But they would do well to remember that civic education, particularly in the United States, is founded upon ideals consistent with those revolutionary principles that Americans, indeed peoples globally, hold dear. And as long as state power continues to expand, those ideals will be threatened by the very educational institutions entrusted with their preservation. That fact is indeed the irony of civic education in the United States.

NOTES

1. James C. Scott, *Seeing Like a State: How Certain Schemes to Improve the Human Condition Have Failed* (New Haven: Yale University Press, 1999); James C. Scott, *The Art of Not Being Governed: An Anarchist History of Upland Southeast Asia* (New Haven: Yale University Press, 2010).

2. David Feith, ed., *Teaching America: The Case for Civic Education* (Lanham: Rowman & Littlefield, Inc., 2011); David E. Campbell, Meira Levinson, and Frederick M. Hess, eds., *Making Civics Count: Citizenship Education for a New Generation* (Harvard Education Press, 2012); and Elizabeth Kaufer Busch and Jonathan W. White, eds., *Civic Education and the Future of American Citizenship* (Lanham: Lexington Books, 2012).

3. Barbara Jacoby and Associates, *Civic Education in Higher Education: Concepts and Practices* (San Francisco: Jossey-Bass, 2009).

4. See Lewis Perry, *Civil Disobedience: An American Tradition* (New Haven: Yale University Press, 2013).

5. In Peter Lassman, ed. *Weber: Political Writings* (Cambridge: Cambridge University Press, 1994 [1919]).

6. See John R. Hibbing and Elizabeth Theiss-Morse, *Stealth Democracy: Americans' Beliefs about How Government Should Work* (Cambridge: Cambridge University Press, 2002).

7. See Benjamin R. Barber, *Strong Democracy: Participatory Politics for a New Age* (Berkeley, CA: University of California Press, 1984).

8. David Graeber, "Occupy and Anarchism's Gift of Democracy," *New York Times*, November 15, 2011. http://www.theguardian.com/commentisfree/cifamerica/2011/nov/15/occupy-anarchism-gift-democracy.

9. Max Stirner. *The Ego and Its Own* (Cambridge: Cambridge University Press, 1995 [1844]).

10. For examples of such practices and communities see Marina A. Sitrin, *Everyday Revolutions: Horizontalism and Autonomy in Argentina* (London and New York: Zed Books, 2012), and Marina A. Sitrin, ed., *Horizontalism: Voices of Popular Power in Argentina* (Edinburgh, Oakland, West Virginia: AK Press, 2006).

11. John Taylor Gatto, (1992; 2000), Paul Goodman (1966), John Holt (1972), Ivan Illich (1971), Herbert R. Kohl (2009), Diane Ravitch (2011; 2013), and Charles E. Silberman (1971)

12. Amy Gutmann, *Democratic Education* (Princeton: Princeton University Press, 1987).

13. John R. Hibbing and Elizabeth Theiss-Morse, "Civics Is Not Enough: Teaching Barbarics in K–12, " *PS: Political Science & Politics* 29, no. 1 (1996).

14. Paulo Freire, *Pedagogy of the Oppressed* (New York: Continuum Publishing Group, Ltd., 2000 [1970]).

15. Henry A. Giroux, *Pedagogy and the Politics of Hope: Theory, Culture, and Schooling: A Critical Reader* (Boulder, CO: Westview Press, 1997).

16. Samuel Bowels and Herbert Gintis, *Schooling in Capitalist America: Educational Reform and the Contradictions of Economic Life* (Chicago: Haymarket Books, [1978] 2011).

17. Sarah M. Stitzlein, *Teaching for Dissent: Citizen Education and Political Activism* (Boulder, CO: Paradigm Publishers, 2013).

18. Cf. Reinhold Hedtke and Tatjana Zimenkova, eds., *Education for Civic and Political Participation: A Critical Approach* (New York: Routledge, 2013); Mordechai Gordon, ed. *Reclaiming Dissent: Civics Education for the 21st Century* (Rotterdam, Netherlands: Sense Publishers, 2009).

19. Stitzlein, *Teaching for Dissent*, 2.

20. Ibid., 63ff.

21. Ibid., 70.

22. Ibid., 77.

23. Ibid., 95.

24. Ibid., 118 ff.

25. Ibid., 184.

26. Max Weber, "Politics as a Vocation," in *Weber: Political Writings,* Peter Lassman, ed (Cambridge: Cambridge University Press, 1995).

27. Cf. David Graeber, *The Democracy Project: A History, a Crisis, a Movement* (New York: Spiegel & Grau, 2013) and David Graeber, *Direct Action: Ethnography* (Edinburgh, Oakland and Baltimore: PM Press, 2009).

28. Bernard E. Harcourt, "Political Disobedience," *Critical Inquiry* 39 (2012): 34.

29. Ibid., 34.

30. See Paul Avrich, *The Modern School Movement: Anarchism and Education in the United States* (Princeton: Princeton University Press, 1980).

31. Ibid., 217 ff.

32. Ibid., 7–8.

33. Robert H. Hayworth, ed. *Anarchist Pedagogies: Collective Actions, Theories, and Critical Reflections on Education* (Oakland: PM Press, 2012).

34. Richard M. Battistoni, "Should Political Scienctists Care about Civic Education?, " *Perspective on Politics* 11, no. 4 (2013).

35. Bent Flyvbjerg. *Making Social Science Matter: Why Social Inquiry Fails and How It Can Succeed Again* (Cambridge: Cambridge University Press, 2001: 53–65).

36. Aristotle. *Nicomachean Ethics*. Trans. C.D.C Reeve (Indianapolis/Cambridge, 2014: 1139b, 18–36; 1140a, 1–23).

37. John Dewey, *Democracy and Education* (New York: The Free Press, 1916), 92–93. For a recent argument along these lines see Dan Sabin, "Democratic/Utopian Education," *Utopian Studies* 23 (2012): 374–405.

38. Jacoby et al., *Civic Education in Higher Education*.

39. James C. Scott, *Two Cheers for Anarchism: Six Easy Pieces on Autonomy, Dignity, and Meaningful Work and Play* (Princeton & Oxford: Princeton University Press, 2012).

40. Foucault, Michel. *Discipline and Punish: The Birth of the Prison* (New York: Vintage, 1995 [1975]).

41. See Avineri, Shlomo and Avner de-Shalit, eds. *Communitarianism and Individualism* (Oxford: Oxford University Press, 1992).

42. For individualist anarchism see Max Stirner, *The Ego and Its Own*. For more community-focused anarchism—by far more common—see various anarchists in Peter Marshall, *Demanding the Impossible: A History of Anarchism* (London, New York, Toronto, and Sydney, 1992).

BIBLIOGRAPHY

Avrich, Paul. 1980. *The Modern School Movement: Anarchism and Education in the United States*. Princeton: Princeton University Press.

Battistoni, Richard, M. 2013. "Should Political Scientists Care about Civic Education?" *Perspectives on Politics* 11, 4: 1135–38.

Bowels, Samuel, and Herbert Gintis. [1978] 2011. *Schooling in Capitalist America: Educational Reform and the Contradictions of Economic Life*. Chicago: Haymarket Books.

Busch, Elizabeth Kaufer, and Jonathan W. White, eds. 2012. *Civic Education and the Future of American Citizenship*. Lanham: Lexington Books.

Campbell, David E., Meira Levinson, and Frederick M. Hess, eds. 2012. *Making Civics Count: Civic Education for a New Generation*. Cambridge: Harvard Education Press.

Chomsky, Noam, and C. P. Otero, ed. 2002. *Chomsky on Democracy and Education*. New York and London: Routledge.

Dewey, John. 1916. *Democracy and Education*. New York: The Free Press.

Feith, David, ed. 2011. *Teaching America: The Case for Civic Education*. Lanham: Rowman & Littlefield Education.

Foucault, Michel. 1995 [1975]. *Discipline and Punish: The Birth of the Prison*. New York: Vintage.

Freire, Paulo. 2000 [1970]. *Pedagogy of the Oppressed*. New York: Continuum Publishing Group, Ltd.

Flyvbjerg, Bent. 2001. *Making Social Science Matter: Why Social Inquiry Fails and How It Can Succeed Again*. Cambridge: Cambridge University Press.

Gatto, John T. 2000. *The Underground History of American Education: A School Teacher's Intimate Investigation into the Problem of Modern Schooling.* New York: Odysseus Group

———. 1992. *Dumbing Us Down: The Hidden Curriculum of Compulsory Schooling.* Gabriola Island, BC, Canada: New Society Publishers.

Giroux, Henry A. 1997. *Pedagogy and the Politics of Hope: Theory, Culture, and Schooling: A Critical Reader.* Boulder, CO: Westview Press.

Godwin, William. [1793] 2013. *An Enquiry Concerning Political Justice.* Oxford: Oxford University Press.

Goodman, Paul. 1966. *Compulsory Mis-Education and the Community of Scholars.* New York: Random House, 1966.

Gordon, Mordechai, ed. 2009. *Reclaiming Dissent: Civics Education for the 21st Century.* Rotterdam, Netherlands: Sense Publishers.

Graeber, David. 2013. *The Democracy Project: A History, a Crisis, a Movement.* New York: Spiegel & Grau.

———. 2011. "Occupy and Anarchism's Gift of Democracy." *New York Times*, November 15. Accessed January 11, 2013. http://www.theguardian.com/commentis-free/cifamerica/2011/nov/15/occupy-anarchism-gift-democracy

———. 2009. *Direct Action: Ethnography.* Edinburgh, Oakland and Baltimore: PM Press.

Gutmann, Amy. 1987. *Democratic Education.* Princeton: Princeton University Press.

Harcourt, Bernard E. 2012. "Political Disobedience." *Critical Inquiry* 39: 33–55.

Hayworth, Robert H., ed. 2012. *Anarchist Pedagogies: Collective Actions, Theories, and Critical Reflections on Education.* Oakland: PM Press.

Hedtke, Reinhold, and Tatjana Zimenkova, eds. 2013. *Education for Civic and Political Participation: A Critical Approach.* New York: Routledge.

Holt, John. 1972. *Freedom and Beyond.* New York: E.P. Dutton & Co., Inc.

Illich, Ivan. 1971. *Deschooling Society.* New York: Harper and Row.

Jacoby, Barbara, and Associates. 2009. *Civic Education in Higher Education: Concepts and Practices.* San Francisco: Jossey-Bass.

Kohl, Herbert R. 2009. *The Herbert Kohl Reader: Awaking the Heart of Teaching.* New York: The New Press.

Landauer, Gustav. *For Socialism.* [1911] 1978. New York: Telos Press.

Marshall, Peter. 1992. *Demanding the Impossible: A History of Anarchism.* London, New York, Toronto, and Sydney.

McIlrath, Lorraine, Ann Lyons, and Ronaldo Munck, eds. 2012. *Higher Education and Civic Engagement: Comparative Perspectives.* New York: Palgrave Macmillan.

Mitchell, W. J. T, Bernard E. Harcourt, and Michael Taussig. 2013. *Occupy: Three Inquires in Disobedience.* Chicago: University of Chicago Press.

Perry, Lewis. 2013. *Civil Disobedience: An American Tradition.* New Haven: Yale University Press.

Ravitch, Diane. 2013. *Reign of Error: The Hoax of the Privatization Movement and the Danger to America's Public Schools.* New York: Knopf.

———. 2011. *The Life and Death of the Great American School System: How Testing and Choice are Undermining Education.* New York: Basic Books.

Sabin, Dan. 2012. "Democratic/Utopian Education." *Utopian Studies* 23: 374–405.

Scott, James C. 2012. *Two Cheers for Anarchism: Six Easy Pieces on Autonomy, Dignity, and Meaningful Work and Play.* Princeton & Oxford: Princeton University Press.

———. 2010. *The Art of Not Being Governed: An Anarchist History of Upland Southeast Asia.* New Haven: Yale University Press.

———. 1999. *Seeing Like a State: How Certain Schemes to Improve the Human Condition Have Failed.* New Haven: Yale University Press.

Silberman, Charles E. 1971. *The Crisis in the Classroom: The Remaking of American Education.* New York: Vintage.

Sitrin, Marina A. 2012. *Everyday Revolutions: Horizontalism and Autonomy in Argentina.* London and New York: Zed Books.

———. ed. 2006. *Horizontalism: Voices of Popular Power in Argentina.* Edinburgh, Oakland, West Virginia: AK Press.

Stevick, E. Doyle, and Bradley A. U. Levinson, eds. 2007. *Reimagining Civic Education: How Diverse Societies Form Democratic Citizens.* Lanham: Rowman & Littlefield Publishers, Inc.

Stirner, Max. [1844] 1995. *The Ego and Its Own.* Cambridge: Cambridge University Press.

Stitzlein, Sarah, M. 2013. *Teaching for Dissent: Citizen Education and Political Activism.* Boulder, CO: Paradigm Publishers.

Weber, Max. [1919] 1994. "Politics as a Vocation," in *Weber: Political Writings,* Peter Lassman, ed. Cambridge: Cambridge University Press.

Chapter Four

Models of Civic Education in America

Gary E. Bugh

How teachers convey basic lessons about living in our representative democracy may help overcome theoretical obstacles to civic education.[1] Fortunately, there are distinct models of civic education that serve as guideposts to teachers navigating civic education through a sea of resistance and irony. It is useful to place "formal pedagogy" and "political participation" at polar ends of an imagined range of civic education approaches.[2] These models, one focusing on teaching objective facts in the classroom and the other on participating directly in politics, provide bearings to identify and evaluate other distinct though less extreme means of civic education. Two such intermediate approaches are "minority dissent" and "civic engagement." These four different "ideal types" of civic education are not necessarily mutually exclusive; nor are they the only ways to impart civic lessons, applicable to all subjects, or used as described in their analytical forms.[3] Yet, teachers may find this continuum useful for aligning their respective civic-education approaches with their goals. In so doing, they will be well-armed to surmount some of the barriers to civic education in America.

THEORETICAL OBSTACLES TO CIVIC EDUCATION IN THE UNITED STATES

There are several obstacles to civic education in America, and those that are theoretical in nature may present the greatest hurdles. Philosophically speaking, one purpose of civic education has long been to develop citizens' "civic virtue"—a set of values and convictions supporting a deep commitment to civil society and other citizens, encouraging participation in public affairs.[4] As an effort to foster civic morality, civic education confronts at least two theoretical impediments.

Resistance to Combining Morality and Government

The first obstacle to civic education in America is a cultural and legal preference to maintain a separation between morality and government. When government becomes involved in promoting civic education, it becomes involved in promoting morality. Modern theorists—including Niccolò Machiavelli and John Locke—pointed out that the intermingling of morality and government provides governing officials a way to justify the abuse of power, and should therefore be avoided. The American constitutional order established in 1789 and defended by the Federalists carries forward this historical resistance to combining government and morality.

The Federalists wanted morality and government detached from one another because they feared rule by the majority of the people. James Madison argued that the "mischiefs of faction" explained why "democracies have ever been spectacles of turbulence and contention; . . . and have in general been as short in their lives as they have been violent in their deaths."[5] Rule by the factious majority would surely result in a "confusion of a multitude" and societal breakdown.[6] After all, "factions" and "sects" had no more morality than "passion or interest," and "neither moral nor religious motives can be relied on as an adequate control" to prevent them from trying to oppress others.[7] Instead of morality or education, Madison held that federalism would keep any faction from becoming strong enough to take over the national government, and separation of powers would encourage ambitious federal officials to keep an eye on each another. Yet, he asserted that congressional representatives would be "a chosen body of citizens, whose wisdom may best discern the true interest of their country, and whose patriotism and love of justice will be least likely to sacrifice it to temporary or partial considerations."[8] Other Federalists gave the same promise about national officials. John Jay contended that presidential electors would be "the most enlightened and respectable citizens" and that presidents would be those "most distinguished by their abilities and virtue."[9] For the Federalists, national officials would govern on behalf of everyone based not on religion, ideology, or interest, but on the individual integrity, wisdom, and merit that they brought to government. However, reflecting their adherence to keep morality and government apart, the Federalists did not address how some Americans would come to have such traits—nor did the proposed constitution.

The body of the Constitution does not establish any institutions specifically designed to develop wisdom or virtue. In the one instance that the Constitution addresses morality, it expressly keeps it out of government with a prohibition on religious tests for public office. The First Amendment clarifies the issue, forever banning Congress from passing any law that would establish a national religion. The Constitution makes no provision for public education, let alone civic education. Presumably, individual character, talent, and knowledge would develop outside the constitutional order, in private. Indeed, Alexis de Tocqueville noted that Americans seem to prefer that education take place in the private sphere and civic morality develop freely, as individuals pursue their own interests, participate in private associations, and experience existing political institutions and practices.[10]

America's institutional separation of morality and government along with the Federalists' defense of this divide fuels a resistance to government involvement in civic education. This opposition is not ill-placed—as Westheimer and Kahne argue, national officials have attempted to implement government-developed civics curricula.[11] They elaborate that what is often left out of government-endorsed "civics" education is teaching students about participation in public affairs, including evaluating and criticizing government and economic structures, practices, and officials.[12] If successful, such education would suppress public resistance to the government's policy goals. However, Benjamin Barber argues that the result of trying to keep morality and government separate is an American educational system that "seems little concerned to provide education on substantive issues. Like most other public responsibilities, this crucial function is left largely in private hands."[13]

Irony of Rights

A second theoretical obstacle to civic education is an educational irony of rights. This refers to the phenomenon that once people see themselves as possessing rights, some may conclude that it is unnecessary to learn anything more about civics. The compelling nature of the concept of rights helps explain this hindrance to civic education.

Rights are powers that citizens equally have regardless of whether they find themselves in the minority, majority, or somewhere in between.[14] Rights provide each citizen ways of participating in collective self-rule, including questioning, criticizing, and renewing government, as well as demanding equal treatment and respect.[15] As such powers, rights exemplify what Robert Dahl calls the "strong principle of equality," which is the belief "that all members of the association are adequately qualified to participate on an equal footing with the others in the process of governing the association."[16] Others—including W. E. B. DuBois, John Dewey, and Peter Bachrach—agree that each citizen has what it takes to participate in politics.[17]

Additionally, some theorists, including the Anti-Federalists and Thomas Jefferson, held that rights are not just an essential and equal aspect of citizenship, they serve an educative function. Along with checking government, this is why they argued for a bill of rights—it would remind citizens that they held unconditional and immutable powers.[18] Jefferson added that civic lessons at the lowest levels of public school would reinforce citizens' knowledge about their rights.[19] He recognized that rights-knowledge was not enough for citizenship; exercising rights through participation in local affairs and election of all officials was necessary to bring forth citizens' "moral sense."[20] Overall, rights in America provide a route for civic education that is able to traverse the constitutional separation of morality and government. In other words, despite the theoretical and institutional barriers to merging morality and government in America, the nation also embraces equal rights, making it possible to bring morality and government together and support civic education.

However, the assertion that citizens possess equal rights ironically dissuades some people from delving deeper into civic knowledge, skills, and practices. Tocqueville recognized this dilemma in his argument that equality encourages each person to believe that there is no higher authority than the individual, in turn isolating citizens from one another.[21] Moreover, knowing that rights serve a civic educative function, an individual might question why we would need to implement civic education in schools. Tocqueville noted, though, that participation in public affairs diminishes the chances that equality would result in withdrawal.[22] The four models of civic education address these and other obstacles.

FORMAL PEDAGOGY APPROACH TO CIVIC EDUCATION

The formal pedagogy approach to civic education focuses on objective facts. Some subjects necessarily cover many factual details and nearly all teaching involves the conveyance of specifics to some extent. Even Benjamin Barber, who advocates direct citizen participation in local politics, acknowledges that "[a] basic knowledge of the nation's constitution and legal system, of its political history and institutions, and of its culture and political practice is obviously indispensable to democracy in any form."[23] Formal pedagogy involves classroom teaching of basic information.

Theoretical Justifications

The formal pedagogy approach reflects the classical liberal concern with keeping government out of morality, which includes keeping it out of education. Rather than morality, the liberal view of education calls for "neutrality." Contemporary liberal theorist John Rawls contends that education provides two functions for individuals: training for a profession and facilitating self-respect.[24] Strengthening a person's self-worth, according to Rawls, prepares the individual to freely choose between different political ideas and theories.[25] Neutrality also avoids inflaming particular factional or religious interests and agitating the existing social order. As Geraint Parry explains, this liberal perspective advocates doctrine-free political education, which a fact-based curriculum seems to accommodate.[26]

However, formal pedagogy may include lessons directed at molding students' character into what Joel Westheimer and Joseph Kahne refer to as the "personally responsible citizen"—someone who "works and pays taxes, obeys laws, and helps those in need during crises."[27] Parry argues that neutral liberal education insists that students eschew privately-learned values and focus instead on being "reasonable."[28] The personally responsible and reasonable citizen fits with the liberal vision of the self-respecting and politically neutral resident. It is reminiscent of Federalist John Adams's argument that history education should emphasize the study of virtuous public figures.[29] Regardless of intent, the fact-based model generally teaches benign information.

Recent Scholarship

Several contemporary scholars study fact-based teaching, although they may examine different kinds of content, such as values or skills.[30] Some of them defend the idea that information-focused pedagogy preserves and propagates society. For example, Amy Gutmann holds that "education must be guided by the principles, not the practices, of a regime."[31] She elaborates that "political education" involves "the cultivation of the virtues, knowledge, and skills necessary for political participation . . . [and] prepares citizens to participate in consciously reproducing their society."[32] Robert Heslep argues that "[e]ducation's moral role in the democratic state . . . is to prepare members of the society to carry out their institutional duties and to help them learn to participate in morally acceptable activities lying beyond their institutional duties," and that this "cannot be performed without the benefit of a curriculum."[33]

Michael Delli Carpini and Scott Keeter's research relates to formal civic pedagogy.[34] Their definition of political knowledge is "the range of factual information about politics that is stored in long-term memory."[35] Analyzing survey questions from 1940–1994, they categorize this information under "the rules of the game," "the substance of politics," and "the people and players."[36] Their research finds that Americans are more knowledgeable about the rarely changing rules of the game and less informed about domestic and foreign issues and specific political actors. Overall, they conclude that most Americans are "generalists," by which they mean people who either know or do not know some facts about many areas of politics; few are "specialists," having extensive knowledge of one or a few areas.[37] Delli Carpini and Keeter therefore contend that it is possible for researchers to measure the political knowledge of any group of Americans with a set of just five "questions about the government in Washington" that they have developed.[38]

Potential Advantages and Possible Problems

Pedantic civics lessons convey specific information, stand against combining government and morality, and, at least at lower educational levels, may contribute to responsible and reasonable citizens. But there are several problems with focusing on seemingly objective facts.

Formal pedagogy lends support to the status quo. Fact-based teaching avoids lessons about diversity, rights, conflict, political participation, criticism, dissent, and abuse of government power. It is likely to focus on contributing to the personally responsible and reasonable citizen. And this neutral aim is susceptible to infiltration by lessons that benefit powers external to citizens, even though the curriculum may do so in the guise of what E. Wayne Ross calls "citizenship education."[39] Ross argues that teaching just the facts can readily transform into political indoctrination. For Ross, the "citizenship transmission" model of social studies appears to be an objective pedagogical fact-based approach, but in actuality it inculcates students with "American" facts and values. Ross explains that

> [i]n this tradition, the purpose of social studies education is to promote student acquisition of certain "American" or "democratic" values via the teaching and learning of discrete, factual pieces of information drawn primarily from the canon of Western thought and culture. Content is based on the beliefs that: certain factual information is important to the practice of good citizenship; the nature of this information remains relatively constant over time; and this information is best determined by a consensus of authorities and experts.[40]

In seeking to reproduce the cultural political heritage of the United States, the formal pedagogy approach tends to advance, as Westheimer argues, "some unified notion of truth that supports—without dissent—officially accepted positions."[41] Historian Howard Zinn shares this conclusion, as he forcefully argues in *Politics and History*.[42] In other words, fact-based pedagogy is not as neutral as some theorists assert because it is prone to teaching the very information that government officials prefer, but without their involvement.

Moreover, an emphasis on objective, pedantic, rote-memorization knowledge is more likely to stymie than stimulate politically active citizenship. With teachers presenting culturally favored lessons to students passively sitting in classrooms, the setting itself is not participatory. Then there is the near absence of lessons concerning active citizenship. Westheimer and Kahne argue that even teaching students to have law-abiding and service-oriented character "can obscure the need for collective and often public sector initiatives; . . . distract attention from analysis of the causes of social problems; and [put forward] volunteerism and kindness . . . as ways of avoiding politics and policy."[43] Fact-based teaching is so likely to suppress active citizenship that some specifically call for it as a way to prevent students from questioning and criticizing power.[44]

When it comes to pedantically teaching civil liberties, the takeaway for some students may be that, since citizens already equally possess rights, there is no need for more civic education. Granted, some research finds that people become more tolerant and efficacious as they become better educated.[45] But, as Doris Graber has argued, there is insufficient evidence that simply being taught facts—the number of stars on the flag, amendments making up the Bill of Rights, or branches of government—contributes to increased levels of political participation or tolerance of minority rights.[46] If anything, just "knowing your rights and knowing the law are concomitants first of all of minimalist or weak democratic politics," Barber contends, since such formal knowledge may present the illusion of citizenship but does not include participation in public affairs.[47]

There are other problems with the formal pedagogy approach. It may benefit students who already have greater advantages than other students. Some see this as a desirable outcome. For example, Rawls holds that education is a distributable resource and because some people may be more intelligent or talented than others, "giving more attention to the better endowed" may be to everyone's benefit, including the least well-off.[48] Translated into practical terms, though, the civics consequence of a formal pedagogical curriculum means that students scoring highest on objective fact-based exams are deemed better citizens. Researchers have found that a focus on neutral institutions and procedures is gender-biased in favor of males.[49] Another issue is that some advocates of formal pedagogy present a false-dichotomy defense, namely, that teachers should either "teach facts" or "leave to chance."[50] For example, Robert Heslep asserts that moral participatory citizenship "cannot be performed without the benefit of a curriculum. It is far too complex for its performance to succeed by happenstance."[51] Yet, there are alternatives to formal pedagogy that are not *de facto*.

POLITICAL PARTICIPATION
APPROACH TO CIVIC EDUCATION

At the other end of a spectrum of civic education models is political participation.[52] Educators rarely if ever use this approach because it concerns direct political activity that takes place not just outside the classroom but entirely outside the curriculum. As Alison Rios Millett McCartney explains, "[p]olitical engagement refers to explicitly politically oriented activities that seek a direct impact on political issues, systems, relationship, and structures."[53] No classroom instruction is necessary in this way of learning political knowledge. According to the political participation model, participants will learn the knowledge relevant to their political goals as they engage in political activity.

Theoretical Justifications

Democratic theory supports the political participation model of civic education. Benjamin Barber envisions an entire democratic civil society essentially built around this extracurricular approach. Barber's "strong democracy" involves an array of participatory structures including neighborhood assemblies and random selection.[54] For Barber, direct political engagement fosters civics knowledge, and therefore civic education is woven throughout his proposed democratic system. He encapsulates the political participation approach with the argument that "knowledge and the quest for knowledge tend to follow rather than to precede direct political participation: give people some significant power and they will quickly appreciate the need for knowledge, but foist knowledge on them without giving them responsibility and they will display only indifference."[55]

Tocqueville's "self-interest rightly understood" is a version of the political participation approach.[56] Tocqueville argued that because participation in public affairs is such an integral aspect of life in America, citizens independently conclude that it is in their self-interest to help others. Through participation in associations and local government, he observed, Americans reason that they may need personal help someday and therefore habitually assist others first. In other words, political participation teaches people a civic morality without any formal classroom instruction.

Recent Scholarship

Doris Graber reflects the political participation approach, at least in her criticism of the formal pedagogy approach. She begins with the premise that human beings are "limited information processors," that is, we are physiologically limited in our ability to remember a lot of detailed information.[57] Therefore, Delli Carpini and Keeter's "factual information about politics," including rules, substance, and players, is not essential for participatory citizenship. Graber argues that citizens do not need to "precisely remember factual knowledge about historically important past and current events."[58] Instead, the knowledge for active citizenship is what people need to know, to borrow Graber's phrasing. Graber's research finds that people already possess sufficient knowledge about issues that concern them in order to participate in politics if they need to do so. The implication is that if there were more opportunities for citizen engagement in politics, especially at the local level, then people would learn what they need as they go.

Potential Advantages and Possible Problems

The political participation approach is a powerful endorsement of Dahl's "strong principle of equality." However, this model presumes that citizens already have basic civics knowledge. Without defending general content to teach, the political participation approach invites parochial-based lessons. It may exacerbate the "mass society" fragmentation of citizens, subjecting individual participants to elite manipulation.[59] It also does not elaborate a transmission mechanism of participatory-relevant knowledge. How are Americans to learn that they have rights? How are Americans to learn about various ways of participating in politics, even if they may not need detailed factual knowledge to begin such engagements? Moreover, the political participation model focuses so much on the exercise of rights that it may discourage the desire to learn more political knowledge. That is to say, the assertion that each person can already participate in politics as needed may prompt some to wonder why they should bother learning anything else about civics.

MINORITY DISSENT APPROACH TO CIVIC EDUCATION

There are other distinct models of civic education in between formal pedagogy and political participation, such as "minority dissent." The minority dissent approach presents stories of resistance to power and struggles for equal citizenship. At a minimum, it conveys the basic lessons that a citizen, even if part of the minority, has and can exercise inviolable and equal rights. The minority dissent approach to civic education offers actual examples of popular participation that did not necessarily depend upon formal civic lessons. In so doing, it brings direct political participation into conventional pedagogical fact-based teaching.

Theoretical Justifications

In a liberal democracy like the United States, citizens' exercise of rights helps guard the individual against government, as well as other forms of power. Government is of particular concern since it has sole legitimate control over many powers that can affect life and death—making laws, punishing individuals, and going to war. Protection of the minority is necessary because a citizen who is part of the minority is more vulnerable to oppression, discrimination, and marginalization than someone who is in the majority. Regardless of where they find themselves, citizens can use their rights to question, criticize, and challenge government, corporations, groups, majority rule, and the status quo, as well as to demand equal respect.

Elizabeth Cady Stanton and W. E. B. DuBois theoretically defended minority resistance to the majority.[60] Both theorists held that marginalized people possess the right to insist on equal standing, and that the shared experience of exclusion informs compelling reasons for inclusion.[61] They also argued that appeals by those in power for virtuous behavior is a way to keep the marginalized from participating in governing.

Several contemporary civic education scholars have defended the minority dissent approach, albeit with different labels.[62] Ross's "informed social criticism" approach to social studies, for example, is "aimed at providing students opportunities for an examination, critique, and revision of past traditions, existing social practices, and modes of problem solving. It is a citizenship education directed toward social transformation as guided by values of justice and equality for determining the direction of social change."[63] Westheimer and Kahne argue for "the justice-oriented citizen" curriculum, which seeks to develop students who will "critically assess social, political, and economic structures and consider collective strategies for change that challenge injustice and, when possible, address root causes of problems."[64] They elaborate that this approach is "likely to teach about social movements and how to affect systemic change."

Various sources provide examples of minority dissent in America. William Bigelow and Norman Diamond offer a useful source of minority dissent in *The Power in Our Hands: A Curriculum on the History of Work and Workers in the United States*.[65] More recently, work by activist Naomi Wolf reviews different areas of life with a critical eye on government power.[66] Several political documentary films—*The Education of Shelby Knox, Sir! No Sir!, The U.S. vs. John Lennon*—present stories about a minority standing against the majority.[67] Government itself may provide minority dissent narratives, such as any given legislative battle in which the minority party resisted an unjust law that the majority party was trying to pass. Perhaps the most notable contemporary scholar in this area is historian Howard Zinn.

Howard Zinn's *A People's History of the United States, The Politics of History*, and more recent offerings under the title *A Young People's History of the United States* provide accessible resources for teachers looking to incorporate the minority dissent approach into their curricula.[68] Howard Zinn's explanation of how he writes history captures the minority dissent approach. Zinn states that

> [m]y history describes the inspiring struggle of those who have fought slavery and racism (Frederick Douglass, William Lloyd Garrison, Fannie Lou Hamer, Bob Moses), of the labor organizers who have led strikes for the rights of working people (Big Bill Haywood, Mother Jones, César Chájvez), of the socialists and others who have protested war and militarism (Eugene Debs, Helen Keller, the Rev. Daniel Berrigan, Cindy Sheehan). My hero is not Theodore Roosevelt, who loved war and congratulated a general after a massacre of Filipino villagers at the turn of the century, but Mark Twain, who denounced the massacre and satirized imperialism.[69]

For Zinn, sharing stories of minority dissent takes students beyond the romanticism that accompanies the political and economic elite-favored traditional version of American history. He contends that "we all have an enormous responsibility to bring to the attention of others information they do not have, which has the potential of causing them to rethink long-held ideas."[70] Zinn describes many historical examples that could be integrated into the minority dissent approach. Telling stories of challenges to power in the United States imparts basic lessons of Americans practicing rights and participating in politics when needed.

Recent Scholarship

There is empirical evidence supporting the minority dissent civic education approach. George Marcus et al. in *With Malice toward Some* find that statements reminding people of the value of free expression and diversity of ideas lead to increased levels of toleration.[71] They favor greater open discussion of democratic principles and practices, especially during minority political activities. For example, when a minority group wants to march in a neighborhood of people who find that group objectionable, presenting the activity in terms of freedom of expression may increase the level of tolerance among those in the majority. As Marcus et al. put it, "[f]raming the issues in terms of a marketplace of ideas, stressing the positive role of dissent, and noting historic freedoms in the United States can increase support for tolerance, even when the group involved is extremely unpopular."[72]

Extending this insight to the classroom, Patricia Avery et al. argue in favor of a "tolerance curriculum," which includes examples of minority dissent to the majority, such as the planned Nazi march in the predominantly Jewish Chicago suburb of Skokie in 1977.[73] They and other scholars contrast the tolerance curriculum with a focus on democratic facts and principles and find that the former approach contributes to increased tolerance of disliked groups, whereas formal pedagogy tends to have no impact on students' levels of tolerance.[74] Westheimer and Kahne's more recent study concludes that what they call a "justice-oriented" curriculum increases students' political efficacy and interest in political issues and participation.[75]

Potential Advantages and Possible Problems

The minority dissent approach provides examples of democratic organization and action, reflecting what Robert Bellah et al. refer to as the "politics of community."[76] Stanton and DuBois held that individuals excluded from politics and society often comprise democratically practicing communities. Susan Herbst in *Politics at the Margin* argues that political activity by marginalized groups often creates "parallel public spheres," which are "worlds of discourse and action beside the mainstream public sphere," and may involve ritual and deep community bonds.[77] One classic example of a democratic community born out of dissent is the Greenham Common women's protest camps against nuclear weapons.[78] Minority dissent stories emphasize the importance of rights for students and that, as citizens, they have powers to participate in politics. They also open up for discussion whether or not the minority needs to possess correct factual information or win. Sharing stories about minority dissent may strengthen the classroom itself as a democratic community.[79]

A conceivable problem with the minority dissent model stems from citizens' use of rights to confront power, especially government. The prospect of teaching students that they can question, challenge, and renew government and other forms of power can be intimidating.[80] Teachers may be apprehensive to present examples of rights practiced knowing that some students would be more comfortable hearing about cooperation, consensus, harmony, or virtue. The topic of privacy, for instance, is practically guaranteed to elicit the folksy wisdom, "If people aren't doing anything wrong, then they don't need to worry about their privacy." This may steer the conversation far away from civil liberties. The minority dissent approach, however, reminds students of some basic reasons for rights, such as "government can legitimately kill you," and "citizens exercise rights to try to stop the abuse of government power." The minority dissent approach teaches about rights through stories of citizen efforts, making the lessons more appealing to everyone.

There may also be the problem that, once minority dissent stories are told, students may never question or criticize power. After all, the narratives demonstrate that any citizen can address the abuse of power and that others have already taken care of many such situations. However, these stories highlight individual and collective political participation, and may serve as points of inspiration.

CIVIC ENGAGEMENT APPROACH TO CIVIC EDUCATION

The "civic engagement" approach also resides somewhere between formal pedagogy and political participation. Civic engagement activities are housed in schools and administered as specific course assignments, entire classes, integral degree requirements, or special activities. Service learning and community activities, such as citizen academies, mock elections, community-oriented internships, and the like, offer experiences outside of—yet indispensably framed by—curricular civic lessons.[81] McCartney explains that

> civic engagement is a catch-all term that refers to an individual's activities, alone or part of a group, that focus on developing knowledge about the community and its political system, identifying or seeking solutions to community problems, pursuing goals to benefit the community, and participating in constructive deliberation among community members about the community's political system and community issues, problems, or solutions.[82]

Definitions by others are similar. For Brian Harward and Dan Shea, civic engagement learning activities "require active student involvement and critical reflection. Engaged forms of learning often use contexts beyond the classroom and involve the application of inquiry, typically (though not exclusively) in collaboration with the larger community."[83]

The results of civic engagement for students, McCartney elaborates, is "knowledge of or connection to the community . . . [and] understanding of the political system or political issues, . . . encourage[ing] the development of capable citizens who have the confidence, knowledge, skills, and motivations to maintain a dynamic, vibrant democracy."[84] Westheimer and Kahne explain that such opportunities seek to develop the "participatory citizen" who will "actively participate in the civic affairs and the social life of the community at local, state, and national levels."[85] The civic engagement approach to political education brings pedagogical fact-based teaching into direct political participation. It uses lessons about participatory democracy, diversity, tolerance, discussion, and reaching agreement to frame students' participation in collective self-rule outside the classroom.

Theoretical Justifications

Democratic theory's endorsement of equal citizen standing supports the civic engagement approach. However, this model recognizes the value and necessity of classroom teaching. John Dewey combined classroom instruction and democratic practice in his defense of civic engagement education. In *Democracy and Education*, Dewey argued that the diversity inherent in a democracy means that "[i]t would be much better to have fewer facts and truths in instruction—that is, fewer things supposedly accepted."[86] He explained that democratic education uses "the method by which one experience is made available in giving direction and meaning to another. . . . the connection of the acquisition of knowledge in the schools with activities, or occupations, carried on in the medium of associated life."[87] Public education, which should be flexible, inquisitive, and discursive, should engage students with their community. For Dewey, the full potential of our intelligence is not possible "until it possesses the local community as its medium."[88]

Today's civic engagement activities take students out of the classroom and frame their activities as learning through experience as participating members of a larger community. The civic engagement approach emphasizes participatory democratic deliberation, highlighting recognition of diversity and ambiguity, and engagement in public discussion and decision-making.[89] Put in such terms, a civic engagement curriculum may help students develop their critical thinking, communication, and consensus-building skills as they engage in collective self-rule.

Recent Scholarship

Integrating the work of several leading civic education scholars, Mike Yawn outlines the best practices for the civic engagement approach. Yawn argues that civic engagement opportunities should (1) directly relate to political or governmental processes, (2) include discussions with students before and after participation in the activity, (3) provide basic professional behavior and leadership lessons, (4) have significant time commitments, and (5) display collaborations among students, teachers, and officials.[90] Others have emphasized the importance of the academic component to the civic engagement model. McCartney argues that along with a connection to community, civic engagement needs to be tied to academic learning, examining "political structures, power relationships, or ideas," and include reflection.[91] The reason for including some in-class contact with civic engagement is that it allows for analytical consideration of civic skills and values, such as community ties, efficacy, participation, and tolerance.[92]

Several studies bear out the idea that civic engagement activities teach civics lessons and values.[93] These studies indicate that along with helping students do better in their scholastic endeavors—improving their writing and critical thinking skills—such classes help build participants' levels of efficacy, tolerance, and social capital. For instance, Westheimer and Kahne found that while the "participatory citizen" approach may not increase students' level of interest in political issues or future political participation as much as the minority dissent model, it nonetheless helps strengthen students' political efficacy.[94] Yawn finds that voluntary citizen academies affect participants' knowledge and attitudes regarding local politics.[95]

Potential Advantages and Possible Problems

By having students directly work with political actors, civic engagement programs and projects help develop not only political knowledge, but also a wide array of civically related skills and values, including analytical thinking, writing, presentation, project coordination, leadership, participation, deliberation, conflict resolution, social capital, tolerance, and efficacy. The civic engagement approach may go a long way in mitigating the educational irony of rights because it merges professional skills with civic morality. Is effective communication, for example, a professional or civic skill? The civic engagement approach does not necessarily place critical thinking, leadership, or writing talents in one category or another but rather allows students to reflect on how these skills overlap with active citizenship. Another advantage of this approach is that integrating civically related lessons into service-learning activities may overcome the transmission issue of the political participation approach.

But there is no guarantee of such incorporation. Moreover, as others have noted, because such activities tend to focus on encouraging cooperative civic values like efficacy and tolerance, they may not delve deeply enough into the conflicts and struggles that reside behind the scenes to comprehensively cover civic education.[96] Along with the democratic theory of Dewey, Dahl, or Barber, however, teaching Madison's theory of factional interests and ambitious public officials may address this potential shortcoming of the civic engagement model.

CONCLUSION

Consideration of ideal civic education models helps orient teaching methods to expectations, strengthening civic teaching to confront several difficulties in America. Perhaps the foremost obstacle to civic education is resistance to government-imposed morality. Another impediment is that focusing on either knowledge or use of rights may ironically discourage students from listening to more factual lessons or participating in political activities. The minority dissent and civic engagement approaches go a long way in overcoming these and other challenges to civic education in America.

Minority dissent and civic engagement are unlike formal pedagogy and political participation models of civic education in several ways. They are directed toward educators rather than legislators or citizens. These approaches are analytical tools for members of a profession rather than demands for either government action or greater citizen participation. By telling stories of minority dissent or facilitating student participation in civic activities, educators contribute to keeping government and morality separate while kindling students' curiosity. These models bridge factual civic lessons and direct political activity. They teach both knowledge and use of rights. Many people may find them more palatable than government-supported civics lessons or direct extracurricular dissent. These moderate approaches do not focus on pedantically defining various aspects of our civil society or on students exercising their rights independently of civics lessons. These are balanced models that pull from both fact-based learning and real political activity without government involvement in civic education. They leave open the possibility of learning more. Both minority dissent and civic engagement are likely to counteract the perception that either learning rights (formal pedagogy) or using rights (political participation) provides sufficient civics knowledge. They may also help create within our educational institutions democratic pockets that remind students of their standing as citizens.

NOTES

1. For discussions of potential systemic challenges to civic education in the United States, see Robert Bellah et al., *Habits of the Heart: Individualism and Commitment in American Life* (New York: Harper & Row, 1985), 293, 298–99; Eva T. H. Brann, *Paradoxes of Education in a Republic* (Chicago: University of Chicago Press, 1979), 111; and John Dewey, *The Public and Its Problems* (1927; Athens, OH: Swallow Press, 1991), 34, 114–16, 141, 203–7.

2. Benjamin Barber also presents these two contrasting models in *Strong Democracy: Participatory Politics for a New Age* (Berkeley: University of California Press, 1984), 233–36. It is not uncommon to organize different civic education approaches with extremes at opposite ends. For example, see E. Wayne Ross, "Negotiating the Politics of Citizenship Education," *PS: Political Science and Politics* 37, no. 2 (April 2004), 249–51.

3. Sociologist Max Weber developed the analytical device of "ideal types," which are acknowledged analytical constructions that aid understanding by explaining likelihoods, not absolutes (Peter Lassman and Ronald Speirs, eds., *Weber: Political Writings* [1944; Cambridge: Cambridge University Press, 1994], 312–13). Among the other possible civic education approaches is "private-sphere social activity," which Barber explains involves local governing institutions and voluntary associations (*Strong Democracy*, 233–35). Robert D. Putnam focuses on private association engagement (*Making Democracy Work: Civic Traditions in Modern Italy* [Princeton, NJ: Princeton University Press, 1993], 167–76). Robert D. Heslep defends informal processes as the alternative to formal civic education (*Education in Democracy: Education's Moral Role in the Democratic State* [Ames: Iowa State University Press, 1989], 220). There is also the "multiculturalist perspective," which focuses on diversity. See Jane Junn, "Diversity, Immigration, and the Politics of Civic Education," *PS: Political Science and Politics* 37, no. 2 (April 2004), 253–34.

4. See, for example, Aristotle, *Nicomachean Ethics*, trans. Terence Irwin (Indianapolis, IN: Hackett, 1985), 1103b3, 1129a17–1130b24; John Dewey, *Democracy and Education* (1916; New York: Free Press, 1944), 179; Dewey, *The Public and Its Problems*, 207; Heslep, *Education in Democracy*, 123; and Thomas Jefferson, "Letter to James Madison December 20, 1787," in *The Portable Thomas Jefferson*, ed. Merrill D. Peterson (New York: Penguin, 1977), 432; "Letter to John Adams October 28, 1813," 537; "Letter to Thomas Law June 13, 1814," 541–43.

5. James Madison, "Federalist Paper No. 10," in *The Federalist Papers: Hamilton, Madison, Jay*, ed. Clinton Rossiter (New York: Mentor, 1961), 81.

6. Ibid., 82.

7. Ibid., 81.

8. Ibid., 82.

9. Jay, "Federalist Paper No. 64," 391; also see Hamilton, "Federalist Paper No. 68," 412, 414.

10. Alexis de Tocqueville, *Democracy in America*, vol. 2, ed. Phillips Bradley (1840; New York: Vintage Books, 1990), 106–20.

11. See, for example, Joel Westheimer, "Introduction—The Politics of Civic Education," *PS: Political Science and Politics* 37, no. 2 (April 2004), 231–32; and Joel Westheimer and Joseph Kahne, "Educating the 'Good' Citizen: Political Choices and Pedagogical Goals," *PS: Political Science and Politics* 37, no. 2 (April 2004), 241.

12. See Westheimer, "The Politics of Civic Education," 232; and Westheimer and Kahne, "Educating the 'Good' Citizen," 243, 246.

13. See Barber, *Strong Democracy*, 234.

14. See Robert A. Dahl's discussion of majority rule, the minority, and rights *Democracy and Its Critics* (New Haven, CT: Yale University Press, 1989), 168–73.

15. For elaboration of this definition of rights, see ibid.; and Ronald Dworkin, *Taking Rights Seriously* (Cambridge, MA: Harvard University Press, 1978), 272, cf., 227.

16. See Dahl, *Democracy and Its Critics*, 31; cf., 97.

17. Peter Bachrach, *The Theory of Democratic Elitism: A Critique* (Boston: Little, Brown, 1967), 3; Dewey, *The Public and Its Problems*, 208–9; and W. E. B. DuBois, *The Souls of Black Folk*, ed. David W. Blight (Boston: Bedford Books, 1997), 20, 50.

18. See, for instance, Jefferson, "Letter to James Madison December 20, 1787," 429; "Letter to John Francis Hopkinson March 13, 1789," 436; "Letter to the President of the United States George Washington September 9, 1792," 458; "Letter to Samuel Kercheval July 12, 1816," 555; and Herbert J. Storing, *What the Anti-Federalists Were For* (Chicago: University of Chicago Press, 1981), 70.

19. See, for example, Jefferson, "Letter to James Madison December 20, 1787," 429; "Letter to John Francis Hopkinson March 13, 1789," 436; "Letter to the President of the United States George Washington September 9, 1792," 458; and "Letter to Samuel Kercheval July 12, 1816," 555.

20. Jefferson, "Letter to Thomas Law June 13, 1814," 541–42; also see "Letter to Samuel Kercheval July 12, 1816," 557.

21. Tocqueville, *Democracy in America*, vol. 2, 99, 287.

22. Alexis de Tocqueville, *Democracy in America*, vol. 1, ed. Phillips Bradley (1835; New York: Vintage Books, 1990), 191–93; Tocqueville, *Democracy in America*, vol. 2, 102–5, 113.

23. Barber, *Strong Democracy*, 234.

24. John Rawls, *A Theory of Justice* (Cambridge, MA: Harvard University Press, 1971), 107.

25. Ibid., 250.

26. Geraint Parry, "Constructive and Reconstructive Political Education," *Oxford Review of Education* 25, no. 1–2 (March–June 1999), 23–38.

27. Westheimer and Kahne, "Educating the 'Good' Citizen," 242. For examples of scholars advocating this view of "citizenship," see Thomas Lickona, "The Return of Character Education," *Educational Leadership* 51, no. 3 (November 1993): 6–11; and Ed A. Wynne, "The Great Tradition in Education: Transmitting Moral Values," *Educational Leadership* 43, no. 4 (December–January 1985–86): 4–9.

28. Parry, "Constructive and Reconstructive Political Education," 34.

29. For example, Adams wrote to his son that "[i]t will become you to make yourself master of all the considerable characters which have figured upon the stage of civil, political, or military life." Lyman H. Butterfield, *Adams Family Correspondence*, vol. 2 (Cambridge, MA: Harvard University Press, 1963), 289–90.

30. See, for instance, James H. Kuklinski et al., "Misinformation and the Currency of Democratic Citizenship," *The Journal of Politics* 62, no. 3 (August 2000): 790–816.

31. Amy Gutmann, *Democratic Education*, 2d ed (1987; Princeton: Princeton University Press, 1999), 19–20.

32. Ibid., 287.

33. Heslep, *Education in Democracy*, 123.

34. Michael X. Delli Carpini and Scott Keeter, *What Americans Know about Politics and Why It Matters* (New Haven, CT: Yale University Press, 1996).

35. Ibid., 10.

36. Ibid., chap. 2. Some of the information addressed by these surveys includes Fifth Amendment rights, branches of government, U.S. membership in the United Nations, Watergate, the greenhouse effect, Glasnost, and specifically named elected officials and political party stands.

37. Ibid., chap. 4.

38. Ibid., 305–6.

39. Ross, "Negotiating the Politics of Citizenship Education."

40. Ibid., 250.

41. Westheimer, "The Politics of Civic Education," 232.

42. Howard Zinn, *The Politics of History*, 2d ed (1970; Urbana: University of Illinois, 1990).

43. Westheimer and Kahne, "Educating the 'Good' Citizen," 243.

44. See James S. Leming et al., eds., *Where Did Social Studies Go Wrong?* (Washington, DC: Thomas B. Fordham Foundation, 2003).

45. See, for example, Delli Carpini and Keeter, *What Americans Know*, chap. 6; Ewa A. Golebiowska, "Individual Value Priorities, Education, and Political Tolerance," *Political Behavior* 17, no. 1 (March 1995): 23–48; Clyde Z. Nunn et al., *Tolerance for Nonconformity* (San Francisco: Jossey-Bass, 1978); James W. Prothro and Charles M. Grigg, "Fundamental Principles of Democracy: Bases of Agreement and Disagreement," *The Journal of Politics* 22, no. 2 (May 1960), 276–94; and Samuel A. Stouffer, *Communism, Conformity, and Civil Liberties: A Cross-Section of the Nation Speaks Its Mind* (Garden City, NY: Doubleday, 1955), chap. 4.

46. See Doris A. Graber, *Processing Politics: Learning from Television in the Internet Age* (Chicago, IL: University of Chicago Press, 2001); and Doris A. Graber, "Why Voters Fail Information Tests: Can the Hurdles Be Overcome," *Political Communication* 11, no. 4 (1994): 331–46.

47. Barber, *Strong Democracy*, 234.

48. Rawls, *Theory of Justice*, 101.

49. See Kathleen Dolan, "Do Women and Men Know Different Things? Measuring Gender Differences in Political Knowledge," *The Journal of Politics* 73, no. 1 (January 2011): 97–107.

50. See Michael T. Rogers, "A Civic Education Crisis," *The Midsouth Political Science Review* (Special Edition on Civic Education and Civic Literacy in the Midsouth) 13, no. 1 (Spring–Fall 2012), 4–6.

51. Heslep, *Education in Democracy*, 123.

52. Others addressing political participation as one of several forms of civic education include Barber, *Strong Democracy*, 233–36; Anne Colby et al., *Educating Citizens: Preparing America's Undergraduates for Lives of Moral and Civic Responsibility* (San Francisco: Carnegie Foundation for the Advancement of Teaching, 2003); Peter Levine, *The Future of Democracy: Developing the Next Generation of American Citizens* (Lebanon, NH: University Press of New England, 2007); and Alison Rios Millett McCartney, "Teaching Civic Engagement: Debates, Definitions, Benefits, and Challenges," in *Teaching Civic Engagement: From Student to Active Citizen*, ed. Alison Rios Millett McCartney et al (Washington, DC: American Political Science Association, 2013).

53. McCartney, "Teaching Civic Engagement," 14.

54. Barber, *Strong Democracy*, chap. 10.

55. Ibid., 234.

56. Tocqueville, *Democracy in America*, vol. 2, 121–24.

57. Graber, *Processing Politics*, chap. 2.

58. Ibid., 7.

59. See, for example, Hannah Arendt, *The Origins of Totalitarianism* (New York: Harcourt Brace, 1951); Bachrach, *Theory of Democratic Elitism*, 7–8, 43; and Dewey, *The Public and Its Problems*, chap. 4 and 6.

60. Ellen Carol DuBois, ed., *Elizabeth Cady Stanton/Susan B. Anthony: Correspondence, Writings, Speeches* (New York: Schoken Books, 1981); and DuBois, *Souls of Black Folk*.

61. See DuBois, ed., *Elizabeth Cady Stanton*, 30–32; and DuBois, *Souls of Black Folk*, 22, 47–48, 50–52.

62. See Katherine Isaac, *Civics for Democracy: The Journey for Teachers and Students* (Washington, DC: Essential Books, 1992).

63. Ross, "Negotiating the Politics of Citizenship Education," 250.

64. Westheimer and Kahne, "Educating the 'Good' Citizen," 243.

65. William Bigelow and Norman Diamond, *The Power in Our Hands: A Curriculum on the History of Work and Workers in the United States* (New York: Monthly Review Press, 1988).

66. See, for example, Naomi Wolf, *Give Me Liberty: A Handbook for American Revolutionaries* (New York: Simon & Schuster, 2008); and Naomi Wolf, *The End of America: Letter of Warning to a Young Patriot* (White River Junction, VT: Chelsea Green, 2007).

67. David Leaf and John Scheinfeld, *The U.S. vs. John Lennon* (Santa Monica: Lionsgate, 2006, DVD, 96 minutes); Marion Lipschutz and Rose Rosenblatt, *The Education of Shelby Knox: Sex, Lies & Education* (New York: Docurama, 2006, DVD, 72 minutes); and David Zeiger, *Sir! No Sir! The Suppressed Story of the GI Movement to End the War in Vietnam* (New York: Docurama, 2005, DVD, 84 minutes).

68. Howard Zinn, *A People's History of the United States: 1492–Present* (New York: Harper Collins, 1980); Howard Zinn and adapted by Rebecca Stefoff, *A Young People's History of the United States* (New York: Seven Stories Press, 2009); Howard Zinn and adapted by Rebecca Stefoff, *A Young People's History of the United States Volume 1: Columbus to the Spanish-American War* (New York: Seven Stories Press, 2007); and Howard Zinn and adapted by Rebecca Stefoff, *A Young People's History of the United States Volume 2: Class Struggle to the War on Terror* (New York: Seven Stories Press, 2007). Also see Howard Zinn, *The Politics of History*.

69. Howard Zinn, "Making History," *The New York Times*, July 1, 2007, http://www.nytimes.com/2007/07/01/books/review/Letters-t-1.html?_r=0.

70. Howard Zinn, "Changing Minds, One at a Time," *The Progressive*, March 2005, 23.

71. George Marcus et al., *With Malice toward Some: How People Make Civil Liberties Judgments* (Cambridge, UK: Cambridge University Press, 1995), 123–24.

72. Ibid., 127.

73. Patricia G. Avery et al., "Exploring Political Tolerance with Adolescents," *Theory and Research in Social Education* 20, no. 4 (Fall 1992): 386–420.

74. Ibid.; and Donald P. Green et al., "Does Knowledge of Constitutional Principles Increase Support for Civil Liberties? Results from a Randomized Field Experiment," *The Journal of Politics* 73, no. 2 (April 2011): 463–76.

75. Westheimer and Kahne, "Educating the 'Good' Citizen," 245.

76. Bellah et al., *Habits of the Heart*, 200, 214–15.

77. Susan Herbst, *Politics at the Margin: Historical Studies of Public Expression outside the Mainstream* (New York: Cambridge University Press, 1994), 181.

78. See Cynthia Enloe, *Bananas, Beaches and Bases: Making Feminist Sense of International Politics* (1990; Berkeley: University of California Press, 2000); and Barbara Harford and Sarah Hopkins, *Greenham Common: Women at the Wire* (London: Women's Press, 1984).

79. Others have also emphasized the value of conveying civic lessons through stories and role-playing. See, for instance, Robert Maranto, "Just the Facts Ma'am (and a Few Stories): What We Need in Civic Education," in *The Midsouth Political Science Review*, 37–51; and Daniel T. Willingham, *Why Don't Students Like School?* (San Francisco: Jossey-Bass, 2009).

80. It is not uncommon for elected officials to regard this approach as a threat to their hold on political power, as Indiana Governor Daniels, who later became president of Purdue University, demonstrated in 2010 with his call for banning the work of Howard Zinn. See Tom LoBianco, "AP Exclusive: Daniels Looked to Censor Opponents," *Associated Press*, July 16, 2013, http://bigstory.ap.org/article/ap-exclusive-daniels-looked-censor-opponents.

81. See, for example, Benjamin Barber and Richard M. Battistoni, "A Season of Service: Introducing Service Learning into the Liberal Arts Curriculum," *PS: Political Science and Politics* 26, no. 2 (June 1993): 235–40; Joseph Y. Howard and Keith A. Nitta, "Helping Students Become Civically Engaged through Service Learning Courses," in *The Midsouth Political Science Review*, 178–85; Levine, *The Future of Democracy*; Alison Rios Millett McCartney et al., eds., *Teaching Civic Engagement: From Student to Active Citizen* (Washington, DC: American Political Science Association, 2013); and Mike Yawn, "Citizen Academies: Promoting Civic Education, Civic Engagement, and Social Capital," in *The Midsouth Political Science Review*, 133–55.

82. McCartney, "Teaching Civic Engagement," 14.

83. Brian M. Harward and Daniel M. Shea, "Higher Education and the Multiple Modes of Education," in McCartney et al., *Teaching Civic Engagement*, 21–40.

84. McCartney, "Teaching Civic Engagement," 13–14.

85. Westheimer and Kahne, "Educating the 'Good' Citizen," 243.

86. Dewey, *Democracy and Education*, 178.

87. Ibid., 344–45.

88. Ibid., 219.

89. See, for example, Westheimer, "The Politics of Civic Education," 231.

90. Yawn, "Citizen Academies," 137. Also see Sidney Verba et al., *Voice and Equality: Civic Voluntarism in American Politics* (Cambridge, MA: Harvard University Press, 1995).

91. McCartney, "Teaching Civic Engagement," 13–14.

92. See, for example, Howard and Nitta, "Helping Students Become Civically Engaged," 179.

93. Janet Eyler and Dwight Giles, Jr., *Where's the Learning in Service-Learning?* (San Francisco: Jossey-Bass, 1999); Janet Eyler et al., "The Impact of Service-Learning on College Students," *Michigan Journal of Community Service Learning* 4 (Fall 1997): 5–15; Richard Niemi and Jane Junn, *Civic Education: What Makes Students Learn* (New Haven, CT: Yale University Press, 1998); Richard Niemi et al., "Community Service by High School Students: A Cure for Civic Ills?" *Political Behavior* 22, no. 1 (March 2000): 45–69; James Youniss and Miranda Yates, *Community Service and Social Responsibility in Youth* (Chicago: University of Chicago Press, 1997); and James Youniss et al., "What We Know about Engendering Civic Identity," *American Behavioral Scientist* 40, no. 5 (March–April 1997): 620–31.

94. Westheimer and Kahne, "Educating the 'Good' Citizen," 245.

95. Yawn, "Citizen Academies," 136–37.

96. Robert Maranto, "Just the Facts Ma'am," 37–51; and Henry Milner, *The Internet Generation: Engaged Citizens or Political Dropouts* (Medford, MA: Tufts University Press, 2010).

BIBLIOGRAPHY

Arendt, Hannah. *The Origins of Totalitarianism*. New York: Harcourt Brace, 1951.

Aristotle. *Nicomachean Ethics*. Translated by Terence Irwin. Indianapolis, IN: Hackett, 1985.

Avery, Patricia G., Karen Bird, John L. Sullivan, and Sandra Johnstone. "Exploring Political Tolerance with Adolescents." *Theory and Research in Social Education* 20, no. 4 (Fall 1992): 386–420.

Bachrach, Peter. *The Theory of Democratic Elitism: A Critique*. Boston: Little, Brown, 1967.

Barber, Benjamin. *Strong Democracy: Participatory Politics for a New Age*. Berkeley: University of California Press, 1984.

Barber, Benjamin R., and Richard M. Battistoni. "A Season of Service: Introducing Service Learning into the Liberal Arts Curriculum." *PS: Political Science and Politics* 26, no. 2 (June 1993): 235–40.

Bellah, Robert N., Richard Madsen, William M. Sullivan, Ann Swidler, and Steven M. Tipton. *Habits of the Heart: Individualism and Commitment in American Life*. New York: Harper & Row, 1985.

Bigelow, William, and Norman Diamond. *The Power in Our Hands: A Curriculum on the History of Work and Workers in the United States*. New York: Monthly Review Press, 1988.

Brann, Eva T. H. *Paradoxes of Education in a Republic*. Chicago: University of Chicago Press, 1979.

Butterfield, Lyman H. *Adams Family Correspondence*, vol. 2. Cambridge, MA: Harvard University Press, 1963.

Colby, Anne, Thomas Ehrlich, Elizabeth Beaumont, and Jason Stephens. *Educating Citizens: Preparing America's Undergraduates for Lives of Moral and Civic Responsibility*. San Francisco: The Carnegie Foundation for the Advancement of Teaching, 2003.

Dahl, Robert A. *Democracy and Its Critics*. New Haven, CT: Yale University Press, 1989.

Delli Carpini, Michael X., and Scott Keeter. *What Americans Know about Politics and Why It Matters*. New Haven, CT: Yale University Press, 1996.

Dewey, John. *Democracy and Education*. 1916. New York: The Free Press, 1944.

Dewey, John. *The Public and Its Problems*. 1927. Athens, OH: Swallow Press, 1991.

Dolan, Kathleen. "Do Women and Men Know Different Things? Measuring Gender Differences in Political Knowledge." *The Journal of Politics* 73, no. 1 (January 2011): 97–107.

DuBois, Ellen Carol, ed. *Elizabeth Cady Stanton/Susan B. Anthony: Correspondence, Writings, Speeches*. New York: Schoken Books, 1981.

DuBois, W. E. B. *The Souls of Black Folk*. Edited by David W. Blight. Boston: Bedford Books, 1997.

Dworkin, Ronald. *Taking Rights Seriously*. Cambridge, MA: Harvard University Press, 1978.

Enloe, Cynthia. *Bananas, Beaches and Bases: Making Feminist Sense of International Politics*. 1990. Berkeley: University of California Press, 2000.

Eyler, Janet, and Dwight Giles Jr. *Where's the Learning in Service-Learning?* San Francisco: Jossey-Bass, 1999.

Eyler, Janet, Dwight Giles Jr., and John Braxton. "The Impact of Service-Learning on College Students." *Michigan Journal of Community Service Learning* 4 (Fall 1997): 5–15.

Golebiowska, Ewa A. "Individual Value Priorities, Education, and Political Tolerance." *Political Behavior* 17, no. 1 (March 1995): 23–48.

Graber, Doris A. *Processing Politics: Learning from Television in the Internet Age*. Chicago, IL: University of Chicago Press, 2001.

Graber, Doris A. "Why Voters Fail Information Tests: Can the Hurdles Be Overcome." *Political Communication* 11, no. 4 (1994): 331–46.

Green, Donald P., Peter M. Aronow, Daniel E. Bergan, Pamela Greene, Celia Paris, and Beth I. Weinberger. "Does Knowledge of Constitutional Principles Increase Support for Civil Liberties? Results from a Randomized Field Experiment." *The Journal of Politics* 73, no. 2 (April 2011): 463–76.

Gutmann, Amy. *Democratic Education*. 2d ed. 1987. Princeton: Princeton University Press, 1999.

Harford, Barbara, and Sarah Hopkins. *Greenham Common: Women at the Wire*. London: Women's Press, 1984.

Harward, Brian M., and Daniel M. Shea. "Higher Education and the Multiple Modes of Education." In *Teaching Civic Engagement: From Student to Active Citizen*. Edited by Alison Rios Millett McCartney, Elizabeth A. Bennion, and Dick Simpson. Washington, DC: American Political Science Association, 2013.

Herbst, Susan. *Politics at the Margin: Historical Studies of Public Expression outside the Mainstream*. New York: Cambridge University Press, 1994.

Heslep, Robert D. *Education in Democracy: Education's Moral Role in the Democratic State*. Ames: Iowa State University Press, 1989.

Howard, Joseph Y., and Keith A. Nitta. "Helping Students Become Civically Engaged through Service Learning Courses." *The Midsouth Political Science Review* (Special Edition on Civic Education and Civic Literacy in the Midsouth) 13, no. 1 (Spring–Fall 2012): 178–85.

Isaac, Katherine. *Civics for Democracy: The Journey for Teachers and Students*. Washington, DC: Essential Books, 1992.

Junn, Jane. "Diversity, Immigration, and the Politics of Civic Education." *PS: Political Science and Politics* 37, no. 2 (April 2004): 253–34.

Kuklinski, James H., Paul Quirk, Jennifer Jerit, David Schwieder, and Robert Rich. "Misinformation and the Currency of Democratic Citizenship." *The Journal of Politics* 62, no. 3 (August 2000): 790–816.

Lassman, Peter, and Ronald Speirs, eds. *Weber: Political Writings*. 1944. Cambridge: Cambridge University Press, 1994.

Leaf, David, and John Scheinfeld. *The U.S. vs. John Lennon*. Santa Monica: Lionsgate, 2006. DVD, 96 minutes.

Leming, James S., Lucien Ellington, and Kathleen Porter, eds. *Where Did Social Studies Go Wrong?* Washington, DC: Thomas B. Fordham Foundation, 2003.

Levine, Peter. *The Future of Democracy: Developing the Next Generation of American Citizens*. Lebanon, NH: University Press of New England, 2007.

Lickona, Thomas. "The Return of Character Education." *Educational Leadership* 51, no. 3 (November 1993): 6–11.

Lipschutz, Marion, and Rose Rosenblatt. *The Education of Shelby Knox: Sex, Lies & Education*. New York: Docurama, 2006. DVD, 72 minutes.

Maranto, Robert. "Just the Facts Ma'am (and a Few Stories): What We Need in Civic Education." *The Midsouth Political Science Review* (Special Edition on Civic Education and Civic Literacy in the Midsouth) 13, no. 1 (Spring–Fall 2012): 37–51.

Marcus, George, John L. Sullivan, Elizabeth Theiss-Morse, and Sandra L. Wood. *With Malice toward Some: How People Make Civil Liberties Judgments*. Cambridge, UK: Cambridge University Press, 1995.

McCartney, Alison Rios Millett. "Teaching Civic Engagement: Debates, Definitions, Benefits, and Challenges." In *Teaching Civic Engagement: From Student to Active Citizen*. Edited by Alison Rios Millett McCartney, Elizabeth A. Bennion, and Dick Simpson. Washington, DC: American Political Science Association, 2013.

McCartney, Alison Rios Millett, Elizabeth A. Bennion, and Dick Simpson, eds. *Teaching Civic Engagement: From Student to Active Citizen*. Washington, DC: American Political Science Association, 2013.

Milner, Henry. *The Internet Generation: Engaged Citizens or Political Dropouts*. Medford, MA: Tufts University Press, 2010.

Niemi, Richard, Mary A. Hepburn, and Chris Chapman. "Community Service by High School Students: A Cure for Civic Ills?" *Political Behavior* 22, no. 1 (March 2000): 45–69.

Niemi, Richard, and Jane Junn. *Civic Education: What Makes Students Learn.* New Haven, CT: Yale University Press, 1998.

Nunn, Clyde Z., Harry J. Crockett Jr., and J. Allen Williams Jr. *Tolerance for Nonconformity.* San Francisco: Jossey-Bass, 1978.

Parry, Geraint. "Constructive and Reconstructive Political Education." *Oxford Review of Education* 25, no. 1–2 (March–June 1999): 23–38.

Peterson, Merrill D., ed. *The Portable Thomas Jefferson.* New York: Penguin, 1977.

Prothro James W., and Charles M. Grigg. "Fundamental Principles of Democracy: Bases of Agreement and Disagreement." *The Journal of Politics* 22, no. 2 (May 1960): 276–94.

Putnam, Robert. *Making Democracy Work: Civic Traditions in Modern Italy.* Princeton, NJ: Princeton University Press, 1993.

Rawls, John. *A Theory of Justice.* Cambridge, MA: Harvard University Press, 1971.

Rogers, Michael T. "A Civic Education Crisis." *The Midsouth Political Science Review* (Special Edition on Civic Education and Civic Literacy in the Midsouth) 13, no. 1 (Spring–Fall 2012): 1–36.

Ross, E. Wayne. "Negotiating the Politics of Citizenship Education." *PS: Political Science and Politics* 37, no. 2 (April 2004): 249–51.

Rossiter, Clinton, ed. *The Federalist Papers: Hamilton, Madison, Jay.* New York: Mentor, 1961.

Storing, Herbert J. *What the Anti-Federalists Were For.* Chicago: University of Chicago Press, 1981.

Stouffer, Samuel A. *Communism, Conformity, and Civil Liberties: A Cross-Section of the Nation Speaks Its Mind.* Garden City, NY: Doubleday, 1955.

Tocqueville, Alexis de. *Democracy in America*, vol. 1. Edited by Phillips Bradley. 1835. New York: Vintage Books, 1990.

Tocqueville, Alexis de. *Democracy in America*, vol. 2. Edited by Phillips Bradley. 1840. New York: Vintage Books, 1990.

Verba, Sidney, Kate L. Schlozman, and Henry E. Brady. *Voice and Equality: Civic Voluntarism in American Politics.* Cambridge, MA: Harvard University Press, 1995.

Westheimer, Joel. "Introduction—The Politics of Civic Education." *PS: Political Science and Politics* 37, no. 2 (April 2004), 231–34.

Westheimer, Joel, and Joseph Kahne. "Educating the 'Good' Citizen: Political Choices and Pedagogical Goals." *PS: Political Science and Politics* 37, no. 2 (April 2004): 241–47.

Willingham, Daniel T. *Why Don't Students Like School?* San Francisco: Jossey-Bass, 2009.

Wolf, Naomi. *Give Me Liberty: A Handbook for American Revolutionaries.* New York: Simon & Schuster, 2008.

Wolf, Naomi. *The End of America: Letter of Warning to a Young Patriot.* White River Junction, VT: Chelsea Green, 2007.

Wynne, Ed A. "The Great Tradition in Education: Transmitting Moral Values." *Educational Leadership* 43, no. 4 (December–January 1985–86): 4–9.

Yawn, Mike. "Citizen Academies: Promoting Civic Education, Civic Engagement, and Social Capital." *The Midsouth Political Science Review* (Special Edition on

Civic Education and Civic Literacy in the Midsouth) 13, no. 1 (Spring–Fall 2012): 133–55.

Youniss, James, Jeffrey A. McLellan, and Miranda Yates. "What We Know about Engendering Civic Identity." *American Behavioral Scientist* 40, no. 5 (March–April 1997): 620–31.

Youniss, James, and Miranda Yates. *Community Service and Social Responsibility in Youth.* Chicago: University of Chicago Press, 1997.

Zeiger, David. *Sir! No Sir! The Suppressed Story of the GI Movement to End the War in Vietnam.* New York: Docurama, 2005. DVD, 84 minutes.

Zinn, Howard. "Changing Minds, One at a Time." *The Progressive*, March 2005, 22–24.

Zinn, Howard. *The Politics of History.* 2d ed. 1970. Urbana: University of Illinois, 1990.

Zinn, Howard. *A People's History of the United States: 1492–Present.* New York: Harper Collins, 1980.

Zinn, Howard, and adapted by Rebecca Stefoff. *A Young People's History of the United States.* New York: Seven Stories Press, 2009.

Zinn, Howard, and adapted by Rebecca Stefoff. *A Young People's History of the United States, Volume 1: Columbus to the Spanish-American War.* New York: Seven Stories Press, 2007.

Zinn, Howard, and adapted by Rebecca Stefoff. *A Young People's History of the United States, Volume 2: Class Struggle to the War on Terror.* New York: Seven Stories Press, 2007.

TWENTY-FIRST-CENTURY INNOVATIONS IN CIVIC EDUCATION

Part A: National Government

Chapter Five

The Role of Congressional Outreach in Civic Engagement

*An Examination of Legislator Websites**

Sally Friedman and Jessica L. Aubin

> Since my retirement from the U.S. Senate in 2005, I have become increasingly involved in the effort to transform civics from a spectator sport into a participatory sport—one in which citizens directly engage in democracy and shape local, state, and federal policies to the betterment of their families and communities.
>
> —Former Florida Senator Bob Graham, *America, the Owner's Manual*

After a long hiatus, the topic of civic engagement has returned to the front burner of scholarly and practical attention. Under the civic engagement rubric, academics and others have been grappling with a variety of thorny questions. What are the best ways to increase voter turnout? How do we encourage the political participation of young people? How might alternative forms of citizen deliberation enhance the quality of discussion in our democracy?

As we debate these questions, many point to the design of political institutions as one of a number of significant reasons for declining levels of civic engagement. This is an important focus and an explanation worthy of our attention. What if we shift the level of analysis from the institutions themselves to include the vantage point of the individuals serving in those institutions? A wide variety of studies suggest that personal contact or appeals on the part of interested activists—campaigners, party officials, interest group leaders—can genuinely make a difference in motivating constituents to increase their civic activity, to become active on an issue or to just plain get out and vote.[1]

Indeed, as former senator Bob Graham (quote above) has shown, the activities of officeholders, as they are serving in those political institutions, can influence the quality of civic engagement in our society. Since his retirement

*We would like to thank Andrew Hodges, Sam McCaffrey, and Robert Spice for their assistance.

from the Senate, Graham has made it a *cause célèbre* to encourage citizens to become more politically active. This work has culminated in his widely regarded book *America, the Owners Manual*.

Based on the idea that the activities of political officeholders can motivate citizens and that members of Congress have some incentive to do so, this chapter explores the roles legislators play in encouraging participation in politics by their constituents. Through an examination of material on member websites, we analyze the civically oriented communications of a random sample of fifty legislators from the 112th Congress. We examine their websites to ascertain the ways they encourage constituents to become politically and civically involved. For example, we ask whether they are encouraging citizens to attend political events, volunteer in their communities, or join efforts toward civic change. Though of an exploratory nature, findings suggest that as a byproduct of their normal interactions with constituents, legislators are encouraging activities we consider to indicate citizen civic engagement, although they may not be framing that communication in an explicitly civic manner.

Questions about the roles legislators play in promoting citizen involvement—with the potential to generalize to other public officials—are important because in an era of declining citizen participation, where citizen evaluations of institutions are at low levels and where feelings of political efficacy and interest have also been waning, it is imperative to find productive ways to encourage enhanced involvement in politics. Thus, members of Congress are in a good position to motivate constituents. As representatives of the branch designed to be closest to the people, they spend considerable time interacting with constituents, and they have a variety of resources designed to promote a constituency connection. Indeed, the same set of tools representatives use to promote reelection and to serve constituents could easily be used to engage in outreach and to promote engagement. By setting the efforts of legislators in a civic engagement context, this study puts a different spin on tried-and-true activities of representatives, demonstrating in the process that though they may not always utilize the explicit words, members of Congress are indeed pointing their constituents toward engaging in a wide variety of civic engagement activities.

A CRISIS OF CIVIC ENGAGEMENT?

The academic and popular literature on civic engagement has poignantly noted what many see as disturbing declines in levels of involvement across the United States. Participation in activities ranging from voting, joining voluntary associations, engaging in campaign activities, etc., has decreased notably over the last fifty years. Robert D. Putnam in his book, *Bowling Alone: The Collapse and Revival of American Community*, suggests that Americans are less involved in family, community, groups, and democratic interactions. This decrease in involvement in bowling leagues (Putnam's metaphor for forming long-term associations with others), community groups, and even visiting with family and friends has lessened our "stock in social capital," which Putnam views as a serious civic problem. According to his research, over the last two to three decades, membership in organizations like the PTA, Red Cross, League of Women Voters, and labor unions have declined by approximately 25 to 50 percent.[2] Additionally, concerning political engagement, Putnam suggests that:

> Americans have perhaps become 10–15 percent less likely to voice our views publicly by running for office or writing to Congress or the local newspaper, 15–20 percent less interested in politics and public affairs, 25 percent less likely to vote, roughly 35 percent less likely to attend public meetings, both partisan and nonpartisan, and roughly 40 percent less engaged in party politics and indeed in political and civic organizations of all sorts. We remain, in short, reasonably well-informed spectators of public affairs, but many fewer of us actually partake in the game.[3]

As is well known, Putnam's findings set off a whirlwind of scholarship identifying significant downturns in a variety of citizen engagement activities. For example, an edited volume, *Democracy at Risk: How Political Choices Undermine Citizen Participation, and What We Can Do about It*, emphasizes "our civic life (is now) impoverished" because of "an erosion of the activities and capacities of citizenship."[4] The authors go on to suggest:

> American democracy is at risk. The risk comes not from some external threat but from disturbing internal trends: an erosion of the activities and capacities of citizenship. Americans have turned away from politics and the public sphere in large numbers, leaving our civic life impoverished. . . . Citizens participate in public affairs less frequently, with less knowledge and enthusiasm, in fewer venues, and less equally than is healthy for a vibrant democratic polity.[5]

Regarding a wide variety of civic activities, the scholarly consensus highlights significant downturns. These range from the electoral-oriented activities of voting, participating in campaigns, and simply acquiring information about political candidates to a variety of ways to participate in the community more generally.[6] These decreases in civic activity are particularly disturbing because they have been so striking among young people.[7]

Explanations for these trends are wide ranging and sometimes speculative. From social and psychological perspectives, explanations focus on education, women in the workplace, apathy, and economic status. Technical and cultural arguments are also proffered, shifting the focus to television, urban sprawl, and the 1960s.[8] Irrespective of theoretical orientation, blame for declining public participation has often been placed on the institutions and rules of the game of American politics. For example, one argument is that a lack of competition in congressional elections provides little incentive for citizens to pay much attention or get involved. The length of presidential campaigns and the front loading of the primary process similarly contribute to lessening interest, and a general perception of too much money in elections serves as a turnoff to many.[9]

While scholars have devoted considerable attention to societal and cultural changes as well as the role of institutions and the need for institutional reform, there has been limited discussion about political leaders. Is there a potential role for officials serving in institutions to motivate the citizenry? In what ways can the activities of officeholders themselves, or the by-product of such activities, encourage citizens to become active?

A ROLE FOR MEMBERS OF CONGRESS?

At first glance, the topic of civic engagement seems fairly disconnected from the daily activities of members of Congress. The academic literature on the U.S. Congress is relatively silent on the topic of civic engagement. There is virtually no mention of the words "civic engagement" in the indices of key texts on the American Congress or to related themes such as promoting democracy, the encouragement of public participation, or specific ways constituents might get involved. Additionally, when one turns to an examination of what Congress itself does to promote civic engagement, little is found. For instance, a search of legislation including the term civic engagement in the 112th Congress produced three bills sponsored by members: H.R. 711 (Youth Corps Act of 2011); H.R. 3464 (Sandra Day O'Connor Civic Learning Act of 2011), which focuses mostly on educational programs that train, develop, and promote civic engagement in the youth; and H.R. 452, which recognizes the importance labor unions play in ensuring a strong middle class by advocating for more equitable wages, humane work conditions, improved benefits, and increased civic engagement by everyday workers. All three of these bills speak to the potential role that Congress as an institution might play. However, considering that approximately 1,600 roll call votes occurred during the 112th Congress (both sessions), three bills on civic engagement seem negligible.[10] The limited reference to civic engagement in both Congress texts and House bills suggests that Congress members might not care about civic engagement.

In addition, much of the Congress literature focuses on the tried-and-true character of legislator goals and characteristics of the legislative environment facilitating or inhibiting those goals. These often cited goals focus on reelection, public policy, and influence.[11] Accordingly, when thinking about these goals, we think about what legislators do in their districts or policies directly affecting constituents (jobs in the districts, services benefiting residents, pork) and key policy issues of the day (foreign policy, the economy). From this vantage point, the topic of civic engagement seems rather remote from the day-to-day activities of the average member of Congress; so we would not expect them to prioritize civic engagement.

However, a closer examination suggests a variety of reasons to hypothesize that activities of legislators might indeed contribute to civic engagement. First, based on what we know about the activities of legislators, it is clear members engage in activities that promote, as a side benefit, citizen participation. For Fenno and other scholars of Congress, legislators cultivate a career in their constituency every bit as much as their career in Washington. As such, they spend considerable time in the district talking to constituents, engaging in service and allocation activities, and developing a home style that keeps them close to the people.[12]

Similarly, members of Congress have long excelled at adapting to new technology and using it to keep in touch with and solicit the input of constituents.[13] Therefore, in the twenty-first century, it is not surprising that members of Congress are taking advantage of modernizing their websites, establishing Facebook pages, Twitter accounts, and other forms of online social interaction.[14] On many of these websites and social media, links letting constituents know they can contact their legislators and information about ways to get involved are prominently featured.

Recent evidence also suggests that citizens are using legislator and government websites. For instance, The Pew Internet and American Life Project reported that in 2004, 29 percent of Americans visited government websites to contact officials. Of those who use the Internet, 72 percent contact government offices with 30 percent of them using email or Internet to do so. A follow-up survey by Pew in 2009 shows an increase by almost 10 percent in the number of individuals who contacted a government official via the Internet.[15] These numbers suggest that constituents are already starting to make virtual connections with political leaders, some of which include members of Congress. If scholars, including Fenno, are correct about the importance of building constituency relationships, clearly the new technologies are allowing members to connect and interact more often and easily, without having to be physically in the district.

Furthermore, there is evidence that if members put out messages highlighting civic engagement, constituents might indeed respond positively.

Thus, Lipinski has shown that member efforts to publicize high-profile votes leads to more accurate perceptions of their stands.[16] Additionally, if citizens become active when asked to do so, this positive response is more likely given the extent that constituents trust their members of Congress more than they trust the legislative institution.[17] Consequently, we would assume that constituents are likely to be receptive to the messages and activities coming from their legislators, whether those messages are delivered in person or through the Internet.

Second, since members of Congress act as policy entrepreneurs on specific issues, it makes sense that some would make civic engagement a priority.[18] Indeed, we know that some legislators (e.g., former senator Bob Graham's work referenced at the beginning), after leaving Congress, have done just that, working diligently by engaging in these sorts of activities. Similarly, former House member Lee Hamilton is "Director of the Center on Congress at Indiana University, a nonpartisan educational institution seeking to improve the public's understanding of Congress and to inspire young people and adults to take an active part in revitalizing representative government in America."[19] The Congress-to-Campus program, created by the U.S. Association of Former Members of Congress, is an "effort to improve college students' understanding of Congress and American government and to encourage them to consider careers in public service."[20]

Why might some members, even while still serving in Congress, choose to become active in these ways? Possible explanations can range from the needs of reelection (it might benefit some members to have involved constituents), to their backgrounds and experiences, and simply the idea that civic participation has been a hot topic in many circles. In addition, regardless of whether they communicate directly to constituents about civic engagement, by virtue of the myriad of interactions they have with citizens, legislators are certainly encouraging people to get involved. Civic engagement may not be the first thing one thinks of when thinking about members of Congress, but it would seem that legislators have some incentives and interests in promoting participation, and their activities in this arena have the potential to make a difference.

RESEARCH DESIGN

As part of their role as civic leaders, do legislators encourage civic engagement activities? We seek to answer this question by focusing on the House of Representatives. Because of its constitutional role as the "people's branch," and because the representative-constituency connection is close, examining the actions of House members is a good starting point.[21] As a first cut, we conceptualized civic engagement from the website developed at Tufts University, The Center for Information and Research on Civic Learning and Engagement (CIRCLE). Established in 2001 to conduct independent research on citizen engagement, CIRCLE has become a premier player in debates on topics including civic education and citizen engagement, with a particular focus on increasing the involvement of youth.

In several publications, CIRCLE researchers divide civic engagement into three types of activities: electoral, civic, and political voice. The researchers argue that: "All electoral activity is political, but political activity includes much more than just the selection of leaders."[22] Thus, the focus by political scientists on only the electoral component of constituent actions misses other ways that citizens can meaningfully participate. For example, the second category of engagement, "Civic activity"—"organized voluntary activity focused on problem solving and helping others," is distinct from electoral activities. Similarly, the third category, labeled as political voice, includes "activities that individuals undertake to give expression to their political opinions."[23] Therefore, using CIRCLE's definition (table 5.1), civic activities include, among other things, community problem solving, regular volunteer activities for nonelectoral organizations, and fund-raising or participating in events—e.g., a walk for a charity. Electoral activities include regular voting, persuading others to vote, wearing buttons, putting up signs, using bumper stickers; and political voice encompasses such actions as contacting officials or the media, signing petitions, protesting, and participating in boycotts and buycotts.[24]

With this framework in mind, we examined the official websites of a random sample of fifty legislators to ascertain the degree to which members of Congress were communicating messages about civic engagement. As one of their primary communication tools and a tool which has become standard

Table 5.1. Measures of Civic Engagement (CIRCLE categories)

Civic	Electoral	Political Voice
Community problem solving	Regular voting	Contacting officials
Regular volunteering for nonelectoral organization	Persuading others to vote	Contacting the print media
	Displaying buttons, signs, stickers	Contacting the broadcast media
	Campaign contributions	Protesting
Active membership in a group association	Volunteering for candidate or political organizations	Email petitions
		Written petitions
Participation in fund-raising run/walk/ride		Boycotting
		Buycotting
Other fund-raising for charity		Canvassing

Table 5.2.   Comparison of Sample Demographic with Entire 112th Congress*

	112th Congress	*Sample*
Party	Republican 243 (55%)	Republican 30 (60%)
	Democrat 198 (45%)	Democrat 20 (40%)
Average length of service	9.8 Years	10.2 Years
Gender	Male 366 (83%)	Male 44 (88%)
	Female 74 (17%)	Female 6 (12%)
Race	Hispanic 29 (6%)	Hispanic 3 (6%)
	Asian 11 (3%)	Asian 1 (1%)
	Black 44 (10%)	Black 2 (4%)
	White 355 (81%)	White 44 (88%)
Region	Midwest 100 (23%)	Midwest 9 (18%)
	Northeast 83 (19%)	Northeast 9 (18%)
	South 154 (35%)	South 21 (42%)
	West 98 (23%)	West 10 (20%)

*Numbers reflect House members and delegates, as both were part of the sample.

Sources: Office of the Clerk, House of Representatives, http://clerk.house.gov/ (August 2014); and Jennifer E. Manning, "Membership of the 112th Congress: A Profile," *Congressional Research Service*, http://www.senate.gov/reference/resources/pdf/R41647.pdf, March 1, 2011.

over the last decade, the official websites of legislators are important. The host of press releases about issue positions and constituency services along with legislative priorities and biographical information expressed on home pages provide a wealth of material to interested constituents.

Several considerations motivated our specific research strategy. Given that—to our knowledge—examining congressional websites in a civic engagement context is relatively unexplored territory, we wanted to balance the need to be systematic with the desire to comprehensively examine the material on these websites. Accordingly, we wanted to work with a sample large enough to allow for the potential of generalization (hence the random sample of 50 out of the 435 House members plus delegates) and to develop somewhat rigorous coding that would be comparable across legislators. The random sample of fifty house members we generated proved to be a reasonably accurate reflection of the general 112th Congress in terms of characteristics including party, seniority, and region/constituency (see table 5.2).

At the same time, we thought it was equally critical to take into account material from diverse sections of these websites (not limiting ourselves, for instance, to just home pages or press release headlines) and to explore in sufficient depth the flavor of the kinds of material legislators were presenting. That being said, in actuality, the large majority of material we did find was covered in the press section of legislator websites.

To achieve these ends, we piloted several member websites for any material that in any way related to the idea of civic engagement. From that examination, we developed a list of nine search words which, when considered in context (see below), proved a reliable way to track instances of the CIRCLE categories described above. Additionally, particularly in the initial stages of our coding process, we checked that our search terms were yielding a satisfactory and representative list of civically-oriented material on legislator websites. The nine words we used for our search terms include: civic engagement, democracy, voter registration, encourage, volunteer, join, contact, boycott, and buycott.

"Civic engagement" and "democracy" are among our list of search words because they reflect the abstract ideas we wish to highlight. "Civic engagement" is a common way that the academic (and some practical) literature highlights messages to get involved; although not an exclusive term, we would argue that it is one of the most frequent and established. Furthermore, searching for the word "democracy" had the potential to bring up references to the importance of our government, Constitution, and the invocation to constituents to engage in conventional democratic traditions. The need to search for "voter registration" is obvious, while the words "join," "encourage," "volunteer," and "contact" seem, to us, to be a reasonable set of words to translate the language of abstract concepts (e.g., civic engagement) into the kind of ordinary language a legislator would use to talk to constituents (e.g., join us), when considered in a civic engagement context. Based on our pilot study, we found searching for these words proved to be a productive way to bring up references to broader remarks on civic engagement. We did not expect there would be many references to buycotts or boycotts, but we included these terms as elements of the political voice category put forth by CIRCLE.[25]

It is clear including some of these words (democracy, voter registration) in search engines is straightforward. However, to understand the connection between words like "encourage" or "join" in the context of civic engagement, we had to read more closely to understand the context of the reference. For instance, a legislator's use of the word "join" could come in the context of asking constituents to join him in writing letters in opposition of a policy such as gun control (political voice), or it could simply mean that that legislator was letting constituents know he himself had "joined" with other members of Congress to vote against a gun control bill. Similarly, a member of Congress could use the word "encourage" to remind constituents to participate in solving a community problem (CIRCLE's community activity), or they could use the term to let people know that they had written a letter to the president encouraging him to support a policy. The data collected and discussed below includes only instances where each word was used in a way that was consistent with a civic engagement context.[26]

At the same time as this research strategy can demonstrate the extent to which legislators communicate about activities we label as civic engagement, we can only speculate about their underlying motivations or intentions. This is particularly important because, as the following sections make clear, by calling for constituents to take action, we think legislator activities are indeed promoting civic engagement, but this promotion may only come about as a by-product of their normal activities. As the examples below will demonstrate, legislators enjoin constituents to get involved on specific issues or community problems. There are not many abstract pronouncements on these websites—though there are a few—urging constituents to participate because participation is an important value in a democracy.

LEGISLATOR PROMULGATION OF CIVIC ENGAGEMENT ACTIVITIES

The data below make clear that very little of the communication from legislators speaks directly to abstract ideas about civic engagement. At first glance, as one reads through the examples documented below, it would be tempting to write these illustrations off as simply instances of partisan politics or reelection motive. Indeed, without directly asking legislators, we lack any sense of either their motivations or the priority each puts on increasing citizen involvement. At the same time, we contend that what is important here is not so much legislator motivations but the results. Members of Congress do routinely try to engage citizens in activities we would generally understand as civic engagement.

As a starting point to examine this data, table 5.3 presents the percentage of times our search terms showed up on legislator websites. While only 6 percent of legislators (three) used the term "civic engagement" directly, large majorities used words like "join," "volunteer," "contact," and "encourage." Just over a third of members said something about "democracy," and a few highlighted the importance of "voter registration." Additionally, legislators frequently used each of these words (in the appropriate context) a number of times, and many legislators used multiple words in a document, leading to a total of almost 900 times these words were cited. In total there were 731 postings on websites—most of them coming from the press release section. Thus the average legislator posted almost 15 entries pointing constituents toward some kind of involvement. If the average legislator also posts approximately 200 press releases in any given year, this would trans-

Table 5.3. Civically Oriented Activity of Legislators

Word	Number and Percent of Members Using Word	Number of Times Word Used
Civic Engagement	6% (3)	5
Voter Registration	16% (8)	8
Encourage	92% (46)	357
Volunteer	62% (31)	105
Boycott	6% (3)	3
Buycott	0% (0)	0
Democracy	38% (19)	39
Join	82% (41)	189
Contact	82% (41)	174
Total N	50	880

late into an approximately 7 percent rate of material encouraging citizens to participate, a finding that is consistent with the analysis of Twitter postings by Evans (chapter 6 in this volume).[27]

Since these words were only flagged in a context where some civically oriented activity was being promoted, their usage indicates a genuine advocacy for the activity described.

Because the specific term (join, encourage, etc.) is less important than the broader context in which it was used, we organize the discussion below in terms of the three CIRCLE categories described above: political voice, electoral activities, and civic/community participation. We arrange our discussion of the categories in this order to identify the ways legislators encourage engagement in the political process (political voice and voting) and their broader push for more general civic involvement (community activities). Due to the exploratory nature of this work, we focus on the qualitative; we flesh out each of the CIRCLE categories by identifying the wide array of examples culled from legislator websites. In sum, our analysis illustrates the differing ways legislator communications, even if somewhat indirectly, promote civic activity.

A NOTE ON THE GENERAL PROMOTION OF CIVIC EDUCATION AND ENGAGEMENT

As mentioned above, there are only a few instances in this data where legislators encourage the abstract promotion of civic engagement. The words "civic engagement" showed up four times on the websites. Perhaps not surprisingly given that legislators, in their role as community leaders, often find themselves speaking to students, several of the examples of general appeals to participate occurred in the context of reminding young people how important it is to get involved in the political process. For example, our sample included press releases entitled "Rep. Roybal-Allard (D-CA) talks to Bell High School students about the importance of a college education, civic engagement, voting, and being informed and active citizens" and "Congressman Sablan (D-NMI) addresses high school students who participated in a Civic Education Program in his district."[28] In a similar vein, "Rep. Scott Tipton (R-CO) asks young people to get politically involved but to do so through engaging the U.S. Constitution." As the call for action says, the congressman "is encouraging students in his district to send his office letters asking about the Constitution as part of Liberty Day."[29]

While similar references, attempting to educate adult constituents about participation in the abstract, are rare, those we found in the following press releases are striking for the amount of detail they include. For example, a press release on the website of Rep. Earl Blumenauer (D-OR), entitled "A Primer of Effective Advocacy," lets constituents know how much their elected officials value their input. Rep. Blumenauer begins by reminding constituents that "civic participation is the cornerstone of a representative democracy." His press release continues, "We {the people} elect people to represent us in local, state and federal offices but our responsibility doesn't end with our votes. If we expect our elected officials to respect our values and represent our points of view, we need to make sure they understand what is important to us. We need to stay involved."[30] The congressman is reiterating to readers that voting is only the starting point, and his press release goes on to explain additional ways citizens can participate, including educating themselves on the issues, providing "solutions not just opposition; and involving others in the political process." Given that citizens do so engage, Blumenhauer ends by arguing that there could be a notable payoff for "individual citizens can make a significant difference in issues that affect their local communities and our nation."[31] Blumenhauer's call for action beyond just electoral activities brings us to the next CIRCLE category, political voice.

Political Voice

The CIRCLE activities listed under political voice include contacting officials, contacting print or broadcast media, email or written petitions, canvassing, protesting, boycotting, and buycotting. Examples of legislators promoting many of these activities can be found in the press releases of our sample. Not surprisingly, but importantly, individual legislators ask citizens to get in touch with their own representatives—that is, themselves. Additionally, they enjoin citizens, in the context of advocating about a community or a national problem, to also contact other officials, and there are a number of examples of legislators soliciting even stronger action—pointing citizens toward signing a petition or participating in a protest. While it is possible to interpret many of these actions as electorally driven with legislators simply looking out for their own partisan self-interest, the result has the consequence of promoting constituent involvement. Moreover, a close examination of these press releases certainly gives the impression that legislators genuinely want to hear from people.

With reference to the CIRCLE category of contacting officials, legislators solicit input from their own constituents. Activities that are common for members of Congress—for instance, holding town meetings, asking constituents to get in touch with their offices or being out and about in the districts—are certainly ways members engage and involve citizens in the political process. So, as we would expect, there were many examples of representatives encouraging constituents to bring their thoughts to town meetings. Some include Rep. Steve Womack's (R-AR) promulgation of his "Coffee with the Congressman," and Rep. Brian Higgins (D-NY) touting his roving "Congress on Your Corner."[32] Among others, Reps. Bill Cassidy (R-LA) and Michele Bachmann (R-MN) held town halls on health care, and Rep. Daniel Webster (R-FL) conducted a series on the federal budget.[33] Scholars have long emphasized the importance of these types of congressional activities as a staple of the job. At the same time, less attention has been paid to the ways these efforts contribute to the promotion of citizen involvement more generally.

What additionally strikes us in the press releases is the number of instances where legislators asked constituents to take their concerns further and to contact additional government officials. Consider the following examples where a representative is advocating about a local problem and asking for constituents' help to do something about it:

- "Congressman Brian Higgins (D-NY) wants to prevent Buffalo Bills blackouts and he's writing to the Federal Communications Commission (FCC) to ask them to change the rules to make that happen. . . . Rep. Higgins particularly urges his constituents to respond."[34]
- "Rep. Walter Jones (R-NC) Pushes Back Against Proposed Ban on Red Snapper Fishing—'I encourage fishermen and others who may be impacted by the proposed interim rule to submit their comments to the National Oceanic and Atmospheric Administration (NOAA).'"[35]

Similarly, Reps. Earl Blumenauer (D-OR) and Sanford Bishop (D-GA) urged constituents to make their voices heard in support of agriculture legislation. As Bishop's press release states:

I cannot over-emphasize how important it is that you as individual growers and as commodity groups constantly and meaningfully stay in contact with your elected officials in the House and the Senate. Keep them aware of what is at stake with agriculture and help them find meaningful ways to help you continue to do what you do better than farmers anywhere in the world.[36]

Likewise, "Rep. [Raul] Grijalva (D-AZ) urged constituents to 'join' him in Tucson For a Public Celebration of Social Security's Birthday And Keep Up The Fight Against Steep Cuts."[37] Rep. Wally Herger (R-CA), after the passage of a bill, which would "strengthen Second Amendment Rights," suggested constituents might want to "contact your United States senators from California to let them know your views on it."[38] In the same vein, Rep. Michele Bachmann (R-MN) let people know that she had "formed the Tea Party Caucus in the House of Representatives in July 2010" and that she wanted people to "encourage your Representative to join us for these important meetings."[39]

A number of Republican legislators went further, acting as a group urging Americans to speak out. For instance, a press release on the website of Rep. John Abney Culberson (R-TX) informed people that in his view, an overly liberal Congress had become out of touch with the average citizen. He consequently expressed that:

I am excited to join my Republican colleagues today to introduce America Speaking Out, a project designed to engage with the American people in a meaningful, new way. Based on the principle that the best ideas are rarely found in Washington, House Republicans are asking Americans for their input in crafting a new agenda. It will be a public forum, where all Americans can propose ideas, debate, and cast votes on them.[40]

What is notable about this later press release is that, contrary to the usual view of legislators speaking for their own constituencies, here a group of Congress members are coming together to publicize their cooperative efforts over the Internet and across congressional district boundaries.

A few representatives wanted constituents to do more than contact government officials, and some asked constituents to identify very specific solutions to issues of the day. For instance, Rep. Joe Wilson (R-SC) requested constituent thoughts on specific ways to lower the national debt, and Rep. Daniel Webster (R-FL) asked constituents to send in their ideas for job creation, which he described as a "community generated outline."[41] In a different vein, Congressman Mark S. Critz (PA-12) announced that he would be holding 'Protect Our Rural Post Offices' events for residents to sign petitions against the targeted closure of local post offices and to file appeals if these offices were closed.[42] For Representative Mike Pence (R-IN), the issue was support of the right-to-life movement, and he let his constituents know that "since he was elected in 2000, Congressman Pence has made it a priority to encourage pro-life Americans who visit the Nation's Capital to stand for life" by participating in an annual march.[43] Lastly, Rep. Michael Grimm (D-NY) even called for a boycott of travel to Mexico by U.S. citizens because of the detainment of U.S. Marine Jon Hammar.[44]

In sum, these examples suggest a variety of ways in which members of Congress encourage political voice. Regardless of the intent of these calls for action, the tried-and-true activities of legislators take on a civic engagement character. Additionally, some members of Congress go further than the traditional activities for which they are known, urging constituents to contact other public officials and become active more generally.

Electoral Activities

The electorally oriented activities highlighted by CIRCLE include regular voting; persuading others to vote; displaying buttons, signs, or stickers; campaign contributions; and volunteering for candidates or political organizations. That said, particularly in contrast to the number of examples we collected with respect to political voice, we are in fact struck by the relatively small number of references to the one electorally oriented activity it might be quite appropriate to find on an official legislator website—urging constituents to register and vote. After all, provisions of the Help America Vote Act (HAVA), changes in types of ballots used at the polls, early voting opportunities, and controversies about voter ID laws certainly put debates about voting front and center.

Nevertheless, the phrase "voter registration" was only flagged on the websites of eight of the fifty members in our sample. Rep. Timothy Walz (R-MN) let constituents know he would bring voter registration forms to his "Saturday store stop."[45] Rep. John Culberson (R-TX) reminded constituents of "absentee voting week," encouraging members of the armed forces to fill out an online ballot if they had not already returned a paper version.[46] Similarly, Rep. Darrell Issa (R-CA) reminded constituents of deadlines to vote in local elections, and Rep. Chaka Fattah (D-PA) expressed concern about voter ID laws, asking for volunteers to get out the vote and letting constituents know procedures and deadlines for voter registration.[47]

One of the most detailed illustrations of a representative attempting to inform voters about election requirements comes from Rep. Mark Critz (D-PA) who launched an Internet application informing people of voting requirements in their states. "It's the responsibility of elected officials to inform constituents and to promote participation in our democratic process," said Congressman Critz. "In the last year, we have witnessed a nationwide assault on American citizens' constitutionally guaranteed right to vote, and little has been done to educate the public about these actions. This new voter registration app. will allow anyone to check the status of their registration, learn about any new requirements, and provide all the information needed to successfully register to vote in Pennsylvania."[48] Finally, a couple representatives did "encourage" constituents to simply get out there to vote.

Although, the examples are limited in the case of electoral activities (due in part to the project's design) they still illustrate ways in which members are encouraging citizens to get involved electorally, in addition to politically and civically, which is illustrated in the following section.

Civic and Community Activities

The CIRCLE category of "civic" activities highlights volunteer and community efforts in local areas, including community problem solving; regular volunteering for a nonelectoral organization; active membership in a group or association; participation in fund-raising or a run, walk, or ride; and other fund-raising for charity. As the CIRCLE researchers intended, this is an expansive list taking our understanding of civic engagement well beyond the simple act of voting and the explicitly political. Elsewhere in this volume, it has been argued that broadening this category even further—to include a wider variety of community-building opportunities—has some utility because a fuller range of pursuits linking citizens to municipal life enhances the quality of the citizen-community connection.[49] Therefore, along with the set of volunteer and community problem-solving opportunities legislators publicize to their constituents, we include in our categorization examples of members promoting a variety of community events and informing people of ways to get involved (e.g., possibilities for grants, internships, and district-wide competitions). Encouraging these types of activities certainly fits the spirit if not the letter of the CIRCLE civic and community involvement category.

Members of Congress asked their constituents to volunteer in several contexts, most consistently in the arena of providing assistance to veterans, 9-11 first responders, or other law enforcement officials. While noncontroversial and therefore safe issues for legislators to publicize, focusing on local "heroes" has the potential to motivate community spirit and to bring people together. An especially poignant example of this support for the military appears as one of several press releases on the subject from Rep. Randy Forbes (R-VA). In language representative of the sentiments expressed by many of his congressional colleagues, he describes veterans as "holiday heroes," and reminds us that:

This weekend, many of us will gather together with family. We will give gifts to those who are important to us. We will hug those loved ones that we do not have the opportunity to see very often. . . . We will sit together in the pews of our churches participating in candlelight Christmas Eve services. . . . But all across the nation, there will be family members who are missing, where an empty seat is found at the dinner table or a Skype conversation takes the place of a hug.[50]

Forbes' press release does much more than focus awareness on those who serve their country; he also wants constituents to take action. Thus, the meat of his invocation to constituents identifies specific ways they can help, including sending care packages, posting messages to troops, or providing "a Christmas tree to say thanks." More generally, he makes it easy for people to get involved, letting them know, "If you want to give your time and talents to support the care of America's veterans, use this form to complete a volunteer application and be contacted by a local Veterans' Affairs Voluntary Service representative."[51] In essence he is asking his constituents to not only value and show thanks for veterans but to also be active in their communities by volunteering their time and energy.

Similarly, legislators as diverse in constituency and ideology as Rep. Scott Garrett (R-NJ), Rep. Ron Kind (D-WI), and Rep. Michele Bachmann (R-MN), among others, issued statements in honor of veterans, particularly on Veteran's day. Their statements encouraged people to participate in a variety of activities, including flying American flags, observing moments of silence, making visits to cemeteries, and urging citizens to write letters to current active duty service members overseas. In a related fashion, Rep. Carolyn McCarthy (D-NY) is one of many congressmembers who used the occasion of an anniversary of the terrorist attacks of September 11 to call constituents to service: "September 11 is a day of remembrance, but we should also make it a day of service. This September 11, volunteer your time to a worthy cause, make a donation to charity offering relief to the victims of Hurricane Katrina, give blood, or participate in any activity that will help those in need."[52]

Furthermore, representatives asked constituents to get involved and volunteer in many settings, including participating in reading programs, fostering the environment, collecting for the needy, and lending a hand in a time of genuine disaster. Consider the following press release headlines on the websites of a diverse set of legislators:

- Congressman Lucille Roybal-Allard (CA-34) "Celebrates Dr. Seuss's 100th Birthday by Reading to Students at Miles Avenue Elementary School in Huntington Park" and by encouraging people to give their time to read to children.[53]

- Rep. Kind Encourages Western Wisconsin Families to Celebrate "Refuge Week" and give their time to protecting the nation's habitats.[54]
- Rep. Dave Camp Designates Offices as Toys for Tots Drop Off Sites.[55]
- Garrett Tours Oakland, Westwood and Hillsdale to Inspect Flood Damage From Hurricane Irene and to urge citizen involvement in recovery efforts.[56]

Finally, some representatives—in this sample, for example, Reps. Carolyn McCarthy (D-NY) and Daniel Webster (R-FL)—make the promotion of a volunteer sector one of the key issues they highlight as part of their work in Congress. Such is the case in the following press release on McCarthy's website:

> One year ago today, President Obama signed into law the Edward M. Kennedy Serve America Act. As the sponsor of the legislation, I was proud to stand with the President as he signed this bill, the first major bipartisan initiative, which launched a new era of American service. . . . This week, as we recognize National Volunteer Week, celebrated from April 18 through April 24, we honor those who have made significant contributions to our communities through volunteerism and public service. The Serve America Act has expanded service opportunities to thousands of Americans and I encourage not only school aged children, but veterans, retirees and senior-citizens to get involved and share their knowledge and skills for the benefit of the community.[57]

This example illustrates that members not only ask constituents to get involved and be civically engaged, but they also, at times, make community involvement and engagement a cornerstone of their policy goals.

In a different vein, legislators solicit constituent action on, as the CIRCLE category labels it, community problem solving. From causes ranging from trading in their guns to calling for observance of Missing Children's Day, to demonstrating concern for the environment, legislators encouraged constituents to "join" and to take part. For example, Rep. Chaka Fattah (D-PA), served as one of the municipal leaders organizing "Groceries for Guns" exchanges in local communities, calling on individuals in Philadelphia to get guns off the streets by trading them in for grocery vouchers.[58] Rep. Dave Camp (R-MI) poignantly reminded his constituents of National Missing Children's Day, urging them to be observant, "Perhaps because they [pictures of missing children] are now so familiar, people don't always stop to look at them as often as they once did."[59] Finally, Rep. John Barrow (R-GA) encouraged constituents to observe "earth hour," as "This is a great example of how a relatively easy act for one family, turning off the lights, multiplied by millions worldwide, can have a positive impact by raising awareness about climate change." Barrow adds, "Maybe it'll also remind folks to turn off lights in their houses when they leave a room or go out for the day, which is good for the environment, and good for the electric bill!"[60]

Members of Congress encourage participation in the community as well, by making constituents aware of events in the district. In some interesting examples of this Rep. Mark Critz (D-PA) let his constituents know of what he termed the "unique opportunity" provided by "the Library of Congress 'Gateway to Knowledge' traveling exhibit."[61] Reps. Michael Grimm (R-NY) and Scott Tipton (R-CO) encouraged constituents to support local businesses by participating in Small Business Saturday.[62] Furthermore, members also hold information sessions, publicize current problems, and notify citizens about grants or other civically oriented opportunities in their communities.

In short, what this vast array of examples suggest is that while members of Congress are not directly using the term civic engagement and though they may not even consciously stop to think that their efforts are encouraging it, their activities do have the consequence of soliciting citizen involvement.

CONCLUSION

Given the modern day crisis in civic engagement highlighted by scholars and practitioners alike, even factors that may push and remind relatively small sets of individuals to get involved can be consequential. In that spirit, we argue that the activities of legislators as they go about their normal business of interacting with constituents can matter. We highlight the relatively low-cost nature of legislators pushing for constituents to become active. Legislators by default are already communicating with constituents and asking for citizen input in a myriad of ways. Their staff and other resources make the job easy, and the increased opportunities afforded by the Internet and additional social media enhance possibilities for two-way dialogue. The encouragement of civic engagement follows as a natural, if understudied, by-product of traditional legislative activities.

In the context of this dearth of attention in the Congress literature, the civic-oriented activities of legislators as elaborated in our data stand out. The amount of information obtained based on our counts of relevant keywords in context and based on our qualitative examples is unmistakable. With the exception of voting and elections, the CIRCLE categories of community activity and political voice are well represented, and our keywords on average turned up a fair amount of examples. As is clear from some of the quoted material throughout the paper, legislators took time to explain why getting involved was important, asked constituents to communicate with additional officials or government agencies and highlighted issues on which constituents could make a difference. In some cases, the press releases were quite detailed as to the nature of the issue in question and the actions it would be helpful for constituents to take. It therefore seems useful to us to put a civic engagement spin on the constituency-oriented activities of members of Congress, and it is important in the modern era to do so. For example, it is easy, as scholars including Putnam have demonstrated, to reminisce about earlier historical eras marked by grassroots party activity, a more active civic life, and yes, even more bowling leagues. But today, perhaps the efforts of members of Congress, as they go about their normal business of traversing their districts and personally engaging constituents, come close to this type of activity, with the difference being in contrast to the past today there is extensive use of new age technology to do so.

At the same time as this data shows members of Congress asking constituents to participate in civically oriented activity, we have no way to know how individual legislators prioritize the importance of civic engagement in the abstract. The specific term "civic engagement" appeared infrequently—though perhaps that it appeared at all is a positive reflection of the penetration of the term into the world of members of Congress. But while some legislators directly spoke about democracy or explained the political process to constituents, most framed concerns in an issue-specific context or simply reacted to events. Electoral involvement, even in the generic version of "go vote on election day," was not particularly prevalent. That said, the things legislators are asking constituents to do seems, to us, to serve an important function in a democracy. They are encouraging citizens to get involved in very concrete ways—to become active on specific issues or to work on better solutions to particular problems in their communities. Perhaps that specificity, in contrast to any abstract exhortations about the need to get involved, is, in the end, the best way of all to motivate constituents. It would be interesting to point out to congressmembers that the activities they already engage in serve the broader function of promoting civic engagement and to ascertain if that would encourage them to take the not so difficult next step of making a more direct link between their work and broader civic engagement principles.

NOTES

1. Donald P. Green and Alan S Gerber, *Get Out the Vote: How to Increase Voter Turnout* (Washington, DC: Brookings Institute Press, 2004); Steven J. Rosenstone and John Mark Hansen, *Mobilization, Participation, and Democracy in America* (New York: Pearson Education Inc., 1993).

2. Robert. D. Putnam, "Tuning In, Tuning Out: The Strange Disappearance of Social Capital in America." *PS: Political Science and Politics* 28, no. 4 (1995): 664–683.

3. Robert Putnam, *Bowling Alone: The Collapse and Revival of American Community* (New York: Simon and Schuster, 2000), 46.

4. Stephen Macedo et al., *Democracy at Risk* (Washington, DC: Brookings Institute Press, 2005), 1.

5. Ibid., 1.

6. Martin P. Wattenberg, *Where Have All the Voters Gone?* (Cambridge: Harvard University Press, 2002); Ruy Teixeira, *The Disappearing American Voter* (Washington D.C.: Brookings Institution Press, 1992); Paul R. Abramson and John H. Aldrich, "The Decline of Electoral Participation in America," *American Political Science Review* 76, no .3 (Sept. 1982), 502–21.

7. Stephen Macedo et al., *Democracy at Risk*; and Eric Plutzer, "Becoming a Habitual Voter: Inertia, Resources, and Growth in Young Adulthood," *The American Political Science Review* 96, no. 1 (March 2002), 41–56.

8. Robert Putnam, "Tuning in, Tuning Out"; and Robert Putnam, "Bowling Alone: America's Declining Social Capital, " *Journal of Democracy* 6, no. 1 (June 1995).

9. Macedo et al., *Democracy at Risk*; Richard J. Ellis and Michael Nelson, eds., *Debating Reform: Conflicting Perspectives on How to Fix the American Political System* (Washington D.C.: Congressional Quarterly Press, 2010).

10. Office of the Clerk: U.S. House of Representatives, http://clerk.house.gov/ (accessed January, 2013).

11. Richard F. Fenno, *Congressmen in Committees* (Boston: Little, Brown & Co., 1973); David R. Mayhew, *Congress: The Electoral Connection* (New Haven: Yale University Press, 1974); John W. Kingdon, *Congressman's Voting Decisions* (Ann Arbor: University of Michigan Press, 1973); R. Douglas Arnold, *The Logic of Congressional Action* (New Haven: Yale University Press, 1992).

12. Richard F. Fenno, *Home Style: House Members in Their Districts* (Boston: Little, Brown & Co., 1978); Mayhew, *Congress: The Electoral Connection*; Morris P. Fiorina, *Congress: Keystone of the Washington Establishment* (New Haven: Yale University Press, 1977); Richard L. Hall, *Participation in Congress* (New Haven: Yale University Press. 1996); Arnold, *The Logic of Congressional Action*; Sally Friedman, *Dilemmas of Representation: Local Politics, National Factors, and the Home Styles of Modern U.S. Congress Members* (Albany: State University of New York Press, 2007).

13. Michael J. Robinson, "Three Faces of Congressional Media," in Thomas E. Mann and Norman J. Ornstein, eds., *The New Congress* (Washington, DC: American Enterprise Institute, 1981); Diana Evans Yiannakis, "House Members' Communication Styles: Newsletters and Press Releases," *Journal of Politics* 44, no. 4 (November 1982), 1049–71; Daniel Lipinski, "The Effect of Messages Communicated by Members of Congress: The Impact of Publicizing Votes," *Legislative Studies Quarterly* 26, no.1 (February 2001), 81–100.

14. E. Scott Adler et al., "The Home Style Homepage: Legislator Use of the World Wide Web for Constituency Contact," *Legislative Studies Quarterly* 23, no. 4 (November 1998), 585–95; Amanda Lenhart, "Twitter and Status Updating: Demographics, Mobile Access and News Consumption," Pew Internet and American Life Project, Pew Research Center, http://www.pewresearch.org, 2009; Jennifer Golbeck et al., "Twitter Use by the U.S. Congress," *Journal of the American Society for Information Science and Technology* 61, no. 8 (2010), 1612–21; C. Lawrence Evans and Walter Oleszeck, "The Wired Congress: The Internet, Institutional Change, and Legislative Work," in James A. Thurber and Colton C. Campbell, eds., *Congress and the Internet* (New Jersey: Prentice-Hall, 2002); Christine B. Williams and Girish Jeff Gulati, "The Political Impact of Facebook: Evidence from the 2006 Midterm Elections and 2008 Nomination Contest," *Politics & Technology Review* (March 2008), 11–21; Jennifer L. Lawless, "Twitter and Facebook: New Ways to Send the Same Old Message?," in Richard L. Fox and Jennifer Ramos, eds., *iPolitics* (New York: Cambridge University Press, 2011).

15. Kay Lehman Schlozman, Aaron Smith, Sidney Verba, and Henry Brady, "The Internet and Civic Engagement," Pew Internet and American Life Project, Pew Research Center, Washington, DC, http://www.pewinternet.org/2009/09/01/the-internet-and-civic-engagement/, 2009.

16. Daniel Lipinski, "The Effect of Messages Communicated by Members of Congress."

17. Stephen C. Craig, *The Malevolent Leaders: Popular Discontent in America.* (Boulder, CO: Westview Press, 1993); John R. Hibbing and Elizabeth Theiss-Morse, *Congress as Public Enemy: Public Attitudes toward American Political Institutions* (Cambridge: Cambridge University Press, 1995); Seymour Martin Lipset and William G. Schneider, *The Confidence Gap* (Baltimore: Johns Hopkins University Press, 1987); John Brehm and Wendy Rahn, "Individual-level Evidence for the Causes and Consequences of Social Capital," *American Journal of Political Science* 41, no. 3 (July 1997): 999–1023.

18. Barry C. Burden, *Personal Roots of Representation* (Princeton: Princeton University Press, 2007); Christine DeGregorio, *Network of Champions: Leadership, Access and Advocacy in the U.S. House of Representatives* (Ann Arbor: University of Michigan Press, 1997); Wendy J. Schiller, "Senators as Political Entrepreneurs: Using Bill Sponsorship to Shape Legislative Agendas," *American Journal of Political Science* 39, no. 1 (1995): 186–203.

19. The Center on Congress at Indiana University, "Lee H. Hamilton: Biography," Indiana University, http://congress.indiana.edu/lee-h-hamilton-biography (accessed January 2013).

20. Stennis Center for Public Service Leadership, "Congress to Campus," Stennis Center for Public Service Leadership, http://www.stennis.gov/programs/congress-to-campus (accessed January 2013).

21. We excluded from our analysis campaign websites because they exist to promote a member's reelection.

22. Scott Keeter et al., "The Civic and Political Health of the Nation: A Generational Portrait," CIRCLE, http://www.civicyouth.org/. Sept. 2002. See also Krista

Jenkins et al., "Is Civic Behavior Political? Exploring the Multidimensional Nature of Political Participation." paper presented at MPSA 2003, Chicago; and Krista Jenkins, "Gender and Civic Engagement: Secondary Analysis of Survey Data," CIRCLE working paper 41, http://www.civicyouth.org/. 2005.

23. Scott Keeter et al., "The Civic and Political Health of the Nation: A Generational Portrait."

24. CIRCLE, http://www.civicyouth.org (August 2012–January 2013).

25. Not all examples/quotations are accompanied by specific dates. Member press releases usually are date specific, but other material on their websites are not.

26. Our strategy of keeping track of words in context turned out to be very labor intensive. Although we do not claim the search to be exhaustive, the initial work to pilot search terms—compare every instance of civic engagement on a few websites to the material turned up by our search terms—along with subsequent checks while coding—leads us to believe our procedures provide a fairly accurate representation of the civically related material on the websites of these legislators.

27. Due to variations in the ways materials were posted and several members leaving office before we could track totals, it proved difficult to track the actual number of releases on each individual legislator's website. However, the estimate of 200 postings per member seems a reasonable approximation.

28. Congresswoman Lucille Roybal-Allard, "Rep Roybal-Allard Talks to Bell High School Students about the Importance of a College Education, Civic Engagement, Voting, and Being Informed and Active Citizens," house.gov, http://roybal-allard.house.gov/news/documentsingle.aspx?DocumentID=224551 (August 2012–January 2013); Congressman Gregorio Sablan, "Dr. Rita Hocog Inos honored in Kilili Fellowship Bill," house.gov, http://sablan.house.gov/press-release/dr-rita-hocog-inos-honored-kilili-fellowship-bill, (August 2012–January 2013).

29. Congressman Scott Tipton, "Tipton Reaffirms Oath to Support and Defend the Constitution," house.gov, http://tipton.house.gov/press-release/tipton-reaffirms-oath-support-and-defend-constitution, (August 2012–January 2013).

30. Congressman Earl Blumenauer, "A Primer for Effective Advocacy," house.gov, http://blumenauer.house.gov/index.php/component/content/article/22-constituent-services/constituent-services/2090-a-primer-of-effective-advocacy, (August 2012–January 2013).

31. Ibid.

32. Congressman Steve Womack, "Coffee with the Congressman," house.gov, http://womack.house.gov/calendar, (August 2012–January 2013); Congressman Brian Higgins, "Congressman Higgins Announces Congress on Your Corner Sites," house.gov, http://higgins.house.gov/services/congress-on-your-corner, (August 2012–January 2013).

33. Congressman Bill Cassidy, "Unanswered Questions from Town Hall on July 16, 2012," house.gov. http://cassidy.house.gov/media-center/press-releases/cassidy-to-host-town-hall-meeting-on-health-care, (August 2012–January 2013). Congresswoman Michele Bachman, "Bachmann Hosts Healthcare Town Hall," house.gov, http://bachmann.house.gov/press-release/bachmann-hosts-healthcare-town-hall (August 2012–January 2013), Congressman Daniel Webster, "Webster

Announces Town Hall Community Discussions," house.gov, http://webster.
house.gov/news/documentsingle.aspx?DocumentID=288505, (August 2012–January 2013); See also Congresswoman Janice Hahn, "Wilmington Congress on Your
Corner," house.gov, http://hahn.house.gov/event/wilmington-congress-your-corner
(August 2012–January 2013).

34. Congressman Brian Higgins, "Higgins Asks FCC to Change the Rules on NFL
Blackouts," house.gov, http://higgins.house.gov/media-center/press-releases/higgins
-asks-fcc-to-change-the-rules-on-nfl-blackouts (August 2012–January 2013).

35. Congressman Walter Jones, "Jones Pushes Back Against Proposed Ban on
Red Snapper Fishing," house.gov, http://jones.house.gov/press-release/jones-pushes
-back-against-proposed-ban-red-snapper-fishing (August 2012–January 2013).

36. Congressman Earl Blumenauer, "Every Oregonian Has a Stake," house.
gov, http://blumenauer.house.gov/index.php/newsroom/in-the-news/2054-qev-
ery-oregonian-has-a-stakeq (August 2012–January 2013); Congressman Sanford
Bishop, Jr., "Congressmen and Senators to help CSU students enter military academies Saturday," house.gov, http://bishop.house.gov/media-center/in-the-news/
congressmen-and-senators-to-help-csu-students-enter-military-academies (August
2012–January 2013).

37. Congressmember Raul M. Grijalva, "Join Rep. Grijalva August 5 in Tucson
For a Public Celebration of Social Security's Birthday And Keep Up The Fight
Against Steep Cuts," house.gov, http://grijalva.house.gov/news-and-press-releases/
join-rep-grijalva-august-5-in-tucson-for-a-public-celebration-of-social-securitys
-birthday-and-keep-up-the-fight-against-steep-cuts/ (August 2012–January 2013).

38. Congressman Walter Herger, "House Votes to Strengthen Second Amendment
Rights," house.gov, http://herger.house.gov/index.php?controller=article&id=15&op
tion=com_tagtrends (August 2012–January 2013).

39. Congresswoman Michele Bachmann, "Tea Party Caucus," house.gov, http://
judicial-discipline-reform.org/docs/RepMBachmann_Tea_Party_Caucus_jul10.pdf
(August 2012–January 2013).

40. Congressman John Abney Culberson, "America, Speak Out!," house.gov,
http://culberson.house.gov/news/documentsingle.aspx?DocumentID=352837 (August 2012–January 2013). See also Congressmember Dave Camp, "Camp Hosts
America Speaking Out Town Hall," house.gov, http://camp.house.gov/news/docu
mentsingle.aspx?DocumentID=189057 (August 2012–January 2013)"; Congressman Jeb Hensarling, "Hensarling to Host Mesquite "America Speaking Out"
Town Hall," house.gov, http://hensarling.house.gov/media-center/press-releases/
hensarling-to-host-mesquite-america-speaking-out-town-hall (August 2012–January
2013); and Jeb Hensarling, "Hensarling Announces "America Speaking Out," house.
gov, http://hensarling.house.gov/media-center/press-releases/hensarling-announces
-america-speaking-out (August 2012–January 2013).

41. Congressman Joe Wilson, "Wilson Seeks to Involve Constituents in Reducing
National Debt," house.gov, http://joewilson.house.gov/media-center/press-releases/
wilson-seeks-to-involve-constituents-in-reducing-national-debt (August 2012–January 2013); and Congressman Dan Webster, "The Webster Wire: Forgotten 21,"

house.gov, http://webster.house.gov/news/email/show.aspx?ID=QMM45DXUSQSG TZ4ZFODTXFCCIM (August 2012–January 2013).

42. Congressman Mark Critz, "Critz Plans Petition/Appeals Events for Local Post Offices Targeted for Closure," house.gov, http://critz.house.gov/press-release/ critz-plans-petitionappeals-events-local-post-offices-targeted-closure (August 2012–January 2013).

43. Congressman Mike Pence, "Pence to Join Pro-Life Americans at Annual March for Life Monday," house.gov, http://mikepence.house.gov/ (August 2012–January 2013).

44. Congressman Michael Grimm, "Rep. Grimm Calls for U.S. Boycott of Travel to Mexico until Detained Marine Jon Hammar is Released," house.gov, http://grimm.house.gov/press-release/rep-grimm-calls-us-boycott-travel-mexico-until-detained -marine-jon-hammar-released (August 2012–January 2013).

45. Congressman Tim Walz, "Rep. Walz to Host Saturday Store Shop," house.gov, http://walz.house.gov/News/DocumentSingle.aspx?DocumentID=84017 (August 2012–January 2013).

46 Congressman John Culberson, "DoD Announces Absentee Voting Week: Sept. 27–Oct. 4," house.gov, https://culberson.house.gov/news/documentsingle .aspx?DocumentID=353185 (August 2012–January 2013).

47. Congressmember Darrell Issa, "Attention San Diego & Riverside Counties: Monday, May 23, is the LAST DAY to register for the June 7th election," house.gov, http://issa.house.gov/district-blog/2011/05/attention-san-diego-a-riverside-coun ties-monday-may-23-is-the-last-day-to-register-for-the-june–7th-election/ (August 2012–January 2013; and Congressmember Chaka Fattah, "Pennsylvania Voter ID Requirements," house.gov, http://fattah.house.gov/, (August 2012–January 2013).

48. Congressman Mark Critz, "Critz Launches New Website App to Ensure all Americans are Aware of their Voting Rights," house.gov, http://critz.house.gov/ press-release/critz-launches-new-website-app-ensure-all-americans-are-aware-their -voting-rights (August 2012–January 2013).

49. See chapter 9 by Armato and Friedman in this volume.

50. Congressman J. Randy Forbes, "Capital Monitor- Holiday Heroes," house.gov, http://forbes.house.gov/news/email/show.aspx?ID=7YSSKMTDVGWFNJNFJZ2 MUC345Y (August 2012–January 2013).

51. Ibid.

52. Congresswoman Carolyn McCarthy, "September 11 Must Be a Day of Remembrance and Service," house.gov, http://carolynmccarthy.house.gov/recent -news/september-11-must-be-a-day-of-remembrance-and-service/ (August 2012–January 2013).

53. Congresswoman Lucille Roybal-Allard, "Congresswoman Lucille Roybal-Allard Celebrates Dr. Seuss's Birthday," house.gov, http://roybal-allard.house.gov/ news/documentsingle.aspx?DocumentID=129441 (August 2012–January 2013).

54. Congressman Ron Kind. "Rep. Kind Encourages Western Wisconsin Families to Celebrate 'Refuge Week,'" house.gov, http://kind.house.gov/latest-news/ rep-kind-encourages-western-wisconsin-families-to-celebrate-refuge-week/ (August 2012–January 2013).

55. Congressman Dave Camp, "Camp Designates Offices as Toys for Tots Drop Off Sites," house.gov., http://camp.house.gov/news/documentsingle.aspx?Doc umentID=121138 (August 2012–January 2013).

56. Congressman Scott Garrett, "Garrett Tours Oakland, Westwood and Hillsdale to Inspect Flood Damage From Hurricane Irene," house.gov, http://garrett.house.gov/ press-release/garrett-tours-oakland-westwood-and-hillsdale-inspect-flood-damage -hurricane-irene (August 2012–January 2013).

57. Congresswoman Carolyn McCarthy, "Rep. McCarthy Recognizes National Volunteer Week and Encourages National Service and Volunteerism," house.gov, http://carolynmccarthy.house.gov/recent-news/rep-mccarthy-recognizes-national -volunteer-week-and-encourages-national-service-and-volunteerism/ (August 2012– January 2013).

58. Congressmember Chaka Fattah, "Rep. Fattah, Councilwoman Reynolds Brown Plan More 'Groceries for Guns' Exchanges," house.gov., http://fattah.house .gov/press/rep-fattah-councilwoman-reynolds-brown-plan-more-groceries-for-guns -exchanges/ (August 2012–January 2013).

59. Congressmember Dave Camp, "Rep. Dave Camp Recognizes National Missing Children's Day," house.gov, http://camp.house.gov/news/documentsingle .aspx?DocumentID=120658 (August 2012–January 2013).

60. Congressman John Barrow, "Barrow Encourages Observance of Earth Hour," house.gov, http://barrow.house.gov/media-center/press-releases/barrow-encourages -observance-of-earth-hour (August 2012–January 2013).

61. Congressman Mark Critz, "Library of Congress Traveling Exhibit in Union- town this Week," house.gov, http://critz.house.gov/press-release/library-congress -traveling-exhibit-uniontown-week (August 2012–January 2013).

62. Representative Michael Grimm, "Rep. Grimm Asks Everyone to 'Shop Small' this Saturday & Support Local Small Businesses," house.gov, http://grimm.house .gov/press-release/rep-grimm-asks-everyone-%E2%80%98shop-small%E2%80%99 -saturday-support-local-small-businesses (August 2012–January 2013); and Con- gressman Scott Tipton, "Tipton Encourages Participation in Small Business Satur- day," house.gov, http://tipton.house.gov/press-release/tipton-encourages-participation -small-business-saturday (August 2012–January 2013).

BIBLIOGRAPHY

Abramson, Paul R., and John H. Aldrich. "The Decline of Electoral Participation in America." *American Political Science Review* 76, no. 3 (1982): 502–21.

Adler, E. Scott, Chariti E. Gent, and Cary B. Overmeyer. "The Home Style Home- page: Legislator Use of the World Wide Web for Constituency Contact." *Legisla- tive Studies Quarterly* 23, no. 4 (November 1998): 585–95.

Arnold, R. Douglas. *The Logic of Congressional Action.* New Haven: Yale University Press, 1992.

Bachmann, Michele. house.gov, http://bachmann.house.gov/. (August 2012–January 2013).

Barrow, John. house.gov, http://barrow.house.gov/. (August 2012–January 2013).

Bilbray, Brian P. house.gov, http://bilbray.house.gov/. (August 2012–January 2013).

Bishop, Sanford D., Jr., house.gov, http://bishop.house.gov/. (August 2012–January 2013).

Blumenauer, Earl. house.gov, http://blumenauer.house.gov/. (August 2012–January 2013).

Brehm, John, and Wendy Rahn. "Individual-level Evidence for the Causes and Consequences of Social Capital." *American Journal of Political Science* 41 (1997): 999–1023.

Burden, Barry C. *Personal Roots of Representation.* Princeton: Princeton University Press, 2007.

Camp, Dave. house.gov, http://camp.house.gov/. (August 2012–January 2013).

Cassidy, Bill. house.gov, http://cassidy.house.gov/. (August 2012–January 2013).

The Center on Congress at Indiana University. "Lee H. Hamilton: Biography." Indiana University. http://congress.indiana.edu/lee-h-hamilton-biography (accessed January 2013).

Craig, Stephen C. *The Malevolent Leaders: Popular Discontent in America.* Boulder, CO: Westview Press, 1993.

Critz, Mark S. house.gov, http://critz.house.gov/. (August 2012–January 2013).

Culberson, John Abney. house.gov, http://culberson.house.gov/. (August 2012–January 2013).

Dalton, Russell. *The Good Citizen: How a Younger Generation Is Reshaping American Politics.* Washington D.C.: Congressional Quarterly Press, 2008.

DeGregorio, Christine. *Network of Champions: Leadership, Access and Advocacy in the U.S. House of Representatives.* Ann Arbor: University of Michigan Press, 1997.

Ellis, Richard J., and Michael Nelson, eds. *Debating Reform: Conflicting Perspectives on How to Fix the American Political System.* Washington D.C.: Congressional Quarterly Press, 2010.

Evans, C. Lawrence, and Walter Oleszeck. "The Wired Congress: The Internet, Institutional Change, and Legislative Work." In *Congress and the Internet,* eds. James A. Thurber and Colton C. Campbell. New Jersey: Prentice-Hall, 2002.

Fattah, Chaka. house.gov, http://fattah.house.gov/. (August 2012–January 2013).

Fenno, Richard F. *Congressmen in Committees.* Boston: Little, Brown & Co., 1973.

Fenno, Richard F. *Home Style: House Members in Their Districts.* Boston: Little, Brown & Co., 1978.

Fiorina, Morris P. *Congress: Keystone of the Washington Establishment.* New Haven: Yale University Press, 1977.

Friedman, Sally. *Dilemmas of Representation: Local Politics, National Factors, and the Home Styles of Modern U.S. Congress Members.* Albany: State University of New York Press, 2007.

Forbes, J. Randy. house.gov, http://forbes.house.gov/. (August 2012–January 2013).

Garrett, Scott. house.gov, http://garrett.house.gov/. (August 2012–January 2013).

Glassman, Matthew Eric, Jacob R. Straus, and Colleen J. Shogun. "Social Networking and Constituent Communication: Member Use of Twitter during a Two Week Period in the 111th Congress." *CRS Report R40823*. Washington D.C.: Congressional Research Service, 2009. http://assets.opencrs.com/rpts/R41066_20100203.pdf

Gohmert, Louie. house.gov, http://gohmert.house.gov/. (August 2012–January 2013).

Golbeck, Jennifer, Justin Grimes, and Anthony Rogers. "Twitter Use by the U.S. Congress." *Journal of the American Society for Information Science and Technology* 61, no. 8 (2010): 1612–21.

Graham, Bob with Chris Hand. *America, The Owner's Manual: Making Government Work for You*. Washington D.C.: Congressional Quarterly Press, 2009.

Graves, Tom. house.gov, http://tomgraves.house.gov/. (August 2012–January 2013).

Green, Donald P., and Alan S. Gerber. *Get Out the Vote: How to Increase Voter Turnout*. Washington D.C.: Brookings Institution Press, 2004.

Grijalva, Raúl M. house.gov, http://grijalva.house.gov/. (August 2012–January 2013).

Grimm, Michael G. house.gov, http://grimm.house.gov/. (August 2012–January 2013).

Hahn, Janice. house.gov, http://hahn.house.gov/. (August 2012–January 2013).

Hall, Richard L. *Participation in Congress*. New Haven: Yale University Press, 1996.

Hanna, Richard L. house.gov, http://hanna.house.gov/. (August 2012–January 2013).

Hastings, Doc. house.gov, http://hastings.house.gov/. (August 2012–January 2013).

Hensarling, Jeb. house.gov, http://hensarling.house.gov/. (August 2012–January 2013).

Herger, Wally. house.gov, http://herger.house.gov/. (August 2012–January 2013).

Hibbing, John R. and Elizabeth Theiss-Morse. *Congress as Public Enemy: Public Attitudes toward American Political Institutions*. Cambridge: Cambridge University Press, 1995.

Higgins, Brian. house.gov, http://higgins.house.gov/. (August 2012–January 2013).

Hochul, Kathleen C. house.gov, http://hochul.house.gov/. (August 2012–January 2013).

Huizenga, Bill. house.gov, http://huizenga.house.gov/ (August 2012–January 2013).

Issa, Darrell E. house.gov, http://issa.house.gov/. (August 2012–January 2013).

Jenkins, Krista, "Gender and Civic Engagement: Secondary Analysis of Survey Data." CIRCLE working paper 41. http://www.civicyouth.org/. 2005.

Jenkins, Krista, Molly W. Andolina, Scott Keeter, and Cliff Zukin. "Is Civic Behavior Political? Exploring the Multidimensional Nature of Political Participation." Paper presented at MPSA 2003. Chicago.

Johnson, Bill. house.gov, http://billjohnson.house.gov/. (August 2012–January 2013).

Jones, Walter B. house.gov, http://jones.house.gov/. (August 2012–January 2013).

Kaptur, Marcy. house.gov, http://www.kaptur.house.gov/. (August 2012–January 2013).

Keeter, Scott, Cliff Zukin, Molly Andolina, Krista Jenkins. "The Civic and Political Health of the Nation: A Generational Portrait." CIRCLE. http://www.civicyouth.org/. Sept. 2002.

Kind, Ron. house.gov, http://kind.house.gov/. (August 2012–January 2013).

Kingdon, John W. *Congressman's Voting Decisions*. Ann Arbor: University of Michigan Press, 1973.

Lankford, James. house.gov, http://lankford.house.gov/. (August 2012–January 2013).

Lawless, Jennifer L. "Twitter and Facebook: New Ways to Send the Same Old Message?" In *iPolitics*, eds. Richard L. Fox and Jennifer Ramos. New York: Cambridge University Press, 2011.

Lipinski, Daniel. "The Effect of Messages Communicated by Members of Congress: The Impact of Publicizing Votes." *Legislative Studies Quarterly* 26, no. 1 (February 2001): 81–100.

Lipinski, Daniel. house.gov, http://www.lipinski.house.gov/. (August 2012–January 2013).

Lenhart, Amanda. "Twitter and Status Updating: Demographics, Mobile Access and News Consumption." Pew Internet and American Life Project, Pew Research Center. http://www.pewinternet.org/2009/02/12/twitter-and-status-updating (accessed January 2013).

Lipset, Seymour Martin, and William G. Schneider. *The Confidence Gap*. Baltimore: Johns Hopkins University Press, 1987.

Macedo, Stephen, Yvette Alex-Assensoh, Jeffrey M. Berry, Michael Brintnall, David E. Campbell, Luis Ricardo Fraga, Archon Fung, William A. Galston, Christopher F. Karpowitz, Margaret Levi, Meira Levinson, Keena Lipsitz, Richard G. Niemi, Robert D. Putnam, Wendy M. Rahn, Rob Reich, Robert R. Rodgers, Todd Swanstrom, and Katherine Cramer Walsh. *Democracy at Risk: How Political Choices Undermine Citizen Participation, and What We Can Do about It*. Washington D.C.: Brookings Institution Press, 2005.

Manning, Jennifer E. "Membership of the 112th Congress: A Profile." Congressional Research Service. http://www.senate.gov/reference/resources/pdf/R41647.pdf, March 1, 2011 (August 2014).

Mayhew, David R. *Congress: The Electoral Connection*. New Haven: Yale University Press, 1974.

McCarthy, Carolyn. house.gov, http://carolynmccarthy.house.gov/. (August 2012–January 2013).

Niemi, Richard G., Herbert F. Weisberg, and David Kimball. *Controversies in Voting Behavior, 5th Edition*. Washington D.C.: Congressional Quarterly Press, 2011.

Office of the Clerk: U.S. House of Representatives. http://clerk.house.gov/ (accessed January 2013 and August 2014).

Palazzo, Steven M. house.gov, http://palazzo.house.gov/. (August 2012–January 2013).

Pence, Mike. house.gov, http://mikepence.house.gov/. (August 2012–January 2013).

Plutzer, Eric. "Becoming a Habitual Voter: Inertia, Resources, and Growth in Young Adulthood." *The American Political Science Review* 96, no. 1 (March 2002): 41–56.

Putnam, Robert. D. "Tuning In, Tuning Out: The Strange Disappearance of Social Capital in America." *PS: Political Science and Politics* 28, no. 4 (1995): 664–683.

Putnam, Robert D. *Bowling Alone: The Collapse and Revival of American Community*. New York: Simon & Schuster, 2000.

Reyes, Silvestre. house.gov, http://reyes.house.gov/. (August 2012–January 2013).

Robinson, Michael J. "Three Faces of Congressional Media." In *The New Congress*, ed. Thomas E. Mann and Norman J. Ornstein. Washington, D.C.: American Enterprise Institute, 1981.

Roby, Martha. house.gov, http://roby.house.gov/. (August 2012–January 2013).

Rogers, Harold. house.gov. http://halrogers.house.gov/. (August 2012–January 2013).

Rosenstone, Steven J., and John Mark Hansen. *Mobilization, Participation, and Democracy in America.* New York: Macmillan, 1993.

Ross, Dennis A. house.gov, http://dennisross.house.gov/. (August 2012–January 2013).

Rothman, Steven R. house.gov, http://rothman.house.gov/. (August 2012–January 2013).

Roybal-Allard, Lucille. house.gov, http://roybal-allard.house.gov/. (August 2012–January 2013).

Sablan, Gregorio Kilili Camacho (Delegate). house.gov, http://sablan.house.gov/. (August 2012–January 2013).

Schiller, Wendy J. "Senators as Political Entrepreneurs: Using Bill Sponsorship to Shape Legislative Agendas." *American Journal of Political Science* 39, no.1 (1995): 186–203.

Schlozman, Kay Lehman, Aaron Smith, Sidney Verba, and Henry Brady. "The Internet and Civic Engagement." Pew Internet and American Life Project. Pew Research Center. Washington, D.C. http://www.pewinternet.org/2009/09/01/the -internet-and-civic-engagement/, 2009.

Shuler, Heath. house.gov, http://shuler.house.gov/. (August 2012–January 2013).

Stennis Center for Public Service Leadership. "Congress to Campus." Stennis Center for Public Service Leadership. http://www.stennis.gov/programs/congress-to -campus (accessed January 2013).

Teixeira, Ruy. *The Disappearing American Voter.* Washington D.C.: Brookings Institution Press, 1992.

Tipton, Scott R. house.gov, http://tipton.house.gov/. (August 2012–January 2013).

Verba, Sidney, Kay Lehman Schlozman, and Henry E. Brady. *Voice and Equality: Civic Voluntarism in American Politics.* Cambridge: Harvard University Press, 1995.

Walz, Timothy J. house.gov, http://walz.house.gov/. (August 2012–January 2013).

Wattenberg, Martin P. *Where Have All the Voters Gone?* Cambridge: Harvard University Press, 2002.

Waxman, Henry A. house.gov, http://waxman.house.gov/. (August 2012–January 2013).

Webster, Daniel. house.gov, http://webster.house.gov/. (August 2012–January 2013).

Whitfield, Ed. house.gov, http://whitfield.house.gov/. (August 2012–January 2013).

Williams, Christine B., and Girish Jeff Gulati. "The Political Impact of Facebook: Evidence from the 2006 Midterm Elections and 2008 Nomination Contest." *Politics & Technology Review* (March 2008): 11–21.

Wilson, Joe. house.gov, http://joewilson.house.gov/. (August 2012–January 2013).

Womack, Steve. house.gov, http://womack.house.gov/. (August 2012–January 2013).

Yiannakis, Diana Evans. "House Members' Communication Styles: Newsletters and Press Releases." *Journal of Politics* 44: 4 (November 1982): 1049–71.

Young, C. W. Bill. house.gov, http://young.house.gov/.(August 2012–January 2013).

Chapter Six

Encouraging Civic Participation through Twitter during (and after) the 2012 Election

Heather K. Evans

As Friedman et al. detail in chapter 5, there has been a renewed push in academic literature toward encouraging civic engagement. Many researchers have published articles dealing with how to increase voter turnout and political participation, especially among young people.[1] Those that seek to increase civic engagement often point to making changes in our institutions to foster greater participation. Friedman et al. examine the individuals within the institution (i.e., members of the U.S. House of Representatives) to see whether they encourage their constituents to get involved in the political process. They find that legislators do talk about civic engagement on their websites; they spend a significant amount of time discussing how their constituents can get involved in their communities.

While the findings in chapter 5 suggest that members of Congress spend time focusing on civic engagement, what we do not know is how much of their total time is spent devoted discussing these activities, and whether certain members of Congress spend more time discussing these activities than others. For instance, members from competitive districts may spend a greater amount of time focusing on civic engagement, especially electoral engagement, since their seats are rarely safe. It is also very difficult to determine how much time each member of Congress devotes to civic engagement by examining their websites. For instance, while the members of Congress examined by Friedman et al. spent some time discussing community activities, we do not know how much of their entire website was devoted to these activities. Were members of Congress also discussing bills they were debating on the floor? Were they talking about important legislation they were sponsoring or their committee memberships? How does the message change depending on the electoral context? Do legislators spend more time discussing civic engagement during an election season than after the election is over?

In this chapter, I examine the messages members of the U.S. House sent to their followers (constituents and others) both during and after the 2012 election on Twitter. By using Twitter as the focus for the analysis, I am able to categorize tweets based on whether they discuss civic engagement and then compare the number of tweets that fit that category to a member's total number of tweets. This is a good measurement of how much time members spend encouraging their followers to engage in the political process. I can also check whether certain types of members spend more time talking about certain types of civic engagement. For instance, are those from competitive districts more likely to talk about voting and registration? Are there any partisan effects (i.e., are Democrats more likely to send certain types of tweets)? I collected data for two months leading up to the 2012 election, and then seven months later. This allows me to discuss whether the electoral context matters for legislators discussing civic engagement.

Recent research on Twitter suggests that individuals exposed to campaign messages are more likely to visit campaign donation pages than those that are not receiving such tweets.[2] This means that what members do on Twitter can affect the behavior of those that follow them. If members of Congress talk about civic engagement on Twitter, their followers should become more politically engaged. Here I explore whether members are actually sending messages that would encourage their constituents to become involved.

This chapter seeks to answer three questions about the types of tweets members of Congress send their followers on their official Twitter pages. Particularly, what this chapter seeks to uncover is (1) whether members of the House spend any time discussing civic engagement with their followers (2) how much of their Twitter time (if any) is spent doing this type of tweeting, and (3) whether particular individuals are more or less likely to encourage their followers to become civically engaged. What I find is that representatives do discuss civic engagement activities on Twitter both before and after their elections, but the amount of time spent tweeting about these activities is minimal compared to their total number of tweets. There is also a partisan bias to civic engagement tweets. Democrats send more tweets aimed at engaging their followers in the civic process.

HYPOTHESES

Given how new the study of social media outreach in politics is, there are few studies on which to draw any hypotheses. We might expect certain members of Congress to be more likely to tweet about civic engagement than others. For instance, competitiveness has been shown in other studies to greatly increase the amount of candidate advertisements to which one is exposed.[3] Along those lines, we might expect that representatives in competitive races would be more likely to tweet about civic engagement activities (especially getting out the vote and volunteering). Previous research has shown that this was the case in the 2010 Senate elections. Haber, for instance, in following the 2010 Senate candidates on Twitter during the last two months of the elections, finds that candidates in competitive contexts were significantly more likely to make what he termed "mobilization" tweets than those in noncompetitive contexts. Mobilization tweets were defined as those "which urge followers to take action in some way . . . voting, urging others to vote, volunteer, donate, or give their time and energy to the campaign in some way."[4] Two years later, Evans et al. also find that candidates for the U.S. House in 2012 in competitive races were significantly more likely to use mobilization tweets.[5] The context of the campaign can therefore affect the likelihood of a candidate focusing on mobilizing their followers.

We might also expect that there would be some personal characteristics of the representatives themselves that would influence how often they spend time addressing civic engagement with their followers on Twitter. Age, for instance, may play a significant role. Younger members of Congress may be more likely to engage with their followers in this manner. Haber also finds in the 2010 Senate race that younger candidates were more likely to post mobilization tweets.[6] This suggests that younger candidates are perhaps more energetic in asking their followers for donations, asking them to volunteer on their campaigns, and to get out and vote. Previous research has also shown that in general, women are more active in civic engagement activities than men.[7] The same has been found with calls on Twitter for political mobilization by political candidates. Evans et al. find that gender matters for mobilization. Female candidates in the 2012 House elections were significantly more likely to send mobilization tweets than male candidates.[8]

Party identification has also been shown to affect the way in which candidates for the U.S. House and Senate tweet. For instance, in 2009 and 2010, Republicans were significantly out-tweeting Democrats and were specifically more likely to send particular types of tweets.[9] In particular, Gainous and Wagner show that in the 2010 House election, Republicans sent significantly more campaign announcements on their Twitter pages than Democrats. Since Republicans did not control the U.S. House, Gainous and Wagner theorize that they used whatever means necessary to increase an electoral advantage through new social media, therefore they were more likely to use Twitter in this manner.[10] Others have made similar arguments. For instance, according to David Karpf's "outparty innovation incentives" theory, the "out-party" (the party currently in the minority) will do whatever necessary to gain a competitive edge against their competition in the upcoming election, particularly through social media.[11] Republicans, then, should have been more likely to pursue Twitter in 2010, and Gainous and Wagner show this to be the case.

Given all of these previous findings, I expect that during the 2012 election, those in competitive races, younger members of Congress, and women will be more likely to encourage their followers to become civically engaged on Twitter. I also expect that Democrats will be more focused on civic engagement on Twitter, since they were currently in the minority party in Congress. I will also examine whether any patterns found during the 2012 election continue during a nonelection time period (June and July 2013). I am specifically interested in whether the trends found in terms of general Twitter use by Evans et al. will hold when I examine specific civic engagement tweets.[12]

METHOD

This project examines whether representatives encourage their followers on Twitter to become active in their political communities, both during and after an election season. Are certain members (Democrats, women) more likely to encourage civic engagement among their followers? To answer these questions, I coded every tweet from the official Twitter pages for the winners of the 2012 House election, for the two months leading up to their election (September 6 to November 6) to determine what they were tweeting about. Specifically, I coded whether the winners of the elections used the key phrases and terms also coded by Freidman and Aubin in chapter 5 which were developed from the categories designated by CIRCLE. CIRCLE divides civic engagement into three types of activities: civic, electoral, and political voice. The three categories are listed below in table 6.1.

I began by examining multiple tweets for instances of legislators discussing civic engagement. After reviewing ten legislator's Twitter pages, the list of phrases and words that I used to code for the occurrence of encouraging civic engagement (which are the same as those used by Freidman and Aubin in chapter 5) were: civic engagement, democracy, voter registration, encourage, volunteer, join, contact, boycott, and buycott.

I also coded for the gender, party, and age of the representative, as well as whether the race was considered competitive two months before the end of the election. In the models that follow, female and Democrat are coded as dummy variables (1 for female, 0 for male; 1 for Democrat, 0 for Republican). Competitiveness is also a dummy variable and is coded from the Cook Political Report. Any race listed as a "toss-up" or "leaning Republican" or

Table 6.1. CIRCLE Indicators of Civic Engagement

Civic	Electoral	Political Voice
Community problem solving	Regular voting	Contacting officials
Regular volunteering for a nonelectoral organization	Persuading others Campaign contributions	Contacting the broadcast media
Active membership in a group or association	Displaying buttons, signs, stickers	Contacting the print media Protesting
Participation in fund-raising run/walk/ride	Volunteering for candidates or political organizations	E-mail petitions Written petitions
Other fund-raising for charity		Boycotting Buycotting Canvassing

"leaning Democratic" by the Cook Political Report on September 13, 2012, was coded as competitive.[13] Age is a continuous variable.

I also coded every tweet representatives made seven months after their elections, in June and July of 2013. This second dataset is used to determine whether any patterns found during the 2012 election continue when an election is not on the horizon. The data examined here is only for those that were tweeting from their official Twitter pages during both time periods (N = 298).

Findings—2012 Election

First, in terms of the sheer number of tweets, overall those that won their elections and were active on Twitter sent approximately 61.5 tweets on average over the two months before their election. Table 6.2 shows the overall results of a first sweep of the data focusing specifically on the key terms also used by Freidman et al. in chapter 5. I included all of the terms (9) in the beginning, but no members were using the terms boycott, buycott, or "civic engagement" during the 2012 elections on their official Twitter pages.

Table 6.2. Representatives Discussing Civic Engagement on Twitter, 2012

	Percent of Representatives	Mean (Standard Deviation)
Volunteer	9.03%	0.15 (0.67)
Encourage	9.36%	0.13 (0.47)
Voter registration	19.13%	0.48 (1.82)
Democracy	8.03%	0.10 (0.37)
Join	43.14%	1.02 (1.87)
Contact	14.72%	0.22 (0.65)

N = 298

Out of the six key phrases that were used by members of Congress, "join" was used by the most members (43.14%), followed by "voter registration" (19.13%) and "contact" (14.72%). On average, those who did discuss these civic activities tweeted more about "joining" than the other activities (tweeting a little over one time on average during the two months). When I verified that these phrases were each used to discuss "civic activities," I found that all but one was truly encouraging those on Twitter to get involved with their communities—that is, democracy. This phrase was used by legislators to not just suggest that their followers get engaged with their democracy, but was also used to discuss the importance of our government and civic traditions. "Join" was also used in two ways: asking followers to "join them" in some type of activity, or as a reference to something that the legislator had done (i.e. "Pleased to join community leaders. . . .").

E,ven though 43.14% of members encouraged their followers to "join" groups and pages, or discussed their own engagement with others, most members spent very little of their total time tweeting about these civic activities. When combining all of the above variations of civic engagement, I find that on average, members of Congress sent 2.12 tweets over the two months before the election about these activities. Given that on average members were sending 61.5 tweets, this means that only about 3.4% of their overall time on Twitter was devoted to promoting civic engagement. Many winners that were tweeting during the 2012 House elections never tweeted about any of these forms of civic engagement (40.9%), and the most any winner tweeted about any of these phrases was thrity-one times (Representative John Garamendi, Democrat, California 3rd District).[14] He spent the most time trying to get his followers on Twitter to register to vote (twenty-three times), which is indicative of the campaign season.

Volunteer

The word "volunteer" was used by a little over 9% of the winners of the 2012 House elections. Out of those that used the phrase "volunteer," most only mentioned it once (66%). Representative Frank Pallone Jr (Democrat, New Jersey 6th District) used the phrase the most in his tweets (eight times).

During the last two months of the 2012 election, all of the tweets sent by members of Congress using the term volunteer were asking their followers on Twitter to give some of their time to help their communities, or were referencing meeting others who volunteer. Kevin Yoder (Republican, Kansas, 3rd District), for instance, sent a tweet asking for individuals to volunteer their time to help kids read on September 13: "Sept is National Literacy Month. Read a book or volunteer at a school or early childhood learning center.

Encourage those learning to read."[15] Many from New York and New Jersey were focused on encouraging individuals to volunteer to help those affected by Hurricane Sandy. For instance, Gregory Meeks (Democrat, New York's 5th District) tweeted on October 30, "If you would like to volunteer for Food Bank for NYC click: http://t.co/O5PuJ72S your help is needed during this trying time #Sandy."[16] Many representatives also sent tweets thanking volunteers for their time and efforts. For instance, Gerry Connolly (Democrat, Virginia's 11th District) tweeted on September 29, "Huge crowd at the Fairfax Kids Fest and beautiful weather. Great to see old friends who volunteer to make this event possible."[17]

To determine whether there are patterns to the usage of the term "volunteer" (as well as the other civic engagement terms), I calculated a Negative Binomial Regression Model while controlling for gender, age, partisanship, and the competitiveness of the race. My findings are given below in table 6.3. The results show that there was a very significant partisan bias in the likelihood of representatives encouraging their followers to volunteer. Democrats were significantly more likely to mention the word "volunteer" in their tweets. Democrats sent approximately two times as many tweets than Republicans about volunteering.[18]

Table 6.3. Negative Binomial Regression Models, Fall 2012

	Volunteer	Encourage	Voter Registration	Democracy	Join	Contact
Female	−0.89	0.46	0.65	−1.41	0.27	0.02
	(0.71)	(0.50)	(0.34)	(0.78)	(0.25)	(0.42)
Age	−0.01	0.01	0.02	−0.00	−0.01	0.00
	(0.02)	(0.02)	(0.02)	(0.02)	(0.01)	(0.02)
Democrat	1.10*	0.70	3.05**	1.39**	0.86**	0.80*
	(0.50)	(0.44)	(0.48)	(0.46)	(0.22)	(0.36)
Competitive	0.65	−1.23	−2.21	−0.19	−0.29	−1.71
	(0.78)	(1.13)	(1.15)	(0.82)	(0.36)	(1.08)
Constant	−1.99	−2.86**	−4.20**	−2.73*	−0.00	−1.91
	(1.44)	(0.13)	(1.09)	(1.23)	(0.58)	(1.04)
Pseudo R^2	0.03	0.03	0.16	0.06	0.03	0.03

N = 298; Standard errors given in parentheses
*$p \leq .05$, ** $p \leq .01$

Encourage

The word "encourage" was used by 9.36% of winners in the 2012 election. The most the term was ever used was only three times, by Representatives Frank LoBiondo (Republican, New Jersey, 2nd District), Charles Rangel (Democrat, New York, 13th District), and Marcia Fudge (Democrat, Ohio's

11th District). The tweets regarding the word "encourage" were about encouraging others to register and to vote in the upcoming election, or encouraging followers to learn more about an important political issue. For instance, on September 10, Charles Rangel (Democrat, New York, 13th District) tweeted "Less than half of young people say that they will definitely vote in November. Before Election Day, encourage 5+ young people to be #VoteReady."[19] As my results in Table 6.3 demonstrate, none of the independent variables was associated with greater use of this word.

Voter Registration

The phrase "voter registration" was the second most commonly occurring term during the two months leading up to the 2012 election. Over 19% of the winners of the House elections used this phrase at least once. The most the term was used was twenty-three times by Representative John Garamendi (Democrat, California's 3rd District). Most of the tweets about voter registration came on September 25, National Voter Registration Day. Some of these tweets were also to let followers know when the deadlines were for voter registration in their states. For instance, on October 9, Representative David Scott (Democrat, Georgia's 13th District) tweeted "Georgia voter registration deadline today http://t.co/LL1HXjlX via @sharethis" to let his followers know that it was the final day to register in the state.[20]

According to the negative binomial regression results reported in table 6.3, there again is a strong partisan effect to the use of this term. Democrats sent 21.10 times more tweets about voter registration than Republicans.[21]

Democracy

The word "democracy" was used by a little over 8% of winners that tweeted during the 2012 House elections. Most of the winners that mentioned democracy only did so once, but three people used the word more than once (Representative Xavier Becerra, Democrat, California, 34th District; Representative John Garamendi, Democrat, California, 3rd District; and Representative Chaka Fattah, Democrat, Pennsylvania, 2nd District). In the two months leading up to the election, one-third of the tweets about democracy were in reference to voting or registration. For instance, on September 10, Representative Gwen Moore (Democrat, Wisconsin's 4th District) tweeted, "In a democracy, decisions are made by a majority of those who make themselves heard and vote. Speak up & be #VoteReady on November 6."[22] Others used the word to talk about our country and those that have made a difference fighting for our freedoms. Representative Scott Rigell (Republican, Virginia's 2nd District) tweeted, "The American flag, no matter where she flies in this world, will continue to be a symbol of democracy, liberty, and the promise of freedom" on September 12.[23]

The results in table 6.3 indicate that Democrats are again significantly out-tweeting Republicans in the use of this term. Democrats use the term "democracy" 3.99 times as often as Republicans.[24]

Join

When it comes to all the ways representatives encouraged their followers on Twitter to become civically engaged, asking them to "join" particular groups and pages was the most frequently occurring word during the last two months of the election. Over 43% of those that were tweeting included this word in at least one of the tweets during the last two months. Representative Mike Quigley (Democrat, Illinois, 5th District) used this term the most at fifteen times over the two months.

Most of the tweets (62%) involving the word "join" were in reference to joining the representative as they met with constituents or were active in the community in other ways. Many of the tweets involved the phrase "join me." For instance, on October 17, Representative Karen Bass (Democrat, California's 37th District) tweeted the following: "Sunday, join me on a community forum/workshop to assist DREAM Act eligible youth. For details visit http://t.co/VAedbDzk."[25] She was asking her followers to come to a community workshop about the DREAM act.

The results in table 6.3 indicate that Democrats were out-tweeting Republicans in the use of this term. Democrats sent 2.35 times as many tweets involving the word "join" than Republicans.

Contact

Almost 15% of the winners of the 2012 House election tweeted a call for their followers to "contact" someone. Most of these tweets asked their followers to contact them or a congressional office. For instance, on October 9, Representative Vicky Hartzler (Republican, Missouri's 4th District) tweeted "There are 39 Jobs Bill awaiting Senate action. Contact your Senator! #4jobs #GOP http://t.co/p79ZvDaK."[26] The most the term was ever used was five times, by Representative Pete Visclosky (Democrat, Indiana's 1st District).

The negative binomial regression results reveal that Democrats again were significantly more likely to use the term "contact" than Republicans (see table 6.3). Incidence rate ratio results demonstrate that Democrats sent 2.22 times as many tweets with the word "contact" than Republicans.

Findings—2013

In the summer of 2013, these representatives were sending on average approximately 124.98 tweets. Out of the civic engagement words and phrases, the word "join" was used the most (see table 6.4). Almost 71% of the N = 298 representatives that were tweeting during the summer used the term "join" in their tweets, and they used it on average 2.14 times. This is almost a 30% increase in the percentage of representatives using this term from the two months leading up to the election, and the usage of the term doubled.

Table 6.4. Representatives Discussing Civic Engagement on Twitter, 2013

	Percent of Representatives	*Mean (Standard Deviation)*
Volunteer	6.38%	0.08 (0.32)
Encourage	13.42%	0.17 (0.50)
Voter registration	1.01%	0.01 (0.14)
Civic engagement	1.68%	0.02 (0.21)
Democracy	11.74%	0.17 (0.56)
Join	70.81%	2.14 (2.62)
Contact	11.41%	0.15 (0.54)

Even though almost 71% of House representatives tweeted the word "join" during the summer of 2013, representatives spent only a little Twitter time talking about these activities. On average, representatives sent only 2.75 tweets about these activities, and since they sent on average 124.98 tweets, this means that only 2.2% of their total Twitter time was dedicated to talking about civic engagement.

Comparing table 6.1 to table 6.4 shows just how important the electoral context is for representatives' Twitter-style. During the election, almost 20% discussed "voter registration" on Twitter, but during the two summer months, only 1% even mentioned it.

To see whether gender, age, partisanship, and competitiveness had any effect on the use of these terms, I calculated negative binomial regression models for each term, and the results for all are given in table 6.5.

The results in table 6.5 show that almost all of the independent variables have an effect on the use of at least one of the engagement terms/phrases. Gender has a significant effect on the use of the word "join." Women were significantly more likely to talk about joining groups and organizations than men in the summer of 2013. Women sent 1.55 times more tweets about joining them in a civic activity than men holding all other variables at their means. Age is significant in only one model. Younger members of Congress sent 5% more tweets about contacting someone than older members of Congress.

Table 6.5. Negative Binomial Regression Models for Summer 2013

	Volunteer	Encourage	Voter Registration	Civic Engagement	Democracy	Join	Contact
Female	-1.02	-0.30	-16.39	-16.42	0.23	0.46**	0.45
	(0.81)	(0.48)	(4049.30)	(2620.98)	(0.45)	(0.18)	(0.57)
Age	-0.00	0.01	-0.12	-0.05	-0.01	-0.01	-0.05**
	(0.02)	(0.02)	(0.08)	(0.05)	(0.02)	(0.01)	(0.02)
Democrat	1.22*	0.10	0.80	2.33*	1.38**	0.28	0.24
	(0.53)	(0.36)	(1.39)	(1.21)	(0.41)	(0.19)	(0.43)
Competitive	0.83	0.18	-16.39	-15.81	-0.69	0.01	-0.39
	(0.69)	(0.56)	(5755.49)	(3212.78)	(0.84)	(0.24)	(0.72)
Constant	-2.95*	-2.34*	1.97	-2.35	-2.03*	1.11**	-0.75
	(1.43)	(0.95)	(4.29)	(2.83)	(1.02)	(0.39)	(0.99)
Pseudo R^2	0.05	0.00	0.12	0.13	0.05	0.01	0.03

Standard errors reported in parentheses.
+p≤.10, *p≤.05, **p≤.01

In this second round of analysis, partisanship continued to be a significant predictor of the use of three of these words/phrases. Democrats were
significantly more likely to talk about volunteering, civic engagement, and
democracy. Democrats sent 10 times as many tweets about civic engagement,
4 times as many tweets about democracy, and 3.5 times as many tweets about
volunteering than Republicans.

DISCUSSION

When it comes to the overall use of the civic engagement words and phrases
during the 2012 election, as expected, Democrats were significantly more
likely to use them than Republicans. The only word that did not produce
significant findings was "encourage." Over 9 percent of representatives used
the word "encourage," and there was not a partisan flavor to the use of the
term. All of the other terms, however, were more likely to be used by Democrats. The largest negative binomial regression difference for the use of the
terms and phrases was "voter registration," where Democrats sent on average
twenty-one times as many tweets regarding registration than Republicans,
holding all other variables at their means.

These partisan findings should not surprise us. Since in 2012 Republicans
held a majority in the U.S. House, we should expect Democrats to make more
of an effort reaching out to their constituents, especially encouraging them to
register for the upcoming election. During the summer of 2013, Democrats
continued to "out-tweet" Republicans for three of these engagement terms/
phrases (volunteer, civic engagement, democracy).

In terms of the other independent variables during the 2012 election, none
were significant predictors of tweet counts. While Evans et al. find that
women were more likely to encourage their followers to get registered for the
upcoming election, in the models reported here, partisanship is the strongest
predictor of tweets about civic engagement.[27] In the summer of 2013, younger
members were more likely to use tweets with the word "contact," while
women were more likely to talk about joining a group or cause.

Overall, the results from both Twitter data collections show that while a
significant number of representatives were tweeting about these civic engagement terms and phrases, they were spending very little of their time on
Twitter encouraging engagement by their followers relative to the number of
tweets they sent. Since other research regarding Twitter has shown that the
average Twitter user is significantly more likely to visit a campaign donation
page than a user that is not on Twitter, especially when they are exposed to
political tweets, it would be useful for politicians to be aware that they pos-

sibly can affect the political engagement of their followers.[28] If representatives spent more time on Twitter talking about volunteering, joining political causes, and contacting their representatives, followers may be more likely to do those activities. Future research should examine this possibility.

NOTES

1. Benjamin Highton, "Voter Registration and Turnout in the United States," *Perspectives on Politics* 2, no. 3 (2004); Alan S. Gerber and Donald P. Green, "Do Phone Calls Increase Voter Turnout? A Field Experiment," *Public Opinion Quarterly* 65, no. 1 (2001); Elizabeth M. Addonizio et al., "Putting the Party Back into Politics: An Experiment Testing Whether Election Day Festivals Increase Voter Turnout," *PS: Political Science and Politics* 40, no. 4 (2007); Tom P. Bakker and Claes H. de Vreese, "Good News for the Future? Young People, Internet Use, and Political Participation," *Communication Research* 38, no. 4 (2011).

2. Peter Greenberger, "How Tweets Influence Political Donations: New Twitter Study with Compete," *The Twitter Advertising Blog*, 2012, https://blog.twitter.com/2012/how-tweets-influence-political-donations-new-twitter-study-with-compete (accessed December 9, 2013).

3. Samuel C. Patterson and Gregory A. Caldeira, "Getting Out the Vote: Participation in Gubernatorial Elections," *American Political Science Review* 77 (1983); James G. Gimpel et al., "Registrants, Voters, and Turnout Variability across Neighborhoods," *Political Behavior* 26, no. 4 (2004); Kim Fridkin Kahn and Patrick J. Kenney, *The Spectacle of U.S. Senate Campaigns* (NJ: Princeton University Press, 1999).

4. Steven Haber, "The 2010 U.S. Senate Elections in 140 Characters or Less: An Analysis of How Candidates Use Twitter as a Campaign Tool," http://aladinrc.wrlc.org/bitstream/handle/1961/10028/Haber,%20Steven%20-%20Spring%20'11.pdf?sequence=1 (accessed July 15, 2014), 15.

5. Evans et al., "Twitter-Style."

6. Haber, "The 2010 U.S. Senate Elections."

7. Kei Kawashima-Ginsberg and Nancy Thomas, "Civic Engagement and Political Leadership among Women—A Call for Solutions," The Center for Information & Research on Civic Learning and Engagement, http://www.civicyouth.org/wp-content/uploads/2013/05/Gender-and-Political-Leadership-Fact-Sheet-3.pdf (accessed July 15, 2014).

8. Evans et al., "Twitter-Style."

9. Jason Gainous and Kevin M. Wagner, *Tweeting to Power: The Social Media Revolution in American Politics* (New York, NY: Oxford University Press, 2014); Matthew Eric Glassman et al., "Social Networking and Constituent Communications: Members Use of Twitter during a Two-Month Period in the 111th Congress," *CRS Report for Congress*, http://www.fas.org/sgp/crs/misc/R41066.pdf (2010); Haber, "The 2010 U.S. Senate Elections."; David S. Lassen and Adam R. Brown. "Twitter: The Electoral Connection?" *Social Science Computer Review* 29, no. 4 (2011): 419–436.

10. Gainous and Wagner, *Tweeting to Power*.

11. David Karpf, *The MoveOn Effect: The Unexpected Transformation of American Political Advocacy* (New York, NY: Oxford University Press, 2014).

12. Evans et al.,"Twitter-Style."

13. This is an improvement over other studies examining competitiveness. Earlier work has used margin of victory as a proxy. This measure was taken at the beginning of the coding cycle since decisions are made early on during a campaign as to whether more or less money will be used. By using this measure, we are able to see if a candidate will tweet differently if the media views their race as competitive two months before the end of their campaigns. Available at http://cookpolitical.com/house/charts/race-ratings/4753.

14. John Garamendi sent 43 tweets that included these key words and phrases, out of a total of 475 tweets during this time period. This means that he devoted approximately 9 percent of his total time on Twitter to encouraging civic engagement, almost three times the average civic-tweet rate of legislators. Most of these instances were regarding voter registration.

15. Kevin Yoder, Twitter post, September 13, 2012, 12:54 p.m., http://twitter.com/RepKevinYoder.

16. Gregory Meeks, Twitter post, October 30, 2012, 7:06 p.m., http://twitter.com/GregoryMeeks.

17. Gerald Connolly, Twitter post, September 29, 2012, 4:49 p.m., http://twitter.com/GerryConnolly.

18. Holding all other variables at their means. Incidence Rate Ratio = 3.01

19. Charles Rangel, Twitter post, September 10, 2012, 10:16 a.m., http://twitter.com/cbrangel.

20. David Scott, Twitter post, October 9, 2012, 8:13 a.m., http://twitter.com/repdavidscott.

21. IRR coefficient = 21.10.

22. Gwen Moore, Twitter post, September 19, 2012, 1:38 p.m., http://twitter.com/RepGwenMoore.

23. Scott Rigell, Twitter post, September 12, 2012, 12:27 p.m., http://twitter.com/repscottrigell.

24. IRR Coefficient = 3.99.

25. Karen Bass, Twitter post, October 17, 2012, 3:49 p.m., http://twitter.com/RepKarenBass.

26. Vicky Hartzler, Twitter post, October 9, 2012, 3:17 p.m., http://twitter.com/RepHartzler.

27. Evans et al., "Twitter-Style."

28. Greenberger, "How Tweets Influence Political Donations."

BIBLIOGRAPHY

Addonizio, Elizabeth M., Donald P. Green, and James M. Glaser. "Putting the Party Back into Politics: An Experiment Testing Whether Election Day Festivals Increase Voter Turnout." *PS: Political Science and Politics* 40, no. 4 (2007): 721–727.

Bakker, Tom P., and Claes H. de Vreese. "Good News for the Future? Young People, Internet Use, and Political Participation." *Communication Research* 38, no. 4 (2011): 451–470.

Evans, Heather K., Victoria Cordova, and Savannah Sipole. "Twitter-Style: An Analysis of How House Candidates Used Twitter in Their 2012 Campaigns." *PS: Political Science and Politics* 47, no. 2 (2014): 454–461.

Gainous, Jason, and Kevin M. Wagner. *Tweeting to Power: The Social Media Revolution in American Politics.* New York, NY: Oxford University Press, 2014.

Gerber, Alan S., and Donald P. Green. "Do Phone Calls Increase Voter Turnout? A Field Experiment." *Public Opinion Quarterly* 65, no. 1 (2001): 75–85.

Gimpel, James G., Joshua J. Dyck, and Daron R. Shaw. "Registrants, Voters, and Turnout Variability across Neighborhoods." *Political Behavior* 26, no. 4 (2004): 343–368.

Glassman, Matthew Eric, Jacob R. Straus, and Colleen J. Shogan "Social Networking and Constituent Communications: Members Use of Twitter During a Two-Month Period in the 111th Congress." *CRS Report for Congress.* (2010) Available here: http://www.fas.org/sgp/crs/misc/R41066.pdf.

Greenberger, Peter. "How Tweets Influence Political Donations: New Twitter Study with Compete." *The Twitter Advertising Blog* (2012). https://blog.twitter.com/2012/how-tweets-influence-political-donations-new-twitter-study-with-compete.

Haber, Steven. "The 2010 U.S. Senate Elections in 140 Characters or Less: An Analysis of How Candidates Use Twitter as a Campaign Tool." (2011). http://aladinrc.wrlc.org/bitstream/handle/1961/10028/Haber,%20Steven%20-%20Spring%20'11.pdf?sequence=1.

Highton, Benjamin. "Voter Registration and Turnout in the United States." *Perspectives on Politics* 2, no. 3 (2004): 507–515.

Kahn, Kim Fridkin, and Patrick J. Kenney. *The Spectacle of U.S. Senate Campaigns* NJ: Princeton University Press, 1999.

Karpf, David. *The MoveOn Effect: The Unexpected Transformation of American Political Advocacy.* New York, NY: Oxford University Press, 2014.

Kawashima-Ginsberg, Kei, and Nancy Thomas. "Civic Engagement and Political Leadership among Women—A Call for Solutions." The Center for Information & Research on Civic Learning and Engagement (2013). http://www.civicyouth.org/wp-content/uploads/2013/05/Gender-and-Political-Leadership-Fact-Sheet-3.pdf.

Lassen, David S., and Adam R. Brown. "Twitter: The Electoral Connection?" *Social Science Computer Review* 29, no. 4 (2011): 419–436.

Patterson, Samuel C., and Gregory A. Caldeira. "Getting Out the Vote: Participation in Gubernatorial Elections." *American Political Science Review* 77 (1983): 675–689.

Chapter Seven

Engagement through the Oval Office

Presidential Rhetoric as Civic Education

Sara A. Mehltretter Drury and
Jeffrey P. Mehltretter Drury

In 1961, President John F. Kennedy boldly declared: "Ask not what your country can do for you, but what you can do for your country."[1] In 1989, President George H. W. Bush spoke of "a Thousand Points of Light, of all the community organizations that are spread like stars throughout the Nation, doing good. We will work hand in hand, encouraging, sometimes leading, sometimes being led, rewarding."[2] Six years later, President Bill Clinton called for government "to give citizens more say" because the nation is "literally a community, an American family that is going up or down together, whether we like it or not."[3] And, in his 2001 Inaugural Address, George W. Bush offered a plea to his audience: "I ask you to be citizens: Citizens, not spectators; citizens, not subjects, responsible citizens building communities of service and a nation of character."[4] These quotations illustrate the proclivity of contemporary presidents to rhetorically emphasize the potential for engaged citizens to be agents of change.

Despite these pleas, presidents do not always offer the resources to facilitate such civic education and civic engagement. On the whole, U.S. institutions increasingly "disaggregate and depoliticize the demands of citizens," Matthew A. Crenson and Benjamin Ginsberg have argued, by situating citizens as "customers" and emphasizing "private rights at the expense of collective action."[5] The president, in particular, is the leader of the nation and often seen as the foremost national voice on matters of policy, foreign and domestic. This leadership role minimizes the president's status as fellow citizen—despite the tradition of the president acknowledging his "fellow citizens" in the opening sentence of nearly every major public address. This is even true on issues about which the public possesses a great deal of experience and knowledge. The president leads by educating citizens on what they should know—and often what actions they should take. As Marc Landy and Sidney M. Milkis have argued, it is ultimately a sign of the president's democratic leadership to take "the public to school."[6]

This chapter takes a different approach, offering a framework for examining presidential leadership from the perspective of civic education and considering to what extent the presidency, as an institution, is equipped to empower citizens by rhetorically enacting such civic education. We argue that the president possesses enormous potential to lead citizens toward greater engagement but, at the same time, he is constrained through the rhetorical norms of the office. To demonstrate how a president's rhetoric represents both opportunities and constraints for civic engagement, we first review the potentials and limits of the presidency and presidential rhetoric. We then use presidential engagement with mental health—and the recent emphasis on civic education in particular—as a case study that reveals these opportunities and challenges.

To develop this case, we examine how past presidents have used their rhetoric primarily to educate, but not engage, the public about mental health issues. We then analyze the Obama administration's rhetoric on mental health, considering his statements after the shooting in Newtown, Connecticut, and his administration's later response with the MentalHealth.gov initiative as models of presidential civic education. Our analysis takes a broad view of presidential rhetoric in the twenty-first century, analyzing the addresses of the president and the public discourse of a president's administration, including statements from significant officials—such as the Vice President or Secretary of Health—and discourse from government websites based in the Executive Branch. This case reveals more than the agenda-setting function of presidential rhetoric insofar as the Obama administration established the broad parameters for the very discussion of mental health and limited partisan outcomes within the framework of information-sharing and public engagement. At the same time, this case also reveals the challenges presidents face in promoting engaged, civic education.

THE PRESIDENT AS (CIVIC) EDUCATOR

Scholars of political communication and U.S. public address have produced a rich literature on the power and struggles of presidential rhetoric. Political scientist Jeffrey Tulis's 1987 book, *The Rhetorical Presidency,* suggested the modern presidency centered on the power of presidents to rally public opinion behind their policy agendas. "Since the presidencies of Theodore Roosevelt and Woodrow Wilson," Tulis argued, "popular or mass rhetoric has become a principal tool of presidential governance."[7] According to Tulis, the rhetorical presidency represented a "new way" of the presidency, a change so radical that it created, in effect, a "second constitution."[8] No longer did the president deliberate with Congress, as envisioned by the Founders, but rather went over the heads of legislators with direct appeals to the people. Indeed, Tulis contended that presidents have come to feel that they "have a *duty* to constantly defend themselves publicly, to promote policy initiatives nation-wide, and to inspirit the population."[9] As a result, the presidency has become an office of symbolic leadership in which "personal or charismatic power" is more important than "the president's constitutional or legal authority."[10]

Other political scientists have argued that, while presidents may feel they have a duty to address the public, presidential rhetoric has few dis-cernable effects on public opinion. George C. Edwards III, for example, has questioned the "potential of persuasive leadership" in the presidency,[11] arguing that a president's rhetoric has little ability to "reshape the political landscape" and "pave the way for change."[12] While he agreed with Tulis that "leading the public is at the core of the modern presidency," Edwards's statistical analysis found the "bully pulpit" to be "ineffective" at changing public opinion.[13] For Edwards, "presidential power is *not* the power to per-suade," but rather, the ability to "facilitate change by recognizing opportu-nities in their environments and fashioning strategies and tactics to exploit them."[14] In other words, Edwards has contended that presidential commu-nication is rarely effective at changing poll results, although presidents can seize opportunities to build their policy initiatives upon the foundation of already existing beliefs and values.

Others have argued that the effects of presidential rhetoric can be better understood within the broader perspective of the president as *rhetor*—someone who educates, persuades, and leads. According to Martin J. Med-hurst, the study of presidential rhetoric entails "how those principles func-tion to allow the speaker or writer—who happens to be a U.S. president—to achieve his or her ends by symbolic means."[15] A rhetorical approach em-phasizes how presidents help set the political agenda for the nation, define the terms of major public debates, and generally influence the character of public discourse about important public issues. David Zarefsky and Erwin C. Hargrove both argue that the president has the power to define reality, thus influencing the way the public views political issues and debates.[16] Ac-cording to Zarefsky, the rhetoric of the president defines "political reality" by shaping how the media and other political actors respond to an issue. "Because of his prominent political position and his access to the means of communication," Zarefsky argued, the president, in "defining a situation," also "might be able to shape the context in which events or proposals are viewed by the public," defining the range of options available "from among multiple possibilities."[17] Similarly, Roderick P. Hart has identified twelve possible effects from presidential speeches and pronouncements that affirm the rhetorical power of the presidency and suggest that presidential discourse does not "fall on deaf ears," but instead has effects that are "broader and deeper than can be captured by paper and pencil measures."[18] Many of these effects point beyond persuasion of policy, demonstrating what Leroy Dorsey has called the president's "rhetorical leadership"—the "process of discovering, articulating, and sharing the available means of influence in order to motivate human agents in a particular situation."[19]

Presidential leadership includes the power not only to define reality and to persuade, but also to educate the public on *which* issues are most important, *why* the issues matter, *who* should address them, and *how* they should do so. This educational power involves more than the agenda-setting function of mediated messages: presidents, as powerful rhetorical leaders, help inform the public, educating citizens to understand their roles, obligations, and opportunities in national politics. As Landy and Milkis have explained, "Presidential words and deeds shape the quality and character of the citizenry . . . a president bears a large share of responsibility for the public's civic education."[20] Backed by the power of the executive, the president is not just a teacher—he is *the* teacher. Thus, while the president serves as commander in chief, and while Sidney Blumenthal has previously identified the president as "communicator in chief,"[21] we submit an additional role—educator in chief.

In attending to the president's status as educator in chief, our purpose is neither to suggest yet another evolution of the presidency nor to claim that this educational role is a fixed institutional feature but rather to emphasize the choices individual presidents face when they rhetorically engage their fellow Americans. Above, we suggested a general choice between advocacy (a persuasive function of rhetoric) and education (an informative function of rhetoric) that presidents face in their efforts to lead the public. Our analysis relies on a further choice within education: the degree to which a president emphasizes the power of citizens to generate political and social change. We agree with Landy and Milkis that presidents "can make the public more passive and self-regarding and submissive, or they can encourage it to be more energetic and public spirited."[22] Presidential invitations to citizen action do not always fall neatly between the two poles of activity or passivity but rather on a continuum between presidential rhetoric as education and as civic education.

Education, as one end of the continuum, represents an informative effort to impart knowledge necessary for governing the nation. Most primetime presidential addresses fall, to varying degrees, on this side of the continuum. In these speeches, presidents inform the audience of policies that they are advocating or decisions that have already been made. These speeches, ranging from State of the Union addresses to war messages, frequently position citizens as spectators and frame presidents and government leaders as the relevant agents of change while offering limited opportunities for citizen involvement. In situations when the public has no legitimate authority or interest, this approach promotes transparency in government while sustaining the president's leadership authority.

Civic education, as the other end of the continuum, involves imparting knowledge and skills about civic behavior and democratic engagement. In its most radical form, presidential civic education would cede complete control to citizens by providing them the tools and resources for change. More moderate forms of civic education focus not on the details related to a single topic or issue in society (which constitutes education) but also or instead on how individuals, as citizens, can tackle these challenging topics and determine particular solutions for their localized political communities.[23] When done properly, civic education can, as Martin Carcasson and Leah Sprain have argued, prepare "citizens with the prerequisite knowledge, skills, and attitudes for the responsibilities of democracy."[24] Civic education bolsters the agency of audience members because it emphasizes, as Harry C. Boyte has explained, that citizens are necessary for governance. This places government officials outside "the center of the civic universe" and stresses that government is not "the only location for democracy's work." Instead, citizens view themselves as "problem solvers and cocreators of public goods," namely localized solutions to pressing political and social problems.[25] Thus, a president moves closer to *civic* education the more he promotes the role of citizens as agents of social change.

Although the president, as educator in chief, may opt for an approach anywhere along the continuum, we contend that most messages fall somewhere in the middle range rather than on either extreme. This is partially because the shift from education to civic education is not easy. One central obstacle for the president is that many public controversies lack straightforward solutions and, consequently, demand substantial time and resources. Scholars have termed these challenges "wicked problems" because there are no permanent solutions, these problems involve multiple stakeholders and therefore multiple stakeholders must be engaged in approaches or strategies, and any approach or strategy will need to be continually reassessed. Horst W. J. Rittel and Melvin M. Webber argued that "nearly all public policy issues—whether the question concerns the location of a freeway, the adjustment of a tax rate, the modification of school curricula, or the confrontation of crime" are wicked problems. Wicked problems are not "ethically deplorable," but rather "malignant," "vicious," "tricky," or "aggressive."[26] In other words, wicked problems are those not easily solved by a single technical or governmental solution, but rather involve a complex network of partners and responses.

Solving these wicked problems might demand that the president more explicitly define the role of citizens in line with deliberative, democratic governance—that is, that presidents treat "citizens as active and engaged problem-solvers working with others to solve community problems" instead of citizens as "taxpayers, consumers, constituents, or voters."[27] While this sort of governance is rarely seen at the national level, a president might model the success of local communities in creating the social capital for collaborative problem solving documented in Robert Putnam and Lewis M. Feldstein's *Better Together: Restoring the American Community.* Putnam, famous for his work on Americans "bowling alone," has also documented the success stories of a variety of local governments and businesses that collaboratively worked to improve challenging social problems such as poor public infrastructure, education disparity, and systemic poverty. Putnam and Feldstein contend, "Society as a whole benefits enormously from the social ties forged by those who choose connective strategies in pursuit of their political goals."[28]

In the case of mental health, we argue that the rhetorical appeals presidents have made are instructive in chronicling the recent efforts of executive leaders to implement a more collaborative approach to complex public controversies. In this context, presidents who inform citizens about the nature and character of mental illness are engaging in *education.* A president engaging in *civic education*, on the other hand, informs citizens about how to individually and collectively promote mental health in their communities and then empowers community members to pursue best practices and solutions for their localities. The change in language from educating about mental illness to promoting mental health is in itself significant, as it suggests a movement from diagnosing the other to collaboration in the community that promotes positive improvements in the quality of life. We will illustrate that President Obama's 2013 mental health initiative represents the most robust integration to date of civic education into the role of educator in chief. To demonstrate this shift as an innovative role for the president, the next section contextualizes how past presidents have prioritized education about mental health.

MODERN U.S. PRESIDENTS AS EDUCATORS ON MENTAL HEALTH

U.S. presidents have long used public rhetoric to tackle the challenge of mental health, from addressing the construction of a government-run mental health institution in 1844 to addressing the reconstruction of a government-

run mental health website in 2013. Given that mental healthcare has been—
and largely remains—the domain of individual states, our history in this section begins with the first half of the twentieth century, when presidents began
taking an active role in mental health. We will demonstrate how presidents
throughout the last century have tended to situate the audience as individuals
who consume information about mental health rather than citizens who collectively address the issue.

Presidents prior to Kennedy dabbled in the discussion of mental health
but did not make it a strong priority for their administrations. For instance,
Presidents Herbert Hoover, Harry S. Truman, and Dwight D. Eisenhower
publicly advocated funding for research into the causes and treatments of
mental illness, usually within their appeals for broader health-related policies.[29] Truman signed into law the National Mental Health Act in 1946 that
established the National Institute on Mental Health (NIMH), for example,
and Eisenhower's "Special Message to the Congress Recommending a
Health Program" in 1955 advocated "new and intensified measures in our
attack on mental health" including funding for early detection and allevia-
tion of mental illness, for personnel to care for those with mental illness,
and for project grants to improve the quality of care for patients.[30] Eisenhower's arguments are representative of other presidents of this era insofar
as his response to the problem situated it with those who could best address
the problem of mental illness, as he relied on the technical sphere of experts
(doctors, scientists, and caregivers). These speeches are also significant for
whom they rhetorically *excluded* as agents of change, namely individuals
in their capacity as citizens.

President John F. Kennedy was the first president to present to Congress
and the citizens at large the challenge of mental illness.[31] In February 1963,
he sent a fourteen-page report to Congress detailing "a bold new approach"
to mental illness and mental retardation in which "governments at every
level—Federal, State, and local—private foundations and individual citizens"
all "face up to their responsibilities in this area."[32] Kennedy's report framed
mental health as a *public* issue affecting citizen taxpayers in addition to identifying its personal toll on families and those who suffer from mental illness.
Beyond invoking citizens in his report, Kennedy addressed them directly
through a three-and-a-half-minute recorded speech on February 5. Kennedy
informed the audience about the frequency and problems of mental health
in the United States and explained why existing state institutions were inadequate—both physically and psychologically—for patients. He concluded by
calling for a "great national effort in this field so vital to the welfare of our
citizens."[33] Unlike his predecessors, Kennedy's rhetoric expanded the sphere
of action beyond the government and medical experts to include the public.

Yet despite Kennedy's oratorical gestures to citizen involvement, the content of his proposals afforded them a limited role. Kennedy placed the federal government in the driver's seat when he explained that his "new approach" is "designed, in large measure, to use Federal resources to stimulate State, local and private action" with the end goal of helping the mentally ill "be successfully and quickly treated in their own communities and returned to a useful place in society."[34] Moreover, Kennedy framed his recorded speech as a preview of "proposed measures" to Congress, implying an effort to educate the public about action on the part of the federal government. The two major initiatives—"to get people out of State custodial institutions and back into their communities and homes, without hardship or danger" and "a new, 5-year program of assistance to States and local health departments to develop comprehensive maternity and child health care programs"—required community action and private financing but seemed unlikely to generate substantial involvement from the average citizen.[35] Kennedy's formulation of the relationship between citizens, government, and mental health is perhaps best captured in the following statement: "The American people, acting through their government where necessary, have an obligation to prevent mental retardation, whenever possible, and to ameliorate it when it is present."[36] Still, his remarks did little to promote the tools and resources citizens needed to tackle the wicked problem of mental illness.

Subsequent presidents largely continued Kennedy's trend as educator when addressing mental health, using live televised speeches as well as communication with Congress to spread information and to find government and private-industry solutions.[37] Nixon, for instance, noted in his 1974 State of the Union message that "research and development funds" would be used to promote "the prosperity, well-being, and health of Americans," because "science will continue to be vital to our efforts . . . to aid in treating mental illness."[38] Carter presented his presidential approach in his remarks upon establishing the President's Commission on Mental Health in February 1977: "Because of a diversity of interest and the complexity of responsible groups who each have an almost fervent commitment to do something for those about whom we are concerned, I want to do a good job as President and I want to be able to achieve some progress in the field of mental health."[39] In line with the rhetorical presidency, Carter situated himself (and the presidency more broadly) as a primary agent and source of progress while recognizing mental health as a specialized "field."

Although Presidents Kennedy through George H. W. Bush supported efforts to research and tackle mental health at a general level, President William J. Clinton gave mental health a public face through the White House Confer-

ence on Mental Health in 1999 and the creation of the www.mentalhealth
.gov website.[40] Clinton previewed the conference in his 1999 annual message
and gestured toward a more communal approach to mental health, remarking,
"Let me say we must step up our efforts to treat and prevent mental illness.
No American should ever be afraid—ever—to address this disease."[41] Leading up to the conference, Clinton announced a "new nationwide campaign,
with Mrs. Gore serving as the honorary chair, to dispel the myths surrounding mental illness and encourage those with mental illness to get help."[42]
The announcement concluded by previewing the scope of the White House
conference: "These facts and myths of mental illness, and the White House's
new nationwide campaign on this issue, will be discussed on Monday at the
first-ever White House Conference on Mental Health, which will involve tens
of thousands of Americans around the country at over 1,000 cites [*sic*] connected to the conference in Washington."[43]

The conference, broadcast over the Internet on June 7, was noteworthy
for how it illustrated the president as educator but also as a budding effort to
get wider citizen involvement. The conference prioritized the educator role
insofar as it used experts through plenary and breakout sessions "to shed
light and understanding on issues surrounding mental illness and its impact
on people of all ages."[44] Yet it also emphasized civic involvement by encouraging people to locally organize a "Down Link meeting" involving "a good
cross section of mental health professionals, consumers, family members,
educators and business, government and community leaders" to "help open
an important discussion within your community on mental health issues."[45]
Clinton's efforts recognized the needs of the local community and the importance of civic involvement, but he framed those efforts as stemming from
education by experts. According to the White House, citizens needed to be
equipped with expert knowledge before the conversation could be productive,
while the personal experience of mental illness was largely neglected.

Clinton's successor, George W. Bush, maintained the focus on the president as educator by emphasizing the importance of accurate information. He
created the New Freedom Commission on Mental Health in order "to confront the hidden suffering of Americans with mental illness."[46] As part of this
effort, Bush signaled civic education when he labeled the stigma of mental
illness as "the first obstacle," calling on "political leaders, health care professionals, and all Americans" to "understand and send this message: Mental
disability is not a scandal; it is an illness."[47] Like Clinton, though, Bush saw
education as a primary tool for combatting the "misunderstanding, fear, and
embarrassment" that attend mental illness.[48] The role of citizens, then, was to
become more informed in order to lessen the stigma.

Beyond addressing stigma, Bush tackled the "fragmented mental health service delivery system."[49] He noted that the commission is "charged to study the problems and gaps in our current system of treatment and to make concrete recommendations for immediate improvements that will be implemented, and these will be improvements that can be implemented and must be implemented by the Federal Government, the State Government, local agencies, as well as public and private health care providers."[50] Consistent with prior presidents, Bush addressed the public at large but remained on the education side of the continuum by emphasizing government action in conjunction with experts and providers.

The Bush administration's online communication—which had become an important extension of executive branch discourse on mental health under Clinton's presidency—made the strongest overtures toward civic education by providing resources for action. In particular, NIMH assumed the mental health website (www.MentalHealth.gov) as its public face and used it as a clearinghouse for information concerning recent research on mental health, relevant events, clinical trials, and opportunities for practitioners and researchers. For instance, the section of the website "for the public" in 2001 greeted users with two questions: "Do you suffer from a mental disorder? Or do you know someone who does? Find out more here." These questions framed members of the "public" not as concerned *citizens* trying to improve their communities but as concerned *consumers* trying to help themselves and loved ones. The user was then told that the webpage "offers information from NIMH about the symptoms, diagnosis, and treatment of mental illnesses. Included are brochures and information sheets, reports, press releases, fact sheets, and other educational materials."[51] Along these lines, the site identified "Public Forums and Dialogues" to be valuable insofar as they were "designed to inform the public of cutting-edge mental health research and to gather input from the community about public health needs."[52] Despite the aesthetic and technological changes to the site between its inception in 1999 and June 2013, the website consistently identified its role as educational,—that is, informing the public about rather than involving the public in mental health.

In sum, while contemporary presidents have become progressively stronger voices in addressing the challenge of mental health and have moved more toward civic education, presidents in a digital age have still prioritized education by situating the public audience as important consumers of knowledge. In the next section, we will demonstrate how Obama's public rhetoric and the restructuring of the mental health website in 2013 have illustrated the potential for the presidency to not just educate about mental health but also to civically educate the public by providing tools for citizens to be sources of knowledge and initiators of change.

FROM EDUCATION TO CIVIC EDUCATION:
OBAMA AND MENTAL HEALTH

President Obama's efforts to address the relationship between mental health and acts of violence began after the shooting at Sandy Hook Elementary School in Newtown, Connecticut, on December 14, 2012. Adam Lanza, a twenty-year-old male, first shot and killed his mother "in her bed," and then went to the school where she taught and killed twenty first graders and six adults in the school, ending his murderous path by turning his weapon on himself.[53] Obama gave a public address on the day of the shooting, and also repeated a substantial portion of those remarks as part of his weekly address. Obama's initial statements offered condolences for the tragic loss of "children, beautiful little kids between the ages of 5 and 10 years old."[54] Yet his move toward action was generic. He first noted that the United States had "been through this too many times," listing past shootings at "a shopping mall in Oregon or a temple in Wisconsin or a movie theater in Aurora or a street corner in Chicago." The president's call to action was exploratory: "We're going to have to come together and take meaningful action to prevent more tragedies like this, regardless of the politics."[55]

In subsequent remarks, Obama built on early references to "meaningful action" by pointing toward the need for better gun control laws and preventive mental health care. The president spoke two days after the shooting at a memorial service in Newtown, and after consoling the community, he promised, "I will use whatever power this office holds to engage my fellow citizens—from law enforcement to mental health professionals to parents and educators—in an effort aimed at preventing more tragedies like this."[56] The president used the power of his office to campaign for gun control legislation—specifically to ban military-style semiautomatic weapons—and to push for better mental health care to help prevent violent, aggressive acts. While Obama initially linked these two agenda items, gun control and mental health later became two separate policy initiatives for his administration.

The first set of responses from the Obama White House focused on top-down structures, largely replicating past presidential efforts to address mental health. This executive-centered approach was evident when, on January 16, the Obama administration officially launched the government-created "Now Is the Time" campaign to address gun violence and mental health awareness. Before signing several executive orders, Obama delivered short remarks that reflected an educational model by situating the White House as the nexus of both information and policies to protect Americans. The president put forward "a specific set of proposals based on the work of Joe [Biden]'s task force," and used "the weight of this office"—the presidency—"to make them a reality." Obama promised that the administration would "make sure mental health professionals know their options for reporting threats of violence, even if we acknowledge that someone with a mental illness is far more likely to be a victim of violent crime rather than the perpetrator."[57] This statement represents traditional public problem-solving and education, when the president and those acting for him (such as Biden) frame the issues, interpret opinions and experiences from the public, and remind the public of constraints in the solutions—such as the idea that those suffering from mental health are more likely to experience crime than perpetrate it against others.

Obama illustrated the ease with which presidents use the power of the office to determine and direct action. On the same day of Obama and Biden's statements, the White House also publicized the "Now Is the Time" White House website,[58] a #NowIsTheTime hashtag for social media, and a "Now Is the Time" fifteen-page plan to "protect our children and our communities by reducing gun violence."[59] The first three components of the plan were closing background check loopholes, banning assault weapons, and making schools safer; the fourth component stressed the importance of mental health in protecting our communities from violence.[60] Many of the suggestions under the fourth directive, "Improving Mental Health Services," involved increasing training around and funding for issues of mental health. These all parallel the initiatives of earlier presidents such as Kennedy, Clinton, and Bush to use the executive branch as a hub and stimulus for mental health resources.

The final bullet point under improving mental health services, however, suggested an action quite different, asserting that we must "Launch a national conversation to increase understanding about mental health: The sense of shame and secrecy associated with mental illness prevents too many people from seeking help. The President is directing Secretaries Sebelius [Health and Human Services] and Duncan [Education] to launch a national dialogue about mental illness with young people who have experienced mental illness, members of the faith community, foundations, and school and business leaders."[61] We will illustrate how, over the course of 2013, this component grew to represent a more comprehensive form of presidential civic education.

The new focus of civic education from the White House emphasized the localized creation of public dialogues about mental health and named the significant roles individual citizens could play in addressing the challenges of mental health. On February 4, Secretary Sebelius revealed the executive branch's emerging emphasis on civic education through an article in *USA Today*. Calling for the audience to "bring mental illness out of the shadows," Sebelius recognized that "we are still a country that frequently confines conversations about mental health to the far edges of our discourse." To rectify this lack of discourse, she previewed Obama's call for "a national dialogue on mental health" that "will challenge each of us to do our part to create communities where young people and their families understand how important mental health is to positive development and feel comfortable asking for help when they need it." The White House, speaking through its Health and Human Services Secretary, invited citizens to directly take part in addressing problems of mental health through community conversations and action.[62]

The campaign then unfolded through traditional means at the same time it pushed the boundaries of presidential engagement with the issue of mental health. In the same vein as prior presidents, President Obama declared May 2013 National Mental Health Awareness Month, and "called upon citizens, government agencies, organizations, health care providers, and research institutions to raise mental health awareness and continue helping Americans live longer, healthier lives."[63] The following month, the White House revived the tradition begun by Clinton to hold a White House Conference on Mental Health. In President Obama's opening remarks for the conference, he noted that the goal "is not to start a conversation" but rather "about elevating that conversation to a national level and bringing mental illness out of the shadows."[64]

In addition to these more traditional modes of engagement, the White House also invited individuals across the country to participate in the initiative. The Department of Health and Human Services in conjunction with Aquilent (a web content company) significantly redesigned the www.mentalhealth.gov website to coincide with the White House conference. The new version of mentalhealth.gov was announced at the White House Conference on Mental Health on June 3, 2013.[65] Statements about the new website point to its emergence from the Obama administration's efforts to address mental health through education.

The redesign of the website demonstrated presidential rhetoric of civic education. For instance, the title slogan on mentalhealth.gov changed from "Transforming the understanding and treatment of mental illness through research" to "Let's talk about it."[66] Rather than focusing on research—a term that implies expert opinion, specialized knowledge, and limited public participation—the website now focused on "talk"—something in which all citizens can partake.

The four scrolling "Features" at the top of the new site further illustrated examples of civic education, rather than informational education. The links to the "Myths and Facts" and "National Conference" features kept the site's traditional role as an information clearinghouse for those wanting to learn about mental health. In particular, the content of the "Myths and Facts" page did not differ substantially from the prior website's content. Yet the redesign oriented this information toward citizen involvement. The subtitle of the

"National Conference" page framed the conference as "answering the call to launch a national conversation," while the "Myths and Facts" page invited the visitor to "Get the facts. Use your knowledge to educate others. Reach out to help others."[67] Thus, the website's framing of information prioritized the actions of citizens, encouraging them to add their lived experiences of living with and addressing mental health in their communities.

This invitation to make a difference is most evident in the third and fourth features of the new site, "Start a Conversation" and "Hope and Recovery." Both of these offer explicit interactions for and between citizens. Whereas earlier presidential efforts privileged medical experts in determining knowledge about mental health, these pages positioned citizens as important bearers of information. The "Hope and Recovery" page, for instance, has "people share personal stories of hope and recovery from mental health problems."[68] The site helps visitors "Start a Conversation" by offering tips for various kinds of people—people with mental health problems, parents and caregivers, friends and family, and educators—to engage interpersonally. These roles (parent, friend, educator, etc.) are motivated by personal rather than civic concerns, but the site also provide tools for starting "Conversations in Your Community" that enable engagement *as citizens* through social media and local interaction.[69] In sum, David Fout, Aquilent CEO, described the redesigned website as "a great example of how a digitally empowered government can be one of the most effective tools in citizen service."[70]

Both the old and new websites educated citizens, but the redesigned mentalhealth.gov invited citizens into a process rather than focusing solely on disseminating information. Even the images stressed this relationship. The redesigned website moved from a primarily text-based interface to a graphic design of citizen-initiatives. Each subtitle—National Conference, Myths and Facts, Start a Conversation, and Hope and Recovery—was paired with human silhouettes and images, inviting the citizens to see themselves as part of the solution.[71] The community conversations page provided links to materials generated by the Substance Abuse and Mental Health Services Administration (SAMHSA), such as a toolkit and discussion guide that offered tips for how to be a discussion facilitator on the topic of mental health. These materials reinforced the communal nature of knowledge, encouraging community groups to begin the conversation by "sharing personal experiences" about what mental health means to the individual and to the community before discussing challenges and solutions as a local collective.[72]

As the White House encouraged community involvement and various "Let's Talk" initiatives, the National Dialogue on Mental Health became a diffuse rather than discrete program. The efforts emerged not from the president or a White House task force, but instead stemmed from a large number of actors beyond the executive branch. The website www.creatingcommunitysolutions.org became a hub through which individuals and organizations might become civically educated and organize their own community conversations about mental health. The site explained its purpose is to "give Americans a chance to learn more about mental health issues—from each other and from research."[73] This statement situated the audience as "Americans," emphasizing a national and civic quality to participation, and prioritized learning from fellow citizens above learning from research.

Along those lines, the website visitor had access to the print documents from SAMHSA in English and Spanish but also sample materials from citizens across the nation who had successfully enacted community conversations. Citizens learned from one another not only about mental health but also about how to have effective deliberations on that topic. Site visitors could access no fewer than ten training videos and webinars, created by a variety of people in a variety of organizations, designed to familiarize them with the process from start to finish and offer some helpful tips concerning face-to-face facilitation and the use of social media.[74] The website also included a national map and calendar of past and future conversations, visually illustrating the communal nature of the project.[75] Many of the organizers have posted the contents of these conversations to further assist civic education and promote change. The website itself recognized its purpose as civic education: "By sharing the outcomes with each other, we can build on each other's strengths and play a part in developing more resilient healthy communities."[76]

In sum, the mental health initiative originated with the executive branch and the White House Conference on Mental Health and relied on traditional presidential education modes of rhetoric, but then expanded into a more collective mode of executive branch civic education. In so doing, the Obama administration has used numerous strategies that counter how presidents have traditionally talked about mental health: emphasizing civic education as a precursor to civic engagement; emphasizing citizens, including those suffering from mental illness, as the producers rather than consumers of knowledge; and emphasizing local efforts at change, enhanced by national resources that assist the individual citizen. In our conclusion, we consider the broader lessons of this case study insofar as they illustrate the opportunities and challenges of the president's emergent role as civic educator.

CONCLUSION

We have demonstrated that President Obama's dialogue initiative on mental health illustrates a tactic of presidential leadership that emphasizes civic education along with more traditional modes of engagement on the topic. We have chronicled how the Obama administration has situated citizens as co-creators of knowledge and solutions, thus encouraging civic involvement at the local level to help create a caring community, rather than merely inform others of expert information. In this conclusion, we consider the lessons of this case for presidential civic education more broadly as it relates to the president's role as national leader.

Presidential civic education aligns with the goals of deliberative democracy, which carries advantages and drawbacks. Our case study in this chapter illustrated the power of civic education to invite engagement with the Oval Office but also through it, as presidents provide a national platform for people to connect with one another and cultivate grassroots change. As of August 2014, communities have organized more than 150 dialogues on mental health.[77] The number of community dialogues on mental health attest to the transformative potential of presidential rhetoric and civic education. In this regard, we confirm the conclusion of other chapters in this volume that such civic education programs—particularly emerging from the highest executive office—are important tools for promoting a democratically engaged citizenry. Yet if this is the case, why did it take more than fifty years of speech on mental health for the president to move toward civic education? Moreover, why have presidents resisted promoting civic engagement on all the wicked problems facing U.S. citizens?

One answer comes down to resources; civic education and the ensuing engagement cost a lot of investment, financial and otherwise. Creating documents, organizing and attending public community dialogues, sifting through the notes from them, and compiling and implementing action steps all require substantial time commitments from citizens, who may be unwilling to take up the president's call to action. This answer certainly explains why citizens do not engage every public controversy. However, it does not offer an entirely satisfactory account for why presidents rarely promote civic education and engagement, especially when such promotion would align with the president's frequent celebration of the nation's democratic heritage and such civic action may, in fact, cost presidents less time and money in the long run than were they to campaign for action in a more top-down approach.

We argue, then, that the president's resistance to civic education results from political rather than material resources. Institutionally speaking, we have shown how presidents seeking to demonstrate leadership and exert their power are inclined toward the role of educator rather than civic educator; educating the audience about political topics such as mental health situates the president as an altruistic leader at the same time he maintains control over the direction of the controversy. This focus fits within the theory of the rhetorical presidency, which emphasizes the president's governance efforts through rhetorical leadership. Presidents have increasingly become policy designers and advocates, working toward securing their own legacies. Our case study concerning mental health has borne this out. Presidents Kennedy, Carter, Clinton, and Bush tended to address mental health as a topic requiring the executive branch's stimulus for research and information sharing. The numerous "I" statements from these presidents emphasized the president's unique position to help lead the nation along the path toward reform or understanding. Apart from Obama, Clinton and Bush alone invited broader citizen involvement, yet even that was under the guise of becoming better informed. For presidents seeking to protect their own authority, there are strong institutional motivations to resist empowerment through civic education.

There are also partisan motivations. Empowering citizens to generate their own ideas about the nature of and solutions to public problems is risky insofar as citizens may come to a different conclusion than the president's desired political outcome. This is especially true for presidents in their first term who are seeking reelection and need to have strong benchmarks or accomplishments on which to base their campaign. Yet even second-term presidents struggle to reconcile the public's attitudes and desires with their own. One might recall Carter's efforts in 1979 to solicit public opinion on the "crisis of confidence" in the United States and his rhetorical dexterity in framing that opinion as supportive of his energy policy despite strong evidence to the contrary.[78] Whereas Carter spoke with a select group of citizens personally invited to Camp David, civic education expands the invitation to people from all political walks of life. It cedes power to the people in determining the course of action at the same time that group of citizens may look to the leaders, such as the president, for resources to implement that action. Civic education may relegate the president to mere executive rather than political leader, and it may produce slower responses—or campaigns too diffuse to measure.

Given this potential, it is unsurprising that presidential civic education most frequently occurs in relation to nonpartisan and community-based problems for which any progress is a boon to the president. As President Obama does not have a partisan stake in the local solutions to mental healthcare and it is unlikely that a substantial number of citizens oppose helping those with mental illness, he faces no political harm in civic education and civic engagement in that arena. Promoting such education may even portray Obama as a compassionate and empowering leader. Yet although Obama appeared to be politically neutral on this topic, he still rendered political choices in the very decision to emphasize civic engagement on this topic and not others.

Ultimately, presidential civic education offers a relatively new yet significant means for presidents to teach people how best to enact their citizenship on a particular topic. Just as the power of the executive branch positions the president to have a significant impact on policy outcomes concerning any given controversy, so too does it enable the president to influence the contours of conversations surrounding that controversy. Franklin Delano Roosevelt articulated this very motivation when campaigning for the presidency in 1932, remarking that "government includes the art of formulating a policy, and using the political technique to attain so much of that policy as will receive general support; persuading, leading, sacrificing, teaching always, because the greatest duty of a statesman is to educate."[79] And yet, as presidents strive to move beyond government to governance—as they strive to equip citizens with the capacity and tools to make a difference—perhaps there is no greater duty of the president than to civically educate and empower his fellow citizens.

NOTES

1. John F. Kennedy, "Inaugural Address," January 20, 1961, in *Public Papers of the Presidents of the United States: John F. Kennedy, 1961–1963*, vol. 1 (Washington D.C.: GPO, 1962), 3.

2. George Bush, "Inaugural Address," January 20, 1989, in *Public Papers of the Presidents of the United States: George Bush, 1989–1993,* vol. 1, bk. 1 (Washington, DC: GPO, 1990), 2.

3. William J. Clinton, "Remarks at Georgetown University," July 6, 1995, in *Public Papers of the Presidents of the United States: William J. Clinton, 1993–2001,* vol. 3, bk. 2 (Washington, DC: GPO, 1996), 1048.

4. George W. Bush, "Inaugural Address," January 20, 2001, in *Public Papers of the Presidents of the United States: George W. Bush, 2001–2009,* vol. 1, bk. 1 (Washington, DC: GPO, 2003), 3.

5. Matthew A. Crenson and Benjamin Ginsberg, *Downsizing Democracy: How America Sidelined Its Citizens and Privatized Its Public* (Baltimore: The Johns Hopkins University Press, 2002), 14.

6. Marc Landy and Sidney M. Milkis, *Presidential Greatness* (Lawrence: University Press of Kansas, 2000), 3–4

7. Jeffrey K. Tulis, *The Rhetorical Presidency* (Princeton, NJ: Princeton University Press, 1987), 4.

8. Ibid., 18.

9. Ibid., 4.

10. Ibid., 190.

11. George C. Edwards, *The Strategic President: Persuasion and Opportunity in Presidential Leadership* (Princeton, NJ: Princeton University Press, 2009), 10.

12. Ibid., 16.

13. George C. Edwards, *On Deaf Ears: The Limits of the Bully Pulpit* (New Haven, CT: Yale University Press, 2006), 4 and 241. Edwards arrived at this conclusion by comparing opinion poll results prior to and after major presidential speeches.

14. Edwards, *The Strategic President*, 188.

15. Martin J. Medhurst, "Introduction, A Tale of Two Constructs: The Rhetorical Presidency versus Presidential Rhetoric," in *Beyond the Rhetorical Presidency*, ed. Martin J. Medhurst (College Station: Texas A&M University Press, 1996), xiv.

16. Erwin C. Hargrove, *The President as Leader: Appealing to the Better Angels of Our Nature* (Lawrence: University Press of Kansas, 1998), 97–98; David Zarefsky, "Presidential Rhetoric and the Power of Definition," *Presidential Studies Quarterly* 34 (2004): 607–19.

17. Zarefsky, "Presidential Rhetoric and the Power of Definition," 611.

18. Roderick P. Hart, "Thinking Harder about Presidential Discourse: The Question of Efficacy," in *The Prospect of Presidential Rhetoric*, ed. James Arnt Aune and Martin J. Medhurst (College Station: Texas A&M University Press, 2008), 244–246. Hart argues that presidential rhetoric may (1) crystallize vague concepts (2) alter the national imagination (3) change definitional habits (4) shift people's presuppositions (5) relocate sources of authority (6) change the arc of time and (7) space (8) shorten the political agenda (9) shift the locus of controversy (10) alter our political metrics (11) model specific attitudes, and (12) instantiate new possibilities.

19. Leroy G. Dorsey, "Introduction," in *The Presidency and Rhetorical Leadership*, ed. Leroy G. Dorsey (College Station: Texas A&M University Press, 2002), 9.

20. Landy and Milkis, *Presidential Greatness*, 3–4.

21. Sidney Blumenthal, "Marketing the President," *New York Times Magazine*, September 13, 1981, 43.

22. Landy and Milkis, *Presidential Greatness*, 3–4.

23. Martin Carcasson and Leah Sprain, "Deliberative Democracy and Adult Civic Education," *New Direction for Adult and Continuing Education* 135 (Fall 2012): 15.

24. Ibid., 15.

25. Harry C. Boyte, "Reframing Democracy: Governance, Civic Agency, and Politics," *Public Administration Review* 65 (2005): 537.

26. Horst W. J. Rittel and Martin Webber,"Dilemmas in a General Theory of Planning," *Policy Sciences* 4 (1973): 160.

27. Martin Carcasson and Leah Sprain, "Key Aspects of the Deliberative Democracy Movement," *Public Sector Digest* (Summer 2010), http://www.publicsector digest.com/articles/view/722.

28. Robert Putnam and Lewis Feldstein, *Better Together: Restoring the American Community* (New York: Simon & Schuster, 2003), 269.

29. Herbert Hoover, "Address to the White House Conference on Child Health and Protection," November 19, 1930, in *Public Papers of the Presidents of the United States: Herbert Hoover, 1929–1933*, vol. 2 (Washington D.C.: GPO, 1976), 489–97; Harry S. Truman, "Special Message to the Congress Recommending a Comprehensive Health Program," November 19, 1945, in *Public Papers of the Presidents of the United States: Harry S. Truman, 1945–1953*, vol. 1 (Washington D.C.: GPO, 1961), 475–91; Dwight D. Eisenhower, "Special Message to the Congress on the Health Needs of the American People," January 18, 1954, in *Public Papers of the Presidents of the United States: Dwight D. Eisenhower, 1953–1961*, vol. 2 (Washington D.C.: GPO, 1960), 69–77; and Dwight D. Eisenhower, "Annual Message to the Congress

180   *Sara A. Mehltretter Drury and Jeffrey P. Mehltretter Drury*

on the State of the Union," January 12, 1961, in *Public Papers of the Presidents of the United States: Dwight D. Eisenhower, 1953–1961,* vol. 8 (Washington D.C.: GPO, 1961), 913–31.

30. Dwight D. Eisenhower, "Special Message to the Congress Recommending a Health Program," January 31, 1955, in *Public Papers of the Presidents of the United States: Dwight D. Eisenhower, 1953–1961,* vol. 3 (Washington D.C.: GPO, 1959), 222.

31. National Institute of Mental Health, "Important Events in NIMH History," *The NIH Almanac,* August 6, 2013, http://www.nih.gov/about/almanac/organization/NIMH.htm.

32. John F. Kennedy, "Special Message to the Congress on Mental Illness and Mental Retardation," February 5, 1963, in *Public Papers of the Presidents of the United States: John F. Kennedy, 1961–1963,* vol. 3 (Washington D.C.: GPO, 1960), 127.

33. John F. Kennedy, "Remarks on Proposed Measures to Combat Mental Illness and Mental Retardation," February 5, 1963, in *Public Papers of the Presidents of the United States: John F. Kennedy, 1961–1963,* vol. 3 (Washington D.C.: GPO, 1960), 138.

34. Kennedy, "Special Message to the Congress on Mental Illness and Mental Retardation," 128.

35. Kennedy, "Remarks on Proposed Measures to Combat Mental Illness and Mental Retardation," 137 and 138.

36. Kennedy, "Special Message to the Congress on Mental Illness and Mental Retardation," 133.

37. For example, see Lyndon B. Johnson, "Address before a Joint Session of the Congress," November 27, 1963, in *Public Papers of the Presidents of the United States: Lyndon B. Johnson, 1963–1969,* vol. 1, bk. 1 (Washington D.C.: GPO, 1965), 8; Lyndon B. Johnson, "Statement by the President upon Signing the Mental Health Amendments of 1967," June 26, 1967, in *Public Papers of the Presidents of the United States: Lyndon B. Johnson, 1963–1969,* vol. 4, bk. 1 (Washington D.C.: GPO, 1968), 653–54; and Jimmy Carter, "Mental Health Systems Legislation: Remarks Announcing the Proposed Legislation," May 15, 1979, in *Public Papers of the Presidents of the United States: Jimmy Carter, 1977–1981,* vol. 4, bk. 1 (Washington D.C.: GPO, 1980), 857–59.

38. Richard M. Nixon, "Annual Message to the Congress on the State of the Union," January 30, 1974, in *Public Papers of the Presidents of the United States: Richard M. Nixon, 1969–1974,* vol. 6 (Washington D.C.: GPO, 1975), 91.

39. Jimmy Carter, "President's Commission on Mental Health: Remarks of the President and Mrs. Carter at the Signing Ceremony of Executive Order 11973," February 17, 1977, in *Public Papers of the Presidents of the United States: Jimmy Carter, 1977–1981,* vol. 2, bk. 1 (Washington D.C.: GPO, 1977), 185.

40. "White House Conference on Mental Health: Working for a Healthier America," *The White House,* October 13, 1999, https://web.archive.org/web/19991013045037/http://mentalhealth.gov/.

41. William J. Clinton, "Address before a Joint Session of the Congress on the State of the Union," January 19, 1999, in *Public Papers of the Presidents of the*

United States: William J. Clinton, 1993–2001, vol. 7, bk. 1 (Washington D.C.: GPO, 2000), 66.

42. "PRESIDENT CLINTON AND TIPPER GORE ANNOUNCE NEW CAM-PAIGN TO COMBAT THE STIGMAS SURROUNDING MENTAL ILLNESS AND ENCOURAGE PEOPLE WITH MENTAL ILLNESS TO GET HELP," *The White House,* June 5, 1999, https://web.archive.org/web/19990824095846/http://www.mentalhealth.gov/campaign.asp.

43. Ibid.

44. "White House Conference on Mental Health: Working for a Healthier America," *The White House,* August 24, 1999, https://web.archive.org/web/19990824065525/http://www.mentalhealth.gov/backgrd.asp.

45. "FACILITATOR GUIDELINES: Your Role," *The White House,* November 4, 1999, https://web.archive.org/web/19991104083152/http://www.mentalhealth.gov/role.asp.

46. George W. Bush, "Remarks at the University of New Mexico in Albuquerque, New Mexico," April 29, 2002, in *Public Papers of the Presidents of the United States: George W. Bush, 2001–2009,* vol. 2, bk. 1 (Washington D.C.: GPO, 2004), 676.

47. Ibid., 677.

48. Ibid., 677.

49. Ibid., 677.

50. Ibid., 678.

51. "FOR THE PUBLIC," *National Institute for Mental Health,* November 27, 2001, https://web.archive.org/web/20020302090158/http://www.mentalhealth.gov/publicat/index.cfm.

52. "NIMH Outreach," *National Institute for Mental Health,* July 15, 2004, https://web.archive.org/web/20041015204449/http://www.mentalhealth.gov/outreach/index.cfm.

53. Joseph Berger and Marc Santora, "Chilling Look at Newtown Killer, but No 'Why,'" *The New York Times* online edition, November 25, 2013, http://www.nytimes.com/2013/11/26/nyregion/sandy-hook-shooting-investigation-ends-with-motive-still-unknown.html.

54. Barack Obama, "DCPD No. 201200946: Remarks on the Shooting in New-town, Connecticut," December 14, 2012, in *Daily Compilation of Presidential Documents* (Washington D.C.: GPO, 2012), 1, http://www.gpo.gov/fdsys/pkg/DCPD-201200946/pdf/DCPD-201200946.pdf.

55. Obama, "DCPD No. 201200946: Remarks on the Shooting in Newtown, Con-necticut," 1.

56. Barack Obama, "DCPD No. 201200953: Remarks at the Sandy Hook Inter-faith Prayer Vigil in Newtown, Connecticut," December 16, 2012, in *Daily Compila-tion of Presidential Documents* (Washington D.C.: GPO, 2012), 1, http://www.gpo.gov/fdsys/pkg/DCPD-201200953/pdf/DCPD-201200953.pdf.

57. Barack Obama, "DCPD No. 201300018: Remarks on Gun Violence," January 16, 2013, in *Daily Compilation of Presidential Documents* (Washington D.C.: GPO, 2013), 3, http://www.gpo.gov/fdsys/pkg/DCPD-201300018/pdf/DCPD-201300018.pdf.

58 "Now Is the Time," *The White House* http://www.whitehouse.gov/now-is-the-time, hyperlinks to http://www.whitehouse.gov/issues/preventing-gun-violence (accessed February 9, 2014).

59. "Now Is the Time," *The White House*, January 16, 2013, 1, http://www.white house.gov/sites/default/files/docs/wh_now_is_the_time_full.pdf.

60. Ibid., 2.

61. Ibid., 15.

62. Kathleen Sebelius, "Sebelius: Bring Mental Illness out of the Shadows," *USA Today*, February 4, 2013, http://www.usatoday.com/story/opinion/2013/02/04/kathleen-sebelius-on-mental-health-care/1890859.

63. Barack Obama, "DCPD Number: DCPD201300290: Proclamation 8696—National Mental Health Awareness Month, 2013, April 30, 2013."

64. Barack Obama, "DCPD No. 201300382: Remarks at the National Conference on Mental Health," June 3, 2013, in *Daily Compilation of Presidential Documents* (Washington D.C.: GPO, 2013), 1, http://www.gpo.gov/fdsys/pkg/DCPD-201300382/pdf/DCPD-201300382.pdf.

65. "National Conference on Mental Health," *The White House*, June 3, 2013, http://www.whitehouse.gov/blog/2013/06/03/national-conference-mental-health.

66. "National Institute of Mental Health," *The White House*, November 1, 2012, https://web.archive.org/web/20121101093601/http://mentalhealth.gov/; "MentalHealth.gov," *The White House*, June 3, 2013, https://web.archive.org/web/20130603231044/http://www.mentalhealth.gov/.

67. "MentalHealth.gov," *The White House*, June 3.

68. "Stories of Hope and Recovery," *The White House*, June 3, 2013, https://web.archive.org/web/20130608081514/http://www.mentalhealth.gov/talk/recovery/index.html.

69. "Talk about Mental Health," *The White House*, June 3, 2013, https://web.archive.org/web/20130614044039/http://www.mentalhealth.gov/talk/index.html; "Conversations in Your Community," *The White House*, June 3, 2013, https://web.archive.org/web/20130615024430/http://www.mentalhealth.gov/talk/community-conversation/index.html.

70. "MentalHealth.Gov, Developed with Support from Aquilent, Goes Live," *Business Wire*, July 9, 2013, http://www.businesswire.com/news/home/20130709005904/en/MentalHealth.Gov-Developed-Support-Aquilent-Live.

71. "MentalHealth.gov," *The White House*, June 3, 2013.

72. Substance Abuse and Mental Health Services Administration, "Community Conversations about Mental Health: Information Brief," HHS Publication No. SMA-13-4763 (Rockville, MD: Substance Abuse and Mental Health Services Administration, 2013), 3.

73. Creating Community Solutions, "Statement of Purpose," February 25, 2014, http://www.creatingcommunitysolutions.org/about.

74. Creating Community Solutions, "Resources," February 25, 2014, http://www.creatingcommunitysolutions.org/resources.

75. Creating Community Solutions, "Community Dialogues," February 25, 2014, http://www.creatingcommunitysolutions.org/events.

76. Creating Community Solutions, "Outcomes," February 25, 2014, http://www.creatingcommunitysolutions.org/outcomes.

77. Creating Community Solutions, "Community Dialogues," October 6, 2014, http://creatingcommunitysolutions.org/events.

78. Jimmy Carter, "Energy and National Goals: Address to the Nation," July 15, 1979, in *Public Papers of the Presidents of the United States: Jimmy Carter, 1977–1981,* vol. 3, bk. 2 (Washington, D.C.: GPO, 1980), 1235–41.

79. Franklin Delano Roosevelt, "'New Conditions Impose New Requirements upon Government and Those Who Conduct Government.' Campaign Address on Progressive Government at the Commonwealth Club," September 23, 1932, in *The Public Papers and Addresses of Franklin D. Roosevelt,* vol. 1, bk. 1 (New York: Random House, 1938), 756.

BIBLIOGRAPHY

Berger, Joseph, and Marc Santora. "Chilling Look at Newtown Killer, but No 'Why.'" *The New York Times* online edition, November 25, 2013. http://www.nytimes.com/2013/11/26/nyregion/sandy-hook-shooting-investigation-ends-with-motive-still-unknown.html.

Blumenthal, Sidney. "Marketing the President." *New York Times Magazine*, September 13, 1981, 42–44.

Boyte, Harry C. "Reframing Democracy: Governance, Civic Agency, and Politics." *Public Administration Review* 65 (2005): 536–46.

Bush, George. *Public Papers of the Presidents of the United States: George Bush, 1989–1993.* Vol. 1. Washington, D.C.: GPO, 1990.

Bush, George W. *Public Papers of the Presidents of the United States: George W. Bush, 2001–2009.* Vols. 1, 2. Washington, D.C.: GPO, 2003, 2004.

Carcasson, Martin, and Leah Sprain. "Deliberative Democracy and Adult Civic Education." *New Direction for Adult and Continuing Education* 135 (Fall 2012): 15–23.

Carcasson, Martin, and Leah Sprain. "Key Aspects of the Deliberative Democracy Movement." *Public Sector Digest* (Summer 2010). http://www.publicsectordigest.com/articles/view/722.

Carter, Jimmy. *Public Papers of the Presidents of the United States: Jimmy Carter, 1977–1981.* Vols. 2, 3, 4. Washington D.C.: GPO, 1977, 1980.

Clinton, William J. *Public Papers of the Presidents of the United States: William J. Clinton, 1993–2001.* Vols. 3, 7. Washington, D.C.: GPO, 1996, 2000.

"Conversations in Your Community." *The White House.* June 3, 2013. https://web.archive.org/web/20130615024430/http://www.mentalhealth.gov/talk/community-conversation/index.html.

Creating Community Solutions. "Community Dialogues." October 6, 2014. http://www.creatingcommunitysolutions.org/events.

Creating Community Solutions. "Outcomes." February 25, 2014. http://www.creatingcommunitysolutions.org/outcomes.

Creating Community Solutions. "Resources." February 25, 2014. http://www.creating communitysolutions.org/resources.

Creating Community Solutions. "Statement of Purpose." February 25, 2014. http://www.creatingcommunitysolutions.org/about.

Crenson, Matthew A., and Benjamin Ginsberg. *Downsizing Democracy: How America Sidelined Its Citizens and Privatized Its Public*. Baltimore: The Johns Hopkins University Press, 2002.

Dorsey, Leroy. "Introduction: The President as a Rhetorical Leader." In *The Presidency and Rhetorical Leadership.* Edited by Leroy Dorsey. College Station: Texas A&M University Press, 2002.

Edwards, George C. *On Deaf Ears: The Limits of the Bully Pulpit*. New Haven, CT: Yale University Press, 2006.

Edwards, George C. *The Strategic President: Persuasion and Opportunity in Presidential Leadership*. Princeton, NJ: Princeton University Press, 2009.

Eisenhower, Dwight D. *Public Papers of the Presidents of the United States: Dwight D. Eisenhower, 1953–1961*. Vols. 2, 3, 8. Washington D.C.: GPO, 1959, 1960, 1961.

"FACILITATOR GUIDELINES: Your Role." *The White House*. November 4, 1999. https://web.archive.org/web/19991104083152/http://www.mentalhealth .gov/role.asp.

"FOR THE PUBLIC." *National Institute for Mental Health*. November 27, 2001. https://web.archive.org/web/20020302090158/http://www.mentalhealth.gov/pub licat/index.cfm.

Hargrove, Erwin C. *The President as Leader: Appealing to the Better Angels of Our Nature*. Lawrence: University Press of Kansas, 1998.

Hart, Roderick. "Thinking Harder about Presidential Discourse: The Question of Efficacy." In *The Prospect of Presidential Rhetoric*. Edited by James Arnt Aune and Martin Medhurst. College Station: Texas A&M University Press, 2008. First presented at the tenth annual meeting of the Conference on Presidential Rhetoric. College Station, Texas, March 2004.

Hoover, Herbert. *Public Papers of the Presidents of the United States: Herbert Hoover, 1929–1933*. Vol. 2. Washington D.C.: GPO, 1976.

Johnson, Lyndon B. *Public Papers of the Presidents of the United States: Lyndon B. Johnson, 1963–1969*. Vols. 1, 4. Washington D.C.: GPO, 1965, 1968.

Kennedy, John F. *Public Papers of the Presidents of the United States: John F. Kennedy, 1961–1963*. Vols. 1, 3. Washington D.C.: GPO, 1960, 1962.

Landy, Marc, and Sidney M. Milkis. *Presidential Greatness*. Lawrence: University Press of Kansas, 2000.

Medhurst, Martin J. "Introduction, a Tale of Two Constructs: The Rhetorical Presidency versus Presidential Rhetoric." In *Beyond the Rhetorical Presidency*. Edited by Martin Medhurst. College Station: Texas A&M University Press, 1996.

"MentalHealth.gov." *The White House*. June 3, 2013. https://web.archive.org/web/20130603231044/http://www.mentalhealth.gov.

"MentalHealth.Gov, Developed with Support from Aquilent, Goes Live." *Business Wire*, July 9, 2013. http://www.businesswire.com/news/home/20130709005904/en/MentalHealth.Gov-Developed-Support-Aquilent-Live.

"National Conference on Mental Health." *The White House*. June 3, 2013. http://www.whitehouse.gov/blog/2013/06/03/national-conference-mental-health.

"National Institute of Mental Health." *The White House*. November 1, 2012. https://web.archive.org/web/20121101093601/http://mentalhealth.gov.

National Institute of Mental Health. "Important Events in NIMH History." *The NIH Almanac*. August 6, 2013. http://www.nih.gov/about/almanac/organization/NIMH.htm.

"NIMH Outreach." *National Institute for Mental Health*. July 15, 2004. https://web.archive.org/web/20041015204449/http://www.mentalhealth.gov/outreach/index.cfm.

Nixon, Richard M. *Public Papers of the Presidents of the United States: Richard M. Nixon, 1969–1974*. Vol. 6. Washington D.C.: GPO, 1975.

"Now is the Time." *The White House*. N.d. http://www.whitehouse.gov/now-is-the-time.

"Now is the Time." *The White House*. January 16, 2013. http://www.whitehouse.gov/sites/default/files/docs/wh_now_is_the_time_full.pdf.

Obama, Barack. *Daily Compilation of Presidential Documents*. Washington D.C.: GPO, 2012, 2013.

"PRESIDENT CLINTON AND TIPPER GORE ANNOUNCE NEW CAMPAIGN TO COMBAT THE STIGMAS SURROUNDING MENTAL ILLNESS AND ENCOURAGE PEOPLE WITH MENTAL ILLNESS TO GET HELP." *The White House*. June 5, 1999. https://web.archive.org/web/19990824095846/http://www.mentalhealth.gov/campaign.asp.

Putnam, Robert D., and Lewis M. Feldstein. *Better Together: Restoring the American Community*. New York: Simon & Schuster, 2003.

Rittel, Horst W. J., and Melvin M. Webber. "Dilemmas in a General Theory of Planning." *Policy Sciences* 4 (1973): 155–69.

Roosevelt, Franklin Delano. *The Public Papers and Addresses of Franklin D. Roosevelt*. Vol. 1. New York: Random House, 1938.

Sebelius, Kathleen. "Sebelius: Bring Mental Illness out of the Shadows." *USA Today*, February 4, 2013. http://www.usatoday.com/story/opinion/2013/02/04/kathleen-sebelius-on-mental-health-care/1890859.

"Stories of Hope and Recovery." *The White House*. June 3, 2013. https://web.archive.org/web/20130608081514/http://www.mentalhealth.gov/talk/recovery/index.html.

Substance Abuse and Mental Health Services Administration. "Community Conversations about Mental Health: Information Brief." HHS Publication No. SMA-13-4763. Rockville, MD: Substance Abuse and Mental Health Services Administration, 2013.

"Talk about Mental Health." *The White House*. June 3, 2013. https://web.archive.org/web/20130614044039/http://www.mentalhealth.gov/talk/index.html.

Truman, Harry S. *Public Papers of the Presidents of the United States: Harry S. Truman, 1945–1953*. Vol. 1. Washington D.C.: GPO, 1961.

Tulis, Jeffrey K. *The Rhetorical Presidency*. Princeton, NJ: Princeton University Press, 1987.

"White House Conference on Mental Health: Working for a Healthier America." *The White House*. October 13, 1999. https://web.archive.org/web/19991013045037/http://mentalhealth.gov/.

Zarefksy, David. "Presidential Rhetoric and the Power of Definition." *Presidential Studies Quarterly* 34 (2004): 607–19.

Part B: State and Local Government

Chapter Eight

An Examination of Judicial Civic Education and Community Outreach Efforts

Brendan Toner

When looking at civic education in the United States, the judicial branch is often left out or discussed less than the executive and legislative branches. This lack of attention is reinforced by the lack of attention the judiciary receives in the popular press. In order to remedy this situation, this chapter examines how court systems throughout the United States seek to educate the public, whose support is essential for the maintenance of the courts' power under the American system of government. To educate the public, the courts have instituted community outreach programs. These outreach and educational activities are necessary considering that trust by the American public in the judiciary has declined since the 1970s.[1]

In addition to declining trust as it relates to the courts, many Americans are not even aware of who sits on the courts, particularly the highest court in the land—the United States Supreme Court. In a 2010 poll conducted by ABC News and the *Washington Post*, most Americans admitted they did not know that John Roberts was the chief justice even though he had held the post for five years prior to the poll being conducted. In fact, instead of simply saying they did not know who the chief justice was many people guessed incorrectly. Some believed Thurgood Marshall, who passed away about twenty years ago, to be the current chief justice. A number of people said that Senate Majority Leader Harry Reid of Nevada was Chief Justice. He has never even been on the Supreme Court. Others incorrectly guessed John Paul Stevens, the oldest Supreme Court justice at the time, but he has never been chief justice.[2]

Poor knowledge of the judiciary parallels the lack of knowledge that Americans have about many other facets of government. This includes less than half of Americans in a Pew Research Quiz knowing that John Boehner was the Speaker of the House in 2011. This number was less than the percentage of Americans who could correctly name Mark Zukerberg as the founder of Facebook. This gap between knowledge of Zukerberg versus Boehner was even higher with younger respondents.[3] Thus polls like the ABC/Washington Post one highlight the poor civic literacy of many Americans, particularly for the leadership of the Supreme Court. This lack of knowledge is even more prevalent for the lower courts—namely for state and local level ones—that are the focus of this chapter. It could be argued that knowledge of state and local courts might be even more important than federal ones. While this overall lack of knowledge is unfortunate, it is even more unfortunate when discussing the judiciary because many Americans are more likely to deal with the judicial branch than either the legislative or executive. These are the courts most Americans are likely to have interactions with, as they deal with the majority of cases that go through the American legal system.[4]

Because of their importance and prevalence in citizens' lives, it is incumbent upon court systems throughout the United States to reach out to the public so the people can garner a better understanding of the courts and what they do. In addition, such activities give the judiciary an opportunity to counteract the often more negative experiences some citizens have in the courts. Finally the need for such civic education and community outreach programs is amplified by the fact the courts need public support in order to maintain their funding from the elected branches. The greater the judiciary's approval by the public, the less likely the branch is to draw the ire of the other branches which face that public periodically in elections. Thus, such programs are increasingly common.

Although now working outside of the court system, former United States Supreme Court Justice Sandra Day O'Connor and others have championed outreach efforts such as iCivics. iCivics is a program that emphasizes activities through interactive games for young people to learn about government. They also provide teachers with lesson plans that facilitate learning. The goal of iCivics is to use the Internet to get young people more aware of how the United States government functions. iCivics has, according to a number of papers, been successful in getting young people more interested in civic education.[5] While iCivics and similar programs may not be perfect, this is the kind of step that could be a template for the courts.

This chapter will highlight the ways that certain local and state court systems throughout the United States have tried to reach out to their community through programs and civic education projects. This is important because most interactions Americans have with government is through the state and local court system, not the federal courts. This should be done even though the courts have historically been passive and reluctant to reach out to the community. While courts do not (and should not) solicit cases (as they only get involved in cases that appear on their docket), this is not and should not be an excuse for avoiding civic education/community outreach programs.

As an overview, first this chapter will take a look at how prevalent it is for state courts, particularly courts of last resorts, to offer community outreach/ civic education programs by examinations of their websites. In addition, there will be a look at how interactive and accessible for the public these courts are by examining their use of social media. Following this, the focus will turn to a case study of three courts—the Arkansas Supreme Court, Michigan Supreme Court, and New York City Civil Court.

PREVIOUS WORK

As Rogers documents (see chapter 1), civic education has been a concern since the founding and again was a major focus of John Dewey and the Progressives early in the twentieth century. In fact, throughout our history many Americans have argued civic literacy and engagement are essential for the continuance of democracy.[6] Today, civic education continues to be a concern of many scholars; some even fear that civic knowledge has declined in the United States over the past fifty years.[7] Robert Putnam may be the most preeminent scholar advocating such claims. He has decried the lack of civic engagement and knowledge in his analysis of the decline of social capital over the last half century.[8] According to Putnam (and others), this is a serious problem that many believe must be rectified before it gets even worse. The extensive social capital literature suggests institutions throughout American society, including schools and government, can fight back against this decline in civic literacy and engagement. While not all scholars agree there is a decline in civic literacy and/or civic engagement, we need to consider that one way to possibly fix any decline is for the courts to act on their own and initiate community outreach and civic education projects.[9]

The academic research on civic education and community outreach programs of courts is not too prolific. The courts seem to have embarked only recently on such projects.[10] For one, previous work has pointed out that these community outreach/civic education efforts are not a luxury but in reality are a very important part of the mission of courts.[11] In fact, court-community communication, which includes civic education, is considered to be one of the ten core competencies of court management.[12] Thus, for the past decade or so there has been a great increase in the number of interactions between court personnel and the community, often done not just to educate the community but to also protect the independence of the judiciary from interference by other branches.[13]

Also, from this literature one can deduce a model best practice for courts to follow when undertaking such activities. First, previous work points out that when conducting this outreach, court personnel must be careful not to comment on pending litigation that they may soon face. This would be an ethical violation and could damage the legitimacy of the courts.[14] Despite such dangers, this does not excuse courts from ignoring community outreach and civic education efforts. Judges and other court personnel are intelligent people and should be able to figure out ways to talk about the courts and their basic functions without commenting on or interfering with pending litigation.

Second, the literature recommends those in the courts be sure that their messages are relevant and audience appropriate.[15] In other words, the message and the topics for an elementary school class should not be the same as the one for people who are residing in a senior center. In addition, certain court services might be more applicable for people of certain ages. For instance, it would make more sense to talk to high school students about the dangers of getting into the juvenile justice system as opposed to a group of adults who are much less likely to deal with this facet of the courts. On the other hand, it would make more sense to talk to older people than to a school-age group about how the courts handle last wills and testaments.

This chapter will build off this previous research and suggest a new avenue for additional research. Thus, this work represents an exploratory first step down this avenue. More study of the courts' civic education and community outreach activities is needed, especially in effectiveness. It will emphasize that judicial education efforts are not just good for citizens who learn more about the functions of the courts, but such activities are also good for the courts themselves, as ways to enhance their popularity and protect their funding. More importantly, this analysis will show such activities take a variety of forms and are easily adaptable to local goals and desires of a court.

METHODOLOGY

Before diving into the data and analysis, it is necessary to lay out the parameters of this study. This is an exploratory analysis of courts and their civic education and community outreach activities. It is a two-part analysis that provides: (1) a survey of civic education and community outreach activities for the fifty state courts (particularly the courts of last resort), plus (2) a more in-depth case study of two state courts (the Arkansas and Michigan Supreme Courts) and one local court (the New York City Civil Court).

First, this work provides an investigation of how common community outreach and civic education efforts are nationwide. This is done by looking at the court websites for all fifty states. More specifically, the websites of courts of last resort (which in most states are called Supreme Courts) are examined followed by a similar analysis of the main websites of the fifty states. The analysis of this section is broken into three components. The core examination is an analysis of the prevalence of community outreach and/or civic education programs by documenting how many of these state court websites mentioned such activities. This required an examination of the websites for all fifty courts of last resort, which was done as of August 15, 2014. If the website discussed community outreach and/or civic education activities or programs, then it was counted as a proactive civic education/engagement court. If it did not have any programs or activities listed, it was counted as being a passive civic education/engagement court. Website tabs and links that were considered to be proactive included titles or phrases like "For the Public," "School and Community Outreach," "Public Resources," etc. The results of this analysis are presented in table 8.1 and mapped in figure 8.1.

To avoid underreporting proactive state court systems, this analysis was repeated for the fifty state court websites. This was done because it was found that some courts of last resort were involved in civic education and/or community outreach programs, but only reported them on the state court website. Replicating the process for courts of last resort, state court websites were coded active and passive based on whether they listed programs of civic education and/or community outreach in the same manner that the courts of last resort were examined. This data is presented in table 8.2. and mapped in figure 8.2

Additionally, this section provides an investigation of any possible correlation between whether the court is elected or appointed and the adoption of civic education or community engagement activities. The expectation is that if the judges are elected (whether through partisan elections, nonpartisan elections, or the Missouri Plan),[16] they will be more likely to undertake these activities. Conversely, if the judges are appointed, one would expect that they will feel less of a need to undertake these activities as they have no reelection incentive. Thus, the coded data from the initial analysis of the websites from the fifty courts of last resort are analyzed based on the mode of selection. Using the American Judicature Society website's classifications, states were categorized by their selection mode. The only difficult state to categorize was Michigan. Michigan has a hybrid system where party leaders nominate and support candidates but their party label is not listed on the ballot. For the purposes of this survey, Michigan is classified as nonpartisan. Given the poor civic literacy of voters as documented earlier, one can intuit most voters probably do not know which party the judicial candidate belongs to, so nonpartisan seems appropriate. While others might argue it should be in its own category or even included with the partisan states since party leaders play a role in the selection process, here Michigan is classified as nonpartisan. The results of this analysis are presented in table 8.3.

For the third component of this analysis, the prevalence of the use of social media by courts of last resort is examined. The question driving this analysis is how accessible is the website given the development of new technologies such as Facebook, Twitter, Flickr, and YouTube. While this does not specifically speak to whether the court has civic education/engagement programs, it will suggest whether or not the court is trying to promote interaction with the community, particularly for youth who are most likely to use social media. For this analysis, again the websites for all fifty courts of last resort were examined as of August 15, 2014. If the court website used the social media listed above, then it was coded as easily accessible and interactive. If the court did not maintain such websites, then it was coded as not readily accessible or interactive. This information is presented in table 8.4.

In the second half of this chapter, a more in-depth discussion of the activities of three courts, two state supreme courts and one local court, is provided. These three courts were selected because they are located in different regions of the United States. Arkansas is in the South, Michigan in the Midwest, and New York City is in the Northeast. They are also diverse in terms of their population and geography with Arkansas being a largely homogeneous state of about three million residents and very rural. Michigan is a mid-sized state with a more heterogeneous population of almost nine million people and largely industrial. New York City is the largest urban area in the United States with a population of over eight million people. This is also one of the most diverse cities in the United States with individuals from just about every part of the nation and world. Thus, this part gives a sense of how a couple of state courts and a city court approach civic education and engagement programs.

Essentially, this chapter offers both a nationwide assessment along with a more in-depth glimpse of how a few courts provide community outreach and civic education. Thus, the first half of this chapter shows that civic education/community outreach is not just an isolated effort of a few courts but is—as Ruth McGregor argues—something taken seriously by numerous courts throughout the United States as part of their core responsibilities.[17] Then, in the second half of this chapter the case studies of Arkansas, Michigan, and New York City courts demonstrates such programs are readily adaptable to state and local needs and interests.

STATE COURTS AND CIVIC EDUCATION/ COMMUNITY OUTREACH PROGRAMS

To see the prevalence of civic education and community outreach programs, table 8.1 and figure 8.1 present the commonality of such activities on websites

Table 8.1. Proactive vs. Passive Courts of Last Resort

Proactive	26 (52%)	CA, DE, MD, MA, NY, RI, UT, VT, AK, FL, HI, IN, IA, KS, MO, MN, NE, WY, KY, NC, OR, MI, IL, LA, OH, WV
Passive	24 (48%)	CT, ME, NH, NJ, SC, VA, AZ, CO, OK, TN, AR, GA, ID, MS, MT, NV, ND, SD, WA, WI, AL, NM, PA, TX

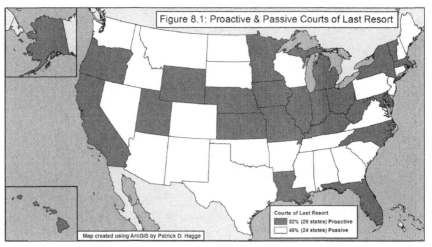

Figure 8.1.   Proactive and Passive Courts of Last Resort
Map created using ArcGIS by Patrick D. Hagge

of courts of last resort. It was found that slightly over half of state courts of last resort had a civic education/community outreach program. More specifically, twenty-six of the states had some sort of program clearly mentioned and easy to find on their website. Of course, on the other hand, that means twenty-four states did not have these programs on their court of last resort website (see figure 8.1).

Amongst the specific outreach programs implemented by the courts of last resort, the Hawaii Supreme Court probably does one of the best, if not the best, job. The Hawaii Supreme Court does this by having a tab devoted to community outreach that include sections on civic education and court tours. These tours can also include attending actual trials and/or other administrative buildings. Also included in the community outreach section is 'how-to' guides dealing with family issues including those involving divorces. The Hawaii Supreme Court also present citizens the chance to ask questions of judicial personnel including judges along with providing volunteer opportunities[18]

Other states which are proactive in their civic education/community outreach projects take a slightly different perspective than Hawaii combining their community outreach tab with education (see Oregon and Indiana). Additionally some states include their community outreach within their educational tabs (see Florida, Illinois, and Vermont). Then, states like Delaware and Alaska included this information on education and outreach within their general information tab on their Supreme Court websites. In Alaska's case there is even an entire website devoted to outreach programs that the court conducted in conjunction with educational institutions throughout the 2013–2014 academic year.[19]

Table 8.2.   Proactive vs. Passive State Court Systems

Proactive	34 (68%)	CA, DE, MD, MA, NY, RI, UT, VT, AK, FL, HI, IN, IA, KS, MO, MN, NE, WY, KY, NC, OR, MI, IL, LA, OH, WV, AR, CT, CO, MT, NV, SD, WA, WI
Passive	16 (32%)	ME, NH, NJ, SC, VA, AZ, OK, TN, GA, ID, MS, ND, AL, NM, PA, TX

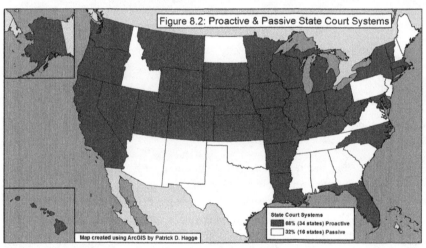

Figure 8.2.   Proactive and Passive State Court Systems
Map created using ArcGIS by Patrick D. Hagge

This, however, is not to say that civic education and community outreach are ignored by all the other twenty-four courts of last resort. Some just do not mention such activities on their court of last resort websites. A more thorough analysis shows a few courts of last resort list such activities on their state court websites as opposed to the court of last resort websites. For instance, Arkansas's Supreme Court (along with seven other states) does not list such activities on their website but do so on the Arkansas state court one. These states, while moving toward civic educational efforts, could probably do more to advertise these services to people not specifically, looking for them or at least add a link connecting them with their main court of last resort websites to make it easier to find. To fully document these activities, table 8.2 contains the results of an analysis of the fifty state court websites. Still, after a search of the fifty state court websites some states such as Georgia and Alabama do not mention any community outreach/civic education programs (see figure 8.2). From table 8.2, it is clear that over two-thirds (thirty-four) of the states have some mention of civic education/community outreach programs. Yet, this still slightly underreports court civic education and community outreach activities. For example, some states do not mention the civic education or community outreach programs its judges have done in conjunction with other governmental actors. For example, in the state of Oklahoma the chief justice took part in community outreach programs in conjunction with the Oklahoma Bar Association.[20] This highlights the fact that most court systems throughout the country do place an emphasis on civic education/community outreach, although some could do a better job of documenting such endeavors.

As a second stab at this data, one interesting question to ponder is whether or not judges who have to face the voters are more likely to have some sort of civic education/community outreach effort prominently mentioned on their website. This would make sense as elected judges have to campaign and worry more about the approval of the public than appointed judges. While probably not directly determining votes, programs in the area of civic education/community outreach can provide a reservoir of goodwill for judges on the court.

To investigate this, states whose judges are elected are compared with states whose judges appointed by the governor or state legislature to see if they were more likely to have some type of civic education/community outreach project on their websites. Those courts of last resort that face the voters are expected to have more civic education/community outreach programs on their websites than states where this is not the case, since such states need the public's support in order to win elections and stay in office.

As can be seen in Table 8.3, courts with the Missouri Plan or the hybrid approach of appointment then reelection are most likely to have civic education/community outreach projects with 77% (10 of 13) of those courts provid-

Table 8.3. Mode of Selection and Civic Education/Community Outreach Activities

Partisan Election	Nonpartisan Election	Missouri Plan (Hybrid)	Appointment
4/8 (50%)	11/15 (73%)	10/13 (77%)	9/14 (64%)
IL, LA, OH, WV	AR, MN, MT, NV, SD, WA, WI, KY, NC, OR, MI	CO, AK, FL, HI, IN, IA, KS, MO, NE, WY	CT, CA, DE, MD, MA, NY, RI, UT, VT

The classification of states by selection mechanism is from the American Judicature Society (www.judicialselection.us/judicial_selection/methods/selection_of_judges.cfm?state=).

ing these types of programs. In states with nonpartisan elections about 73% (11 of 15) included a civic education/community outreach activities on their websites, while only 50% (4 of 8) of states with partisan elections were found to include such activities. As for appointed courts, it was found that 64% (9 of 14) included this information. The lowest percentage, though, came from courts with partisan elections. It was found that only 50% of them included a civic education/community outreach section. Thus, unexpectedly the lowest percentage came from states with partisan elections. Still, two of the three selection mechanisms with an election component are about 10% more likely to display such activities.

Generally speaking, the thirty-six state courts where the judges faced some type of election were slightly more likely to be active on their websites in the area of civic education/community outreach than in states where the judges did not face electoral consequences (69% or 25 of 36 versus 64% or 9 out of 14). However, it should be noted again that in courts were judges are elected by partisan means this number dropped dramatically. This could be because in these states judges rely on their party label in order to get elected instead of focusing on civic education and community outreach efforts.

Another way to investigate the courts' community outreach would be to see if state court systems are present on social media applications such as Twitter, Facebook, etc. The question is: Are courts encouraging community interaction and involvement through social media? Having a social media presence is definitely a way to reach out to citizens, especially younger people. It is also a mechanism promoting direct community feedback. Thus, a social media presence promotes both interaction with the community and accessibility by it.

As can be seen from table 8.4, state courts are much less likely to have a social media presence (again based on their court of last resort websites) compared with the executive and legislative branches from their states. This is to be expected since the executive and legislative branches tend to be much more political and more oriented to routine interaction with the public. Of the thirteen courts of last resort who had a social media presence on their website, twelve (or 92%) of them are justices who face the voters periodically. Thus, most states currently do not have a social media presence, but for those that do, they are all, except for one state, elected by the people through one form or another. In addition, unlike the findings earlier, states where judges are elected through partisan contests were just as, if not more, likely percentage-wise to use social media than were states were judges are selected by other means. Still, since less than 30% of courts of last resort nationwide have social media accounts, this may be an area that both elected and nonelected courts can explore to improve their interaction with and accessibility by the public. They are probably likely to do so, as a new generation which is more

Table 8.4. Court of Last Resort Websites Use of Social Media

Court Social Media Use	Frequency (percent)	Type of Court	Frequency (percent)	States
Use Social Media	13 (26%)	**Partisan**	3/8 (38%)	PA, WV, IL
		Nonpartisan	5/15 (33%)	MI, MT, KY, ID, WA
		MO Plan (Hybrid)	4/13 (31%)	IN, IA, HI, TN
		Appointment	1/14 (7%)	CT
Do Not Use Social Media	37 (74%)	**Partisan**	5/8 (62%)	AL, NM, TX, LA, OH
		Nonpartisan	10/15 (67%)	GA, MS, ND, AR, MN, NV, SD, WI, NC, OR
		MO Plan (Hybrid)	9/13 (69%)	AZ, OK, CO, AK, FL, KS, MO, NE, WY
		Appointment	13/14 (93%)	ME, NH, NJ, SC, VA, CA, DE, MD, MA, NY, RI, UT, VT

comfortable with social media enters the judicial ranks. Due to this it would not be surprising to see the number of state courts of last resort using social media at least double over the next five years.

Overall, whether judges are elected or not, a number of courts (but not all) are getting involved in these community outreach/civic education projects throughout the United States. This involvement is readily advertised through many of their websites. The use of social media by courts, however, is much less prevalent and an avenue many courts are likely to explore in the future.

CASE STUDY OF THREE COURTS

For the second half of this work, the focus is on how three specific courts are promoting civic education and/or community outreach. It will be noticed all three courts deal with issues of civic education and court outreach in one manner or another but through a variety of programs suited to their state or local interest.

Arkansas Courts

One court which vocalizes the logic for reaching out to the public through civic education/community outreach is the Arkansas Supreme Court. It should be noted, however, that for all of its interest in the subject, one cannot get to the community outreach page directly through its court of last resort (Supreme Court) website. Instead, an Internet user who wants to find out about these initiatives must go through the main judiciary web page. This makes Arkansas one of the eight states who have civic education/ community outreach programs on their state court website but not on their court of last resort website.

The story of community outreach/civic engagement in the Arkansas Supreme Court begins with Chief Justice James Hannah. In the fall of 2013, Chief Justice Hannah announced that the court was beginning a comprehensive public relations program to engage the community with the court system in a positive way. This effort began with a Judicial Branch Leadership Council developing plans to reach out toward the community through tours, educational presentations, and other activities.[21] More recently, Chief Justice Hannah has continued to speak out on this issues through his 2014 State of the Judiciary Address.[22]

If one is interested in Chief Justice Hannah's motives for such activities, they are two-fold. First, this outreach/educational effort was initiated in large part because the state has seen recent attacks on the independence of the judicial branch from the state legislature, especially as it related to the issue of tort reform. This occurred because the Arkansas Supreme Court struck down features of a bill on tort reform passed by the state legislature. This decision has led to calls by some elected officials in the state to take away powers from the judicial branch.[23] Chief Justice Hannah believes civic education/ community outreach programs are one very important way to gain support for the judiciary from the public, as voters can pressure their legislators to tone down their criticisms of the courts or even possibly encourage them to provide more funding for the courts.

In addition, Chief Justice Hannah seems personally concerned with civic, particularly judicial, illiteracy. Considering that many in the public do not understand the unique role that the judiciary plays in our separation of powers system, his concern seems well-founded.[24] The expectation is that once people know more about the courts they will be more likely to support the judiciary. Others, however might contend that public support for the judiciary comes from its neutrality and the fact that it does not have a very visible public profile. Despite such concerns, Hannah argues civic education/community outreach is not an optional effort. The judicial branch in Arkansas is doing this because it needs the trust and the confidence of the people in order to survive.[25] The importance placed on judicial outreach can even be seen when looking at the Arkansas Supreme Court's rules for their judges. Included in the rule on promoting confidence in the judiciary is a discussion on how judges should initiate and participate in community outreach activities in order to increase the public's confidence in the courts. Of course, this is combined with one caveat—not commenting on specific cases before the court.[26]

Thus, the Arkansas Supreme Court has launched a number of civic education/community outreach programs. Included in this outreach effort is a program that encourages students throughout the state to visit the state justice building. Likely most courts have a similar program, so this can be thought of as the baseline of civic education/community outreach programs. However, the Arkansas Courts take this a step further by going to where people live with programs like Appeals on Wheels. In this program, judges reach out and go to citizens throughout the state, not just where the court is located in Little Rock.[27] This can be important in a poor, rural state such as Arkansas where much of the population lives over an hour from Little Rock. It may be more difficult (but not impossible) to conduct programs such as field trips for school children from cities hours away.

The Arkansas courts provide an interesting template for court community outreach/civic education projects. It is clear that the courts and the individuals who make them up, particularly Chief Justice Hannah, realize outreach is not just something that should be done in the interest of citizens. It is also done in the interest of the courts to protect their funding sources from attack by other political actors and institutions. This self-preservation motive alone is reason enough for courts around the country to begin and/or expand such efforts. In the case of Arkansas, however, it will be interesting to see the direction the effort goes in the next few years when Hannah is no longer on the court.[28] Will it be a continuation and expansion of the programs discussed or will it be a step back away from these civic education/community outreach activities because it is his personal interest?

Michigan Courts

It is not just the Arkansas courts that have placed an emphasis on civic education and community outreach. The Michigan state court system, particularly its Supreme Court, has also instituted a number of programs related to this area. These programs include Constitution Day efforts on September 17, leading high school tours, juror appreciation days, and other activities, such as Law Day and Adoption Day.[29]

First of all, like Arkansas, the Michigan courts emphasize community visits throughout the state by court personnel. Judges normally based in Lansing (the state capitol) have hosted events for high school students in cities and towns throughout the state (such as Dearborn, Saginaw, and Auburn Hills). During these sessions high school students get a firsthand point of view of the issues faced by the Michigan Supreme Court, something to which they would otherwise not be exposed.[30]

Also, jury duty—while not specifically civic education/community outreach—is important to discuss. For one, this may be the only time average citizens interact with or experience the court system. Therefore, it is incumbent upon the courts to provide a positive experience in order to facilitate positive views about the judicial system from the public. Yet, court systems have become stricter in forcing jurors to report for duty since many people try to avoid it, considering that the pay can be quite low and people have to miss work.[31] There is, therefore, an incentive for court systems to find some ways to make jurors feel welcome as many do not want to be there. In Michigan, they go out of their way to make sure that jurors feel appreciated and know that they value their time. This is done through having an entire month dedicated to juror appreciation and an entire page on their website expressing their gratefulness for those who serve.[32] It would be interesting to see if other courts across the United States are so proactive in promoting jury duty.

Then, Michigan Courts actively promote Constitution Day, which is part of the nationwide effort to recognize and celebrate the United States Constitution by a number of civic institutions throughout the United States. This is required by a law that was passed in 2004 to publicize the signing of the Constitution by convention delegates on September 17.[33] The Michigan courts participate by providing an easily accessible website similar to iCivics that provide learning activities for students of different grade levels. It also includes links to other websites that may be helpful in promoting the understanding of the basics of the Constitution by young people.

Another program conducted by the Michigan Courts is that of Law Day. This is a national holiday held on May 1 since the 1950s when it was signed into law by President Eisenhower. It celebrates the rule of law in the United States and advertises how it contributes to our freedom as Americans. While programs that commemorate this occasion are often hosted by youth groups, bar associations, etc., the Michigan courts are unique for the courts themselves actively leading such programs.[34] To help with this celebration, the court has voluntarily taken it upon itself to provide historical contexts, legal definitions, lesson plans, and other information to help community organizations mark this day in a,n appropriate manner. This is really important to do considering that many people do not even know the day exists.[35]

An additional outreach project the Michigan Courts provide is Adoption Day. Adoption Day, which is observed by the Michigan Courts on the Tuesday before Thanksgiving, is when the courts perform a number of functions to assist people who have or are trying to adopt children. These include finalizing adoptions, holding parties, and providing other services for adopting families. This involves generally educating the public about the adoption process, which can often be costly and time-consuming.[36] While this program focuses on facilitating adoptions, it has the added benefit of showing citizens how helpful and caring the court system can be. Another benefit of this specific outreach effort is that it involves the courts working with and not against other governmental agencies, in this case the Michigan Department of Human Services and the Michigan Adoption Resource Exchange. This also more generally educates the citizens participating in the program about the court and its functions. In addition, the media attention from events such as these gives the public a positive image of the court system as a service provider, all of which likely facilitates an increase in the court's public approval.[37]

As can be seen, Michigan has been proactive to educate and inform the public, demonstrating the exceptional potential of the courts as community service providers about how the judiciary plays an important role in the state constitutional system. In particular, the Michigan courts are uniquely proactive in providing programs like Constitution Day, Law Day, and Adoption Day which are typically left to schools, professional organizations, and other nonprofits to provide. This is in addition to the more routine activities of field trips to the courts or sending out court representatives into the community.

NEW YORK CITY CIVIL COURT

While the previous two examples focused on state courts, it is also important to look at a local court that is attempting to reach out and create closer ties with their community. The final court examined in terms of community engagement and civic education is located in New York City. Despite only being a city, New York City has a larger population than Arkansas and almost as large as that of Michigan.[38] This court is important to examine since it gives a different perspective, considering this is a local court.

The Civil Court is where New Yorkers go when dealing with everyday legal problems involving cases where the dollar amount is less than $25,000.[39] These may include landlord/tenant disputes or disagreements with merchants. Disputes such as these can be very important for those who are involved. Litigants and defendants would appreciate having an understanding court system to assist them through the process, along with knowing that they are being treated in a fair manner. One way to enhance such experiences for citizens is through civic education and community outreach projects.

One avenue the Civil Court uses, which is similar to Arkansas and Michigan, is that they have speakers who work in the court system (including judges) visiting community groups. Again, though, it is mentioned and strictly adhered to that court personnel should stick to making general points as opposed to speaking about specific cases that the court is facing or may face in the near future. This service is available to schools and other community organizations.[40]

As with the previous two courts already discussed, the New York City Civil Courts also provide tours for interested members of the public. This is important because it can give people, especially young people, a greater understanding of how the system works. It can also be valuable because it can expose people to possible career opportunities in the court system that they may have never thought of before. By educating these young people, they are more likely to become supporters of the court system and continue to be supportive of the courts as they reach adulthood.

Yet, the city courts combine these routine court activities with community seminars. These are conducted at the court once a month and are offered to provide residents with information on how to deal with situations that may arise in the courts. Another important feature of this program is that they make sure to advertise these seminars in a number of sources including fliers and newspapers so that community members are aware of these seminars.

Amongst the most pressing problems for city courts is hostility between some minority groups and the legal system in general. Considering that minority groups make up about two-thirds of New York City's overall population, outreach toward minority communities is very important for the Civil Court.[41] As the United States is by 2050 going to be a majority-minority nation, demographic changes toward a larger minority population in the United States will make it important for other courts throughout the country to replicate such efforts.[42] In the New York City Civil Courts, outreach to minority groups and others is done in part by what is known as Community Law Days. This program, similar to the one that was discussed in Michigan, involves court personnel reaching out to targeted groups such as those from minority groups and providing information about the court. In addition, the court provides food and sets up other activities to get the community involved. These types of court projects have been occurring in New York City for many years.[43]

Mediation Settlement Days are also offered by the courts. This allows for the general public to learn about the mediation process, which is important since in the last two decades there has been a move in courts away from the adversarial process and toward mediation.[44] This serves two purposes. One, it allows people to settle their disputes without having to resort to an adversarial process. It also frees up time for the courts to be involved with other projects and show that they are being wise stewards of taxpayers' money by saving on trial costs. This could be considered civic education since citizens are learning about ways to navigate the often complicated judicial system, highlighting the fact that not every judicial situation has to end up in a time-consuming and expensive trial.

As can be seen, the Civil Courts in New York City have many similarities with their counterparts in Arkansas and Michigan. All of them offer the routine programs of visiting the court or sending representatives of the court out into the communities. However, where the New York City Civil Court is unique is in its outreach targeting minority groups in particular.

PATTERNS IN THE CIVIC EDUCATION/COMMUNITY OUTREACH PROGRAMS OF COURTS

From this two-part investigation, it appears that civic education/community outreach efforts are not just a passing fad but something that is increasingly taken seriously by courts throughout the nation. Over half of the states throughout the country have such initiatives in their state courts of last resort, and over two-thirds mention civic education/community outreach programs on their state court websites. That said, specific examination of the civic education/community outreach programs in three diverse jurisdictions (Arkansas, Michigan, and New York City) has shown that, while these programs share some key similarities, there are also significant differences based on state and local interests and needs.

Similarities in all three of these courts include educational tours of their facilities for school groups throughout their jurisdictions. This type of outreach is a two-way street since all three of these courts not only invite people to them, but today they have projects by which court personnel leave the courtroom and visit people within their communities. Another similarity between these court systems is the targeting of specific days for civic education and/or community outreach. Some days, like Constitution Day or Law Day (Michigan), were instituted by the national government, and courts have voluntarily chosen to develop programs to honor them. Other days have been created by the individual courts themselves, such as Adoption Day (Michigan) and Mediation Settlement Day or Community Law Days (New York City). Such court activities provide a reoccurring date on the calendar every year that focuses attention on civic education/community outreach periodically. However these efforts are isolated to said dates.

While all three of the courts discussed have these similarities, they also provide civic education/community outreach that is unique to their locality. This is not to be a negative since not all jurisdictions are the same. Civic education/community outreach programs that may be perfect for one place may be woefully miscast in another. For instance, the New York City Civil Courts may be able to conduct more outreach programs since they are more geographically compact. More importantly, given their larger minority population than their counterparts in Arkansas and Michigan, they also have a stronger minority emphasis in their programs. Of course, with immigration trends minority outreach may become a more important part of court projects throughout the country in the years ahead.

Then, one great feature of the federalist system of the United States is that states can create programs that get implemented by others once they are seen as successful. As it relates to the three courts that were discussed in this paper, programs emphasized by individual courts that could be replicated throughout the nation include the Michigan Courts highlighting their role in helping people to adopt children. The Michigan courts have also taken the lead in providing an interactive, technologically advanced programming by which young people can learn more about the judicial system.

Overall, the courts have reoriented their thinking by being less passive and more assertive in civic education/community outreach efforts. This is not natural since the courts by law are often in the position of being passive and waiting for cases to appear before them. This idea of civic education/community outreach also may be difficult for many judges since this is not an issue in their legal training. Despite these obstacles, this assertiveness needs to be put forward by the courts because there is probably not anyone (lawyers, ABA, or other interest groups) or any other branches of government (which may resent the courts for some of their decisions) who will try to improve the image of the courts if they themselves do not take the first step. As the courts become more proactive, they should also realize that the other branches of government do not have to be an enemy in the process. The courts can work with other government institutions on important civic education/outreach projects (as the Michigan Courts demonstrate with their Adoption Day program). Besides gaining public trust, this may gain the trust of the other parts of government and is likely to make the government work better.

Of course, in the future there needs to be new avenues opened in the civic engagement process. One way is through technology, namely the Internet. This can be helpful at engaging younger citizens. This youth outreach is obviously not just necessary for the courts but for all types of institutions inside and outside of government. This should include the use of social media that is becoming pervasive with people under the age of twenty-five. They often use mediums such as Facebook and Twitter to communicate and find out information about what is happening in the world. Already, as was documented, over ten state supreme courts have taken steps toward this throughout the nation. This is a number that is likely to and should grow in the future. As for now, however, more can be done in this area. This can be highlighted best when comparing the judicial against the state executive branches where forty-six states (92 percent) have a social media presence and state legislatures where twenty-one of these states (42 percent) have either a Twitter or Facebook presence for their State Senate and House websites to keep citizens up to date on what is taking place in those legislative chambers.[45]

More generally, there is a need for judicial scholars to empirically study and test the courts' civic education/community outreach programs. Then, this knowledge could be shared with other court systems in the United States to see what outreach/educational programs work as well as which ones do not so that they are not repeated. This could be done and has been done to some extent already but not by scholars. For example, there are mentions of certain programs throughout the states on the American Bar Association website and/or at the meetings at the federal level with the Judicial Conference of the United States, or at conferences sponsored by the American Bar Association or other like-minded groups which take place on a regular basis.[46]

Future work in this area over the next decade could look to see if the numbers of courts participating in civic education/community outreach programs has increased. This appears to be the case. From this analysis we know there is already a large number of states that get involved in such efforts. However, given the minimal literature on court civic education/community engagement, this needs to be more thoroughly investigated. Also, most would probably agree that social media use by the courts will increase significantly over the next decade, but if we do not see this, it means such activities are not becoming a part of what the judiciary does in the twenty-first century.

Other investigations could examine other courts beyond Arkansas, Michigan, and New York City to see if they have similar programs or if they differentiate the way they employ their civic education/community outreach efforts. On the other hand, though less likely, it may be found that other courts do not take these efforts seriously. It would be interesting for those studying the courts and/or civic education/community outreach to see where there are and are not similarities throughout the United States, as well as what does and does not work. Finally, work needs to be done to assess the effectiveness of such programs, particularly to see if such activities meet Chief Justice Hannah's (Arkansas) expectation of increased public approval of the institution.

CONCLUSION

Possibly the best and most important outcome of these civic education projects initiated by the judiciary are that they are a win-win for both the courts and society at large. These kind of projects are important for the courts because they help to build legitimacy and public support at a time when the courts are facing assaults from the other branches of government. These other government institutions have the ability to take away some of the powers of the courts along with controlling their continued funding. In addition, many of these civic education and community outreach programs empower people, increasing their civic literacy and even saving them time and money (by, for example, educating them on the use of mediation). In other words, this is not just an altruistic mission, though it has many altruistic features. It is essential for twenty-first-century courts to maintain their authority and build their public approval.

In general, just as other civic education/community outreach efforts such as iCivics benefit society as a whole, such programs by courts help people to better understand government, as well as why having an independent judiciary is worthwhile. It is also incumbent upon the people who run the court systems in the United States at all levels to get this message of the importance of the American judiciary out to the public. This should be an effort that everyone in the judicial system rallies around in order for the judicial branch to legitimate and enhance its role in the American political system.

NOTES

1. Jeffrey Jones, "Americans' Trust in Government Generally Down This Year," *Gallup,* September 26, 2013.

2. Chris Cillizza, "The Most Amazing Supreme Court Chart Ever," *Washington Post,* June 28, 2012.

3. Chris Good, "Just 43% Know That Boehner Is Speaker," *The Atlantic,* April 1, 2011.

4. Sara Benesh and Wendy Martinek, "Lower Court Compliance with Precedent," in Kevin McGuire, ed., *New Directions in Judicial Politics* (New York: Routledge, 2012).

5. Karon LeCompte, Brandon Moore, and Brooke Blevins, "The Impact of iCivics on Students' Core Civic Knowledge," *Research in the Schools* 18, no. 2 (2011): 57–73; Kei Kawashima-Ginsberg, "CIRCLE Working Paper #76: Summary of Findings From the Evaluation of iCivics Drafting Board Intervention," The Center for Information & Research on Civic Learning and Engagement, http://www.civicyouth .org/wp-content/uploads/2012/12/WP_76_KawashimaGinsberg.pdf, 2012.

6. Thomas Ehrlich, "Civic Education: Lessons Learned," *PS: Political Science and Politics* 32, no. 2 (1999): 245–50.

7. See, for example: Richard Niemi and Jane Junn, *Civic Education: What Makes Students Learn* (New Haven: Yale University Press, 1998); Laura McNabb, "Civic

Outreach Programs: Common Models, Shared Challenges and Strategic Recommendations" *Denver University Law Review* 90, no. 4 (2013): 871–900.

8. Robert Putnam. "Bowling Alone: America's Declining Social Capital," *Journal of Democracy* 6, no. 1 (1995): 65–78.

9. For scholarship that questions the decline in civic literacy, see Michael Delli Carpini and Scott Keeter, *What Americans Know about Politics and Why it Matters* (New Haven: Yale University Press, 1996). Alternatively, for scholarship that questions the decline in civic engagement, see Theda Skocpol and Morris Fiorina, eds., *Civic Engagement in American Democracy* (Washington, DC: Brookings Institution Press, 1999)

10. John Sweeney et al., "Courts Connecting with Their Communities: Judicial Outreach Comes of Age," in Gordon Griller et al., eds., *Improvement of the Administration of Justice* (Chicago: American Bar Association, 2002).

11. Sweeney et al., "Courts Connecting with Their Communities."

12. Roger Hartley and Kevin Bates, "Meeting The Challenge of Educating Court Managers," *Judicature* 90, no. 2 (2006): 81–88.

13. McGregor, "State Courts and Judicial Outreach."

14. Ronald D. Rotunda, "Judicial Comments on Pending Cases: The Ethical Restrictions and the Sanctions—A Case Study of the Microsoft Litigation," *University of Illinois Law Review* (2001): 611.

15. Sweeney et al., "Court Connecting With Their Communities: Judicial Outreach Comes of Age."

16. The Missouri Plan is a hybrid form of judicial selection that includes initial political appointments with retention elections for judges.

17. McGregor, "State Courts and Judicial Outreach."

18. Hawaii Supreme Court, "Community Outreach," Hawaii Courts, http://www.courts.state.hi.us/outreach/community_outreach.html

19. Alaska Supreme Court, "General Information," Alaska Courts, http://www.courts.alaska.gov/outreach.htm.

20. Oklahoma Bar Association, "Law Day 2013: Annual Celebration to Highlight Equality," http://www.okbar.org/news/Recent/2013/LawDayCelebration.aspx.

21. Roby Brock, "Justice Hannah Notes Threat to Judicial System," *The City Wire,* June 17, 2013.

22. James Hannah, "State of the Judiciary," *Friends of the Court,* June 13, 2014.

23. Rob Moritz, "Lawmakers Struggle With Tort Reform," *Arkansas News,* April 15, 2013.

24. Ibid.

25. John Lyon, "Chief Justice: Public Understanding of Judicial Branch Lacking," *Arkansas News,* June 30, 2013.

26. Arkansas Supreme Court, *Judicial Rules* (Little Rock, AR, 2014).

27. Ibid.

28. It should be noted, though, that Hannah's term as chief justice ends in 2016 and may have to give up his pension to run again. See Max Brantley "Arkansas Supreme Court: Another Sign of Fracturing," *Arkansas Times,* August 13, 2014.

29. Michigan Supreme Court, "Community Outreach," Michigan Courts, http://courts.mi.gov/courts/michigansupremecourt/publicinfooffice/publicoutreach/pages/default.aspx.

30. Michigan Supreme Court, "Community Outreach."

31. Casey Mulligan, "Just Compensation for Jurors," *New York Times,* January 22, 2014.

32. Michigan Supreme Court, "Community Outreach."

33. Valerie Strauss and Lori Aratani, "Law Requires Lessons on the Constitution," *Washington Post,* July 19, 2005.

34. Mark Cohen, ed., *2013 Law Day Planning Guide.* American Bar Association.

35. Ibid.

36. Ibid.

37. Peg McNichol, "Families Welcome Children on Adoption Day," *Holland Sentinel,* November 27, 2013.

38. Sam Roberts, "Slower Racial Change Found in Census of City," *New York Times,* July 28, 2011.

39. New York City Civil Courts, "Community Outreach," NYCourts.gov, http://www.nycourts.gov/COURTS/nyc/civil/outreach.shtml.

40. Ibid.

41. Sam Roberts, "Slower Racial Change Found in Census of City."

42. Jeffrey S. Passel and D'Vera Cohn, "U.S. Population Projections: 2005–2050," *Pew Research Center,* February 11, 2008.

43. Greg Berman and David Andersen, *Drugs, Courts and Neighborhoods: Community Reintegration and the Brooklyn Treatment Court* (New York: Center for Court Innovation, 1999), http://www.courtinnovation.org/pdf/drugs_courts_neighborhoods.pdf.

44. Louraine Arkfield and John Greco, "Rethinking Limited Jurisdiction: What Are They, and What Must They Do to Improve," in Gordon Griller et al., eds., *Improvement of the Administration of Justice (*Chicago: American Bar Association, 2002).

45. This is based on data I collected from state legislative and executive websites as of August 15, 2014.

46. American Bar Association, "Judicial Outreach Resource Center," American Bar Association, http://www.americanbar.org/groups/judicial/committees/judicial_outreach_network/judicial_outreach_resource_center.html.

BIBLIOGRAPHY

Alaska Supreme Court. "General Information." Alaska Courts. http://www.courts.alaska.gov/outreach.htm (accessed July 14, 2014).

American Bar Association. "Judicial Outreach Resource Center." American Bar Association, http://www.americanbar.org/groups/judicial/committees/judicial_out reach_network/judicial_outreach_resource_center.html (accessed July 14, 2014).

Arkansas Supreme Court. "Court Rules." Arkansas Judiciary. https://courts.arkansas.gov/rules-and-administrative-orders/court-rules (accessed January 25, 2014).

Arkfield, Louraine, and John Greco. "Rethinking Limited Jurisdiction: What Are They, and What Must They Do to Improve." In *Improvement of the Administration of Justice,* edited by Gordon Griller and E. Keith Stott and John Fallahay. Chicago: American Bar Association, 2002.

Benesh, Sara, and Wendy Martinek. "Lower Court Compliance with Precedent." In *New Directions in Judicial Politics,* edited by Kevin McGuire, p. 259–77. New York: Routledge, 2012.

Berman, Greg, and David Andersen. *Drugs, Courts and Neighborhoods: Community Reintegration and the Brooklyn Treatment Court.* New York: Center for Court Innovation, 1999. Available at http://www.courtinnovation.org/pdf/drugs_courts _neighborhoods.pdf (accessed February 7, 2014).

Brantley, Max. "Arkansas Supreme Court: Another Sign of Fracturing." *Arkansas Times,* August 13, 2014. http://www.arktimes.com/ArkansasBlog/archives/2014/08/13/ arkansas-supreme-court-another-sign-of-fracturing (accessed August 21, 2014).

Brock, Roby. "Justice Hannah Notes Threat to Judicial System." *The City Wire,* June 17, 2013. https://www.thecitywire.com/node/28279 (accessed February 7, 2014).

Cillizza, Chris. "The Most Amazing Supreme Court Chart Ever." *Washington Post,* June 28, 2012. http://www.washingtonpost.com/blogs/the-fix/post/what-people -dont-know-about-the-supreme-court--in-one-chart/2012/04/18/gIQA5w6gQT _blog.html (accessed January 26, 2014).

Cohen, Mark, ed. *2013 Law Day Planning Guide.* American Bar Association, 2013. http://www.americanbar.org/content/dam/aba/images/public_education/lawday -guide-2013.pdf (accessed July 8, 2014).

Delli Carpini, Michael, and Scott Keeter. *What Americans Know about Politics and Why It Matters.* New Haven, CT: Yale University Press, 1996.

Ehrlich, Thomas. "Civic Education: Lessons Learned." *PS: Political Science and Politics* 32, no. 2 (1999): 245–50.

Gladwell, Malcolm. *David and Goliath: Underdogs, Misfits and the Art of Battling Giants.* New York: Little, Brown and Company, 2013.

Good, Chris. "Just 43% Know That Boehner Is Speaker." *The Atlantic,* April 1, 2011. http://www.theatlantic.com/politics/archive/2011/04/just-43-know-boehner -is-speaker/73341 (accessed February 7, 2014).

Hannah, James. "State of the Judiciary." *Friends of the Court,* June 13, 2014.

Hartley, Roger, and Kevin Bates. "Meeting the Challenge of Educating Court Managers," *Judicature* 90, no. 2 (2006): 81–88

Hawaii Supreme Court. "Community Outreach." Hawaii Courts. http://www.courts .state.hi.us/outreach/community_outreach.html (accessed July 14, 2014).

Hibbing, John, and Elizabeth Theiss-Morse. *Congress As Public Enemy.* Cambridge, Cambridge University Press, 1995.

Jones, Jeffrey M. 2013. "Americans' Trust in Government Generally Down This Year." *Gallup.* September 26, 2013. http://www.gallup.com/poll/164663/americans -trust-government-generally-down-year.aspx (accessed July 14, 2014).

Kawashima-Ginsberg, Kei. "CIRCLE Working Paper #76: Summary of Findings from the Evaluation of iCivics Drafting Board Intervention." The Center for Information

& Research on Civic Learning and Engagement, 2012. Available at http://www.civic
   youth.org/wpcontent/uploads/2012/12/WP_76_KawashimaGinsberg.pdf.

LeCompte, Karon, Brandon Moore, and Brooke Blevins. "The Impact of iCivics
   on Students' Core Civic Knowledge." *Research in the Schools* 18, no. 2 (2011):
   57–73.

Lyon, John. "Chief Justice: Public Understanding of Judicial Branch Lacking." *Arkansas News,* June 30, 2013. http://arkansasnews.com/sections/news/arkansas/chief
   -justice-public-understanding-judicial-branch-lacking.html (Accessed January 25,
   2014).

McGregor, Ruth. "State Courts and Judicial Outreach." *Daedalus* 137, no. 4 (2008):
   129–38.

McNabb, Laura. "Civic Outreach Programs: Common Models, Shared Challenges
   and Strategic Recommendations." *Denver University Law Review* 90, no. 4 (2013):
   871–900.

McNichol, Peg. "Families Welcome Children on Adoption Day." *Holland Sentinel,* November 27, 2013. http://www.hollandsentinel.com/article/20131127/
   NEWS/131129266/10924/NEWS?template=printart (accessed February 1, 2013).

Michigan Supreme Court. "Community Outreach." Michigan Courts. http://courts.
   mi.gov/courts/michigansupremecourt/publicinfooffice/publicoutreach/pages/de
   fault.aspx (accessed February 8, 2014).

Miroff, Bruce, Raymond Seidleman, Todd Swanstrom, and Tom DeLuca. *The Democratic Debate: American Politics in an Age of Change.* Stamford, CT: Cengage,
   2014

Moritz, Rob. "Lawmakers Struggle with Tort Reform," *Arkansas News,* April
   15, 2013. http://arkansasnews.com/sections/news/lawmakers-struggle-tort-reform
   .html (accessed July 8, 2014).

Mulligan, Casey. "Just Compensation for Jurors." *New York Times,* January 22, 2014.
   http://economix.blogs.nytimes.com/2014/01/22/just-compensation-for-jurors/
   ?_php=true&_type=blogs&_r=0 (accessed February 1, 2014).

New York City Civil Courts. "Community Outreach." NYCourts.gov. http://www
   .nycourts.gov/COURTS/nyc/civil/outreach.shtml (accessed February 8, 2014).

Niemi, Richard, and Jane Junn. *Civic Education: What Makes Students Learn.* New
   Haven: Yale University Press, 1998.

Oklahoma Bar Association. "Law Day 2013: Annual Celebration to Highlight Equality" http://www.okbar.org/news/Recent/2013/LawDayCelebration.aspx.

Pasek, Josh, Kate Kenski, Daniel Romer, and Katherine Hall Jamison. "America's
   Youth and Community Engagement: How Use of Mass Media Is Related to Civic
   Activity and Political Awareness in 14- to 22-Year Olds." *Communications Re-
   search* 33, no. 3 (2006): 115–35.

Passell, Jeffrey S., and D'Vera Cohn. "U.S Population Projections: 2005–2050." *Pew
   Research Center* February 11, 2008. http://www.pewhispanic.org/files/reports/85
   .pdf (accessed February 1, 2014).

Putnam, Robert. "Bowling Alone: America's Declining Social Capital." *Journal of
   Democracy* 6, no. 1 (1995): 65–78.

Roberts, Sam. "Slower Racial Change Found in Census of City." *New York Times,* July 28, 2011. http://www.nytimes.com/2011/07/29/nyregion/census-finds-slight -stabilizing-in-new-york-city-racial-makeup.html (accessed January 25, 2014).

Rotunda, Ronald D. "Judicial Comments on Pending Cases: The Ethical Restrictions and the Sanctions—A Case Study of the Microsoft Litigation." *University of Illinois Law Review* (2001): 611.

Skocpol, Theda, and Morris Fiorina. "Making Sense of the Civic Engagement Debate." In *Civic Engagement in American Democracy,* edited by Theda Skocpol and Morris Fiorina. Washington, DC: Brookings Institution, 1999.

Strauss, Valerie, and Lori Aratani. "Law Requires Lessons on the Constitution." *Washington Post,* July 19, 2005. http://www.washingtonpost.com/wp-dyn/content/article/2005/07/18/AR2005071801585.html (accessed February 7, 2014).

Sweeney, John, Richard Fruin, and Rebecca Fanning. "Courts Connecting with Their Communities: Judicial Outreach Comes of Age." In *Improvement of the Administration of Justice,* edited by Gordon Griller, E. Keith Stott, and John Fallahay. Chicago: American Bar Association, 2002.

Chapter Nine

The Civically Oriented Activities of Big City Mayors

The View from Website Press Releases

Michael A. Armato and Sally Friedman

Local institutions are to liberty what primary schools are to science; they put it within the people's reach; they teach people to appreciate its peaceful enjoyment and accustom them to make use of it. Without local institutions a nation may give itself a free government, but it has not got the spirit of liberty.

> —Alexis de Tocqueville, *Democracy in America*[1]

The office of mayor, like the presidency and the governorship, is an institution of many purposes, the object of many expectations from the city's citizens, officials, party leaders, bureaucrats, and interest groups, and the source of both rewards and frustrations for its incumbent.

> —Wallace Sayre and Herbert Kaufman,
> *Governing New York City; Politics in the Metropolis*

As a large body of literature (including work in this volume) demonstrates, declining levels of civic engagement are well documented.[2] These trends are concerning because they raise questions about the overall quality of the American democracy, specifically pointing to lower levels of citizen empowerment, narrower participation in decision making, and less confidence in the political system.

Since, as the Tocqueville quote above suggests, the character of civic engagement certainly begins at the local level, it makes sense to focus on activities in this arena as a starting point for understanding ways to enhance the vibrancy of our communities. Thus, recent scholarship identifies a variety of municipal efforts to expand the role of citizens and to assess factors that have the potential to impact the degree of citizen participation.[3] Largely overlooked in this literature has been cross-city comparisons of the efforts of specific public officials to encourage citizen engagement. As indicated by the quote from Sayre and Kaufman's influential work on New York City above, such officials have the potential to make a positive difference.

Using the nation's largest cities as the backdrop, this chapter provides an exploration of the role mayors play in encouraging civic engagement. Through a study of the headlines of website press releases of the mayors of twenty-six of the nation's largest cities (populations greater than 500,000) over the course of 2012, we examine the role of the mayor—whose executive powers, use of the bully pulpit, and ability to set the tone for the administration—could substantially impact the degree of citizen engagement.

Findings generally demonstrate that mayors are indeed using their press releases as a tool to involve citizens; they also indicate that these officials do a better job of encouraging general community-building activity than they do of motivating citizens to practice explicitly political participation. While this latter finding may not be surprising, we argue that an expansive definition of the term "civic engagement" allows us to better understand the ways such activities are promoted in large urban areas.

CIVIC ENGAGEMENT AND THE ROLE OF MAYORS

Since the pioneering work of Robert Putnam pointed scholars' attention toward significant declines in social capital, researchers have observed a concomitant decay of civic engagement.[4] As has been well documented across the academy and in essays throughout this volume, such deteriorations have been noted in diverse areas of political life including voting, campaign activity, and participation in interest groups.

These changes are no less striking at the level of municipal politics. Thus, the proportion of adults indicating they had "always" voted in local elections has declined from almost half (47 percent) in 1967 to just over a third of citizens (35 percent) in 1987.[5] These shifts have been particularly evident in urban centers featuring high concentrations of poverty.[6] Beyond voting, "between 1973 and 1994, the percentage of people attending a public meeting on town or school affairs declined from 22 to 12 percent."[7]

As modern-day participation in local politics has been waning, we also know that involvement in that arena is important. Thus, as long ago as the Anti-Federalists, a body of scholarship within the American political tradition has highlighted the importance of local level politics in fostering civic engagement and representation.[8] Accordingly, many scholars and practitioners alike look to the municipal level of government as a logical starting place to involve citizens. With over 90,000 municipalities in existence in 2012 and with over 96 percent of elected officials serving at this level, "cities and their surrounding localities provide a vast array of opportunities for civic engagement."[9] Additionally, the immediate impact of community problems on the citizenry, the closeness of the people to government, and the ability to tailor parochial forums to the needs of diverse environments point to the importance of local level communities as arenas for enhancing and motivating citizen involvement. Thus, the literature is replete with examples documenting a wide array of efforts in this domain of government to increase various forms of civic engagement.[10]

What of the role of mayors? The systematic study of the efforts of city chief executives to promote civic engagement has been largely ignored, but one does not have to delve deeply into the literature on urban politics to get the idea that, as the focal point for the public affairs of their municipalities, these chief executives are perfectly positioned to take the lead in encouraging their citizens to get involved. Mayors generally possess significant formal powers in terms of their level of control over a city's bureaucracy, budget, and legislative process.[11] Even more, they often play a key role in agenda setting and in establishing priorities for their communities. By virtue of their office, they enjoy considerable media attention, and in turn, they can focus citizen's attention on the areas they consider most important.

Finally, there is as well an important symbolic aspect to the activities of mayors. As is the case with the U.S. president, a mayor can serve as a beacon of unity. "The mayor and his office are the visible expression of the city, its personification as an organized community, its leading ceremonial figure on occasions of state."[12] In short, it is certainly the case that "in any major city, whoever holds the position of mayor can make a difference—in citizen mobilization, in policy innovation, in equity."[13]

Thus, case study evidence from the literature demonstrates that some mayors have in fact made a difference in the area of civic engagement.[14] But, what led these mayors to promote citizen involvement, and especially in the types of big cities under examination in this chapter, why should we expect mayors to use the prerogatives of their office to promote civic education and engagement? A complete answer to this question is beyond the scope of this chapter, but given that civic engagement has been on the front burner for so many academics and practitioners alike, it is logical to assume that mayors (especially of the nation's biggest cities) would either face some external pressure or simply feel the need to jump on the bandwagon. In this context, as is true for other political actors, individual mayors have policy goals, and for some promoting civic engagement might be of value.

In line with these possibilities, it is worth noting that the official organization of U.S. mayors—the U.S. Conference of Mayors—has recently provided some strong demonstration of their commitment to the promotion of civic engagement. According to their website, they describe themselves as "one of the nation's leading organizations dedicated to community building, civic engagement and the promotion of volunteerism."[15] To stress this, at the occasion of his swearing-in as head of the conference in 2012, Philadelphia's "Mayor Nutter also announced a new program through Bloomberg Philanthropies for mayors across the United States to encourage volunteerism in America."[16] Suggesting that this is a matter of personal as well as organizational importance, Mayor Nutter added: "'Civic engagement is one of America's greatest strengths. . . . We need to tap into this extraordinary resource—and I know many cities are doing just that,' explained Nutter when sharing the news with the mayors."[17]

Further, the noncontroversial nature of promoting civic engagement activities certainly allows mayors an opportunity to claim credit with citizens. At a time when so many of the issues they face are divisive and contentious, it would likely be in their interest to promote some good old-fashioned citizenship activities: reminding citizens to get out and vote, urging residents to contact them about a local problem, or even encouraging locals to participate in a city competition or parade. In the digital age, all that is involved in doing so comes down to asking a staff member to simply post a press release.

In addition, that same digital age which might make it easier for public officials to get the word out to citizens also has the potential to fundamentally transform and enhance a role for citizens themselves. For example, in his inaugural address as head of the U.S. Conference of Mayors—delivered as recently as June 20, 2014—Mayor Kevin Johnson of Sacramento put forth the concept to his fellow mayors that we are entering into a new era that he labeled as "Cities 3.0."[18] Describing this time as one where transactions are "paperless, wireless and cashless," he also highlighted the possibility for a more active and engaged role for citizens:

> In Cities 2.0, city crews would drive around looking for reported potholes to fill them. It could sometimes take weeks or months for a response. In Cities 3.0 here's what it would look like: That pothole on my street? I should be able to take a picture of it with my phone, and upload it through a city app that will tag it with its GPS location. Providers throughout the city could instantaneously be dispatched to fill the pothole on the same day. It's quicker, easier, and more efficient. And active, connected citizens become part of the city's network to solve problems.[19]

Additionally, though likely to be the case for some mayors more than others, a host of factors—electoral, cultural, and demographic—might point certain mayors in the direction of promoting civic engagement. Electoral incentives

(as well as disincentives) figure in as we clearly have examples in the literature where even small increases in voter turnout have the potential to change
an election outcome.[20] For example, perhaps mayors promote civic activities
in particular areas of a city in order to bolster their own electoral fortunes.
Similarly, scholars argue that cultural traditions impact a mayor's propensity
to engage citizens and that demographic characteristics of the cities themselves could affect the degree to which mayors promote civic involvement.[21]
In sum, a review of the literature demonstrates that mayors possess the powers and the platform to encourage citizen civic engagement and that many
have some incentives to do so.

DEFINING CIVIC ENGAGEMENT

As much as the phrase "civic engagement" has been discussed and debated
over the last several decades, it is important before we specify what we
count for purposes of this chapter as civic engagement to emphasize that
scholars offer numerous alternative conceptualizations of the term. Many
point to a political component, identifying a broad range of activities—
voter turnout, partisan and campaign activities, and the direct input of citizens in the policymaking process.[22]

Others frame civic engagement more broadly, employing the term to include the wide range of volunteer and service activities taking place in local
communities. Campbell, for example, distinguishes between political and
civic engagement. He identifies "political" participation efforts as those in
which citizens encourage the government to make or change public policy or
where they play a role in the choosing of government actors. He alternatively
defines "civic" participation as actions that "are not motivated by the desire
to affect public policy." To illustrate the dichotomy, he compares the participation of a hypothetical citizen campaigning for a candidate who vows to
change policies about homelessness (political activity) with the same resident
working at a soup kitchen to help a homeless person (civic activity).[23]

Similarly, in his broader study of citizenship, Dalton divides civically oriented activities into duty-based and engaged citizenship.[24] The activities he
considers to be duty-based include the explicitly political activities of voting
and belonging to a political party. Activities promoting engaged citizenship
include participation in voluntary associations and volunteer efforts. Thus,
building on the idea that civic engagement includes voluntary and service
opportunities, a host of scholars have identified participation in voluntary
organizations, religious entities, nonprofits, and neighborhood associations
as a hallmark of civic engagement.[25]

Finally, Putnam's 1995 article employs the broadest definition of all, defining "'civic engagement' to refer to people's connections with the life of their communities, not merely with politics."[26] Apparently, he (and others) interpret this idea of "connection with the life of the community" broadly as in *Bowling Alone* he observes:

> American Society, like the continent on which we live, is massive and polymorphous, and our civic engagement historically has come in many sizes and shapes. A few of us still share plowing chores with neighbors, while many more pitch in to wire classrooms to the Internet. Some of us run for Congress, and others join self-help groups. Some of us hang out at the local bar association and others at the local bar. Some of us attend mass once a day, while others struggle to remember holiday greetings once a year.[27]

In this spirit, Kent Portney introduces readers to what he labels the concept of community building. He defines this as "efforts aimed at promoting greater interpersonal interaction, greater participation in civic organizations, and, in short, fostering civil society."[28] As an example, he cites the goals of Seattle's sustainability program that attempts to incorporate residents into "community and neighborhood life," works toward residents "achieving a sense of belonging," and promotes "volunteerism and community service."[29]

The categories we develop below include all these aspects of civic engagement. We code mayor press releases for the extent to which they urge citizens to become involved in political and volunteer activities. In line with the broader net cast by Putnam and Portney, we also create a category of "community building" which concentrates on the aspect of Portney's definition geared toward "fostering civil society" to help residents feel connected and integrated into city life. For example, mayors asking citizens to attend a local parade, to go to an event, or to participate in an art contest we believe fall into Portney's definition of community building. All these instances help to foster community life, and therefore, we assert are building blocks of civic engagement if not actual civic engagement itself.

RESEARCH DESIGN

This chapter provides an examination of how big-city mayors encourage the civically oriented activities of their constituents. To what extent and in what kinds of ways do mayors solicit citizen involvement, and what kinds of factors explain variation in their efforts? To explore these questions, we conducted a content analysis of the press release headlines on the mayoral websites of twenty-six of thiryt-four of the nation's largest cities (populations greater than 500,000 people) for the year 2012. We describe our coding procedures below, but first we explain our focus on mayor press releases and our selection of specific cities for the analysis.

It is clear that mayors have considerable latitude when deciding in what venues and with what degree of effort they choose to promote citizen civic engagement. In-person contact, the use of a host of traditional and social media, and government websites are all obvious ways to spread the word. As well, mayors make choices as to what to delegate to their staffs, which (if any) specific groups should be targeted, and the level of intensity of any particular mobilization effort. In addition to the obvious value of providing a systematic source of data, the utility of examining website press releases as we do in this chapter has to do with their potential to get the word out to citizens. From the perspective of the mayor, the promotion of the presumably noncontroversial nature of civically oriented efforts provides an opportunity to publicize actions enhancing the possibility for public approval. This should be especially true in the case of the kinds of large cities under examination here where mayors can use their work in a noncontroversial area to counter their actions on presumably more divisive issues.

In addition, as hinted at above, for citizens it is a digital age, and technology has started to change the way people engage in civic activities.[30] As more and more people become virtually connected, it is increasingly likely that, perhaps even as a first point of entry, citizens will find out what government is doing through the information provided on official websites. Alternatively, as is seen from Evans in chapter 6 and Gelbman in chapter 11 of this volume, social media including Twitter provide another technological medium that politicians and constituents are utilizing for political information. Such information is, after all, just a smartphone or couple of mouse clicks away.

But, what about any disconnect between what mayors say they do and what they actually do? Recent scholarship on another set of elites, members of the U.S. Congress, has demonstrated a strong correlation between what legislators put forward on their websites and their actual legislative priorities.[31] This positive press release/priority relationship, at least for one group of politicians, builds our confidence that in the overall scheme of their activities, information on mayoral websites will be reflective of the things they most want to promote. That said, we speculate that the view from mayor press releases might nonetheless provide an overrepresentation of their civically oriented activities because the noncontroversial nature of these undertakings might make them efforts mayors particularly want to publicize.

So, why the focus on the nation's largest cities? We chose this group because quite simply, they are flagship cities. They are where most people live, their populations are diverse, and other localities look to them as models for what is possible in service provision. Even more, setting these large cities in the context of the fuller range of city size, we think that these areas represent a hard case as a test for civic engagement. For example, a Baltimore or a Philadelphia or a San Francisco may not represent the kind of small town New England model Tocqueville had in mind in the quote opening this chapter where he expressed that "local institutions are to liberty what primary schools are to science."[32] To the extent that this view is correct, if we find mayors encouraging civic engagement in these large cities, how much more likely might they be to do so in even smaller communities?

Specifically, according to the Weismann Center for International Business at Baruch College, in 2012 thirty-four U.S. cities had populations upwards of 500,000.[33] We collected press releases from websites of the mayors of the twenty-six cities where such information was available (table 9.3 includes a list of these cities and their mayors). We confined our data collection to only those press releases listed on what was explicitly labeled as the official mayor's page or where there was an indicator in a search engine that the press release came directly from the mayor's office, and we coded only the headline of each press release.[34]

As argued in the previous section of this chapter, we believe that encouraging participation in community activity in localities is as valuable for the fabric of democracy as is promoting explicitly political or volunteer engagement. Thus, as we explain our coding procedures (see table 9.1), we operationalize civic engagement to include all these aspects of involvement.

To examine citizen participation in the political arena, we adapted categories put forward by Macedo et al.[35] The authors classified aspects of local politics in terms of electorally oriented activities (voting, campaigning, and running for office) and those actions taking place between elections. The latter category was further broken down into three subcategories:

- encouraging citizen participation on any type of board, committee, neighborhood association, or council;
- soliciting citizen input or citizen deliberation as part of the process of making important city decisions;
- encouraging citizen coproduction of services; processes whereby citizens are asked to become "active participants in the *production* of" city services such as promoting public safety and security.[36]

As specified above, we also coded press release headlines for the extent that they encouraged community building activities outside of the political arena, creating three subcategories. Thus, in line with the host of scholars pointing to the importance of volunteer activities, the first of these categories coded the extent to which mayors were asking citizens to engage in some kind of service within their communities. Second, following Putnam and Portney, we found it useful to code the extent to which mayors encourage citizens to take part in more general community-building activities. These include participation in local events, celebrations, and contests. Also, because references to the digital age kept showing up in our analysis, we coded press releases for the extent to which mayors were promoting new "tools," generally new Internet resources, designed to make city services more accessible.

In sum, we coded for mayor encouragement in the following categories:

Table 9.1. Explanation of Coding

Political	
Elections	Voting, campaigning, and running for office
Nominations for Local Boards	Encouraging citizen participation on any type of board, committee, neighborhood association, or council
Citizen Input/Deliberation	Soliciting citizen-input or citizen-deliberation as part of the process of making important city decisions
Citizen Coproduction of Services	Encouraging citizen coproduction of services; processes whereby citizens are asked to become involved in the implementation of city services such as promoting public safety and security
Community	
Volunteering	Service within the community
Civic Tool	Instruments, generally new Internet resources, designed to make city services more accessible
Community Building	Participation in community events, celebrations, or contests

Lastly, we note that while it was easy to sort press releases as to whether they pointed to either of our broad categories of political or community engagement, in approximately 5 percent of our cases, we engaged in discussion and collaborated to decide which of the particular political or community-oriented categories a press release fits.

DO BIG CITY MAYOR PRESS RELEASES ENCOURAGE CIVIC ENGAGEMENT?

Tables 9.2–9.6 furnish readers with an overview of the extent to which mayor press releases encourage political and community-oriented engagement. Of the

**Table 9.2. Mayoral Encouragement of Civic Engagement
(Website Press Release Headlines)**

Mayoral Encouragement of Civic Engagement (Website Press Release Headlines)	Number of Civic Engagement Press Releases by Category	Percent of All Press Releases Including Civic Engagement	Percent of Civic Engagement Press Releases by Category
Political	265	7.1%	30.1%
Elections	10	0.3%	1.10%
Nominations For Local Boards	21	0.6%	2.40%
Citizen Input/Deliberation	96	2.6%	10.90%
Citizen Coproduction of Services	138	3.7%	15.70%
Community	615	16.6%	69.89%
Volunteering	96	2.6%	10.90%
Civic Tool	101	2.7%	11.50%
Community Building	418	11.3%	47.50%
Totals	880	23.7% (N=3,714)	100% (N=880)

3,714 press releases coded, 265 (7.1%) asked citizens to get involved directly in some form of political activity, and another 615 (16.6 %) promoted participation in the community (see table 9.2). Fully 880 of the 3,714 press releases (23.7%) reference some kind of civic engagement activity. While we lack a baseline for comparison, given the many demands on the time and energy of big city mayors and the many urban and suburban problems these mayors face on a daily basis, these figures provide a preliminary indication that, in the aggregate, mayors are indeed promoting civic engagement activities.

But what kind of activities are they promulgating, and which mayors are encouraging involvement? Tables 9.2, 9.3, and 9.4 make clear that promoting general community-building sorts of activities is notably more likely than asking citizens to become active in a political context, accounting for almost three-quarters of the civic engagement content on these websites. Of the additional press releases that did feature political content, it is worth noting that the most frequent category of engagement found in this data is coproduction (15.7% of press releases that encourage civic engagement). Coproduction involves people in the provision of government services only to the extent of asking citizens to be vigilant about things relevant to their daily lives (e.g. reminding them to obey traffic or fire safety regulations or asking them to look out for the safety of their neighborhood and neighbors). To follow through, citizens need not venture particularly far out of their ordinary routines.

Mayors also ask citizens to participate more directly in the political process. Almost 11% of press releases that encourage civic engagement (ninety-six in total) solicit political input, and only thirty-one press releases deal with electoral participation or the solicitation of nominations to government boards and commissions (see table 9.2).

In terms of community-building activities themselves, in the aggregate, volunteering is a staple of community engagement, accounting for 10.9% of all the civically oriented press releases. Our tools category accounts for another 11.5%. By far the largest percentage (47.5%) of civically oriented press releases fall into the category of general community building (see Table 9.2).

Table 9.3 arranges these cities in terms of the propensity of their mayors to solicit citizen involvement. The table provides confirmation of the overall patterns, and it also demonstrates variation in the extent to which big city mayors encourage their citizens to take part. In fourteen of the twenty-six cities, or over half, the percent of press releases we coded for civic engagement was above the 23.7% average; several cities were within a few percentage points

Table 9.3.   Civic-Engagement-Oriented Press Releases by Mayor and City

City	Mayor	Total # of Press Releases	# of Press Releases Encouraging CE	% of Press Releases Encouraging CE
Las Vegas, NV	Carolyn G. Goodman	9	9	100.0%
Fort Worth, TX	Betsy Price	57	34	59.6%
Louisville, KY	Greg Fischer	79	43	54.4%
Boston, MA	Thomas Menino	341	135	39.6%
Detroit, MI	David Bing	167	61	36.5%
Charlotte, NC	Anthony Foxx	14	5	35.7%
Nashville, TN	Karl Dean	64	19	29.7%
Philadelphia, PA	Michael Nutter	325	96	29.5%
Indianapolis, IN	Gregory A. Ballard	59	16	27.1%
Milwaukee, WI	Thomas Barrett	16	4	25.0%
Columbus, OH	Michael Coleman	33	8	24.2%
Denver, CO	Michael B. Hancock	125	30	24.0%
Albuquerque, NM	Richard J. Berry	130	31	23.8%
Phoenix, AZ	Greg Stanton	101	24	23.8%
Jacksonville, FL	Alvin Brown	102	24	23.5%
Los Angeles, CA	Antonio Villaraigosa	120	28	23.3%
Seattle, WA	Michael McGinn	181	38	21.0%
Portland, OR	Sam Adams	11	2	18.2%
Houston, TX	Annise Parker	89	16	18.0%
Chicago, IL	Rahm Emanuel	410	72	17.6%
Washington, DC	Vincent Gray	411	69	16.8%
San Francisco, CA	Edwin Lee	224	35	15.6%
San Diego, CA	Jerry R. Sanders	46	7	15.2%
New York, NY	Michael R. Bloomberg	428	57	13.3%
Baltimore, MD	Stephanie Rawlings-Blake	154	17	11.0%
San Jose, CA	Charles R. Reed	18	0	0.0%
TOTAL/*AVE*		**26**	**3714**	**880**	**23.7%**

below that mark, and a few exhibited notably higher rates. For example, of the twenty-one mayors that published more than thirty press releases, four encouraged civic engagement over one-third of the time, including Mayors Price (Fort Worth, 60%), Fischer (Louisville, 55%), Menino (Boston, 40%), and Bing (Detroit, 37%). At the other extreme, Mayors Rawlings-Blake (Baltimore) and Bloomberg (New York City) called for citizen involvement in just 11 and 13 percent of press releases respectively.

As was true in the aggregate, mayors in individual cities are more likely to encourage general community building rather than direct political involvement (table 9.4). Thus, in eighteen of the twenty-five cities featuring press releases encouraging civic engagement, the balance of soliciting community building over explicitly political activity was above the three-quarter mark. Conversely, in only seven cities (Fort Worth, Detroit, Philadelphia, Milwaukee, Columbus, Seattle, Portland) the balance was closer, in some cases even constituting a fifty–fifty split.

These findings are displayed graphically in figure 9.1. The map provides a visual description of the percentages of community and politically oriented press releases by city, as well as the percent of press releases not related to citizen engagement (all other releases).

Finally, tables 9.5 and 9.6 provide an even more detailed breakdown of the types of civic engagement activities these mayors encourage. Ranking cities from highest to lowest in terms of the propensity of their mayors to publicize directly political engagement, Table 9.5 shows the mix of activities these mayors promote. Table 9.6 provides a similar breakdown of the community engagement category.

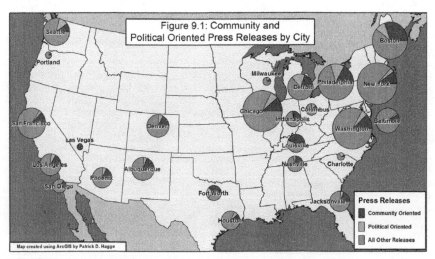

Figure 9.1.   Community and Political Oriented Press Releases by City
Map created using ArcGIS by Patrick D. Hagge

Table 9.4. Percentage of Civic Engagement (CE) Press Releases That Are Political versus Community Oriented by Mayor and City

City	Mayor	# of Press Releases Encouraging CE	# of CE Oriented Press Releases Coded Political	% of CE Press Releases Coded Political	# of CE Press Releases Coded Community	% of CE Press Releases Coded Community
Las Vegas, NV	Carolyn G. Goodman	9	1	11.1%	8	88.9%
Fort Worth, TX	Betsy Price	34	13	38.2%	21	61.8%
Louisville, KY	Greg Fischer	43	8	18.6%	35	81.4%
Boston, MA	Thomas Menino	135	31	23.0%	104	77.0%
Detroit, MI	David Bing	61	29	47.5%	32	52.5%
Charlotte, NC	Anthony Foxx	5	4	80.0%	1	20.0%
Nashville, TN	Karl Dean	19	4	21.1%	15	78.9%
Philadelphia, PA	Michael Nutter	96	40	41.7%	56	58.3%
Indianapolis, IN	Gregory A. Ballard	16	1	6.3%	15	93.8%
Milwaukee, WI	Thomas Barrett	4	2	50.0%	2	50.0%
Columbus, OH	Michael Coleman	8	4	50.0%	4	50.0%
Denver, CO	Michael B. Hancock	30	8	26.7%	22	73.3%
Albuquerque, NM	Richard J. Berry	31	6	19.4%	25	80.6%
Phoenix, AZ	Greg Stanton	24	6	25.0%	18	75.0%
Jacksonville, FL	Alvin Brown	24	5	20.8%	19	79.2%
Los Angeles, CA	Antonio Villaraigosa	28	8	28.6%	20	71.4%
Seattle, WA	Michael McGinn	38	19	50.0%	19	50.0%
Portland, OR	Sam Adams	2	1	50.0%	1	50.0%
Houston, TX	Annise Parker	16	6	37.5%	10	62.5%
Chicago, IL	Rahm Emanuel	72	25	34.7%	47	65.3%
Washington, DC	Vincent Gray	69	19	27.5%	50	72.5%
San Francisco, CA	Edwin Lee	35	6	17.1%	29	82.9%
San Diego, CA	Jerry R. Sanders	7	1	14.3%	6	85.7%
New York, NY	Michael R. Bloomberg	57	14	24.6%	43	75.4%
Baltimore, MD	Stephanie Rawlings-Blake	17	4	23.5%	13	76.5%
San Jose, CA	Charles R. Reed	0	0	0.0%	0	0.0%
TOTAL/AVE	**26**	**880**	**265**	**30.1%**	**615**	**69.9%**

When big city mayors do encourage directly political engagement (table 9.5), as was also true in the aggregate, they are most likely to encourage coproduction and citizen input/deliberation. For example, sixteen of twenty-four mayors that highlight politically oriented civic engagement only discuss coproduction and citizen input. In terms of community involvement, mayors clearly encourage general community building most often (table 9.6). However, they also advocate for residents to volunteer in their communities and to utilize public channels of communication (civic tools).

From this first cut at the data, should we consider the glass of civic engagement as promoted by big city mayors half empty or half full? We think the approximately 7 percent of press release headlines including promotion of directly political involvement—a percentage in line with findings from other chapters

Table 9.5.   Breakdown of Politically Oriented Press Releases by Category*

City	# Politically Oriented Press Releases	Elections	Nomination for Local Boards	Citizen Input/ Deliberation	Citizen Coproduction of Services
Charlotte, NC	4	0.0%	0.0%	100.0%	0.0%
Columbus, OH	4	0.0%	25.0%	50.0%	25.0%
Milwaukee, WI	2	0.0%	0.0%	0.0%	100.0%
Portland, OR	1	0.0%	0.0%	100.0%	0.0%
Seattle, WA	19	0.0%	73.7%	15.8%	10.5%
Detroit, MI	29	6.9%	0.0%	55.2%	37.9%
Philadelphia, PA	40	7.5%	5.0%	25.0%	62.5%
Fort Worth, TX	13	0.0%	0.0%	30.8%	69.2%
Houston, TX	6	0.0%	0.0%	33.3%	66.7%
Chicago, IL	25	0.0%	0.0%	64.0%	36.0%
Los Angeles, CA	8	0.0%	0.0%	12.5%	87.5%
Washington, DC	19	0.0%	5.3%	36.8%	57.9%
Denver, CO	8	0.0%	12.5%	37.5%	50.0%
Phoenix, AZ	6	0.0%	0.0%	66.7%	33.3%
New York, NY	14	7.1%	0.0%	14.3%	78.6%
Baltimore, MD	4	0.0%	0.0%	25.0%	75.0%
Boston, MA	31	12.9%	3.2%	25.8%	58.1%
Nashville, TN	4	0.0%	0.0%	0.0%	100.0%
Jacksonville, FL	5	0.0%	0.0%	80.0%	20.0%
Albuquerque, NM	6	0.0%	0.0%	33.3%	66.7%
Louisville, KY	8	0.0%	0.0%	25.0%	75.0%
San Francisco, CA	6	0.0%	0.0%	50.0%	50.0%
San Diego, CA	1	0.0%	0.0%	0.0%	100.0%
Las Vegas, NV	1	0.0%	0.0%	100.0%	0.0%
Indianapolis, IN	1	0.0%	100.0%	0.0%	0.0%
San Jose, CA	0	0.0%	0.0%	0.0%	0.0%
TOTAL/AVE	**265**	**3.8%**	**7.9%**	**36.2%**	**52.1%**

*Percentages refer to percent of each city's politically oriented press releases that fall into a specific category.

Table 9.6. Breakdown of Community-Oriented Press Releases by Category*

City	# of Community Oriented Press Releases	Volunteering	Civic Tool	Community Building
Indianapolis, IN	15	40.0%	13.3%	46.7%
Las Vegas, NV	8	0.0%	25.0%	75.0%
San Diego, CA	6	0.0%	16.7%	83.3%
San Francisco, CA	29	13.8%	24.1%	62.1%
Louisville, KY	35	34.3%	5.7%	60.0%
Albuquerque, NM	25	28.0%	24.0%	48.0%
Jacksonville, FL	19	26.3%	5.3%	68.4%
Nashville, TN	15	33.3%	20.0%	46.7%
Boston, MA	104	9.6%	3.8%	86.5%
Baltimore, MD	13	7.7%	15.4%	76.9%
New York, NY	43	7.0%	34.9%	58.1%
Phoenix, AZ	18	11.1%	27.8%	61.1%
Denver, CO	22	9.1%	13.6%	77.3%
Washington, DC	50	6.0%	10.0%	84.0%
Los Angeles, CA	20	5.0%	10.0%	85.0%
Chicago, IL	47	14.9%	34.0%	51.1%
Houston, TX	10	10.0%	10.0%	80.0%
Fort Worth, TX	21	19.0%	9.5%	71.4%
Philadelphia, PA	56	17.9%	25.0%	57.1%
Detroit, MI	32	34.4%	9.4%	56.3%
Columbus, OH	4	25.0%	0.0%	75.0%
Milwaukee, WI	2	0.0%	50.0%	50.0%
Portland, OR	1	0.0%	0.0%	100.0%
Seattle, WA	19	5.3%	15.8%	78.9%
Charlotte, NC	1	0.0%	100.0%	0.0%
San Jose, CA	0	0.0%	0.0%	0.0%
TOTAL/AVE	**615**	**15.6%**	**16.4%**	**68.0%**

*Percentages refer to percent of each city's community oriented press release that fall into a specific category.

in this volume—shows mayors using this tool in a way that suggests they are trying to get the word out to their constituents.[37] While it may not be surprising that general community-building activity trumps the political, we argue above that this kind of community building is essential to a vibrant democracy.

WHAT KINDS OF ACTIVITIES ARE MAYORS ENCOURAGING?

Looking at the numbers is one thing, but equally important is the specific content of the 880 press release headlines in which mayors are encouraging citizen involvement. More than an abstract idea, civic engagement means that specific policies are affected and real people are brought into contact with political and civic processes. Engaging even a few more citizens in civic life, as any individual press release has the potential to do, can genuinely make an on-the-ground difference.

So, what are these press releases actually about? What types of activities do they cover? It turns out that a wide range of examples is included in even the most straightforward of these categories. To illustrate the breadth of material included here, we focus below on the political processes of encouraging citizen input and citizen coproduction (the most frequent types of political engagement mayors promote) as well as highlight the scope of community-building activities so prevalent in the data.[38]

Citizen Input

Citizen input, of course, literally involves asking for citizen comments, feedback, or suggestions on some aspect of the political or policy process. While many of the instances of these kinds of forums in this data simply mean that a mayor, or government official closely connected with the mayor, would be engaging in public discussions, there are also examples of mayors going out of their way to initiate such forums with the public. Thus, Houston's Mayor Parker informed citizens that the "Gulfgate Area" would be the "Next Stop for Three Minutes with the Mayor Neighborhood Office Hours."[39] Mayors Foxx (Charlotte) and Bing (Detroit) held constituent meetings at accessible locations including high schools or churches.[40] Mayor Hancock (Denver) held a meeting of the "first 'Cabinet in the Community,'" and Mayor Price (Fort Worth) asked constituents to "Walk! Fort Worth" while providing citizen input.[41]

While dialog with constituents often encompassed wide-ranging discussions (as in the examples above), sometimes the focus highlighted a specific area of public policy. This included education as Mayor Emanuel of Chicago urged citizens to submit questions for his Facebook town hall and Mayor Brown announced that comedian Bill Cosby would help kick off an education summit in Jacksonville.[42] Several mayors offered citizens the opportunity to suggest proposals for insertion in the city budget or to submit their own numbers that would balance the budget.[43] Chicago even sent out workers to clean up graffiti in response to specific citizen requests.[44]

Finally, though many of these news releases focused on providing direct means for communicating citizen input to officials, there are certainly examples in the data of interactions that take on a more deliberative character. Thus, Mayor Price of Fort Worth invited constituents to "Come be a part of the Big Brainstorm" and let them know that "SteerFW will unveil its plans for 2013 at the Big Brainstorm, 11:30 a.m. Friday, Jan. 11, at the Cendera

Center."[45] More poignantly, Mayor Emanuel (Chicago) emphasized the importance of work to help the integration of new immigrants: "Mayor Emanuel Unveils First-Ever Chicago New Americans Plan—New Plan, Developed over Months of Community Conversations, Outlines 27 Distinct Initiatives That Can Create Thousands of Jobs and Boost the Ability of Chicago's 560,000 Foreign-Born Residents to Fully Contribute to the City's Growth."[46]

Coproduction

In what they cite as an understudied aspect of local politics, Macedo et al. argue that "citizens should be not just *consumers* of public services but active participants in the *production* of those services as well."[47] Similarly, Marschall adds that coproduction of services is "both an arrangement and a process, wherein citizens and government share 'conjoint responsibility' in producing public services."[48] In this regard, what strikes us about these press releases is the frequency and variety of ways in which citizens are asked to assist with the provision of some kind of governmental service. We see some degree of coproduction in all but five cities in our data set (table 9.5), and what officials ask citizens to do covers a range of governmental activities.

As has been suggested, perhaps the most common way citizens are asked to help out comes in the context of a broad range of safety concerns.[49] Some requests are relatively simple and require little of citizens. For instance, Detroit residents were asked to participate in fire prevention week activities.[50] Philadelphians were reminded to "Set Your Clocks, Check Your Stocks" to change smoke alarm batteries, and in Columbus people were warned to take steps to avoid the Shigella outbreak that was described as reaching epidemic proportions.[51]

From these three examples, we begin to see the range of public safety issues in which citizens were asked to take part. In addition, there are instances in these press releases where citizens were urged to become involved to an even greater degree. For example, in Albuquerque, caregivers of Alzheimer's patients were given jump drives to keep track of the locations of their charges.[52] Philadelphians were encouraged to alert officials in the case of a "code blue" should they find people in need or homeless on the streets in especially cold weather.[53] Residents of Los Angeles were reminded of the importance of a gun buyback program, and in a different context, they were given the opportunity to join emergency response teams.[54]

Nor were mayor requests for assistance from citizens confined to public safety concerns; participation was solicited in areas including recycling for environmental purposes, beautifying neighborhoods, and even adopting a hydrant to make sure snow was shoveled correctly:

- "Boston's new Recycling Clear Plastic Bags are now available at neighborhood stores. . . . The Mayor is encouraging residents to "Recycle More" to help keep Boston neighborhoods clean."[55]
- "Mayor Dave Bing Announces Expansion of White Picket Fence Program. . . . The initiative provides an opportunity for property owners to purchase adjacent, vacant city-owned lots for only $200. The residents receive a $200 gift card for the purchase of supplies to fence and beautify the lots."[56]
- "Mayor Menino Invites Residents to 'Adopt-A-Hydrant' this Winter. From shoveling out cars to building snowmen, Boston residents know that the challenges and joys of winter are best handled when people work together."[57]

In short, the study of coproduction may be relatively overlooked in the urban politics literature, but even the limited set of examples described here indicate the range of possibilities for citizens to become involved.

Community Building

As discussed earlier in the chapter, diverse scholars identify alternative definitions of civic engagement, with some focusing on the directly political, others adding in a strong community service element, and still others casting a broad net for activities that enrich the fabric of society more generally. Given their importance to the creation of vibrant communities and given the frequency of community-building activities, we document below the ways mayors in the largest American cities appear to offer a wide variety of opportunities to involve citizens (see table 9.6 for the breakdown of community-oriented activities by city).

Thus, community-building activity begins with bringing people together, and it is easy in these press releases to find examples of events centering on national holidays or key groups in the community. For example, there are mayoral press releases honoring veterans, remembering Martin Luther King, commemorating September 11, and celebrating groups important to the historical development of a particular city such as Latinos in Los Angeles.[58] In some instances, cities have fairly long traditions of conducting these kinds of ceremonies. In others, the establishment of such events is more recent so that "after an overwhelming response last year, Mayor Greg Fischer today announced that the service and sacrifices of veterans and active duty military will again be honored with a Veteran's Day Parade and other activities in downtown Louisville."[59] In a very different context, and in a press release that stands out for its unusual degree of partisanship, even as he participated in Memorial Day events in Washington, DC, Mayor Gray reminded his constituents that although it is important to honor the efforts of servicemen and women of the military, it is also vital to remember his constituents were "Being Denied Rights at Home."[60]

Other types of unifying activities included asking citizens to wear specific colors, dress in a certain style, or in some way come together to support an event or cause. Thus, "Orange Friday" marked the football accomplishments of the Denver Broncos, and residents of Baltimore were urged to "light the city purple" in support of the Baltimore Ravens.[61] New York City held one of its traditional ticker tape parades to celebrate the success of the Giants, and it is worth noting that even a few parades were held in honor of high school or college sports teams.[62]

Nor was this kind of display limited to sports; there are surprisingly poignant examples in these press releases where unity was being called for to show support for important causes. Thus, Denver residents were asked to "'Paint the City Blue' for Child Abuse Prevention."[63] Louisville held "college colors day" to inspire increased college attendance, and in the course of the year Philadelphians were asked to take part in diverse activities including America Recycles Day, "Peace Day Philly" to highlight the value of nonviolence, and LGBT History Month.[64]

Residents were encouraged to participate in a wide variety of additional community activities covering the gamut from recreation, to entertainment, to health events.[65] It is worth noting in this regard that many cities put a particular premium on activities to engage youth. Given the high poverty levels prevalent in so many of these areas, the extent to which mayors publicize efforts to enhance the opportunities of the young is heartening. First and foremost, these include recreational activities.[66] Additionally, these encompass promoting reading, encouraging school attendance, and soliciting grants to simply make the lives of young people better.[67]

Another instance of community building, and one which is more prevalent than we might have expected, has to do with the promotion of community challenges. Residents are asked to get involved in a competitive process, and winners receive public recognition. Thus, city residents are asked to come up with general logos, to "Deck the Windows of Boston," or to participate in making a "welcome video" contest.[68] Sometimes, the challenge is more issue-oriented: "City Of Philadelphia Encourages Applications for Green Infrastructure Competition" or "Phoenix Animal Cruelty Task Force Poster Contest Winners Announced."[69]

Finally, some cities simply showed off their uniqueness:

• "Historic Albuquerque Rail Yards Hosts Open House and Tours. . . . For the first time since purchasing the historic Rail Yards site south of downtown in 2007, the City of Albuquerque will be inviting the general public onto the property . . . as part of the process to develop a Master Plan for the site;"[70]

- "Celebrate 200 Day with the Columbus Clippers. . . . Join The Columbus Clippers as we celebrate the 200th day of our city's bicentennial;"[71]
- "Mayor Lee Announces Second Annual Chinatown Sunday Streets & Ping Pong Tournament;"[72]
- "Only in Seattle highlights shopping and dining in local neighborhoods."[73]

In short, the publicizing of the variety of community-building activities taking place in these large urban areas seems alive and well. To downplay this piece of civic engagement would be to miss some of the vibrancy occurring in some of the biggest cities of the nation.

CROSS-CITY VARIATION, SOME PRELIMINARY ANALYSIS

What factors might account for the considerable variation in mayor promulgation of civic engagement demonstrated in tables 9.3 to 9.6? To get a preliminary handle on some possible explanations, we examined relationships between a number of potential independent variables with several measures of the percent of civically oriented press releases. Our group of independent variables comprised a set of demographics including city population, education levels (percent graduating high school or college), income (median household income and percentage living below the poverty line), and measures of the racial makeup of a city's population (percent Caucasian).[74] We also examined the potential for differences by region, city form of government, and political culture.

For the most part, relationships were small or inconsistent, and obviously, the small number of cases limits our ability to draw firm conclusions. Thus, the higher the percent of citizens with a bachelor's degree, the lower the percent of mayor press releases encouraging civic engagement ($r = -.39$); yet there is virtually no relationship ($r = -.06$) between the percentage with a high school degree and a mayor's propensity to encourage civic engagement. There is some suggestion that the five mayors in a council-manager form of government issue more civically oriented press releases (44%) than the twenty-one strong mayors (24%) and some indication that mayors from the South and Midwest are more likely to solicit civic engagement.[75] Similarly, there is a moderate correlation ($r = .19$) between percent Caucasian and a mayor's promotion of civic engagement. However, many of these relationships are marginal, numbers are small, and some mayors fail to issue many press releases.[76]

One consistent finding that did in fact emerge from an exploration of these relationships is that measures of the income level of a city impacted a mayor's propensity to promote civic engagement. Thus, as a city's median household income increased, both the percent of mayor press releases soliciting any form of civic engagement and the percentage promoting direct political engagement decreased ($r = -.25$ for both relationships). The converse holds true for the percent below the poverty line. The poorer the city, the more likely mayors were to solicit political involvement ($r = .47$), though not overall engagement ($r = .05$).

We suggest that this linkage deserves additional exploration, and we speculate that several factors could play a role in this connection. First off, we might expect that the needs of citizens living in economically less well-off cities are simply greater than those in other types of cities. Hence there should be greater pressure on local governments to provide services. At the same time, it is exactly these lower income cities that we would expect to have a lower tax base. By virtue of their role as chief executive, these mayors then are literally being asked to do more with less. No wonder they might be more likely to reach out to encourage citizen involvement.

CONCLUSION

We have argued that mayors of big cities are well positioned to educate their constituents on civic affairs and have incentives to promote citizen involvement. The data analysis above suggests that this is indeed the case.

We are struck by the extent to which civically oriented activities are found throughout these press releases whether in an explicitly political context or in the promotion of more general volunteer or community-building activities. Approximately 7 percent of the press releases encouraged citizens to participate politically; adding in volunteer and community activities, almost one-quarter address public involvement. Even more, these findings describe what is happening in most cities; twenty-five of twenty-six mayors use a portion of their press releases to promote citizen engagement.

Politically, the types of activities solicited by mayors focus most on citizen coproduction and citizen input. The finding that press releases asking for citizen participation in the provision of government services (coproduction) show up so often in this data is intriguing because of the understudied nature of these kinds of activities and because increasing digital connections between citizens and government will only enhance the possibility for these types of interactions. The finding of press releases inviting citizen input and deliberation is relevant because such input is after all what the democratic process is all about.

On the other hand, the large percentage of press releases identifying community-oriented activities at one level may not be surprising. It is easy to publicize city competitions, parades, and other events highlighting summer fun. At the same time, that these kinds of events show up so frequently on these websites, we think adds in important ways to an understanding of what civic engagement entails. Simply, by encouraging these citizens to participate in such a rich array of community events and activities, mayors are truly inviting citizens to take part in city life, thus reinforcing the importance of the expansive definition of civic engagement put forth by Portney and Putnam.

Similarly, assuming mayors indeed want to encourage the civic engagement of their citizens, we argue that they are also missing opportunities to do so. In light of the fact that civic engagement has been such a hot button issue, we are surprised that there is not even more of this type of material on websites. Why in a nonpartisan manner are mayors not reminding constituents, for example, to turn out on Election Day and to remember their sacred obligation to vote? Why are there not more postings letting citizens know about opportunities to serve on city boards or commissions or publicizing opportunities to attend forums to provide input on city problems? In this digital age, posting a few more press releases each week or each month seems something citizens could reasonably expect of their political leaders.

That said, the major implication of our somewhat exploratory analysis is that there is a vast array of opportunities for civic engagement across the nation's largest cities. Given the myriad of problems facing big city mayors and the idiosyncrasies of the content of their websites, mayors, actors with considerable potential to set the tone for their constituents, are indeed key facilitators and promoters of civic engagement.

NOTES

1. As quoted in Stephen Macedo et al., *Democracy at Risk: How Political Choices Undermine Citizen Participation, and What We Can Do about It* (Washington, DC: Brookings Institute Press, 2005), 68–69.

2. Robert Putnam, *Bowling Alone: The Collapse and Revival of American Community* (New York: Simon and Schuster, 2000); Macedo et al., *Democracy at Risk*; Robert D. Putnam, "Tuning In, Tuning Out: The Strange Disappearance of Social Capital in America," *PS: Political Science and Politics* 28, no. 4 (1995): 664–683.

3. J. Eric Oliver, "City Size and Civic Involvement in Metropolitan America," *The American Political Science Review* 94, no. 2 (2000); Peter Dreier et al., *Place Matters: Metropolitics for the Twenty-First Century*, Second ed. (Lawrence, KS: University Press of Kansas, 2004), 101; Carol Ebdon and Aimee L. Franklin, "Citizen Participation in Budgeting Theory," *Public Administration Review* 66, no. 3 (2006): 438–439.

4. Putnam, "Tuning In, Tuning Out"; *Bowling Alone*.

5. Macedo et al., *Democracy at Risk*, 66.

6. Ester R. Fuchs et al., "Social Capital, Political Participation and the Urban Community," in Susan Saegert et al., eds., *Social Capital and Poor Communities* (New York: Russell Sage Foundation) 2001, 290.

7. Macedo et al., *Democracy at Risk*, 91.

8. "Centinel, Number I," in Ralph Ketcham, ed., *The Anti-Federalist Papers and the Constitutional Convention Debates* (New York, NY: New American Library, 1986); Herbert J. Storing, *What the Anti-Federalists Were For* (Chicago, IL: The University of Chicago Press, 1981).

9. Macedo et al., *Democracy at Risk*, 68; United States Census Bureau, "American Fact Finder," U.S. Census Bureau, http://factfinder2.census.gov/faces/tableser vices/jsf/pages/productview.xhtml?src=bkmk (accessed Aug. 5, 2014).

10. Susan S. Fainstein and Clifford Hirst, "Neighborhood Organizations and Community Planning: The Minneapolis Neighborhood Revitalization Program," in W. Dennis Keeting et al., eds., *Revitalizing Urban Neighborhoods* (Lawrence, KS: University of Kansas Press, 1996); Beth Gazley and Jeffrey L. Brudney, "Volunteer Involvement in Local Government after September 11: The Continuing Question of Capacity," *Public Administration Review* 65, no. 2 (2005); Elaine B. Sharp, "Political Participation in Cities," in John P. Pelissero, ed., *Cities, Politics and Policy* (Washington, DC: CQ Press, 2003).

11. David N. Ammons and Charldean Newell, *City Executives Leadership Roles, Work Characteristics, and Time Management* (Albany, NY: State University of New York Press, 1989); Richard M. Flanagan, *Mayors and the Challenge of Urban Leadership* (Lanham, MD: University Press of America, 2004).

12. Wallace Stanley Sayre and Herbert Kaufman, *Governing New York City: Politics in the Metropolis* (New York, NY: Russell Sage Foundation, 1960, 657).

13. Lana Stein, "Mayoral Politics," in John P. Pelissero, ed., *Cities, Politics and Policy* (Washington, DC: CQ Press, 2003), 148.

14. Cathy J. Cohen, "Social Capital, Intervening Institutions, and Political Power," in Susan Saegert et al., eds., *Social Capital and Poor Communities* (New York: Russell Sage Foundation, 2001), 267–68; Peter Dreier, "Urban Politics, and Progressive Housing Policy: Ray Flynn and Boston's Neighborhood Agenda," in W. Dennis Keating et al., *Revitalizing Urban Neighborhoods* (Lawrence, KS: University of Kansas Press, 1996), 80; Richard Edward DeLeon, *Left Coast City: Progressive Politics in San Francisco, 1975–1991* (Lawrence, KS: University Press of Kansas, 1992), 96.

15. U.S. Conference of Mayors, "Supporting The Peace Corps," U.S. Conference of Mayors, http://www.usmayors.org/resolutions/80th_conference/jobs14.asp (accessed Aug. 4, 2014).

16. U.S. Conference of Mayors, "Philadelphia Mayor Michael Nutter Sworn in as 70th President of the U.S. Conference of Mayors," U.S. Conference of Mayors, http://usmayors.org/pressreleases/uploads/2012/0616-NutterSwornIn.pdf (accessed Aug. 4, 2014).

17. Ibid.

18. U.S. Conference of Mayors, "USCM President Sacramento Mayor Kevin Johnson 82nd Annual Meeting Inaugural Address," U.S. Conference of Mayors,

http://www.usmayors.org/82ndAnnualMeeting/media/0620-release-kjinauguration speech.pdf (accessed Aug. 4, 2014).

19. Ibid.

20. John Hull Mollenkopf, *A Phoenix in the Ashes* (Princeton, NJ: Princeton University Press, 1992).

21. As an example of the influence of culture, see Daniel J. Elazar, *American Federalism: A View from the States* (New York: Crowell, 1966).

22. Yvette M. Alex-Assensoh, "Social Capital, Civic Engagement and the Importance of Context," in Scott L. McLean et al., eds., *Social Capital: Critical Perspectives on Community and "Bowling Alone,"* 203–17 (New York, NY: New York University Press, 2002); Macedo et al., *Democracy at Risk*; Ester R. Fuchs et al., "Social Capital, Political Participation and the Urban Community."

23. David E. Campbell, *Why We Vote: How Schools and Communities Shape Our Civic Life* (Princeton, NJ: Princeton University Press, 2006), 16–17.

24. Russell J. Dalton, *The Good Citizen: How a Younger Generation Is Reshaping American Politics* (Washington, DC: CQ Press, 2008).

25. Kim Quaile Hill and Tetsuya Matsubayashi, "Church Engagement, Religious Values, and Mass-Elite Policy Agenda Agreement in Local Communities," *American Journal of Political Science* 52, no. 3 (2008); Wendy M. Rahn et al., "National Elections as Institutions for Generating Social Capital," in Theda Skockpol and Morris P. Fiorina, eds., *Civic Engagement in American Democracy* (Washington, DC: Brookings Institution Press / New York, NY: Russell Sage Foundation, 1999).

26. Putnam, "Tuning In, Tuning Out," 665.

27. Putnam, *Bowling Alone*, 27.

28. Kent Portney, "Civic Engagement and Sustainable Cities in the United States," *Public Administration Review* 65, no. 5 (2005): 587.

29. Ibid.

30. Marcella Ridlen Ray, "Technological Change and Associational Life," in Theda Skocpol and Morris P. Fiorina, eds., *Civic Engagement in American Democracy* (Washington, DC: Brookings Institution Press / New York, NY: Russell Sage Foundation, 1999); Alina Oxendine et al. "The Importance of Political Context for Understanding Civic Engagement: A Longitudinal Analysis, " *Political Behavior* 29, no. 1 (2007); James K. Scott, "'E' the People: Do U.S. Municipal Government Web Sites Support Public Involvement?," *Public Administration Review* 66, no. 3 (2006).

31. Justin Grimmer, *Representational Style in Congress: What Legislators Say and Why It Matters* (New York, NY: Cambridge University Press, 2013).

32. Stephen Macedo et al., *Democracy at Risk*, 68–69.

33. The Weissman Center for International Business Zicklin School of Business, "Top 100 Cities—Ranked by Population 2012 Estimates," Baruch College, http://www.baruch.cuny.edu/nycdata/world_cities/largest_cities-usa.htm (accessed Dec. 20, 2013).

34. We excluded postings on the websites of specific city departments that sometimes were interlinked and mixed in with mayor postings. Further, in instances where the mayor's term was completed or to double-check accuracy, we used Wayback-machine to collect the data. Three months of data was not available for the City of

Columbus, the closest thing to a press release available in Fort Worth was labeled as "Mayor's Messages," and no press releases were published for New York City in December of 2012. Data was collected between December 20, 2013, and January 13, 2014. Data was not available for the following eight cities with populations over 500,000: Austin, TX; Dallas, TX; Tucson, AZ; Fresno, CA; Oklahoma City, OK; Memphis, TN; El Paso, TX; and San Antonio, TX.

35. Macedo et al., *Democracy at Risk*, 67–115.

36. Ibid., 95; Melissa J. Marschall, "Citizen Participation and the Neighborhood Context: A New Look at the Coproduction of Local Public Goods," *Political Research Quarterly* 57, no. 2 (2004).

37. See Friedman and Aubin (chapter 5) and Evans (chapter 6) in this volume.

38. We leave for another paper a fuller discussion of the other categories we coded: volunteer activity, nominations for municipal boards, encouraging electoral participation, and civic tools.

39. Annise Parker, "Gulfgate Area Next Stop for Three Minutes with the Mayor Neighborhood Office Hours," City of Houston, http://www.houstontx.gov/mayor/press/index.html (accessed Jan. 4, 2014).

40. David Bing, "Mayor Bing to Host District Community Meeting September 13," City of Detroit, https://www.detroitmi.gov/News.aspx (accessed Dec. 31, 2013); Anthony Foxx, "Mayor Foxx to host town hall at Mallard Creek High School," City of Charlotte, http://web.archive.org/web/20130628114840/http://charmeck.org/city/charlotte/mayor/news/Pages/default.aspx (accessed Dec. 31, 2013).

41. Michael B. Hancock, "Mayor Hancock holds first 'Cabinet in the Community," City of Denver, http://www.denvergov.org/mayor/MayorsOffice/Newsroom/tabid/442244/cmd504977/arch/Default.aspx (accessed Jan. 2, 2014); Betsy Price, "Come take a walk with us with 'Walk! Fort Worth,'" City of Fort Worth, http://fortworthtexas.gov/mayor/message.aspx?id= (accessed Jan. 13, 2014); while the vast majority of press releases have posting dates, a few do not.

42. Rahm Emanuel, "Mayor Emanuel Asks Chicagoans to Submit Education-Related Questions for His Second #AskChicago Facebook Town Hall," City of Chicago, http://www.cityofchicago.org/city/en/depts/mayor/press_room/press_releases.html?startDate=01%2F01%2F2012&endDate=12%2F31%2F2012&submit-press-release-search=Go&numPerPage=10 (accessed Jan. 4, 2014); Alvin Brown, "Mayor Brown Announces 2013 Education Summit," City of Jacksonville, http://www.coj.net/mayor/headlines.aspx?page=6 (accessed Jan. 2, 2014).

43. Stephanie Rawlings-Blake, "Mayor Rawlings-Blake Launches Citizen Budget-Balancing Website," City of Baltimore, http://www.baltimorecity.gov/OfficeoftheMayor/NewsMedia/tabid/66/articleType/Archives/Default.aspx (accessed Jan. 7, 2014); Michael B. Hancock, "Mayor Hancock launches new website to gain input on Denver's Financial Future," City of Denver, http://www.denvergov.org/mayor/MayorsOffice/Newsroom/tabid/442244/cmd504977/arch/Default.aspx (accessed Jan. 2, 2014).

44. Rahm Emanuel, "Mayor Emanuel Announces Significant Expansion of Graffiti Program In 2013 Budget," City of Chicago, http://www.cityofchicago.org/city/en/depts/mayor/press_room/press_releases.html?startDate=01%2F01%2F2012&

endDate=12%2F31%2F2012&submit-press-release-search=Go&numPerPage=10 (accessed Jan 4, 2014).

45. Betsy Price, "Come be a part of the Big Brainstorm," City of Fort Worth, http://fortworthtexas.gov/mayor/message.aspx?id= (accessed Jan. 13, 2014).

46. Rahm Emanuel, "Mayor Emanuel Unveils First-Ever Chicago New Americans Plan," City of Chicago, http://www.cityofchicago.org/city/en/depts/mayor/press _room/press_releases.html?startDate=01%2F01%2F2012&endDate=12%2F31%2F2 012&submit-press-release-search=Go&numPerPage=10 (accessed Jan 4, 2014).

47. Macedo et al., *Democracy at Risk*, 95.

48. Marschall, "Citizen Participation and the Neighborhood Context," 232.

49. Macedo et al., *Democracy at Risk*, 95; Marschall, "Citizen Participation and the Neighborhood Context."

50. David Bing, "The City of Detroit Fire Department will host its annual Fire Prevention Week from October 8–13," City of Detroit, https://www.detroitmi.gov/ News.aspx (accessed Dec. 31, 2013).

51. Michael Nutter, "Set Your Clocks, Check Your Stocks," City of Philadelphia, http://cityofphiladelphia.wordpress.com/2012/12/ (accessed Jan. 4, 2014); Michael Coleman, "Shigella Outbreak Reaches Ten Year High for Columbus," City of Columbus, http://web.archive.org/web/20130226141455/http://mayor.columbus .gov/pressreleases.aspx?menu_id=450&id=36&menu_id=450 (accessed Jan. 5, 2014).

52. Richard J. Berry, "Mayor Richard J. Berry Launches New Program to Help Find People With Alzheimer's Who Go Missing," City of Albuquerque, http://www .cabq.gov/mayor/news/current-news/folder_summary_view?b_start:int=280&-C= (accessed Jan. 7, 2014).

53. Michael Nutter, "Code Blue Issued," City of Philadelphia, http://cityofphila delphia.wordpress.com/2012/12/ (accessed Jan. 4, 2014).

54. Antonio Villaraigosa, "Mayor Villaraigosa, Chief Beck Announce Gun Buyback Program Has Collected Over 7,942 Firearms From Across The City in Four Years," City of Los Angeles, http://web.archive.org/web/20130116230615/ http://mayor.lacity.org/PressRoom/index.htm (accessed Jan. 3, 2014); Antonio Villaraigosa, "Mayor Villaraigosa Announces Volunteer Opportunities in City's Crisis Response Team," City of Los Angeles, http://web.archive.org/web/20130116230615/ http://mayor.lacity.org/PressRoom/index.htm (accessed Jan. 3, 2014).

55. Thomas Menino, "Boston's new Recycling Clear Plastic Bags are now available at neighborhood stores," City of Boston, http://www.cityofboston.gov/news/press_ search.aspx?search=1&sel_month=null&sel_year=2012&type_press=on&page=1 (accessed Dec. 20, 2013).

56. David Bing, "Mayor Dave Bing Announces Expansion of White Picket Fence Program—City Highlights Success of Neighborhood Initiative in Southwest Detroit," City of Detroit, https://www.detroitmi.gov/News.aspx (accessed Dec. 31, 2013).

57. Thomas Menino, "Mayor Menino Invites Residents to 'Adopt-A-Hydrant' this Winter," City of Boston, http://www.cityofboston.gov/news/press_search. aspx?search=1&sel_month=null&sel_year=2012&type_press=on&page=1 (accessed Dec. 20, 2013).

58. Alvin Brown, "Mayor Alvin Brown Kicks Off the Week of Valor," City of Jacksonville, http://www.coj.net/mayor/headlines.aspx?page=6 (accessed Jan. 2, 2014); Stephanie Rawlings-Blake, "Mayor Rawlings-Blake Announces Details Of Baltimore's 12th Annual Dr. Martin Luther King, Jr. Parade," City of Baltimore, http://www.baltimorecity.gov/OfficeoftheMayor/NewsMedia/tabid/66/articleType/Archives/Default.aspx (accessed Jan. 7, 2014); Vincent Gray, "Mayor Vincent C. Gray Encourages District Residents to Remember Sacrifices for Freedom on September 11 Anniversary," District of Columbia, http://mayor.dc.gov/newsroom?field_date_value[min][date]=2012-01-01&field_date_value[max][date]=20121231&keys=&field_release_type_tid=All&sort_by=field_date_value&sort_order=ASC&page=40 (accessed Jan. 5, 2014); Antonio Villaraigosa, "Mayor Villaraigosa Honors Contributions Of Latino Americans At Heritage Month Opening Ceremonies," City of Los Angeles, http://web.archive.org/web/20130116230615/http://mayor.lacity.org/PressRoom/index.htm (accessed Jan. 3, 2014).

59. Greg Fischer, "Louisville Veteran's Day Parade Set for Nov. 11," City of Louisville, http://www.louisvilleky.gov/Mayor/News/default.htm?newsmode=archive&newsyear=2012 (accessed Jan. 5, 2014).

60. Vincent Gray, "Mayor Vincent C. Gray Salutes Fallen Heroes and DC Military for Fighting for Democracy Overseas While Being Denied Rights at Home," District of Columbia, http://mayor.dc.gov/newsroom?field_date_value[min][date]=2012-01-01&field_date_value[max][date]=2012-1231&keys=&field_release_type_tid=All&sort_by=field_date_value&sort_order=ASC&page=40 (accessed Jan. 5, 2014).

61. Michael B. Hancock, "Mayor Hancock Proclaims 'Orange Friday,'" City of Denver, http://www.denvergov.org/mayor/MayorsOffice/Newsroom/tabid/442244/cmd504977/arch/Default.aspx (accessed Jan. 2, 2014); Stephanie Rawlings-Blake, "Mayor Rawlings-Blake Urges Baltimore To 'Light The City Purple' For The Ravens," City of Baltimore, http://www.baltimorecity.gov/OfficeoftheMayor/NewsMedia/tabid/66/articleType/Archives/Default.aspx (accessed Jan. 7, 2014).

62. Michael R. Bloomberg, "Mayor Bloomberg Announces New York City Will Host A Ticker-tape Parade And Ceremony For The Super Bowl XLVI Champions New York Giants," City of New York, http://www1.nyc.gov/office-of-the-mayor/news.page#page-1 (accessed Dec. 20, 2013); Rahm Emanuel, "Mayor Emanuel Congratulates Mount Carmel Caravan Football Team On Winning the State Championship," City of Chicago, http://www.cityofchicago.org/city/en/depts/mayor/press_room/press_releases.html?startDate=01%2F01%2F2012&endDate=12%2F31%2F2012&submit-press-release-search=Go&numPerPage=10 (accessed Jan. 4, 2014).

63. Michael B. Hancock, "Denver to 'Paint the City Blue' for Child Abuse Prevention Month,'" City of Denver, http://www.denvergov.org/mayor/MayorsOffice/Newsroom/tabid/442244/cmd504977/arch/Default.aspx (accessed Jan. 2, 2014).

64. Greg Fischer, "Mayor Declares Friday 'College Colors Day' to Inspire Going to College," City of Louisville, http://www.louisvilleky.gov/Mayor/News/default.htm?newsmode=archive&newsyear=2012 (accessed Jan. 5, 2014); Michael Nutter, "City Of Philadelphia to Celebrate America Recycles Day on November 15," City of Philadelphia, http://cityofphiladelphia.wordpress.com/2012/12/ (accessed Jan. 4, 2014); Michael Nutter, "Mayor Nutter Encourages Philadelphians To Ob-

serve Peace Day Philly," City of Philadelphia, http://cityofphiladelphia.wordpress
.com/2012/12/ (accessed Jan. 4, 2014); Michael Nutter, "Mayor Nutter, City Officials To Celebrate LGBT History Month With The Raising Of The Rainbow Flag,"
City of Philadelphia, http://cityofphiladelphia.wordpress.com/2012/12/ (accessed
Jan. 4, 2014).

65. Karl Dean, "Second Annual Mayor's 5K Draws More than 5,000 Walk-
ers, Runners," City of Nashville, https://www.nashville.gov/News-Media.
aspx?sid=403&category=Mayor-Office-Press-Releases (accessed Jan. 5, 2014);
Michael Nutter, "Event. Mayor Nutter Provides Update on Details for Live Nation
Budweiser Made in America Music Festival," City of Philadelphia, http://cityof
philadelphia.wordpress.com/2012/12/ (accessed Jan. 4, 2014); Vincent Gray, "Mayor
Vincent C. Gray Marks World AIDS Day 2012," District of Columbia, http://mayor
.dc.gov/newsroom?field_date_value[min][date]=2012-01-01&field_date_value
[max][date]=2012-1231&keys=&field_release_type_tid=All&sort_by=field_date
_value&sort_order=ASC&page=40 (accessed Jan. 5, 2014).

66. Thomas Menino, "Boston Centers for Youth & Families' Swim League Seeking Youth Participants," City of Boston, http://www.cityofboston.gov/news/press
_search.aspx?search=1&sel_month=null&sel_year=2012&type_press=on&page=1
(accessed Dec. 20, 2013); David Bing, "Youth Can Still Enter the Hershey's Track
& Field Games Presented by the Detroit Recreation Department," City of Detroit,
https://www.detroitmi.gov/News.aspx (accessed Dec. 31, 2013).

67. Greg Stanton, "Storytime with the Stantons at Phoenix Public Library," City
of Phoenix, http://web.archive.org/web/20120512112345/http://www.phoenix.gov/
news/mayor/index.html (accessed Jan. 3, 2014); Rahm Emanuel, "Mayor Emanuel
and School Leaders Join Students, Teachers, Principals and Parents to Kick-Off the
First School Day for Chicago's Schools," City of Chicago, http://www.cityofchi
cago.org/city/en/depts/mayor/press_room/press_releases.html?startDate=01%2F01
%2F2012&endDate=12%2F31%2F2012&submit-press-release-search=Go&numPer
Page=10 (accessed Jan. 4, 2014); Sam Adams, "Youth Action Grants Celebrated
at City Hall on Friday; 11 Winners Include Programs about Bullying, Slavic Community Building, Farming, and Racial Stereotypes," City of Portland, http://web
.archive.org/web/20121021171722/http://www.portlandonline.com/mayor/index
.cfm?c=49434 (accessed Jan. 13, 2014).

68. Antonio Villaraigosa, "Mayor Villaraigosa Opens Market Week By Unveiling
Designed/Made In Los Angeles Logo," City of Los Angeles, http://web.archive.org/
web/20130116230615/http://mayor.lacity.org/PressRoom/index.htm (accessed Jan.
3, 2014); Thomas Menino, "Mayor Menino Announces Winners of the 'Deck the
Windows of Boston Main Streets' Contest," City of Boston, http://www.cityofbos
ton.gov/news/press_search.aspx?search=1&sel_month=null&sel_year=2012&type
_press=on&page=1 (accessed Dec. 20, 2013); Rahm Emanuel, "Mayor Emanuel An-
nounces Winners of NATO Welcome Video Contest," City of Chicago, http://www
.cityofchicago.org/city/en/depts/mayor/press_room/press_releases.html?startDate
=01%2F01%2F2012&endDate=12%2F31%2F2012&submit-press-release-search
=Go&numPerPage=10 (accessed Jan 4, 2014).

69. Michael Nutter, "City Of Philadelphia Encourages Applications for Green Infrastructure Competition," City of Philadelphia, http://cityofphiladelphia.wordpress .com/2012/12/ (accessed Jan. 4, 2014); Greg Stanton, "Phoenix Animal Cruelty Task Force Poster Contest Winners Announced," City of Phoenix, http://web.archive.org/ web/20120512112345/http://www.phoenix.gov/news/mayor/index.html (accessed Jan. 3, 2014).

70. Richard J. Berry, "Historic Albuquerque Rail Yards Hosts Open House and Tours," City of Albuquerque, http://www.cabq.gov/mayor/news/current-news/ folder_summary_view?b_start:int=280&-C= (accessed Jan. 7, 2014).

71. Michael Coleman, "Celebrate 200 Day with the Columbus Clippers," City of Columbus, http://web.archive.org/web/20130226141455/http://mayor.columbus.gov/ pressreleases.aspx?menu_id=450&id=36&menu_id=450 (accessed Jan. 5, 2014).

72. Edwin Lee, "Mayor Lee Announces Second Annual Chinatown Sunday Streets & Ping Pong Tournament," City and County of San Francisco, http://www .sfmayor.org/index.aspx?page=943 (accessed Jan. 8, 2014).

73. Michael McGinn, "Only in Seattle highlights shopping and dining in local neighborhoods," City of Seattle, http://www.seattle.gov/news/results.asp (accessed Dec. 31, 2013).

74. United States Census Bureau, "Census Bureau Quick Facts," U.S. Census Bureau, http://quickfacts.census.gov/qfd/index.html (accessed Jan. 15, 2014).

75. The percentages by region are: South 33 percent, Midwest 32 percent, Northeast 22 percent, West 21 percent.

76. We also conducted a preliminary test of the connection between Daniel Elazar's classic categorization of states into moralistic, individualistic, and traditionalistic political cultures with the percentages of civically oriented press releases. Cities in states coded as traditionalistic had somewhat higher than average rates of positive mayor press releases.

BIBLIOGRAPHY

Adams, Sam. "Mayor Sam Adams Latest News." City of Portland, OR. Accessed Via Internet Archive Wayback Machine, January 13, 2014. http://web.archive.org/ web/20121021171621/http://www.portlandonline.com/mayor/index.cfm?c=49278.

Alex-Assensoh, Yvette M. "Social Capital, Civic Engagement and the Importance of Context." In *Social Capital: Critical Perspectives on Community and "Bowling Alone,"* edited by Scott L. McLean, David A. Schultz, and Manfred B. Steger, 203–17. New York, NY: New York University Press, 2002.

Ammons, David N., and Charldean Newell. *City Executives Leadership Roles, Work Characteristics, and Time Management.* Albany, NY: State University of New York Press, 1989.

Ballard, Gregory A. "Mayor's Office News Releases." City of Indianapolis, IN. Accessed December 31, 2013. http://www.indy.gov/eGov/Mayor/pressroom/Pages/ default.aspx.

Barrett, Thomas. "Mayor Tom Barrett News." City of Milwaukee, WI. Accessed January 5, 2014. http://city.milwaukee.gov/News400.htm.

Berry, Richard J. "News from the Mayor's Office." City of Albuquerque, NM. Accessed January 7, 2014. http://www.cabq.gov/mayor/news/currentnews/folder_summary_view?b_start:int=280&-C=.

Bing, David. "Mayor's Office News." City of Detroit, MI. Accessed December 31, 2013. https://www.detroitmi.gov/News.aspx.

Bloomberg, Michael R. "Office of the Mayor News." City of New York, NY. Accessed December 20, 2013. http://www1.nyc.gov/office-of-the-mayor/news.page#page-1.

Brown, Alvin. "Mayor Headlines." City of Jacksonville, FL. Accessed January 2, 2014. http://www.coj.net/mayor/headlines.aspx?page=6.

Campbell, David E. *Why We Vote: How Schools and Communities Shape Our Civic Life*. Princeton, NJ: Princeton University Press, 2006.

"Centinel, Number I." In *The Anti-Federalist Papers and the Constitutional Convention Debates,* edited by Ralph Ketcham, 227–37. New York, NY: New American Library, 1986.

Cohen, Cathy J. "Social Capital, Intervening Institutions, and Political Power." In *Social Capital and Poor Communities,* edited by Susan Saegert, J. Phillip Thompson, and Mark R. Warren, 267–89. New York: Russell Sage Foundation, 2001.

Coleman, Michael B. "Michael B. Coleman Media Center." City of Columbus, OH. Accessed Via Internet Archive Wayback Machine January 5, 2014. http://web.archive.org/web/20130226141455/http://mayor.columbus.gov/pressreleases.aspx?menu_id=450&id=36&menu_id=450.

Dalton, Russell J. *The Good Citizen: How a Younger Generation Is Reshaping American Politics*. Washington, DC: CQ Press, 2008.

Dean, Karl. "Mayor's Office Press Releases." City of Nashville, TN. Accessed January 5, 2014. https://www.nashville.gov/News-Media.aspx?sid=403&category=Mayor-Office-Press-Releases.

DeLeon, Richard Edward. *Left Coast City: Progressive Politics in San Francisco, 1975–1991*. Lawrence, KS: University Press of Kansas, 1992.

Dreier, Peter. "Urban Politics, and Progressive Housing Policy: Ray Flynn and Boston's Neighborhood Agenda." In *Revitalizing Urban Neighborhoods,* edited by W. Dennis Keating, Norman Krumholz, and Peter Star, 63–82. Lawrence, KS: University of Kansas Press, 1996.

Dreier, Peter, John Mollenkopf, and Todd Swanstrom. *Place Matters: Metropolitics for the Twenty-First Century*. Second ed. Lawrence, KS: University Press of Kansas, 2004.

Ebdon, Carol, and Aimee L. Franklin. "Citizen Participation in Budgeting Theory." *Public Administration Review* 66, no. 3 (2006): 437–47.

Elazar, Daniel J. *American Federalism: A View from the States*. New York: Crowell, 1966.

Emanuel, Rahm. "Mayor's Press Releases." City of Chicago, IL. Accessed January 4, 2014. http://www.cityofchicago.org/city/en/depts/mayor/press_room/press_re

leases.html?startDate=01%2F01%2F2012&endDate=12%2F31%2F2012&submit
-press-release-search=Go&numPerPage=10.

Evans, Heather K. "Encouraging Civic Participation on Twitter during (and after) the 2012 Election." This volume.

Fainstein, Susan S., and Clifford Hirst. "Neighborhood Organizations and Community Planning: The Minneapolis Neighborhood Revitalization Program." In *Revitalizing Urban Neighborhoods,* edited by W. Dennis Keating, Norman Krumholz, and Peter Star, 96–111. Lawrence, KS: University of Kansas Press, 1996.

Fischer, Greg. "Mayor Greg Fischer News Room—2012 Archive." City of Louisville, KY. Accessed January 5, 2014. http://www.louisvilleky.gov/Mayor/News/default.htm?newsmode=archive&newsyear=2012.

Flanagan, Richard M. *Mayors and the Challenge of Urban Leadership.* Lanham, MD: University Press of America, 2004.

Foxx, Anthony. "Mayor Anthony Foxx News Releases." City of Charlotte, NC. Accessed Via Internet Archive Wayback Machine, December 31, 2013. http://web.archive.org/web/20130628114840/http://charmeck.org/city/charlotte/mayor/news/Pages/default.aspx.

Friedman, Sally, and Jessica L. Aubin, "The Role of Congressional Outreach in Civic Engagement: An Examination of Legislator Websites." This volume.

Fuchs, Ester R., Robert Y. Shapiro, and Lorraine C. Minnite. "Social Capital, Political Participation and the Urban Community." In *Social Capital and Poor Communities,* edited by Susan Saegert, J. Phillip Thompson, and Mark R. Warren, 290–324. New York: Russell Sage Foundation, 2001.

Gazley, Beth, and Jeffrey L. Brudney. "Volunteer Involvement in Local Government after September 11: The Continuing Question of Capacity." *Public Administration Review* 65, no. 2 (2005): 131–42.

Gelbman, Shamira M. "Interest Groups, Twitter, and Civic Education." This volume.

Goodman, Carolyn G. "Mayor Carolyn G. Goodman." City of Las Vegas, NV. Accessed January 5, 2014. http://www.lasvegasnevada.gov/Government/mayor_carolyn_g_goodman.htm.

Goodman, Carolyn G. "Mayor Carolyn G. Goodman." City of Las Vegas, NV. Accessed Via Internet Archive Wayback Machine, January 5, 2014 http://web.archive.org/web/20120902014355/http://www.lasvegasnevada.gov/Government/mayor_carolyn_g_goodman.htm.

Gray, Vincent. "Executive Office of the Mayor News Room." The District of Columbia. Accessed January 5, 2014. http://mayor.dc.gov/newsroom?field_date_value[min][date]=2012-01-01&field_date_value[max][date]=20121231&keys=&field_release_type_tid=All&sort_by=field_date_value&sort_order=ASC&page=40.

Grimmer, Justin. *Representational Style in Congress: What Legislators Say and Why It Matters.* New York, NY: Cambridge University Press, 2013.

Hancock, Michael B. "Mayor Michael B. Hancock News Archives." City of Denver, CO. Accessed January 2, 2014. http://www.denvergov.org/mayor/MayorsOffice/Newsroom/tabid/442244/cmd504977/arch/Default.aspx.

Lee, Edwin. "Office of the Mayor 2012 News Releases." City and County of San Francisco, CA. Accessed January 8, 2014. http://www.sfmayor.org/index.aspx?page=943.

Macedo, Stephen, and others. *Democracy at Risk: How Political Choices Undermine Citizen Participation and What We Can Do about It.* Washington, DC: Brookings Institution Press, 2005.

Marschall, Melissa J. "Citizen Participation and the Neighborhood Context: A New Look at the Coproduction of Local Public Goods." *Political Research Quarterly* 57, no. 2 (2004): 231–44.

McGinn, Michael. "Office of the Mayor Newsroom." City of Seattle, WA. Accessed December 31, 2013. http://www.seattle.gov/news/results.asp.

Menino, Thomas. "News & Press Releases." City of Boston, MA. Accessed December 20, 2013. http://www.cityofboston.gov/news/press_search.aspx?keywords=&search=1&sel_month=null&sel_year=2012&type_press=on&department=55&department=31.

Mollenkopf, John Hull. *A Phoenix in the Ashes.* Princeton, NJ: Princeton University Press, 1992.

Nutter, Michael. "Mayor's Press Releases." City of Philadelphia, PA. Accessed January 4, 2014. http://cityofphiladelphia.wordpress.com/category/press-release/.

Oliver, J. Eric. "City Size and Civic Involvement in Metropolitan America." *The American Political Science Review* 94, no. 2 (2000): 361–73.

Oxendine, Alina, and others. "The Importance of Political Context for Understanding Civic Engagement: A Longitudinal Analysis." *Political Behavior* 29, no. 1 (2007): 31–67.

Parker, Annise. "Mayor's Office Press Releases." City of Houston, TX. Accessed January 4, 2014. http://www.houstontx.gov/mayor/press/index.html.

Portney, Kent. "Civic Engagement and Sustainable Cities in the United States." *Public Administration Review,* 65, no. 5 (2005): 579–91.

Price, Betsy. "Mayor's Message Archive." City of Fort Worth, TX. Accessed January 13, 2014. http://fortworthtexas.gov/mayor/message.aspx?id=.

Putnam, Robert D. *Bowling Alone: The Collapse and Revival of American Community.* New York: Simon & Schuster, 2000.

Putnam, Robert D. "Tuning In, Tuning Out: the Strange Disappearance of Social Capital in America." *PS: Political Science and Politics* 28, no. 4 (1995): 664–83.

Quaile Hill, Kim, and Tetsuya Matsubayashi. "Church Engagement, Religious Values, and Mass-Elite Policy Agenda Agreement in Local Communities." *American Journal of Political Science* 52, no. 3 (2008): 570–84.

Rahn, Wendy M., John Brehm, and Neil Carlson. "National Elections as Institutions for Generating Social Capital." In *Civic Engagement in American Democracy,* edited by Theda Skocpol and Morris P. Fiorina, 111–60. Washington, DC: Brookings Institution Press / New York, NY: Russell Sage Foundation, 1999.

Rawlings-Blake, Stephanie. "Office of Mayor Stephanie Rawlings-Blake News & Media." City of Baltimore, MD. Accessed January 7, 2014. http://www.baltimorecity.gov/OfficeoftheMayor/NewsMedia/tabid/66/articleType/Archives/Default.aspx.

Reed, Charles R. "Office of Mayor Chuck Reed 2012 Press Release Archive." City of San Jose, CA. Accessed December 31, 2013. http://www.sanjoseca.gov/index.aspx?NID=3621.

Ridlen Ray, Marcella. "Technological Change and Associational Life." In *Civic Engagement in American Democracy*, edited by Theda Skocpol and Morris P. Fiorina, 297–329. Washington, DC: Brookings Institution Press / New York, NY: Russell Sage Foundation, 1999.

Sanders, Jerry R. "Mayor Jerry Sanders In the News Archives." City of San Diego, CA. Accessed Via Internet Archive Wayback Machine, January 4, 2014. http://web.ar chive.org/web/20121029172050/http://www.sandiego.gov/mayor/news/2012.shtml.

Sayre, Wallace Stanley, and Herbert Kaufman. *Governing New York City: Politics in the Metropolis*. New York, NY: Russell Sage Foundation, 1960.

Scott, James K. "'E' the People: Do U.S. Municipal Government Web Sites Support Public Involvement?" *Public Administration Review* 66, no. 3 (2006): 341–53.

Sharp, Elaine B. "Political Participation in Cities." In *Cities, Politics and Policy*, edited by John P. Pelissero, 68–96. Washington, DC: CQ Press, 2003.

Stanton, Greg. "Mayor News Releases." City of Phoenix, AZ. Accessed Via Internet Archive Wayback Machine, January 3, 2014. http://web.archive.org/web/20121005064237/http://phoenix.gov/news/mayor/index.html.

Stanton, Greg. "Office of the Mayor." City of Phoenix, AZ. Accessed Via Internet Archive Wayback Machine, January 3, 2014. http://web.archive.org/web/20130113112240/http://phoenix.gov/mayor/index.html.

Stein, Lana. "Mayoral Politics." In *Cities, Politics and Policy*, edited by John P. Pelissero, 148–68. Washington, DC: CQ Press, 2003.

Storing, Herbert J. *What the Anti-Federalists Were For*. Chicago, IL: The University of Chicago Press, 1981.

United States Census Bureau, "American Fact Finder." United States Census Bureau. Accessed August 5, 2014. http://factfinder2.census.gov/faces/tableservices/jsf/pages/productview.xhtml?src=bkmk.

United States Census Bureau. "Census Bureau Quick Facts." United States Census Bureau. Accessed January 15, 2014. http://quickfacts.census.gov/qfd/index.html.

U.S. Conference of Mayors. "Philadelphia Mayor Michael Nutter Sworn in as 70th President of the U.S. Conference of Mayors." U.S. Conference of Mayors. Accessed August 4, 2014. http://usmayors.org/pressreleases/uploads/2012/0616 -NutterSwornIn.pdf.

U.S. Conference of Mayors. "Supporting The Peace Corps." U.S. Conference of Mayors. Accessed August 4, 2014. http://www.usmayors.org/resolutions/80th_confer ence/jobs14.asp.

U.S. Conference of Mayors. "USCM President Sacramento Mayor Kevin Johnson 82nd Annual Meeting Inaugural Address," U.S. Conference of Mayors. Accessed August 4, 2014. http://www.usmayors.org/82ndAnnualMeeting/media/0620-re lease-kjinaugurationspeech.pdf.

Villaraigosa, Antonio. "Mayor Antonio Villaraigosa Press Room." City of Los Angeles, CA. Accessed Via Internet Archive Wayback Machine, January 3, 2014. http://web.archive.org/web/20130207162718/http://mayor.lacity.org/PressRoom/index .htm?region7_element1_NextRow=41.

Weissman Center for International Business Zicklin School of Business. "Top 100 Cities—Ranked by Population 2012 Estimates." Baruch College. http://www.baruch .cuny.edu/nycdata/world_cities/largest_cities-usa.htm. Accessed December 20, 2013.

Chapter Ten

Encouraging Civic Participation of Citizens through County Websites

A Case Study of Arkansas

Barbara Warner*

Encouraging civic participation by citizens does not just happen through time-honored traditional vehicles. It can also be done at various levels through e-government. As defined by Curtin et al., e-government is "governing populations through the use of online information and services."[1] One of the vehicles for this is county websites. Counties are not only an important level of government in terms of the activities they oversee and manage, but they are an understudied area when it comes to e-government. As Aroon Manoharan points out, the literature on e-government offers little relating specifically to the adoption of websites by county governments in the United States.[2]

Of the fifty U.S. states, forty-eight have operational county governments.[3] Although the 3,069 counties differ in their governance, structure, and responsibilities, they provide and administer numerous services that include elections, transportation and infrastructure, public facilities and utilities, education, justicial and correctional services, healthcare, coordination with other levels of government and nonprofit organizations, record-keeping and more.[4] What is more, counties serve as geographical approximations for congressional redistricting.

County governments are also the loci of the evolution of great societal trends in the nation, especially in regions that have seen dramatic population increases that have resulted in a fight for expanded governing powers.[5] Moreover, counties as a whole have more than 19,300 elected board members and elected executives, they invest $482.1 billion a year in providing services for 296 million residents, and they rely upon 3.3 million employees; yet they face limited resources.[6] Finally, counties are seen as the most flexible, locally responsive and creative of the various types of governance systems in

*I wish to thank my former graduate assistant, Joshua Colvin, Dr. Rollin Tusalem, and the many semesters of students taking my Public Information Management class at Arkansas State University.

249

the United States. Their politics and policies are seen as typifying the idea of thinking globally and acting locally.[7]

Despite the reach, power, and potential of counties, the types of e-government communication currently used by local governments are rarely monitored or analyzed.[8] And yet, as Chadwick notes, when it comes to community deliberation and participation, the Internet appears to offer both increasing and decreasing opportunities for political participation. Chadwick concludes that "e-democracy in communities is producing more complex, rather than simply more or less . . ., political participation."[9] Yet Curtin et al. say that necessary components of e-government include governmental accountability, accessibility, transparency, and collaboration, which include the ability of citizens to vote and to monitor their government. They are strong advocates of e-government for increasing civic participation and highlight the significant advancement by counties in this area.[10]

Given the importance of e-government and of counties, this chapter uses Arkansas county websites as a case study to analyze counties as drivers of civic participation, in particular the promotion of citizen voting and monitoring of their government. Arkansas is a fruitful source for the study of county e-government because it has three of the fastest growing counties in the nation, according to the U.S. Census Bureau. It is also a growing economic force (home to the largest retailer in the world [Walmart] and the nation's largest poultry and meat processor [Tyson Foods]. It is the largest rice producer in the nation.[11] Additionally, it is home to former President Bill Clinton and a boyhood home of legendary entertainer Johnny Cash. The state has other claims to fame and is rich in natural resources. Arkansas is increasingly diverse in its population.[12] Still, many areas are remote and rural, some areas are quite poor, some areas experience high unemployment, and some areas do not have high Internet access. Given these variables, it seemed fitting to analyze all seventy-five Arkansas county governments to try to ascertain how much they are promoting such civic participation, in particular encouraging voter turnout, through e-government.

While Curtin et al. say that citizens want the ability to register to vote online,[13] that appears to be well beyond the present capacity of all seventy-five Arkansas counties. But one would hope that, at the least, these counties would provide their citizens with the means to be civic participants by informing them about voter registration and giving them information on budgetary matters and county meetings to help them make good voting decisions. Indeed, access to such information is here considered important to the quality of a county website, particularly in terms of whether or not it encourages voter participation.

To even begin to encourage such participation via e-government, a county must have a website, and that website must be informative. Provision of a county website and the quality of that site are considered here as a public good (or a good or service provided by government) that can be enjoyed by everyone, even if they do not contribute to its provision.[14] Such a provision can also enhance social capital. Putnam defines social capital as the "features of social organization, such as trust, norms and *networks* that can improve the efficiency of society by facilitating coordinated actions."[15] As Putnam sees it, those who have social capital tend to get more of it, just like with conventional capital.[16] And social trust can arise from networks of civic engagement, among other factors.[17] Further, Putnam says, "norms and networks of civic engagement contribute to economic prosperity and are in turn reinforced by that prosperity." In short, citizens in what Putnam calls "civic communities" "expect better government and, in part through their own efforts, they get it. They demand more effective public service, and they are prepared to act collectively to achieve their shared goals."[18] This is the demand side. On the supply side, the social infrastructure of civic communities, combined with the democratic values of citizens and officials, promote better performance by government.[19] Thus, as Putnam points out, various social science observers as far back as Alexis de Tocqueville in *Democracy in America* have highlighted the influence of socioeconomic factors on the performance of democratic institutions, including economic well-being.[20] Robert Dahl and Seymour Martin Lipset further have stressed the importance of wealth and education in effective democratic government.[21] In summary, Putnam and others suggest that economic development spurs the development of civic culture and places more demands for participatory democracy and accountability on government.

One way for counties to contribute to a civic culture is by providing viable websites that give citizens information on voting and educate them on how to be more informed voters by providing them with information on budgetary matters and county meetings, given that more educated citizens are more likely to embrace all forms of civic engagement and place more demands upon government.[22] Such citizen expectations are seen as providing an impetus to create new public goods through better Internet infrastructure and accessibility via vehicles such as county e-government sites. And one would hope that voter turnout would be a high priority, seeing as it is counties that supervise elections.

METHODOLOGY

In light of this discussion, this study therefore examines the relationship between civic participation and the quality of e-government in a couple of ways. It asks two questions. The first is: Does the quality of e-government affect civic participation? The second is: What factors contribute to counties developing websites and to providing overall quality and accessible websites?

The first hypothesis is that civic participation (as operationalized by voter turnout) will be higher in counties with an official website that provides helpful information. Quality is defined here as websites being officially present and providing voter information, as well as budgetary and meeting information. The presumption is that such information might help citizens be better civic participants and that the presence of such information might even reflect demands by citizens for such civic services.

The second hypothesis is that population and economic affluence have a role in influencing the presence of a website and its quality. Population matters because a larger mass of citizens typically demand more information, have a greater potential for affluence, and produce more tax revenue. More populous, affluent populations also are likely to have more access to the Internet and to seek more information from it.

The research questions are therefore twofold: (1) Does the quality of Arkansas county websites yield higher voting rates among citizens? (2) Does the population and affluence of a county affect the presence and quality of a website?

The independent variable for the first research question is a website's overall quality, based upon a 0 to 12 scale.[23] The dependent variable is voter turnout in a county. For the first research question, the study also employs other control variables, such as population, median household income, percent of the population with a bachelor's degree, and Arkansas' congressional districts (Districts 1, 2, and 4 were compared, and District 3 was used as the reference category).

For the second research question, the independent variables are population and affluence (as measured by median household income) of a county, while the dependent variables are the presence and quality of a website.

Of Arkansas' seventy-five counties, thirty-three had a website as of the time of this study in 2012 (see figure 10.1). Of these, only thirty-one were stand-alone county websites that were not integrated into the Arkansas.gov state portal website (meaning they were solely provided by the county). Those that were integrated into the Arkansas.gov state portal website were subdomains of the state portal and used some services from that portal. Two counties did not have websites at all—Lafayette County and Sharp County. Nevertheless, all seventy-five counties were part of this study.

For this study, the presence of a website is a dichotomous variable—either a county has one or it does not. As mentioned, the quality of the website is

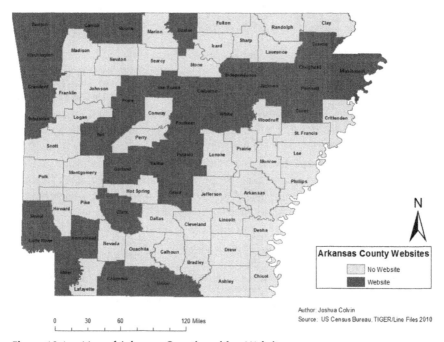

Figure 10.1.   Map of Arkansas Counties with a Website
Arkansas county government websites and 2010 U.S. Census Bureau data

defined as providing voting information and providing county budgetary and official meeting information.[24] Voting information is defined as informing citizens through the county website how to register (although it was found at the time of this study that none in Arkansas actually allow them to vote online). Budgetary information is defined as information about the county's finances. Official meeting information is defined as the publication online of official meeting agendas and minutes where citizens can learn about the activities of their county government.

The study involved searching each Arkansas county government website for information on voter registration, county budgets, and official meeting notifications and minutes. This data was accumulated in 2012. Voter turnout data came from the Arkansas Secretary of State's 2008 Presidential Preferential Primary Election site, which gives the name of the county, the number of registered voters, the total numerical votes, and the voter turnout by percentage.[25] The presumption was that voter participation data is fairly consistent from year to year.

RESULTS

Null Effect of County e-Government on Voter Turnout

Perhaps surprisingly, the regression results indicate that voter behavior in Arkansas counties is not driven by the presence of a website or the quality of a county's website. These variables do not achieve statistical significance. In fact, the findings in table 10.1 indicate instead that it is the median household income variable that has a direct effect promoting higher voter turnout, significant at p<.05. This reinforces the literature on voter turnout. As Michael R. Roskin et al. note, "High income people vote more than the less affluent, the well-educated more than high-school dropouts. These two characteristics often come together (good education leads to good incomes) and reinforce each other. High income gives people a stake in election outcomes, and education raises levels of interest and sophistication."[26]

Table 10.1. Does E-Government Affect Voter Turnout?

	Unstandardized Coefficient	Robust Standard Error	t-statistic	p-value
Presence of Website	−.6770602	1.572034	−0.43	0.668
Population (Natural Log)	−1.297779	1.245216	−1.04	0.301
Median Household Income	.0003043*	.0001225	2.48	0.015
% Population w/ Bachelor's Degree	−.156112	.2069304	−0.75	0.453
Congressional District 1	−4.291759*	1.843817	−2.33	0.023
Congressional District 2	−.5293045	2.008574	−0.26	0.793
Congressional District 4	−4.044534*	1.717972	−2.35	0.021
Constant	42.69165**	10.76629	3.97	0.000
F	2.71*			
Root MSE	5.1078			

OLS regression with the dependent variable as voter turnout by Arkansas county and the main independent variable as presence of a website (coded dichotomously as 0 = no website and 1 = presence of website). The n size is all 75 Arkansas counties. For congressional districts, district 3 is the reference category because it is the most affluent district in Arkansas. Significance levels are reported at p<.01 (**) and p<.05 (*), based on a two-tailed test.

However, interesting district patterns emerge. Using Congressional District 3 of Arkansas as the reference category, the regression results show that District 1 and District 4 have lower voter turnouts.[27] These two districts tend to have poorer counties than does District 3. Notably, both Districts 1 and 4 are closer to the poorer Mississippi Delta (home to many African Americans) than Districts 2 and 3. The literature historically has shown that redistricting, which Arkansas underwent in 2011, especially drives down voting rates among African Americans, which make up nearly 16 percent of Arkansas residents.[28] Thus, there is room for more study in this area.

Table 10.2 also indicates that the overall quality of a website has no statistical relationship to voter turnout. Similar to table 10.1, this regression shows that a county's median household income exerts a positive relationship on voter turnout, significant at $p<.05$. Congressional Districts 1 and 4 have lower voter turnout than the reference category, which is District 3 (both are significant at $p<.05$)

Table 10.2. Does the Quality of e-Government Affect Voter Turnout?

	Unstandardized Coefficient	Robust Standard Error	t-statistic	p-value
Overall Quality of Website	−.0723657	.1585706	−0.46	0.650
Population (Natural Log)	−1.280513	1.243557	−1.03	0.307
Median Household Income	.0003024*	.0001202	2.51	0.014
% Population w/ Bachelor's Degree	−.141277	.2084363	−0.68	0.500
Congressional District 1	−4.349656*	1.849107	−2.35	0.022
Congressional District 2	−.5559726	1.984587	−0.28	0.780
Congressional District 4	−4.117422*	1.728283	−2.38	0.020
Constant	42.46134**	10.82289	3.92	0.000
F	2.80			
Root MSE	5.1067			

OLS regression with the dependent variable as voter turnout by Arkansas county and the main independent variable as overall quality of the website (measured on a scale of 0 to 16, considering all aspects of what constitutes a quality website according to this study). The n size is all 75 Arkansas counties. For congressional districts, district 3 is the reference category because it is the most affluent district in Arkansas. Significance levels are reported at $p<.01$ (**) and $p<.05$ (*), based on a two-tailed test.

Additionally, when we look at what determines the presence or nonpresence of a county website in Arkansas, we find that counties with high populations are 3.7 times more likely to have a website than counties with a low population (significant at $p<.01$) (see table 10.3).

Finally, when we look at what determines good quality websites in the seventy-five Arkansas counties, we find again population is primarily driving quality (significant at $p<.01$). But having a higher education, a bachelor's degree in particular, also drives website quality, though to a lesser degree (significant at $p<.05$) (see table 10.4).

In summary, the results show that population size increases the odds that an Arkansas county will have a county website and that a larger population with a higher education level increases the likelihood of a quality county website. Affluence is often associated with higher levels of education. While e-government may not influence voter turnout in Arkansas counties, further

Table 10.3. Determinants of the Presence of County Websites in Arkansas

	Unstandardized Coefficient	Robust Standard Error	Odds Ratio	t-statistic	p-value
Population	1.334774	1.849349	3.799138	2.74	0.006**
Median Household Income	.0000966	.0001018	1.000097	0.95	0.343
% Population w/ Bachelor's Degree	.1701599	.1260553	1.185494	1.6	0.110
Congressional District 1	−.0867264	.8239335	.916928	−0.10	0.923
Congressional District 2	.655232	2.292985	1.925589	0.55	0.582
Congressional District 4	−.9796063	.2827677	.3754589	−1.30	0.193
Constant	−19.13896	3.255e-08	4.88e-09	−2.87	0.004**
Wald Chi Square	14.97*				
Pseudo R-Square	0.3501				

Logistic regression with the dependent variable: Presence or nonpresence of a website (coded dichoto-mously as 0 = no website and 1 = presence of website). Odds ratios appear in column 3. The n size is all 75 Arkansas counties. For congressional districts, district 3 is the reference category because it is the most affluent district in Arkansas. Significance levels are reported at p<.01 (**) and p<.05 (*), based on a two-tailed test.

Table 10.4. Determinants of the Quality of Website for Seventy-five Arkansas Counties

	Unstandardized Coefficient	Robust Standard Error	t-statistic	p-value
Population	2.031346	.8743638	2.32	0.023*
Median Household Income	.0001137	.0001284	0.89	0.379
% Population w/ Bachelor's Degree	.3114122	.14988	2.08	0.042*
Congressional District 1	−1.453403	1.748015	−0.83	0.409
Congressional District 2	−.235071	2.016339	0.12	0.908
Congressional District 4	−2.539067	1.596701	−1.59	0.116
Constant	−22.98521	7.378464	−3.12	0.003**
Pseudo R-Square	0.4902			

OLS regression with the dependent variable: Overall quality of a website (0–12 scale). The n size is all 75 Arkansas counties. For congressional districts, district 3 is the reference category because it is the most affluent district in Arkansas. Significance levels are reported at p<.01 (**) and p<.05 (*), based on a two-tailed test.

study needs to be done to see if it influences other forms of civic participation or social capital goods, such as trust in government, etc.

Examples of Strong and Weak County e-Governments in Arkansas

A sampling of counties from the data also can illustrate strong and weak county e-governments in Arkansas. For instance, Washington and Faulkner counties, which rank as the top two counties in quality, have the highest number of residents with bachelor's degrees. They also contain the major urban centers of Fayetteville and Little Rock (the state capital), respectively, which buttress their population. And they provide a web presence and the most information relating to high quality.[29]

Washington County, home to the flagship University of Arkansas and the growing cities of Fayetteville and Springdale, is in Congressional District 3, one of the more affluent of the four congressional districts in Arkansas. Washington County has a comparatively high voter turnout of 36.68 (on a scale ranging from 20.98 to 45.90 of the seventy-five Arkansas counties surveyed). It also has a comparatively high median income of $42,303 (on a scale ranging from $21,676 to $51,589 for the seventy-five Arkansas counties surveyed).Also, Washington County has a population of 203,065 as of the 2010 census.[30] Its website provides information on who can vote, who can register to vote, how and when to register to vote, when citizens can vote, and absentee and early voting. It lists when the polls are open. Washington County also provides times and places of official county meetings in a hyperlinked calendar fashion that is kept up to date. And it provides the minutes from these meetings, as well as an archive of past meeting minutes, committees, court videos, and the minutes of the Protected Agricultural and Rural Areas Task Force. There are many options to learn about this county's history, including a historic interactive map. There is information about the county's time capsule, statues and memorials, judges and sheriffs, plus news of the county and other citizen information.[31]

Similarly, Faulkner County, population 113,237 as of the 2010 census, contains three colleges and is home to Conway, from which many people commute to the state capital of Little Rock.[32] It provides official city and statewide election results. Residents can view their personal voter registration information, register or update their registration information, view dates and places of upcoming elections, find out where to vote, view voting machine instructions, request an absentee ballot form, learn about the county board's responsibilities in an election, and learn how to be a poll worker, among other information.[33] There is also information about the history of the county, although not to the extent of the Washington County site. Faulkner County also provides meeting times and places for the Quorum Court members, the names and contacts of the court's officials, and the court's committees and their members. Additionally, it provides the times of the court's meetings; its journals, agendas, proposed ordinances and resolutions; its personnel manual; its budgets; its ordinances; and, at this writing, meeting information for 2011–2013. Much additional information is provided, including that on the Water-works and Sewer Public Facilities Board members.[34] Thus, both Washington and Faulkner county websites are up to date on most of their information and provide extensive links, although Washington County provides the most.

In contrast, Poinsett County, population 24,583 as of 2010 census,[35] has the lowest number of residents with a bachelor's degree. While it provides a web presence, it has the lowest-quality e-government website.[36] For exam-ple, the website for Poinsett County, which is home to Harrisburg, Marked Tree, and Trumann and is part of the Jonesboro Metropolitan Statistical Area, as well as branches of Arkansas State University, has an election commission link that provides only the names and home towns of the mem-bers, with no contact information. It directs visitors to the county clerk's of-fice for more information, which provides no substantial directions regard-ing voting. There is a confusing link on the clerk's site to another Poinsett County site that has a link to voter information, but it links to the Arkansas Secretary of State's office.[37] As regards the Quorum Court, there are only lists of officials, the towns they reside in and their districts, with no way to contact them. The election commission officials are listed by names, cities or towns, party and title only, again with a link to the county clerk's office for more information. Various county officials are listed, along with their addresses, phones, and fax numbers (resting on the assumption that most citizens have fax machines). Some have website links; others have email links that connect users to Microsoft Outlook, which residents may not have set up. There is no indication of meetings, time and places, or meeting minutes. There is a brief history of the county.[38]

EXPLAINING THE PRESENCE OF COUNTY e-GOVERNMENT

In this study, I have looked at Arkansas counties as a case study in regards to progress, or lack of it, when it comes to certain variables that might be indica-tive of promoting civic engagement, in particular encouragement by citizens to vote. The results show that voter turnout in Arkansas counties is influenced primarily by median household income and variations in congressional dis-tricts (with affluence being a factor in these districts). And the results show that population size increases the odds that an Arkansas county will have a county website and that a population with a higher education level increases the likelihood of a quality website, with affluence often associated with higher levels of education. The research, however, did not find that county e-government increased voter turnout.

What then can we say about these results? Since e-government is a fairly new phenomenon, these results make sense primarily because of e-government's nascent nature. But as populations grow, become more educated and affluent, we should see further development of e-government in Arkansas counties.

And perhaps one day, such sites will become significant drivers of civic participation and even online voting, especially if this trend is reinforced by other levels of government. Other factors influencing this may be awareness of citizens of the importance of county government in their lives (especially regarding elections, public policymaking, and expenditures of their tax money), the provision by counties of greater transparency, better access by citizens to the Internet, and counties marketing themselves more vigorously as the purveyors of quality information.

Arkansas counties vary in affluence and citizen Internet access.[39] Affluence can affect feelings of political efficacy, including civic participation through voting. Indeed, a significant amount of literature exists indicating that poverty can exacerbate feelings of political inefficacy.[40] Questions about political efficacy and affluence also bring up the effects of redistricting, especially as it relates to African American populations (historically poorer and less politically engaged) as subjects for future study as they relate to e-government. While it is anticipated that as Arkansas counties grow in population, education levels and affluence also will grow, the presumption is not that this will happen equally. But this study shows these factors can be drivers of a quality website presence that motivates civic participation.

As has been pointed out, when it comes to the study of e-government, much of the research has focused at the country level. Curtin et al. saw impressive but varied progress as regards e-democracy when they first compiled their study of country websites.[41] Susan Khazaeli and Daniel Stockemer also saw potential for improved governance among 170 counties when they studied Internet penetration rates. They saw possibilities for greater access to government information, enhanced pluralism and more political discourse, as well as heightened transparency and accountability of governments.[42] Other advocates of "cyber democracy" view the Internet as a way to boost civic engagement.[43]

But are these hopes too lofty? Steven Clift sees the Internet as having had little impact on democracy to date, but does foresee it having great potential for the future through a public Internet that he believes will reshape democracy.[44] Others fear cyber democracy will become merely a "new technocracy that will be dominated by computer and software companies."[45] Still others view politics on the Internet as featuring merely traditional components.[46] Finally, others envision political actors using the Internet to accelerate pluralism and alter political power structures, while not really advancing democracy.[47] And recently, issues of net neutrality have raised new potential barriers for access, potentially creating a tiered system for those who pay more to get more information and better speed of access. As one of my students astutely pointed out, even when e-government exists, citizens may need an in-person governmental guide to help them navigate it, necessitating perhaps centers for governmental assistance.

Counties remain entities where much of the work of government takes place and where many services are provided, including (most importantly for this study) information on elections and some key information needed to make good election decisions. Yet Arkansas counties vary greatly as to whether they even have a web presence, the quality of their sites and whether they provide the kind of information voters need to hold their governments accountable for their tax dollars.

Nevertheless, one sees improvement. When this study of Arkansas county websites first began in 2011, there was such significant variation in the quality of sites that it appeared some counties had just thrown up a brochure-type entity online to meet some expectation or compliance issue, and had not paid much attention to it since.[48] Some Arkansas county websites were treated like small-town cafés where everyone knew what was going on and even wanted officials' recipes and pictures of their office parties. In other cases, a site did not exist. And in at least one case, in the absence of an official site, someone put up a site that contained county information of various sorts and even his own views, including those on abortion. Recently, at least one county (Benton) was noticed to have taken a glitzy trend, to the point that students studying county websites complained that this interfered with its usefulness, while another county (Jackson) was found to have completely situated itself within the site of its major town of Newport, rather than establish its own county website presence. Not only did this make this county's information hard to find, but the minimal county information provided gave the impression that the county's primary existence resided in its major city. This minimized the importance of other population areas in the county.

Despite the important roles counties play, they may be perceived as weak governmental entities, as compared with cities and states. And there appears to be insufficient literature on the perception by citizens of the importance of county governments. For instance, Glen Whitley—a former president of the organization that represents counties—the National Association of Counties (NACo)—initiated a 2010–2011 "Initiative to Raise Awareness and Understanding of Counties."[49] Noting that counties nationwide were "facing tough times in a troubled economy," he said that "now more than ever it is crucial that counties develop dynamic ways to promote essential and effective county services available to residents who are struggling to make ends meet." He noted that "many families, seniors and veterans have fallen on hard times" and that "promoting available county services can help foster goodwill and strengthen communities." He particularly highlighted efforts by selected counties to do coordinated publicity efforts to promote their services. However, the new president of NACo, Riki Hokama, made no mention in his 2014 introductory press release about county's electronic presence or enhancing civic participation, focusing instead on infrastructure and transportation priorities.[50] One can hope that "infrastructure" also includes Internet availability, but it does not seem as such when presented in connection with transportation.

In short, Arkansas counties need to educate their citizens more about their website existence and the important roles counties play in citizen lives. They need to establish a standard level of quality and transparency, provide citizen efficiencies, and pay attention to user-friendly design. Finally, they need to better market themselves to their citizens (and to visitors and potential residents). If counties want to play a more high-profile role in governance, they need to take more seriously their equally important role in e-governance, the wave of the future, and invest in their websites. They need to accommodate themselves to their demographics, including their citizens' languages, changing ethnicity, and levels of connectivity. In all cases, they need to think of themselves as vehicles for civic participation and make themselves better known as conduits for that participation.

This means Arkansas county officials (and their nationally representative organization) need to think globally, not just locally, especially as their populations, diversity, and Internet sophistication grow. This maturation process needs to occur in the technological infrastructure of the county to accommodate e-government, e-commerce, and e-participation, as well as in physical infrastructure.

Matthew Symonds describes four stages of e-government. The first is rudimentary and entails simple information, similar to an online brochure. The second is a weak form of interactivity that begins to use the potential of new technology by allowing users to enter information, make requests, and even update some details. The third approaches an e-commerce model, allowing for online transactions and purchases. The fourth stage is more customer oriented and transcends bureaucratic structures by integrating government services, providing a sophisticated search engine and incorporating metadata.[51] Alternatively, Curtin et al. provide a fifth stage that is user-driven, offers many options for feedback, and allows for civic dialogue and participation. This is seen as a truly democratic model. It views government as a catalyst and helpful consultant that also transparently manages money.[52]

Arkansas county websites (and other states' county sites) need this larger vision of their role. They need to connect citizens to their governments in a secure way, make information and tasks more available and easy to use to promote efficiency, and empower citizens so that they can enjoy greater political participation, even for those who live in more remote or underdeveloped areas of the state, and those who may have only limited technological access. This effort therefore involves a state and perhaps even a federal commitment as well.

In the parameters of this study, the ideal Arkansas county website would officially and prominently exist, and would provide complete information about the county and about voting. Voting information would include when elections are to be held, for whom and where (with an interactive function that allows citizens to find their precincts). It would explain the requirements for being allowed to vote and how voting is done, whether electronically or by other means. And it would include the candidates and their party affiliations. If there are any issues to vote on, those should be identified. A sample ballot could be provided. In a brave new world, county e-government would even allow voters to register online and perhaps one day allow voting to be done online, given the proper verification techniques.

Moreover, in connection with helping their citizens be informed voters, ideal sites should provide budgetary information, including a citizen-friendly version or summary. Meeting information should include all public meetings held by county officials, as well as the time, location, and the issues to be discussed. Citizens should be allowed input. All of this information should be kept up to date, and there should be no broken links. There need to be easy ways for citizens to ask questions and get prompt answers. All the above information should be prominent and easy to find. And there should be a designated person—a chief information manager, so to speak—who oversees the website as a full-time job, as exists at other levels of government.

Since the study by Curtin et al., the United Nations has developed reports on county e-government. Its 2014 report ranks the Republic of Korea as the top e-government provider in the world, while the United States ranks seventh (down two ranks since the 2012 survey). In discussing "e-participation," the U.N. said governments would benefit from engaging citizens in public policy decision-making and service delivery. While it emphasized that e-participation did not replace traditional public participation, the United Nations said that e-participation expands the ways government engages people and that governments should especially try to reach various social groups, encourage "peaceful and constructive social engagement," and incorporate social media that "collect and take into account people's views and feedback."[53]

Thus the United States needs to make its development of e-government a priority at the federal level and improve its ranking, setting an example for lower levels of government such as counties. It should also encourage state and local governments to seriously engage in e-government and e-participation, connecting, and perhaps partnering, with them.

To date, municipal governments, especially at the county level, have not been studied to the extent of other larger government entities in terms of their provision of e-government services, especially those that might encourage civic participation. This chapter has been an attempt to expand that dialogue.

NOTES

1. Gregory Curtin et al., *The World of E-Government* (New York: Haworth Press, 2003), 215.

Curtin et al. define e-government as rethinking "all aspects of governance and service delivery to see how it can take advantage of technology and new business models to improve the efficiency of internal processes, as well as change the nature and quality of government interactions with both individuals and businesses" (20–21).

2. Aroon Manoharar, "A Study of the Determinants of County E-Government in the United States," *The American Review of Public Administration* 43, no. 2 (March 2013), 159–78.

3. "Overview of County Government," National Association of Counties, 2014, http://www.naco.org/Counties/learn/Pages/Overview.aspx (accessed July 7, 2014).

4. Emilia Istrate and Anya Nowakowski, "Why Counties Matter: Five Things to Know about Counties," National Association of Counties, July 2013; http://www.naco.org/Counties/countiesdo/Pages/Why-Counties-Matter2_5.aspx; http://www.naco.org/Counties/countiesdo/Pages/Why-Counties-Matter2_1.aspx; http://www.naco.org/Counties/countiesdo/Pages/Why-Counties-Matter2_2.aspx; http://www.naco.org/Counties/countiesdo/Pages/Why-Counties-Matter2_3.aspx, and http://www.naco.org/Counties/countiesdo/Pages/Why-Counties-Matter2_4.aspx (accessed July 7, 2014).

5. "History of County Government Part I—Introduction," National Association of Counties, 2014, http://www.naco.org/Counties/learn/Pages/HistoryofCountyGovernmentPartI.aspx (accessed July 8, 2014).

6. Istrate and Nowakowski, "Why Counties Matter," http://www.naco.org/Counties/countiesdo/Pages/Why-Counties-Matter2_1.aspx (accessed July 8, 2014).

7. "History of County Government Part I—Introduction."

8. Wayne Williamson and Bruno Parolin, "Review of Web-Based Communications for Town Planning in Local Government," *Journal of Urban Technology* 19, no. 1 (January 2012), 43–63.

9. Andrew Chadwick, *Internet Politics: States, Citizens, and New Communications Technologies* (New York: Oxford University Press, 2006), 112–13.

10. Curtin et al., *The World of E-Government*.

11. "Arkansas Farming Facts," Arkansas Farm Bureau, http://www.arfb
.com/for-consumers/arkansas-ag-facts/ (accessed October 25, 2014).

12. "Resident Population Estimates for the 100 Fastest Growing U.S. Counties with 10,000 or More Population in 2010: April 1, 2010 to July 1, 2013," U.S. Census Bureau, Population Division, March 2014, http://factfinder2.census.gov/faces/tableservices/jsf/pages/productview.xhtml?src=bkmk (accessed July 8, 2014). Note: Benton County ranked 69, Saline County 86 and Washington County 94 (accessed August 24, 2014).

13. Curtin et al., *The World of E-Government*.

14. Campbell R. McConnell and Stanley L. Brue, *Macro-Economics: Principles, Problems, and Politics*, 3rd ed (New York: McGraw-Hill Inc.), G17.

15. Robert D. Putnam, *Making Democracy Work: Civic Traditions in Modern Italy*. (Princeton, NJ: Princeton University Press, 1993), 167. Italics added to original quote for emphasis.

16. Ibid., 169.

17. Ibid., 171.

18. Ibid., 180.

19. Ibid., 182.

20. Ibid., 11.

21. See Robert Dahl's *Polyarchy: Participation and Opposition* (New Haven: Yale University Press, 1971); and Seymour Martin Lipset's *Political Man: The Social Bases of Politics* (New York: Doubleday, 1960).

22. Larry M. Bartels, "Economic Inequality and Political Representation," unpublished paper presented at the Annual Meeting of the American Political Science Association, Boston, MA, August 2002; Warren E. Miller and Donald E. Stokes, "Constituency Influence in Congress," *American Political Science Review* 57 (1963): 45–56; John L. Sullivan and Eric M. Uslaner, "Congressional Behavior and Electoral Marginality," *American Journal of Political Science* 22 (1978): 536–53; Sidney Verba, Kay Lehman Schlozman and Henry Brady, *Voice and Equality: Civic Voluntarism in American Politics* (Cambridge: Harvard University Press, 1995); Gerald Wright Jr. and Michael B. Berkman, "Candidates & Policy in U.S. Senate Elections," *American Political Science Review* 80 (1986): 567–88; and Eric M. Uslaner, "Civic Engagement in America: Why People Participate in Political and Social Life," Knight Foundation's Civic Engagement Project, 2002 (September), unpublished.

23. The measures of a quality website in this study are availability of a website ("presence"), as well as twelve selected features of the website: voting information, property assessment information, online bill or fine payment options, county road development information, adherence to W3C disability standards, Flesch-Kincaid readability levels, a Spanish-language option, availability of a search bar, provision of budgetary and official meeting information, e-mail response time to standard inquiries ,and contact information.

24. Inherent in the quality of a website is whether one is present at all. Therefore, presence is defined as whether or not an Arkansas county government has a stand-alone website. Only stand-alone websites were used. A stand-alone website is defined

as a site that is provided by the county government, has its own domain name, and is not part of a different website, such as the Arkansas state government website.

25. "Voter Turnout—2008 Presidential Preferential Primary Election," Arkansas Secretary of State, http://www.sos.arkansas.gov/electionresults/index.php?ac:show:tu rnout=1&elecid=151 (accessed August 25, 2014).

26. Michael G. Roskin, et al., *Political Science: An Introduction*, 13th edition (Upper Saddle River, NJ: Pearson, 2014), 189.

27. Congressional District 3 was chosen as a reference category because of its perceived affluence, considering the high-level and number of industries located there (Walmart, the largest retailer in the world, and Tyson Foods, to name just two). It is also home to the flagship University of Arkansas and such cities as Bentonville, Fayetteville, Fort Smith, and Springdale. Finally, it is growing very fast and experiencing suburban sprawl. While its median household income ranks slightly lower than District 2 ($44,405 compared to $46,493), simply removing the capital of Little Rock from the district would make District 3 the most affluent. District 1 has a median household income of $35,995 and District 4 of $35,470, according to "Fast Facts for Congress: My Congressional District, U.S. Census Bureau, 2013 (accessed November 24, 2014) at http://www.census.gov/fastfacts/.

28. Arkansas underwent redistricting of its U.S. House seats in 2011, but unlike North Carolina, increasing minority votes was not a priority topic. In a 2011 study, Danny Hayes and Seth C. McKee, while confirming the literature historically showing that redistricting drives down voting rates, showed this effect was strongest among African Americans. However, they found that this negative effect on civic participation was reversed if precincts with large numbers of that ethnic group were redrawn into a district represented by an African American. It is worth noting that 15.6 percent of Arkansas is populated by African Americans, slightly higher than the 13.2 percent nationally. Additional research on the effects of redistricting on the African American voter turnout may be warranted. As it stands, Arkansas U.S. House districts will be represented by all white males in 2015. The same is true for the state's two senators and its new governor. See Danny Hayes and Seth C. McKee, "The Intersection of Redistricting, Race, and Participation," *American Journal of Political Science* 56 (1) (January 2012): 115–30, http://home. gwu.edu/~dwh/intersection.pdf (accessed November 24, 2014), as well as State and County Quick Facts: Arkansas http://quickfacts.census.gov/qfd/states/05000.html (accessed November 24, 2014).

29. Washington County (Arkansas), http://www.co.washington.ar.us/ (accessed August 25, 2014); Faulkner County (Arkansas), http://www.faulknercounty.org/ (accessed October 25, 2014).

30. "Washington County, Arkansas—State and County QuickFacts—Population 2010," U.S. Census Bureau, http://quickfacts.census.gov/qfd/states/05/05045.html (accessed October 19, 2014).

31. Washington County (Arkansas), http://www.co.washington.ar.us/ (accessed August 25, 2014).

32. "Faulkner County, Arkansas—State and County QuickFacts—Population 2010," U.S. Census Bureau, http://quickfacts.census.gov/qfd/states/05/05045.html (accessed October 19, 2014).

33. Faulkner County (Arkansas), http://www.faulknercounty.org/ (accessed August 25, 2014).

34. Ibid.

35. State and County Quick Facts: Poinsett County, http://quickfacts.census.gov/qfd/states/05/05111.html (accessed December 3, 2014).

36. Ibid.

37. Poinsett County (Arkansas), http://www.poinsettcounty.us/ (accessed August 25, 2014).

38. Ibid.

39. Indeed, annual surveys of a sampling of Arkansas county websites by my MPA students continue to show variation in Internet access by citizens, when this information is provided by the counties.

40. For an initial study of how some segments of society, including the affluent, are more likely to participate in politics, see Sidney Verba and Norman H. Nie, *Participation in America: Political Democracy and Social Equality* (New York: Harper and Row, 1972); Angus Campbell, Philip E. Converse, Warren E. Miller, and Donald E. Stokes, *The American Voter* (New York: John Wiley and Sons, 1960); Steven J. Rosenstone and John Mark Hansen, *Mobilization, Participation and Democracy* (New York: Macmillan, 1993); Sidney Verba, Kay Lehman Schlozman, and Henry Brady, *Voice and Equality: Civic Voluntarism in American Politics* (Cambridge, MA: Harvard University Press, 1995); and M. Margaret Conway, *Political Participation in the United States*, 3rd edition (Washington, DC: Congressional Quarterly Press, 2000). Additionally, in their study of the relationship between Internet access and online exposure to information, as correlated with political efficacy, knowledge and participation in the 2000 presidential election, Kate Kenski and Natalie Jomini Stroud found that small, but statistically significant associations, even when taking into consideration such sociodemographic variables as party identification, partisan strength and other media exposure. See Kate Kenski and Natalie Jomini Stroud, "Connections between Internet Use and Political Efficacy, Knowledge, and Participation," *Journal of Broadcasting & Electronic Media* (June 2006), 173–92, http://sspa.boisestate.edu/communication/files/2010/05/Kenski-and-Stroud-Connections-Between-Internet-Use.pdf (accessed November 25, 2014).

41. Curtin et al., *The World of E-Government.*

42. "Susan Khazaeli and Daniel Stockemer, The Internet: A New Route to Good Governance," International Political Science Review, 34, no. 5 (July 5, 2013), 463–482, http://ips.sagepub.com/content/34/5/463.full.pdf+html (accessed August 26, 2014).

43. Esther Dyson et al., "Cyberspace and the American Dream: A Magna Carta for the Knowledge Age," The Progress Freedom Foundation, August 22, 1994, http://www.pff.org/issues-pubs/futureinsights/fi1.2magnacarta.html (February 16, 2014); Lawrence K. Grossman, *The Electronic Republic: Reshaping American Democracy in the Information Age* (New York: Penguin Books, 1996).

44. Steven Clift, "The e-Democracy e-Book: Democracy Is Online 2.0," Democracy Online Newswire, 2000, http://www.publicus.net/ebook/edemebook.html (accessed February 16, 2014).

45. Darin Barney, *Prometheus Wired: The Hope for Democracy in the Age of Network Technology* (Chicago: University of Chicago Press Books, 2000).

46. Michael Margolis and David Resnick, *Politics as Usual: The "Cyberspace Revolution"* (Thousand Oaks, CA: Sage Publications, 2000).

47. Bruce Bimber, "The Internet and Political Transformation: Populism, Community, and Accelerated Pluralism," *Polity* 31(1) (1998). See also Kenneth M. Winneg's unpublished 2009 dissertation titled "Online Political Participation in the 2008 U.S. Presidential Election: Mobilizing or Reinforcing?" http://repository.upenn.edu/cgi/viewcontent.cgi?article=1073&context=edissertations (accessed November 24, 2014). He notes that the research has been mixed as to whether the Internet mobilizes new or marginalized electoral participants or whether it just reinforces the activity of those already engaged. He found that in some cases, Internet usage can motivate certain groups to politically engage, with online campaign contact being a strong predictor for participation. He also affirmed studies showing that political participation is more robust among those who are more educated, affluent, and skilled in civic participation.

48. This study of Arkansas counties continues as my graduate students each semester present their evaluations of various counties in terms of e-government potential and ease of use. For some students, the idea that a county website could be useful and a way to learn about their communities, involve them in their government, keep them informed, do business more efficiently and entice them to visit is a novel one. Although students come to realize they do considerable business with counties, many are not aware of a county e-government presence and have not considered counties as an e-government option. However, once alerted to this fact, they are both laudatory and critical consumers. They want more information, better information and more useful information. They want ease of use and transparency. They are also alarmed by some of the private information made available, by the informality of some websites, by the lack of standardization of information and by the lack of attention to updating information. They want more integration of social media. Some counties do the latter to a large or small extent (e.g., Benton and Craighead counties). Some counties use Facebook (e.g., Clark, Columbia), while some do not. Further study of the use of social media by county governments seems warranted.

49. Glen Whitley, "An Initiative to Raise Awareness and Understanding of Counties: Examples of How Your County Can Raise County Awareness," n.d., http://www.naco.org/Counties/countiesdo/Documents/Examples%20of%20Public%20Awareness%20Programs.pdf (accessed November 11, 2014).

50. "Hokama Becomes NACo President: Vows to Help Strengthen County Transportation and Infrastructure Services," National Association of Counties press release, July 14, 2014 http://www.naco.org/newsroom/Documents/Press%20Release%20Documents/Hokama2014.pdf (accessed November 19, 2014).

51. Matthew Symonds, "Government and the Internet—The Next Revolution," *The Economist* 355 (June 24, 2000), http://ezproxy.library.astate.edu/login?url=http://search.proquest.com/docview/224059494?accountid=8363 (accessed October 25, 2014).

52. Curtin et al., *The World of E-Government*, p. 216, 229.

53. United Nations E-Government Survey 2014: E-Government for the Future We Want, 2014, http://unpan3.un.org/egovkb/portals/egovkb/documents/un/2014 -survey/e-gov_complete_survey-2014.pdf (accessed August 25, 2014), pp. 15, 60–61.

BIBLIOGRAPHY

"About Counties." National Association of Counties, http://www.naco.org/COUN TIES/Pages/default.aspx (accessed October 26, 2014).

Barney, Darin. *Prometheus Wired*. Chicago: University of Chicago Press, 2000.

Bimber, B. "The Internet and Political Transformation: Populism, Community, and Accelerated Pluralism." *Polity* 31 (1998), 133–60.

Chadwick, Andrew. *Internet Politics: States, Citizens, and New Communications Technologies*. New York: Oxford University Press, 2006.

Clift, Steven. "The e-Democracy e-Book: Democracy Is Online 2.0." Democracy Online Newswire, 2000. Available at http://www.publicus.net/ebook/edemebook .html (accessed February 16, 2014).

Curtin, Gregory, Michael H. Sommer, and Veronika Vis-Sommer. *The World of E-Government*. New York: Haworth Press, 2003.

Dahl, Robert A. *Polyarchy, Participation and Opposition*. New Haven: Yale University Press, 1971.

Davis, Richard. *The Web of Politics*. New York: Oxford University Press, 1999.

Dyson, Esther, George Gilder, George Keyworth, and Alvin Toffler. "Cyberspace and the American Dream: A Magna Carta for the Knowledge Age." The Progress Freedom Foundation, August 22, 1994. Available at http://www.pff .org/issues-pubs/futureinsights/fi1.2magnacarta.html (accessed February 16, 2014).

Faulkner County (Arkansas). http://www.faulknercounty.org/ (accessed October 25, 2014).

Grossman, Lawrence K. *The Electronic Republic: Reshaping Democracy in the Information Age*. New York: Viking, 1995.

"History of County Government Part I." National Association of Counties, 2013. Available at http://www.naco.org/Counties/learn/Pages/HistoryofCountyGovern mentPartI.aspx (accessed August 27, 2014).

Istrate, Emilia and Anya Nowakowski "Why Counties Matter: Counties are a $482 Billion Network of Public Service Providers." *National Association of Counties*, July 2013. Available at http://www.naco.org/Counties/countiesdo/Pages/Why -Counties-Matter2_2.aspx (accessed February 18, 2014).

Istrate, Emilia and Anya Nowakowski (1b). "Why Counties Matter: Counties Are a $482 Billion Network of Public Service Providers." National Association of Counties, July 2013. Available at http://www.naco.org/Counties/countiesdo/Pages/ Why-Counties-Matter2_1.aspx (accessed February 18, 2014).

Khazaeli, Susan and Daniel Stockemer. "The Internet: A New Route to Good Governance." *International Political Science Review* 34, no. 5 (July 5, 2013): 463–82.

Lipset, Seymour Martin. *Political Man*. New York: Doubleday, 1960.

Manoharan, Aroon, "A Study of the Determinants of County E-Government in the United States," *The American Review of Public Administration* 43, no. 2 (March 2013), 159–78.

Margolis, Michael and David Resnick. *Politics as Usual: The "Cyberspace Revolution."* Thousand Oaks, CA: Sage Publications, 2000.

Poinsett County (Arkansas). http://www.poinsettcounty.us/ (accessed August 25, 2014).

Putnam, Robert D. *Making Democracy Work: Civic Traditions in Modern Italy*. Princeton, NJ: Princeton University Press, 1993.

David M. Simpson, "Use of Web Technologies by U.S. Planning Agencies: Results from a National Benchmarking Survey," 2005, pp. 22–26, Washington, DC: U.S. Municipal Year Book 2005, https://www.urbaninsight.com/files/sites/default/files/articles/us-planning-agencies/2005-tech-survey.pdf (accessed August 30, 2014).

Matthew Symonds. "Government and the Internet—The Next Revolution." *The Economist*, 355 (June 24, 2000), http://ezproxy.library.astate.edu/login?url=http://search.proquest.com/docview/224059494?accountid=8363 (accessed October 25, 2014).

United Nations E-Government Survey 2014: E-Government for the Future We Want. 2014. http://unpan3.un.org/egovkb/portals/egovkb/documents/un/2014-survey/e-gov_complete_survey-2014.pdf (accessed August 25, 2014).

"Voter Turnout: 2008 Presidential Preferential Primary Election." Arkansas Secretary of State Mark Martin. Arkansas.gov. Available at http://www.sos.arkansas.gov/electionresults/index.php?ac:show:turnout=1&elecid=151.

Washington County (Arkansas). http://www.co.washington.ar.us/ (accessed August 25, 2014).

Williamson, Wayne, and Bruno Parolin. "Review of Web-Based Communications for Town Planning in Local Government." *Journal of Urban Technology* 19, no. 1 (January 2012): 43–63.

Part C: Private Institutions

Chapter Eleven

Interest Groups, Twitter, and Civic Education

Shamira M. Gelbman

Though often maligned for promoting narrow concerns and injecting negativity into political discourse, interest groups can contribute in important ways to democratic vitality. In particular, they fill the representational vacuum left by the decline of political parties and stimulate political participation, albeit often in less-than-optimally robust forms.[1] Furthermore, both as key producers and keepers of expert information and as linkage institutions connecting citizens and government, interest groups harbor the potential to play a pivotal role in promoting civic education.

As Karpf highlights, the rise of the Internet in recent years has recast the mobilization landscape, particularly for "legacy" interest groups that flourished during the twentieth century and have had to bring their traditional advocacy practices in line with contemporary modes of political communication and interaction. For Karpf, the major effect of these developments has been the rise of "Internet-mediated" and "netroots" organizations, which are inherently poised to capitalize on new modes of civic interaction and communication.[2] Obar and his coauthors nevertheless show that traditional interest groups have begun to adapt to the new media environment. Most, if not all, of the fifty-three organizations that responded to their survey predate the digital era, and all but a few of the very smallest—that is, those with fewer than five staff members—report using a variety of social media and networking platforms to share information about political issues and governmental processes with grassroots supporters and encourage their civic participation.[3]

The finding that interest groups today perceive social media as key instruments for educating and mobilizing citizens is bolstered by recent efforts to assess the extent to which new media have permeated political communication in the United States. Rapidly increasing numbers of Americans have come to rely on social media for access to political information, and social platforms such as Facebook and Twitter have been fixtures of the American campaign scene since the 2008 election season.[4] Thus, according to a 2013 report by the Pew Research Center's Internet & American Public Life Project, social media and networking tools have become especially popular means for civic engagement in recent years. The proportion of Americans reporting such activities as posting political information, "friending" public officials, or joining political groups on social networking sites quadrupled between 2008 and 2012, and young adults in particular are more inclined to partake in political activity through social media than in traditional formats.[5]

This chapter investigates the extent to which traditional interest groups have acclimated to this new media environment by examining eight national organizations' use of Twitter for civic education and mobilization.[6] Through an exploratory content analysis of their tweets over the course of a month, it finds that, by and large, the groups do actively use Twitter to educate followers on their issue causes and the governmental processes they seek to influence. Far less emphasis is placed on mobilization, however, and public interaction with the organizations' Twitter content is limited.

THE USE OF TWITTER BY INTEREST GROUPS FOR CIVIC EDUCATION

Previous research demonstrates that interest groups sense that they need to shift the locus of their civic engagement efforts to the digital arena and that interest groups of all sizes perceive benefit from the use of social media. This nevertheless begs a variety of questions pertaining to interest groups' actual use of these platforms. For example, what proportion of interest groups' social media activity is in fact devoted to civic education? How do interest groups use social media platforms to promote civic education? Are social media users generally responsive to civic education and attempts to mobilize them for civic engagement?

Data and Methods

To begin answering these questions, this study builds directly on Obar et al.'s survey research to examine interest groups' actual use of Twitter for civic education during the calendar month of November 2013. Whereas the federal government shutdown had dominated political media for most of the previous month, November was a relatively mundane month politically and is thus apt to provide a window into organizations' routine use of Twitter. Although election day occurred during this month, the dearth of prominent races in this "off year" meant that the organizations were not consumed with electioneering pursuits. Nevertheless, there was some opportunity to observe how interest groups use social media for electoral mobilization based on their Twitter activity, especially in the high-profile Virginia and New Jersey gubernatorial contests.

The Twitter feeds of eight of the fifty-three interest groups that responded to Obar et al.'s survey on the use of social media technologies for advocacy tasks were selected for content analysis: AARP, American Civil Liberties Union (ACLU), Alliance for Justice (AFJ), Family Research Council (FRC), Friends Committee on National Legislation (FCNL), Human Rights Campaign (HRC), NAACP, and National Council of La Raza (NCLR). As table 11.1 indicates, all of these organizations are "large groups" by Obar et al.'s definition of having at least 21 employees.[7] Nevertheless, recent financial reports show substantial variation in their size, ranging from Alliance for Justice's 34 employees (and zero volunteers) to AARP's 293 employees (and nearly 40,000 volunteers) in 2011. All eight interest groups were founded prior to the emergence of digital social media—that is, they are what Karpf calls "legacy" interest groups—and therefore would have had to incorporate social media communications strategies into established organizational routines.[8] Still, they vary considerably in their longevity: The NAACP, founded in 1909, is more than a century old; at the other extreme, the FRC was formed on the cusp of the mass Internet age in 1992. The selected groups also represent a mix of issue foci and ideological positions, and include both 501(c)3 and 501(c)4 organizations.

For purposes of this study, content analysis was limited to the Twitter profiles that are available through one-click access from the eight interest groups' website homepages. To be sure, the interest groups' Twitter presence

Table 11.1.   Interest Group Features

Organization	Founding Year	Tax Status	Employees	Volunteers
AARP	1961	501(c)(3)	293	39609
ACLU	1920	501(c)(4)	96	10
Alliance for Justice (AFJ)	1974	501(c)(3)	34	0
Family Research Council (FRC)	1992	501(c)(3)	88	10
Friends Committee on National Legislation (FCNL)	1943	501(c)(4)	38	1100
Human Rights Campaign (HRC)	1982	501(c)(4)	269	5320
NAACP	1909	501(c)(3)	157	5000
National Council of La Raza (NCLR)	1968	501(c)(3)	165	50

Data are from the organizations' IRS Forms 990 for 2011, which are available through the "990 Finder" feature on the Foundation Center's website, http://foundationcenter.org/findfunders/990finder/.

is not limited to these official profiles; rather, all of them have additional accounts through the profiles of state and local affiliates, administrative and issue-oriented units within the national organization, and/or key staff members. The focus here is nevertheless only on the Twitter activity of the main official accounts—that is, the ones advertised on the homepages of the interest groups' websites—since it is these that have the widest popular reach.

To organize the interest groups' Twitter activity for analysis, a coding protocol with seven categories was developed based on Obar et al.'s operational definitions of civic engagement and collective action.[9] Thus, the first coding category, "Education—Issues" corresponds to the Obar et al. survey's prompt for respondents to evaluate each social media technology's effectiveness for "educating the public about issues that matter to our organization."[10] Unsurprisingly, most tweets in this category (or the off-Twitter content to which they directed followers) were not neutral or objective in their framing or presentation of issue information. To ensure that this category was in fact capturing the organizations' use of Twitter to educate rather than to advertise their stances, a distinction was drawn between tweets offering followers background information or insight into an issue and tweets engaged in mere position taking. The former were coded into this category regardless of their bias, while the latter were not coded at all.

Another question in the survey, regarding the utility of social media technologies for "informing citizens about relevant dates, events, government deliberations, etc.," yielded two categories.[11] "Education—Government" comprised tweets that inform followers of the progress or outcome of government action on an issue of interest to the organization or explain how a governmental process works. "Events," meanwhile, was used to code tweets that apprised followers of significant dates related to the interest group's issue foci (e.g., National Caregivers Month, Transgender Day of Remembrance) and upcoming events. These included in-person events like local meetings and presentations, job fairs, and grassroots lobbying days, online events such as virtual town hall meetings and webinars, and media appearances by interest group leaders.

Whereas the "Education—Issues," "Education—Government," and "Events" categories relate to interest groups' use of Twitter to convey information to their followers, the remaining four deal with interest groups' use of Twitter to solicit participation from their followers. Corresponding to the Obar et al. survey question about the utility of social media technologies for "giving citizens a place to voice their opinion,"[12] the fourth category, "Voice," includes tweets that encourage followers to ask questions, relate their experience, offer their opinion, or partake in an online discussion forum. The fifth category, "Petition," was derived straightforwardly from a survey question about social media technologies' usefulness for "collecting petition signatures,"[13] and encompasses tweets that direct followers to add their names to petitions. This included both petitions sponsored by the interest group itself and those initiated by third parties. The sixth category, based on a survey question about the usefulness of social media technologies for "submitting citizens' comments to government,"[14] was "Comments," and was intended to capture tweets that solicited followers' statements for transmission to public officials. In practice, however, not a single tweet ended up in this category, perhaps because this function is carried out behind the scenes based on the accumulation of social media feedback rather than through discrete calls for user comments.[15]

Finally, "Mobilization," corresponding to the Obar et al. survey question regarding social media technologies' usefulness for "mobilizing citizens,"[16] was used as an umbrella category for tweets encouraging followers to take any action not encompassed by the "Voice," "Petition," and "Comments" categories. The solicited actions ranged widely from traditional calls for followers to vote or contact their senators and representatives to a whole host of Twitter-centered activities—whether retweeting or otherwise sharing interest group-supplied content about focal issues, posting self-photographs with designated hashtags in support of an interest group position, or engaging in one-day "Twitter storm" events to raise awareness about specific issues. Tweets requesting users to make monetary donations to fund-raising campaigns were included in this category, as were those explicitly urging followers to become interest group members.

Findings

As table 11.2 summarizes, all eight organizations established their Twitter accounts more than three years prior to the November 2013 study period. While all of the groups have set their profile page colors to match their organizational logos, their static content is generally limited to the organization name, a brief mission statement, and contact information. Only two groups (NCLR and HRC) have taken the additional step of maintaining a customized sidebar with action links. And, although all of the organizations maintain substantial Twitter followings, there is considerable variation, ranging from just shy of 2,500 to more than 330,000 subscribed followers.

All together, the eight organizations produced 1906 tweets between November 1 and November 30, 2013. The most active was AARP, whose 583 tweets account for more than 30 percent of the total. At the other extreme, FCNL posted a meager 47 tweets over the course of the month. Setting aside these outliers, the groups ranged from 117 to 289 tweets, with no apparent

Table 11.2. Interest Groups on Twitter

Organization	Twitter Handle	Twitter Join Date	Twitter Followers on Nov. 30, 2013	Total Tweets in Nov. 2013
AARP	@AARP	10/7/2009	70,398	583
ACLU	@ACLU	2/12/2008	187,933	289
Alliance for Justice (AFJ)	@AFJustice	6/30/2010	2,468	137
Family Research Council (FRC)	@FRCdc	12/16/2008	9,991	238
Friends Committee on National Legislation (FCNL)	@FCNL	5/7/2009	2,869	47
Human Rights Campaign (HRC)	@HRC	1/27/2009	331,495	208
NAACP	@NAACP	6/5/2009	61,379	117
National Council of La Raza (NCLR)	@NCLR	3/26/2008	26,733	287

correspondence between tweet volume and organization size or number of followers. The Pearson's r for the correlation between tweet volume and number of followers is just 0.13. The Pearson's r for the correlation between tweet volume and organization size (as measured by the number of employees) is a more robust 0.68. A scatter plot of this relationship, shown in figure 11.1, suggests strong correlation at the extremes (that is, for the smallest and largest organizations), but weak correlation for the middle of the pack.

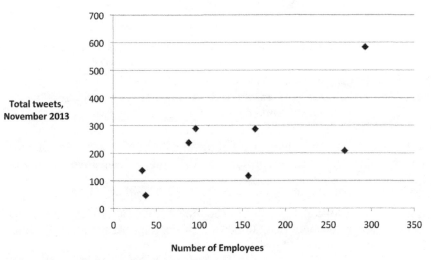

Figure 11.1. Correlation between Organization Size and Tweet Volume
Shamira Gelbman

Figure 11.2 presents the daily tweet volume for each group between November 1 and 30, 2013. Most, but not all, Twitter activity was conducted on weekdays, which accounts for the subtle "surge and decline" pattern that is evident across the board over the course of the month. Otherwise, there is a good deal of day-to-day variation, as holidays (e.g., Veterans Day on November 11 and Thanksgiving on November 28), organizational events and campaigns (e.g., FCNL's Lobby Day on November 14 and NCLR's #thunderclap fundraising campaign toward the end of the month), and political developments (e.g., the Senate vote to pass the Employment Non-Discrimination Act on November 4 and the Supreme Court's grant of certiorari in the *Hobby Lobby* case on November 26) yielded considerable fluctuation rather than consistent posting behavior by the organizations.

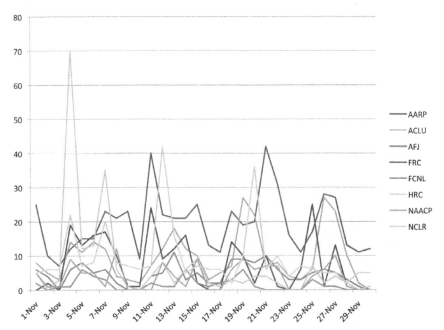

Figure 11.2.   Daily Tweet Volume
Shamira Gelbman

Many of the interest groups' tweets were readily coded as described in the previous section. Nearly 45 percent of the 1,906 total tweets fit into one of the civic education or mobilization categories, but this summary statistic masks the inordinately depressing effect of one outlier. Although AARP's total tweet volume far exceeds that of any other of the other groups, the vast majority of its nearly 600 tweets had no civic education or mobilization content, and thus could not be classified. Excluding the AARP, nearly 60 percent of the remaining seven organizations' 1,323 tweets were coded and, among them, only one (FRC) had fewer than 50 percent code-able tweets.[17] As such, these data suggest that, by and large, traditional interest groups have indeed taken to social media to facilitate their civic education and engagement activities.

As figure 11.3 suggests, however, the coded tweets were not evenly spread across the seven categories. On the contrary, more than 40 percent of the coded tweets (N=385) were classified as "Education—Issues," while not a single tweet fell into the "Comments" category and only six were coded as "Petition." Generally speaking, the organizations were far more prone to use Twitter as a means for conveying information to followers than for mobilizing them; in fact, among all the groups only HRC came even close to parity between informational and mobilization tweets, and quite a few of its 58 tweets in the latter category are retweets of celebrity endorsements of its "Love Conquers Hate" campaign against Russia's 2013 antipropaganda law.

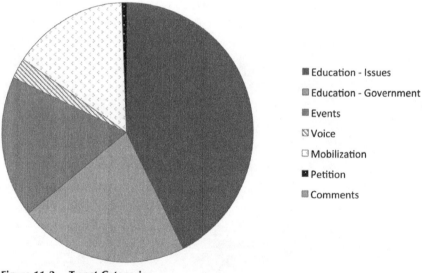

Figure 11.3.   Tweet Categories
Shamira Gelbman

How Did Interest Groups Educate Followers?

As suggested earlier, a considerable amount of Twitter activity conducted by the interest groups in this study is devoted to civic education. In fact, more than 60 percent of the coded tweets (and more than 30 percent of all tweets) provided followers with background information, newly released updates and reports, and analytical discussions about a variety of issues and government proceedings. The prevalence of such instructional tweets by interest groups raises questions as to how this civic education is carried out. For example, do interest groups tend to present information about issues and government proceedings in raw form, or do they predigest it for ease of consumption by followers who may lack the savvy or forbearance to decipher it themselves? And to what extent do they incorporate, whether wittingly or not, pedagogical best practices that seek to engage followers in "active learning" or take pains to make issue information and governmental developments personally relevant to their followers?

It bears noting at the outset of this discussion that, in contrast to other social media platforms, Twitter's 140-character length limit for user postings places a substantial constraint on the capacity for elaborate explanation in tweets themselves.[18] As such, only a few of the "Education—Issues" and "Education—Government" tweets directly conveyed information, usually a newly published statistic (e.g., "Who opposes the #HHS mandate? Women. 54% of likely women voters 18 to 54 oppose") or an announcement of the outcome of a governmental proceeding (e.g., "Illinois Governor Signs #MarriageEquality Into Law").[19] Far more frequently, "civic education" was conducted off-medium, with the tweets themselves serving as inducements for followers to click on links to informational reports, the interest groups' own blog posts, YouTube videos, or traditional media outlets' article coverage.

In some cases, the interest groups used Twitter simply as a means for transmitting governmental process outputs in essentially as-is form. Toward the end of the month, for example, ACLU retweeted its National Security Project Director's posting of the link to a full-text PDF of a district court opinion with just a bare statement of the ruling's bottom line.[20] More typically, though, the organizations took care to repackage information in user-friendly formats. Thus, tweets very often contained links to YouTube videos and organizational blog posts with plain-language explanations of issue information and governmental developments. Similarly, the interest groups occasionally posted or linked to infographics with visual representations of complex processes. In one, FRC offered a flow chart of the progress and future steps of a multifaceted campaign to secure a "military religious freedom" provision in 2014 defense spending legislation.[21] Another, posted by NCLR, presented English and Spanish depictions of a "Yellow Brick Road" of deadlines for open enrollment in health insurance plans under the Affordable Care Act.[22]

In addition to presenting information in accessible formats, many tweets in the two "Education" categories suggest efforts to make seemingly arcane information personally engaging. For instance, an ACLU update on the growing roster of congressional sponsors of an NSA reform bill prompted followers to follow the link embedded in the tweet in order to answer the question, "Is your rep on the list?"[23] Similarly, an AARP tweet prompted followers to "learn something new" by taking an online quiz about Social Security benefits.[24]

From Education to Action

As noted earlier, a fairly small proportion of the interest groups' tweets prompted followers to take action in support of their causes or otherwise engage in political activity. Indeed, only about 18 percent of coded tweets (and less than 9 percent of all tweets) fell into the "Voice," "Mobilization," and "Petition" categories. Nevertheless, the 164 tweets that do include or link to some exhortation for participation shed light on both interest groups' adaptation to the new world of digital activism and followers' responsiveness to their mobilization appeals.

Particularly in response to the hype surrounding social media use during the 2009 election protests in Iran and the Arab Spring of 2011, popular and scholarly observers have engaged in considerable debate over the nature of activism promoted on Twitter and other social media. While some have celebrated the democratizing and revolutionary potential of social media,[25] critics have alleged that social media-based mobilization yields only "clicktivism" and "slacktivism," deprecating references to Internet users involvement in feel-good but materially inconsequential activist activities—for example, "liking" (on Facebook) or "favoriting" (on Twitter) cause-related content, weighing in on a pseudo-poll, or replacing one's avatar or profile photograph with a cause-related image.[26] A recent study, moreover, found that "slacktivism" is not merely inconsequential, but actually detrimental to citizens' subsequent propensity for meaningful activism.[27]

There is some evidence to suggest that the legacy interest groups in this study are joining the "clicktivism" bandwagon. ACLU, for example, asked for "a #Thanksgiving RT" as part of a campaign to encourage President Obama to review and commute long sentences for nonviolent offenders.[28] Other organizations likewise encouraged followers to upload and share images or use particular hashtags in tweets in support of their causes. Nevertheless, while the encouragement of "slacktivism" is certainly evident in some tweets from some groups, it is far from the only sort of activity promoted by most organizations in this study. Some, in fact, only urged relatively traditional forms of political action, including contacting congressmen, making financial contributions to causes, attending community meetings, and becoming card-carrying interest group members. A few of the organizations also used Twitter for "get out the vote" purposes, both for the gubernatorial elections in New Jersey and Virginia early in the month and for a pro-life ballot initiative in Albuquerque, New Mexico on November 19.[29]

As with the "Education-Issues" and "Education-Government" tweets, the interest groups' mobilization tweets also featured creative efforts to engage followers. Drawing on celebrities' social capital was especially prevalent in tweets in this category. AARP, for example, tweeted a short YouTube video featuring racecar driver Jeff Gordon to promote action steps in a campaign against hunger.[30] NAACP likewise partnered with singer-songwriter John Legend to advance its voter registration and voting rights initiatives.[31] The most extensive celebrity-based mobilization effort was HRC's "Love Conquers Hate" campaign, which in November 2013 alone featured retweets of more than fifty celebrity postings in opposition to Russia's anti-gay propaganda law, most containing mobilization language encouraging followers to take part as well.

On the other hand, the relatively small number of tweets in the four mobilization categories insinuates probable missed opportunities for activating followers. For example, although FRC linked to an informational article about the Albuquerque abortion ballot initiative, it did not overtly encourage followers to take part in the vote.[32] A number of tweets in the "Events" category in particular suggest that using Twitter to encourage participation is often an afterthought, if it is thought of at all. FCNL, for example, held its semiannual "Lobby Day" in Washington, DC, on November 14. The first Twitter reference to the event was posted just three days earlier, and that retweeted posting by the Committee's Executive Secretary was essentially a "countdown" message with no call for participation.[33] Quite a few other announcements were made within hours of event start times, likely too late for interested followers to make arrangements to attend.

Do Followers Respond?

Web 2.0 platforms—that is, Internet technologies that facilitate active contribution by users rather than just their passive consumption of information—are lauded for their transformation of mass communication from the traditional one-way conveyance of information to dynamically interactive sites of relatively egalitarian interchange. Research on nonprofit organizations' use of new media technologies has not generally shown them to promote very much interaction between organizations and supporters, however. Both Bortree and Seltzer and Waters et al., for example, found that advocacy groups have not generally been successful at promoting "dialogic" or otherwise interactive relationships with users on Facebook.[34] In an analysis of forty national environmental organization blogs, Merry likewise found that, despite interest groups' active use of blogs to educate the public, there was disappointingly little interactivity between organizations and citizens in these forums.[35] There is, nevertheless, reason to suspect that Twitter might differ from other social media in this respect. After all, as Murthy emphasizes, Twitter is "designed to facilitate interactive multicasting" through its prominent hashtagging and retweeting features.[36] Thus, unlike Facebook, a social networking interface based on pre-existing friendship ties, and standard blogs, which open space for relatively linear blogger-reader conversation in comments sections, Twitter seems designed to foster spontaneous and rapid interaction across complex user networks.

So, do Twitter's "multicasting" features in fact lend themselves to greater interactivity between interest groups and rank-and-file supporters? The short answer to this question seems to be no; in fact, perhaps the most striking finding of this study is just how infrequently interest group content is retweeted, "favorited," or replied to by other users. Despite their thousands of subscribed followers, coded tweets by interest groups were retweeted just thirty-three times on average. When HRC—the organization with the greatest number of followers (well over 300,000 at the end of the data collection period) and the only one in the study to have any of its content retweeted more than five hundred times—is excluded, the average number of retweets drops to eleven. More than a third of all coded tweets were retweeted fewer than five times, including nearly a hundred that were not retweeted at all, and, again excluding HRC, only a small handful of tweets were retweeted more than fifty times. Across all groups, moreover, retweets were far more prevalent than other observable user reactions to Twitter content such as favoriting tweets or replying to them, as shown in figure 11.4.

It also bears noting that the civic education postings that enjoy the most retweets tend to be those highlighting news or information that is already salient or well-known. For example, the single most recirculated tweet in the study—an

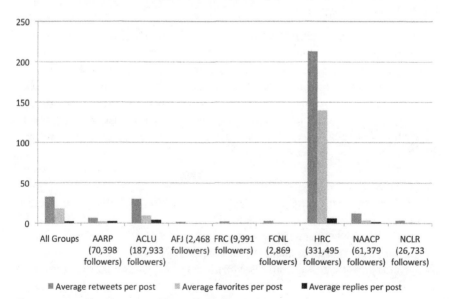

Figure 11.4. Retweets, Favorites, and Replies
Shamira Gelbman

HRC announcement of the Illinois House of Representatives' vote to legalize same-sex marriage that was retweeted more than three thousand times—reported a widely broadcast news story. Not a week later, a tweet by the same organization on the progress of an initiative to facilitate discharge document amendments by transgender veterans was retweeted a mere fifty-eight times.[37] Thus, even as interest groups are using Twitter to educate the public about lesser-known aspects of their focal issues and less salient governmental developments, they do not seem to be successful at piquing followers' interest in these matters.

CONCLUSION

The preceding discussion suggests a mixed bag of conclusions regarding the use of social media by interest groups to promote civic education and engagement. On the one hand, even "legacy" organizations seem to have embraced Twitter, among other social media, as an important means to advance their civic education efforts. Large proportions of their tweets are devoted to promulgating information about issues and governmental processes, often with eye-catching graphics and sometimes with innovative modes of presentation and novel ways for followers to engage with new information, interest group staffers, and government officials. On the other hand, the public does not appear to be well engaged by interest groups' civic education efforts. While some organizations do have very large numbers of followers, their audience does not seem inclined to interact with these interest groups on Twitter after having made the initial decision to subscribe to their tweets. Nor do the interest groups themselves consistently use Twitter as effectively as they might to apprise citizens of new developments and engage them in productive political activity. Thus, while interest groups are clearly using social media for civic education, it is also evident that there is considerable room for improvement, particularly in actuating the dynamic and interactive potential of new media.

NOTES

1. See, for example, Grant Jordan and William Maloney, *Democracy and Interest Groups: Enhancing Participation?* (Basingstoke and New York: Palgrave Macmillan, 2007); David K. Ryden, *Representation in Crisis: The Constitution, Interest Groups, and Parties* (Albany, NY: SUNY Press, 1996); Jack L. Walker Jr. *Mobilizing Interest Groups in America: Patrons, Professions, and Social Movements* (Ann Arbor: University of Michigan Press, 1991).

2. David Karpf, *The MoveOn Effect: The Unexpected Transformation of American Political Advocacy* (Oxford: Oxford University Press, 2012), chap. 1.

3. Obat et al., "Advocacy 2.0: An Analysis of How Advocacy Groups in the United States Perceive and Use Social Media as Tools for Facilitating Civic Engagement and Collective Action," *Journal of Information Policy* 2 (2012).

4. Christine B. Williams and Girish J. "Jeff" Gulati, "Social Networks in Political Campaigns: Facebook and the Congressional Elections of 2006 and 2008," *New Media & Society* 15 (2012).

5. Aaron Smith, "Civic Engagement in the Digital Age," *Pew Research Center*, 2013, http://pewinternet.org/Reports/2013/Civic-Engagement.aspx (accessed August 11, 2014).

6. While social media use for political communication is on the rise across age groups, there also seems to be an emerging generation gap in social media platform preferences such that young adults are gravitating to Twitter even as Facebook is gaining popularity among older cohorts. As such, an analysis of "legacy" interest groups' use of this particular new media technology lends additional insight into the prospects of their continued role in the civic engagement arena.

7. Obar et al., "Advocacy 2.0," 10. Two of the organizations (AFJ and HRC) are listed in Obar et al.'s "Other" category of surveyed groups that did not provide information about the size of their staff.

8. Karpf, *The MoveOn Effect.*

9. Obar et al., "Advocacy 2.0," 13.

10. Ibid., 13.

11. Ibid.

12. Ibid.

13. Ibid.

14. Ibid.

15. Twitter would probably serve especially well for this purpose due to the system of "hashtags," or keywords (or unspaced phrases) preceded by the # symbol and placed in the body of a tweet, that can be used to identify all nonprivate postings on a topic or theme. Indeed, a few tweets examined in this study hint at this sort of comment aggregation strategy by urging followers to include a particular hashtag in tweets related to an interest group campaign. See, for example, ACLU National, Twitter post, November 19, 2013, 4:25 p.m., http://twitter.com/ACLU; NCLR, Twitter post, November 20, 2013, 11:47 a.m. http://twitter.com/NCLR.

16. Obar et al., "Advocacy 2.0," 13.

17. Whereas most of the AARP's uncoded tweets were unrelated to political advocacy or civic engagement, most of the FRC's were "thank you notes" to individual followers who had retweeted or otherwise shared the organization's Twitter content.

18. Serial tweets, or a series of numbered tweets that comprise a single communication when strung together, can be used to circumvent the 140-character limit. However, only two instances of serial tweeting occur in this study's tweet set.

19. FRC, Twitter post, November 27, 2013, 9:46 a.m., http://twitter.com/FRCdc; Human Rights Campaign, Twitter post, November 21, 2013, 3:12 p.m., http://twitter.com/HRC.

20. Hina Shamsi, Twitter post, November 25, 2013, 12:31 p.m., http://twitter.com/HinaShamsi.

21. FRC, Twitter post, November 26, 2013, 11:13 a.m., http://twitter.com/FRCdc.

22. NCLR, Twitter post, November 14, 2013, 6:10 p.m., http://twitter.com/NCLR.

23. ACLU National, Twitter post, November 22, 2013, 2:37 p.m., http://twitter.com/ACLU.

24. AARP, Twitter post, November 17, 2013, 5:00 p.m., http://twitter.com/AARP.

25. For example, see Simon Lindgren, "The Potential and Limitations of Twitter Activism: Mapping the 2011 Libyan Uprising," *Communication, Capitalism & Critique* 11 (2013): 207–20; Stephanie Vie, "In Defense of 'Slacktivism': The Human Rights Campaign Logo as Digital Activism," *First Monday* 19 (2014), accessed August 10, 2014, doi: http://dx.doi.org/10.5210.fmv19i4.4961.

26. See, for example, Malcolm Gladwell, "Small Change: Why the Revolution Will Not Be Tweeted," *The New Yorker*, October 4, 2010, www.newyorker.com/reporting/2010/10/04/101004fa_fact_gladwell; Evgeny Morozov, "Iran: Downside to the 'Twitter Revolution,'" *Dissent* 56 (2009). There is some resonance between new concerns about "slacktivism" and somewhat older apprehension regarding the transformation of American civic life such that "checkbook activism" has replaced meaningful associational membership. See, for example, Theda Skocpol, *Diminished Democracy: From Membership to Management in American Civic Life* (Norman: University of Oklahoma Press, 2003).

27. Kirk Kristofersson et al., "The Nature of Slacktivism: How the Social Observability of an Initial Act of Token Support Affects Subsequent Prosocial Action," *Journal of Consumer Research* (forthcoming).

28. ACLU National, Twitter post, November 27, 2013, 2:42 p.m., http://twitter.com/ACLU.

29. For example, NAACP, Twitter post, November 4, 2013, 7:31 p.m., http://twitter.com/NAACP; NAACP, Twitter post, November 4, 2013, 8:31 p.m., http://twitter.com/NAACP; ACLU National, Twitter post, November 19, 2013, 7:54 p.m., http://twitter.com/ACLU.

30. AARP, Twitter post, November 1, 2013, 1:25 p.m., http://twitter.com/AARP.

31. John Legend, Twitter post, November 4, 2013, 2:53 p.m., http://twitter.com/johnlegend.

32. FRC, Twitter post, November 18, 2013, 12:45 p.m., http://twitter.com/FRCdc.

33. Diane Randall, Twitter post, November 11, 2013, 6:20 p.m., http://twitter.com/DianeFCNL.

34. Denise Bortree and Trent Selter"Dialogic Strategies and Outcomes: A Review of Environmental Advocacy Groups' Facebook Profiles," *Public Relations Review* 35 (2009); Richard Waters et al., "Engaging Stakeholders through Social Networking: How Nonprofit Organizations Are Using Facebook," *Public Relations Review* 35 (2009).

35. Melissa Merry, "Blogging and Environmental Advocacy: A New Way to Engage the Public?" *Review of Policy Research* 27 (2010).

36. Dhiraj Murthy, *Twitter: Social Communication in the Twitter Age* (Cambridge: Polity Press, 2013), 6.

37. Human Rights Campaign, Twitter post, November 5, 2013, 5:06 p.m., http://twitter.com/HRC; Human Rights Campaign, Twitter post, November 11, 2013, 10:38

a.m., http://twitter.com/HRC. Unsurprisingly, perhaps, the single most retweeted posting by an organization other than HRC was the ACLU's tweet on the Illinois House vote on same-sex marriage. See ACLU National, Twitter post, November 5, 2013, 5:05 p.m. http://twitter.com/ACLU.

BIBLIOGRAPHY

Bortree, Denise S. and Trent Seltzer. "Dialogic Strategies and Outcomes: A Review of Environmental Advocacy Groups' Facebook Profiles." *Public Relations Review* 35 (2009): 317–319.

Gladwell, Malcolm. "Small Change: Why the Revolution Will Not Be Tweeted." *The New Yorker* (October 4, 2010), retrieved from www.newyorker.com/reporting/2010/10/04/101004fa_fact_gladwell.

Guo, Chao and Gregory D. Saxton. "Tweeting Social Change: How Social Media Are Changing Nonprofit Advocacy." *Nonprofit and Voluntary Sector Quarterly* 43 (2014): 57–79.

Jordan, Grant and William Maloney. *Democracy and Interest Groups: Enhancing Participation?* Basingstoke and New York: Palgrave Macmillan, 2007.

Karpf, David. *The MoveOn Effect: The Unexpected Transformation of American Political Advocacy*. Oxford: Oxford University Press, 2012.

Kristofersson, Kirk, Katherine White, and John Peloza. "The Nature of Slacktivism: How the Social Observability of an Initial Act of Token Support Affects Subsequent Prosocial Action." *Journal of Consumer Research* (forthcoming).

Lindgren, Simon. "The Potential and Limitations of Twitter Activism: Mapping the 2011 Libyan Uprising." *Communication, Capitalism & Critique* 11 (2013): 207–20.

Merry, Melissa K. "Blogging and Environmental Advocacy: A New Way to Engage the Public?" *Review of Policy Research* 27 (2010): 641–56.

Morozov, Evgeny. "Iran: Downside to the 'Twitter Revolution.'" *Dissent* 56 (2009): 10–14.

Murthy, Dhiraj. *Twitter: Social Communication in the Twitter Age*. Cambridge: Polity Press, 2013.

Obar, Jonathan A., Paul Zube, and Clifford Lampe. "Advocacy 2.0: An Analysis of How Advocacy Groups in the United States Perceive and Use Social Media as Tools for Facilitating Civic Engagement and Collective Action." *Journal of Information Policy* 2 (2012): 1–25.

Ryden, David K. *Representation in Crisis: The Constitution, Interest Groups, and Political Parties*. Albany: SUNY Press, 1996.

Skocpol, Theda. *Diminished Democracy: From Membership to Management in American Civic Life*. Norman: University of Oklahoma Press, 2003.

Smith, Aaron. "Civic Engagement in the Digital Age." *Pew Research Center*, 2013, retrieved from http://pewinternet.org/Reports/2013/Civic-Engagement.aspx.

Vie, Stephanie. "In Defense of 'Slacktivism': The Human Rights Campaign Logo as Digital Activism." *First Monday* 19 (2014). Accessed August 10, 2014. doi: http://dx.doi.org/10.5210.fmv19i4.4961.

Walker, Jack L., Jr. *Mobilizing Interest Groups in America: Patrons, Professions, and Social Movements.* Ann Arbor: University of Michigan Press, 1991.

Waters, Richard D., Emily Burnett, Emily Lamm, and Jessica Lucas. "Engaging Stakeholders through Social Networking: How Nonprofit Organizations Are Using Facebook." *Public Relations Review* 35 (2009): 102–106.

Williams, Christine B., and Girish J. "Jeff" Gulati. "Social Networks in Political Campaigns: Facebook and the Congressional Elections of 2006 and 2008." *New Media & Society* 15 (2012): 52–71.

Cited Tweets

AARP. "Twitter / @AARP: RT @Drive2EndHunger: VIDEO: . . ." November 1, 2013, 1:25 p.m. https://twitter.com/AARP/status/396327128238927872.

AARP. "Twitter / @AARP: How well do you know Social . . ." November 17, 2013, 5:00 p.m. https://twitter.com/AARP/status/402194476351107072.

ACLU National. "Twitter / @ACLU: BREAKING: The freedom to marry . . ." November 5, 2013, 5:05 p.m. https://twitter.com/ACLU/status/397847149355888640.

ACLU National. "Twitter / @ACLU: Say NO to border militarization . . ." November 19, 2013, 4:25 p.m. https://twitter.com/ACLU/status/402910582669467651.

ACLU National. "Twitter / @ACLU: New Mexico: Today vote AGAINST . . ." November 19, 2013, 7:54 p.m. https://twitter.com/ACLU/status/402963195960098816.

ACLU National. "Twitter / @ACLU: Yesterday, the true #NSA reform . . ." November 22, 2013, 2:37 p.m. https://twitter.com/ACLU/status/403970593105539072.

ACLU National. "Twitter / @ACLU: .@Jezebel This mom wants her . . ." November 27, 2013, 2:42 p.m. https://twitter.com/ACLU/status/405783643554996225.

FRC. "Twitter / @FRCdc: Operation #ProLife Cities, . . ." November 18, 2013, 12:45 p.m. https://twitter.com/FRCdc/status/402492798303481857.

FRC. "Twitter / @FRCdc: A helpful look at what supporters . . ." November 26, 2013, 11:13 a.m. https://twitter.com/FRCdc/status/405368668378660864.

FRC. "Twitter / @FRCdc: Who opposes the #HHS mandate? . . ." November 27, 2013, 9:46 a.m., https://twitter.com/FRCdc/status/405709158831652864.

Human Rights Campaign. "Twitter / @HRC: Congrats to Illinois! Marriage . . ." November 5, 2013, 5:06 p.m. https://twitter.com/HRC/status/397847331447382017.

Human Rights Campaign. "Twitter / @HRC: Trangender Service Members . . ." November 11, 2013, 10:38 a.m. https://twitter.com/HRC/status/399924217317036033.

Human Rights Campaign. "Twitter / @HRC: Illinois Governor Signs . . ." November 21, 2013, 3:12 p.m. https://twitter.com/HRC/status/403616940263866368.

Legend, John. "Twitter / @johnlegend: I'm proud to join the @NAACP . . ." November 4, 2013, 2:53 p.m. https://twitter.com/johnlegend/status/397451477964161024.

NAACP. "Twitter / @NAACP: Tomorrow is Election Day in . . ." November 4, 2013, 7:31 p.m. https://twitter.com/NAACP/status/397521405736398848.

NAACP. "Twitter / @NAACP: Virginia's Election Day is . . ." November 4, 2013, 8:31 p.m. https://twitter.com/NAACP/status/397536555516305408.

NCLR. "Twitter / @NCLR: Following the Road to Enrollment . . ." November 20, 2013, 6:10 p.m. https://twitter.com/NCLR/status/401125003401252864.

NCLR. "Twitter / NCLR: Join the #fast4families and . . ." November 14, 2013, 11:47 a.m. https://twitter.com/NCLR/status/403202877042470912.

Randall, Diane. "Twitter / @DianeFCNL: Only 3 more days until @FCNL . . ." November 11, 2013, 6:20 p.m. https://twitter.com/DianeFCNL/status/400040290968678400.

Shamsi, Hina. "Twitter / @HinaShamsi: Court rejects #NYPD defense . . ." November 25, 2013, 12:31 p.m. https://twitter.com/HinaShamsi/status/405025934580801536.

Section III

CIVIC EDUCATION IN INSTITUTIONS OF HIGHER EDUCATION

Part A: Classroom-based Studies

Chapter Twelve

Dude, Where's the Civic Engagement?

The Paradoxical Effect of Civic Education on the Probability of Civic Participation*

Donald M. Gooch and Dr. Michael Rogers

Scholars have long emphasized the importance of civic education in build-ing citizen capacity for democracy. As Rogers explains in chapter 1, there is quite an extensive history of calls for civic education in the West generally and in the United States particularly. The idea dates to at least Plato and Aristotle in Ancient Greece.[1] In fact, in *Politics* Aristotle identifies participa-tion in the governance of the state as a criterion of virtuous citizens. As he explains, "the *polis* . . . is an aggregate of many members; and education is therefore *the* means of making it a community and giving it unity."[2] Aristotle establishes the important role civic education plays in a regime. Similarly, America's founders placed a lot of stock in civic education. Noah Webster viewed civic education as a vital tool for social engineering; it was a means for instilling civic values in citizens. Alternatively, Jefferson saw civic educa-tion as essential in staving off the tyranny and corruption of the state; it was a means for educating citizens in how to protect themselves from government encroachments.[3] Generally, as Rogers explains in chapter 1, the Founders be-lieved civic education is the key to preserving America's democratic repub-lic. This belief recurs throughout America's history, from Mann's common school movement of the nineteenth century to Dewey and the Progressives' educational reforms in the twentieth century to the Civic Mission of Schools Movement today. Converse puts it best when he claims civic education is the universal solvent of political behavior.[4]

---

*This study of civic education, civic literacy, and civic engagement at three universities expands on our earlier study of civic education and civic literacy at one university. For the original study, see Donald M. Gooch and Michael T. Rogers, "A Natural Disaster of Civic Proportions: College Students in the Natural State Falls Short of the Naturalization Benchmark," *Midsouth Political Science Review* 13, no. 1 (2012).

In this chapter, we study the interrelationships between civic education, civic literacy, civic participation, and civic efficacy. Consistent with the results of our earlier study in 2012, we find the overall state of college student civic knowledge is low. We also argue civic education in the form of a college class on American government yields substantial improvements in it.[5] We take a multifaceted approach to investigate the causal mechanisms that influence levels of civic knowledge and engagement. Utilizing a pretest/posttest quasi-experimental research design implemented at three universities (two in Texas and one in Arkansas) over multiple semesters from 2012 to 2013, we assess the impact of civic education, civic efficacy, and political interest on civic participation. We use a multivariate statistical analysis that models likely civic participation using civic education, civic participation, civic efficacy, and political interest as determinants.

We find a paradoxical relationship between civic literacy and likely civic participation. One the one hand, there is a significant and positive relationship between political interest, civic efficacy, and past civic participation with likely civic participation. On the other hand, we find no such relationship between civic literacy and likely civic participation. Indeed, some models show higher levels of civic literacy are negatively correlated with likely civic participation. Apparently, civic education does tend to improve civic knowledge and provide citizens with a greater capacity to participate in political decision-making. Yet, it is higher levels of political interest and feelings of civic efficacy as well as past civic participation that drive the likelihood of citizens to participate in civic activities. In fact, civic knowledge has a countervailing effect on likely participation in some models. This means civic education is not an unmitigated good. As a tool for promoting civic engagement, civic education may sometimes be ineffective, even counterproductive. Given the complexity of the interrelationship between civic-mindedness and civic activity, we caution against a myopic approach to civic education. The complex interrelationships between civic literacy, civic efficacy, and civic participation suggest a multifaceted, multipedagogical, and overlapping approach to civic education is necessary, especially if the goal is to improve civic literacy *and* civic engagement.

CIVIC EDUCATION: A GROWING FIELD OF EMPIRICAL INQUIRY

Systematic empirical study of civic education and its effects is minimal given its long history. This is changing given widespread concern over a "civic crisis" or "recession" today.[6] A central impetus for this concern is Putnam's groundbreaking work on America's decline in social capital since the mid-1900s.[7] The academic response to this crisis has been substantial. While the pervasive civic illiteracy of Americans has been well-documented, there has been renewed vigor in such empirical inquiries. Secondly, there has been increased scrutiny of the ability of formal civic education to produce competent citizens.

America's Poor Civic Literacy

Given America's concern over a civics crisis, there has been extensive research of American civic illiteracy. America's minimal knowledge of politics has long been known, as our earliest political surveys from the mid-twentieth century established it. More recent studies continue to confirm it.[8] In fact, Dudley and Gitelson observe recent scholarly research "has often taken the character of a race to discover the most appalling lack of knowledge."[9] For example, the McCormick Tribune Freedom Museum did a civic survey in 2006. Most major media outlets (including *USA Today*, the *Boston Globe*, and Foxnews.com among others) seized on their survey findings, which showed Americans knew more members of the Simpsons cartoon family than first amendment rights.[10] Then, there are annual, large-n studies of civic literacy conducted by the Intercollegiate Studies Institute (ISI) since 2005. Beyond their provocative titles are equally disturbing statistics, as ISI claims students manage little better than a coin-flip or around 50 percent correct on civics exams, that a subset of officeholders do no better but actually worse (44 percent) than the general public (49 percent), and that college education is no panacea as college seniors (54.2 percent) typically performed only slightly better than freshmen (50.4 percent).[11] These findings fuel the sense of a civics crisis and reinforce some established scholarly insights. Foremost, their findings buttress the conventional view that students who exhibit greater understanding of politics are significantly more likely to engage in citizenship activities.[12]

Unfortunately, this scholarly triage fails to correct a faulty popular belief that civic literacy is in decline. On the contrary, time series inquiries show civic literacy today is no worse than in the past. As Delli Carpini and Keeter observe, "Americans are essentially no more or less informed about politics than they were fifty years ago."[13] They argue there are three general types of voters—the ignorant, the generalist, and the specialist.[14] They conclude Americans are not ignorant but also not highly informed; what Americans know is a reflection of what they are exposed to, and they are best categorized as generalists.[15] Given their finding, one understands why the American Political Science Association's Task Force on Civic Education for the 21st Century concluded the problem of ignorance in the American electorate has proved as difficult to eradicate as cancer.[16]

Debating the Effectiveness of a Civics Curriculum

Given America's poor civic literacy, United States' educational institutions have seen increased scrutiny. Many political figures (e.g., former Supreme Court Justice O'Connor and former Senator Graham) have pointed to the decline in America's formal curriculum, particularly at the high school level.[17] Yet, scholars disagree on whether a civics curriculum, per se, matters. In the earliest studies in the mid-twentieth century, the conventional view to emerge was educational levels generally improve civic literacy but civics courses have negligible effect. Contrary to common sense, Langton and Jennings's 1960s seminal study of the subject found civics courses had no real effect on civic literacy. While they acknowledge most studies show mixed results, their investigation "offers strikingly little support for the impact of [a civics] curriculum."[18] They offer the "redundancy theory as explanation," that once a person meets a basic threshold of knowledge in a subject additional instruction has negligible impact.[19] As a corollary they offer the "sponge theory." Based on the data for African Americans, they argue demographics not saturated in politics had greater aptitude for gains from a civics curriculum. Essentially, people with low information have more room to soak up new content. For such people, a civics course can have an impact.[20] Overall, Langton and Jennings conclude unless "a radical restructuring of the courses" occurs, "[o]ur findings certainly do not support the thinking of those who look to the civics curriculum in American high schools as even a minor source of political socialization."[21]

Today, Langton and Jennings's view persists. Many scholars question if an enhanced civics curriculum is the solution. For example, Conover and Searing argue taking a course in civics has "virtually no relationship to the students' sense of citizenship," except in one area. They concede "having a civics course makes students more aware of their legal duties as citizens."[22] There is, however, a growing literature challenging this view. Although the impact is weak, Delli Carpini and Keeter find self-reported higher levels of study of government in high school increased knowledge of "the rules of the game"—that is, better understanding of government structures and processes.[23]

For the collegiate level, Nie and Hillygus provide indirect evidence a civics curriculum matters. Examining collegiate degrees, they find a strong, positive correlation between increased social science credit hours and political engagement and participation. In contrast, increased humanities and education credits show no real effect, and increased credits in business, the sciences, and engineering all had a negative impact on civic engagement. The point is, social sciences—where civics courses are housed—mattered.[24] Likewise, in an earlier version of our study we find a small but significant growth in civic knowledge (particularly of government structures) among college students through one civics course in college.[25] Of course, this could be a confirmation of Langton and Jennings's sponge theory as our study was of largely Arkansas natives who typically last had a civics course in ninth grade.

Still, the strongest case curriculum matters is in Niemi and Junn's work. Studying secondary education, they find it is a combination of the amount of civics curriculum with how recent it was taken that matters. They claim, "having had a civics or American government course in twelfth grade gives a student a 2 percentage-point edge over someone whose last course was earlier, and an additional 2 points over students who have had no civics courses."[26] Their observations suggest an alternative to the redundancy theory, what we dub the exposure theory. More akin to the sponge theory, the exposure theory holds a civics curriculum matters most depending on the amount of previous civics exposure combined with how recent that exposure occurred. Following the logic of the exposure theory, Niemi and Junn found students with no or little previous civics instruction are the most prone to a sizable increase in civics literacy through a civics curriculum. The key difference from the sponge theory is Niemi and Junn continue to find a meaningful, though minimal increase in civic knowledge as a student moves from one civics course to more.[27] Their work suggests exposure matters, but the endurance of increased knowledge is probably short-term unless used. It also seems likely the growth decreases rapidly with the number of civic courses taken.

In this study as in our earlier inquiry, we confirm the poor civic literacy of one group of Americans, college students.[28] However, this inquiry greatly expands our previous 2012 one by increasing the inquiry to two new universities (Stephen F. Austin State and Sam Houston State) while continuing to collect data for Arkansas Tech University. It also adds a whole new affective measurement not part of the original survey mechanism. Now, on top of measuring what affect one college civic course has on civic literacy, we have a battery of questions measuring the civic engagement and likely future civic participation of students.

CIVIC EDUCATION, CIVIC LITERACY, CIVIC EFFICACY, AND CIVIC INTEREST

Since scholarship holds political knowledge in America is low and has changed little over time, the question becomes: Is this a problem? Although research suggests the 'reasoning voter' needs few informational cues to participate in elections,[29] many academics believe the average American citizen lacks an adequate level of political information for effective participation.[30] Voters require some information and an ability to employ it to make satisficing decisions. Citizens lacking political or civic efficacy may find it prohibitively difficult to participate effectively.[31] Popular participation anchors policies and decisions by government actors in authoritative consent and acts as a check on government when it strays from public assent. It nourishes the political system through pluralistic institutions and in competitive campaigns. As we have previously argued, democratic societies depend on a politically efficacious electorate to produce responsive public policy, to constrain and influence government, and to hold government accountable retrospectively and prospectively.[32]

That said, a large body of theoretical work hypothesizes a link between civic education, interest, and participation. Yet, there exists a dearth of empirical study of their interplay. To promote such empirical research, in 1996 the American Political Science Association (APSA) organized a Task Force on Civic Education for the 21st Century. Some important ramifications of this task force were the development of new measurements of civic education and the establishment of objectives for achieving higher levels of civic efficacy.[33] Although this task force has since been disbanded, APSA replaced it with the first ever Standing Committee on Civic Education and Engagement. Even with this new vigor in academic research of civic education and engagement, the interrelationship between civic literacy, civic interest, civic education, and civic participation remains largely theoretical with few studies systematically examining their interplay

Behaviorally, we know the dimensions of civic participation and civic engagement through the literatures on civic literacy, civic interest, and civic efficacy. Civic knowledge is defined as retention of the information essential for active citizens to participate in politics. This entails knowledge of candidates, political issues, party positions, and political events.[34] Civic literacy empowers citizens to hold officeholders accountable for their policies and political decisions. Civic interest and civic efficacy are affective dimensions that motivate individuals to acquire and retain civic knowledge and to participate in the community.[35] Given that citizens are cognitive misers with strong disincentives for acquiring civic knowledge, civic interest is a significant component in citizens acquiring higher levels of civic literacy and civic efficacy.[36] Undoubtedly civic interest encourages citizens to broaden their civic knowledge base. However, it does not necessarily follow that increased civic knowledge will result in higher levels of civic interest, nor more civic participation.[37]

While conventional wisdom and behavioral studies suggest civic participation, civic interest, and civic efficacy are natural by-products of improved civic literacy, there is a dearth of empirical studies to prove it. Assessing the relationship between civic knowledge, civic interest, and political participation is of prime importance to attempts to improve American civic literacy and engagement. This study starts to unpack the complicated interrelationship of these variables.

Methodology

Utilizing a pretest/posttest quasi-experimental research design, we are able to examine the impacts of civic literacy and knowledge, civic participation and likely participation, as well as political interest and civic efficacy with strong internal validity. We assess longitudinal changes in these civic characteristics from the start to finish of a four month course. This study also tests the robustness of the findings we reported previously.[38] More importantly, we examine trends in civic literacy and assess the effect civic education has on civic participation. For policymakers, our work provides invaluable information on how a civics course in college impacts civic literacy and political participation. For civic educators, our work enhances current academic knowledge by showing the impact teachers can have on improving the civic literacy, engagement, and likely future participation of college students.

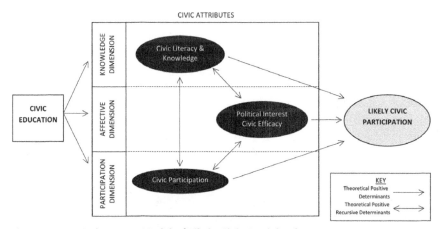

Figure 12.1.   Endogenous Model of Likely Civic Participation
Don Gooch and Mike Rogers

In our 2012 study, we posited that these influences—while conceptually distinct—are endogenous and self-supporting. Here, we extend and update our model of civic education and likely civic participation (Figure 12.1). The endogenous model of civic education posits that civic education has an indirect effect on likely civic participation through the medium of civic attributes in three primary dimensions: the knowledge dimension, the affective dimension, and the participation dimension. The knowledge dimension includes civic knowledge (retained information about civic institutions, leaders, and political institutions) and civic literacy (the understanding of civic processes and pathways for political activism). The affective dimension involves a citizen's feelings about civics. This includes both their level of interest in politics and their beliefs about the political process (i.e., whether it can produce effective solutions to political problems, is open to participation, and includes a democratic cache). Lastly, the participation dimension is necessary, as those who have participated in civic/political activities are more likely to participate again.

We hypothesize all three dimensions are influenced by civic education and higher levels of each dimension are correlated with one another and with the likelihood to participate in a recursive, near exponential relationship. Just as a multitude of waves in the ocean coalesce into a rising tide crashing into the shore, higher levels in one civic attribute dimension redound in the others to produce a more active, effective citizen. Apathetic citizens are typically not motivated to learn or participate in politics. Likewise, a deficit in political knowledge can be a barrier to citizen participation. Conversely, participating in politics and/or learning about civics may generate a greater interest in politics and/or produce an increased likelihood of participation. The simultaneity of civic literacy, political interest, civic efficacy, civic participation, and likely future civic engagement suggests that civic educators have multiple points of entry to improve civic efficacy and political participation but also that improvements in one area may have complex, even counterproductive, effects on other areas. It is a challenging social process to model, understand, and manipulate.[39]

To measure civic literacy, we employ questions from the citizenship exam instrument (Appendix A) we used previously.[40] A version of the citizenship exam has been given to Arkansas Tech University (ATU) American Government courses since 2007. The study here is restricted to data collected since spring 2012 when we added a battery of questions on political participation, political interest, and civic efficacy to the instrument. This survey was also implemented at two additional Texas institutions, Stephen F. Austin State University (SFASU) and Sam Houston State University (SHSU). Thus, data was collected over three semesters at ATU and SFASU, and for one semester at SHSU. This broadens the scope of the assessment and improves the generalizability of the study. The assessment uses a pretest/posttest research design. At all three institutions the instrument was implemented in standard American Government courses.[41] The home towns of the students in the sample are illustrated in figure 12.2. The sample draws from students across Arkansas and East Texas, with large subsamples from the Dallas-Fort Worth and Houston areas in Texas and from the I-40 corridor from Little Rock to Fayetteville in Arkansas.

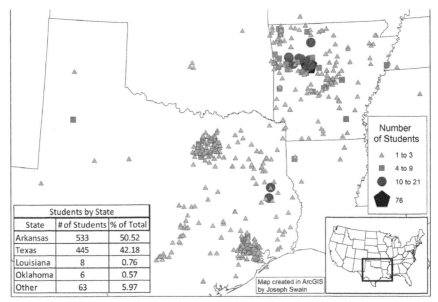

Students by State		
State	# of Students	% of Total
Arkansas	533	50.52
Texas	445	42.18
Louisiana	8	0.76
Oklahoma	6	0.57
Other	63	5.97

Number of Students

△ 1 to 3
■ 4 to 9
● 10 to 21
⬠ 76

Map created in ArcGIS by Joseph Swain

Figure 12.2. Concentration of Students by High School
Joseph Swain

The Citizenship Exam Survey Measures and Data

In the pretest-posttest procedure, the survey was administered at the beginning of the semester and then again at the end when students had either completed the course or were within the final two weeks of doing so. Unique identifiers were assigned to students to protect confidentiality and to match pretests with posttests. For the pretest and posttest comparisons, students who did not complete the exam in either implementation were dropped from the sample.[42]

As for the instrument, it includes questions on demographics, political characteristics, and behavioral measures, in addition to an assessment of civic knowledge through the "citizenship exam." The instrument opens with a demographic battery, collecting data on citizenship, race, gender, family income, and age. We use a standard two-question branching measure for determining party identification and ideology along a seven-point scale. We collect college-student specific data on intended major, high school and college grade point average, as well as the number of semesters of government the respondent has taken in high school and college.

Thus, the instrument includes composite variables to assess civic literacy, civic participation, likely civic participation, and political interest. Civic efficacy is sourced to a single item on the survey. In order to assess participation and likely participation, we use the ANES political participation and likely political participation question batteries from the cumulative file.[43] We employed a measure of attentiveness to politics using a frequency count across four separate mediums: television, in-person conversations, online social media, and visits to websites. We also include a political interest and a news attentiveness item. The instrument concludes with a battery measuring civic literacy using twenty-six questions from the bank of United States Citizenship and Immigration Services (USCIS) naturalization test questions. We have three separate measurements of civic literacy on the citizenship exam. The first measurement treats each required answer as a 'separate' question and rates students accordingly. We label this their "CS" for citizenship score. So, while there are twenty-six questions on the citizenship exam, there are three multi-answer questions that mean the CS score ranges from zero to thirty-three possible points. We prefer this measure because it counts every correct answer given by respondents. As a second measure, students must get multipart questions completely correct in order to be a correct answer. We label this "CS—26" for citizenship score–26, as it ranges from zero to twenty-six possible points. To illustrate the difference, consider the question asking for the three branches of government. If a student names only the executive and legislative branches, that student gets the branches question wrong and receives no point for the CS-26 measurement while he/she gets two of three possible points on the CS measurement.

As a third measurement of civic knowledge, we provide a count of the number of blanks on the citizenship exam portion of the survey. We label this "Blanks Percentage." This measure does not distinguish between right and wrong answers; as long as the respondent wrote a legible answer, they get credit for a response. This measure is counted like the CS measure, so it ranges from zero (attempt given for every possible answer) to thirty-three (no attempt given for any possible answers). Through this measure, we assess the relative confidence each respondent has in their civic knowledge. The logic is that if one leaves the answer blank, they are admitting political apathy. Plausibly, low-knowledge/high-confidence citizens may behave in ways comparable with citizens who have high levels of civic knowledge and attempt to answer questions they do not know. However, those who are apathetic will show little knowledge and are expected to avoid answering most questions. We combine all three measures together in a composite variable we label civic literacy.

Next, the survey contains a battery of questions to assess the current and likely participatory activities of respondents. We combine them into separate composite variables: civic participation and likely civic participation. These questions ask whether the respondent has voted, signed a petition, contacted a public official, or participated in a protest, and whether the respondent is likely to do these in the future. Each of these participation activities exists on a continuum of civic involvement. Voting is the lower end of absolute civic participation while participation in a protest or volunteering for a campaign are the higher end. Given the sample is college students, the likely participation battery may provide more interesting information in terms of civic participation than the actual participation rate. The results from both the actual and likely participation batteries are combined into two summary participation variables. In this analysis, we use an equal-weighting scheme for each participation item. Our measures of civic efficacy and political interest are single survey items. However, the political interest measure we employ in our likely civic participation models is a summary measure of political interest. It combines the political interest measure with activities by respondents to access political information, such as reading a newspaper, watching a political TV show, or reading a political blog.

Again, this study investigates the impact civic education has on likely civic participation as mediated through the civic attributes of civic literacy, civic participation, political interest and civic efficacy. Our analysis examines both absolute levels of civic characteristics and relative changes in those characteristics. A relative civic characteristic is conceptually defined as the level of a civic attribute of a citizen relative to some established benchmark, in this case our pretest survey. An absolute civic characteristic is defined as the level of a civic attribute of a citizen on an established scale. We accomplish that here by examining the levels of civic literacy, civic efficacy, political interest, and civic participation in our posttest sample. Our discussion of absolute civic participation, literacy, efficacy, and political interest examines the pretest and posttest samples separately.

We use two measures of absolute civic literacy as defined in our previous work.[44] Borrowing from the logic of the ISI studies, we use the common educational grade-based standard (100 point scale) where the baseline for civic literacy is a C average or 70% or better in correct responses. The second measure of absolute civic literacy uses the standard of the United States government for the United States Citizenship and Immigration Service (USCIS) Naturalization Test. For individuals applying to become American citizens, they must get six out of the ten randomly selected citizenship questions right in order to pass.[45] For civic efficacy and political interest, we limit our inquiry to comparisons within the study.

For the civics exam portion of the instrument, we drew twenty-six questions from the one hundred question United States Naturalization Test. We grouped these items into four conceptual areas of citizenship:

1. American Political Heritage (APH)—questions covering political symbols and facts like how many stripes are on the flag or how many states are in the Union.
2. Current Politics (CP)—questions on topical political information like who the president is or who the mayor of their town is.
3. Government Structure (GS)—questions on the institutions and processes of American politics like who elects the president or what institution makes laws.
4. Constitution (CON)—questions on the Constitution and its provisions like what is the Bill of Rights or what are changes to the Constitution.

The citizenship exam is weighted mostly toward current politics (33 percent), with a number of questions asking students to name who their current representatives are at the local, state, or federal level. This overrepresentation is intentional, as it is information of much practical utility for active citizen participation, as it is difficult to hold representatives accountable if you do not know who they are.[46] American political heritage questions are underrepresented. While such information is important, it is likely correlated with desire and capacity to participate. It is of the least practical use to active citizens, hence fewer questions were included in this category. There are a relatively equal number of questions on government structure and the Constitution. Both categories are of equal import in terms of utility for active citizens and as indicators of civic knowledge and political interest. These two categories are also often a focus of American Government courses. Together, they comprise about half the citizenship exam.

Sample Characteristics

The demographic data from pretest, posttest, and pre-post samples are similar across the samples and representative of the student bodies from which they are drawn. While ATU has added 2,274 additional students over the course of the data collection period (2007–2013), for a current undergraduate, main-campus student population of 7,688, the relative breakdown of students into gender, racial, and age categories has not changed significantly over this period.[47] The proportion of Whites in this data collection is 81.6%. They are only slightly overrepresented in our pretest sample in comparison to ATU demographics (table 12.1) and close to the state population figure (80.6%) but somewhat below the Pope County population demographics (92% White).[48] The most significant difference between the ATU student population demographics and those of the pretest sample is the three-point overrepresentation of males (47.5%). Since males tend to be underrepresented nationally on

Table 12.1. Comparison of Student & Local Populations to Sample Characteristics by University

Demographic Characteristics		ATU School Population	ATU Pope County Pop.	ATU Pretest Sample	SFA School Population	SFA Nacogdoches County Pop.	SFA Pretest Sample	SHS School Population	SHS Walker County Pop.	SHS Pretest Sample
RACE	White	80.9%	89.5%	81.6%	57.2%	58.3%	64.7%	58.0%	57.4%	66.2%
	Black	7.5%	2.9%	8.4%	21.9%	15.5%	24%	17.0%	19.3%	18.2%
	Hispanic	4.3%	6.8%	6.1%	13.8%	14.9%	8.4%	17.0%	14.4%	11.7%
	Other	7.3%	0.8%	3.9%	7.1%	11.3%	2.9%	8.0%	8.9%	3.9%
GENDER	Male	44.4%	49.6%	47.5%	37.2%	47.4%	35.6%	42.0%	58.9%	35.1%
	Female	55.6%	50.4%	52.5%	62.8%	52.3%	64.3%	58.0%	41.1%	64.9%
INCOME	Median	—	$39,055	40K–60K	—	$38,347	60K–80K	—	$42,589	60K–80K
CITIZEN	U.S. Citizen	95.7%	97.5%	98.1%	99.0%	93.1%	99.4%	98.2%	94.6%	98.7%
	Other	4.3%	2.5%	0.9%	1.0%	6.9%	0.6%	1.8%	5.4%	1.3%

undergraduate campuses, this difference works in favor of the general representativeness of the sample rather than against it.

The SFASU and SHSU samples are similar given their proximity and that both schools are in East Texas. One advantage of including these schools is both student populations are much more diverse than ATU's (table 12.1). The White student populations for SFASU and SHSU are 57.2% and 58% respectively.[49] Both pretest samples have an overrepresentation of Whites relative to their student populations, with Whites accounting for 64.7% and 66.2% of the SFASU and SHSU pretest samples (table 12.1). Whites are significantly overrepresented in both student populations from the two Texas schools and in the pretest samples relative to the Texas state population (43.4%).[50] Still, both pretest samples are much more racially diverse than ATU's, hence diversifying the sample and providing a more representative set of results. The pretest samples from the Texas schools underrepresent males relative to the student populations, which themselves underrepresent males with respect to state and county populations. However, there are a sufficient number of males in each school sample to assess gender differences. The average age of respondents in the full, combined sample is twenty years of age and in line with expectations for a sophomore-level college course. The age of respondents ranges from seventeen to seventy-one; the bulk (92%) falls between the ages of seventeen and twenty-one. Citizenship in all three school samples is near-universal (98% or above, see table 12.1).

Of all demographic variables, income bias most undermines the representativeness of all three samples. All three school samples have reported family incomes well in excess of the median incomes of their counties. This is an unavoidable problem in using college student samples, as nationally college student populations are skewed toward more wealthy families. The reported family incomes across the samples are consistent with expectations for a student body drawn largely from the rural and small-to-moderate cities of Central Arkansas and East Texas. The median household income for Pope County is $39,055, while the median household income for ATU students at pretest falls in the $40,000–$60,000 range. This suggests ATU students come from considerably more affluent households than the average citizen in Pope County. We see a similar pattern with SFASU and SHSU pretest samples, as the median student at both schools reported a family income of $60,000–$80,000 while Nacogdoches County (SFASU) and Walker County (SHSU) have median household incomes of $38,347 and $42,589 respectively.

Only students who took both the pretest (N=904) and the posttest (N=677) are included in the pre-post sample (N=506). This reduced sample somewhat vitiates the mortality threat due to the number of student drops from the course.[51] While attrition is likely stratified by grade point average, the fact the rate is below 30% suggests the reduced sample remains representative of school populations. Buttressing this contention is the fact that demographic splits between the pretest, posttest, and pre-post samples are relatively equivalent. The pre-post sample is, within a couple percentage points, consistent with those in previous data collections. Table 12.2 shows the sample demographics for the pretest sample are relatively equivalent to those of the posttest. There are a few notable exceptions. The pretest sample is more heavily drawn from Arkansans by about eight percentage points. There is also a significant increase in the income category, with about a five-percentage-point

Table 12.2. Sample Demographics

Demographic Characteristics		Prettest Sample		Posttest Sample		Pre-Post Combined Sample	
Variables	Categories	%	N	%	N	%	N
State	AR Resident	54.70	518	47.39	336	46.59	246
	TX Resident	40.76	386	48.10	341	49.24	260
School	ATU	60.10	595	59.96	542	51.13	272
	SFASU	31.52	312	30.86	279	40.23	214
	SHSU	8.38	83	9.18	83	8.65	46
College Standing	Freshman	43.70	416	37.06	265	40.49	215
	Sophomore	36.97	352	41.54	297	40.11	213
	Junior / Senior	19.32	184	21.39	153	19.40	103
Ideology	Conservative	46.03	325	44.92	283	43.69	218
	Moderate	22.38	158	22.86	144	24.05	120
	Liberal	31.58	223	32.22	203	32.26	161
Party ID	Republican	55.65	415	54.74	352	55.44	270
	Independent	15.32	114	7.15	46	14.58	71
	Democrat	29.04	216	38.10	245	29.98	146
Race	White	74.81	707	73.74	525	76.08	404
	Black	14.29	135	15.03	107	12.81	68
	Hispanic / Other	10.90	103	11.24	80	11.11	59
Gender	Male	42.50	391	41.31	278	41.75	220
	Female	57.50	529	58.69	395	58.25	307
Income	$20K & under	16.12	142	15.25	104	10.87	56
	$21–$40K	23.38	206	20.82	142	20.19	104
	$41–$60K	19.18	169	16.86	115	21.55	111
	$61–$80K	13.96	123	16.28	111	15.34	79
	$81–$100K	13.05	115	12.90	88	14.95	77
	$101K & above	14.30	126	17.89	122	17.09	88
US Citizenship		98.43	938	98.47	707	98.87	526

drop in respondents reporting incomes at or below $20,000 and a concomitant increase in the percentage of respondents between $20,000 and $40,000. The percentage of Republicans is consistent across all three samples. However, there is a significant dip in the sample of students who just took the posttest (15.32% for the pretest to 7.5% for the posttest). Still, the percentage of independents recovers to pretest levels in the pre-post sample (14.58%). Small intersample differences are likely the result of random variation in the characteristics of students that dropped the sections of the American Government course or were not in attendance for the pretest or posttest administrations.

On a seven point ideological scale with seven indicating "strongly conservative," respondents averaged just over five in the full pretest sample. This hardly changes in the posttest sample or the pre-post sample, as approximately 45% of the students in the three samples identify as conservatives (table 12.2). The conservative ideological bent of the sample reflects the general political inclinations of these regions and states.

While these are convenience samples and hence nonrandom, we suspect the representativeness of these samples goes beyond that of the classes and schools in which they were conducted. The sample demographics are relatively similar to the county and state population demographics. Furthermore, as a general education requirement at ATU and state core curriculum requirement for SFASU and SHSU, these courses contain a healthy cross-section of school majors. Still, the school populations do contain a larger percentage of Arts & Humanities majors, so some caution in generalizing these findings is warranted.

CIVICS EXAM RESULTS

Across all semesters, the average student performance is remarkably consistent in the pretest sample, whether one considers the overall citizenship score (figure 12.3a) or the score by conceptual area (figure 12.3b). While average scores are lower than those of national studies (such as ISI's), this is undoubtedly a combination of differences in instruments (ISI and many civics-based surveys employ multiple choice questions, but we employ fill-in-the-blank) and regional demographics (Central Arkansas and East Texas are typical of the rural South—regions with poorer school systems and where people are generally less politically engaged). Figures 12.3c and 12.3d show the differences in pretest civic literacy and pre-posttest improvement by school. There are significant differences in the improvement in civic literacy between the schools (figure 12.3d), as SFASU had the lowest improvement while SHSU had the highest (students raised their citizenship score by 20%). However, the

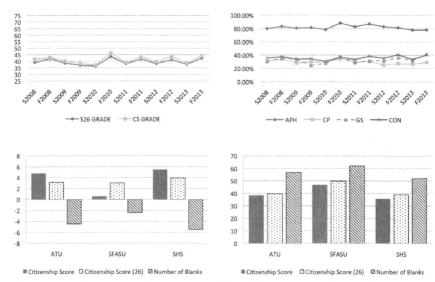

Figure 12.3. Average Performance Overall and by Conceptual Categories as well as Civic Literacy Improvements by School
Don Gooch and Mike Rogers

magnitude of improvement is directly related to the overall levels of citizenship improvement in the pretest, suggesting these differences may largely be a function of regression to the mean. Alternatively, SHSU may simply have had lower initial levels of civic literacy and thus, consistent with the "sponge" and "exposer" theories advanced by Langton and Jennings and Niemi and June, SHSU had more room to gain. Therefore, SHSU students got more from the civic education curriculum.[52] SHSU had the lowest pretest citizenship score, while SFASU bested SHSU by nearly twenty percentage points (figure 12.3c). Furthermore, the SHSU sample is relatively small (one class of students for one semester). Thus one must exercise caution in drawing conclusions based on comparisons of it with the other schools. We do not anticipate these differences significantly impacting the combined sample results.[53]

THE PARADOX OF CIVIC LITERACY AND EFFICACY ON CIVIC PARTICIPATION AND INTEREST

Consistent with our early study, we fine one semester of American government improves civic literacy.[54] On average, there is substantial improvement in all four citizenship measures from the pretest to the posttest (figure 12.4). Most students improved both citizenship score measures; most students also

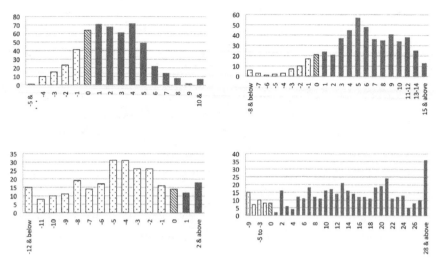

Figure 12.4.   Pre-Post Differences in Citizenship Measures
Don Gooch and Mike Rogers

left fewer blank questions in the posttest than the pretest (figures 12.4a, 12.4b, and 12.4c).[55] The composite civic literacy score for the three citizenship measures reflects the same pattern we see in the individual measures (figure 12.4d).[56] Figure 12.5 shows a paired T-Test between the pretest and posttest citizenship scores. Note the difference between pretest and posttest citizenship scores are mostly above zero and the mean of paired comparisons is higher in the posttest than the pretest. Also, the agreement graph shows that most respondents had posttest scores higher than their pretest scores, with the bulk of the points found in the lower quadrant above zero (figures 12.5a, 12.5b, & 12.5c). The Q-Q plot of the respective quantiles for the pretest and posttest citizenship scores shows the bulk of the outliers are in the citizenship improvement quantiles. In other words, more students exhibited outlier improvements than exhibited outlier regressions. Also, these outliers were on average larger than those in the negative quantiles (figure 12.5d).

Then, figure 12.6 demonstrates student civic literacy improved in all four conceptual categories. Students exhibited the most significant improvement in Government Structure. This is to be expected. Most political scientists and most American government textbooks weight instruction toward the structure and function of government. The second largest area of growth is on the Constitution. Again, this is a subject weighted heavily in instruction and textbooks. American Political Heritage is the strongest area for most students to begin with, so—following Langton and Jennings's redundancy theory—being saturated on the topic probably explains the small growth. The Current

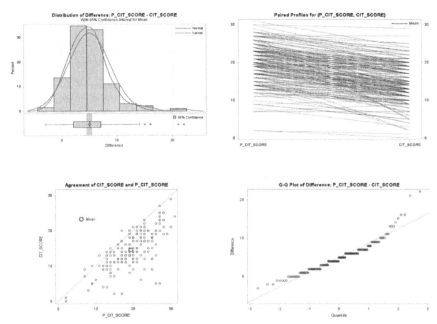

Figure 12.5. Citizenship Scores Paired Comparisons
Don Gooch and Mike Rogers

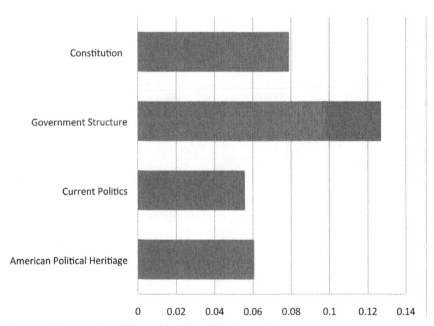

Figure 12.6. Pre-Post Change in Citizenship Categories
Don Gooch and Mike Rogers

Politics course, an area where low pretest scores offer an opportunity for great growth, shows the least improvement. This may be because instructors do not emphasize memorizing who is currently in office, and unless these figures are in the media often (as per Niemi and Junn's exposure theory), students may just not value this information. What is most encouraging about these results is the improvement across the board. It is also promising that the greatest growth occurs in Government Structure. Being an emphasis of instruction and textbooks, it appears a course in American government while in college can lay an important foundation for a student's future participation. After all, you have to know the rules of the game to play.

Overall, there is a statistically significant improvement in civic literacy from a one-semester government class (figure 12.7). Over 85% (86.67% to be exact) of students showed increased civic literacy and over half of students in the sample experienced significant improvement (three or more additional correct responses). While most students "fail" the naturalization exam, those results change dramatically by the posttest. For the pretest, 87% of the students failed to meet the naturalization benchmark of 60% correct and that percentage balloons to 98.89% if the requirement was a "C" or 70% or better. By the posttest, these failure rates drop to 61.8% for the naturalization benchmark and 71.82% for the standard of a C. Interestingly, these numbers for the three universities were marginally worse than the average performance (86% and 91% respectively) from previous administrations to just ATU students (2007–2012). Still, these results reinforce our previous findings; a one semester civics course in college is an effective ameliorative for civic literacy deficits.[57]

Student improvement is not just in their overall scores. Figure 12.8 demonstrates growth in almost every question on the survey. Only the minimum voting age question saw regression. Figure 12.8 reports the pre-post mean differences for the survey items, while table 12.3 reports the results of paired comparison T-tests. The T-tests evaluate the statistical significance of the difference between the means on the pretest and posttest for each question on the exam. Both figure 12.8 and table 12.3 show the one-semester American government course produced improvement on almost all of the citizenship exam items across the universities. Those improvements are statistically significant at either the .10, .05, or .01 alpha levels.

There were a few exceptions, mostly in the Current Politics category. For example, there is no statistically significant improvement in those identifying the current president (0.318). Most were able to identify Barack Obama on the pretest. So, the redundancy and the exposure theories suggest the lack of improvement in this item is due to high saturation on the question. Yet, the other two items failing to achieve statistical significance do not follow this

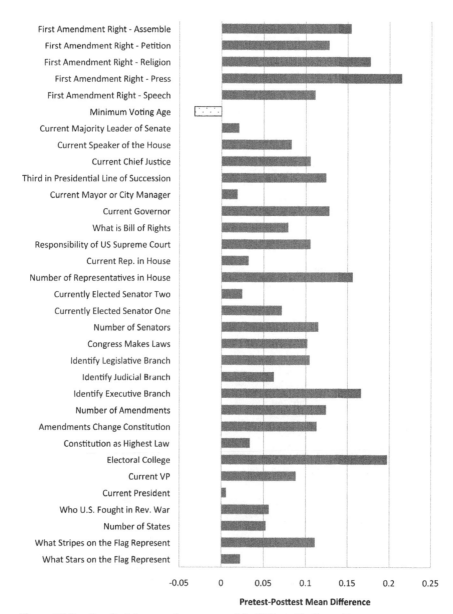

Figure 12.7. Pre-Post Average Improvement in Citizenship Exam Items

Don Gooch and Mike Rogers

Table 12.3. Citizenship Measures Pre-Post Mean Difference T-Tests

Variable	Pretest-Posttest Mean Difference	T-Test P-Value
Civic Literacy (summary)	13.8434***	< .001
Citizenship Score (grade%)	17.5733***	< .001
Citizenship –26 Score (grade%)	8.1109***	< .001
Number of Blanks (grade%)	12.172***	< .001
American Political Heritage (summary)	0.0606***	< .001
What Stars on the Flag Represent	0.0226**	0.019
What Stripes on the Flag Represent	0.1109***	< .001
Number of States	0.0526***	< .001
Who U.S. Fought in Rev. War	0.0564***	0.001
Current Politics (summary)	0.0558***	< .001
Current President	0.0056	0.318
Current VP	0.0883***	< .001
Number of Senators Identified	0.0977***	< .001
Both Senators Identified	0.0207**	0.041
Current Rep. in House	0.0320**	0.019
Current Governor	0.1278***	< .001
Current Mayor or City Manager	0.0188	0.182
Current Chief Justice	0.1053***	< .001
Current Speaker of the House	0.0827***	< .001
Current Majority Leader of Senate	0.0207**	0.041
Government Structure (summary)	0.1270***	< .001
Electoral College	0.1974***	< .001
Constitution as Highest Law	0.0338	0.175
Number of Branches Identified	0.3233***	< .001
All Three Branches Identified	0.1805***	< .001
Congress Makes Laws	0.1015***	< .001
Number of Senators	0.1147***	< .001
Number of Representatives in House	0.1560***	< .001
Responsibility of US Supreme Court	0.1053***	< .001
Constitution (summary)	0.0789***	< .001
Amendments Change Constitution	0.1128***	< .001
Number of Amendments	0.0883***	< .001
What is Bill of Rights	0.0789***	< .001
Third in Presidential Succession	0.1241***	< .001
Minimum Voting Age	–0.0320**	0.017
Number of 1st A Rights Identified	0.7820***	< .001
All Five 1st A Rights Identified	0.1015***	< .001

* P < .10, ** P < .05, *** P<.01

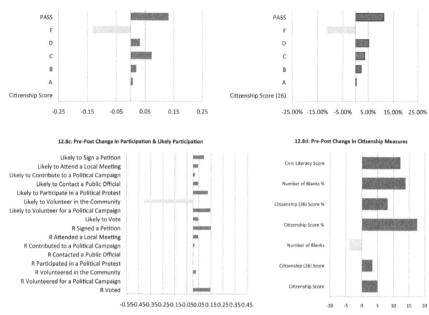

Figure 12.8.   **Pre-Post Differences in Citizenship and Participation Measures**
Don Gooch and Mike Rogers

pattern. Few students identified their current mayor in the pretest, and there was no statistically significant improvement in students able to do so on the posttest. Of course, the mayors of localities are not typically covered in an American government class. Thus, there is a lack of exposure likely explaining this result. The truly troubling result is the lack of students identifying the Constitution as the highest law in the land. While there was a raw improvement in this score, it was not statistically significant (0.175). This is troubling because it is a point of emphasis in most American Government courses. As for the only item where students regressed, it was the minimum voting age question. Students did worse on this question in the posttest than the pretest, and the difference is statistically significant (0.017). Why this was the case is not apparent, but some information presented in the course may lead students in a wrong direction on this question.[58] On a more positive note, the most substantial improvements were in identifying First Amendment rights, identifying the branches of government, recognizing the purpose of the Electoral College, and knowing the number of representatives in the U.S. House of Representatives (table 12.3).

Turning to table 12.3, it reports T-Tests for the citizenship measures and the citizenship score categories. The pre-post differences between the citizenship measures are illustrated in figure 12.7, while the pre-post differences for the citizenship score categories are shown in figure 12.6. For each of the citizenship measures and for each of the citizenship score categories, the mean difference between the pretest and the posttest shows a statistically significant improvement in civic literacy (P-value is less than .001). Students improved the most on the Citizenship Score, the more forgiving of the two measures of correctness. Overall, students improved by nearly eighteen percentage points on this measure. The least improvement was observed on the most stringent of the citizenship score measures, the Citizenship –26 Score (+ 8.11%).[59]

In table 12.4, T-Test statistics for four different categories of items (sample demographics, political participation, interest in politics, and political characteristics) on the survey are reported. If no demographic information changed from pretest to posttest as should be the case, items in the sample demographics category should have a mean difference of zero and a P-value of 1.0. As can be seen, the items for citizenship, race, gender, and family income are near zero and have P-values approaching 1.0. The one exception is citizenship, but this is a category which theoretically could shift due to changes in citizenship status and an increased awareness of who qualifies as a citizen. Still, the mean difference is close to zero and not statistically significant. We also fail to observe significant differences in party identification or ideology. Given that these tend to be relatively stable political characteristics, this result is unsurprising. It suggests the presentation of materials in these courses was not significantly biased in a partisan or ideological direction. If it was, it had no meaningful effect on students' partisanship and ideological beliefs.

In figure 12.8c, the pre-post mean differences between political participation and likely to participate are illustrated. The T-Test statistics for the mean differences on these items are in table 12.4. Most measurements of actual participation rates show very little change from pretest to posttest, as is understandable given only a few months elapsed between the two surveys. The largest change is the significantly higher number of students reporting they voted by the posttest. However, we should be cautious in concluding this is a civic education effect as it may in part be due to the number of respondents who became eligible and voted for the first time in the 2012 election held between the fall 2012 pretest and posttest administrations.

Individually, the mean difference in the political participation items between the pretest and the posttest is statistically significant for only three items. These were voting, attending a local meeting, and signing a petition; all three increased from the pretest to the posttest. A decline in reports should not occur, assuming students responded to the pretest honestly, and we find none. The mean difference in the political protest item is essentially zero, despite the negative coefficient, and the P-value is near 1.0 (0.828). Again, the statistically significant result for voting is the easiest to explain, as a presidential

Table 12.4. Demographic & Political Characteristics Pre-Post Mean Difference T-Tests

Variable	Pretest—Posttest Mean Difference	T-Test P-Value
Sample Demographics		
U.S. Citizenship	−0.0018	0.318
White	0.0019	0.763
Male	0.0021	0.931
Family Income of R	−0.0021	0.957
Political Participation		
Participation (summary)	0.4436***	< .001
R Voted	0.1443***	< .001
R Volunteered for a Political Campaign	0	1.000
R Volunteered in the Community	0.0247	0.304
R Participated in a Political Protest	−0.0020	0.828
R Contacted a Public Official	0.0020	0.895
R Contributed to a Political Campaign	0.0103	0.318
R Attended a Local Meeting	0.0412***	0.014
R Signed a Petition	0.1485***	< .001
Likely Participation (summary)	−0.7888***	0.019
Likely Participation 2 (summary)¥	0.5321***	
Likely to Vote	0.0437	0.194
Likely to Volunteer for a Political Campaign	0.1438***	0.005
Likely to Volunteer in the Community	−0.4093***	< .001
Likely to Participate in a Political Protest	0.1237**	0.022
Likely to Contact a Public Official	0.0440	0.380
Likely to Contribute to a Political Campaign	0.0148	0.669
Likely to Attend a Local Meeting	0.0420	0.433
Likely to Sign a Petition	0.0919**	0.048
Interest in Politics		
Political Efficacy	0.1227*	0.038
Political Interest (summary)	−0.0839	0.189
Political News Interest (summary)	0.1715	0.213
TV Show on Politics	0.0474	0.413
Discuss Politics with a Friend	−0.0513	0.367
Write an Online Political Message	0.0474	0.434
Visit a Political Website	0.1460**	0.020
Level of Interest in Politics	−0.1355**	0.023
News Attentiveness	−0.1022	0.141
Political Characteristics		
Party Identification (summary)	−0.0882	0.167
Ideology	0.0157	0.817

* P < .10, ** P < .05, *** P<.01
¥ excludes "Likely to Volunteer in Community" item

election occurred in the fall of 2012. A number of students took advantage of their first opportunity to participate in a national election. The election may also account for the increased number who reported attending a local meeting and signing a petition. It is also possible that students increased their participation rates in these activities as a result of their American government courses. It is difficult to disentangle the two plausible explanations. Overall, largely driven by an increase in the number who had voted, the composite measure of participation shows students participated more (0.44).

With table 12.4 and figure 12.8c, the results of the battery on the likelihood to participate are presented. Students are asked to report the likelihood they will participate in activities in the future. Theoretically, a semester spent learning about civics and being educated in the nuts and bolts of the political process should increase the likelihood of future participation by students, especially in cases where rational ignorance of the political process previously stymied such participation. We observe three statistically significant increases in this battery: likely to volunteer for a political campaign (+0.14), likely to participate in a political protest (+0.12), and likely to sign a petition (+0.09). The increases are statistically significant at the .01 level for volunteering for a political campaign and for participating in a political protest and the .05 level for signing a petition. These increases are despite the fact that students on the whole reported relatively high likely-to-participate rates in the pretest. Thus, large increases in such items, particularly low-transaction-cost civic activities like voting, were unlikely.

Interestingly, improvements in the likelihood to participate are not confined to low-transaction-cost activities. Volunteering for campaigns and participating in protests are considered relatively high-commitment activities. Furthermore, the coefficients for all of the items but one are positive. As figure 12.8c shows, students reported they were more likely to participate in civic activities in the posttest than the pretest for all but one question. Overall, most students only slightly changed. That said, two-thirds of the students fall within the 1–4 absolute point change categories, and both "more likely" categories exceed the counts in the corresponding "less likely" categories. The only decrease in the probability to participate occurred in the likelihood to volunteer in the community. This was also the largest difference (−0.41) observed in this battery, and the P-value for the mean difference is less than .001. In fact, the decline in likelihood to volunteer in the community dwarfs the other items' moderate to small increases. Why students were significantly less likely to volunteer in their communities after taking the government course is puzzling. No immediate explanation is apparent. One possibility (untested through this instrument) is focusing on transaction costs and collective actions problems in a course on American government may discourage some students from community volunteering. Studies have shown students exposed to game theoretic concepts (like free-riding) are more likely to behave as the models predict.[60] Given the size of the decrease in likelihood to volunteer in the community, we generate two likely participation composite measures—one including and one excluding the volunteer in the community item. As can be seen, including the item creates a net decline in overall participation (−0.79), while excluding it results in a net mean positive coefficient for likely participation (0.59).

For political interest, we have a mixed bag of indicators, some showing a decrease in interest in politics while others suggesting an increase. There is a statistically significant decline in the level of interest in politics, though it is a relatively small mean change (−.136). The summary measure for political interest also has a negative coefficient, though the mean decline is not statistically significant. Conversely, more students reported they would visit a political website in the posttest wave (0.146). We use this as a proxy for increased interest in or attention to politics. The only negative coefficient among the political news interest items was "discuss politics with a friend;" that mean difference is statistically insignificant. Figures 12.9a and 12.9b give these mean differences, while the T-Test statistics are reported in table 12.4. On the one hand, students reported they were less interested in politics (−0.14). On the other, they reported higher levels of political efficacy (0.12) and an increase in confidence that the political process and participation in it makes a difference in achieving policy change. These shifts are statistically significant at the .01 or .05 levels. Students also reported an increased attentiveness to news, but it is not statistically significant.

All in all, three consistent findings are evident: (1) civic literacy and civic efficacy improved as a consequence of an American government course; (2) some participation activities and the likelihood of participation in civic ac-

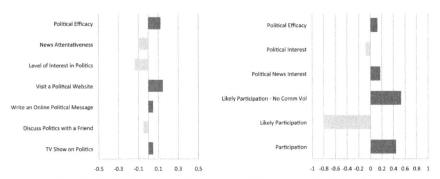

Figure 12.9. Pre-Post Changes in Civic Interest, Efficacy, and Participation Measures
Don Gooch and Mike Rogers

tivities increased but others decreased; (3) beyond some increase in political news attentiveness, political interest either declined or remained constant. Despite being better informed and having an increased confidence in the effectiveness of political activism after the course, students were not uniformly more likely to participate, nor did they exhibit greater interest in politics.

To assess the impact of civic learning, efficacy, participation, and political interest on likely participation, we go beyond simple binary mean comparisons and evaluate civic attributes as determinants of likely civic participation in a multivariate analysis. Two distinct regression analyses are provided to assess the effects of civic attributes on likely participation as a consequence of taking a course on American government. The first examines the determinants of likely civic participation in the pretest and posttest samples for the four measures of civic literacy: Citizenship Score, Citizenship-26 Score, Blank Percentage, and the composite Civic Literacy measure (table 12.5). The second evaluates the effect that changes in participation, likely participation, political interest, and civic efficacy had on the likelihood to participate from the pretest to the posttest (table 12.6). Demographic characteristics (race, gender, and family income), political characteristics (partisanship and ideology), college performance (G.P.A. and standing), political interest, political efficacy, and the composite measures for political participation, likely political participation, and political news interest are included in the analyses as independent variables. An interaction term for partisanship and ideology is included in all models to account for colinearity. In all models, non-civic attribute measures (such as the demographic variables) use posttest results for the analysis. These variables remain relatively constant and there is no theoretical reason why changes in such measures would determine the likelihood of participation in civic activities.

In table 12.5, we report ordinary least squares regression coefficients and standard errors for pretest and posttest analyses of likely civic participation regressed against civic attributes and the demographic and political factors. The models vary based on the three measures of civic literacy and the composite civic literacy variable. The models have reasonably good fits, with improvements over the mean that account for between 29 and 37 percent of the variation in civic literacy. The only demographic or political characteristic that was a statistically significant predictor of pretest or posttest likelihood to participate was gender. Males consistently reported lower probabilities of participation vis-à-vis females.[61] Also, past civic participation is a stable, robust, and substantively large factor in likely civic participation across all models. Students who had already participated reported substantially higher probabilities of future civic activity. Beyond past civic participation, the strongest predictors of higher levels of likely civic participation in the pretest

Table 12.5. Pre-Post Determinants of Likely Participation with Alternative Measures of Civic Literacy

LIKELY TO PARTICIPATE MODELS

VARIABLES	CS Pretest Parameter Estimate (Standard Error)	CS Posttest Parameter Estimate (Standard Error)	CS-26 Pretest Parameter Estimate (Standard Error)	CS-26 Posttest Parameter Estimate (Standard Error)	Blank% Pretest Parameter Estimate (Standard Error)	Blank% Posttest Parameter Estimate (Standard Error)	Civic Lit Pretest Parameter Estimate (Standard Error)	Civic Lit. Posttest Parameter Estimate (Standard Error)
Intercept	16.855*** (2.211)	14.655*** (3.149)	16.748*** (2.205)	15.111*** (3.053)	17.995*** (2.262)	17.810*** (2.680)	17.267*** (2.230)	14.345*** (3.174)
Ideology	-0.281 (0.209)	0.072 (0.278)	-0.276 (0.209)	0.097 (0.275)	-0.291 (0.204)	0.034 (0.234)	-0.283 (0.209)	0.102 (0.276)
Party ID	0.075 (0.218)	-0.168 (0.280)	0.074 (0.218)	-0.161 (0.280)	0.044 (0.214)	-0.080 (0.249)	0.076 (0.217)	-0.190 (0.280)
White	0.750 (0.756)	-0.257 (0.943)	0.787 (0.761)	-0.211 (0.935)	0.991 (0.744)	0.061 (0.897)	0.821 (0.756)	-0.188 (0.973)
Male	-1.227** (0.591)	-1.100 (0.821)	-1.207** (0.595)	-0.988 (0.816)	-1.129** (0.586)	-0.717 (0.702)	-1.135** (0.594)	-1.106 (0.824)
Family Income	0.062 (0.178)	0.077 (0.229)	0.045 (0.177)	0.040 (0.226)	0.065 (0.174)	0.098 (0.291)	0.063 (0.177)	0.059 (0.229)
College GPA	-0.362 (0.388)	-0.601 (0.624)	-0.375 (0.388)	-0.761*** (0.618)	-0.369 (0.375)	-0.949 (0.514)	-0.327 (0.386)	-0.700 (0.622)
College Standing	-0.577 (0.346)	0.033 (0.423)	-0.575 (0.346)	0.075 (0.421)	-0.544 (0.341)	-0.093 (0.383)	-0.573 (0.345)	0.041 (0.424)
Participation	1.458*** (0.261)	1.230*** (0.320)	1.447*** (0.261)	1.137*** (0.314)	1.458*** (0.257)	1.238*** (0.270)	1.499*** (0.262)	1.164*** (0.311)
Civic Education Measure	-0.028 (0.019)	-0.021 (0.021)	-0.028 (0.020)	-0.009 (0.027)	-0.039** (0.017)	0.001 (0.010)	-0.039** (0.020)	-0.011 (0.020)
Political Interest	0.425*** (0.068)	0.464*** (0.095)	0.438*** (0.068)	0.470*** (0.095)	0.435*** (0.067)	0.435*** (0.085)	0.436*** (0.068)	0.467*** (0.097)
Civic Efficacy	1.090*** (0.309)	0.856* (0.466)	1.110*** (0.308)	0.668 (0.441)	1.072*** (0.305)	0.224 (0.375)	1.080*** (0.307)	0.867* (0.468)
PID*IDEOLOGY	-0.030 (0.083)	0.085 (0.111)	-0.032 (0.083)	0.092 (0.111)	-0.034 (0.081)	0.040 (0.097)	-0.029 (0.083)	0.082 (0.112)
R2	.366	.329	.365	.322	.370	.294	.369	.327
N	286	216	286	220	291	271	286	216

* $P < .10$, ** $P < .05$, *** $P < .01$

and the posttest were political interest and civic efficacy. Students with higher levels of political interest and civic efficacy were more likely to participate in a civic activity in both samples.

In contrast, however measured civic literacy (the "Civic Education Measure" in the table) fails to obtain statistical significance in most models. In all but one of the pretest and posttest models, civic literacy (Civic Lit) has a negative coefficient. Controlling for the other factors, those with higher levels of civic literacy were less likely to participate in civic activities before and after receiving civic education. This factor achieves statistical significance in the blank percentage (Blank%) and civic literacy pretest models, though it drops out in the posttest. This likely is due to the range of civic literacy across-the-board improvements from the pretest to the posttest. The average magnitude was relatively small, constricting the range of improved civic literacy, thus limiting its capacity to serve as a factor in likely participation. Combined with the negative coefficients for college GPA (college GPA obtains statistical significance in only one model—the Citizenship–26 posttest (CS–26) and college standing, it means that the better students in the class were less likely to participate, and the class in American government did not substantially affect the propensity to participate. This is both a puzzling and paradoxical finding. Controlling for political interest and efficacy, variation in civic literacy has the opposite effect one expects. Furthermore, the better performing and more civically literate students reported lower levels of likely civic participation. This suggests that increased levels of civic literacy as a consequence of civic education may actually drive *down* both the likelihood to participate and civic efficacy. One possible explanation is the "political science effect," where an academic inquiry into politics can sour students on the actual practice of politics. Much as watching the process of sausage-making can turn someone off to eating sausage, so too can a political science education, in exposing the true underbelly of the political system, dissuade students from getting involved.

In table 12.6, we take the analysis a step further. We model changes in civic attributes as determinants of changes in the reported likelihood to participate. These models assess directly the change in likelihood to participate after a course in American government as a function in the changes of civic attributes that occurred from pretest to posttest. As reported earlier, the bulk of changes in the likelihood to participate were small (and for volunteering in the community in the opposite direction). This is also true for political interest and civic efficacy on the whole. It is not the case with civic literacy, which underwent a substantial improvement from pretest to posttest. Given these factors, poor delta model fits are expected and, indeed, are seen in table 12.6. Less than 10 percent of the variance in likelihood to participate is explained by the model parameters. However, despite the poor fit, the coefficients for

Table 12.6. Pre-Post Demographic & Difference Determinants of Pre-Post Likely to Participate Difference Measure

	LIKELY TO PARTICIPATE PRE-POST DIFFERENCE MODELS			
	CS Pre-Post	CS-26 Pre-Post	Blank% Pre-Post	Civic Lit Pre-Post
COMBINED & DIFFERENCE VARIABLES	Parameter Estimate (Standard Error)	Parameter Estimate (Standard Error)	Parameter Estimate (Standard Error)	Parameter Estimate (Standard Error)
Intercept	-2.625 (2.941)	-2.519 (2.868)	-1.752 (2.967)	-2.617 (3.026)
Ideology	0.063 (0.344)	0.018 (0.321)	0.030 (0.322)	0.105 (0.343)
Party ID	-0.009 (0.335)	-0.002 (0.324)	-0.008 (0.325)	-0.043 (0.335)
White	1.085 (1.235)	1.078 (1.190)	0.758 (1.255)	0.888 (1.268)
Male	0.017 (0.883)	-0.024 (0.858)	-0.066 (0.862)	0.029 (0.888)
Family Income	-0.198 (0.271)	-0.157 (0.261)	-0.129 (0.267)	-0.190 (0.276)
College GPA	-0.368 (0.592)	-0.465 (0.577)	-0.613 (0.589)	-0.443 (0.602)
College Standing	0.443 (0.524)	0.552 (0.523)	0.471 (0.519)	0.427 (0.526)
Participation (difference)	0.402 (0.421)	0.364 (0.403)	0.280 (0.404)	0.311 (0.417)
Civic Education Measure (difference)	-0.031 (0.029)	-0.039 (0.037)	0.005 (0.012)	-0.007 (0.024)
Political Interest (difference)	0.345*** (0.123)	0.360*** (0.121)	0.355*** (0.122)	0.343*** (0.124)
Civic Efficacy (difference)	0.068 (0.447)	0.065 (0.422)	0.051 (0.423)	0.080 (0.449)
PID*IDEOLOGY	0.048 (0.124)	0.036 (0.123)	0.038 (0.123)	0.043 (0.124)
R2	.091	.098	.093	.084
N	159	162	162	159

* P < .10, ** P < .05, *** P<.0

participation, political interest, civic efficacy, and civic literacy measures are in the same direction as the models of table 12.5.

On the whole, increases in civic participation and civic efficacy were associated with higher civic participation likelihoods, though these factors were statistically insignificant. Political interest, however, was highly statistically significant, and the coefficients were substantively large, with an average of 0.35 increases in political interest associated with a single unit increase in the likelihood to participate. Thus the most significant and substantively large predictor of a higher likelihood to participate in civic activities was an increase in interest in politics. The fact that those students who improved their civic literacy were not more likely to participate (in fact, the coefficient for civic literacy is negative across all models) is puzzling and disappointing. While civic education through an American government course substantially improved the civic literacy of students, it did not make them more likely to participate. Indeed, controlling for other factors, they were less likely to do so.

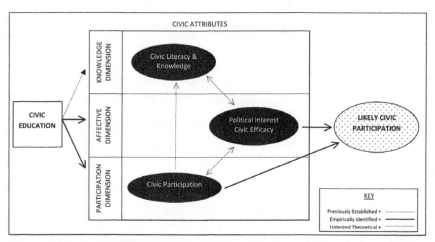

Figure 12.10.   Updated Model of Likely Civic Participation Based on Empirical Findings
Don Gooch and Mike Rogers

Given our findings here and from our previous work, we have updated our model of civic education (see figure 12.10). We do not model the endogenous, recursive relationships between civic attributes posited in our base theoretical model; we did test for multi-collinearity between the independent predictors, and no model assumptions are violated in these analyses. Assessing these factors in a statistical model that accounts for endogenous relationships between civic attributes is a future task for study. Figure 12.10 depicts the findings presented here that civic education impacts both the affective and participation dimensions of civic attributes. It needs to be emphasized that the effect of civic education is not consistently in one direction. Civic education mostly produced an increase in likely civic participation activities. The one exception is volunteering in the community, where students were less likely to volunteer after the course in American government. Figure 12.10 shows the strong, statistically significant, and positive relationship we found between past civic participation, political interest, and civic efficacy on likelihood to participate in civic activities. Students who felt more efficacious and were more interested in politics were more likely to participate in the pretest, and this effect was accentuated with the course. Given the statistically insignificant or significantly negative effects we obtain for civic literacy across our models, we eliminate civic literacy and civic knowledge as independent determinants of civic participation and likely civic participation in our updated theoretical model (figure 12.10).

DISCUSSION: CIVIC ILLITERACY AND THE PARADOX OF CIVIC EDUCATION AND CIVIC ENGAGEMENT

All in all, this study produces as many questions as it answers. Foremost, we accept without question that civic literacy is a necessary prerequisite of informed civic participation. Also, this study and our earlier one have consistently demonstrated—in contradiction to the conventional academic view—that a one-semester American government course matters; it increases civic knowledge and literacy (at least in the short term). Then, we have learned that growth in political participation and civic engagement do not follow necessarily from increased political knowledge. Put succinctly, it is not clear improved civic literacy leads to citizens sustaining democratic institutions through greater political participation and/or civic engagement.

To illustrate the importance of this paradoxical finding, consider what it means for the current civic education movement in the United States. Luminaries like former Supreme Court Justice Sandra Day O'Connor and former Florida governor and retired United States Senator Robert Graham argue today's civics crisis is the result of a decreased and inadequate civics curriculum. They lament America's civics curriculum in secondary education went from three one-semester courses in the mid-1900s to one today.[62] Their argument reflects the commonsense view that more civics instruction produces more civically literate citizens and more civically literate citizens then become more engaged in government and society. As O'Connor rhetorically writes, "How can we expect the next generations to care about, to cherish and sustain our democratic institutions when they don't know what they are or how they work?"[63] Our paradoxical findings on civic knowledge and participation fly in the face of this commonsense, linear understanding of civic education. Our findings undermine the logic and strategy of this national movement, which treats civic education as a monolith for all civic ills.

In figure 12.11, we illustrate the commonsense model of civic education, which assumes a functionally linear and positive relationship between civic literacy and the likelihood of participation. Yes, there is substantial surface validity to this assumption. It is reasonable to expect a greater understanding of civics and the political process to (1) reduce the information costs associated with political participation and (2) reveal avenues for reducing the transaction costs of political participation. For example, a citizen would experience reduced information costs to his or her voting decision on a ballot initiative if they already know what ballot initiatives are and what changes to the law they can make. Also, a citizen would have lower transaction costs associated with participatory politics if he/she has a better understanding of where specific policies (like zoning policy) are made. That citizen can better target his/her participatory activities at the appropriate level of government to achieve the desired policy change.

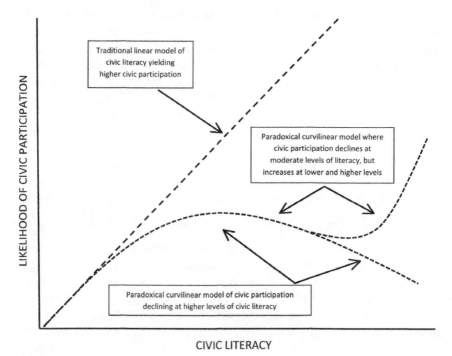

Figure 12.11.   The Paradox of Civic Literacy and Civic Participation
Don Gooch and Mike Rogers

The logic of this commonsense view appears sound but the presumption that civic knowledge will, on the whole, turn citizens on to civic engagement is faulty. Increased knowledge of politics may just as well increase citizen apathy. As citizens become more aware of inherent collective action problems associated with politics, the significant barriers Madisonian constitutional government erects to political activism, or the money involved in elections, they may just be more turned off to participating. Instead of encouraging participation or enhancing civic efficacy, increased civic knowledge may frustrate citizens and discourage them from being engaged. There are infinite functional forms the relationship between civic literacy and likely civic participation can take. In figure 12.11, we suggest two possibilities. First, we hypothesize a paradoxical curvilinear relationship between civic literacy and likely participation. The first depicts civic literacy improving civic participation up to a plateau point. At that inflection point, more civic literacy results in lower and lower probabilities of civic participation. Alternatively, we hypothesize participation increases at lower and higher levels of civic literacy, but declines at moderate levels of civic literacy. Thus, it may be a curvilinear relationship where moderate levels of civic literacy are associated with lower likelihood of participation, but lower and higher levels result in higher participation rates. Of course, other functional relationships are possible. The question as to the exact functional relationship between civic participation and civic literacy is a subject ripe for future research.

Essentially, the findings on civic education, civic literacy, and civic engagement reported here suggest the commonsense linear model underlying the current civic education movement is too simplistic. Our findings suggest it is unlikely to deliver the civic goods expected. Increased civic literacy will likely result, but the results for civic engagement are likely to be mixed, even negative. The model fundamentally misperceives what drives civic participation. Civic education—to the extent it is provided through a lecture-based one-semester course on American government—can increase civic literacy but does little to improve civic involvement and political participation; it may have no or even the opposite effect.

So, what does this mean for civic activists? First, we need to revise our thinking and model. We facilitate this rethinking with our two alternative models in Figure 12.11. Rather than the one-to-one positive correlation between civic literacy and civic participation of the commonsense view, it juxtaposes two theoretical possibilities consistent with the paradoxical relationship between civic knowledge and civic literacy and the likelihood of political participation. Most likely, different levels of civic literacy yield different effects on the likelihood of civic participation, as some levels actually cause citizens to be less involved. In short, civic education is no universal balm for civic participation.

All in all, we know the common assumption that increased civic education leads to improved civic literacy that leads to a higher rate of civic participation is faulty. The first half holds up consistently to empirical testing in a one-semester American government course, but the latter does not. For institutions of higher education, this raises important questions about civic education and what it can and cannot accomplish. While some scholars (see Hilmer's argument in chapter 3) question if formal civic education through state sponsored schools is ever the solution, most scholars, politicians, and the public find schooling as central to the civic education fight.[64] If the paradoxical relationship between civic knowledge and participation as found holds, it has important implications for schools, civic educators, and policy makers. All should take a step back and ask themselves a more fundamental question: Is civic knowledge the end in and of itself, or merely the means to the end of greater civic efficacy and political participation? If it is the latter, then our findings suggest civic education—at least in its traditional lecture-based form—may be counterproductive to those ends.

Given our results, we believe future research is needed. Scholars need to look at various factors that can affect and explain this paradox; a number come to mind. First, research has not adequately exhausted the importance of curriculum. For example, while Langton and Jennings suggested in the 1960s that more civics is not better, we need additional research that confirms our findings that they are wrong.[65] We also need further testing of the redundancy theory versus the sponge and exposure theories. We believe the exposure theory is the most promising but need other studies of the effect of a civics curriculum to confirm it. In the future, one way we plan to test this is by examining Texas's two-semester civics curriculum requirement for college. Is it more effective than Arkansas's one? Additionally, it would be helpful to know how timing of courses matters. For example, scholars could examine if it is detrimental that Arkansans typically have their high school civics course in ninth grade while the norm for most states is twelfth.[66] These are questions of curriculum that can add insight into the nonlinear relationship of civic literacy and participation.

Also, there are equally pressing questions on pedagogy. Curriculum may help civic literacy as this and our earlier work show, but what if the goal is civic engagement?[67] The scholarship of teaching and learning (SoTL) suggests best civic education practices for promoting civic knowledge and civic engagement. James Youniss notes research shows the best practice is not traditional lecture, writing, "Among several classroom practices, discussion proved the strongest predictor of civic knowledge. The findings, which tran-

scend national differences in educational approaches, indicate that expressing ideas and listening to others' expressions spark a feedback dynamic that
enhances cognitive understanding."[68] On the civic engagement side, Youniss
argues service and service learning are best practices when the goal is enhancing *both* civic knowledge and engagement.[69] Campbell agrees, arguing
the youth civic engagement literature finds deliberation, service-learning,
and video game simulations are the tools of the classroom oriented toward
producing participatory citizens.[70] Then, Levinson seems to be more about
practice than content in curriculum. In a vein similar to Bugh's minority dissent pedagogy (chapter 4), she recommends a democratic theory of change
that is built on a classroom that combines intentionality, transparency, reflection, and authenticity.[71] Fundamentally, she advocates education *within* and
for democracy, not education *in* democracy.[72] She claims educators should
be activists with youth, not for them.[73] Put simply, future research needs to
continue to investigate how pedagogy affects civic literacy and engagement,
but it needs to do so across schools and not just in our own. Hence, the value
of Strachan and Bennion's research consortium (chapter 14). In particular,
American government classes remain traditionally lecture-based but we need
comparative study of different pedagogies used in it to see if they have a more
positive impact on participation and likely participation.[74]

Next, this discussion of formal education needs to be expanded to address
its connection with the larger civic ecology of America. Some work has
already been done in this area. For example, Campbell convincingly demonstrates how school environment matters.[75] Likewise, Youniss emphasizes
programs beyond classroom instruction are essential, noting studies find
participation in student government and other high school organizations are
what increase the likelihood of civic engagement after it.[76] Certainly, this
volume reinforces this finding for colleges with Rackaway and Campbell's
arguments about the virtual university (chapter 15) and Yawn's citizen
academies (chapter 16). Similarly, we need to know if the type of educational institution matters. At the primary and secondary level, Campbell has
been integral in the debate over public versus private education, giving a
slight "private edge" because private (Catholic) schools do somewhat better than public ones.[77] Yet, this question needs to be better addressed at the
collegiate level. Is there a difference in the ability of community colleges
versus colleges versus university in promoting civic education? What about
public versus private at this level? Certainly, ISI suggests so, but more research is needed.[78]

As a final issue, we need more empirical study of civic identity formation.
At the turn of the twenty-first century, Conover and Searing lament the state
of disarray and decline in political socialization research.[79] Over a decade later,

one often has to turn to other disciplines to gain insight into civic identity formation, and that insight is not promising. For example, Malin (a psychologist) summarizes the literature on American identity formation and how it is a problem, particularly for youth. She notes literatures that show (1) youth distance themselves from their role as American citizens, (2) they have a high distrust of government, (3) they lack pride in citizenship, and (4) they tend to be apathetic about politics. She notes this is even more so the case for minority youth. These findings likely are a part of the story of the paradoxical relationship of civic literacy and participation. We need to rethink if the traditional pedagogy of lecture is exacerbating the identity formation struggles of our youth. Lecture may be enough to increase youth knowledge of politics, but it may not nurture them into engaged, participatory citizens.

We hope our research has begun to fill the void in curricular research on civic education, but more work is needed. We have found a one-semester American government course as a civics requirement can increase civic literacy. However, the story on whether that increased civic literacy leads to more civic engagement and political participation is cloudier. Through a case study of the impact of American government courses on civic literacy at three Southern universities, we add to the literature arguing a civics curriculum matters. Our case for civic literacy producing more participation is less successful. It may be that the answer to the riddle of civic education, civic efficacy, and civic engagement (i.e., the puzzle of encouraging an informed and engaged civic identity) may be found in a fundamental restructuring of how and in what environment we teach civics.

NOTES

1. For the history of civic education, see Derek Heater, *A History of Education for Citizenship* (New York: RoutledgeFalmer, a Taylor & Francis Group, 2004).

2. Aristotle, *Politics* (Oxford: Claredon Press, 1948), 1263b.

3. R. Freeman Butts, *The Revival of Civic Learning: A Rationale for Citizenship Education in American Schools* (Akron: Phi Delta Kappa Educational Foundation, 1980); Ian Lister, "Civic Education for Positive Pluralism in Great Britain," in *Education for Democratic Citizenship: A Challenge for Multi-Ethnic Societies*, ed. Roberta S. Sigel and Marilyn Hoskin (New Jersey: Lawrence Erlbaum Associates, Inc., 1991); Diane Ravitch, "Education and Democracy," in *Making Good Citizens: Education and Civil Society*, ed. Diane Ravitch and Joseph P. Viteritti (New Haven: Yale University Press, 2001).

4. Philip E. Converse, "Change in the American Electorate," in *The Human Meaning of Social Change*, ed. Angus Campbell and Philip E. Converse (New York: Russell Sage Foundation, 1972), 324.

5. Gooch and Rogers, "A Natural Disaster of Civic Proportions."

6. Bob Graham and Chris Hand, *America, the Owner's Manual: Making Government Work for You* (Washington, DC: CQ Press, 2010); Sam Dillon, "Failing Grades on Civics Exam Called a 'Crisis,'" *The New York Times* 2011, http://www.nytimes.com/2011/05/05/education/05civics.html?_r=0 (accessed October 15, 2014); Michael C. Johanek, "Preparing Pluribus for Unum: Historicial Perspectives on Civic Education," in *Making Civics Count: Citizenship for a New Generation,* ed. David E. Campbell, Meira Levinson, and Frederick M. Hess (Cambridge: Harvard Education Press, 2012).

7. Robert Putnam, *Making Democracy Work: Civic Traditions in Modern Italy* (Princeton, NJ: Princeton University Press, 1993); Robert Putnam, "Bowling Alone: America's Declining Social Capital," *Journal of Democracy* 6, no. 1 (1995); Robert Putnam, "Tuning in, Tuning Out: The Strange Disappearance of Social Capital in America," *PS: Political Science and Politics* 28, no. 4 (Dec. 1995); Robert Putnam, *Bowling Alone: The Collapse and Revival of American Community* (New York: Simon and Schuster, 2000); Robert Putnam, "Community-Based Social Capital and Education Performance," in *Making Good Citizens: Education and Civil Society,* ed. Diane Ravitch and Joseph P. Viteritti (New Haven: Yale University Press, 2001).

8. Michael X. Delli Carpini and Scott Keeter, *What Americans Know about Politics and Why It Matters* (New Haven: Yale University Press, 1996); Richard G. Niemi and Jane Junn, *Civic Education: What Makes Students Learn?* (New Haven: Yale University Press, 1998); Henry Milner, *Civic Literacy: How Informed Citizens Make Democracy Work* (London: University Press of New England, 2002); Ilya Somin, *Democracy and Political Ignorance: Why Smaller Government Is Smarter* (Stanford: Stanford University Press, 2013); Richard G. Niemi, "What Students Know about Civics and Government," in *Making Civics Count: Citizenship Education for a New Generation,* ed. David E. Campbell, Meira Levinson, and Frederick M. Hess (Cambridge: Harvard Education Press, 2012); Gooch and Rogers, "A Natural Disaster of Civic Proportions."

9. Robert L. Dudley and Alan R. Gitelson, "Political Literacy, Civic Education, and Civic Engagement: A Return to Political Socialization?," *Applied Development Science* 6, no. 4 (2002): 176.

10. "Characters from 'the Simpsons' More Well Known to Americans Than Their First Amendment Rights, Survey Finds," 2006, http://www.mccormickfoundation.org/news/2006/pr030106.aspx (accessed October 15, 2014); "Study: More Know 'the Simpsons' Than First Amendment Rights," *USA Today*, 3/1/2006 http://usatoday30.usatoday.com/news/nation/2006-03-01-freedom-poll_x.htm (accessed October 15, 2014); "Study: More Know 'Simpsons' Than Constitution," FoxNews.com, http://www.foxnews.com/story/2006/03/01/study-more-know-simpsons-than-constitution/ (accesed October 15, 2014).

11. ISI, "The Coming Crisis in Citizenship" (Wilmington, DE: Intercollegiate Studies Institute's National Civic Literacy Board, 2006), http://www.americancivicliteracy.org/2006/summary.html (accessed October 15, 2014); "Failing Our Students, Failing America: Holding Colleges Accountable for Teaching America's History

and Institutions" (Wilmington, DE: Intercollegiate Studies Institute's National Civic Literacy Board, 2007), http://www.americancivicliteracy.org/2007/summary_sum mary.html (accessed October 15, 2014); "Our Fading Heritage: Americans Fail a Basic Test on Their History and Institutions," (Wilmington, DE: Intercollegiate Studies Institute's National Civic Literacy Board, 2008), http://www.americancivicliteracy .org/2008/summary_summary.html (accessed October 15, 2014).

12. ISI, "Failing Our Students;" "Our Fading Heritage."

13. Delli Carpini and Keeter, *What Americans Know about Politics and Why It Matters,* 105–106. In addition, America's low civic literacy has been documented over time by the political knowledge questions in the United States National Election Survey—see Donald Kinder and David Sears, "Public Opinion and Political Action," in *The Handbook of Social Psychology,* ed. G. Lindzey and E. Aronson (Oxford: Oxford University Press, 1985); Milner, *Civic Literacy.* For an analysis of civic literacy at the secondary level, see Niemi and Junn, *Civic Education.* For collegiate civic literacy see Gooch and Rogers, "A Natural Disaster of Civic Proportions." For a few works suggesting American civic literacy levels are acceptable, see Niemi, "What Students Know about Civics and Government"; Peter Levine, "Education for a Civil Society," in *Making Civics Count: Citizenship Education for a New Generation,* ed. David E. Campbell, Meira Levinson, and Frederick M. Hess (Cambridge: Harvard Education Press, 2012).

14. Delli Carpini and Keeter, *What Americans Know about Politics,* 50.

15. Ibid., 74, 98, and 103–04.

16. APSA, "Task Force to Set Agenda for Civic Education Program," *PS: Political Science and Politics* 30, no. 4 (1997); "APSA Task Force on Civic Education in the 21st Century: Expanded Articulation Statement: A Call for Reactions and Contributions," *PS: Political Science and Politics* 31, no. 3 (1998).

17. Sandra Day O'Connor, "The Democratic Purpose of Education: From the Founders to Horace Mann to Today," in *Teaching America: The Case for Civic Education,* ed. David Feith (Lanham: Rowman & Littlefield Education, 2011), 6; Bob Graham and Chris Hand, "A Failure of Leadership: The Duty of Politicians and Universities to Salvage Citizenship," in *Teaching America: The Case for Civic Education,* ed. David Feith (Lanham: Rowman & Littlefield Education, 2011), 22; and Graham and Hand, *America, the Owner's Manual.* Another advocate for increasing the civics curriculum is Jason Ross, "The Wisdom of Twenty Thousand Teachers: Strengthen State Requirements, Stop Marginalizing the Founders," in *Teaching America: The Case for Civic Education,* ed. David Feith (Lanham: Rowman & Littlefield Education, 2011). For a study of secondary changes in civics coverage, see Richard G. Niemi and Julia Smith, "Enrollment in High School Government Classes: Are We Short-Changing Citizenship and Political Science Training?," *PS: Political Science and Politics* 34, no. 2 (2001).

18. K. Langton and M. K. Jennings, "Political Socialization and the High School Civics Curriculum in the United States," *American Political Science Review* 62 (1968): 853, 58.

19. Ibid., 854.

20. Ibid., 857–58, 60.

21. Ibid., 865–67.

22. Pamela Johnson Conover and Donald D. Searing, "A Political Socialization Perspective," in *Rediscovering the Democratic Purposes of Education,* ed. Lorraine M. McDonnell, P. Michael Timpane, and Roger Benjamin (Lawrence: University of Kansas Press, 2000), 115.

23. Delli Carpini and Keeter, *What Americans Know about Politics,* 144.

24. Norman Nie and D. Sunshine Hillygus, "Education and Democratic Citizenship," in *Making Good Citizens: Education and Civil Society,* ed. Diane Ravitch and Joseph Viteritti (New Haven: Yale University Press, 2001).

25. See Figure 6 of Gooch and Rogers, "A Natural Disaster of Civic Proportions," 73.

26. Niemi, Richard G. and Jane Junn, *Civic Education: What Makes Students Learn?* (New Haven: Yale University Press, 1998), 121.

27. Ibid., 67.

28. Gooch and Rogers, "A Natural Disaster of Civic Proportions."

29. Samuel L. Popkin, *The Reasoning Voter: Communication and Persuasion in Presidential Campaigns* (Chicago: University of Chicago Press, 1994).

30. For example, see Somin, *Democracy and Political Ignorance*; Stephen Macedo et al., *Democracy at Risk: How Political Choices Undermine Citizen Participation, and What We Can Do about It* (Washington, DC: Brookings Institution Press, 2005).

31. Popkin, *The Reasoning Voter.*

32. Gooch and Rogers, "A Natural Disaster of Civic Proportions."

33. APSA, "Task Force to Set Agenda for Civic Education Program."

34. Delli Carpini and Keeter, *What Americans Know about Politics*; Milner, *Civic Literacy*; Niemi, "What Students Know about Civics and Government."

35. William A. Galston, "Civic Knowlege, Civic Education, and Civic Engagement: A Summary of Recent Research," *International Journal of Public Administration* 30, no. 6 (2007). "Civic Education and Political Participation," *PS: Political Science and Politics* 37, no. April (2004); Steven E. Finkel, "Civic Education and the Mobilization of Political Participation in Developing Democracies," *The Journal of Politics* 64, no. 4 (2002); Alan Acock, Harold D. Clarke, and Marianne C. Stewart, "A New Model for Old Measures: A Covariance Structure Analysis of Political Efficacy." *The Journal of Politics* 47, no. 4 (1985).

36. Popkin, *The Reasoning Voter*; Jonathan Bendor, Daniel Diermeier, and Michael Ting, "A Behavioral Model of Turnout," *The American Political Science Review* 97, no. 2 (2003); Conover and Searing, "A Political Socialization Perspective;" Cindy D. Kam, "When Duty Calls, Do Citizens Answer?," *The Journal of Politics* 69, no. 1 (2007); William H. Riker and Peter C. Ordeshook, "A Theory of the Calculus of Voting," *The American Political Science Review* 62, no. 1 (1968); Paul F. Whiteley, "Rational Choice and Political Participation. Evaluating the Debate," *Political Research Quarterly* 48, no. 1 (1995).

37. Thomas Ehrlich, "Civic Education: Lessons Learned," *PS: Political Science and Politics* 32, no. 2 (1999); John R. Hibbing and Elizabeth Theiss-Morse, "Civics Is Not Enough: Teaching Barbarics in K–12," *PS: Political Science & Politics* 29, no.

1 (1996); Pamela Martin, Holley Tankersley, and Min Ye, "Are They Living What They Learn?: Assessing Knowledge and Attitude Change in Introductory Politics Courses," *Journal of Political Science Education* 8, no. 2 (2012); Robert Putnam, "Bowling Alone: America's Declining Social Capital;" Jennie E. Brand, "Civic Returns to Higher Education: A Note on Heterogeneous Effects," *Social Forces* 89, no. 2 (2010); Mark Bauerlein, "Don't Believe the Hype: Young Voters Are Still Disengaged, and Universities Have Few Incentives to Fix It," in *Teaching America: The Case for Civic Education*, ed. David Feith (Lanham: Rowman & Littlefield Education, 2011); Steven E. Finkel and Amy Erica Smith, "Civic Education, Political Discussion, and the Social Transmission of Democratic Knowledge and Values in a New Democracy: Kenya 2002," *American Journal of Political Science* 55, no. 2 (2011).

38. Gooch and Rogers, "A Natural Disaster of Civic Proportions."

39. For possible alternative models, see D. Sunshine Hillygus, "The Missing Link: Exploring the Relationship between Higher Education and Political Engagement," *Political Behavior* 27, no. 1 (2005): 27–30. Reviewing the civic education literature, Hillygus argues three models are implied: the Civic Education Hypothesis (Niemi and Junn; Rosenstone and Hansen; Wolfinger and Rosenstone; Galston, etc.), the Social Network Hypothesis (Brody; Nie, Junn and Stehlik-Barry), and the Political Meritocracy Hypothesis (Hess and Torney, Neuman). Our endogenous model of civic education is most akin to the Civic Education Hypothesis, although our study can speak to the Political Meritocracy Hypothesis as well because we collected self-reported data on high school GPA.

40. Gooch and Rogers, "A Natural Disaster of Civic Proportions."

41. At SFASU, the instrument was implemented in PSC 142-Introduction to American Government (Structure & Function). This is part of a two-course core curriculum requirement in Texas. Texas mandates coverage of federal and Texas state government. We are giving the instrument to students in both courses. We plan to report the effect of a two-course sequence in the future.

42. The mortality threat to pretest-posttest designs employed in a college course is potentially significant. Dropouts may not be randomly distributed. Students doing poorly in the class are more likely to drop and miss the posttest. However, the data vitiates concerns regarding sample mortality. First, the pretest and posttest samples evince no significant demographic differences (see table 12.1). Even differences in college standing and G.P.A. are similar, suggesting the pretest and posttest samples are sufficiently similar to guard against false positives and false negatives from sample mortality. Second, for civic literacy the sample mortality bias would work against finding improvement. According to redundancy theory, better students who tend to stay in the class come in with a higher floor of civic knowledge and hence less room for improvement. While sample mortality cannot be wholly dismissed, given these numbers it does not present a significant threat to the validity and reliability of the data presented here.

43. American National Election Studies, "American National Election Studies (ANES) Cumulative Data File," (Ann Arbor, MI: Inter-university Consortium for Political and Social Research, 1948–2008), http://doi.org/10.3886/ICPSR08475.v14 (accessed October 15, 2014).

44. Gooch and Rogers, "A Natural Disaster of Civic Proportions."

45. Per Section 312 under the Immigration & Naturalization Act of 1952, applicants filing Form N-400 to become naturalized citizens must complete an interview with the USCIS where their English skills and knowledge of civics are tested. Naturalized citizens must possess "a knowledge and understanding of the fundamentals of the history, and of the principles and form of government, of the United States." See *Immigration and Naturalization Act*, 82-414 (1952). The USCIS draws these questions from a list of one hundred. See United States Citizenship and Immigration Services, "The Naturalization Test," Department of Homeland Security, http://www.uscis.gov/us-citizenship/naturalization-test (accessed October 15, 2014).

46. Gooch and Rogers, "A Natural Disaster of Civic Proportions."

47. For example, Whites were 84.55 percent of the ATU student body in 2007, and they were 80.87 percent as of 2013. See Wyatt Watson, "Arkansas Tech University Student Demographics: All Main Campus Students" (Russellville, AR: Arkansas Tech University, 2015), http://www.atu.edu/ir/docs/enrollment/enrollment-fall/student_demographics_overview_main_campus_fall.pdf (accessed October 15, 2014).

48. Arkansas and Pope County demographics reported from the U.S. Census Bureau's 2010–2015 American Community Survey five-year estimates, available at: http://factfinder.census.gov/ (accessed October 10, 2014)

49. The demographics of SFASU are available through the Office of Institutional Research, "Fast Facts for Lumberjacks 2013–2014" (Nacogdoches, TX: Stephen F. Austin State University, 2014), http://www.sfasu.edu/research/docs/FastFacts.pdf (accessed October 15, 2014). For SHSU, see "Sam Houston State University College Portrait" (Huntsville, TX: Sam Houston State University, 2014), http://www.collegeportraits.org/TX/shsu/print (accessed October 15, 2014).

50. Texas demographics came from the Texas Department of State Health Services, "Texas Population, 2013 (Projections)" (Texas Department of State Health Services, 2014), http://www.dshs.state.tx.us/chs/popdat/ST2013.shtm (accessed October 15, 2014).

51. Five hundred six respondents completed the pretest and a posttest, resulting in an attrition rate of 44 percent. About a third of that rate (18.2 percent) is due to students in the posttest sample not taking the pretest, leaving an effective mortality rate of 25.8 percent.

52. Niemi and Junn, *Civic Education;* Langton and Jennings, "Political Socialization and the High School Civics Curriculum in the United States."

53. This is a nonrandom sample. An appropriate level of caution must be exercised when using these results to make inferences about larger populations. We believe this sample speaks best to college students, a population that tends to be from families with higher incomes and education levels than those of the general population that house those institutions. That said, these school populations—even after adding diversity with two schools from Texas—remain drawn from largely poorer rural, White, and politically conservative populations.

54. Gooch and Rogers, "A Natural Disaster of Civic Proportions."

55. For figures 12.4a and b, most of the change is increased scores (i.e., to the left of zero). For figure 12.4c we want and get change in the other direction (i.e., to the right of zero) meaning students left fewer answers blank.

56. The composite measure of civic literacy (range = 0–100) is an average of the summary variable which combines the three civic knowledge scores: citizenship score, citizenship score 26, and blank percentage grade (range = 0–300).

57. Gooch and Rogers, "A Natural Disaster of Civic Proportions."

58. For example, most American government courses cover the history of suffrage. They likely note the lowering of the voting age from twenty-one to eighteen. Maybe some students become confused by this additional information and think the minimum voting age is still twenty-one.

59. The difference is likely due to the fact that students received credit for improving on the multipart questions in the Citizenship Score when they did not answer all parts correctly. Remember, this is not the case for Citizenship–26, where students only received credit if all parts are correct in multipart questions.

60. See, for example, Gerald Marwell and Ruth E. Ames, "Economists Free Ride, Does Anyone Else?," *Journal of Public Economics* 15, no. 3 (1981).

61. This runs contrary to national studies that typically find gender equality or higher male participation rates. Still, differences tend to be small. See "Who Votes, Who Doesn't, and Why: Regular Voters, Intermittent Voters, and Those Who Don't," (Pew Research Center, October 18, 2006), http://www.people-press.org/2006/10/18/who-votes-who-doesnt-and-why/ (accessed October 15, 2014). On the other hand, some studies show the gender gap has flipped in Millennials, with women more likely to report higher rates of participation. See "Trends by Race, Ethnicity, and Gender," (The Center for Information & Research on Civic Learning and Engagement, August 11, 2014), http://www.civicyouth.org/quick-facts/235-2/ (accessed October 15, 2014). Regardless, the result is robust across pretest and posttest models. However, the coefficient is attenuated in the posttest models because the variable drops out as a statistically significant predictor. Civic education may have to some extent a leveling effect on participation rates, serving to ameliorate some of the structural factors that lead to differences in civic participation.

62. Graham and Hand, *America, the Owner's Manual*, 22; O'Connor, "The Democratic Purpose of Education," 3–6.

63. American Enterprise Institute for Public Policy Research, "Civic Engagement through Education," in *AEI Program on American Citizenship* (American Enterprise Institute for Public Policy Research, September 23, 2013), http://www.citizenship-aei.org/2013/09/civic-engagement-through-education/#.VMcOoC4sC68 (accessed October 15, 2014).

64. Terry M. Moe, "The Two Democratic Purposes of Public Education," in *Rediscovering the Democratic Purposes of Education*, ed. Lorraine M. McDonnell, P. Michael Timpane, and Roger Benjamin (Lawrence: University of Kansas Press, 2000), 127 and 29; Lorraine M. McDonnell, "Defining Democratic Purposes," in *Rediscovering the Democratic Purposes of Education*, ed. Lorraine M. McDonnell, P. Michael Timpane, and Roger Benjamin (Lawrence: University of Kansas Press, 2000), 10; O'Connor, "The Democratic Purpose of Education," 6; David Feith, "Preface: Keeping the Republic," in *Teaching America: The Case for Civic Education*, ed. David Feith (Lanham: Rowman & Littlefield Education, 2011), xix; Michael T. Rogers, "A Civic Education Crisis," *Midsouth Political Science Review* 13, no. 1 (2012).

65. Langton and Jennings, "Political Socialization and the High School Civics Curriculum in the United States."

66. Rogers, "A Civic Education Crisis"; Niemi and Smith, "Enrollment in High School Government Classes."

67. Gooch and Rogers, "A Natural Disaster of Civic Proportions."

68. James Youniss, "How to Enrich Civic Education and Sustain Democracy," in *Making Civics Count: Citizenship Education for a New Generation*, ed. David E. Campbell, Meira Levinson, and Frederick M. Hess (Cambridge: Harvard Education Press, 2012), 120.

69. Youniss warns the kind of service matters if the goal is increased civic knowledge and political engagement. He argues students gravitate to service with no political component, which is not likely to have any effect on political knowledge and participation. He laments only "[a]n estimated 5 percent of all the service done by college-age students pertains to policy or political issues." He adds there is no reason to think the percentage is higher for high school students. See ibid., 127.

70. David E. Campbell, "Introduction," in *Making Civics Count: Citizenship Education for a New Generation*, ed. David E. Campbell, Meira Levinson, and Frederick M. Hess (Cambridge: Harvard Education Press, 2012), 8–9; David E. Campbell, "Voice in the Classroom: How an Open Classroom Climate Fosters Political Engagement among Adolescents," *Political Behavior* 30, no. 4 (2008).

71. Meira Levinson, *No Citizen Left Behind* (Harvard University Press, 2012), 186–91.

72. Ibid., 284–85.

73. Ibid., 293.

74. One recent article doing such research is Craig Douglas Albert and Marha Humphries Ginn, "Teaching with Tocqueville: Assessing the Utility of Using 'Democracy' in the American Government Classroom to Achieve Student-Learning Outcomes," *Journal of Political Science Education* 10, no. 2 (April–June 2014).

75. Ibid., 172.

76. Ibid., 124.

77. Campbell, "Civic Education in Traditional Public, Charter and Private Schools."

78. ISI, "Failing Our Students, Failing America."

79. Conover and Searing, "A Political Socialization Perspective."

BIBLIOGRAPHY

Acock, Alan, Harold D. Clarke, and Marianne C. Stewart. "A New Model for Old Measures: A Covariance Structure Analysis of Political Efficacy." *The Journal of Politics* 47, no. 4 (1985): 1062–84.

Albert, Craig Douglas, and Marha Humphries Ginn. "Teaching with Tocqueville: Assessing the Utility of Using 'Democracy' in the American Government Classroom to Achieve Student-Learning Outcomes." *Journal of Political Science Education* 10, no. 2 (April–June 2014): 166–85.

American Enterprise Institute for Public Policy Research, "Civic Engagement through Education." In *AEI Program on American Citizenship*: American Enterprise Institute for Public Policy Research, September 23, 2013. (http://www.citizenship-aei.org/2013/09/civic-engagement-through-education/#.VMcOoC4sC68).

American National Election Studies, "American National Election Studies (ANES) Cumulative Data File." Ann Arbor, MI: Inter-university Consortium for Political and Social Research, 1948–2008 (http://doi.org/10.3886/ICPSR08475.v14).

APSA. "APSA Task Force on Civic Education in the 21st Century: Expanded Articulation Statement: A Call for Reactions and Contributions." *PS: Political Science and Politics* 31, no. 3 (1998): 636–37.

———. "Task Force to Set Agenda for Civic Education Program." *PS: Political Science and Politics* 30, no. 4 (1997): 744.

Bauerlein, Mark. "Don't Believe the Hype: Young Voters Are Still Disengaged, and Universities Have Few Incentives to Fix It." In *Teaching America: The Case for Civic Education*. Edited by David Feith. Lanham: Rowman & Littlefield Education, 2011.

Bendor, Jonathan, Daniel Diermeier, and Michael Ting. "A Behavioral Model of Turnout." *The American Political Science Review* 97, no. 2 (May, 2003): 261–80.

Brand, Jennie E. "Civic Returns to Higher Education: A Note on Heterogeneous Effects." *Social Forces* 89, no. 2 (December 2010): 417–33.

Busch, Elizabeth Kaufer, and Jonathan W. White. "Introduction." In *Civic Education and the Future of American Citizenship*. Edited by Elizabeth Kaufer Busch and Jonathan W. White. Lanham: Lexington Books, 2013.

Butts, R. Freeman. *The Revival of Civic Learning: A Rationale for Citizenship Education in American Schools*. Akron: Phi Delta Kappa Educational Foundation, 1980.

Campbell, David E. "Civic Education in Traditional Public, Charter and Private Schools: Moving from Comparison to Explanation." In *Making Civics Count: Citizenship Education for a New Generation*. Edited by David E. Campbell, Meira Levinson, and Frederick M. Hess. Cambridge: Harvard Education Press, 2012.

Campbell, David E. "Introduction." In *Making Civics Count: Citizenship Education for a New Generation*. Edited by David E. Campbell, Meira Levinson, and Frederick M. Hess. Cambridge: Harvard Education Press, 2012.

Campbell, David E. "Voice in the Classroom: How an Open Classroom Climate Fosters Political Engagement among Adolescents." *Political Behavior* 30, no. 4 (2008): 437–54.

Carter, Lief H., and Jean Bethke Elshtain. "Task Force on Civic Education Statement of Purpose." *PS: Political Science and Politics* 30, no. 4 (1997): 745.

"Characters from 'the Simpsons' More Well Known to Americans Than Their First Amendment Rights, Survey Finds." (2006). (http://www.mccormickfoundation.org/news/2006/pr030106.aspx).

Conover, Pamela Johnson, and Donald D. Searing. "A Political Socialization Perspective." In *Rediscovering the Democratic Purposes of Education*. Edited by Lorraine M. McDonnell, P. Michael Timpane, and Roger Benjamin. Lawrence: University of Kansas Press, 2000.

Converse, Philip E. "Change in the American Electorate." In *The Human Meaning of Social Change*. Edited by Angus Campbell and Philip E. Converse. New York: Russell Sage Foundation, 1972.

Delli Carpini, Michael, and Scott Keeter. *What Americans Know about Politics and Why It Matters*. New Haven: Yale University Press, 1996.

Dillon, Sam. "Failing Grades on Civics Exam Called a 'Crisis.'" *The New York Times*, 2011 (http://www.nytimes.com/2011/05/05/education/05civics.html?_r=0)

Dudley, Robert L., and Alan R. Gitelson. "Political Literacy, Civic Education, and Civic Engagement: A Return to Political Socialization?" *Applied Development Science* 6, no. 4 (2002): 175–82.

Ehrlich, Thomas. "Civic Education: Lessons Learned." *PS: Political Science and Politics* 32, no. 2 (Jun., 1999): 245–50.

Feith, David. "Preface: Keeping the Republic." In *Teaching America: The Case for Civic Education*. Edited by David Feith. Lanham: Rowman & Littlefield Education, 2011.

Finkel, Steven E. "Civic Education and the Mobilization of Political Participation in Developing Democracies." *The Journal of Politics* 64, no. 4 (November, 2002 2002): 994–1020.

Finkel, Steven E., and Amy Erica Smith. "Civic Education, Political Discussion, and the Social Transmission of Democratic Knowledge and Values in a New Democracy: Kenya 2002." *American Journal of Political Science* 55, no. 2 (April, 2011): 417–35.

Galston, William A. "Civic Education and Political Participation." *PS: Political Science and Politics* 37, no. April (April, 2004 2004): 263–66.

———. "Civic Knowledge, Civic Education, and Civic Engagement: A Summary of Recent Research." *International Journal of Public Administration* 30, no. 6 (2007): 623–42.

———. "A Natural Disaster of Civic Proportions: College Students in the Natural State Falls Short of the Naturalization Benchmark." *Midsouth Political Science Review* 13, no. 1 (2012): 54–82.

Graham, Bob, and Chris Hand. *America, the Owner's Manual: Making Government Work for You*. Washington, DC: CQ Press, 2010.

Graham, Bob, and Chris Hand. "A Failure of Leadership: The Duty of Politicians and Universities to Salvage Citizenship." In *Teaching America: The Case for Civic Education*. Edited by David Feith. Lanham: Rowman & Littlefield Education, 2011.

Heater, Derek. *A History of Education for Citizenship*. New York: RoutledgeFalmer, a Taylor & Francis Group, 2004.

Hibbing, John R., and Elizabeth Theiss-Morse. "Civics Is Not Enough: Teaching Barbarics in K–12." *PS: Political Science & Politics* 29, no. 1 (March 1996): 57–62.

Hillygus, D. Sunshine. "The Missing Link: Exploring the Relationship between Higher Education and Political Engagement." *Political Behavior* 27, no. 1 (2005): 25–47.

Immigration and Naturalization Act. 82–414. 1952.

ISI. "The Coming Crisis in Citizenship." Wilmington, DE: Intercollegiate Studies Institute's National Civic Literacy Board, 2006. (http://www.americanciviclit eracy.org/2006/summary.html).

———. "Failing Our Students, Failing America: Holding Colleges Accountable for Teaching America's History and Institutions." Wilmington, DE: Intercollegiate Studies Institute's National Civic Literacy Board, 2007. (http://www.americancivic literacy.org/2007/summary_summary.html).

———. "Our Fading Heritage: Americans Fail a Basic Test on Their History and Institutions." Wilmington, DE: Intercollegiate Studies Institute's National Civic Literacy Board, 2008. (http://www.americancivicliteracy.org/2008/summary_sum mary.html).

Johanek, Michael C. ""Preparing Pluribus for Unum: Historicial Perspectives on Civic Education." In *Making Civics Count: Citizenship for a New Generation*. Edited by David E. Campbell, Meira Levinson, and Frederick M. Hess. Cambridge: Harvard Education Press, 2012.

Kam, Cindy D. "When Duty Calls, Do Citizens Answer?" *The Journal of Politics* 69, no. 1 (2007): 17–29.

Kinder, Donald, and David Sears. "Public Opinion and Political Action." In *The Handbook of Social Psychology*. Edited by G. Lindzey and E. Aronson. Oxford: Oxford University Press, 1985.

Langton, K., and M. K. Jennings. "Political Socialization and the High School Civics Curriculum in the United States." *American Political Science Review* 62 (1968): 862–67.

Levine, Peter. "Education for a Civil Society." In *Making Civics Count: Citizenship Education for a New Generation*. Edited by David E. Campbell, Meira Levinson, and Frederick M. Hess. Cambridge: Harvard Education Press, 2012.

Levinson, Meira. *No Citizen Left Behind*: Harvard University Press, 2012.

Lister, Ian. "Civic Education for Positive Pluralism in Great Britain." In *Education for Democratic Citizenship: A Challenge for Multi-Ethnic Societies*. Edited by Roberta S. Sigel and Marilyn Hoskin. New Jersey: Lawrence Erlbaum Associates, Inc., 1991.

Macedo, Stephen, Yvette Alex-Assensoh, Jeffrey M. Berry, Michael Brintnall, David E. Campbell, Luis Ricardo Fraga, Archon Fung, William A. Galston, Christopher F. Karpowitz, Margaret Levi, Meira Levinson, Keena Lipsitz, Richard G. Niemi, Robert D. Putnam, Wendy M. Rahn, Rob Reich, Robert R. Rodgers, Todd Swanstrom, and Katherine Cramer Walsh. *Democracy at Risk: How Political Choices Undermine Citizen Participation, and What We Can Do about It*. Washington, DC: Brookings Institution Press, 2005.

Martin, Pamela, Holley Tankersley, and Min Ye. "Are They Living What They Learn?: Assessing Knowledge and Attitude Change in Introductory Politics Courses." *Journal of Political Science Education* 8, no. 2 (2012): 201–23.

Marwell, Gerald, and Ruth E. Ames. "Economists Free Ride, Does Anyone Else?" *Journal of Public Economics* 15, no. 3 (1981): 295–310.

McDonnell, Lorraine M. "Defining Democratic Purposes." In *Rediscovering the Democratic Purposes of Education*. Edited by Lorraine M. McDonnell, P. Michael Timpane, and Roger Benjamin. Lawrence: University of Kansas Press, 2000.

Milner, Henry. *Civic Literacy: How Informed Citizens Make Democracy Work*. London: University Press of New England, 2002.

Moe, Terry M. "The Two Democratic Purposes of Public Education." In *Rediscovering the Democratic Purposes of Education*. Edited by Lorraine M. McDonnell, P. Michael Timpane, and Roger Benjamin. Lawrence: University of Kansas Press, 2000.

Nie, Norman, and D. Sunshine Hillygus. "Education and Democratic Citizenship." In *Making Good Citizens: Education and Civil Society*. Edited by Diane Ravitch and Joseph P. Viteritti. New Haven: Yale University Press, 2001.

Niemi, Richard G. "What Students Know about Civics and Government." In *Making Civics Count: Citizenship Education for a New Generation*. Edited by David E. Campbell, Meira Levinson, and Frederick M. Hess. Cambridge: Harvard Education Press, 2012.

Niemi, Richard G., and Jane Junn. *Civic Education: What Makes Students Learn?* New Haven: Yale University Press, 1998.

Niemi, Richard G., and Julia Smith. "Enrollment in High School Government Classes: Are We Short-Changing Citizenship and Political Science Training?" *PS: Political Science and Politics* 34, no. 2 (2001): 281–87.

O'Connor, Sandra Day. "The Democratic Purpose of Education: From the Founders to Horace Mann to Today." In *Teaching America: The Case for Civic Education*. Edited by David Feith. Lanham: Rowman & Littlefield Education, 2011.

Office of InstitutionalResearch, "Fast Facts for Lumberjacks 2013–2014." Nacogdoches, TX: Stephen F. Austin State University, 2014. (http://www.sfasu.edu/research/docs/FastFacts.pdf).

Popkin, Samuel L. *The Reasoning Voter: Communication and Persuasion in Presidential Campaigns*. Chicago: University of Chicago Press, 1994.

Putnam, Robert. *Bowling Alone: The Collapse and Revival of the American Community*. New York: Simon and Schuster, 2000.

———. "Bowling Alone: America's Declining Social Capital." *Journal of Democracy* 6, no. 1 (1995): 65–78.

———. "Community-Based Social Capital and Education Performance." In *Making Good Citizens: Education and Civil Society*. Edited by Diane Ravitch and Joseph P. Viteritti. New Haven: Yale University Press, 2001.

———. *Making Democracy Work: Civic Traditions in Modern Italy*. Princeton, NJ: Princeton University Press, 1993.

———. "Tuning in, Tuning Out: The Strange Disappearance of Social Capital in America." *PS: Political Science and Politics* 28, no. 4 (Dec. 1995).

Ravitch, Diane. "Education and Democracy." In *Making Good Citizens: Education and Civil Society*. Edited by Diane Ravitch and Joseph P. Viteritti. New Haven: Yale University Press, 2001.

Riker, William H., and Peter C. Ordeshook. "A Theory of the Calculus of Voting." *The American Political Science Review* 62, no. 1 (1968): 25–42.

Rogers, Michael T. "A Civic Education Crisis." *Midsouth Political Science Review* 13, no. 1 (2012): 1–36.

Ross, Jason. "The Wisdom of Twenty Thousand Teachers: Strengthen State Requirements, Stop Marginalizing the Founders." In *Teaching America: The Case for*

Civic Education. Edited by David Feith. Lanham: Rowman & Littlefield Education, 2011.

"Sam Houston State University College Portrait." Huntsville, TX: Sam Houston State University, 2014 (http://www.collegeportraits.org/TX/shsu/print).

Somin, Ilya. *Democracy and Political Ignorance: Why Smaller Government Is Smarter.* Stanford: Stanford University Press, 2013.

"Study: More Know 'the Simpsons' Than First Amendment Rights." *USA Today*, 3/1/2006 (http://usatoday30.usatoday.com/news/nation/2006–03–01-freedom-poll_x.htm).

"Study: More Know 'Simpsons' Than Constitution." FoxNews.com, accessed October 15, 2014. (http://www.foxnews.com/story/2006/03/01/study-more-know-simpsons-than-constitution/).

Texas Department of State Health Services, "Texas Population, 2013 (Projections)." Texas Department of State Health Services, 2014 (http://www.dshs.state.tx.us/chs/popdat/ST2013.shtm).

"Trends by Race, Ethnicity, and Gender." The Center on Information & Research on Civic Learning and Education, August 11, 2014. (http://www.civicyouth.org/quick-facts/235-2/).

United States Citizenship and Immigration Services, "The Naturalization Test." Department of Homeland Security, accessed October 15, 2014 (http://www.uscis.gov/us-citizenship/naturalization-test).

Watson, Wyatt. "Arkansas Tech University Student Demographics: All Main Campus Students." Russellville, AR: Arkansas Tech University, 2015. (http://www.atu.edu/ir/docs/enrollment/enrollment-all/student_demographics_overview_main_campus_fall.pdf).

Whiteley, Paul F. "Rational Choice and Political Participation: Evaluating the Debate." *Political Research Quarterly* 48, no. 1 (1995): 211–33.

"Who Votes, Who Doesn't, and Why: Regular Voters, Intermittent Voters, and Those Who Don't." Pew Research Center, October 18, 2006. (http://www.people-press.org/2006/10/18/who-votes-who-doesnt-and-why/).

Youniss, James. "How to Enrich Civic Education and Sustain Democracy." In *Making Civics Count: Citizenship Education for a New Generation.* Edited by David E. Campbell, Meira Levinson, and Frederick M. Hess. Cambridge: Harvard Education Press, 2012.

Chapter Thirteen

Educating Students about the National Debt

A Multiyear Study of Civic Education in the University Core Curriculum

Steven E. Galatas and Cindy Pressley

What do students know about the national debt and budget deficit issues? Does this knowledge reflect factual information about these issues, is it at a basic level of information, or are students largely misinformed? Does exposure to basic factual information and classroom experiences about the national debt and budget deficit shift basic cognitive knowledge? Does the classroom experience also shift affective learning, cognitive evaluation, and problem solving?

To address these questions, this chapter offers an examination of a multiyear study of students enrolled in an introductory level political science course required of all students pursuing any degree at Stephen F. Austin State University (SFASU). Students participated in a pretest of basic factual information, affective knowledge, and evaluative knowledge questions. Students then received instruction on the national debt and budget deficit issues. Finally, students answered a posttest survey, duplicating questions from the pretest to determine the extent to which the educational intervention changed their basic, affective, and evaluative knowledge.

The introductory political science course and module on the national debt and budget deficit issues included a student writing assignment associated with a state legislative mandate to assess the university general education, core curriculum assessment process. This assessment process also served as a component of SFASU's participation in the America's Future Initiative of the American Democracy Project sponsored by the Association of American State Colleges and Universities. In some years, such classroom experiences coincided with co-curricular activities like on-campus speakers, screening of movies like *I.O.U.S.A* or *Inside Job*, and student-government-ponsored programs. While co-curricular activities and course assessment processes are important to the promotion of civic awareness of the national debt and budget deficit, these aspects of the America's Future Initiative have been addressed elsewhere.[1]

We begin with an overview of the literature on civic engagement and student learning, including a discussion of the link between civic education, basic factual knowledge, and learning about economic and public policy issues. Then, we present an overview of the context of the political science course and its role in the university's general education, core curriculum. As part of this discussion, we review the state-mandated core curriculum assessment process as implemented for political science courses at SFASU. Finally, we provide analysis of the data collected from pretests and posttests of students' basic cognitive, affective, and evaluative knowledge associated with classroom experiences involving the national debt and budget deficit issues. Finally, we offer conclusions about the impact of our educational intervention on student knowledge.

CIVIC ENGAGEMENT AND STUDENT LEARNING

In 2000, Robert Putnam published the now classic *Bowling Alone: The Collapse and Revival of American Community* that placed the changing nature of American involvement in civic life in the spotlight.[2] Americans had traditionally been active in various forms of civic life. However, declines in civic involvement in recent decades reflect generational, not cohort, effects.[3] Because an active citizenry plays an essential role in a well-functioning democracy, it is essential that scholars examine this downward trend in the hopes of altering it.

One way to re-energize the American public's involvement in civic life is through civic education. Historically, scholars and civic leaders linked the maintenance of order in society and self-interested freedom to civic education.[4] While recent scholarship has addressed the need to increase education in civics at multiple education levels, it is important to first look at the role civic education has historically played in the United States.[5]

At the turn of the nineteenth and twentieth century, the United States was facing rapid changes resulting from industrialization and immigration. These changes led educators to focus on civic education as a means to promote the democratic system.[6] For political scientists of the time, civic education was initially connected to the study of history. However, the focus later switched to current rights and duties of the state.[7] Furthermore, the role of civic education in American society was not only to help manage changes associated with industrialization and immigration but was also meant to control the behavior and actions of children.[8] Civic education served to instill shared values associated with traditional morals and instill specific habits associated with being a good citizen.[9] The basic goal of civic education then was to build political knowledge within young people in order to cultivate civic values deemed important in American society. Eventually, Progressives of the late 1800s and early 1900s tended to take issue with this perspective on civic education as it was seen as a form of indoctrination. If civic education oscillated between enforcing traditional values and more Progressive concepts over the subsequent decades, by the 1980s and 1990s civic education shifted to a new model. Civic experiences and values became the major focus, with explicit focus on political and civic knowledge and skills, without a focus on moral or character development.[10] Civics education was once again part of the education spectrum, but it has not yet reached a point where it is considered a requirement by the education system.[11]

In examining recent scholarship on civic knowledge, education, and engagement, Galston concludes "that civic knowledge is an important determinant of civic capability and character. Moreover, recent findings suggest that formal, classroom-based civic education provides an effective means of teaching civic knowledge."[12] While traditional classroom civics education is important, recent scholarship shows faculty are experimenting with a range of pedagogical tools in order to increase student knowledge.

Pedagogical tools have included simulations, overlapping concept areas during instruction, and use of national newspapers.[13] Rankin found that the use of multiple types of knowledge (textbook and multimedia current events) can be used to enhance student understanding of public policy issues, especially when those issues are dramatic and newsworthy.[14] Ehrlich extends this argument into the realm of higher education, advocating traditional classroom civic education with experiential learning in the larger world to prepare students for life-long citizenship, decision-making, and democratic deliberation.[15] Based on Ehrlich's own service-learning teaching experiences, he argues that civic education encompasses academic, social, moral, and civic goals.[16] Ehrlich found that a combination of strategies that included problem-based, collaborative, and community service learning are promising pedagogical tools to increase civic learning and overall civic education in the higher education classroom.

Omelicheva and Avdeyeva study the use of lecture versus alternative formats of learning (specifically debate) in the political science college classroom.[17] They found that lecture is an inappropriate method for higher-level learning, whereas alternative formats such as debate may allow students to connect more with the material, including greater comprehension of complex concepts, application to new settings, and critical evaluation skills.[18] The increased use of forms of deliberation and discussion may be one way of combating criticism of the civics instruction currently provided in secondary and higher education.[19]

While innovation in curriculum and instruction are important, the positive relationship between higher levels of education and civic engagement is more critical.[20] Emphasizing this connection, Beaumont et al. offer evidence from their research that demonstrates increases in political engagement through college experiences while ensuring that they did not change the students' own political persuasions.[21] The research used a variety of means of examination, such as student and faculty surveys, interviews, and writing exercises. Using a pretest-posttest format, they examine changes in student engagement across five scales: "a sense of politically engaged identity, foundational political knowledge, skills of political influence and action, intentions to participate in conventional electoral activities, intentions to participate in activities expressing political voice."[22] The research determined that those with higher levels of interest improved their engagement slightly while those with lower initial interest demonstrated more significant increases in political engagement; students gained knowledge, skills, and motivation to be more regularly involved in a wide variety of political activities including leadership and activism.[23] This broader view of political engagement helps to inform the activities promoted by colleges and universities in developing politically engaged citizens of the future.

There are struggles, however, in providing civic education. One struggle that appears is when citizens hold on to incorrect information as though it were factually correct. Kuklinski et al. discuss the issue of a misinformed rather than noninformed American public, including confidently holding wrong beliefs.[24] The authors note that knowledge of facts is essential to having an informed public, and citizens must have access to factual knowledge and must use the knowledge to inform their decisions and opinions. A problem arises in the first condition in that factual knowledge is not well disseminated by the American political system. If citizens do receive factual knowledge, however, will they use this knowledge to inform their decisions and opinions? Kuklinski et al. offer. This is problematic given the tendency of citizens to resist facts and the challenge of inducing citizens to use correct information. The authors extend this observation to public policy, noting that citizens do not necessarily lack information, but they hold consistently to the wrong information and then make choices about policy based upon the misinformation.[25] Ultimately, collective decisions vary significantly from those that occur when the public holds factually correct information.

A second struggle requires a return to Farr's discussion of the historically rooted understanding of civic education in the United States.[26] The United States is undergoing a demographic shift, including rapid growth of the Hispanic population especially in states like Texas and California. Kiasatpour and Lasley discuss the difficulties of teaching core curriculum political science courses in colleges and classrooms that serve a largely Hispanic population in Texas. Key challenges included communication skills, assignment deadlines, and inexperience with academic culture.[27] Other challenges included poverty, lesser level of academic preparation, student learning styles, and large class size. If civic educators are to provide appropriate instruction to actively engage citizens in civic life, it is essential that they recognize and attempt to adjust their styles to meet the needs of the changing American population, thus taking into account issues of diversity.

A final struggle to discuss is the changing technology available to citizens and educators, and how these tools can help to improve overall engagement of students if used properly.[28] For example, Gagnier discusses a survey conducted among the millennial generation, those born post-1978, and how they perceive themselves and the state of American governance and politics. It is important for educators to take this type of research into account when considering ways to promote civic engagement among the younger generations. Millennials tend to favor instruction and assignments that favor self-definition and problem-solving especially when coupled with technology and social networking.[29]

Civic education, tools that can be used for civic education, and the struggles that educators may face are important components to consider when examining specific concerns of civic knowledge, such as fiscal policy. In general, students are not receiving information to become informed citizens in the areas of economics, federal budgeting, and deficit/debt management.[30] Parker and Deane analyzed how closely the public paid attention to five hundred news stories over a ten-year period (1986–1996) and found 30 percent of Americans followed business and economic stories including gas prices and the stock market crash of 1987.[31] The study also looked at knowledge of the news and found that they were given correct responses 81 percent of the time for the question regarding whether "the federal government spends more money than it takes in."[32] An informed public can help make decisions regarding public policy that could get the United States back on track economically.[33] Research has shown that public opinion about economic policy has an impact on economic policy decision-making.[34] A problem arises, however, when the citizens are attempting to make decisions without being educated on what those decisions may mean for civic life.

In general, the American public is not well educated on issues of economic policy, especially when compared to economic experts. Blendon et al. examine whether there are overlaps and/or differences in the way the public and economists view economic policy issues. They base their research on a set of surveys conducted in 1996, concluding that a large part of the public believed the economy was performing less well than official government data.[35] Blendon et al. also note that Americans with a college degree have opinions that are more aligned to government data than those of Americans without college degrees. Furthermore, opinions between the public and economists depend on the issue. For example, the public and economists were provided with a set of reasons commonly given as to why the economy is not doing better. The public chose seven of these general reasons, including the federal budget is too big, too many people on welfare, foreign aid spending is too high, education and job training are inadequate, taxes are too high, people place too little value on hard work, and people are not saving enough. Economists agreed with the inadequacy of education and job training as well as the low rate of personal savings.[36] To explain these differences between the public and economists, Blendon et al. suggest personal experience trumps actual data, distrust of government data by the public, poor reporting by the media on these issues, and use of different sources of data among the two groups. The authors conclude that Americans lack a good foundation about how the economy operates and thus have a difficult time assessing economic performance.[37]

Caplan uses the 1996 Survey of Americans and Economists on the Economy to determine that the views of the public and of economists regarding the economy are different even when controlling for concerns such as the possible self-serving nature of economists' opinions. Caplan notes that "controlling for all other variables, economists' differences with the public can be decomposed into two effects: the first is a general effect of education, the second a specific product of economic training. Rather than merely eliminating random errors, both education and economic training actually seem to *debias* individuals, though economic training is usually the more potent of the two."[38] Caplan criticizes the explanations offered by Blendon et al. (1997) and points out they have not tested their hypotheses.[39] Caplan does argue that there are marked differences in opinion between the public and economists and this may be based on systematically biased beliefs rather than self-serving bias, ideology, or education. He explains that first impressions by the public matter for economic beliefs. Moreover, when controlling for ideology, the gap between economists and the public increase, while education diminishes the gap, as does the level of economic training.[40]

Blinder and Krueger conducted a random sample, random digit dialing telephone survey of those in the United States who were over eighteen in 2003 with a 26 percent response rate, interviewing 1,002 persons.[41] They used a different survey instrument than Blendon et al. and Caplan to examine public opinion on the economy. They argue that respondents desire to be informed on economic policies, with television as their dominant source of information. Ideology is the most important variable on major economic policy issues like social security in the general public, with self-interest variables the least important.[42] When inquiring about the desire to be well-informed about economic policy, the survey results indicated while ideology (liberal, conservative, moderate, other, nonpolitical) made little difference, when asking about political engagement using a question about whether the person voted in the 2000 presidential election, the survey results signified that those who indicated they voted desired to be well-informed on economic policy issues.[43] The survey also queried the basic economic policy knowledge of respondents on several economic issues. Results indicate that the average responses were roughly correct, with one exception—the federal budget deficit.[44] Blinder and Krueger find it positive that a percentage of Americans desire to be well-informed on economic policy issues and have a reasonable amount of correct information on economic policy. Yet, they express concern that economic knowledge is not significantly higher among those using more sources of information, using information more intensively, or desiring to be informed. According to the research, this does not necessarily bode well "for those of us engaged in economic education and/or economic policy—or for economic theorists who use *homo economicus* as the backbone of their models of political economy."[45]

An emerging literature examines the impact of knowledge of the national debt and budget deficit, as well as curricular and co-curricular activities among American university students. In a symposium from the journal *PS: Political Science and Politics,* several articles examine campus experiences associated with the American Democracy Project's "America's Future" initiative. Catlett notes a positive impact on student learning when discussion of the national debt and budget deficit in the classroom was supplemented with curricular and co-curricular activities including intergenerational dialogues regarding entitlement programs.[46] Martin reviews experiences associated with using a political theory course to provide political and economic context for debates over the national debt and budget deficit. He finds that a personal-budget-making exercise, analytical essays, and a national-government-budget exercise enhanced student learning and retention of course information about the national debt and budget deficit.[47] In reviewing the attempt to embed teaching about the national debt and budget deficit in the university's general education, core curriculum, Galatas and Pressley stress the need to explain why these issues matter on a personal level to the student, the need to ensure information is accurate and up-to-date, and the need to overcome student predispositions so that students engage the facts and move toward evaluative learning.[48]

Moving beyond this symposium, Levy and Orr utilized a deliberative simulation of the federal budget to engage students in active learning. The authors find generally that students entering an introductory level American government class lack knowledge about the federal budget and budget deficit. While students participating in their budget simulation experienced some gains in knowledge, the gains were relatively minor. Moreover, students in the simulation moderated their preferences as a result of participation in the simulation at rates similar to those students receiving instruction using a traditional lecture format.[49] The lack of significant gains in factual knowledge about the budget are similar to those of Baranowski, and contrast with a local school district budget simulation by Wakelee and Itkonen in which students demonstrated significant gains in student knowledge as a result of participation.[50]

The purpose of this literature review was to introduce the problems faced with civic education today, to examine pedagogical tools to potentially increase civic education, and to then explain the specific civic education problem—knowledge of economic policy—addressed by the research conducted in this chapter. Civic education has been a historical part of American democracy; however, recent years have seen interest in civic engagement and civic life fade. This decline is particularly notable in complex public policy areas such as economic policy. The research conducted here connects concepts of civic education, civic engagement, and economic policy using higher education as its focus point.

SETTING THE CONTEXT FOR "AMERICA'S FUTURE" AT SFASU

Texas is one of five states that require the study of both federal and state constitutions for college and university students.[51] The Texas requirement is a product of state legislation that mandates six hours of university course credit to receive an associate or baccalaureate degree from a state university or community college in Texas.[52] At SFASU the six hours of course credit are spread across two courses that integrate the study of Texas and U.S. governments using a topical or thematic approach.[53] One of the courses at SFASU, Political Science 142, includes a substantive focus on key state and national policies such as defense and security policy, fiscal and monetary policy, education policy, and social welfare policy.[54] In addition, discussion of the national debt and budget deficit issues is compatible with the goals for social science education for general education, core curriculum courses identified by the Texas Higher Education Coordinating Board.[55] For social and behavioral sciences twelve such standards, called Exemplary Educational Objectives (EEOs), exist. One of the guidelines involves developing and communicating explanations for social problems. Another specifically mentions public policy.[56] Thus, Political Science 142 offers an appropriate setting to examine civic engagement and student learning associated with the national debt and budget deficit issues.[57]

By the fall of 2006, the THECB mandated that all core curriculum, general education courses develop an assessment plan to measure student learning and to demonstrate student mastery of the EEOs. While institutions and university systems were given freedom to develop plans unique or tailored to their setting, all students in general education classes were required to be assessed.[58] The political science faculty at SFASU agreed to link PSC 142 and its core curriculum assessment process with the America's Future Initiative of the American Democracy Project (ADP) of the Association of American State Colleges and Universities (AASCU). Launched in the Fall of 2009, nine institutions across the United States accepted an invitation to join the America's Future Initiative, partnering with Public Agenda (a non-partisan organization based in Washington, DC) to develop programs aimed at educating students about the national debt and budget deficit issues. In doing so, the SFASU political science faculty agreed to embed a writing assignment that addressed the national debt and budget deficits into the general education, core curriculum assessment process for one political science course, Political Science 142. While most of the nine institutions have ceased participation in the "America's Future Initiative," the program is still listed as one of the "Civic Engagement in Action Series" sponsored by the ADP.[59] The ADP at SFASU retains its commitment to educating students on the national debt and budget deficit issues.

As part of the America's Future Initiative, the national debt and budget deficit were added to the PSC 142 course materials. Faculty were given freedom to determine the manner in which the national debt and public policy issues were presented in their classrooms beyond the general education, core curriculum assessment process. We followed Cain by working with faculty to develop a short, intensive overview of the national debt and budget deficit issues with examples and applications.[60] One of the more common methods of instruction was to include lectures on fiscal policy. Professors were given information created by Public Agenda.[61] Professors could use the exact tools, including PowerPoint slides and discussion guides, or could modify materials to coincide with individual learning styles. Some faculty incorporated short videos, websites (e.g., the debt clock), and news clips on the state of the economy. When faculty covered the national debt and budget deficits during the semester varied, with some faculty teaching the material in the first weeks of the semester, while others waited until the end of the semester.

In some years, like 2010, the teaching of the national debt and budget deficit issues coincided with co-curricular activities. On a number of occasions, students could elect to attend a viewing of the movie *I.O.U.S.A* or *Inside Job*. Through the America's Future Initiative, guest speakers from Public Agenda and the Concord Coalition (another nonpartisan organization in Washington, DC) were brought to campus in 2010 and 2011. The ADP at SFASU co-sponsored "Debt Week" with the Student Government Association in 2009 and 2010. During these co-curricular events, displays illustrating the size of the national debt and budget deficit as well as other information were placed around the campus. Workshops on entitlement reform occurred in the evenings during "Debt Week" in 2010 and 2011. In 2012, "Democracy Wall," a free-speech response board on which individuals may post comments, asked passersby to comment on the national debt and budget deficit, including possible ways to reduce the deficit and debt. Thus, co-curricular activities offered opportunities to reinforce classroom instruction.

To examine the impact of the classroom experience directly on student knowledge of the budget deficit and national debt issues, faculty teaching PSC 142 were asked to allow their students to participate in a pretest, posttest research design. Faculty agreed voluntarily to permit the students to participate in the survey prior to the beginning of classroom instruction on the budget deficit or national debt issues. When the module on the national debt and budget deficit is finished, the posttest is administered, typically within a week of the end of the module. While most faculty teaching individual sections of PSC 142 agreed, the decision was ultimately left to the faculty member as to whether to devote the classroom time to the surveys.[62] In addition, individual students were informed of their right to opt out of the surveys. For the 2010 survey, a total of fourteen sections, taught by six different faculty participated in the project, and in 2012, seven sections, taught by four different instructors participated. The 2013 survey included seven sections from five different faculty; in 2014 twelve sections taught by five different instructors were surveyed.

The pretest and posttest consists of twenty-five questions broken into four categories.[63] First, the surveys gather information about the respondents' level of concern and awareness of the national debt and budget deficit issues. Next, respondents answer questions about their knowledge of the issues, including size of the national debt. Then a set of questions addressed the proportions of the U.S. government's budget devoted to spending on various broad areas of policy including entitlements, national defense, and interest payments of the debt. A final question in this section asks respondents which foreign government holds the largest share of the U.S. government's national debt. A third set of questions asks about possible solutions to the debt. These questions ask respondents to rate on a four-point Likert-scale whether each of four possible solutions is the "only" solution to the national debt and budget deficit. A final set of questions asks for the demographic characteristics of the respondents.

Findings throughout this chapter reflect results only from those students who completed the pretest and posttest waves of the surveys. While a large number of surveys were conducted each year, there were significant attrition rates from pretest to posttest. Table 13.1 presents information about the total number of students surveyed, either pretest or posttest, and the total number of students who completed both waves by year. In 2010, 638 students completed at least one wave of the survey, while 290 (45.5%) completed both the pretest and the posttest in 2010. In 2012, 511 students completed at least one wave, and 236 (46.2%) completed both waves. For 2013, a total of 638 students participated in at least one wave, with 233 (36.5%) completing both. Finally, in 2014, 538 students filled out at least one wave, and 379 (70.4%) finished both the pretest and the posttest.[64]

Table 13.1. Survey Respondents by Wave of Survey

Year	Both Waves	Total Surveys
2010	290	638
	(45.5%)	(100.0%)
2012	236	511
	(46.2%)	(100.0%)
2013	233	638
	(36.5%)	(100.0%)
2014	379	538
	(70.4%)	(100.0%)

IMPACT ON BASIC KNOWLEDGE

To assess the impact of instruction on basic cognitive knowledge of the national debt and related issues, we compared the pretest and posttest answers on the surveys. These questions asked about student knowledge of the size of the national debt, the percentage of the national government's budget devoted to entitlements, the percentage of the budget devoted to defense, the percentage of the budget devoted to interest on the national debt, and percent of the national debt owed to foreign countries. For each question, respondents chose from four possible answers. For example, regarding the size of the national debt, possible answers were $100 billion, $1 trillion, $17 trillion, and $50 trillion. For each knowledge question, we reduced the answers from the survey respondents to a dichotomous variable measuring if the respondent selected the correct answer from a choice of four on the survey instruments.

Then, we compared whether the pretest and posttest answers were correct. A cross-tabulation contingency table was calculated, and a Pearson Chi-square test was used as a test of significance.

Table 13.2 provides the results of the comparison of the pretest and posttest surveys by year for each of the four basic knowledge questions. Generally,

Table 13.2.   Comparison of Knowledge Questions Pretest and Posttest

	Incorrect on Both	Correct Pre, Incorrect Post	Incorrect Pre, Correct Post	Correct on Both	Chi-Squared	N
Size of National Debt						
2010	56 (19.3%)	29 (10.0%)	57 (19.7%)	148 (51.0%)	36.63***	290
2012	29 (12.3%)	16 (6.8%)	52 (22.0%)	139 (58.9)	22.38***	236
2013	35 (15.0%)	11 (4.7%)	38 (16.3%)	149 (63.0%)	53.37***	233
2014	44 (11.7%)	37 (9.8%)	68 (18.0%)	228 (60.5%)	29.92***	377
% Budget–Entitlements						
2010	126 (43.4%)	26 (9.0%)	91 (31.4%)	47 (16.2%)	11.04***	290
2012	138 (58.5%)	27 (11.4%)	41 (17.4%)	30 (12.7%)	18.16***	236
2013	86 (36.9%)	48 (20.6%)	47 (20.2%)	52 (22.3%)	6.49**	233
2014	184 (48.9%)	65 (17.3%)	72 (21.0%)	55 (14.6%)	11.42***	376
% of Budget–Defense						
2010	98 (33.8%)	45 (15.5%)	83 (28.6%)	64 (22.1%)	4.50*	290
2012	110 (46.6%)	44 (18.6%)	43 (18.2%)	39 (16.5%)	8.46**	236
2013	102 (43.8%)	45 (16.7%)	50 (21.5%)	42 (18.0%)	7.95*	233
2014	171 (45.4%)	68 (18.0%)	79 (21.0%)	59 (15.6%)	7.99**	377
% of Budget–Interest						
2010	121 (41.7%)	44 (15.2%)	76 (26.2%)	49 (16.9%)	5.13*	290
2012	105 (44.5%)	42 (17.8%)	45 (19.1%)	44 (18.6%)	10.42**	236
2013	123 (52.8%)	48 (20.6%)	31 (13.3%)	31 (13.3%)	9.77*	233
2014	191 (50.5%)	76 (20.1%)	70 (18.5%)	111 (29.4%)	2.63	378

* $p < 0.05$; ** $p < 0.01$; *** $p < 0.001$

the results are statistically significant for every question in 2010, 2012, and 2013. In 2014 only the question on the percent of the national government budget devoted to interest payments on the national debt fails to show statistically significantly results on the posttest compared to the pretest.

Turning to the results for the individual questions, the most basic question on the surveys is that of the size of the national debt. On this question, table 13.2 shows the majority of students demonstrated correct knowledge on both the pretest and posttest across all four years of the surveys, ranging from a low of 51.0% in 2012 to a high of 63.9% in 2013. Thus, students have general knowledge of the size of the national debt. This finding most likely results from extensive media and political attention placed on the national debt and budget deficit as a result of the economic downturn from the Great Recession and the ensuing attempts by the U.S. government to stimulate the economy. By 2014, issues like the Affordable Healthcare Act (ACA), or Obamacare, received attention in Texas due to its potential to explode the size of the budget as a result of expected Medicare/Medicaid expansion. Because the question was closed-ended, the expected percentage giving this answer is 25.0%, yet the results for all four waves of the survey are more than double this figure. However, the second largest category of responses is those students who shifted from an incorrect answer on the pretest to the correct answer on the posttest, ranging from a low of 16.3% in 2013 to a high of 22.0% in 2012. Thus, teaching about the national debt and budget deficit reinforces knowledge of the size of the debt and encourages students to acquire factual information regarding the size of the debt. Of course, this result may only be a short-term effect.

On the size of the U.S. government budget devoted to entitlements, the general pattern is for the largest share of students to answer incorrectly on both waves of the surveys, as shown on table 13.2. The results range from a low of 36.9% of students answering incorrectly on both waves in 2013 to a high of 58.5% incorrect in 2012. While this pattern appears as a failing to impart knowledge on students, a larger percentage of students shift from an incorrect answer on the pretest to a correct answer on the posttest for three of the four years of the study. For example, in 2010, 31.4% of students shifted to the correct answer on the posttest, compared with only 9% of students who shifted to an incorrect answer. Comparable figures for 2012 are 17.4% versus 11.4%, for 2013 are 20.2% versus 20.6%, and for 2014 are 19.1% versus 17.3%. However, students tend to underreport the size of the budget associated with entitlements across all years, typically choosing the answers of 10% or 20%. Given that entitlements account collectively for the largest share of the budget at approximately 40% of the budget annually, this finding creates a possible barrier to helping students address how to solve the national debt and budget deficit issues in the long run. These findings also reinforce the discussion of the general lack of knowledge about economic issues and public policies in the general public and among university students, as well as the lack of student learning after exposure to these issues.[65] Both sets of literature also point to the role of ideological predispositions as limiting the impact of factual information on learning about the budget deficit and national debt.

Similarly, table 13.2 shows the largest share of students incorrectly reported the proportion of the budget devoted to national defense on both waves of the survey each year. The percentage of students incorrectly reporting the size of the defense budget ranges from a low of 33.8% in 2010 to a high of 46.6% in 2012. However, in 2010, 2013, and 2014 a higher proportion of students shifted to the correct answer regarding the percentage of the budget devoted to national defense on the post-survey than shifted from the correct to incorrect answer. In 2012, 18.2% of students shifted from an incorrect answer to the correct one, while 18.6% shifted from the correct answer to an incorrect one. Among the incorrect answers, students consistently—over all years of the surveys—overreported the size of the national budget devoted to defense. Again, this misperception of the size of defense spending may interfere with attempts to understand the national debt and budget deficit issues. These findings again suggest that the general lack of knowledge among students mirrors findings about the general public. Economic and public policy issues and the role of predispositions limit the impact of factual information on learning.

The final basic knowledge question involved the percentage of the budget devoted to interest on the national debt. Consistent with the literature on student and general public knowledge of economic issues and public policy, the largest share of students across all years of the study incorrectly answered this question across both waves of the study, ranging from a low of 41.7% in 2010 to a high of 52.8% in 2013. In 2010, more students (26.2%) shifted from the incorrect answer to the correct answer by the posttest, while 15.2% shifted from the correct to the incorrect answer. In 2012, the comparable figures were 19.1% and 17.8%. However, in 2013 and 2014, the trend reverses with more students shifting from correct to incorrect answers (20.6% in 2013 and 20.15% in 2014) than from incorrect to correct answers (13.3% in 2013 and 18.5% in 2014.) Misperceptions of this aspect of the national government's budget are important since increases in the interest payments on the national debt ultimately place strains on the attempts to balance the budget.

Overall, the knowledge questions provide some evidence that our efforts to address the national debt and budget deficit issues in a general education, core curriculum courses have some limited effects, with the most success on the issue of the size of the national debt. On the positive side, movement between the pretest and the posttest generally and consistently is in the correct direction, with significantly larger numbers of students shifting from incorrect to correct answer from the pretest to posttest. Still, basic factual information is the most simplistic level of cognitive learning. Cognitive knowledge also includes the ability to evaluate a problem and make judgments about it. This so-called "higher level" learning is considered more essential to fostering critical thinking skills of students.[66]

The pretest and posttest surveys contained a series of questions about possible solutions to the national debt and budget deficit issues. These questions address cognitive knowledge and evaluation. Four possible solutions included reducing defense spending, reducing spending on entitlements, cutting nondefense discretionary spending, or raising taxes. If students engage in learning about the national debt and budget deficit issues, then ideally the learning process allows students to begin to critically think and to evaluate possible solutions. We expect students to begin seeing the complexity of the issues of the national debt and budget deficit and the need for a multifaceted approach to solve these public policy issues. We expect, therefore, to see students shifting from their pretest disposition toward the "Disagree" and "Strongly disagree" side of the scale. To test this possible shift, we compared the pretest and posttest answers on the surveys, measuring if students moved one or more response levels from the disagreement side of the scale.

As shown in table 13.3, a clear majority of students across all years of the survey demonstrated no change in response from the pretest to the posttest across all four possible solutions to the national debt and budget deficit issues. Again, these results are consistent with the literature on student learning about the national debt and budget deficit, as well as federal government budgeting in general.[67] Student predispositions, coupled with a general lack of basic factual information limit the impact of teaching on public policy and economic issues on student learning. While these results are somewhat disappointing, a larger proportion of students shifted away from each of the four solutions as the only solution than students who shifted toward the solution as the only solution to these public policy issues. Therefore, among those students who did experience greater evaluative learning, the tendency was to shift toward greater understanding of the complexity of the issue, rather than a shift to the more simplistic, single or "only" solutions.

This pattern is most evident in 2010, where larger percentages of students move away from each of the four possible solutions as the only solution. Likewise, in 2012, more students shifted away from reducing discretionary spending (22.1%) and raising taxes (21.6%) as the only solutions than shifted the other direction, 18.6% and 17.7% respectively. In 2013, more students shifted away from raising taxes as the only solution (22.0%) than in the other

Table 13.3.   Effect of Educational Intervention on Solutions to National Debt and Budget Deficit

Year	Solution	Moved Away from As Only Solution	No Change	Moved Toward As Only Solution	N
2010	Reduce Defense Spending	62 (21.7%)	178 (62.2%)	46 (16.1%)	286
	Entitlement Reform	87 (30.4%)	149 (52.1%)	50 (17.5%)	286
	Reduce Discretionary Spending	68 (23.9%)	162 (57.0%)	54 (19.0%)	284
	Raise Taxes	63 (22.1%)	170 (59.6%)	52 (18.2%)	285
2012	Reduce Defense Spending	50 (22.5%)	127 (55.0%)	54 (23.4%)	231
	Entitlement Reform	49 (21.4%)	122 (53.3%)	58 (25.3%)	229
	Reduce Discretionary Spending	51 (22.1%)	137 (59.3%)	43 (18.6%)	231
	Raise Taxes	50 (21.6%)	140 (60.6%)	41 (17.7%)	231
2013	Reduce Defense Spending	49 (21.1%)	130 (56.0%)	53 (22.8%)	232
	Entitlement Reform	51 (22.0%)	118 (50.9%)	63 (27.2%)	232
	Reduce Discretionary Spending	48 (20.8%)	134 (58.0%)	49 (21.2%)	231
	Raise Taxes	51 (22.0%)	138 (59.5%)	43 (18.5%)	232
2014	Reduce Defense Spending	107 (28.8%)	195 (57.4%)	70 (18.8%)	372
	Entitlement Reform	112 (30.3)	190 (51.4%)	58 (15.7%)	370
	Reduce Discretionary Spending	92 (25.0%)	191 (51.9%)	85 (23.1%)	368
	Raise Taxes	68 (18.5%)	233 (63.3%)	73 (19.8%)	368

direction (18.5%). In 2014, more students shifted away from reducing defense spending (28.8%), entitlement reform (30.3%), and reductions in discretionary spending (25.0%) as the only solution, compared with those students who shifted toward each solution as the only solution (18.8%, 15.7%, and 23.1% respectively). Thus, there is evidence that students acquired knowledge of the issues to the extent that typically regardless of year or proposed solution one-in-five to one-in-four students were able to demonstrate evaluative learning regarding the complexity of the issues of the national debt and budget deficits. If the goal of higher education is to promote critical thinking and evaluation among students, including such skills in the area of politics, public policy, and civic life, we have achieved success in this area.

Yet, taxonomies of knowledge do not simply focus on learning as a cognitive process; learning occurs also in other domains including affective contexts. Shifts in attitudes, values, and awareness of policy information are essential to the learning process and educational experience.[68] To assess this level of learning, two questions on the pretest and posttest provide direct tests of affective learning. These questions ask students about the importance of the issues of the national debt and budget deficit and about their level of worry associated with these issues. One additional question attempts to connect the national debt and budget deficit issues to affective learning; this question links the issues of the national debt and budget deficit to the student's personal well-being.

Similar to the questions regarding evaluative learning, the pretest and posttest survey's questions regarding affective learning offered respondents four possible responses on a modified Likert-scale. (see table 12.4.) For these questions, we subtracted the pretest survey answers from the posttest survey answers, giving us a scale that ranges from 3 to –3 where the highest value indicates a shift from the least affective learning of "not important at all" or "not worried at all" or "not harmful at all" to the highest level of affective learning of "very important" or "very worried" or "very harmful." Consistently across all years in table 13.4 a solid majority of students reported the same level of affective response on both the pretest and posttest surveys regarding their perception of the importance of the national debt and budget deficit issues, ranging from a low of 58.8% of respondents in 2010 to a high of 64.2% in 2012. Similar results occurred for the perceived level of worry, ranging from as few as 54.1% in 2010 to as many as 64.1% in 2013 reporting no change in the level of worry. For the perceived effect of the national debt and budget deficit on personal well-being, a low of 51.7% in 2010 reported no change in perceived effect, while 2013 showed a high of 58.4% for this category. However, the general pattern among those who shifted in their affective learning indicated a shift toward greater concern over the issues of the national debt and budget deficit issues. For the questions on importance and worry, this pattern held consistent across all four years of the surveys. Moreover, approximately one in four or more students reported an increase in the importance or awareness of the issue. The shift in perception among students from the pretest to the posttest regarding the effect of the national debt and budget deficit issues on personal

Table 13.4. Effect of Educational Intervention on Affective Knowledge of the National Debt Issue

Year	Effect	Unit Shift in Perception							N
		3	2	1	0	−1	−2	−3	
2010	Importance	1 (0.3%)	8 (2.8%)	89 (30.8%)	170 (58.8%)	21 (3.3%)	0 (0.0%)	0 (0.0%)	289
	Worry	3 (1.0%)	8 (2.8%)	76 (26.5%)	157 (54.7%)	42 (14.6%)	1 (0.3%)	0 (0.0%)	287
	Effect Personal Well-being	0 (0.0%)	14 (4.9%)	70 (24.5%)	148 (51.7%)	52 (18.2%)	2 (0.7%)	0 (0.0%)	286
2012	Importance	0 (0.0%)	5 (2.2%)	47 (20.3%)	149 (64.2%)	31 (13.4%)	0 (0.0%)	0 (0.0%)	232
	Worry	0 (0.0%)	2 (0.9%)	49 (21.0%)	142 (60.9%)	37 (15.9%)	3 (1.3%)	0 (0.0%)	233
	Effect Personal Well-being	0 (0.0%)	6 (2.6%)	45 (19.2%)	127 (54.3%)	53 (22.6%)	3 (1.3%)	0 (0.0%)	234
2013	Importance	0 (0.0%)	6 (2.6%)	65 (28.1%)	138 (59.7%)	20 (8.7%)	2 (0.9%)	0 (0.0%)	231
	Worry	0 (0.0%)	4 (1.7%)	56 (24.2%)	148 (64.1%)	21 (9.1%)	2 (0.9%)	0 (0.0%)	231
	Effect Personal Well-being	0 (0.0%)	3 (1.3%)	47 (20.3%)	135 (58.4%)	44 (19.0%)	2 (0.9%)	0 (0.0%)	231
2014	Importance	0 (0.0%)	4 (1.1%)	103 (27.2%)	227 (59.9%)	44 (11.6%)	1 (0.3%)	0 (0.0%)	379
	Worry	0 (0.0%)	10 (2.6%)	86 (22.7%)	232 (61.2%)	49 (12.9%)	2 (0.5%)	0 (0.0%)	379
	Effect Personal Well-being	0 (0.0%)	13 (3.5%)	83 (22.3%)	196 (52.5%)	70 (18.8%)	10 (18.8%)	1 (0.3%)	373

well-being is less consistent. In 2010 and 2014, more than one in four students reported a shift toward greater concern over the effect on personal well-being; these shifts were larger than the reverse direction. About one in five students reported greater concern over the effect on personal well-being on the posttest in 2013. However, in 2012, the level of the shift between the pretest and post-test was similar to 2013, but slightly more students reported less concern over the effect of the national debt and budget deficit in 2012.

While the number of students across questions and years who showed affective learning was small, the movement was generally in the desired direction. In general, these findings about affective learning may reflect the limitations of the classroom experience as the primary delivery format for affective learning. For example, the literature on civic engagement and service learning suggests that acquisition of multiple types of knowledge is enhanced by strategies of active and experiential learning whether through co-curricular activities or simulations and similar classroom pedagogical tools.[69] The extent to which teaching about the national debt and budget deficit at SFASU coincided with varying pedagogical strategies varied over year and instructor. In addition, exposure to extra-classroom activities such as Debt Week in 2010, guest speakers in classes, screening of movies like *I.O.U.S.A.*, and other events occurred in a nonsystematic manner. Often these activities were outside the control of the faculty, depending on student interest, time commitments, and willingness to attend events. Nonetheless, we have demonstrated an impact on affective learning by students as a result of classroom instruction about the national debt and budget deficit issues.

IMPACT OF TEACHING ABOUT THE NATIONAL DEBT AND BUDGET DEFICIT ISSUES ON STUDENTS

While the national debt and budget deficit issues are daunting subjects to include in a university's general education, core curriculum courses, the experiences at SFASU offer some tentative evidence that these issues have an impact on student learning, especially in higher levels of cognitive evaluation of problems and in the area of affective learning. While most students remained unchanged in the basic level of knowledge about the issues of the national debt and budget deficits, we find some evidence of students acquiring additional basic information about the national debt and budget deficit issues. More importantly, students are able to assess possible solutions to the national debt and budget deficit, with one in every four or five students acquiring the ability to evaluate the complexities of the national debt and budget deficit issues. Moreover, some students express deeper evaluations of the national debt and budget deficit issues by moving away from simplistic solutions, such as "raising taxes" as the only answer to these public policy problems. Equally important, there is a consistent pattern of shifting students in a positive affective learning direction as well. A substantial minority of students (approximately one in four) began to see the national debt and budget deficit issues as more important, as something that they should worry about, and as something that may affect their personal well-being. More students are affected in this direction than in the opposite direction. Thus, teaching the national debt and budget deficit issues have influenced, if in limited ways, the higher-order cognitive evaluations and affective learning of students.

These results are more impressive, perhaps, when considering the relatively high degree of turnover among the faculty who teach Political Science 142 in a given spring semester. Some of these sections of the course are taught by adjunct faculty. Lacking a permanent attachment to the university, adjunct faculty vary significantly from year to year. In addition, some professors and instructors shift from PSC 142 to the other general education, core curriculum course, Political Science 141. Finally, some faculty leave SFASU as a result of retirement, to take faculty positions at other universities, or to leave academia for other employment.[70] In the future, greater efforts need to be made to communicate with new faculty teaching PSC 142 as to the importance of the national debt and budget deficit modules and to provide greater consistency in the content that students receive during classroom instruction and discussion, especially since these modules are also part of the course's core curriculum assessment. Another issue is the relatively high proportion of students who do not complete both waves of the survey. Greater efforts need to be made to ensure students participate across both waves of the survey, especially given the much larger percentage of students who completed both waves in 2014 (70.4%) compared to earlier years (45.5% in 2010, 46.2% in 2012, and 36.5% in 2013).

In addition, we need to review the survey instruments themselves to align better the knowledge questions with the classroom experience. We need to work with faculty to emphasize the complexity of the national debt and budget deficit issues and the necessity of a multifaceted approach to reducing the debt and deficit over time. For example, we could move from simple solutions to more complex solutions combining entitlement reform, spending control, and tax increases.

Nonetheless, the America Future Initiative at SFASU has attempted to link education involving the national debt and budget deficit issues in a general education, core curriculum course and to link learning on these public policy issues to assessment processes associated with undergraduate education. We also followed the model of Beaumont and of Omelicheva and Avdeyeva by deepening student understanding and skills regarding a policy issue.[71] We have also attempted—with limited success—to integrate Rankin's strategy of multiple types of knowledge to enhance understanding of public policy issues.[72] We have demonstrated that the America's Future Initiative embedded in a general education, core curriculum class changes students' affective knowledge and cognitive evaluation of a major public policy problem: the national debt and budget deficit.

APPENDIX A

Selected questions from both the Pretest Survey and Posttest Survey:

1) How important is the national debt and budget deficit to you?

| Very important | Somewhat important | Not very important | Not important at all |

2) How worried are you about the size of the national debt?

| Very important | Somewhat important | Not very important | Not important at all |

4) What effects do you think that the growing national debt will have on your personal economic well-being in the coming decades?

| Very harmful | Somewhat harmful | A little harmful | Not harmful at all |

5) Approximately, how large do you think the national debt is currently?*

| $100 billion | $1 trillion | $17 trillion | $50 trillion |

6) Approximately, what percent of the current national government budget do you think goes to pay for Medicare, Medicaid, and Social Security?

| 10% | 20% | 40% | 80% |

7) Approximately what percent of the current national government budget goes to defense spending, including the war in Afghanistan?

| 10% | 20% | 40% | 80% |

8) Approximately what percent of the current national government budget do you think that the US government will pay in interest on the national debt in 2014?

| 2% | 9% | 12% | 15% |

11) The national debt and budget deficit issues may be solved by:

   a) Cutting defense spending only

      Strongly   Agree   Disagree   Strongly
      Agree   Disagree

   b) Reforming programs like Medicare, Medicaid and Social Security only

      Strongly   Agree   Disagree   Strongly
      Agree   Disagree

   c) Cutting discretionary spending on things like transportation, public assistance programs, and border security only

      Strongly   Agree   Disagree   Strongly
      Agree   Disagree

   d) Raising taxes only

      Strongly   Agree   Disagree   Strongly
      Agree   Disagree

NOTES

1. Rob Catlett, "Blending Elements of Economics and Political Science: Intergenerational Dialogue, Civic Engagement, and Related Student Scholarly Activity," *PS: Political Science and Politics* 43, no. 2 (2010); Steven E. Galatas and Cindy Pressley, "Teaching about America's Fiscal Future in the University's Core Curriculum," *PS: Political Science and Politics* 43, no. 2 (2010); J. Wesley Martin, "Practical Theory: Teaching Political and Economic Citizenship," *PS: Political Science and Politics* 43, no. 2 (2010); Jennifer A. Stollman, "America's Financial Future, Civic Engagement," *PS: Political Science and Politics,* 43, no. 2 (2010).

2. (New York: Simon & Schuster Paperbacks, 2000).

3. William A. Galston, "Political Knowledge, Political Engagement, and Civic Education," *Annual Review of Political Science* 4, no. 1 (2001): 219.

4. Susan Hunter and Richard A. Brisbin Jr., "Civic Education and Political Science: A Survey of Practices," *PS: Political Science and Politics* 36, no. 4 (October 2003): 759.

5. See Melvin J. Dubnick, "Nurturing Civic Lives: Developmental Perspectives on Civic Education—Introduction," *PS: Political Science and Politics* 36, no. 2 (April 2003); Constance Flanagan, "Developmental Roots of Political Engagement," *PS: Political Science and Politics* 36, no. 2 (April 2003); William A. Galston, "Civic Education and Political Participation," *PS: Political Science and Politics* 37, no. 2 (April 2004).

6. James Farr, "The Science of Politics: As Civic Education: Then and Now," *PS: Political Science and Politics* 37, no. 1 (January 2004): 38.

7. Ibid.

8. Dubnick, "Nurturing Civic Lives," 253–255.

9. Ibid., 253.

10. Ibid., 254.

11. Anand R. Marri et al., "Analyzing Social Issues Related to Teaching about the Federal Budget, Federal Debt, and Budget Deficit in Fifty State High School Social Studies Standards," *The Social Studies* 103, no. 4 (2012): 133–139.

12. William A. Galston, "Civic Knowledge, Civic Education, and Civic Engagement: A Summary of Recent Research," *International Journal of Public Administration* 30, no. 6–7 (2007): 639.

13. For simulations, see Daniel Wakelee and Tiina Itkonen, "The Politics of School District Budgeting: Using Simulations to Enhance Student Learning," *Journal of Political Science Education* 9, no. 2 (April 12, 2013); Dena Levy and Susan Orr, "Balancing the Books: Analyzing the Impact of a Federal Budget Deliberative Simulation on Student Learning and Opinion," *Journal of Political Science Education* 10, no. 1 (January 21, 2014): 75. For the use of overlapping concept areas, see Monica Cain, "Teaching Health Policy in an Economic Framework to Non-majors," *Journal of Public Affairs Education* 15, no. 2 (2009): 245. For the use of newspapers, see Juan C. Huerta and Joseph Jozwiak, "Developing Civic Engagement in General Education Political Science," *Journal of Political Science Education* 4, no. 1 (February 29, 2008): 44

14. David M. Rankin, "Processing the War in Iraq While Learning about American Politics," *Journal of Political Science Education* 3, no. 6 (2010).

15. Thomas Ehrlich, "Civic Education: Lessons Learned," *PS: Political Science and Politics* 32, no. 2 (June 1999): 245.

16. Ibid., 245.

17. Mariya Y. Omelicheva and Olga Avdeyeva. "Teaching with Lecture or Debate? Testing the Effectiveness of Traditional versus Active Learning Methods of Instruction," *PS: Political Science and Politics* 41, no. 3 (July 2008).

18. Ibid., 606.

19. See John Gastil, "Adult Civic Education through the National Issues Forums: Developing Democratic Habits and Dispositions through Public Deliberation," *Adult Education Quarterly* 54 no. 4 (August 2004); John Gastil and James P. Dillard, "The Aims, Methods, and Effects of Deliberative Civic Education through the National Issues Forums," *Communication Education* 48, no. 3 (May 18, 2009): 189.

20. Jeremy Brooke Straughn and Angie L. Andriot, "Education, Civic Patriotism, and Democratic Citizenship: Unpacking the Education Effect on Political Involvement," *Sociological Forum* 26, no. 3 (September 2011).

21. Elizabeth Beaumont et al., "Promoting Political Competence and Engagement in College Students: An Empirical Study," *Journal of Political Science Education* 2, no. 3 (2006).

22. Ibid., 253.

23. Ibid., 264.

24. James H. Kuklinski et al., "Misinformation and the Currency of Democratic Citizenship," *The Journal of Politics* 62, no. 3 (August 2000): 790.

25. Ibid., 792.

368 *Steven E. Galatas and Cindy Pressley*

26. Farr, "The Science of Politics," 37–40.

27. James H. Kuklinski, et al., Misinformation and the Currency of Democratic Citizenship," *The Journal of Politics*, 62 no. 3 (August 2000): 156

28. See Stephen Goldsmith, "Service 2.0 and Cities," *National Civic Review* 97, no. 3 (Fall 2008); Stephen B. Deloach and Steven A. Greenlaw, "Do Electronic Discussions Create Critical Thinking Spillovers?" *Contemporary Economic Policy* 23, no. 1 (January 2005).

29. Christina M. Gagnier, "Democracy 2.0: Millennial-generated Change to American Governance," *National Civic Review* 97, no. 3 (Fall 2008): 36. For the potential truth of this insight, see Rackaway's chapter 15 of this volume.

30. See "Survey of the States: Economic and Personal Finance Education in our Nation's Schools 2014," Council for Economic Education, http://www.councilforeconed.org/wp/wp-content/uploads/2014/02/2014-Survey-of-the-States.pdf, accessed 11/15/2014; Anand R. Marri et al., "Analyzing Social Issues Related to Teaching about the Federal Budget, Federal Debt, and Budget Deficit in Fifty State High School Social Studies Standards," 133–139.

31. Kimberly Parker and Claudia Deane, "Ten Years of the Pew News Interest Index," The Pew Research Center for The People and The Press (report presented at the meeting of the American Association for Public Opinion Research 1997): 4.

32. Ibid., 9.

33. See Daniel W. Rossides, "Understanding Deficits and Debt or Putting America on a Real Budget," *Social Policy* (Winter 2011): 3–6.

34. Robert J. Blendon et al., "Bridging the Gap between the Public's and Economists' Views of the Economy," *The Journal of Economic Perspectives* 11, no. 3 (Summer 1997): 105–118.

35. Ibid., 107.

36. Ibid., 113.

37. Ibid., 116.

38. Bryan Caplan, "Systematically Biased Beliefs about Economics: Robust Evidence of Judgmental Anomalies from the Survey of Americans and Economists on the Economy," *The Economic Journal* 112, no. 479 (April 2002): 434.

39. Ibid.

40. Ibid., 456.

41. Alan S. Blinder and Alan B. Krueger, "What Does the Public Know about Economic Policy, and How Does It Know It? Working Paper 10787," NBER Working Paper Series, National Bureau of Economic Research, September, 2004, http://www.nber.org/papers/w10787 (accessed 11/15/2014).

42. Ibid., 2.

43. Ibid., 9.

44. Ibid.,16.

45. Ibid., 42.

46. Rob Catlett, "Blending Elements of Economics and Political Science.

47. J. Wesley Martin, "Practical Theory: Teaching Political and Economic Citizenship.

48. Steven E. Galatas and Cindy Presley, "Teaching about America's Fiscal Future in the University's Core Curriculum."

49. Dena Levy and Susan Orr, "Balancing the Books: Analyzing the Impact of a Federal Budget Deliberative Simulation on Student Learning and Opinion."

50. Michael K. Baranowski, "Simulations and Student Understanding of the Budget Process" (paper presented as the annual meeting of the American Political Science Association, APSA 2011 Annual Meeting Paper, January 22, 2012), http://ssrn.com/abstract=1903284 (accessed October 28, 2014); Daniel Wakelee and Tiina Itkonen, "The Politics of School District Budgeting: Using Simulations to Enhance Student Learning," *Journal of Political Science Education* 9, no. 2 (2013).

51. Karen Kedrowski, "Civic Education by Mandate: A State-by-State Analysis," *PS: Political Science and Politics* 36, no. 2 (2003).

52. Tex. Education Code Ann. § 51.301 (Vernon 2013).

53. Individual universities or systems of universities are free to implement the two-course, six-hour requirement as they choose. Community colleges, however, are required to teach the courses as a three-hour U.S. government course and a three-hour Texas government course.

54. Political Science 142 includes institutional arrangements such as the U.S. Congress, U.S. presidency, Texas legislature, Texas executive, etc., as well as various national and state policies. The other course, Political Science 141, covers the U.S. and Texas constitutions, political behavior, civil rights, and civil liberties.

55. "Core Curriculum: Assumptions and Defining Characteristics (Rev. 1999)," Texas Higher Education Coordinating Board, 1999, http://www.thecb.state.tx.us/index.cfm?objectid=7ED36862–993C-10F2-C64CA9C9EDF26C4C (accessed September 5, 2009).

56. Specifically, EEO #4 for social and behavior sciences states, "To develop and communicate alternative explanations for solutions to contemporary social issues." EEO #10 states, "To analyze, critically assess, and develop creative solutions to public policy." Ibid.

57. Faculty are generally free to choose which policy areas to cover in PSC 142. However, the linkage of PSC 142 to general education, core curriculum assessment meant that all faculty teaching PSC 142 must cover the national debt and budget deficit issues. Most faculty embedded this discussion into a broad examination of the national government's economic policies, like fiscal and monetary policy.

58. The fragmented nature of higher education in Texas creates a challenge to implementing THECB policies and recommendations. Texas has five university systems that govern institutions of higher education: the University of Texas System, the Texas A and M University System, the Texas Tech University System, the University of Houston System, and the Texas State University System. Each of these systems is headed by a board of regents appointed by the governor; each system is comprised of multiple campuses located in various communities around the state or a specific region of the state. In addition, several institutions are outside a system and are governed by a board of regents appointed to oversee their specific campus. SFASU is

such an institution. Community colleges in Texas are governed by a board of trustees elected by residents in the community college's area of jurisdiction.

59. Association of American Colleges and State Universities, "Civic Engagement in Action Series: Creating New Models for Student Understanding," Association of American Colleges and State Universities, http://www.aascu.org/programs/adp/civic-series/ (accessed March 12, 2013).

60. Monica Cain, "Teaching Health Policy in an Economic Framework to Non-majors."

61. Public Agenda, "Facing Up to the Nation's Finances: A Nonpartisan Project on the Long-term Challenges of the Federal Budget," Public Agenda, 2011, http://FacingUp.org/students (accessed January 10, 2014).

62. While PSC 142 is taught every semester throughout the academic year, the largest enrollments occur in the spring semesters. Because resources are limited, we chose to limit our project to consecutive spring semesters. Due to technical issues, data from 2011 is not available.

63. To match respondents' pretest and posttest, a unique survey identification number is generated for each respondent based upon a portion of his or her student identification number.

64. The attrition rate may limit the accuracy and reliability of the surveys, especially in 2010, 2012, and 2013. However, the attrition among high school students in surveys concluding that the magnitude of the problem in proportional to the rate of attrition, see David Burkam and Valerie Lee, "Effects of Monotone and Nonmonotone Attrition on Parameter Estimates in Regression Models with Educational Data: Demographic Effects on Achievement, Aspirations, and Attitudes." They argue high levels of attrition may not be problematic when attrition is selective, not systematic. Similarly, no evidence of bias may exist when attrition is a result of selective attrition; see Jeffrey Zabel, "An Analysis of Attrition in the Panel Study of Income Dynamics and the Survey of Income and Program Participation with an Application to a Model of Labor Market Behavior." Finally, meta-analysis of research on attrition in developed societies finds again that selective attrition has minimal impact on survey results; see Una Lee, "Panel Attrition in Survey Data: A Literature Review." Thus, we have no reason to believe the rates of attrition in this survey are a product of anything other than selective attrition by the participants.

65. For works debating the lack of knowledge on economics, see Robert J. Blendon et al., "Bridging the Gap between the Public's and Economists' Views of the Economy;" Bryan Caplan, "Systematically Biased Beliefs about Economics;" Alan S. Blinder and Alan B. Krueger, "What Does the Public Know about Economic Policy, and How Does It Know It? Working Paper 10787;" James H. Kuklinski et al., "Misinformation and the Currency of Democratic Citizenship." For scholars debating the lack of learning among students, see Michael K. Baranowski, "Simulations and Student Understanding of the Budget Process;" Steven E. Galatas and Cindy Pressley, "Teaching about America's Fiscal Future in the University's Core Curriculum;" Dena Levy and Susan Orr, "Balancing the Books: Analyzing the Impact of a Federal Budget Deliberative Simulation on Student Learning and Opinion."

66. Benjamin S. Bloom et al., *Taxonomy of Educational Objectives: The Classification of Educational Goals. Handbook I: Cognitive Domain* (New York: David McKay Company, 1956); Lorin W. Anderson and David A. Krathwohl, eds., *A Taxonomy for Learning, Teaching, and Assessing: A Revision of Bloom's Taxonomy of Educational Objectives* (New York: Addison Wesley Longman, 2001).

67. Steven E. Galatas and Cindy Pressley, "Teaching about America's Fiscal Future in the University's Core Curriculum;"; Dena Levy and Susan Orr, "Balancing the Books."

68. D. R. Krathwohl et al., *Taxonomy of Educational Objectives: The Classification of Educational Goals. Handbook II: Affective Domain* (New York, NY: David McKay Co., 1973).

69. Robert Catlett, "Blending Elements of Economics and Political Science"; I Thomas Ehrlich, "Civic Education: Lessons Learned;" J. Wesley Martin, "Practical Theory: Teaching Politics and Economic Citizenship;" Mariya Y. Omelicheva and Olga Avdeyeva, "Teaching with Lecture or Debate? Testing the Effectiveness of Traditional versus Active Learning Methods of Instruction;" David M. Rankin, "Processing the War in Iraq While Learning about American Politics;" Jennifer A. Stollman, "America's Financial Future, Civic Engagement."

70. In 2010, six different faculty members taught sections of PSC 142 and participated in the America's Future Initiative. In 2012, four faculty members who participated in the project taught the course; all four of those faculty members taught the course in 2010. By 2013, only two of the four faculty members participating in the project had taught the course the year before. Moreover, the two new faculty in 2013 taught a significant majority of the students who completed both waves of the surveys. In 2014, only one of the original faculty members from the 2010 surveys was still teaching sections of PSC 142; one other faculty member teaching the course in the spring of 2013 also taught the course in the spring of 2014. An additional faculty member returned in 2014 to teaching the course; this faculty member had taught the course in 2010 and 2012.

71. Beaumont et al., "Promoting Political Competence and Engagement in College Students;" Omelicheva and Avdeyeva. "Teaching with Lecture or Debate?"

72. Rankin, "Processing the War in Iraq While Learning about American Politics."

BIBLIOGRAPHY

Anderson, Lorin W., and David A. Krathwohl, eds. *A Taxonomy for Learning, Teaching, and Assessing: A Revision of Bloom's Taxonomy of Educational Objectives.* New York: Addison Wesley Longman, 2001.

Association of American Colleges and State Universities. "Civic Engagement in Action Series: Creating New Models for Student Understanding." Association of American Colleges and State Universities. http://www.aascu.org/programs/adp/civicseries/ (accessed March 12, 2013).

372 *Steven E. Galatas and Cindy Pressley*

Baranowski, Michael K. "Simulations and Student Understanding of the Budget Process." APSA 2011 Annual Meeting Paper, January 22, 2012. Accessed October 28, 2014. http://ssrn.com/abstract=1903284.

Beaumont, Elizabeth, Anne Colby, Thomas Ehrlich, and Judith Torney-Purta. "Promoting Political Competence and Engagement in College Students: An Empirical Study." *Journal of Political Science Education* 2, no. 3 (2006): 249–270.

Bentley, Colleen, Richard H. Dunfee, and Beth Olsen. *Advancing a Civic Engagement Agenda: A Guide to Marketing, Management and Money.* New York: American Association of State Colleges and Universities, 2009.

Blendon, Robert J., John M. Benson, Mollyann Brodie, Richard Morin, Drew E. Altman, Daniel Gitterman, Mario Broussard, Matt James. "Bridging the Gap between the Public's and Economists' Views of the Economy." *The Journal of Economic Perspectives* 11, no. 3 (Summer 1997): 105–118.

Blinder, Alan S. and Alan B. Krueger. "What Does the Public Know about Economic Policy, and How Does It Know It? Working Paper 10787." NBER Working Paper Series. National Bureau of Economic Research (September, 2004). http://www.nber.org/papers/w10787.

Bloom, B. S., M. D. Engelhart, E. J. Furst, W. H. Hill, and D. A. Krathwohl, *Taxonomy of Educational Objectives: The Classification of Educational Goals*; *Handbook I: Cognitive Domain.* New York: David McKay Company, 1956.

Burkam, David T., and Valerie E. Lee. "Effects of Monotone and Nonmonotone Attrition on Parameter Estimates in Regression Models with Educational Data: Demographic Effects on Achievement, Aspirations, and Attitudes." *Journal of Human Resources* 33, no. 2 (1998): 555–574.

Cain, Monica. "Teaching Health Policy in an Economic Framework to Non-majors." *Journal of Public Affairs Education* 15, no. 2 (2009): 243–250.

Caplan, Bryan. "Systematically Biased Beliefs about Economics: Robust Evidence of Judgmental Anomalies from the Survey of Americans and Economists on the Economy." *The Economic Journal* 112, no. 479 (April 2002): 433–458.

Catlett, Rob. "Blending Elements of Economics and Political Science: Intergenerational Dialogue, Civic Engagement, and Related Student Scholarly Activity." *PS: Political Science and Politics* 43, no. 2 (2010): 337–342.

Council for Economic Education. "Survey of the States: Economic and Personal Finance Education in Our Nation's Schools 2014." Accessed 11/15/2014. http://www.councilforeconed.org/wp/wp-content/uploads/2014/02/2014-Survey-of-the-States.pdf.

Deardorff, Michelle D., and Paul J. Folger. "Assessment That Matters: Integrating the 'Chore' of Department-based Assessment with Real Improvements in Political Science Education." *Journal of Political Science Education* 1, no. 3 (September 1, 2006): 277–287.

Deloach, Stephen B., and Steven A. Greenlaw. "Do Electronic Discussions Create Critical Thinking Spillovers?" *Contemporary Economic Policy* 23, no. 1 (January 2005): 149–163.

Dubnick, Melvin J. "Nurturing Civic Lives: Developmental Perspectives on Civic Education—Introduction." *PS: Political Science and Politics* 36, no. 2 (April 2003): 253–255.

Ehrlich, Thomas. "Civic Education: Lessons Learned." *PS: Political Science and Politics* 32, no. 2 (June 1999): 245–250.

Farr, James. "The Science of Politics: As Civic Education: Then and Now." *PS: Political Science and Politics* 37, no. 1 (January 2004): 37–40.

Flanagan, Constance. "Developmental Roots of Political Engagement." *PS: Political Science and Politics* 36, no. 2 (April 2003): 257–261.

Gagnier, Christina M. "Democracy 2.0: Millennial-generated Change to American Governance." *National Civic Review* 97, no. 3 (Fall 2008): 32–36.

Galatas, Steven E., and Cindy Pressley. "Teaching about America's Fiscal Future in the University's Core Curriculum." *PS: Political Science and Politics* 43, no. 2 (2010): 323–326.

Galston., William A. "Political Knowledge, Political Engagement, and Civic Education." *Annual Review of Political Science* 4, no.1 (2001): 217–234.

Galston, William A. "Civic Education and Political Participation." *PS: Political Science and Politics* 37, no. 2 (April 2004): 263–266.

Galston, William A. "Civic Knowledge, Civic Education, and Civic Engagement: A Summary of Recent Research." *International Journal of Public Administration* 30 no. 6–7 (2007): 623–642.

Gastil, John. "Adult Civic Education through the National Issues Forums: Developing Democratic Habits and Dispositions through Public Deliberation." *Adult Education Quarterly* 54, no. 4 (August 2004): 308–328.

Gastil, John, and James P. Dillard. "The Aims, Methods, and Effects of Deliberative Civic Education through the National Issues Forums." *Communication Education* 48, no. 3 (May 18, 2009): 179–192.

Goldfinger, Johnny, and John W. Presley, eds. *Educating Students for Political Engagement: A Guide to Implementation and Assessment for Colleges and Universities.* New York: American Association of State Colleges and Universities, 2010.

Goldsmith, Stephen. "Service 2.0 and Cities." *National Civic Review* 97, no. 3 (Fall 2008): 52–55.

Grummel, John A. "Using Simulation to Teach Decision-making within the Policy Process." *PS: Political Science and Politics* 36, no. 4 (October 2003): 787–789.

Huerta, Juan C., and Joseph Jozwiak. "Developing Civic Engagement in General Education Political Science." *Journal of Political Science Education* 4, no. 1 (February 29, 2008): 42–60.

Hunter, Susan, and Richard A. Brisbin Jr. "Civic Education and Political Science: A Survey of Practices." *PS: Political Science and Politics* 36, no. 4 (October 2003): 759–763.

Kedrowski, Karen. "Civic Education by Mandate: A State-by-State Analysis." *PS: Political Science and Politics* 36, no. 2 (2003): 225–227.

Kiasatpour, Soleiman, and Scott Lasley. "Overcoming the Challenges of Teaching Political Science in the Hispanic-serving Classroom: A Survey of Institutions of Higher Education in Texas." *Journal of Political Science Education* 4, no. 2 (2008): 151–168.

Krathwohl, D. R., B. S. Bloom, and B. B. Masia. *Taxonomy of Educational Objectives: The Classification of Educational Goals. Handbook II: Affective Domain.* New York, NY: David McKay Co., 1973.

Kuklinski, James H., Paul J. Quirk, Jennifer Jerit, David Schwieder, and Robert F. Rich. "Misinformation and the Currency of Democratic Citizenship." *The Journal of Politics* 62, no. 3 (August 2000): 790–816.

Lee, Una. 2003. "Panel Attrition in Survey Data: A Literature Review." Centre for Social Science Research Working Paper #41, Centre for Social Science Research, University of Capetown. Accessed October 30, 2014. http://www.cssr.uct.ac.za/sites/cssr.uct.ac.za/files/pubs/wp41.pdf.

Levy, Dena, and Susan Orr. "Balancing the Books: Analyzing the Impact of a Federal Budget Deliberative Simulation on Student Learning and Opinion." *Journal of Political Science Education* 10, no. 1 (January 21, 2014): 62–80.

Malone, Christopher, and Gregory Julian. "Democratic Action Research (DARE) and Large Scale Simulations: Teaching Political Literacy and Civic Engagement at Pace University's Presidential Convention 2004." *PS: Political Science and Politics* 38, no. 4 (October 2005): 771–776.

Marri, Anand R., Margaret S. Crocco, Jay Shuttleworth, William Gaudelli, and Maureen Grolnick. "Analyzing Social Issues Related to Teaching about the Federal Budget, Federal Debt, and Budget Deficit in Fifty State High School Social Studies Standards." *The Social Studies* 103 (2012): 133–139.

Martin, J. Wesley. "Practical Theory: Teaching Political and Economic Citizenship." *PS: Political Science and Politics* 43, no. 2 (2010): 327–331.

Meisel, Wayne. "Connecting Cocurricular Service: A Movement Toward Civic Engagement." *Liberal Education* (Spring 2007): 52–57.

Omelicheva, Mariya Y., and Olga Avdeyeva. "Teaching with Lecture or Debate? Testing the Effectiveness of Traditional versus Active Learning Methods of Instruction." *PS: Political Science and Politics* 41, no. 3 (July 2008): 603–607.

Parker, Kimberly, and Claudia Deane. "Ten Years of the Pew News Interest Index." The Pew Research Center for The People and The Press. Paper presented at the 1997 meeting of the American Association for Public Opinion Research.

Public Agenda. "Facing Up to the Nation's Finances: A Nonpartisan Project on the Long-term Challenges of the Federal Budget." Public Agenda. January 10, 2011. http://FacingUp.org/students.

Rankin, David M. "Processing the War in Iraq While Learning about American Politics." *Journal of Political Science Education* 3, no. 6 (2010): 258–273.

Rossides, Daniel W. "Understanding Deficits and Debt or Putting America on a Real Budget." *Social Policy* (Winter 2011): 3–6.

Stollman, Jennifer A. "America's Financial Future, Civic Engagement." *PS: Political Science and Politics* 43, no. 2 (2010): 343–346.

Straughn, Jeremy Brooke, and Angie L. Andriot. "Education, Civic Patriotism, and Democratic Citizenship: Unpacking the Education Effect on Political Involvement." *Sociological Forum* 26, no. 3 (September 2011): 556–580.

Texas Higher Education Coordinating Board. "Core Curriculum: Assumptions and Defining Characteristics (Rev. 1999)." Texas Higher Education Coordinating Board. Accessed September 5, 2009. http://www.thecb.state.tx.us/reports/pdf/5934.pdf?CFID=17951433&CFTOKEN=16100485.

Texas Higher Education Coordinating Board. Accessed March 10, 2014. http://www
.thecb.state.tx.us/.

Wakelee, Daniel, and Tiina Itkonen. "The Politics of School District Budgeting: Using Simulations to Enhance Student Learning." *Journal of Political Science Education* 9, no. 2 (April 12, 2013): 236–248.

Wallin, Bruce A. "A Federal Deficit Reduction Simulation: Learning Politics and
Policy in a Budgetary Context." *PS: Political Science and Politics* 38, no. 3 (July
2005): 407–409.

Weimer, Maryellen. *Improving Your Classroom Teaching*. Newbury Park, CA: Sage
Publications, 1993.

Zabel, Jeffrey E. "An Analysis of Attrition in the Panel Study of Income Dynamics and the Survey of Income and Program Participation with an Application to a
Model of Labor Market Behavior." *Journal of Human Resources* 33(2): 479–506.

Chapter Fourteen

Moving Civic Education Research Forward

The Inter-Campus Consortium for SoTL Research

J. Cherie Strachan and Elizabeth Bennion

Political scientists are increasingly called upon to enhance our students' levels of political knowledge, as well as to encourage them to more fully engage in civic and political life. Demonstrating that these efforts, both in the classroom and across campus, are effective in transforming students into informed citizens is a challenging task. Many political scientists, however, now regularly engage in the scholarship of teaching and learning (SoTL) as they apply the research methods of our discipline to assess the impact of our pedagogy and civic engagement efforts.

Most faculty members—especially those at teaching institutions—do not have the time or resources to conduct systematic collection of data beyond a single campus, or perhaps even a single classroom. Cross-campus data collection is essential to discern whether the impact of teaching and programming efforts generalize across different contexts and students. In response to these methodological concerns, the authors welcome you to join a new research consortium, which will facilitate the type of data collection needed to advance the scholarship of teaching and learning in our discipline.

THE ASSESSMENT MOVEMENT

As increasing numbers of diverse students pursue college degrees, higher education in the United States has come under pressure to demonstrate that students are learning substantive knowledge and marketable skills. By the 1980s, several influential reports on the academy called for institutionalized feedback as an important way to mark improvements in student learning.[1] In response, regional accrediting agencies began to require member institutions to implement outcome assessments. Most colleges and universities now develop assessment plans and systematically collect data about student performance. By 2009, for example, 94 percent of the member campuses of the Association of American College and Universities (AAC&U) assessed, or planned to assess, general education outcomes across several classes. These assessments focus on important skills, such as writing, critical thinking, quantitative reasoning, and oral communication, as well as substantive knowledge in disciplines ranging from humanities and social sciences to the natural sciences and mathematics.[2] A majority of these institutions (68 percent) also reported student learning was already being assessed at the department level, indicating that assessment has made deep inroads into academic practices. In response to this trend, the American Political Science Association (APSA) now provides a number of resources to guide political science departments' assessment efforts, including offering workshops for chairs, providing access to sample assessment plans online, and publishing an edited volume on the topic.[3]

Initial calls for assessment reassuringly argued that the faculty should be in control of such endeavors. By being transparent about their goals and collecting data on student learning, professors could engage in continuous improvement, while also satisfying their external audiences' demands for evidence. Indeed, assessment done well helps institutions and departments enhance their endeavors to serve students well.[4] Moreover, external pressure to provide outcome data of student learning shows no signs of diminishing. The combination of skyrocketing tuition, diminishing financial support for public institutions, and declining employment opportunities for college graduates have led both the general public and prominent politicians to question the value of a college degree.[5] With the humanities and social sciences recently under attack, political scientists face heightened pressure to demonstrate the value of our instruction.[6]

Provosts and deans now provide financial rewards not simply to programs with high enrollments, but also to those with well-developed assessment plans and convincing data on student learning. Similarly, just as President Obama's Race to the Top program ties funding to assessment data in K–12 education, many governors and state legislatures have proposed linking funding for public colleges and universities to student learning outcomes and graduation rates.[7] The task of assessment is too important to be left to others, especially as recent efforts to assess student learning led to indictments denigrating the academy's ability to promote learning and critical thinking or to increase political knowledge and participation.[8] To respond to critics whose controversial claims are frequently based on questionable methodological choices, faculty must step into the assessment role initially occupied by educational reformers. It is no longer enough to claim that students learn in the classroom, one must document this learning using rigorous and defensible assessment techniques.

Moreover, assessment provides an opportunity to be *explicit* about desired learning outcomes, to measure effectiveness in achieving these outcomes, and to improve teaching when learning outcomes fall short of our expectations. Unlike elementary and secondary teachers, academics are recognized experts, who still retain the ability to define the specific learning objectives associated with our classrooms and our discipline. Political scientists can set the standards for the substantive knowledge that we expect students in our classrooms to master. We can also use our expertise to establish expectations for the level of civic literacy and civic skills required for effective citizenship. Yet if we fail to do so, others most certainly will. As Edelman and coauthors noted, "If political science does not govern its own discipline with respect to assessment, someone else would."[9]

THE CITIZEN ENGAGEMENT MOVEMENT

Political scientists seek to increase substantive knowledge about the political process and to encourage our students to more fully engage in civic and political life. The crisis of purpose in higher education triggering calls for assessment in the 1980s, also brought renewed attention to the civic mandate of colleges and universities. While American institutions have always been expected to "foster enlightened civic and political leadership," this priority was marginalized after World War II, as the number of institutions proliferated and the type of students they served became more diverse.[10] By the 1990s, these trends, in combination with young people's declining interest in traditional means of political participation, spurred a call to action among educational reformers, who believed that traditional civic education practices were no longer an effective means of transforming students into active citizens.[11]

The civic engagement movement, grounded in John Dewey's experiential approach to cultivating good citizens, emerged through various outlets over the past three decades.[12] Perhaps the most visible contemporary examples of the movement's agenda are reflected in the work of Campus Compact and the American Association of State College and University's American Democracy Project.[13] Those reformers most committed to the agenda of explicit political socialization are not satisfied with the accomplishments of the citizen engagement movement. For a review of these concerns, see Saltmarsh and Hartley's edited collection, where the contributors argue for renewed vigor, new approaches and even new terminology in an effort to democratize the culture of higher education.[14] One measure of the movement's success is the increasing awareness and use of pedagogies—such as service learning and experiential learning—designed to increase social consciousness and political activity among students. Campus Compact, for example, was launched in 1985 to support higher education institutions dedicated to such work. The organization now has 1,100 members, and approximately one-third of the student body on these member campuses enroll in service learning courses each year.[15] Meanwhile, the Carnegie Foundation for the Advancement of Teaching (CFAT) first solicited applications for its Community Engagement classification in 2010. Since that time, 196 campuses across the country have demonstrated an institutional commitment to such approaches, allowing them to earn this CFAT classification.[16]

The civic engagement movement often targeted administrators under the assumption committed college presidents and provosts could do far more to promote change on their campuses than individual faculty members. When these administrators look for partners on campus, they often turn to political science, where department mission statements (not to mention the personal convictions of individual professors) emphasize the role of civic education in cultivating informed, active citizens. Political scientists were quick to respond to the calls for more engaged pedagogy, filling an important gap on their college campuses.[17] These approaches are grounded in normative concerns over the quality of civic learning on college campuses. Such efforts may become important, for pragmatic reasons, in the near future. Although Saltmarsh and Hartley lack empirical evidence to fully document their claims, they argue strapped state budgets are not the only threat to academia's future. Rather, Saltmarsh and Hartley express concern about the connection between declining public support for higher education and higher education's distance from average citizens' concerns.

According to Saltmarsh and Hartley, the ivory tower's increasing emphasis on specialization and professional publications means that the work of the academy now rarely intersects with the communities that it is intended to serve. This concern is echoed by *New York Times* columnist Nicholas Kristof in a much-discussed column entitled, "Professors, We Need You!"[18] Kristof laments what he sees as a decline in the number of public intellectuals, noting that "Ph.D. programs have fostered a culture that glorifies arcane unintelligibility while disdaining impact and audience. This culture of exclusivity is then transmitted to the next generation through the publish-or-perish tenure process." Faculty research productivity affects individual advancement and reputation within academe, as well as departmental and institutional prestige.[19] Kristof is concerned that university research does not matter in solving real-world problems. As evidence, Kristof notes that in the late 1930s and early 1940s, one-fifth of articles in *The American Political Science Review* focused on policy prescriptions; at last count, the share was down to 0.3 percent. Saltmarsh and Hartley go further, arguing that university professors and their students should be actively engaged in the community, working with local communities to solve problems.[20]

Positioning academics as experts who dole out knowledge and advice to their clients among the general public may not be enough to foster deeply rooted support for higher education. Increasingly, a college education is seen as vocational training required for certain types of employment. Given public concerns over access to higher education, this training is often framed as a private benefit for individual students rather than a public good for society overall. As this mind-set spreads, the potential threat to public colleges and universities is dire. While some people perceive a tension between professional training and broader liberal arts training, in reality, many of the skills developed through high-impact pedagogy in the liberal arts develop precisely the skills that employers are seeking. A summary of research findings conducted by Peter D. Hart Research Associates, Inc., found that business executives listed strong work habits, self-discipline, critical thinking skills, communication skills, problem-solving skills, computer skills, and cultural/global awareness as the most important outcomes of college. While business leaders did not identify "civic responsibility" as a "most important outcome" of college, the general public placed such engagement among their top three priorities.[21] A follow-up study based on focus group interviews with business leaders found that very few business leaders discussed the challenges of finding recent college graduates who have the specific job or technical skills needed for a given job.[22] In contrast, participants were much more frustrated with recent graduates' deficiencies in more general skills and abilities, most notably perceived deficits in communication skills, teamwork skills, and work ethic—all skills that can be developed through high-impact approaches to teaching and learning including collaborative internships and research, as well as team-based civic leadership projects that require students to work together in teams and to communicate with multiple campus and community stakeholders.

If colleges and universities do not engage in authentic efforts to engage the community—a process that Saltmarsh and Hartley prefer to call democratic engagement—average citizens are apt to wonder what their tax dollars are supporting.[23] Practicing pedagogies of engagement not only connects political scientists to the communities that their institutions serve, it enables the community to help set the discipline's research agenda. Moreover, the tangible outcomes of such approaches not only serve the common good, but help to raise the profile of political science departments both on campus and across our communities during a time of ever-shrinking resources and fiscal constraint.

THE SoTL MOVEMENT

While the citizen engagement movement and efforts to increase assessment occurred at the same time, the citizen engagement movement's emphasis on engaged pedagogy is even more closely linked to a third development that first emerged in the 1990s—the scholarship of teaching and learning (SoTL). Educational reformers concerned with student learning outcomes were also aware that implementing and assessing engaged student-centered pedagogies would take a substantial amount of time and energy. Yet by the 1980s, an increasing number of colleges and universities required research excellence as a criterion for tenure and promotion.[24] In an effort to enhance the value of teaching activities in an environment where professional advancement was increasingly tied to research productivity, reformers proposed a new understanding of scholarly activity.

The most articulate and widely cited defense of this approach was published by CFAT. CFAT president Ernest Boyer's *Scholarship Reconsidered: The Priorities of the Professoriate* (published in 1990), offered a new academic paradigm where public, systematic reflection on teaching practices should fall within the definition of scholarly work. In short, Boyer argued that professors should use the methodological approaches appropriate to their disciplines to reflect on the effectiveness of their pedagogies, and this process should be undertaken with appropriate scholarly rigor. Findings from such work, he argued, should be publicly available so that the most effective practices could be identified and shared.[25]

The data collection techniques recommended by Boyer sound quite similar to those of the assessment movement, with the major difference that producing assessment data was largely a response to external pressures, while support for the SoTL came primarily from within the professoriate. With institutional support from CFAT, which also founded the Carnegie Academy for the Scholarship of Teaching and Learning, Boyer's initial recommendations have had a dramatic influence on academia. Most institutions now have centers dedicated to teaching and learning, and some have adjusted their tenure and promotion guidelines to accommodate work grounded in SoTL, though this conversation is still ongoing and linked to a larger conversation about the purpose of universities in the twenty-first century.[26] Meanwhile, new professional organizations and peer-reviewed journals were founded to provide professional outlets for SoTL activities and findings.[27] A recent assessment of SoTL's impact on academia, aptly titled *The Scholarship of Teaching and Learning Reconsidered*, concludes that "the movement has, of course, gone far beyond the Carnegie circle itself—so far in fact that no one person or group can speak for all who use the term."[28]

Within our own discipline, SoTL has made slow and steady inroads. In the 1990s, the American Political Science Association (APSA) founded the Teaching and Learning Division, and the number of SoTL articles appearing in *PS: Political Science and Politics* began to increase until they became a regular feature in "The Teacher" section. Between 1991 and 2013, 246 teaching-related articles had been published in *PS*.[29] In 1997, professors engaged in SoTL research founded their own division, the Undergraduate Education Section, since renamed the Political Science Education Section, to extend the focus of SoTL research to graduate education. Within a decade, these commitments grew to include the 2005 launch of a peer-reviewed section journal, *The Journal of Political Science Education* (which had published 165 articles by 2013) and, beginning in 2004, an annual APSA Teaching & Learning Conference. These outlets guarantee the increasing numbers of political scientists engaged in SoTL research have an outlet for their work.[30]

THE CONSORTIUM AS AN IMPORTANT NEXT STEP

While these accomplishments are substantial, efforts to assess our civic engagement and pedagogical accomplishments in the discipline of political science have hit a plateau. Many of the professors engaged in this research work at institutions where their primary responsibility is teaching. They often do not have access to multiple sections of large (150–750 students) lecture courses to use for the purpose of collecting quantitative data on student learning outcomes. They usually lack the time or resources required to conduct systematic data collection beyond a single campus, or perhaps even a single classroom—which can limit the type of cases selected for in-depth, qualitative research. Innovative and thoughtful SoTL scholars are frequently constrained, not by faulty research designs or methodological flaws, but by limited resources.[31] Intriguing preliminary findings cannot be verified or expanded without collaboration with teacher-scholars at other institutions. Systematic cross-campus data collection is essential to discern whether specific teaching and programming efforts are uniformly successful, or whether their influence is contextual and affected by intervening variables such as student demographics, campus climate, and geographic region.

To address these concerns, the Inter-Campus Consortium for SoTL Research will provide a structure and procedure for identifying, strengthening, and executing SoTL projects using a broad network of dedicated teachers and researchers. Political scientists collecting assessment data of their pedagogy and civic engagement efforts will now have an easier way to collaborate with one another. Those who join the Consortium will have the opportunity to participate in an on-going research project and to learn about new Consortium-sponsored projects in the future. Those who collect data for a Consortium-sponsored project will have access to the raw data collected from their own campus or regions, as well as a summary report of findings relevant to their campuses. In addition, they will be eligible to submit an original project to the Advisory Board for permission to use the Consortium's database and resources.

The Consortium provides an array of benefits to individual members and participants. For instance, teacher-scholars interested in conducting original SoTL research will gain access to students, classes, and campuses beyond their own. These resources will enhance publication and grant opportunities, enabling individual scholars to gain respect and visibility for their research. Furthermore, Consortium members can participate in ongoing projects to gain access to data about their own campuses and students. This data will be useful for internal assessment reports, as well as for academic presentations and publications focused on a single classroom or campus. Participation in the Consortium will help enable political scientists to meet teaching, research, and service requirements for tenure and promotion.

Participation in a national colloquium dedicated to the scholarship of teaching and learning demonstrates the seriousness with which a faculty member approaches his or her teaching. A scholarly approach to teaching, and to evidence-based, effective pedagogy, is designed to improve a faculty member's teaching methods and student learning outcomes. As Lee Shulman notes, for a scholarship of teaching, we need scholarship that makes our work public and thus susceptible to critique. It then becomes community property, available for others to build upon.[32] Participation in the Colloquium demonstrates the faculty member's commitment to such teaching and learning goals, and a willingness to engage in cooperative inquiry as a service to the discipline. From an instrumental perspective, the Consortium provides an excellent networking opportunity. The Consortium allows participants to keep up-to-date on cutting edge SoTL research, and to share teaching and research ideas. Moreover, Consortium members can serve as external reviewers for fellow faculty seeking tenure and/or promotion. Finally, both primary investigators and project participants will have opportunities to publish findings in appropriate outlets, demonstrating an active scholarly agenda.

Furthermore, the Consortium provides a number of benefits to the discipline of political science, especially as the number of political scientists working at four-year teaching institutions and at community colleges continues to increase. For example, the Consortium will facilitate SoTL large N research designs and provide data on more diverse populations of subjects for small N research design. This will increase the number of significant and substantively important findings from our scholarly efforts. Such work will enhance the external validity of SoTL research, producing more generalizable knowledge. We anticipate that these strengths of the Consortium will increase the amount of high-quality, publishable SoTL research produced. This will enhance the profile of political science SoTL research within our own discipline and across the social sciences.[33]

One of the Consortium's explicit goals is to make it feasible for teacher-scholars at colleges with heavy teaching loads to participate in cutting-edge SoTL research. Professors who take their teaching seriously and seek like-minded colleagues—whether they work at liberal arts colleges, regional comprehensive universities, community colleges, or research universities—will find a home in the Consortium. The Consortium and the high-quality research it produces will enhance teacher-scholars' visibility within the discipline's journals and at its professional meetings. The emphasis on SoTL will also provide insight into best practices, with the potential to improve teaching effectiveness across the discipline.

Join the Consortium

Political scientists now have a way to cooperate with one another to conduct cutting-edge, cross-campus scholarship of teaching and learning (SoTL). The Consortium is designed to facilitate the completion of high-quality, multi-campus SoTL research assessing the effectiveness of political scientists' efforts to develop the skills, knowledge, and dispositions necessary for effective citizenship in a democracy. Join the Consortium to participate in a current project or to learn about exciting new projects in the future. Gain access to data collected on your own campus. Submit a project of your own to the Advisory Board. Most importantly, visit the Consortium web page to learn more about joining and participating in cross-campus SoTL research.

Joining the Consortium is as simple as providing your contact information, as well as descriptive information about your institution, department, and interests, to the codirectors. Joining does not require participation in every Consortium-sponsored project. Rather, working closely with the American Political Science Association's Political Science Education Section, the Consortium provides an organized network of teacher-scholars interested in SoTL research. The Consortium's board will screen proposals and offer suggestions for strengthening both research questions and research design. The directors will recruit participants for Consortium-approved projects, allowing researchers access to a wide range of political scientists teaching at diverse institutions. In short, being a member of the Consortium ensures that you will be offered the opportunity to participate in an array of projects—but also have the freedom to select which projects fit your own schedule and agenda. Visit the Consortium's web page at (www.tinyURL.com/JoinSotl) and begin collaborating with colleagues on exciting new projects that will help to shape our discipline's future research agendas and teaching practices.

NOTES

1. Association of American Colleges and Universities, *Integrity in the College Curriculum, A Report to the Academic Community* (Washington, DC: Association of American Colleges and Universities, 1985); William J. Bennet, *To Reclaim a Legacy: A Report on the Humanities in Higher Education* (Washington, DC: National Endowment for the Humanities, 1984); Fletcher McLellan, "An Overview of the Assessment Movement" in Michelle Deardoff et al., eds., *Assessment in Political Science* (Washington, DC: American Political Science Association, 2009); National Institute of Education, *Involvement in Learning: Realizing the Potential of American Higher Education* (Washington DC: Author, 1984); Southern Education Board Commission for Educational Quality, *Access to Quality Undergraduate Education* (Atlanta, GA: Southern Education Board, 1985).

2. Hart Research Associates, *Learning and Assessment: Trends in Undergraduate Education: A Survey among Members of the Association of American Colleges and Universities* (Washington, DC: Association of American Colleges and Universities, 2009), http://www.aacu.org/membership/documents/2009MemberSurvey_Part1.pdf (accessed September 30, 2012).

3. Michelle Deardorff et al., eds., *Assessment in Political Science* (Washington, DC: American Political Science Association, 2009).

4. Michelle Deardorff and Paul Folger, "Making Assessment Matter: Structuring Assessment, Transforming Departments," in Michelle Deardorff et al., eds., *Assessment in Political Science* (Washington, DC: American Political Science Association, 2009).

5. Of course, these concerns underscore competing conceptualizations of the type of value a college degree is expected to provide. Politicians and members of the general public are more likely to focus on the material gains (such as employment and a higher standard of living) that should accompany a college degree. Professors, who are charged with undertaking such assessments, typically have a broader definition of "value" that encompasses intellectual development and capacity for critical thinking.

6. Craig Brandon, *The Five-Year Party: How Colleges Have Given Up on Educating Your Child and What You Can Do about It* (Dallas: Ben Bella Books, Inc., 2010); Paul Fain, "College for All?" *Inside Higher Ed*, 29, 2012, http://www.insidehighered.com/news/2012/06/29/politicians-and-pundits-ramp-questions-about-value-degrees (accessed September 30, 2012); Charles Lane, "Congress Should Cut Funding for Political Science Research," *The Washington Post*, June 4, 2012, http://www.washingtonpost.com/opinions/congress-should-cut-funding-for-political-science-research/2012/06/04/gJQAuAJMEV_story.html (accessed Septem-

ber 30, 2012); Robert J. Samuelson, "It's Time to Drop the College-for-All Crusade," *The Washington Post*, May 27, 2012, http://www.washingtonpost.com/opinions/its-time-to-drop-the-college-for-all-crusade/2012/05/27/gJQAzcUGvU_story.html (accessed September 30, 2012); Naomi Schaeffer Riley, *The Faculty Lounges, and Other Reasons Why You Won't Get the College Education You Pay For* (Lanham, MD: Rowman & Littlefield, 2012). Such criticisms range from pop-culture books such as those published by Schaeffer Riley and Brandon to more serious efforts to influence higher education policy found at Richard Vedder's Center for College Affordability and Productivity, which can be located at the following link: http://centerforcollegeaffordability.org/

7. For an update of such efforts, see Jon Marcus, "Will New Funding Rules Improve Dismal University Graduation Rates?" *Time*, April 25, 2012, http://www.time.com/time/nation/article/0,8599,2113097,00.html (accessed September 30, 2012). The push for performance-based funding was part of the Compete to Complete initiative sponsored by the National Governor's Association in 2010–2011. For a description of this initiative, see http://www.subnet.nga.org/ci/1011/.

8. Richard Arum and Josipa Roksa, *Academically Adrift: Limited Learning on College Campuses* (Chicago: The University of Chicago Press, 2011); Intercollegiate Studies Institute, *Enlightened Citizenship: How Civic Knowledge Trumps a College Degree in Promoting Active Civic Engagement* (Wilmington, DE: Intercollegiate Studies Institute, 2011), http://www.americancivicliteracy.org (accessed September 30, 2012).

9. Paul Edelman et al., "Assessment/Learning Outcomes II Track Summary," *PS: Political Science & Politics* 39, no. 3 (2006): 538.

10. Matthew Hartley, "Idealism and Compromise and the Civic Engagement Movement," in John Saltmarsh and Matthew Hartley, eds., *"To Serve a Larger Purpose": Engagement for Democracy and the Transformation of Higher Education* (Philadelphia: Temple University Press, 2011), 28.

11. Anne Colby et al., *Educating Citizens: Preparing America's Undergraduates for Lives of Moral and Civic Responsibility* (San Francisco: Jossey-Bass, 2003); Anne Colby et al., *Educating for Democracy, Preparing Undergraduates for Responsible Political Engagement* (San Francisco: Jossey-Bass, 2007); Martin Wattenberg, *Is Voting for Young People?* 3rd ed. (New York: Pearsons, 2012); Cliff Zukin et al., *A New Civic Engagement?* (New York: Oxford University Press, 2006).Pe

12. John Dewey, *Democracy and Education* (New York: The Macmillan Co., 1916). For a full account of the various associations and foundations associated with the civic engagement movement, see Hartley, "Idalism and Compromise," 2011.

13. A description of Campus Compact's history and current activities can be found on the organization's web page at http://www.compact.org/, while updates about the AASC&U's American Democracy Project are provided at http://www.aascu.org/programs/ADP/.

14. John Saltmarsh and Matthew Hartley, eds., *"To Serve a Larger Purpose": Engagement for Democracy and the Transformation of Higher Education* (Philadelphia: Temple University Press, 2011).

15. Campus Compact, "Who We Are," Campus Compact, http://www.compact .org/about/history-mission-vision/ (accessed 08/01/2014).

16. Carnegie Foundation for the Advancement of Teaching, "Community Engagement Classification," http://classifications.carnegiefoundation.org/descriptions/com munity_engagement.phparnegie (accessed September 30, 2012).

17. For a review of the full array of citizen engagement approaches that have emerged in political science, see Allison Rios Millet McCartney et al., eds., *Teaching Civic Engagement: From Student to Active Citizen* (Washington, DC: American Political Science Association, 2013).

18. Nicholas Kristof, "Professors, We Need You!," *New York Times*, Sunday Review, February 15, 2014, http://www.nytimes.com/2014/02/16/opinion/sunday/ kristof-professors-we-need-you.html?_r=0 (accessed 8/1/2014).

19. E. G. Creamer, *Assessing Faculty Publication Productivity: Issues of Equity*. ASHEERIC Higher Education Report No. 26. (Washington, DC: ASHE-ERIC/ George Washington University, Graduate School of Education and Human Development, 1998).

20. The emergence of public policy as a distinct discipline and the corresponding proliferation of public policy schools and journals may have influenced this reduction in political scientists publishing policy-related work in traditional political science journals.

21. Peter D. Hart Research Associates, Inc., *Summary of Existing Research on Attitudes toward Liberal Education Outcomes for the Association of American Colleges and Universities*, Association of American Colleges and Universities, August 2004, https://www.aacu.org/sites/default/files/files/LEAP/HartExistingResearchRe port.pdf (accessed 8/1/14).

22. Peter D. Hart Research Associates, Inc., *Report of Findings Based on Focus Groups among Business Executives*, Association of American Colleges and Universities, January 31, 2006, http;//www.aacu.org/leap/documents/PrivateEmployersFind ings.pdf (accessed 8/1/14).

23. Saltmarsh and Hartley, eds., *"To Serve a Larger Purpose."* These arguments are made throughout the contributions to this edited volume, but especially in the introductory and concluding chapters.

24. Jack H. Shuster and Howard R. Bowen, "The Faculty at Risk," *Change* 17, no 5 (1985): 13–21.

25. Ernest Boyer, *Scholarship Reconsidered: The Priorities of the Professoriate* (Stanford, CA: The Carnegie Foundation for the Advancement of Teaching, 1990).

26. For a discussion of continued barriers in recognizing SoTL as scholarship in the promotion process see, for example, Roger Bashier, "Why Is the Scholarship of Teaching and Learning Such a Hard Sell?" *Higher Education Research & Development* 28, no. 1 (March 2009) http://matsusemi.saloon.jp/wp-content/uploads/2012/07/ Boshier-Roger20091.pdf (accessed 08/01/2014). Also, for a study of faculty attitudes at a campus that has worked to revise the promotion and tenure review process to include the scholarship of teaching and learning, see *Recognition and Reward: SoTL and the Tenure Process at a Regional Research University* 2009 (https://www.iupui .edu/~josotl/archive/vol_11/no_3/v11n3secret.pdf, accessed 08/01/2014).

27. For a listing of key SOTL conferences, interdisciplinary journals, and disciplinary journals, see Cathy Bishop-Clark and Beth Dietz-Uhler, *Engaging in the Scholarship of Teaching and Learning: A Guide to the Process, and How to Develop a Project from Start to Finish* (Sterling, VA: Stylis, 2012) .

28. Pat Hutchings et al., *The Scholarship of Teaching and Learning Reconsidered: Institutional Integration and Impact* (Stanford, CA: The Carnegie Foundation for the Advancement of Teaching, 2011), xiv.

29. For an analysis of articles published in "The Teacher," see Elizabeth Bennion and Hanna Dill, "Civic Engagement Research in Political Science Journals: An Overview of Assessment Techniques," in Alison Rios Millet McCarthy et al., eds., *Teaching Civic Engagement: From Student to Active Citizen* (Washington, DC: American Political Science Association, 2013), 423–436.

30. For an overview of the types of scholarship emerging from these new outlets, see ibid.

31. All of these observations are based on the coauthors' professional experiences as program chairs for APSA's Political Science Education Section, discussants on Political Science Education panels, track participants at APSA's Teaching & Learning Conference, and manuscript reviewers for the *Journal of Political Science Education*.

32. Lee S. Shulman, "Taking Teaching Seriously," *Change* 31, no. 4 (July/August 1999): 10–17. Republished online by the Carnegie Foundation for the Advancement of Teaching, http://www.carnegiefoundation.org/elibrary/taking-learning-seriously (accessed 08/01/2014).

33. The discipline of sociology has five well-known journals dedicated to SoTL research: *International Studies in Sociology of Education, Learning and Teaching in the Social Sciences, Sociology of Education, Teaching and Learning Matters,* and *Teaching Sociology.* The field of psychology has twelve such journals. In contrast, political science has two journals in which political scientists can publish their SoTL work, a small "Political Science Teacher" section within *PS Political Science and Politics* and the *Journal of Political Science Education.*

BIBLIOGRAPHY

Arum, Richard, and Josipa Roksa. *Academically Adrift: Limited Learning on College Campuses.* Chicago: University of Chicago Press, 2011.

Bennett, William J. *To Reclaim a Legacy: A Report on the Humanities in Higher Education.* Washington, DC: National Endowment for the Humanities, 1984.

Bennion, Elizabeth, and Hanna Dill. "Civic Engagement Research in Political Science Journals: An Overview of Assessment Techniques." In *Teaching Civic Engagement: From Student to Active Citizen,* 423–436. Washington DC: American Political Science Association, 2013.

Bishop Clark, C., and B. Dietz-Uhler. *Engaging in the Scholarship of Teaching and Learning: A Guide to the Process, and How to Develop a Project from Start to Finish.* Sterling: Stylus Publishing, 2012.

Boshier, Roger. "Why Is the Scholarship of Teaching and Learning Such a Hard Sell?" *Higher Education Research and Development* 28, no.1 (March 2009): 1–15. http://matsusemi.saloon.jp/wp-content/uploads/2012/07/Boshier-Roger20091.pdf.

Boyer, E. *Scholarship Reconsidered: Priorites of the Professoriate.* Stanford: The Carnegie Foundation for the Advancement of Teaching, 1990.

Brandon, Craig. *The Five-Year Party: How Colleges Have Given Up on Educating Your Child and What You Can Do about It.* Dallas, TX: BenBella Books, 2010.

Campus Compact. "Who We Are." Accessed August 1, 2014. http://www.compact.org/about/history-mission-vision/.

Carnegie Foundation for the Advancement of Teaching. "Community Engagment Classification." The Carnegie Foundation. Accessed August 1, 2014. http://classifications.carnegiefoundation.org/descriptions/community_engagement.phparnegie.

Colby, Anne, Elizabeth Beaumont, and Thomas Ehrlich. *Educating for Democracy: Preparing Undergraduates for Responsible Political Engagement.* San Francisco: Jossey-Bass, 2007.

Colby, Anne, Thomas Ehrlich, Elizabeth Beaumont, and Jason Stephens. *Educating Citizens: Preparing America's Undergraduates for Lives of Moral and Civic Responsibility.* San Francisco: Jossey-Bass, 2003.

Creamer, E. "Assessing Faculty Publication Productivity: Issues of Equity." =ERIC Digest, 1999. http://www.ericdigests.org/1999-1/equity.html.

Cruz, Laura, Jill Ellern, George Ford, Hollye Moss, and Barbara Jo White. "Recognition and Reward: SOTL and the Tenure Process at a Regional Comprehensive University." *Mountain Rise: The International Journal of the Scholarship of Teaching and Learning* (Summer 2009). https://www2.viu.ca/integratedplanning/documents/RecognitionandReward.pdf

Deardorff, Michelle, and Paul Folger. "Making Assessment Matter: Structuring Assessment, Transforming Departments." In *Assessment in Political Science.* Washington DC: American Political Science Association, 2009.

Deardorff, Michelle, Kerstin Hamann, and John Ishiyama. *Assessment in Political Science.* Washington DC: American Political Science Association, 2009.

Dewey, John. *Democracy and Education.* New York City: Macmillan, 1916.

Edelman, Paul, Jocelyn Evans, Halima Khan, Jessica Schattschneider, and Michelle Williams. "Assessment/Learning Outcomes II Track Summary." *PS: Political Science & Politics* 39, no. 3 (2006): 538.

Fain, Paul. "College for All?" *Inside Higher Ed.* June 29, 2012. Accessed September 30, 2012. https://www.insidehighered.com/news/2012/06/29/politicians-and-pundits-ramp-questions-about-value-degrees.

Hartley, Matthew. "Idealism and Compromise and the Civic Engagement Movement." In *"To Serve a Larger Purpose": Engagement for Democracy and the Transformation of Higher Education,* 28. Philadelphia: Temple University Press, 2011.

Hutchings, Pat, Mary Taylor Huber, and Anthony Ciccone. *The Scholarship of Teaching and Learning Reconsidered: Institutional Integration and Impact.* Stanford: The Carnegie Foundation for the Advancement of Teaching, 2001.

Integrity in the College Curriculum: A Report to the Academic Community. The findings and recommendations of the Project on Redefining the Meaning and Purpose of Baccalaureate Degrees. Washington, DC: Association of American Colleges and Universities, 1985.

Intercollegiate Studies Institute. *Enlightened Citizenship: How Civic Knowledge Trumps a College Degree in Promoting Active Civic Engagement.* American Civic Literacy. January 1, 2011. Accessed September 30, 2012. http://www.ameri cancivicliteracy.org.

Kristof, Nicholas. "Professors, We Need You!" *The New York Times.* February 15, 2014. Accessed August 1, 2014. http://www.nytimes.com/2014/02/16/opinion/ sunday/kristof-professors-we-need-you.html?_r=0

Lane, Charles. "Congress Should Cut Funding for Political Science Research." *The Washington Post,* June 4, 2012. Accessed September 30, 2012. http://www.wash ingtonpost.com/opinions/congress-should-cut-funding-for-political-science-re search/2012/06/04/gJQAuAJMEV_story.html

Lanning, Sharon, Monica Leisey, Susan Polich, Joseph Schuab, and Mary Secret. "Faculty Perceptions of the Scholarship of Teaching and Learning: Definition, Activity Level and Merit Considerations at One University." *Journal of the Scholarship of Teaching and Learning* 11, no. 3 (2011): 1–20. Accessed November 6, 2014. https://www.iupui.edu/~josotl/archive/vol_11/no_3/v11n3secret.pdf.

Learning and Assessment: Trends in Undergraduate Education: A Survey among Members of the Association of American Colleges and Universities. Association of American Colleges and Universities. January 1, 2009. Accessed September 30, 2012. http://www.aacu.org/membership/documents/2009MemberSurvey_Part1.pdf.

Marcus, Jon. "Will New Funding Rules Improve Dismal University Graduation Rates?" *Time,* April 25, 2012.

McLellan, Fletcher. "An Overview of the Assessment Movement." In *Assessment in Political Science.* Washington DC: American Political Science Association, 2009.

National Institute of Education. *Involvement in Learning: Realizing the Potential of American Higher Education.* Washington DC: National Institute of Education, 1984.

Peter D. Hart Research Associates Inc. *Report of Findings Based on Focus Groups among Buiness Executives Conducted on Behalf of The Association of American Colleges and Universities.* The Association of American Colleges and Universities. January 31, 2006. http://www.aacu.org/leap/documents/PrivateEm ployersFindings.pdf.

Peter D. Hart Research Associates Inc. *Summary of Existing Research on Attitudes toward Liberal Education Outcomes for the Association of American Colleges and Universities.* Association of American Colleges and Universities. 2004. http://www .aacu.org/sites/default/files/files/LEAP/HartExistingResearchReport.pdf.

Rios Millett McCartney, Allison, Elizabeth Bennion, and Dick Simpson, eds. *Teaching Civic Engagement: From Student to Acitive Citizen.* Washington DC: American Political Science Association, 2013.

Saltmarsh, John, and Matthew Hartley, eds. *"To Serve a Larger Purpose": Engagement for Democracy and the Transformation of Higher Education.* Philadelphia: Temple University Press, 2011.

Samuelson, Robert. "It's Time to Drop the College-for-All Crusade." *The Washington Post,* May 27, 2012. Accessed September 27, 2012. http://www.washington

post.com/opinions/its-time-to-drop-the-college-for-all-crusade/2012/05/27/gJQA
zcUGvU_story.html.

Schaeffer Riley, Naomi. *The Faculty Lounges, and Other Reasons Why You Won't
Get the College Education You Pay For*. Lanham: Rowman & Littlefield, 2012.

Shulman, Lee S. "Taking Teaching Seriously." *Change* 31, no. 4 (July–August 1999):
10–17. http://www.carnegiefoundation.org/elibrary/taking-learning-seriously.

Shuster, Jack H., and Howard R. Bowen. "The Faculty at Risk." *Change* 17, no. 5
(September–October 1985): 13–21.

Southern Education Board Commission for Educational Quality. *Access to Quality
Undergraduate Education*. Atlanta: Southern Education Board, 1985.

Wattenberg, Martin. *Is Voting for Young People?* 3rd ed. New York City: Pearsons,
2012.

Zukin, Cliff, Scott Keeter, Molly Andolina, Krista Jenkins, and Michael Carpini. *A
New Engagement? Political Participation, Civic Life, and the Changing American
Citizen*. New York City: Oxford University Press, 2006.

Part B: Initiatives beyond the Classroom

Chapter Fifteen

Democratizing Information

Web 2.0 Tools at Fort Hays State University

Chapman Rackaway and Carolyn Campbell

Online tools are changing the way college teachers strive to inspire civic engagement and build civic leadership skills in students.[1] Galston catalogs the difficulties college educators face in teaching students, how declining civic knowledge among incoming freshmen increases the remedial needs for citizenship education at the college level.[2] Well-functioning democracies require informed, educated, and active participants within the citizenry.[3] Educating students on facts, current events, and constitutional design is not enough, and faculty members across the country have been engaged in efforts both curricular and co-curricular that build knowledge of civic leadership opportunities and the skills to apply that knowledge. New online tools that allow media users to create content as well as consume it have provided a new environment in which those skills can be built and harnessed.[4] By developing media consumers that also create their own content, we make engagement an integral part of news and media consumption today.

Fort Hays State University (FHSU) has been involved in the American Association of State Colleges and Universities' (AASCU) American Democracy Project (ADP) efforts to bolster student civic engagement since the initiative began in 2003.[5] When ADP began the eCitizenship initiative in 2008, FHSU was one of the charter institutions. Online tools and community building are mission friendly for institutions such as FHSU, with both in-person and online colleges. In fact, as an early adopter of online education, FHSU features twice the number of students studying online as those studying on campus.

FHSU's mission has long focused on first-generation and underserved college students. The students who come to FHSU have often experienced little in the way of civic education in their precollegiate curriculum. Most come from rural schools in western Kansas or other rural areas within three hundred miles of the campus. Therefore FHSU has embraced AASCU's desire to build civic engagement, recognizing that our students would benefit particularly from ADP's efforts.

A longtime innovator in civic engagement programming, FHSU has become a leader in curricular and co-curricular civic engagement through ADP, using existing initiatives as well as creating programs of our own. FHSU boasts the first implementation of "Times Talk" brownbag news discussions at an ADP institution, and is a national leader in subinitiatives such as the online social media-focused eCitizenship, and global problem-focused 7 Revolutions/Global Challenges.[6] FHSU approached online tools with the same focus and intent, and as a result has a significant set of embedded online curricular and co-curricular efforts to expand civic engagement in an online world.

CIVIC ENGAGEMENT AT FHSU

Fort Hays State University defines "civic engagement" as an educational activity (curricular and co-curricular) that is designed to develop civic knowledge, skills and values resulting in action that has a direct impact on the quality of life in a community.[7] FHSU prioritizes civic engagement for the twofold purpose of promoting civic knowledge and improving our community connectedness.

First, civic engagement promotes student learning objectives that are consistent with civic knowledge, skills, and values. Active and engaged citizens must have an understanding of social and political issues and their historical contexts, be knowledgeable about public structures and processes, and have the skills and motivation to put that knowledge into action.

Second FHSU's civic engagement efforts must strive to achieve the ultimate goal of improving the greater community (this can mean local, state, national, and/or global communities). Our public work is designed for the purpose of addressing and solving community and societal problems and ultimately improving the human condition.

The underlying goal of FHSU's civic engagement efforts is thus to engage students in a dialog amongst themselves and with their communities on problems, aspirations, and other needs in their communities and beyond. It can be easy for students to become cocooned in their own microcommunities on campus and not connect to the world beyond. To break through those barriers, FHSU has focused on building stronger connections between students and the community. Historically, classes in the Department of Leadership Studies have been tasked with not only responding to community needs but seeking out and developing projects that would address these needs. Service learning has long been a substantial focus of the FHSU faculty's curriculum as well.[8] In 2009, the university's efforts were recognized with the Carnegie Foundation's Community Engaged Campus specialty designation. The emergence of online tools for social connectedness provided FHSU a new opportunity to carry its mission forward.

ONLINE TOOLS IN THE CLASSROOM

Technology is significantly influencing civic education inside and outside the classroom. Almost all undergraduate students have broadband Internet access and more than three-quarters of them regularly use online and social media.[9] Almost any element of traditional university teaching and co-curricular life can be adapted to or changed by technological tools. A variety of different tools exist, and it is important to match the tool to desired student outcomes. Grade books have been joined by spreadsheets, testing happens in both Blue Books and on Blackboard, and educational institutions now deliver entire programs both in-person and online. Students live in a technological world, and so attempting to engage students means using that technology.[10] More specifically, some have started to use Web 2.0 tools to achieve specific pedagogical goals. For instance, the open-sourced web encyclopedia known as Wikipedia has been used in lieu of textbooks in some classes, despite controversy over its appropriateness.[11] One professor has students submit papers to an internal class-only wiki within his course management system for peer review prior to submitting final drafts.[12]

Social media sites such as Twitter are communication tools that help promote and improve civic engagement efforts.[13] Ari Kohen shows how Twitter can be adapted to the classroom in order to build a student community inside and outside of the classroom setting, as well as advance teaching. Kohen's use of Twitter began by posting questions to allow students who missed class to keep up with the coursework. Over time Kohen used Twitter as a mechanism for students to briefly summarize important points within the site's 140-character limit. Far from limiting students, Kohen found that Twitter became a vital teaching tool for political theory classes. The use of Twitter transformed in-class discussions to continuing discussions outside of the classroom, let students develop the ability to concisely share their opinions, and built community among the students and interested outsiders who participated in the Twitter threads. Methods of properly assessing student learning from such tools remain unresolved, however.[14]

As digital natives, college students of the Millenial age are generally more accustomed to using computer-based tools than their older cohorts.[15] From texting to time on social media, students live immersed in a sea of technology. Students can become detached from the learning at hand if technology is not used, or if it is used inappropriately. Technology is merely an apparatus, neither entirely beneficial nor detrimental in nature. Potential benefits of technology include enhanced learning, community building, and increased student engagement in learning materials. On the other hand, technology can be detrimental by distracting students from learning goals or by interfering with learning if students experience technical difficulties. As Bauerlein posits, overreliance on technology can suppress student learning and development by allowing them to completely forego reading books.[16] However, what Bauerlein tacitly admits is that the benefit or detriment of technology is in its use. If technology supplements and enhances reading, it can increase reading comprehension and student learning.[17] Literature on successful technological instruction integration displays a common thread: strategic goals guide the application of technology to teaching.

Yuen and Hung reinforce the point about intentional application of technology. Surveying students about social networking in the classroom, their results suggest most students' attitudes toward the use of class social networks were positive. Social networking in the observed classrooms was helpful for promoting communities of practice among students. Information sharing, both class-relevant and not, reinforced a shared experience that built social capital.[18]

For a variety of reasons, blogging is very promising for college teaching and civic engagement. Blogging by students weaves numerous important skills into a single activity set. Reading and consuming information as a base source, analyzing the source material, composing and writing the post, and maintaining the conversation in replies in order to build community, all satisfy pedagogical goals. Critical thinking, collaboration, media literacy, and writing skills are all put to the test by tasking students with blogging. Students must come to understand political issues, synthesize them with other information, and then clearly share their analysis. Students can produce quality opinion-editorial pieces in a blog, and with an equally committed body of students providing comments, build an active community of strong critical thinkers.[19]

WEB 2.0

The Internet, taken as a communication medium, is completely different from any other media developed since the printing press. Just as the printing press was a revolutionary development in information dissemination, the Internet has provided a knowledge distribution revolution. What separates the Internet of today from twentieth-century broadcast media such as radio and television is the ability of the end-user to produce content in addition to consume subject matter. The early days of the Internet, or Web 1.0, featured one-way communication much like traditional media. But social media would put content creation in the hands of consumers, revolutionizing online communication and becoming a new interactive phenomenon in Web 2.0.

The significant barriers to entry of broadcast radio and television such as cost of equipment and licensure are obviated by the Internet's low cost of content dissemination. The effect of putting content creation in the hands of the general public has been revolutionary in the realm of broadcast media. Web 2.0 has resulted in drastic changes to newspapers and television, as well as changing the culture in subtle yet significant ways.[20]

Skeptical views of the power of Web 2.0-driven civic engagement persist. Pasek and colleagues and Bennett et al. cast doubt on the ability of asynchronous digital communication to build stable connections between people for constructive political action.[21] Despite those warnings, other studies of Web 2.0 use have shown it to have a significant and positive impact on student engagement and civic participation. Leung showed that three basic senses of self-esteem and orientation could be built via social media usage: self-efficacy, perceived competence, and desire for control. In other words, the more one connected with others online, the more capable of making important decisions and following through with constructive action one felt he or she was. Thus social media's great value is in building community among students to reinforce learning values, make learning more student-driven than faculty-driven, and create the social capital needed to mobilize citizens.[22] Cogburn and Espinoza-Vasquez found that three million donors and five million voters were activated and mobilized by the online social media efforts of the Obama campaign, effectively showing that a well-designed Web 2.0 outreach effort could mobilize as effectively as traditional in-person outreach campaigns.[23]

The list of Web 2.0 tools is vast and includes text, graphical, social, audio, and video content. Text tools are the most common element of the Web 2.0 milieu, such as blogs. Comments on news websites, blogs and their comments features, and collaboration sites all allow the individual consumer to interact with the writer and material and create their own material to share. Take a single story on a given day of a regional newspaper, for instance, a story in Wichita, Kansas's *Eagle*. A story on debt downgrades posted at 7:00 a.m. had thirty-six comments from Kansans offering their own analysis of the story by 2:00 p.m. that same day.[24] As keyboards have been the main input source for computers from the beginning, it makes sense that text tools were the first and are the longest-lasting web 2.0 tools. They require no more equipment other than those needed to operate the computer.

While graphical tools can be powerful pedagogical instruments, they are generally for more advanced users. Graphical tools require moderate technical skills to use; however, free software is now readily available online to combine photos into video slideshow presentations and websites that allow the manipulation and captioning of photos.[25] Many people are highly familiar with the social Web 2.0 tools of today: Facebook, Twitter, Google Plus, LinkedIn, and other online communities where individuals and groups post profiles and share links, personal content, and interact are examples of the social Web 2.0 world. The stable profiles of such sites give the social network continuity. Having a profile, where one's content and personal information are shared, is an important part of the Web 2.0 phenomenon. The identity that comes from the ability to post personal information and photos online in a stable and personalized interactive environment is an extension of the individual and allows for community building.[26]

Consider a newspaper's comments section. If any individual can post and not leave any identifying information, it not only allows them the freedom to make up falsehoods, attack other posters on a personal basis, and generally disrupt the conversation; it also prevents them from developing an identity on the site. By having profiles, people become known for their posts and content. The university can attempt to ensure that students follow practices of civility and decorum in their communication, setting the stage for constructive disagreement in the future. The posters develop reputations and a community of sorts can be built on a much wider scale than ever before possible. Local communities can emerge from such comments sections, whether it is a newspaper and its city, or a class and its students.

The new Web 2.0 environment allows for the creation of living texts that can expand, contract, and change over time. The dynamic nature of Web 2.0 also allows for a communal construction of content. The ability to build community is another of the great strengths of Web 2.0. As engagement and senses of community are intrinsically connected and concepts are reinforced, Web 2.0 is a natural engagement tool for community building.

SOCIAL CAPITAL

The Internet has allowed for citizens to be more empowered in their media consumption and the political process generally. Political candidates connect directly to voters through social media, and organizations like AmericansElect.com seek to move the nominating process online. The Web 2.0 phenomenon similarly allows teachers to put more power in the hands of students to create and disseminate knowledge—expanding the toolkit of skill-building strategies available. Further, Web 2.0 tools may provide an answer to one of the great challenges of political science education in the last two decades: building and reinforcing social community.

Robert Putnam pointed out in his seminal *Bowling Alone* that social capital, a sense of connectedness between individuals and the larger community, has been on the wane for forty years and is especially acute among the youngest citizens. Declining social capital has implications for political science faculty, as citizen engagement in the political process is part of the core of the material we teach. A society less connected is one that, by definition, is less participatory.[27] Reacting to Putnam's work, many colleges entered into co-curricular arrangements, such as the American Democracy Project with the express purpose of building social capital among college students.[28] Engaging students with curricular and co-curricular empowerment became high priorities in the classroom, conveniently at the same time Web 2.0 tools were being developed.

Putnam identifies a number of aspects of social capital in *Bowling Alone,* but the two most important elements are bonding and bridging social capital. Bridging social capital involves bringing people from disparate and distant communities together, while bonding social capital refers to strengthening connections within a geographically concentrated community.[29] Puntam's work was developed prior to the Internet's rise and ubiquity, so the concept of geography as an element (and challenge) for social capital is important. During the pre-Internet era, it was difficult to mobilize and develop social capital among distant communities; now, however, the geographic distance between communities is lessened if not entirely eliminated. Web 2.0 tools, especially the social media sites, allow a sustained and direct connection between people and provide the opportunity to build both types of social capital. Social capital is important for pedagogy because group learning has been shown to be highly effective. To make authentic group learning, some form of community building is necessary.[30]

Do Web 2.0 tools boost in-person social capital, represent a threat to it, or have they created a unique form of social capital? *Bowling Alone* is highly skeptical of the possibility of online social capital in any form. As more people eschew the bowling alley or playing cards with friends in a basement for MMOs on Playstation or online poker, Putnam posits that social capital suffers.[31] Wasko and Faraj claim that without existing strong connections and commitment to a network, online participation does not build social capital.[32]

Morozov's work joins in Putnam's skepticism. In his work, *The Net Delusion: The Dark Side of Internet Freedom,* he posits that the Internet actually boosts the individual over the community and as a result threatens the community-building nature of online participation advocated by others. Morozov points to the unrest in Iran that Sullivan claimed was the beginning of regime change in Tehran. He shows how those protestors did not accomplish their goals of overturning their government, and in fact their use of social media allowed them to subsequently be terrorized by the government. Morozov concluded the promise of the Internet is not as limitless as its supporters claim.[33]

On the other hand, Wellman et al. argue that online participation can build community as a rejoinder to critics such as Wasko et. al and Morozov.[34] Pfeil and colleagues present a more nuanced view of social networking's benefits. Significantly, Pfeil et. al find that social capital gains are strongest among the young.[35] Community building, whether in person or online, makes for an improved learning environment.[36]

But Web 2.0 tools can build social capital, as Ellison and colleagues found. Especially among college-aged students, online tools as examined by the Ellison study did show increased social capital among participants. Social capital is an important element not just for community building but for learning in general. Engagement by students, whether with communities or class material, increases student commitment and, as a by-product, should improve learning outcomes through group reinforcement. Web 2.0 media are thus particularly effective at building bridging social capital and maintaining offline relationships and connections that can be translated into classroom-relevant material.[37] Blogging is one accessible Web 2.0 tool for the classroom, and it has the added advantage of being similar to an assignment that many instructors have used before: the media journal.

One of the most important potential benefits of Web 2.0 civic engagement is drawing new and inactive citizens into politics for the first time. Neblo et al. show that people who are disaffected by politics or frustrated with "politics as usual" that otherwise pay little attention to politics can be enticed by friends to deliberate on political issues and indeed cast ballots on Election Day.[38] Most importantly, Gil de Zuniga et al. showed that online social capital can be built, and that frequency of online participation predated synchronous, in-person political participation with a high degree of correlation. In short, using social media can be a very effective method of building civic engagement skills and activating those skills among the participants.[39]

Web 2.0 has therefore provided the opportunity to expand civic engagement into the online world beyond the usual on-campus efforts. Fort Hays State University has a long-standing dedication to civic engagement. There is no shortage of civic leadership both in and out of the classroom, and technological advancements have led to an increase in the use of Web 2.0.

ONLINE LEARNING

FHSU has been a virtual learning provider for more than a decade and a half, with well-developed and widely used online learning programs serving nearly ten thousand students. Because students from every corner of the world have begun taking advantage of FHSU's Virtual College, it is important for Web 2.0 to be used not only on campus, but also as a resource for virtual students to gain a more developed experience with online learning. Many of the tools described below are available for both on-campus students and virtual learners worldwide.

Because so many of the courses offered on-campus are also offered online, it is important for both instructors and students to utilize different Web 2.0 tools to ensure the fullest potential of the courses. These tools, such as video lectures and discussion groups, have made it much easier for students to experience distance-learning—including study abroad programs—and ensure they are getting the attention they need from their instructors. As Mutz and Young show, engaging communication media can have a significant impact on learning. Using such technologies in the classroom therefore can directly impact active engagement by students.[40]

Tiger Talkback

One of the most widely used and longest-running methods for civic engagement (commonly referred to as eCitizenship) at FHSU is called Tiger Talkback, which is a basic form of Web 2.0. The leaders of the FHSU American Democracy Project began Tiger Talkback in order to create conversations about current world issues. This basic tool began as a whiteboard in a common area of the campus known as the Memorial Union. Every day in the Union, students can eat lunch, shop at the bookstore, or study in the lounge; as an area of high traffic, the Memorial Union is the perfect place to begin a civic conversation. Each week, ADP and Union staff change the topics and questions on the board, keeping the conversation topical and relevant to current local, national, or international events. Many of the questions can be controversial, so as to engage students and faculty in conversations that would allow them to step out of their "comfort zones" and be opened to diverse opinions and thoughts.[41] In the past, topics have included the death of Osama Bin Laden, the tenth anniversary of the September 11 terrorist attacks, and whether or not the government should be given any control over the distribution of contraceptives. The conversations featured varied perspectives and often significant disagreement. Concerns among campus leadership that inappropriate material or off-topic discussion would appear seem unfounded as conversations have focused on the topics at hand.

The Tiger Talkback board is an extremely popular and effective tool. Dahlgren's work enhances the belief that guided conversations online can turn passive nonparticipants into budding public intellectuals.[42] It is clear that even in a more technologically savvy world, students still find using a physical visual aid as a method of content creation intriguing. The basic idea of a physical discussion board was derived from similar ideas at Indiana University Purdue University, Indianapolis (IUPUI); Stephen F. Austin University; and Towson University. IUPUI uses a very unique structure known as "Democracy Plaza." Democracy Plaza is more than just a wall or a gathering place. Democracy Plaza is a network created for the purpose of getting students and faculty to come together to discuss issues of the day, ask questions, and find common ground.[43] Similarly, Towson University's "Freedom Square" blackboard allows members of the university to speak freely about the issues that matter to them. Freedom Square has expanded from a physical structure on campus to an online blogging site that allows participants around the world to join the conversation.[44]

The Tiger Talkback board at FHSU is constantly filled with thoughts and discussion points based on the question of the week, which often leads to more discussion on a related topic. It is not uncommon to find that, by the end of the week, the conversation has become so stimulating that there is no room left on the board.

Tiger Talkback has transformed over the years at FHSU from a simple whiteboard to a social media tool. One of the first tools used to make this transformation happen was a site similar to Twitter, called Wiffitti. Wiffitti is a unique social media tool that is sometimes used for blogging in classes at other schools. After posting the Tiger Talkback question of the week, the ADP team would release the selected Wiffitti URL to students and faculty so they could respond to the topic and engage each other in an interactive web-based discussion.

It became clear after several weeks that Wiffitti was not the ideal way to use Tiger Talkback. Students were unfamiliar with the website, and therefore found it difficult to respond. The ADP team, knowing how important social media is in our society, sought out another social media tool and eventually decided that Twitter would be the ideal medium for Tiger Talkback. In Spring 2012, the university fully invested in Twitter as the online discussion forum for Tiger Talkback. Twitter had reached a level of ubiquity among students, and the common presence of Twitter on smartphones meant its mobility was an advantage over other sites. Three monitors were installed with dedicated

Twitter displays on campus (in the Memorial Union, the Library's Learning Commons, and the dining center of the campus' largest residence hall).

Use of the Twitter tool since the 2010–2011 academic year has shown significant progress. A rush of users began following the ADP and Tiger Talkback Twitter accounts (@adpfhsu and @tigertalkback), with 209 followers in the first year and a smaller number of new followers each year after. However, replies using the #tigertalkback hashtag increased slowly but steadily from the beginning year. (See table 15.1.) As more students come to college with existing Twitter accounts, the numbers should increase and continue to grow the online conversation. As more students have come to college with active Twitter accounts, encouraging students to participate has become easier. As a number of faculty have begun to provide course credit for participation, numbers have also grown, but an area for significant improvement is in convincing students to regularly participate in the Twitter dialog even when they are not given course credit for their interactions.

Table 15.1. Use of Twitter

Academic Year	2010–2011	2011–2012	2012–2013	Total
Followers	209	167	69	445
Tweets	54	87	66	207

Talking Democracy

Fort Hays State University's KFHS broadcasting channel has been home to another popular civic engagement tool, a weekly television show called *Talking Democracy*. Every week, *Talking Democracy* focuses on a new guest who discusses a topic with the host in an effort to begin a diverse conversation based on current events. Popular guests have included state representatives discussing current events at the Kansas Statehouse, and representatives from the FHSU Student Government Association discussing student allocations and current bills on the floor.

Talking Democracy's Twitter feed is an important tool for the broadcasting crew before, during, and after each episode. Just like any other television program, *Talking Democracy* can receive feedback from its viewers regarding topics and guests. Viewers and followers submitted questions for guests, show topics, and guideline ideas for a student government debate televised by *Talking Democracy*. Park and colleagues show that the key to introducing new participants to politics that are not already interested is by focusing on their desire for entertainment and connecting it to political content.[45] While official ratings are not available for *Talking Democracy*, through the two dominant cable companies in western Kansas, the program is available in more than one hundred thousand homes throughout the region.

Times Talk

One of the most popular civic engagement programs at Fort Hays State University is the ADP's Times Talk. Times Talk is a program that actually began at FHSU and, due to its success, has spread to other universities throughout the country (such as Georgia College and the University of Missouri in St. Louis). Times Talk is an on-campus public forum for any student, staff or faculty member, or member of the public to enjoy hearing different perspectives on current events highlighted in recent editions of the *New York Times*. The ADP invites any individual or group of individuals to present information about topics that have included elections, the environment, and prescription drug use. The presentations are conducted in comfortable settings in which members of the audience are welcome to listen, take notes, ask questions and begin conversations about anything related to the topic. Pettingill's work suggests that such events are strong drivers of civic engagement.[46]

In 2011, ADP began collaborating with FHSU's Forsyth Library, experimenting with technology that would allow Times Talk presentations to reach those who are unable to attend the event in person. These viewers are able to dial in using a method similar to a conference call in order to ask their own questions. Virtual students could not only watch the Times Talk; now they could actively participate by making points ahead of time and asking questions during the presentations. Times Talk presentations have had great success in drawing participants and viewers. (See table 15.2.) During a period when fewer Times Talk were offered in 2012 participation declined, but when the talks are offered regularly, FHSU routinely draws more than three hundred in-person participants each academic year. Times Talk has become one of FHSU's most attended civic engagement events, and therefore ADP has begun leveraging Times Talk participation to increase participation in other areas such as encouraging participants to live-tweet Times Talk to integrate Tiger Talkback better into the events.

Table 15.2.   Times Talk Attendance

Academic Year	2010–2011	2011–2012	2012–2013	Total
Attendance	340	170	361	871

Be Heard: Online Voter Registration

Fort Hays State University knows that the most direct way to be civically engaged is to participate in local, statewide, and nationwide elections. In order to do this, citizens must be registered to vote. The Be Heard Project is an American Democracy Project initiative that aims to convey the importance of being a responsible citizen by participating in elections. Before Election Day, ADP provides materials that help students register, including registration cards and information about what to bring to the polls, such as ID cards. The Be Heard Project is crucial because one of the most common reasons students are not registered to vote is because they are unaware of the registration process and often think it is too difficult. ADP helps to ease the confusion by answering questions and providing helpful voting tips.

Online voter registration has been a difficult transition, but the FHSU ADP webpage included online voter registration links since 2008 and for 2010 expanded to include an effort to engage online students in the administration and promotion of a mock presidential election on campus. Research indicates that aggressive outreach campaigns combining in-person and social media components are up to two times as effective at mobilizing turnout as in-person only effort.[47] Through the last three election cycles, a significant number of students have participated in FHSU Be Heard drives, with more than half of the new-student population signing up to vote during the last two presidential election years and just over half that number during the 2010 midterms. (See table 15.3.)

Table 15.3.　Be Heard Project New Registrants

Year	2008	2010	2012	Total
New registrants	600	291	518	1409

Mock Elections

Along with ensuring students understand their right to vote and the need to become registered, the ADP at FHSU also aims to help students understand the importance of actually *exercising* those rights. One of the many ways this takes place is through mock elections held in election years. Becoming a registered voter is only the first step in the civic engagement process. The mock elections are available both online and through traditional paper ballots, and results are announced via campus-wide email. The email includes the results of the election and the number of total voters. Participating in the process of casting a ballot provides an important insight to students; it allows students to realize the importance of practicing responsible civic engagement. A small number of students participated in the initial 2012 mock election (fifty-two voters). Although this number seems insignificant, the process is constantly being reviewed and improved, keeping in mind the goal of gaining substantially more participants over the next few years—something FHSU has experienced with the creation and improvement of other similar activities.

Blogging in the Classroom

Web 2.0 is used throughout FHSU in a number of ways. Several classes use online blogging as a form of regular classwork. Typically, the classes that use blogging focus on current issues, including politics, international affairs, and the environment. The blogs serve multiple purposes. First, they enhance the knowledge of current affairs. Students writing blogs usually need to have a deep understanding of the topic. Second, they enhance communication. With blogging comes conversation. In many classes, students receive grades for their blog posts; additionally, they might receive grades based on their responses to posts of other classmates. This ensures that students not only understand what they are writing about, but that they are also able to communicate different perspectives to each other. Finally, they help students gain a better understanding of their own thoughts and opinions about issues. Engaging in important discussions allows students to develop creative insights and diverse opinions about the world around them.

Twitter

Twitter is an important tool in the FHSU Web 2.0 civic engagement effort. Although not all of the students at FHSU currently use a Twitter account, using Twitter is becoming a more popular tool in many areas of campus, including ADP events and student government events. Some of the most prominent examples of the use of Twitter include the Tiger Talkback weekly questions, student government elections, the student government allocations process, and even pre-enrollment and new student orientation.

The idea to use Twitter for Tiger Talkback discussions produced the strongest results during the 2011–2012 school year when a television monitor was mounted in a popular corner of the Memorial Union. The screen is available for students, faculty, and visitors to view the conversations taking place on the Tiger Talkback feed, making it easy to follow the tweets of the Twitter users.

During the 2012 student government elections, Twitter became increasingly popular due to the competitive nature of the election. For the first time in several years, the race for president/vice president was contested, allowing the students the chance to really get to know the candidates before making the important decision at the polls. Two very different debates took place between the candidates: one took place in front of a very large crowd of interested students and the second on a special edition of *Talking Democracy*. Both debates yielded an opportunity for the students to be involved in the campaign process, highlighting key issues and asking their own questions of the candidates. Between Twitter, Facebook groups, and the on-campus efforts of the candidates and their supporters, more than seven hundred students cast their votes for their student leaders, the highest turnout in years.

Other Social Media

Students around the world have turned to social media as a main form of civic engagement, which means that institutions such as FHSU must continue their efforts to reach out to students in a positive way, encouraging them to get more involved. Facebook pages, Twitter accounts, blogs, and YouTube channels have been created to connect with students. Students and faculty have contributed more than 259 likes to the ADP Facebook page since 2010–2011 (see table 15.4). The ADP blog and Facebook pages serve to keep students up-to-date with different events sponsored around campus and with other ADP events around the country. Students can participate in Tiger Talkback discussions both on Facebook and Twitter, and keep up with recent discussions on the blog as well. As mentioned earlier, regular growth in event participation has been used to leverage increasing participation in online engagement events such as Tiger Talkback.

Table 15.4.   Facebook Interactions

Year	2011	2012	2013	Total
Likes	115	82	62	259

CONCLUSION

Although providing students with the tools to participate in civic engagement activities is crucial, higher education institutions must strive to do more. Students must know about the elements and make the conscious decision to participate. Select groups of faculty that have added blogging, Twitter, or Facebook to their courses have helped expand the presence of Web 2.0 tools on campus and off. Posters and regular notes on the student web portal have helped as well.

Students are now responding to online tools as a part of their collegiate lives. At first students seemed to bristle at participating in social media as part of their learning process. However, the ubiquity of Web 2.0 has made avoidance all the more difficult for students. As a result, a cadre of students regularly participate in all of the Web 2.0 activities on campus.

It has become evident that Web 2.0 is not only useful in the extracurricular lives of students; it has also become increasingly crucial in the classroom environment. It is also obvious that the Web 2.0 tools available today are not at the apex of their development. Web 2.0 tools are constantly evolving, undergoing revision, improvement, and becoming more accessible. For the modern mobile student wishing to become more informed and engaged is easier than it has ever been. Encouraging students to become more engaged has been the main focus of civic engagement efforts in institutions like FHSU. The world is becoming smaller thanks to the ease of communication and accessibility of information, but it is also becoming more complex as today's great web developers continue to improve the way people connect and interact. The phenomenon of Web 2.0 has led to worldwide revolutions, allowing citizens to improve the way they engage in the political process, and it is not about to stop anytime soon.

FHSU has developed a wide system of Web 2.0 tools, so that any student with a free moment and an urge to participate has an avenue. The result is a more engaged campus that overcomes divisions between in-person and online students while encouraging the skills of critical thinking, community, media literacy, and civic leadership that form the core of community-engaged institutions.

NOTES

1. Michael X. Delli Carpini, and Steven Keeter, *What Americans Know about Politics and Why It Matters* (New Haven, CT: Yale University Press, 1996); Melvin Dubnick, "Nurturing Civic Lives: Developmental Perspectives on Civic Education," *PS: Political Science and Politics* 36, no. 2 (2003).

2. William Galston, "Civic Education and Political Participation," *PS: Political Science and Politics* 37, no. 2 (April 2004).

3. Henry Milner, *Civic Literacy: How Informed Citizens Make Democracy Work* (Nashua, NH: UPNE, 2002); Jeremy Brooke Straughn and Angie L. Andriot, "Education, Civic Patriotism, and Democratic Citizenship: Unpacking the Education Effect on Political Involvement," *Sociological Forum* 26, no. 3 (September 2011).

4. Stephen Deloach and Steven Greenlaw, "Do Electronic Discussions Create Critical Thinking Spillovers?" *Contemporary Economic Policy* 23, no. 1 (February 2005); Ari Kohen, "Teaching Political Theory with Twitter: The Pedagogy of Social Networking," in Robert Glover and Daniel Tagliarina, eds., *Teaching Politics beyond the Book: Film, Texts, and New Media in the Classroom* (New York, NY: Continuum, 2009); Derrick Cogburn and Fatima K. Espinoza-Vasquez, "From Networked Nominee to Networked Nation: Examining the Impact of Web 2.0 and Social Media on Political Participation and Civic Engagement in the 2008 Obama Campaign," *Journal of Political Marketing* 10, no. 1–2 (2011); Indira Nair, Marie Norman, G. Richard Tucker, and Amy Burkert, "The Challenge of Global Literacy: An Ideal Opportunity for Liberal Professional Education," *Liberal Education* 98, no.1 (Winter 2012).

5. For further explanation of the American Democracy Project, see Cecilia Orphan, "About ADP," American Association of State Colleges and Universities, October 11, 2003, http://www.aascu.org/programs/ADP/ (accessed September 19, 2011).

6. "eCitizenship: New Tools, New Strategies, New Spaces," American Association of State Colleges and Universities, http://www.aascu.org/programs/adp/eCitizen ship/ (accessed July 27, 2014); "Global Challenges," American Association of State Colleges and Universities, http://www.aascu.org/GlobalChallenges/ (accessed July 27, 2014).

7. See Curtis Brungardt, "ADP at FHSU," 2008, http://www.fhsu.edu/adp/ (accessed July 26, 2014).

8. See Cheryl Hofstetter Duffy, "Going Public with the Research Paper," *Ohio Journal of English Language Arts* 51, no. 1 (Winter/Spring 2011); C. L. Brungardt, et al., "Improving, Expanding, and Institutionalizing Civic Learning and Community Engagement," NASPA Civic Learning and Democratic Engagement (CLDE) Conference, Philadelphia, PA, June 2013.

9. Aaron Smith, Lee Rainie, and Kathryn Zikuhr, "College Students and Technology," July 9, 2011, http://www.pewinternet.org/Reports/2011/College-students -and-technology/Report.aspx (accessed February 1, 2014).

10. Joseph Kahne et al., "Digital Opportunities for Civic Education," in David E. Campbell et al., eds., *Making Civics Count: Citizenship Education for a New Generation* (Cambridge: Harvard University Press, 2012).

11. John Orlando, "Wikipedia in the Classroom: Tips for Effective Use," *Faculty Focus*, May 26, 2010, http://www.facultyfocus.com/articles/effective-teaching-strat egies/wikipedia-in-the-classroom-tips-for-effective-use/.

12. Heather Havenstein, "Wiki Becomes Textbook in Boston College Classroom," *Computerworld*, August 15, 2007, http://www.computerworld.com/s/article/9030802/Wiki_becomes_textbook_in_Boston_College_classroom?taxonomyId =16&intsrc=hm_topic (accessed October 2, 2011).

13. James Youniss, "How to Enrich Civic Education and Sustain Democracy," in David E. Campbell et al., *Making Civics Count: Citizenship Education for a New Generation* (Cambridge: Harvard Education Press, 2012).

14. Ari Kohen, "Teaching Political Theory with Twitter."

15. Erin Gemmil and Michael Peterson, "Technology Use among College Students: Implications for Student Affairs Professionals," *NASPA Journal* 43, no. 2 (July 2006).

16. Mark Bauerlein, "The Peer Bubble," in *Civic Education and the Future of American Citizenship*, eds. E. K. Busch and J. W. White (Lanham, Lexington Books, 2013).

17. Chapman Rackaway, "Video Killed the Textbook Star?: Use of Multimedia Supplements to Enhance Student Learning," *Journal of Political Science Education* 8, vol. 2 (2012).

18. See Steve Yuen and Hsiu-Ting Hung, "Exploring the Use of Social Networking in the College Classroom," paper presented at the Society for Information Technology & Teacher Education, 2010.

19. Susanna Davis, "What Web 2.0 Looks Like in My Classroom," *Teaching College English: The Glory and Challenges*, http://www.teachingcollegeenglish

.com/2011/02/25/what-web-2–0-looks-like-in-my-classroom/ (accessed September 20, 2011).

20. Roger Burrows and David Beer, "Sociology and, of and in Web 2.0: Some Initial Considerations," *Sociological Research Online* 12, no. 5 (2007).

21. Josh Pasek et al., "Realizing the Social Internet? Online Social Networking Meets Offline Civic Engagement," *Journal of Information Technology & Politics* 6 (September 30, 2007); W. Lance Bennett et al., "Communicating Civic Engagement: Contrasting Models of Citizenship in the Youth Web Sphere," *Journal of Communication* 61, no. 5 (October 2011).

22. Louis Leung, "User-generated Content on the Internet: An Examination of Gratifications, Civic Engagement and Psychological Empowerment," *New Media & Society* 11, no. 8 (December 2009).

23. Derrick Cogburn and Fatima K. Espinoza-Vasquez, "From Networked Nominee to Networked Nation.

24. Bryan Lowry, "S&P Downgrades Kansas Bond Rating; Brownback Pushes Back," *The Wichita Eagle*, August 7, 2014, http://www.kansas.com/2014/08/06/3584491/sp -downgrades-kansas-bond-rating.html (accessed August 7, 2014).

25. See "Slideshare," LinkedIn Corporation, 2014, http://www.slideshare.net/ (accessed July 27 2014); "Let's Get You Set Up with Google Drive," Google Drive, http://drive.google.com (accessed July 27 2014); "Be a Great Presenter: Create Zooming Presentations That Make You More Engaging and Memorable," Prezi Inc., 2014, http://www.prezi.com (accessed July 27 2014); "PIXLR," Autodesk, http:// pixlr.com (accessed July 27 2014); "PicMonkey: Photo Editing Made of Win," Pic-Monkey, 2014, http://picmonkey.com (accessed July 27 2014).

26. Soraya Mehdizadeh, "Self-Presentation 2.0: Narcissism and Self-Esteem on Facebook," *Cyberpsychology, Behavior, and Social Networking* 13, no. 4 (2010).

27. Robert Putnam, *Bowling Alone: The Collapse and Revival of American Community* (New York, NY: Simon & Schuster, 2000).

28. Cecilia Orphan, "The American Democracy Project," http://www.aascu.org/ programs/ADP/. Accessed July 27 2014.

29. Putnam, *Bowling Alone*, 23.

30. Leonard Springer et al., "Effects of Small-Group Learning on Undergraduates in Science, Mathematics, Engineering, and Technology: A Meta-Analysis," *Review of Educational Research* 69, no. 1 (Spring 1999): 35.

31. Putnam, *Bowling Alone*, 266.

32. Molly Wasko and Samer Faraj, "Why Should I Share?: Examining Social Capital and Knowledge Contribution in Electronic Networks of Practice," *MIS Quarterly: Management Information Systems* 29 (2005).

33. Evgeny Morozov, *The Net Delusion: The Dark Side of Internet Freedom* (New York, NY: Public Affairs, 2011).

34. Barry Wellman et al., "Does the Internet Increase, Decrease, or Supplement Social Capital?: Social Networks, Participation, and Community Commitment," *American Behavioral Scientist* 45, no. 3 (November 2001).

35. Ulrike Pfeil et al., "Age Differences in Online Social Networking—A Study of User Profiles and the Social Capital Divide among Teenagers and Older Users in MySpace," *Computers in Human Behavior* 25 (2009).

36. Gert Jan Hofstede et al., "Why Simulation Games Work-In Search of the Active Substance: A Synthesis," *Simulation and Gaming* 41, no. 6 (December 2010).

37. Nicole Ellison et al., "The Benefits of Facebook 'Friends:' Social Capital and College Students' Use of Online Social Network Sites," *Journal of Computer-Mediated Communication* 12, no. 4 (July 2007): 1.

38. Michael Neblo et al., "Who Wants to Deliberate—And Why?" *The American Political Science Review* 104, no. 3 (August 2010).

39. Homero Gil de Zuniga et al., "Social Media Use for News and Individuals' Social Capital, Civic Engagement and Political Participation," *Journal of Computer-Mediated Communication* 17, no. 3 (April 2012).

40. Diana Mutz and Lori Young, "Communication and Public Opinion: Plus Ça Change?" *The Public Opinion Quarterly* 75, no. 5 (2011).

41. Julie Hatcher, "Assessing Civic Knowledge and Engagement," *New Directions for Institutional Research* 149 (Spring 2011).

42. Peter Dahlgren, "Public Intellectuals, Online Media, and Public Spheres: Current Realignments," *International Journal of Politics, Culture, and Society* 25, no 4 (December 2012).

43. "Democracy Plaza," The Trustees of Indiana University, https://dplaza.usg.iupui.edu/Default.aspx (accessed July 27, 2014).

44. "TU Freedom Square," Towson University, http://tufreedomsquare.com/ (accessed July 27, 2014).

45. Namsu Park et al., "Being Immersed in Social Networking Environment: Facebook Groups, Uses and Gratifications, and Social Outcomes," *Cyberpsychology & Behavior* 12, no. 6 (December 2009).

46. Linsay Pettingill, "Engagement 2.0? How the New Digital Media Can Invigorate Civic Engagement," *Good Work Project Report Series,* no. 50, https://www.thegoodproject.org/pdf/50-Engagement-2.0.pdf (accessed October 19, 2011).

47. Allison Dale and Aaron Strauss, "Don't Forget to Vote: Text Message Reminders as a Mobilization Tool," *American Journal of Political Science* 53, no. 4 (October 2011).

BIBLIOGRAPHY

American Association of State Colleges and Universities. "eCitizenship: New Tools, New Strategies, New Spaces." Accessed March 10, 2014. http://www.aascu.org/programs/adp/eCitizenship/.

American Association of State Colleges and Universities. "Global Challenges." Accessed March 10, 2014. http://www.aascu.org/GlobalChallenges/.

Bauerlein, Mark. "The Peer Bubble." In *Civic Education and the Future of American Citizenship.* Edited by E. K. Busch and J. W. White. Lanham, Lexington Books, 2005.

Bennett, W. Lance, Chris Wells, and Deen Freelon. 2011. "Communicating Civic Engagement: Contrasting Models of Citizenship in the Youth Web Sphere." *Journal of Communication* 61 (2011): 835–856.

Brungardt, Curtis. "ADP at FHSU." 2008. Accessed July 26, 2014. http://www.fhsu.edu/adp/.

Brungardt, C. L, J. Arensdorf, C. J. Brungardt, B. Bruner, and R. Ochs. "Improving, Expanding, and Institutionalizing Civic Learning and Community Engagement." NASPA Civic Learning and Democratic Engagement (CLDE) Conference, Philadelphia, PA, June 2013.

Burrows, Roger, and David Beer. "Sociology and, of and in Web 2.0: Some Initial Considerations." *Sociological Research Online* 12 (2007).

Cogburn, Derrick, and Fatima K. Espinoza-Vasquez. "From Networked Nominee to Networked Nation: Examining the Impact of Web 2.0 and Social Media on Political Participation and Civic Engagement in the 2008 Obama Campaign." *Journal of Political Marketing* 10 (2011).

Dahlgren, Peter. "Public Intellectuals, Online Media, and Public Spheres: Current Realignments." *International Journal of Politics, Culture, and Society* 25 (2012).

Dale, Allison, and Aaron Strauss. 2011. "Don't Forget to Vote: Text Message Reminders as a Mobilization Tool," *American Journal of Political Science* 53 (2011).

Davis, Susanna. "What Web 2.0 Looks Like in My Classroom" *Teaching College English: The Glory and Challenges.* Accessed September 20, 2011. http://www.teachingcollegeenglish.com/2011/02/25/what-web-2-0-looks-like-in-my-classroom/.

Delli Carpini, Michael X., and Steven Keeter. *What Americans Know about Politics and Why It Matters*. New Haven, CT: Yale University Press, 1996.

Deloach, Stephen, and Steven Greenlaw. "Do Electronic Discussions Create Critical Thinking Spillovers?" *Contemporary Economic Policy* 23 (2005): 149–163.

Dubnick, Melvin. (2003) "Nurturing Civic Lives: Developmental Perspectives on Civic Education." *PS: Political Science and Politics* 36 (2): 253–255.

Duffy, Cheryl Hofstetter. "Going Public with the Research Paper." *Ohio Journal of English Language Arts* 51, no. 1 (Winter/Spring 2011): 39–43.

Ehrlich, Thomas. *Educating Citizens: Preparing America's Undergraduates for Lives of Moral and Civic Responsibility*. New York: Jossey Bass, 2003.

Ellison, Nicole, Charles Steinfeld, and Cliff Lampe. "The Benefits of Facebook 'Friends:' Social Capital and College Students' Use of Online Social Network Sites." *Journal of Computer-Mediated Communication* 12 (2007): 1143–1168.

Galston, William. "Civic Education and Political Participation." *PS: Political Science and Politics* 37, no. 2 (April 2004): 263–266.

Gemmil, Erin and Michael Peterson. "Technology Use among College Students: Implications for Student Affairs Professionals." *NASPA Journal* 43, no. 2 (2006): 280–300.

Gil de Zuniga, Homero, Nakwon Jung, and Sebastian Valenzuela. "Social Media Use for News and Individuals' Social Capital, Civic Engagement and Political Participation." *Journal of Computer-Mediated Communication* 17, no. 3 (April 2012): 319–336.

Goldsmith, Steven. "Service 2.0 and Cities." *National Civic Review* 97, no. 3 (2008): 52–55.

Hatcher, Julie. "Assessing Civic Knowledge and Engagement." *New Directions for Institutional Research* 149 (Spring 2011): 81–92.

Havenstein, Heather. "Wiki Becomes Textbook in Boston College Classroom." *Computer World* (August 15, 2007). Accessed October 2, 2011. http://www.computer

world.com/s/article/9030802/Wiki_becomes_textbook_in_Boston_College_class
room?taxonomyId=16&intsrc=hm_topic.

Hofstede, Gert, Leon De Caluwe, and Vincent Peters. "Why Simulation Games
Work-In Search of the Active Substance: A Synthesis." *Simulation and Gaming*
41, no. 6 (December 2010): 824–843.

Kahne, Joseph, Jacqueline Ullman and Ellen Middaugh. "Digital Opportunities for
Civic Education." In *Making Civics Count: Citizenship Education for a New Gen-
eration.* Edited by David E. Campbell, Meira Levinson, and Frederick M. Hess.
Cambridge: Harvard University Press, 2012.

Kohen, Ari. "Teaching Political Theory with Twitter: The Pedagogy of Social Networking. " In *Teaching Politics beyond the Book: Film, Texts, and New Media in
the Classroom.* Edited by Robert Glover and Daniel Tagliarina. New York, NY:
Continuum, 2009.

Leung, Louis. "User-generated Content on the Internet: An Examination of Gratifications, Civic Engagement and Psychological Empowerment." *New Media & Society*
11, no. 8 (2009): 1327–1347.

Mehdizadeh, Soraya. "Self-Presentation 2.0: Narcissism and Self-Esteem on Facebook,"
Cyberpsychology, Behavior, and Social Networking 13, no. 4 (August 2010): 357–364.

Milner, Henry. *Civic Literacy: How Informed Citizens Make Democracy Work.*
Nashua, NH: UPNE, 2002.

Morozov, Evgeny. *The Net Delusion: The Darks Side of Internet Freedom* (Public
Affairs: New York, NY: 2012).

Mutz, Diana, and Lori Young. 2011. "Communication and Public Opinion: Plus Ça
Change?" *The Public Opinion Quarterly* 75, no. 5 (2011): 1018–1044.

Nair, Indira, Marie Norman, G. Richard Tucker, and Amy Burkert. "The Challenge of
Global Literacy: An Ideal Opportunity for Liberal Professional Education." *Liberal
Education* 98, no.1 (Winter 2012): 56–61.

Neblo, Michael, Kevin Esterling, Ryan Kennedy, David Lazer, and Anand Sokhey.
"Who Wants to Deliberate—And Why?" *The American Political Science Review*
104, no. 3 (2010): 566–583.

Orlando, John. 2010. "Wikipedia in the Classroom: Tips for Effective Use." *Faculty
Focus.* Accessed July 27, 2014. http://www.facultyfocus.com/articles/effective
-teaching-strategies/wikipedia-in-the-classroom-tips-for-effective-use/.

Orphan, Cecilia. "The American Democracy Project," American Association of State
Colleges and Universities. 2003. Accessed September 19, 2011. http://www.aascu
.org/programs/ADP/.

Park, Namsu, Kerk Kee, and Sebastian Valenzuela. "Being Immersed in Social
Networking Environment: Facebook Groups, Uses and Gratifications, and Social
Outcomes." *Cyberpsychology & Behavior* 12, no. 6 (December 2009): 729–733.

Pasek, Josh, eian more, and Daniel Romer. "Realizing the Social Internet? Online
Social Networking Meets Offline Civic Engagement." *Journal of Information
Technology & Politics* 6 (2009): 197–215.

Pettingill, Lindsay. "Engagement 2.0? How the New Digital Media Can Invigorate
Civic Engagement." *Good Work Project Report Series.* no. 50, Accessed October
19, 2011. https://www.thegoodproject.org/pdf/50-Engagement-2.0.pdf.

Pfeil, Ulrike, Raj Arjan, Panayiotis Zaphiris. "Age Differences in Online Social Networking—A Study of User Profiles and the Social Capital Divide among Teenagers and Older Users in MySpace." *Computers in Human Behavior* 25 (2009): 643–665.

Putnam, Robert. *Bowling Alone: The Collapse and Revival of American Community.* New York, NY: Simon & Schuster, 2000.

Rackaway, Chapman. "Video Killed the Textbook Star?: Use of Multimedia Supplements to Enhance Student Learning." *Journal of Political Science Education* 8:2 (2012): 189–200.

Smith, Aaron, Lee Rainie, and Kathryn Zikuhr. 2011. "College Students and Technology." July 9, 2011. http://www.pewinternet.org/Reports/2011/College-students -and-technology/Report.aspx (accessed February 1, 2014).

Springer, Leonard, Mary Elizabeth Stanne, and Samuel S. Donovan. "Effects of Small-Group Learning on Undergraduates in Science, Mathematics, Engineering, and Technology: A Meta-Analysis." *Review of Educational Research* 69 (Spring 1999): 21–51.

Straughn, Jeremy Brooke, and Angie L. Andriot. "Education, Civic Patriotism, and Democratic Citizenship: Unpacking the Education Effect on Political Involvement." *Sociological Forum* 26, no. 3 (September 2011): 556–580.

Wasko, Molly, and Samer Faraj. "Why Should I Share?: Examining Social Capital and Knowledge Contribution in Electronic Networks of Practice," *MIS Quarterly: Management Information Systems* 29, no. 1 (2005): 35–57.

Wellman, Barry, Annabel Haase, James Witte, and Keith Hampton. "Does the Internet Increase, Decrease, or Supplement Social Capital?: Social Networks, Participation, and Community Commitment." *American Behavioral Scientist* 45, no. 3 (November 2001): 436–455.

Youniss, James. "How to Enrich Civic Education and Sustain Democracy," In *Making Civics Count: Citizenship Education for a New Generation.* Edited by David E. Campbell, Meira Levinson, and Frederick M. Hess. Cambridge: Harvard Education Press, 2012.

Yuen, Steve, and Hsiu-Ting Hung. "Exploring the Use of Social Networking in the College Classroom." Paper presented at the Society for Information Technology & Teacher Education, 2010.

Chapter Sixteen

Teaching Local

*Civic Engagement & Local Government**

Mike Yawn

Numerous studies reveal that the American public fails to live up to the lofty ideals of democratic theorists, with individuals falling short on measures of civic knowledge and civic engagement.[1] While most of these studies focus on citizens' knowledge of national government and procedures, the few studies addressing civic engagement at the local level reveal even more dispiriting findings.[2] In short, citizens increasingly show little engagement at all levels of government.

In response to these studies, various programs have been implemented in the hopes of reversing this trend. One such effort is the "citizen academy," a program initiated by local governments to promote knowledge of local government, stronger relations between elected officials and citizens, and local leadership.[3] This research employs an experimental design to examine the impact of one "citizen academy" offered by Walker County in Texas. The results indicate such programs have the potential to increase participants' knowledge about local government, enhance participants' social capital, and, more anecdotally, develop a core of mid-level activists at the local level.

LITERATURE

The importance of citizen engagement and education have long been central to democratic theory. For John Stuart Mill, the "practical part of the political education" freed people from the "narrow circle of personal and family selfishness," allowing them to comprehend and manage "joint interests" and "joint

---

*This is a continuation of my research on citizen academies. For an initial investigation of the subject, see "Citizens Academies: Promoting Civic Education, Civic Engagement, and Social Capital," *The Midsouth Political Science Review* Volume 12 Number 1 (2012).

concerns."[4] Writing more recently, Michael Sandel echoes and emphasizes the importance of *community* education, arguing that proper self-governance "requires a knowledge of public affairs and also a sense of belonging, a concern for the whole, a moral bond with the community whose fate is at stake."[5]

Empiricists, on the other hand, have found little evidence that the American public has the type of "knowledge of public affairs" democratic theory demands. A recent report sponsored by the American Political Science Association and the Brookings Institution, for example, concludes that today's citizens "participate in public affairs less frequently, with less knowledge and enthusiasm, in fewer venues, and less equally than is healthy for a vibrant democratic polity."[6] This is especially disturbing because political knowledge correlates with political sophistication, increased levels of political engagement, enhanced political efficacy, and a respect for democratic values.[7] Moreover, a person's perceived knowledge enhances her persuasiveness on matters of vote choice or even, perhaps, on democratic orientations.[8]

Political knowledge also correlates with social capital, a topic of ever-increasing salience to scholars and to administrators interested in "citizen academies." On the individual level, social capital increases trust in government and in others and enhances rates of political participation.[9] On a macrolevel, social capital is associated with government efficiency, enhanced representation and accountability, and overall government performance.[10]

Unfortunately, most social capital studies indicate it, like civic knowledge, is on the decline. But it is perhaps this decline that has spurred an increase of scholarly interest in civic education, particularly at the secondary and higher-education levels.[11] In addition to the long-standing civics classes of government or social studies, classes or programs promoting experiential learning, internships, and community service appear to be increasing in high schools and on campuses across the United States.[12]

Few measures of the impact of civic education programs on nonstudent populations exist. Public administrators initiated most nonstudent programs. These programs are, in turn, studied by public administrators for the purpose of improving the efficacy of the program's future iterations. Their analyses offer a list of best practices to guide the development of programs designed to engage the general public in, typically, local government-related programs.[13]

Interestingly, the principles or "best practices" adopted by public administrators in implementing these programs correspond with some of the leading scholarly works on civic education. According to the civic voluntarism model offered by Verba, Schlozman, and Brady, probably the most widely accepted of the civic engagement models, participation depends largely on three related variables: interest, recruitment, and resources, with the latter including time, money, and skills.[14] In addition, such work tends to overlap broadly with the work of Delli Carpini and Keeter, who argue that Americans are in particular need of content knowledge relating to (1) the rules of the game (2) the substance of politics, and (3) people and parties.[15] The present work combines both theoretical and applied approaches, using experimental methods to examine the impact of a government-initiated program designed to promote civic education.

DEVELOPMENT AND IMPLEMENTATION OF A CITIZENS ACADEMY PROGRAM

Citizen Academies go by different names. In Decatur, Georgia, it is "Decatur 101." In Hickory, North Carolina, the program goes by "Hickory Neighborhood College." And for the town of La Plata, Maryland, it was the ungainly "Citizen's Academy for La Plata's Water and Sewer Systems" (the program closed in 2009 owing to lack of interest).[16]

The program formats also vary. Generally, the programs include 5–10 meetings, with enrollment frequently capped at 20–30 participants. As one program coordinator shared, "We want individuals to have the chance to participate, so we keep it small."[17] The smaller size also lowers the cost. Most of the programs are free to citizens, with the costs covered by either sponsors or the local government.

For city government programs, topics often include government structure, finance, public works, public safety, parks and recreation, economic development, and the like. Counties are less likely to offer such programs, but according to one county program director, they are more needed at that level:

> Cities have an identity—Fire trucks, a police force, garbage trucks. Counties have a wider variety of services, but they aren't seen as *county* services. The jail. Courts. Law enforcement. We don't have the same kind of visible identity. And in our case, people ask, "what are we getting for our tax dollars?" And our county program allows us to explain that to them.

As the above reflection suggests, county governments focus on slightly different topics than cities (e.g., commissioners' court, law enforcement, and voter registration).

Whether city or county, the programs emphasize practical concerns: promoting transparency; increasing residents' knowledge of local government operations, resources, and constraints; recruiting for boards and commissions or other leadership roles; strengthening community relations; and the like. The "Citizen Academy" that serves as the direct subject of this research was originally conceived as a city program. In fact, it was initiated by the Com-

munity Services Director of a Texas city and was successfully operated for
two years, before staff and council turnover jeopardized the program.

At that point, it was shifted to the county level and I, along with county
staff and volunteers, continued the program. The program, "County U,"
was offered annually from 2009 to 2012. Twenty participants attended five
weekly sessions addressing (1) County Overview and Commissioners Court
(2) District Attorney and the Justice System (3) Administration and Non-
Profits (4) Public Safety, and (5) Emergency Services. The program included
a total of 12.5 contact hours, incorporated various presentations by county
officials, question-and-answer sessions, group activities, interactive lessons
with the presenters, and tours of county facilities and local venues. The sessions also integrated informal dinners, allowing citizens to dine with the
presenters—mostly elected officials.

Over the four-year period the program was offered, more than ninety
individuals enrolled. The participants were split largely between males and
females, retired and working, student and local resident, and the age range
spanned from eighteen to eighty. This diversity offers promising opportunities for bridging social capital, which Putnam describes as "especially valuable" for democracies.[18] Moreover, the participants' interaction, occurring
in governmental facilities over discussions of governmental procedures with
governmental officials, fits La Due Lake and Huckfeldt's definition of "politically relevant social capital" as a "consequence of political expertise and
information that is regularly communicated within an individual's network
of social relations" and which "facilitates political engagement."[19] Moreover,
the program's design was consistent with findings that citizen-centered programs work best when the program curriculum emphasizes "cooperation with
rather than independence from" local government.[20] In short, the program
offered a test of the "best practices" of local citizen academies, while also
providing a natural setting for systematically examining the effect of civic
education on political knowledge and social capital.

DATA AND METHODOLOGY

To assess the effectiveness of "County U," staff created two separate evaluation tools. First, there were anonymous week-to-week surveys assessing
the participants' ratings of speakers, venues, exercises, and topics. These
surveys, administered from 2010 to 2012, allowed the coordinator to tweak
the program annually in response to calls for improvement.

In addition, a diagnostic test of individual participants' knowledge of local government was administered just prior to the first session. Following
the five-week program, participants took a posttest asking the same political

knowledge items as on the pretest. The posttest also included questions concerning the respondents' perceptions about (1) gains in knowledge (2) community connections, and (3) the overall value of the program. This pretest/posttest diagnostic quiz was administered from 2009 to 2012.

Although the questions are limited, the experimental design of the study is elegant and tight. Despite the absence of a control group, there seems little chance that participants' knowledge over the course of the program was affected by external factors. County governments operate in a low-information environment generally, and this is especially true in the county in which the program was administered.[21]

In all pretest/posttest experimental designs, researchers choose between a "testing effect" and an "instrumentation effect." By using the same questions on the diagnostic tests, the testing effect—in which gains reflect participants' skill at the specific test rather than substantive changes—is a possible threat to this study. Given we administered short tests separated by five weeks and many speakers and experiences, the priming or memorization potential was reduced. Moreover, there was little threat of "teaching to the test." While the tests were prepared with a general idea of the broad topics to be addressed each week (e.g., "Fire Safety"), there was no explicit foreknowledge of the points to be stressed by the presenters. In addition, the weekly presenters had no knowledge of the tests, making it impossible for them to direct their presentations to the test material.

Attrition and attendance are also potential threats to the program's internal validity. Regarding attrition, if the uninterested or the difficult-to-teach drop out of the program, the gains of the remaining participants can exaggerate the program's impact. In this case, however, there was little to no attrition, with only two of the ninety-four-plus participants actually dropping out. Regarding attendance, it was high (see the findings section below).

We expect the diagnostic tests—lacking in-depth measures of efficacy, trust, or the richness of individuals' experiences—actually underestimate the full impact of the program, although items tapping respondents' perceptions and qualitative data help fill in such gaps. In terms of external validity, the results presented below are not generalizable to larger populations. We do argue, however, that the results are typical for mid-level and potential mid-level activists at the local level.[22]

FINDINGS

With any program designed to promote engagement, making the program itself engaging is essential. In addition to reviewing objectives, timetables, and topics to avoid (e.g., electioneering) with elected officials, we tracked participants' attendance rates and their evaluations of venues, speakers, and exercises. Attendance was measured by unobtrusively recording who was and was not present at each meeting and then calculating the percentage of classes attended. For the four-year program period, participants attended 92 percent of the meetings, an attendance record likely to produce envy in most college professors. In addition, after each meeting, participants were asked to rate (anonymously) each speaker, venue, and exercise on a five-point scale, with five being the highest rating. These evaluations were incorporated into the program in 2010, 2011, and 2012. Participants were explicitly reminded that the anonymous evaluations were used to improve the program. The results are presented in table 16.1.

Table 16.1. Program Evaluation

Item	Mean (sd)	n[1]
Speaker Ratings	4.67 (.24)	455
Venue Ratings	4.54 (.26)	362
Exercise Ratings	4.53 (.22)	67

[1]Although the number of participants for each program was typically around 20, the sample sizes for these evaluations is much higher. Participants rated multiple speakers, multiple venues, and multiple exercises. In a given year, for example, an average of 18 participants might evaluate 10 different speakers, providing a pooled n of 180. The "Exercise Ratings" has a smaller sample size because there were fewer exercises than speakers or venues, and not all exercises were included on the evaluation form.

As the results indicate, the evaluations were high, with participants rating each category with a score greater than a 4.5. The ratings were generally consistent across the various years, showing uniformly positive scores. Participants were also asked for written comments, and their comments were consistent with the quantitative scores. A majority of comments, for example, highlighted how much participants enjoyed spending time with the presenters.

With its emphasis on hands-on learning, the discussion of timely issues, and collaboration, this citizen academy shares an element of the town hall meeting or "school of democracy."[23] As with all schools, the primary objective is education, and it is no different in "County U." Although the diagnostic surveys differed from year-to-year, eight questions were consistently asked on the pretest and posttest surveys across all four years.

These questions include multiple-choice and open-ended items concerning (1) the duties of the County Clerk (2) the county population (3) the number of County Commissioners (4) the length of the District Attorney's term (5) which officials are elected and unelected (6) the capacity of the county jail (7) the number of firefighters employed by the county, and (8) the size of the county's budget.

As expected, the results indicate participants began with a low level of county government knowledge. Across the program's four years, the mean of pre-test questions answered correctly never reached four. Only one of the seventy-six total respondents answered six of the pretest questions correctly.

These scores changed dramatically, however, following participation in "County U" (see table 16.2). The mean number of correct answers on the posttest typically exceeded six items, and never fell below five. In some years, the number of questions answered correctly on the posttest was more than twice the number answered correctly on the pretest. As the paired T-tests show, the results were significant at the .01 level for each individual year and, *a fortiori*, for the pooled set encompassing all four years.

Table 16.2.   Effects of County U Program on Civic Knowledge

Knowledge Sum	N	Mean, Pre	Mean, Post	Change (se)	T
2009	17	3.00	6.06	3.06 (.30)	10.10***
2010	18	3.11	6.39	3.28 (.40)	8.14***
2011	18	3.67	6.89	3.22 (.29)	11.25***
2012	23	3.00	5.55	2.55 (.32)	7.24***
All Years	**76**	**3.18**	**6.12**	**2.94 (.17)**	**17.26***

***indicates change is significant at the .01 level

To guard against the possibility that these gains reflect the acquisition of isolated facts, staff also asked participants to self-evaluate the effectiveness of the program. Across all four years, participants used a five-point scale to rank their level of agreement with the following statements: (1) "I feel more knowledgeable about the operation of county government following the County U program," and (2) "I feel more connected with my county officials following the County U program." A final item asked respondents to indicate on a four-point scale how "rewarding" the County U program was for them.

Table 16.3.   Perceptions about County U Experience

Item	Scale	Mean (sd)	n
Feel More Knowledgeable	Five-point	4.87 (.34)	77
Feel More Connected	Five-point	4.72 (.48)	78
Rewarding	Four-point	3.95 (.23)	19[1]

[1]The smaller sample size for the "rewarding" question stems from the fact that it was not asked following the 2011 program.

The results, as presented in table 16.3, suggest that at the very least, the participants found the program rewarding, expanded their social connections, and helped them gain knowledge. One hundred percent of the participants marked the highest or second highest value for each of these items. To measure the overall value of the program, participants were also asked to (anonymously) rate the "overall experience" of each week in County U from 2010 to 2012. The mean score for all weeks from 2010 to 2012 was a 4.77, measured on a five-point scale, reinforcing the findings on the "Rewarding" item in table 16.3.

For the coordinators of the program, the program's efficacy in expanding networks and building relationships was especially apparent. For example, in comments following the final session, approximately 75 percent of the participants indicated "meeting officials" or "interacting with the people" were the highlights of the program. Moreover, as the coordinator of the program, I enjoyed a privileged observational position, watching relationships develop across racial, gender, and life-cycle lines. Such relationships forge "bridging social capital" and should be a key component of future research on such programs. Although this study does not systematically track participants' activities following the program, increases in social capital—particularly political capital—increase "the likelihood that an individual will be engaged in politics," suggesting that such programs have the potential of plugging what one program coordinator called "a hole in civic education."[24] Tracking such involvement is a key topic for future research.

Finally, qualitative data strongly supports the quantitative results described above. In addition to the participants' overwhelmingly positive comments about the program, a cursory examination of "County U" rosters indicates that at least eighteen participants took jobs or internships with the city, county, or state government following their completion of the program; another five participants ran for office (with one winning); six enrolled in a graduate program specializing in public administration; and at least seventeen later served in some kind of official capacity (e.g., boards or regular volunteer) for the county government or one of the other organizations incorporated into "County U."

Taken together, the qualitative and quantitative results suggest citizen academies increase civic knowledge considerably and provide rewarding opportunities for civic engagement. This program also provides clues to how similar programs might be implemented and managed to maximize gains in political knowledge and civic engagement.

CONCLUSIONS AND DISCUSSION

"County U" was established with the practical purpose of strengthening community bonds and promoting local leadership,[25] but it was also designed to increase participants' civic knowledge, social capital, and level of civic engagement. Accordingly, it touches on the three types of content knowledge needed by American citizens as identified by Delli Carpini and Keeter: (1) the rules of the game (2) the substance of politics, and (3) people and parties.[26] The material covered in the five weekly sessions and the opportunities for interaction were explicitly set up to provide: (1) information on government structure (i.e., the rules of the game), (2) explanations of local policies, resources, and constraints (i.e., the substance of politics), and (3) the opportunity to connect with elected officials (i.e., people and the parties).

The program also includes the three conditions described in Verba, Schlozman, and Brady's "civic voluntarism" model.[27] The program reinforces and extends participants' already active interest in government, presents opportunities for entry into the political and civic world, and provides the resources and skills needed to participate effectively in local politics.

Residents who sign up for citizen academies undoubtedly differ systematically from typical residents. They are, typically, more interested in local politics and government, have higher rates of civic literacy, and presumably have larger social networks. Accepting these assumptions, however, makes the participants' gains in civic knowledge and social connections all the more impressive. At minimum, the program facilitated the opportunity for greater knowledge and politically relevant interaction. Moreover, studies show additional civic education (albeit at the high school and college level) leads to greater civic engagement even when controlling for preexisting interest, suggesting that the findings here are not sample bound.[28]

Moreover, the program brought a diverse group of potential or actual mid-level activists in touch with each other and with elected officials. Students, local residents, county staff, and elected officials participated together, allowing collaboration to cut across socioeconomic, age, and occupational lines. Diverse subgroups interacted constructively, helping create "bridging social capital" which, in turn, engenders trust and cooperation.[29]

Programs targeting nonschool populations (e.g., "County U") are understudied in the scholarly literature. The results presented here suggest that many of the same gains achieved through school-related programs (e.g., internships, experiential learning, community service, etc.) are achievable in the community. Further, the results indicate drawing participants from a cross-section of the community enhances social capital growth and strengthens relationships between the "town and gown." Programs targeting nonschool populations promote community education, providing, as Michael Sandel advocated, "a knowledge of public affairs and also a sense of belonging, a concern for the whole, a moral bond with the community whose fate is at stake."[30]

NOTES

1. Michael X Delli Carpini and Scott Keeter, *What Americans Know about Politics and Why It Matters* (New Haven: Yale University Press, 1996); Alexander Astin et al., *The American Freshman: Thirty Year Trends* (Los Angeles: Higher Education Research Institute, UCLA, 1997); Richard Niemi and Jane Junn, *Civic Education: What Makes Students Learn* (New Haven: Yale University Press, 1998); Robert Dudley and Alan Gitelson, "Civic Education, Civic Engagement, and Youth Civic Development," *PS: Political Science and Politics* 36 (2003): 263–67.

2. Amy Carter and Ryan Teten, "Assessing Changing Views of the President: Revisiting Greenstein's 'Children and Politics,'" *Presidential Studies Quarterly* 32 (2002): 456; Delli Carpini and Keeter, *What Americans Know*, 78.

3. No full national inventory of these programs exists. Probably the most complete list is offered by the University of North Carolina's School of Government, which seeks "to create a community of local government practitioners working with citizens academies in their communities." They list ninety-one such programs nationally, although many of the programs appear to no longer be operational. The programs can be found at: http://www.sog.unc.edu/programs/citizensacademies.

4. John Stuart Mill, *On Liberty* (Indianapolis: Bobbs-Merrill, 1956), 133–34.

5. Michael Sandel, *Democracy's Discontent: America in Search of a Public Policy* (Cambridge: Harvard University Press, 1996), 5–6.

6. Stephen Macedo et al., *Democracy at Risk: How Political Choices Undermine Citizen Participation, and What We Can Do about It* (Washington, DC: Brookings Institution Press, 2005), 1.

7. Delli Carpini and Keeter, *What Americans Know*; Russell Neuman, *The Paradox of Mass Politics: Knowledge and Opinion in the Mass Electorate* (Cambridge: Harvard University Press, 1986); Jane Junn, "Participation and Political Knowledge," in *Political Participation and American Democracy*, ed. William Crotty (New York: Greenwood Press, 1991); Sidney Verba, Kate L. Schlozman, and Henry E. Brady, *Voice and Equality: Civic Voluntarism in America* (Cambridge: Harvard University Press, 1995); Robert C. Luskin, "Measuring Political Sophistication," *American Journal of Political Science* 31 (1987); Norman Nie, Jane Junn, and Kenneth Stehlik-Barry, *Education and Democratic Citizenship in America* (Chicago: University of Chicago Press, 1996); Angus Campbell, Gerald Gurin, and Warren E. Miller, *The Voter Decides* (New York: Wiley, 1954); George Balch, "Multiple Indicators in Survey Research:

'The Concept of Political Efficacy,'" *Political Methodology* 1 (1974); Samuel Stouffer, *Communism, Conformism, and Civil Liberties* (Garden City: Doubleday, 1955); John L Sullivan, James E. Piereson, and George E. Marcus, *Political Tolerance and American Democracy* (Chicago: University of Chicago Press, 1982); Herbert McCloskey and John Zaller, *The American Ethos: Public Attitudes toward Capitalism and Democracy* (Cambridge: Harvard University Press, 1984); Paul Sniderman et al., "Principled Tolerance and American Values," *British Journal of Political Science* 19 (1989); George E. Marcus et al., *With Malice toward Some: How People Make Civil Liberties Judgments* (New York: Cambridge University Press, 1995).

8. Robert Huckfeldt, P. E. Johnson, and John Sprague, *Political Disagreement: The Survival of Diverse Opinions within Communication Networks* (Cambridge: Cambridge University Press, 2004); Sean Richey, "The Autoregressive Influence of Social Network Political Knowledge on Voting Behavior," *British Journal of Political Science* 38 (2008); Steven Finkel and Howard Ernst, "Civic Education in Post-Apartheid South Africa: Alternative Paths to the Development of Political Knowledge and Democratic Values," *Political Psychology* 26 (2005).

9. Robert Putnam, "Bowling Alone: America's Declining Social Capital," *Journal of Democracy* 6 (1995); John Brehm and Wendy Rahn, "Individual-Level Evidence for the Causes and Consequences of Social Capital," *American Journal of Political Science* 41 (1997); Wendy Rahn and John E. Transue, "Social Trust and Value Change: The Decline of Social Capital in American Youth, 1976–1995" *Political Psychology* 19 (1998); Eric Uslaner, "Social Capital, Television, and the 'Mean World': Trust, Optimism, and Civic Participation," *Political Psychology* 19 (1998); Sean Richey, "Manufacturing Trust: Community Currency and the Creation of Social Capital," *Political Behavior* 1 (2007); Luke Keele, "Social Capital and the Dynamics of Trust in Government," *American Journal of Political Science* 51 (2007); Ronald La Due Lake and Robert Huckfeldt, "Social Capital, Social Networks, and Political Participation," *Political Psychology* 19 (1998); Ellen Quintelier, Dietland Stolle, and Allison Harrell, "Politics in Peer Groups: Exploring the Causal Relationship between Network Diversity and Political Participation," *Political Research Quarterly* 65 (2012).

10. Robert Putnam, *Making Democracy Work: Civic Traditions in Modern Italy* (Princeton: Princeton University Press, 1993); Stephen Knack, "Social Capital and the Quality of Government: Evidence from the States," *American Journal of Political Science* 46 (2002); Johnny Goldfinger and Margaret Ferguson, "Social Capital and Governmental Performance in Large American Cities," *State and Local Government Review* 41 (2009); Alex Inkeles, "Measuring Social Capital and Its Consequences," *Policy Sciences* 33 (2000); Michael Claibourn and Paul S. Martin, "The Third Face of Social Capital: How Membership in Voluntary Associations Improves Policy Accountability," *Political Research Quarterly* 60 (2007).

11. Niemi and Junn, *Civic Education*; Norman Nie and Sunshine Hillygus, "Education and Democratic Citizenship," in *Making Good Citizens: Education and Civil Society*, eds. Diane Ravitch and Joseph P. Viteritti (New Haven: Yale University Press, 2001); Sunshine Hillygus, "The Missing Link: Exploring the Relationship between Higher Education and Political Engagement," *Political Behavior* 27 (2005); Steven Finkel, "Civic Education and the Mobilization of Political Participation in

Developing Democracy," *The Journal of Politics* 64 (2002); Finkel and Ernst, "Civic Education in Post-Apartheid South Africa."

12. Richard Niemi, Mary A. Hepburn, and Chris Chapman, "Community Service by High School Students: A Cure for Civic Ills," *Political Behavior* 22 (2000).

13. For example, Mike Yawn, "Management Minute: Connecting with Citizen Academies," *PM Magazine* 95: 10 (2013).

14. Verba, Schlozman, and Brady, *Voice and Equality*.

15. Delli Carpini and Keeter, *What Americans Know*, 78.

16. Again, for these and other programs see: http://www.sog.unc.edu/programs/citizensacademies.

17. As part of my research on citizen academies, I conducted semistructured and confidential interviews with a half-dozen coordinators of these programs across the country. The unattributed quotes used throughout the research were the products of these confidential interviews.

18. Robert Putnam, "Community-Based Social Capital and Educational Performance," in *Making Good Citizens: Education and Civil Society*, eds. Diane Ravitch and Joseph P. Viteritti (New Haven: Yale University Press, 2001), 86.

19. La Due Lake and Huckfeldt, "Social Capital, Social Networks, and Political Participation," 570.

20. Richard L. Cole, "Citizen Participation in Municipal Politics," *American Journal of Political Science* 19 (1975): 778. See also James Sundquist and David Davis, *Making Federalism Work* (Washington, DC: The Brookings Institution, 1969).

21. A cursory content analysis of the local newspaper over the four years in which the program was administered suggests that, on average, about 2.5 stories were written on county government during the span of a given year's County U program. This typically involved a bullet-point coverage of the Commissioners Court meetings.

22. Although most Citizen Academies do not study changes in participants as systematically as the program described here, my interviews with program coordinators from across the country suggested that their experiences were consistent with the findings presented below. All of the coordinators with whom I spoke expressed satisfaction with their program's effectiveness. Moreover, most coordinators indicated that a significant percentage of the participants emerged as community leaders, particularly with regard to their service on local boards and commissions, a finding consistent with the program studied here.

23. James Bryce, *The American Commonwealth* (New York: MacMillan, 1912): 601.

24. La Due Lake and Huckfeldt, "Social Capital, Social Networks, and Political Participation," 581.

25. For examples of practical concerns with running such programs, see Mike Yawn, "Management Minute: Connecting with Citizen Academies."

26. Delli Carpini and Keeter, *What Americans Know*, 65.

27. Verba, Schlozman, and Brady, *Voice and Equality*.

28. For example, see Pam Conover and Donald Searing, "A Political Socialization Perspective," in *Rediscovering the Democratic Purposes of Education*, ed. L. McDon-

nel, P. Timpane, and R. Benjamin (Lawrence: University of Kansas Press, 2000); Nie
and Hillygus, "Education and Democratic Citizenship"; Hillygus, "The Missing Link."

29. See, for example, Luke Keele, "Social Capital and the Dynamics of Trust in
Government."

30. Sandel, *Democracy's Discontent*, 5–6.

BIBLIOGRAPHY

Astin, Alexander W., Sarah Parrott, William Korn, and Linda Sax. *The American Freshman: Thirty Year Trends.* Los Angeles: Higher Education Research Institute, UCLA, 1997.

Balch, George. "Multiple Indicators in Survey Research: 'The Concept of Political Efficacy.'" *Political Methodology* 1 (1974): 1–43.

Brehm, John, and Wendy Rahn. "Individual-Level Evidence for the Causes and Consequences of Social Capital." *American Journal of Political Science* 41 (1997): 999–1023.

Bryce, James. *The American Commonwealth.* New York: MacMillan, 1912.

Campbell, Angus, Gerald Gurin, and Warren E. Miller. *The Voter Decides.* Evanston, IL: Row, Peterson, 1954.

Carter, Amy, and Ryan Teten. "Assessing Changing Views of the President: Revisiting Greenstein's 'Children and Politics.'" *Presidential Studies Quarterly* 32 (2002): 453–62.

Claibourn, Michael, and Paul S. Martin. "The Third Face of Social Capital: How Membership in Voluntary Associations Improves Policy Accountability." *Political Research Quarterly* 60 (2007): 192–201.

Cole, Richard L. "Citizen Participation in Municipal Politics." *American Journal of Political Science* 19 (1975): 761–81.

Conover, Pam and Donald Searing. "A Political Socialization Perspective." In *Rediscovering the Democratic Purposes of Education*, edited by L. McDonnel, P. Timpane, and R. Benjamin. Lawrence, 91–125. Kansas City: University of Kansas Press, 2000.

Delli Carpini, Michael X., and Scott Keeter. *What Americans Know about Politics and Why It Matters.* New Haven: Yale University Press, 1996.

Dudley, Robert, and Alan Gitelson. "Civic Education, Civic Engagement, and Youth Civic Development." *PS: Political Science and Politics* 36 (2003): 263–67.

Finkel, Steven E. "Civic Education and the Mobilization of Political Participation in Developing Democracies." *The Journal of Politics* 64 (2002): 994–1020.

Finkel, Steven E., and Howard Ernst. "Civic Education in Post-Apartheid South Africa: Alternative Paths to the Development of Political Knowledge and Democratic Values." *Political Psychology* 26 (2005): 333–64.

Goldfinger, Johnny, and Margaret Ferguson. "Social Capital and Governmental Performance in Large American Cities." *State and Local Government Review* 41 (2009): 25–36.

Hillygus, Sunshine. "The Missing Link: Exploring the Relationship between Higher Education and Political Engagement." *Political Behavior* 27 (2005): 25–47.

Huckfeldt, Robert, P. E. Johnson, and John Sprague. *Political Disagreement: The Survival of Diverse Opinions within Communication Networks*. Cambridge: Cambridge University Press, 2004.

Inkeles, Alex. "Measuring Social Capital and Its Consequences." *Policy Sciences* 33 (2000): 245–68.

Junn, Jane. "Participation and Political Knowledge." In *Political Participation and American Democracy*, edited by William Crotty, 193–212. New York: Greenwood Press, 1991.

Keele, Luke. "Social Capital and the Dynamics of Trust in Government." *American Journal of Political Science* 51 (2007): 241–54.

Knack, Stephen. "Social Capital and the Quality of Government: Evidence from the States." *American Journal of Political Science* 46 (2002): 772–85.

La Due Lake, Ronald, and Robert Huckfeldt. "Social Capital, Social Networks, and Political Participation." *Political Psychology* 19 (1998): 567–84.

Luskin, Robert C. "Measuring Political Sophistication." *American Journal of Political Science* 31 (1987): 856–99.

Marcus, George E., John L. Sullivan, Elizabeth Theiss-Morse, and Sandra Wood. *With Malice toward Some: How People Make Civil Liberties Judgments*. New York: Cambridge University Press, 1995.

Macedo, Stephen, Jeffrey M. Berry, Michael Brintnall, David E. Campbell, Luis Ricardo Fraga, Archon Fung, William A. Galston, Christopher F. Karpowitz, Margaret Levi, Meira Levinson, Keena Lipsitz, Richard G. Niemi, Robert D. Putnam, Wendy M. Rahn, Rob Reich, Robert R. Rodgers, Todd Swanstrom, Katherine Cramer Walsh. *Democracy at Risk: How Political Choices Undermine Citizen Participation, and What We Can Do about It*. Washington, DC: Brookings Institution Press, 2005.

McCloskey, Herbert, and John R. Zaller. *The American Ethos: Public Attitudes toward Capitalism and Democracy*. Cambridge: Harvard University Press, 1984.

Mill, John S. *On Liberty*. Ed. Currin V. Shields. Indianapolis: Bobbs-Merrill, 1956.

Nie, Norman, and Sunshine Hillygus. "Education and Democratic Citizenship." In *Making Good Citizens: Education and Civil Society*, edited by Diane Ravitch and Joseph P. Viteritti, 30–57. New Haven, CT: Yale University Press, 2001.

Nie, Norman, Jane Junn, and Kenneth Stehlik-Barry. *Education and Democratic Citizenship in America*. Chicago: University of Chicago Press, 1996.

Niemi, Richard, and Jane Junn. *Civic Education: What Makes Students Learn*. New Haven: Yale University Press, 1998.

Niemi, Richard, Mary A. Hepburn, and Chris Chapman. "Community Service by High School Students: A Cure for Civic Ills?" *Political Behavior* 22 (2000): 45–69.

Neuman, Russell. *The Paradox of Mass Politics: Knowledge and Opinion in the Mass Electorate*. Cambridge, MA: Harvard University Press, 1986.

Putnam, Robert. *Making Democracy Work: Civic Traditions in Modern Italy*. Princeton, NJ: Princeton University Press, 1993.

Putnam, Robert. "Bowling Alone: America's Declining Social Capital." *Journal of Democracy* 6 (1995): 65–78.

Putnam, Robert. "Community-Based Social Capital and Educational Performance." In *Making Good Citizens: Education and Civil Society*, edited by Diane Ravitch and Joseph P. Viteritti, 58–95. New Haven: Yale University Press, 2001.

Quintelier, Ellen, Dietland Stolle, and Allison Harrell. "Politics in Peer Groups: Exploring the Causal Relationship between Network Diversity and Political Participation." *Political Research Quarterly* 65 (2012): 868–81.

Rahn, Wendy, and John E. Transue. "Social Trust and Value Change: The Decline of Social Capital in American Youth, 1976–1995." *Political Psychology* 19 (1998): 545–65.

Richey, Sean. "Manufacturing Trust: Community Currency and the Creation of Social Capital." *Political Behavior* 1 (2007): 69–88.

Richey, Sean. "The Autoregressive Influence of Social Network Political Knowledge on Voting Behavior." *British Journal of Political Science* 38 (2008): 527–42.

Sandel, Michael. *Democracy's Discontent: American in Search of a Public Policy.* Cambridge: Harvard University Press, 1996.

Sniderman, Paul, Philip E. Tetlock, James M. Glaser, Donald Phillip Green, and Michael Hout. "Principled Tolerance and American Political Values." *British Journal of Political Science* 19 (1989): 25–46.

Stouffer, Samuel. *Communism, Conformism, and Civil Liberties.* Garden City, NY: Doubleday, 1955.

Sullivan, John L., James E. Piereson, and George E. Marcus. *Political Tolerance and American Democracy.* Chicago: University of Chicago Press, 1982.

Sundquist, James, and David Davis. *Making Federalism Work.* Washington, DC: The Brookings Institution, 1969.

Uslaner, Eric. "Social Capital, Television, and the 'Mean World': Trust, Optimism, and Civic Participation." *Political Psychology* 19 (1998): 441–67.

Verba, Sidney, Kate L. Schlozman, and Henry E. Brady. *Voice and Equality: Civic Voluntarism in American Politics.* Cambridge: Harvard University Press, 1995.

Yawn, Mike. "Management Minute: Connecting with Citizen Academies." *PM Magazine* Vol. 95:10 (2013), page 23.

Chapter Seventeen

Partnering with Your Local PBS Station to Promote Civic and Political Engagement

Elizabeth A. Bennion

This chapter describes an experiential learning project that simultaneously benefits students, the university, and the community. As a political science faculty member and Campus Director of IU South Bend's American Democracy Project, I host a weekly public affairs program called *Politically Speaking*, which is broadcast live each Sunday (re-airing each Monday) to a twenty-two-county area containing 1.2 million viewers. As part of the program, I interview national and state legislators, along with local politicians, academics, practitioners, and political activists. Recent guests have included U.S. Senator Dan Coats (IN), U.S. Senator Joe Donnelly (IN), U.S. Representative Jackie Walorski (IN-2), and U.S. Representative Fred Upton (MI-15). Other recent guests have included Mayor Pete Buttigieg (South Bend, IN), Mayor Dave Wood (Mishawaka, IN), Mayor Dick Moore (Elkhart, IN), Mayor Gregg Kauffman (Goshen, IN), and Mayor Karen Freeman-Wilson (Gary, IN), along with numerous state legislators, law enforcement officials, political activists, researchers, and civic leaders. Topics have included Indiana and Michigan state legislative updates, and a discussion of contemporary policy debates such as education reform, drug policy, school safety, gun control, immigration policy, health care reform, same-sex marriage, domestic violence, and more. The program focuses on the impact of public policy decisions on people in the Michiana region—including southern Michigan and northern Indiana.

This high visibility partnership between Indiana University South Bend and the local public television station includes the creation of a political science research team as part of a three-credit applied research seminar. Employing students as researchers, call screeners, episode critics, and amateur videographers, my work on the TV show is a way to further the civic education and engagement mission of the political science department, the American

Democracy Project, and the campus, increasing the visibility of the university, promoting student learning, and strengthening campus-community partnerships. As a public, regional comprehensive university, this partnership with our regional public television station is particularly appropriate as our missions coincide with both organizations seeking to serve the people of the region by providing educational opportunities and programming.

By offering a small applied research seminar each semester, capped at fifteen students, I can offer students a rich hands-on experience in creating a live public affairs television program. With eight to twelve (instructor-approved) students enrolled each semester, I rely upon these students for ideas, research, and feedback, while they learn about a wide variety of policy issues they may have never considered, gain tangible research and media production skills, and experience the joy of seeing the results of their efforts aired live each week.[1] This ability to develop knowledge and skills through the experience of preparing for a weekly television broadcast is an example of experiential learning that simultaneously benefits the students, instructor, university, and community. Like other projects highlighted in this book, it uses the *experience* of civic engagement to promote lifelong civic knowledge, skills, and dispositions among students. It is a model that could be replicated on other campuses while answering Nick Kristof's urgent call for professors to engage in contemporary policy debates that matter to people outside the academy.[2]

LEARNING THROUGH EXPERIENCE: THE VALUE OF EXPERIENTIAL EDUCATION

Experiential education is based on the belief that students learn best when participating actively in hands-on opportunities that connect content to *application* in the real world. *Experiential education is an approach to learning in which educators "purposefully engage with learners in direct experience and focused reflection in order to increase knowledge, develop skills, clarify values, and develop people's capacity to contribute to their communities."*[3] The concept of experiential learning is not new. John Dewey originally wrote about the benefits of experiential education in 1938, explaining, "there is an intimate and necessary relation between the processes of actual experience and education."[4] If designed properly, experiential approaches to student learning maintain high academic standards while promoting *academic* engagement through critical reflection linking theory and practice. Through a combination of concrete experience and critical reflection, students can make new discoveries, take responsibility for their learning, give and receive constructive feedback, and understand why specific lessons are beneficial to their personal and professional lives.

Students in the "Politically Speaking: Make Live TV" course illustrate the value of this approach to learning. Their comments about the course reflect an awareness of the knowledge and skills they are gaining, as well as their growing realization that they can make a positive difference in their communities. Post-course student reflections indicate that they were particularly pleased to be able to share what they were learning with others. Students appreciated the ability to "learn about the newest and most current issues that are happening in [their lives], state, and city," noting that course topics were "relevant" enough to provoke out-of-class conversations and even to "go home and discuss with my family." They also raved about the ability to conduct research that "directly impact[s] the real life public policy debate."[5]

Students also recognize that the combination of experience and critical reflection in the course enhance the learning experience while providing tangible professional skills: Students appreciate the "hands on experience," while also viewing their participation on the show as a "resume builder." In their end-of-semester reflection papers, students reported that the class provided them with "research skills that cannot be simulated by other courses."[6] Mass communications students especially appreciated the applied nature of the research, providing practical experience to those interested in the broadcast industry. In sum, students appreciate the value of this learning experience both because of the skills they gain and because these skills can be documented, utilized, and appreciated by people outside of the academy.

Why Experiential Education Works: Lessons from Neuroscience

There is extensive research about how young adults learn and how educators can have a long-term impact on students' understandings of the world.[7] The conceptual model of the brain as fixed has been replaced by new evidence that the architecture of the brain is constantly shaped by experience.[8] If a neuron fires often, it grows and extends out toward other neurons, connects with them, and sends signals back and forth through synapses, creating a network of active neurons. Changes in the connections that make up these networks define learning. Two things cause networks to form: practice and emotion. Lasting learning is motivated by emotion and solidified by practice.[9] A lecture can motivate students and stimulate emotion, but it does not give them much practice at forming their own explanations and networks.[10] Students may learn enough facts and definitions in a class to pass exams, but lecture-based pedagogy does not always succeed in teaching students to think critically and analytically.[11] Lasting learning requires more than just new facts; it is motivated by "forcing students to confront, analyze, and articulate compelling discrepancies that require change in what they believe."[12] Deep learning takes place when students really are required to fully examine their current views and to change something about their current understanding of the way the world works. This does not mean moving from a liberal to a conservative perspective on a specific political debate (or vice versa). However, it does mean thinking about things in a new, deeper, more analytic—more complex—way. One can learn new facts and quickly forget them, but when one changes something about his or her thought process or worldview, this is a form of learning that endures and shapes future knowledge and decisions. Testing beliefs through experience is one way to learn that existing beliefs are incomplete or that they do not "work" in the real world.

Again, Politically Speaking seminar students seem to confirm the validity of this research. Student comments suggest that emotions—even negative emotions—produce memorable learning experiences. For example, one student described herself as a quote "shy person" and noted that the course made her "step out of" her "comfort zone." As a result, she reported a gain in self-confidence and interpersonal communication skills, noting: "I can do more than I gave myself credit for." Another student indicated that working a camera during the live show made her feel a lot of pressure ("OMG . . . such pressure!"), but that with practice she felt more at ease and is grateful for a "memorable" learning experience.[13] These emotionally charged learning experiences left students with a new understanding of the work required to produce a live weekly affairs program. As the above quotations demonstrate, students' anxieties often resulted in tangible, memorable learning experiences. Despite the difficulty and discomfort of the situation—or perhaps because of this difficulty—students pushed themselves to do more than they originally thought possible.

Similarly, students recognize the value of confronting diverse viewpoints that challenge their own beliefs—both during class discussions and when viewing the show. Students appreciated the opportunity to confront ideas they "never would have thought about," to "speak openly about topics," and to "compare and contrast competing arguments." As one student noted in his final reflections, working with students "from different backgrounds [who hold] different viewpoints" made the course "a great learning experience" and "forced" some students, on both sides of the aisle, to "adjust their partisan views."[14] Students recognized the importance of this exchange of ideas, noting that "those who thought they knew about a certain topic could easily gain more information by conducting independent research and by talking with peers." Another student commented more directly on her own personal learning experience, noting that, although she "often disagreed very strongly with my peers' opinions," she "always learned something new." Through class discussions and debates students practice the skills of civic dialogue, including critical thinking, respectful disagreement, and evidence-based argumentation. Students not only observed guests model this behavior each week, they also gained personal experience through "thought provoking" class discussions that added to "the excitement of the course."[15]

Experiential Education at Its Finest: Implications for Civic Education

Civic engagement can be defined as "a catch-all term that refers to an individual's activities, alone or as part of a group, that focus on developing knowledge about the community and its political system, identifying or seeking solutions to community problems, pursuing goals to benefit the community, and participating in constructive deliberation among community members about the community's political system and community issues, problems and solutions."[16] Given that civic engagement, by definition, requires active *engagement with* the community, experiential education is an ideal way to develop the knowledge and skills required for active citizenship. When it comes to civic education, civic engagement is both a means and an ends. Students learn the skills of engagement by *practicing* that engagement. Active experiential learning is, therefore, an ideal pedagogy for promoting civic knowledge, skills, and dispositions.

A REPLICABLE MODEL: PARTNERING WITH YOUR LOCAL TV STATION

In his recent keynote address during the American Political Science Association's 2014 Teaching and Learning Conference, APSA President John Aldrich encouraged political scientists to find ways to make their work more visible to stakeholders outside the academy. While not all political scientists can aspire to gain a national following like Melissa Harris-Perry or Rachel Maddow, a smaller, regional audience is well within the reach of many political scientists. An added advantage of this local or regional approach is that political science faculty can continue their work on campus, including their work with students. Students can work with faculty to practice public intellectual engagement—gaining tangible research and production skills, while also learning about politics, public policy, public opinion, and mass media.

Background: Connecting Campus and Community

The idea for this partnership came from the community partner, WNIT public television. Angel Hernandez, Vice President of Production for WNIT, had been tracking my work for several years and had, from time-to-time, mentioned finding a way to "match your skills to our needs." In addition to my work organizing public forums and candidate debates on campus, I had appeared as a guest on *Politically Speaking* a couple of times, had moderated a segment on student attitudes toward politics, and had served as the lead organizer for three congressional debates televised on WNIT. When journalist Jim Wensits retired, Mr. Hernandez invited me to host the program. Knowing that I had never expressed an interest in a broadcasting career, and being familiar with my work, he took a different approach toward "selling me" on the idea. He noted that this was an opportunity to continue to do what I was already doing while bringing my civic education and engagement programming and messaging to a bigger audience. Rather than suggesting that I change my self-defined mission, he (wisely) stressed that hosting a weekly television program broadcast to viewers in twenty-two counties would give me an opportunity to further that mission to promote civil dialogue and civic engagement, while gaining positive recognition for my work, my students, and my campus. Because I have written, spoken, and published on the importance of civic education, campus-community partnerships, experiential learning, and the public purpose of higher education, this was the ideal "pitch."[17]

Community Impact

The full community impact of the partnership between IU South Bend and WNIT is difficult to measure. However, several benefits seem clear. First, a professor-moderator brings research-based knowledge to the discussion of public policy issues. There have been several occasions on which I have shared political science research findings with the panelists and viewers. I provide background information or ask guests to offer a hypothesis about how the current situation fits, or defies, well-established research findings (which I summarize on air). Second, involving students in the project provides additional (semiskilled) labor that allows for the introduction of special features that would otherwise be cost-prohibitive, particularly for an underfunded public television station. "Man-on-the-street"-style citizen videos and on-screen "fast facts" providing additional information about guests, legislation, institutions, and policies are two regular features that were added due to the partnership between the university and the TV station. This partnership includes a university-funded research seminar and WNIT Politically Speaking internship.[18] In addition, the station gets free labor in the form of a call screener, a camera operator, and Chyron operator each week.[19] This cost savings on labor allows the paid WNIT staff to save hours to properly format and upload the fast facts and videos prepared by the students, thus allowing additional features to be added without going over budget for the program.

Campus Costs

This arrangement is not without costs to the campus. A campus must be committed to the civic mission of higher education in order to sustain this type of partnership. In the case of IU South Bend's partnership with WNIT television, the university allows the host to teach a small (underenrolled, instructor-consent-required) research seminar each semester. This costs tuition dollars. In addition, the College of Liberal Arts and Sciences pays $1,500 to $2,250 for the student intern who supervises all student video shoots, finalizes all fast facts, and operates the Chyron machines every Sunday. The intern also attends all class sessions, putting in a total of ten to fifteen hours per week (most often fifteen). In addition, the host has a reduced (2–2) teaching load due to her work as the Campus Director of the American Democracy Project (ADP), leading campus-wide civic education and engagement efforts. It is under the umbrella of the ADP that I situate my work with WNIT. In fact, I state my affiliation with the IU South Bend American Democracy Project at the beginning of each episode. This is a good opportunity for visibility for the ADP and the campus, but does not *directly* produce additional grants or donors in ways that compensate for the investment that the campus has made into civic education and engagement outreach on campus and beyond.

Campus Benefits

Although there are costs involved for the campus, there are also benefits. Anecdotally, it seems that faculty and staff at other campuses have taken notice of our university's public outreach efforts. Numerous people at other local campuses (e.g., St. Mary's College, University of Notre Dame, Bethel College, Holy Cross College, Andrew University, Ivy Tech Community College, etc.) have commented on the amazing work that IU South Bend is doing in the area of civic education. One goal of such highly visible educational outreach efforts is to make the community aware of the seriousness with which the campus takes its public education mission and the high quality of the educational experiences the campus offers to students. Additionally, the "prestige" of the campus is enhanced by having a "local celebrity" broadcasting high-quality programming to a 1.2 million person, twenty-two-county viewing area each week. The episode topic, along with host information, is featured in local papers every week, and several episodes have resulted in follow-up newspaper and broadcast media stories, providing additional positive media coverage for the university.[20] Moreover, the College of Liberal Arts and Sciences, which funds this partnership, can point to the ways in which it is living up to its stated mission to "collaborate with peers and students in free inquiry to create new knowledge and provide transformative learning experiences, leading students to become engaged, informed, creative, and adaptive contributors to the local and global society."[21] Similarly, local political leaders recognize the importance of getting local academics engaged in community outreach. In April 2014 the South Bend City Council recognized my civic education and engagement work with a special resolution. Both the Chancellor of IU South Bend and WNIT's Vice President for Production spoke at this event.

COURSE DETAILS: THE SYLLABUS AND BEYOND

Learning Objectives

This course is designed to produce students who are able to:

- demonstrate Internet-based research skills,
- explain how the policy-making process works in Indiana and Michigan state government,
- identify state and local elected officials from the region, including party identification and key issue priorities,
- compare and contrast competing arguments and sponsored legislation in a variety of policy areas,
- create relevant on-screen facts pertaining to an assigned policy topic,
- describe the general direction and diversity in public opinion surrounding controversial policy proposals,
- analyze a policy discussion identifying strengths and weaknesses in guest arguments and performance,
- and evaluate a television program identifying strengths and weaknesses in the content and production value of each episode.

Each of these skills is developed through weekly episode preparation and episode review assignments; all of which received written and verbal instructor feedback. In addition, through their studio experiences, it is expected that students will develop (modest) technical skills in the area of video production, call screening, interviewing, professional conduct, and interpersonal relations. Finally, it is hoped that students will display an enhanced interest in local, state, and regional politics; an increased sense of political efficacy (after recognizing that politicians are, in fact, accessible to them); and an increased willingness to participate actively in the political system.

Student expectations for this unusual course are set through the course description, which is shared in the course bulletin; on the all-campus electronic bulletin board; and in email messages to political science and mass communication majors and minors. The brief description is as follows: "Students in this unique course will help Professor Bennion prepare for a LIVE weekly television show!" Students are not only reminded that "topics and assignments are not all pre-determined," but also that they will have an episode review due every Monday and an episode preparation due every Wednesday in addition to two required video production assignments and four in-studio call screening or camera operation sessions. Students are told, up front, what kinds of things they will be expected to do throughout the semester, including:

- Conduct background research on TV guests.
- Conduct background research on state and local political issues.
- Craft questions for guests.
- Conduct on-location interviews with Michiana residents.
- Screen calls at WNIT during the live episodes.
- Run the host camera during live episodes at WNIT.
- Post questions on Facebook and encourage others to "like" and post, too.
- Help develop materials for the Facebook page and website.
- Share ideas regarding show content, design, and production value.
- Watch all episodes and provide constructive feedback to strengthen the program.

The course is worth 600 points total. Students submit fifteen episode reflections (150 points total). In these assignments students discuss the most and least interesting parts of each episode. Students point out anything that detracted from the quality of each episode, offer ideas for improvement, and indicate whether or not guests should be invited to participate in future episodes. Students also submit fifteen episode preparation assignments (150 points total). These assignments require students to conduct background research on the issues and guests appearing on the show, as well as provide suggested questions, background information for the host, legislative updates on specific bills authored or sponsored by our guests, and "fast facts" for the screen. All sources must be documented and URLs provided where the instructor can find more information, if needed. Four call-screening or camera-work sessions are required in the WNIT studio (25 points each; 100 points total). Two video production assignments are also required (25 points each; 50 points total). Students are required to respond to a series of questions about their learning experiences in a structured reflection paper accompanying each of these hands-on learning activities. The final 150 points in the course are earned through active participation in our class sessions. To receive full credit, students must attend all sessions and provide continuous, active, and insightful feedback. Each of these assignments is designed to further specific learning objectives.

STUDENT PERSPECTIVES:
FROM STUDENTS TO RESEARCH TEAM

Overall, students have performed very well in this (instructor-consented) course. Grades have varied by student, but 100 percent of the students completing the course have indicated that they enjoyed the course, learned new things, and would recommend the course and the instructor to their friends. Even those who scored a grade of "C" brought research notes to class sessions and contributed to class discussions and studio productions.[22]

As noted earlier, student reflections and evaluations often focused on the hands-on/applied nature of the research and assignments in this course. Students praised the course for developing their research skills and interpersonal skills while also requiring them to think about issues and perspectives they otherwise might not have considered. Though students' reflections often centered on the value of the *knowledge* and *skills* they gained through their participation in the course, several also suggested that the course had a transformative effect on their *attitudes*.

For example, this student is passionate when discussing his new knowledge, skills, connections, and outlook.

> I was able to meet many politicians since coming into the class. I know almost 100% more than I did before the class. During this class, I learned more about the American public and how it views politics. The class also offered insights and front row looks at policy creation and procedures. I have gained vital policy researching skills in the class that I feel would otherwise take years to learn how to accomplish. I gained a personal and business connection to a policy-maker because I was connected with the class. And, the course gave me more information about how to contact policy makers that allows me, and the people I mentor in my fraternity, to make our voices heard.[23]

For this student, the course not only offered new insights, research skills, and professional networking opportunities, but also changed his own understanding of his role as a political actor.

Seeing and speaking to the instructor and the policy makers gave me a belief that I can make a difference and made it a personal goal. Since entering the class I have convinced myself I would like to be elected to some form of office. I now watch most political debates on TV and listen to them on radio. I consider myself a political enthusiast, something that was not true before taking the course.[24]

Other students articulated similar perspectives demonstrating the value of this approach in developing civic knowledge, skills, attitudes, and identity.

FACULTY PERSPECTIVE:
FROM PROFESSOR TO MEDIA HOST

Because I contend that my partnership with the local public television station is one that could be replicated by other political science faculty members, it is important to discuss the costs and benefits of such an arrangement for the individual faculty members who might decide to take up this challenge.

Applicable Skills

Importantly, I have found that many skills developed as a classroom teacher are transferable to the position as media host. Creating a "lesson plan" or deciding how to convey the most important information to your audience in the time allotted is required in both situations. Facilitating respectful and meaningful conversation that furthers participants' understanding of the topic of the day is also required in both situations. Similarly, both "jobs" require the facilitator to be able to respectfully limit the total talk time of verbose participants while encouraging less talkative participants to contribute their voices and ideas. The ability to rephrase or reframe a student's remarks—or a caller's question—is also useful in moving the conversation forward.

As a classroom teacher I am frequently required to seek clarification, request additional evidence, or point out logical fallacies and inconsistencies in ways that clear up misconceptions and increase understanding while simultaneously not embarrassing any individual speaker. This skill is certainly useful during live television when getting to the heart of the arguments surrounding a specific policy proposal or in separating rhetoric and talking points from genuine information and evidence regarding public policy. The best college teachers have well-developed skills in the areas of logic, argumentation, and oral communication. They also have a firm (and constantly expanding) knowledge base related to their academic field. Obviously, such knowledge and skills are useful when hosting policymakers and political activists as part of an educational public affairs program. Fortunately, these many transferable skills make the transition from professor to host a relatively easy one (though learning to read 'naturally' from the teleprompter is a different matter entirely).

Benefits

Simply because the skills of a teacher-scholar are applicable to the job of hosting a public affairs program does not mean that all professors should become television hosts. Each professor will have to consider the benefits he or she might derive from this considerable commitment. From a faculty perspective, there are many benefits to hosting a local public affairs television show. First, hosting *Politically Speaking* furthers my own civic education as well as my civic education goals for my students and the larger community. I am able to learn more about my community, about state and local politics, and about important policy debates while also educating others on these topics. Second, my work on the television program combines scholarship, teaching, and service in ways that enhance the quality of my work in all three areas, while strengthening my "case" for excellence in teaching and service. In fact, the television program became a final "feather in my cap" when making my case for promotion to full professor based on *excellence* in both teaching and service (while also exceeding requirements for scholarship). Third, hosting a weekly television program provides a high level of visibility assuring that others—both on campus and in the community—are familiar with my work. This level of visibility is important not only for the university, but also for the individual faculty member. This is particularly true for faculty who are committed to civic education and to university-community partnerships. It is easier to leverage resources (e.g., internship funding and low enrollment caps) when the value of your work is well-documented and widely recognized.

Another way to consider the benefits to the individual faculty host is to use the language of "selective benefits" often associated with interest group membership; selective benefits are benefits one acquires only if he or she joins a particular group.[25] However, this framework is useful in other contexts. A full range of selective benefits stems from my partnership with WNIT public television. First, hosting the program provides some *material benefits*. Material benefits are tangible things like money, goods, or services. In this case, I am paid a small host stipend for each episode (while also accessing free goods and services including suits, hairstyling, and makeup application services).[26] Second, hosting the program provides some *purposive benefits*. Purposive benefits are psychological in nature—the benefits from a feeling that one is furthering a noble purpose or "doing the right thing." In this case, my commitment to public information, civil dialogue, and an educated citizenry is affirmed and achieved through my participation in an informative, hour-long, policy-focused program accessible to all households—regardless of whether or not they have cable TV.[27] Third, my role on the program provides me with *informational benefits*; I have access to research assistants (students/interns) and an incentive to seek out information that I might otherwise ignore. My own knowledge of local and state politics, as well as the regional impact of national politics, has increased dramatically since taking on the role of TV host. Hosting the show also provides some *solidarity benefits*; it provides me with an opportunity to expand my social and professional network and to meet others who share my commitment to civic engagement and public service.[28]

Costs

Although hosting the program provides numerous benefits for a civic-minded faculty member, it is difficult to calculate whether these benefits outweigh the costs. For me they do at the present time, but this would not be true in all cases and is undoubtedly dependent upon individual circumstances including both resources and other commitments. The primary cost of hosting a live, one-hour, weekly public affairs program is *time*. The program is aired live every Sunday from 2–3 p.m. requiring a three-hour commitment each Sunday, including transportation (half hour), hair/makeup (one hour), rehearsal (half hour), and taping (one hour). Because I have to be at the television studio at noon each Sunday, my family had to discontinue our tradition of going to brunch, running errands, and then having some family fun time each Sunday after church. This is a considerable sacrifice given our busy lives the rest of the week and the many years we had devoted to making the Sabbath a day of rest for our family. Most of the time spent on hosting duties is expended throughout the week in preparing and/or editing on-screen fast facts, conducting background research on the guests, relevant legislation and policy areas, writing the introductory and closing remarks, and developing a talking points agenda and host notes for each episode. During my first semester as host, for a variety of reasons, I also spent about fifteen hours a week lining up guests for the program. Throughout my year-and-a-half hosting the program I have become much more efficient in conducting my research. My official host notes, once ten single-spaced pages, now fit on a single piece of paper containing a checklist of topics written in 18- to 20-point font. I write only the topics, plus critical facts, figures, statistics, or bill numbers uncovered during my research. The research process itself provides me with all of the background information I need; allowing me to "jog" my memory with a

446 *Elizabeth A. Bennion*

single word or phrase. Although, with practice I have become much more efficient in preparing for each episode, there is still a significant amount of time involved in such preparation. This is unavoidable given the fact that each week's program features new guests and new topics, requiring new research on education policy, healthcare policy, gun control, same-sex marriage, the minimum wage, or some other topic of the week.

Another "cost" associated with this work—or, perhaps, a required adjustment—involves the relative lack of autonomy involved in producing a television show. As a college professor, I am used to having almost complete autonomy over my work. The quality of my product—whether a class session, a presentation, or a manuscript for publication—is almost exclusively dependent on the work of one person: me. Like many professors, I value this autonomy immensely. This point cannot be overstated. Autonomy-seeking individuals like to have full control over the final product, including its quality. This model does not work in the world of television. I can recommend that the director and camera operators include certain shots while avoiding others, but these recommendations are easily ignored. I can encourage the use of specific "fast facts" or graphics, but cannot ensure that they will be used. I can encourage the control room to put through as many good questions as possible, but cannot ultimately determine which (or how many) questions they put through and which they put aside. I can register my opinion about the set (too dark), the table (too big), and the program open (outdated), and the name keys (too rare), but these opinions are merely advisory and are easily overridden by production executives. This adjustment remains extremely difficult for me. Academics who do not share my tendencies toward control and perfectionism might not find this transition as difficult, but I suspect that many academics entered the academy, in part, because of their desire for autonomy over their creative work. On the plus side, working outside of the academy is a good way to gain a greater appreciation for the autonomy we experience as academics and the good fortune we have to be so thoroughly in control of our own work product.

Reducing Costs

There are several ways to reduce the *time* commitment required to prepare for a weekly program. An *intern* can be tasked to provide a draft version of the on-screen fast facts for each episode, and students in a *small research seminar* designed to support the program can also propose fast facts based on weekly research assignments.[29] The same is true for background research on the guests, relevant legislation, and basic policy knowledge. Although the host ultimately has to read all of this material, edit it for clarity, and check it for accuracy, having a team of research assistants minimizes the total time invested in background research. Requiring students to cite their sources and to provide URL links to additional information, while also assigning more than one student to research each set of research questions, reduces the time required for accuracy audits.

Students can also be used to suggest key topics of conversation for the show based on their independent research. Another great way to make sure that the topic list includes the most important issues related to each week's topic and maximizes the value of the on-screen guests is to have each guest suggest three or four topics that he or she would like to discuss during the show. An alternative approach is to provide a tentative topics list to guests and ask them if there is anything missing from the list that they would really like to discuss, or if there are topics they are unable to discuss on air. This pre-episode guest feedback provides additional comfort for both moderator and guests during the live broadcast. Taking the extra step to get this feedback (which can be solicited by the producer) also *saves time* when making final determinations about what topics make the final list—and in what order. Rather than conducting extensive background research to determine the most important issues to discuss related to each week's topics, let the expert guests who will appear on the program do it for you.

A high-quality producer also helps to reduce the host's time commitment. A good producer will ask for recommendations for possible guests, but will do all of the legwork for you: finding contact information, tracking people down, and getting recommendations for replacement guests if the invited guests are unable to participate. Often, contacting and recontacting high-profile guests until they finally respond, and then confirming and reconfirming participation, are required to book quality guests on a live show. A station commitment of fifteen to twenty-five hours per week should be allotted for the producer to work on the program. The producer should also coordinate all communications with the crew, passing along host concerns, suggestions, and ideas and making sure that others followup on the best, or most essential, of these ideas. Regular team meetings, though difficult to schedule, are also recommended to cut down on the frustration that comes with relying on others for the overall quality of a product with which you are associated.

Benefits are significant. Costs are also significant. However, costs can be mitigated through the judicious use of college student researchers and a strong producer and production crew. Moreover, involving students in the project does more than simply provide a source of free labor that reduces the host's time commitment while increasing the overall quality of the program; it also furthers the civic education and engagement mission of the host and the university, thereby magnifying the benefits of this university-community partnership.

APPLICATIONS BEYOND THE CASE STUDY:
MAKING YOUR WORK VISIBLE

Developing a relationship with your local public television station to produce a live one-hour public affairs program is only one way to expand the reach of civic education and engagement efforts. Hosting small TV segments on public or commercial television stations is another option (e.g., "A Sustainability Minute").[30] Appearing on local television programs and granting media interviews to local print and broadcast reporters are other ways to act as a public intellectual who informs the public discourse.[31] I have granted hundreds of interviews; they are listed under the "Service to the Community" section of my CV. I have also hosted televised segments featuring my students talking about their views on politics and have encouraged reporters who attend our American Democracy Project events to interview students. It is important for students to develop their public speaking and media skills; it is equally important for the community to see our students actively engaged in politics and community service.

Another option for public engagement includes writing op-eds for the local paper—and encouraging your students to do so—or hosting live issue forums and candidate debates. I do this as director of our American Democracy Project, generating dozens of positive news stories about our campus outreach efforts each semester. Some faculty members also maintain their own blogs, or write for well-known national blogs dealing with important real-world policy issues and political debates. Blogging is another activity that both faculty and students can engage in at multiple levels.

The common thread underlying all of these approaches is that they develop the skills of citizenship by *practicing* these skills. They promote *experiential learning* for both the instructor and the students. They allow both students and instructors to combine scholarship, teaching, and service. Faculty members committed to civic education and to their role as public intellectuals are ideally situated to conduct research that promotes public education and serves community needs.

APPENDIX A: PAST EPISODE TOPICS

—past episodes are available at wnit.org/politicallyspeaking—

SEASON 16: October 2013–May 2014
  1. Meet the Sheriffs
  2. The Politics of Sustainability

3. Government Shutdown
4. Affordable Care Act: What Obamacare Means for You
5. Pets or Property?
6. What You Need to Know about Congress Right Now
7. Michigan Legislature Update
8. Indiana State Legislature Preview
9. Legislators Tell All: The Importance of Public Policy
10. The War on Drugs
11. The War on Drugs 2
12. The State of the Union Review
13. Indiana General Assembly Review
14. Interview with Congressman Fred Upton
15. Domestic Violence
16. Children and Public Policy
18. Affordable Care Act Update
19. A Conversation with Fr. Jenkins
20. Raising the Minimum Wage
21. IN (2nd District) Democrat Primary Candidates
22. Indiana Senators
23. Indiana/Michigan Legislative Update
24. Politics of Higher Education
25. 25th Anniversary Show

SEASON 15: January 2013–May 2013
8. Indiana State Legislature
9. Presidential Inauguration
10. Third Parties
11. Incarceration and Re-Entry
12. Student Thoughts on Politics
13. Legislative Update: Indiana Senate
14. Legislative Update: Jim Arnold
15. Michigan State Legislature
16. Gun Violence and Public Policy
17. Immigration and Beyond
18. Education Reforms
19. Women in American Politics
20. Meet the Mayors
21. School Safety
22. Same-Sex Marriage
23. 2013 Session Wrap

APPENDIX B: POLS Y380 POLITICALLY
SPEAKING—COURSE DESCRIPTION

Students in this unique course will help Professor Bennion prepare for a LIVE weekly television show!
   Topics and assignments are not all pre-ordained. Students in this course will:

* Conduct background research on TV guests.
* Conduct background research on state and local political issues.
* Craft questions for guests.
* Conduct on-location interviews with Michiana residents.
* Participate in the studio audience—asking or answering questions on live TV.
* Post questions on Facebook and encourage others to "like" and post, too!
* Help develop materials for the Facebook page and website.
* Share ideas regarding show content, design, and production value.
* Watch all episodes and provide constructive feedback to strengthen the program.

Assignments:
Reflections & Critiques: 150 points

15 @ 10 points each
   ➢ Episode Preparations: 150 points

15 @ 10 points each
   ➢ Studio or Production Work: 150 points

6 @ 25 points
   ➢ Two citizen videos @ 25 points each
   ➢ Four studio sessions call screening or running camera @ 25 points each

Attendance & Participation: 150 points
   ➢ % of sessions attended sets maximum points possible
   ➢ Score is adjusted to reflect participation level.

NOTES

1. Students have been helping with the program since I began hosting in January 2013. The program runs September (or October) through November and January through May, making it a good fit with the academic calendar. To date, three sections of the course have been offered, one per semester.

2. Nicholas Kristof, "Professors, We Need You!," *The New York Times*, Feb. 15, 2014, http://www.nytimes.com/2014/02/16/opinion/sunday/kristof-professors -we-need-you.html?_r=0 (accessed August 1, 2014).

3. "Frequently Asked Questions," *Association for Experiential Education: A Community of Progressive Educators & Practitioners,* http://www.aee.org/member ship/FAQs (accessed August 1, 2014).

4. John Dewey. *Experience and Education* (New York: Macmillan Co., 1997 [1938]), 7.

5. Words in quotation marks are taken directly from students' end-of-the-semester reflection paper (Fall 2013).

6. Ibid.

7. For a good review of this literature see Antonio Bowen, *Teaching Naked: How Moving Technology out of Your College Classroom Will Improve Student Learning* (San Francisco: Jossey-Bass, 2012).

8. James E. Zull, "The Art of Changing the Brain," *Educational Leadership* 62, no. 1 (Sept. 2004), 68–72.

9. Antonio Damasio, *Descartes' Error: Emotion, Reason, and the Human Brain* (New York: Avon Books, 1994).

10. Bowen, *Teaching Naked.*

11. Danny Damron and Jonathan Mott, "Creating an Interactive Classroom: Enhancing Student Engagement and Learning in Political Science Courses," *Journal of Political Science Education* 1 no.3 (2005): 367–383.

12. Bowen, *Teaching Naked.*

13. All quoted material is cited verbatim from student reflection papers fall 2013.

14. Ibid.

15. Ibid.

16. Alison Rios Millett McCartney, "Teaching Civic Engagement: Debates, Definitions, Benefits, and Challenges," in Alison Rios Millett McCartney et al., *Teaching Civic Engagement: From Student to Active Citizen* (American Political Science Association, 2013), 14.

17. As an academic who is pleased not to have to think *too much* about professional appearance, there was just one more matter, peculiar to television, to settle. After agreeing that WNIT would put the names of hair, makeup, and wardrobe professionals in the credits if my students or I could secure these (free) service agreements, we had a deal!

18. The intern supervises student video production each week and finalizes the fast facts, while also displaying them on screen using the Chyron machine during the live episodes. Students in the course take turns interviewing local citizens, screening calls in the studio, and running the (primarily stationary) host camera each week. Students also help compile background information on the guests and relevant "fast facts" as part of their weekly episode preparation assignments.

19. The Chyron is used to display guest name keys, the station phone number, and "fast facts" on the screen.

20. I proposed that we issue weekly press releases about each week's episode the same way that I do with all of my on-campus ADP events or community-based ser-

vice projects. This partnership with commercial media has been very successful. Our local newspaper, *The South Bend Tribune*, runs a community brief about the show every week, encouraging citizens to call in. And, because local commercial news stations face resource constraints, the opportunity to interview pre-arranged guests at the WNIT studio and to use footage from the program provides a valuable resource in creating easy, yet informative, stories about 'hot topics' and current policy debates. The only requirement to use the station or the footage is that other media outlets mention WNIT *Politically Speaking* in their original news stories.

21. College of Liberal Arts and Sciences mission statement, IU South Bend University website, https://www.iusb.edu/clas/mission/index.php (accessed August 15, 2014).

22. During the first two semesters, students earned 10 A's, 7 B's, and 2 C's.

23. All quoted material is cited verbatim from student reflection papers fall 2013.

24. Ibid.

25. For more about selective benefits see Mancur Olson, *The Logic of Collective Action: Public Goods and the Theory of Groups* (Cambridge, MA: Harvard University Press, 1971 [1965]); and James Q. Wilson, *Political Organization* (Princeton: Princeton University Press, 1995).

26. It is important to note that the rate of pay (totaling approximately $4,375 annually), if broken down to account for the number of hours devoted, is not sufficient to make material benefits a primary incentive for this type of work. Sacrificing time each day throughout the week as well as family time every Sunday is not something that can be compensated through the small weekly stipend offered by a regional public television station. And, of course, the hairstyling, clothing, and professional makeup application all take time and would not be necessary if it were not for my role as a TV host.

27. The program airs twice on public television before being posted to the Internet where it is accessible free of charge to anybody who can access a computer with Internet service.

28. If a political scientist is considering running for public office, the visibility of the position and expanded professional network might be particularly useful in building support and adding credibility to her/his candidacy.

29. Although grading weekly assignments for all students adds to the total time devoted to program-related matters throughout the week, it is important to remember that this course replaces another non-program-related course that would also take up instructor time without contributing to the program. Moreover, the research assistance, production assistance, and diverse weekly feedback on every episode are extremely valuable.

30. IU South Bend's Center for a Sustainable Future hosts regular five-minute segments on WNIT.

31. Encourage your university to develop both a speaker's bureau and a media contact list available to local civic and media organizations.

BIBLIOGRAPHY

Association for Experiential Education. "Frequently Asked Questions," *Association for Experiential Education: A Community of Progressive Educators & Practitioners.* Accessed 1, 2014. http://www.aee.org/membership/FAQs.

Bowen, Antonio. *Teaching Naked: How Moving Technology out of Your College Classroom Will Improve Student Learning.* San Francisco: Jossey-Bass, 2012.

College of Liberal Arts and Sciences mission statement, Indiana University South Bend University website. Accessed August 15, 2014. https://www.iusb.edu/clas/mission/index.php.

Damasio, Antonio. *Descartes' Error: Emotion, Reason, and the Human Brain.* New York: Avon Books, 1994.

Damron, Danny, and Jonathan Mott. "Creating an Interactive Classroom: Enhancing Student Engagement and Learning in Political Science Courses" *Journal of Political Science Education* 1, no. 3 (2005): 367–83.

Dewey, John. *Experience and Education* New York: Macmillan Co., 1997 [1938], 7.

Kristof, Nicholas. "Professors, We Need You!," *The New York Times*, Feb. 15, 2014. Accessed August 1, 2014. http://www.nytimes.com/2014/02/16/opinion/sunday/kristof-professors-we-need-you.html?_r=0.

Olson, Mancur. *The Logic of Collective Action: Public Goods and the Theory of Groups.* Cambridge, MA: Harvard University Press, 1971 [1965].

Rios Millett McCartney, Alison. "Teaching Civic Engagement: Debates, Definitions, Benefits, and Challenges." In Alison Rios Millett McCartney et al., *Teaching Civic Engagement: From Student to Active Citizen.* American Political Science Association, 2013.

Wilson, James Q. *Political Organization.* Princeton: Princeton University Press, 1995.

Zull, James E. "The Art of Changing the Brain." *Educational Leadership* 62, no. 1 (Sept. 2004): 68–72.

Conclusion: The Dimensions of Civic Education in the Twenty-first Century

A Path Forward to Better Theory, Analysis, and Practice

Donald M. Gooch

> The greatness of America lies not in being more enlightened than any other nation, but rather in her ability to repair her faults.
>
> —Alexis de Tocqueville, *Democracy in America*

A DIVERSE PEDAGOGICAL AND INSTITUTIONAL RESPONSE TO AMERICA'S DECLINING CIVIC ECOLOGY

This volume began by exploring the comprehensive macro- and micro-analysis of American civic life in Alexis de Tocqueville's magnum opus, *Democracy in America*. Tocqueville champions the diversity of civic involvement that has been a continual source of civic renewal in the United States. As Tocqueville makes clear, the dynamism of civic engagement by the American people is sustenance for the republic—nurturing the capacity for self-governance. The methods developed to promote civic engagement and early American civic participation paved the way for the innovative and cutting-edge civic pedagogies and civic engagement strategies of the twenty-first century. These are timeless lessons for civic educators irrespective of era. Yet, in the twenty-first century, new challenges to civic education and the health of the civic ecology of America require original, unique, diverse, and overlapping modalities to address the inequities and deficiencies of the body public's civic attributes.

Civic capacities are the white blood cells of a well-functioning civic immune system. When they are numerous and strong, the American social fabric can weather a host of harmful exogenous shocks. But today, apathy, divisiveness, polarization, social fragmentation, technology-induced social isolation, and other civic disease vectors have weakened the body politic. The resulting civic ignorance, civic disinterest, nonparticipation, and lack of engagement have left the American political community brittle and vulnerable. Yet Tocqueville, quoted above, was prescient in recognizing America's ability to introspectively and creatively self-heal civic wounds. We have the capacity to improve civic efficacy, civic engagement, and the overall civic ecology of America through self-diagnosing, solution-oriented research and the development of pedagogical innovations that rely upon the improving body of knowledge on civic education. The tools and resources necessary to repair the damage wrought by civic disease, boosts for the civic immune system, are attained through civic education. Like antibodies proliferating to fight a cancer, educated citizens are the balm to civic ignorance, the booster-shot for civic participation, and the key to rehabilitating civic engagement. But just as drug researchers must adapt treatments to adjust for antibiotic-resistant viruses, so too must civic educators adapt, improve, and innovate civic education to meet the evolving technological, pedagogical, and cultural challenges of the twenty-first century.

Throughout, we have surveyed the lion's share of the literature on civic education, from Tocqueville, Dewey, and Putnam, to Galston and Delli Carpini and Keeter.[1] But two recent works highlight both the extent of the democratic dilemma that civic ignorance and apathy represent and the twenty-first-century innovations necessary for mitigating their deleterious effects. In *Democracy and Political Ignorance*, Ilya Somin casts doubt on the democratic minimalists who argue little knowledge is necessary to rationally participate in political processes and that citizens are able to use cognitive shortcuts to overcome widespread and systematic political ignorance.[2] Somin surveys political and civic knowledge data from a cross section of national surveys and concludes that voter knowledge levels fall well short of that called for by deliberative democracy theorists. For example, on most basic questions related to key issues in the 2010 election, such as Obama's 2009 stimulus bill, the majority of Americans were serially uninformed. While most Americans identified "the economy" as the most important issue facing the nation, 67 percent were unaware the economy grew in 2009. Fifty-seven percent were unaware Obama's stimulus bill contained tax cuts. Sixty percent of the public were unable to identify Harry Reid, the Senate Majority Leader, a key political actor and the person who shepherded the stimulus bill through the Senate.[3] Echoing Downs, Somin argues that democratic accountability is hampered by widespread civic illiteracy, particularly given that it is 'rational' for citizens to be politically ignorant. People are cognitive misers, the acquisition of political knowledge on an individual basis is plagued by the free-rider collective action problem, the low likelihood of casting a decisive vote hobbles civic learning just as it does turnout, and acquiring accurate and unbiased information about public policy issues is exceedingly difficult.[4] Somin's thesis is confirmed by extensive scholarship on the civic literacy of Americans.[5]

While Somin is not sanguine about efforts to reduce political ignorance, Christopher Ansell, in *Pragmatist Democracy*, argues that public agencies are up to the task as mediating institutions between citizens and democratic government and an educative force for citizens in the body politic.[6] Ansell suggests that problem-solving, particularly at the local level, is possible through a process of evolutionary learning, organization, and developed avenues of consent and accountability. Public agencies, newly imagined and constructed as pragmatic intermediaries between the public and shareholders in democratic politics, rather than as the endpoint of a chain of delegated authority via the elective branches, serve as the "lynchpin of democracy."[7] In this capacity they develop policy competencies through evolutionary learning, facilitate communication between stakeholders, and bind publics together in collaborative problem-solving.[8] Thus for Ansell, the solution to the problem so ably documented by Somin is institutions. Where public agencies are free to engage in joint problem-solving with the public, institutions can serve as a critical medium for public learning, repositories of experience and knowledge, and as tools for problem solving. In eschewing the Weberian hierarchical model of bureaucratic organization and its "iron cage" boogieman, Ansell adopts an ecological approach to problem-solving through "strange loop" iterative exchanges across hierarchical levels that facilitate communication between them in a communicative problem-solving meta-community.[9] Ansell focuses on bureaucratic agencies, particularly at the local governmental level, i.e. police departments. But a corresponding case can be made for other governmental institutions such as county governments (Warner, chapter 10), mayors (Armato and Friedman, chapter 9), and as high an institutional level as the presidency (Drury and Drury, chapter 7). Institutional innovations in civic education and engagement have been precisely the focus of the seven chapters of Section II. And our contributors have collectively emphasized the importance of bridge-building between policy-makers and participatory communities across the institutionally layered democratic environment in the United States. Thus in these two works by Somin and Ansell, we can see both the challenges of twenty-first-century civic education and the innovations necessary to respond, ameliorate, and revitalize its civic ecology. They combine to set these challenges in stark relief. The contributors to *Civic Education in the Twenty-first Century* have identified overlapping and multiple modes of civic education, reported on research into new tools and pedagogical approaches to civic education, and discussed new ways to engage citizens, civic entrepreneurs, and public officials in the process of improving and maintaining the civic ecology of the twenty-first century.

This volume, a comprehensive treatment of innovations and developments in twenty-first-century civic education, provides a unique opportunity to bring together theoretical and empirical researchers to engage in a focused study of civic education. The authors here have simultaneously engaged in theory-building, conducted empirical analyses, and focused on practical problem-solving in order to advance our understanding of civic education in the twenty-first century. In so doing, the contributors here have described, diagnosed, and developed potential solutions to the three factors of the civic education crisis in modern America: the paucity of civic literacy, the decline in formal civic education, and the growing generational gap in civic participation and engagement between Millennials and the older generations of American citizens. To some extent, all the authors in this volume address these three fundamental civic education issues; however, there are chapters that either bring more theoretical leverage to bear on one over the others, or where the findings bear more clearly on, for instance, the civic literacy problem as opposed to the gap between participation and civic engagement. In so doing, they have done much to develop solutions to the political knowledge problem documented by Somin and, with few exceptions, have done so within frameworks consistent with the pragmatic local institutionalism paradigm elaborated by Ansell.

While most recent research has focused on documenting the civics crisis, normatively and empirically, few scholars have attempted to explain the nuts and bolts of twenty-first-century civic education in America. We have thus assessed the strengths and weaknesses of the diverse civic education tools available to today's civic educators. In fact, the bulk of previous civic education works have too often been singular in focus, narrowly assessing formal, lecture-based civic education in the classroom as if it is the totality of our civic educative tools and the core of civic education in America. Though formal education is essential to the civic education process, this edited volume and the authors who have contributed to it demonstrate that civic education is a multifaceted project occurring through overlapping environments that span the political and social institutions of America and require the leadership and efforts of civic leaders, public officials, and civic educators across America.

Civic Education in the Twenty-first Century has mined the civic education literature for faults in current civic education and engagement and explored a wealth of new ideas for repairing the civic health of the nation. Section I featured an unprecedented comprehensive history of civic education in America, the two sides of the central philosophical debate on civic education, and the organization of these and other arguments into a spectrum of civic education pedagogy. Section II authors first addressed the capacity of national and state political institutions and public officials to act as civic education entrepreneurs and leaders in encouraging and inducing civic engagement. Secondly, they investigated further down the vertical hierarchy of democratic institutions in America, showing how 'street-level' civic educators address a different, though complementary, set of public policy issues on which citizens can act and engage. Finally, Gelbman demonstrated the potential of private institutions to complement public institutions as mediators of civic engagement. In Section III, contributors conducted groundbreaking, methodologically innovative and rigorous studies of civic education at the collegiate level that advance considerably our understanding of the current state of civic literacy, efficacy, and participation among today's college students. Collectively, these chapters illustrate the importance of employing multiple modalities of civic education in order to maximize improvements in civic attributes that improve the civic ecology in America.

THEORY-BUILDING, EMPIRICAL ANALYSIS, AND PRACTICAL PROBLEM-SOLVING

In exploring the state of civic literacy, the decline in formal civic education, and the gap between generations in participation and engagement, our civic education researchers deploy the aforementioned three-pronged attack on the problem of twenty-first-century civic education to assess civic literacy along multiple, civically relevant dimensions of affect and behavior in order to find possible solutions to civic knowledge and efficacy deficits that plague the body politic and endanger civic ecology. Rogers confirms a historical oscillation in civic educational priorities among civic actors and institutions that underlies an episodic approach to civic education in America. Bugh takes on the theory-building task of describing and assessing the various models of civic education in America. He identifies four "ideal type" pedagogical approaches to civic instruction: formal instruction, political participation, minority dissent, and civic engagement. Each emphasizes different civic attributes and makes differing contributions to the civic ecology. Thus one or more may be more appropriate for certain civic education goals than others. Bugh argues that formal civic education may be the best model for improving civic knowledge, but other models may better serve other civic attributes, such as participation. Thus our contributors have developed two important theoretical insights into civic education in America: an oscillation in the programmatic efforts in civic education and inconsistent effects for certain civic education

pedagogies on civic attributes and civic ecology. I use Bugh's civic education typology to elucidate the innovative pedagogical tools and to highlight
the important findings on civic education and civic engagement found in this
volume later in this chapter.

Taking up the baton from the theory-builders, Gooch and Rogers conduct
an empirical investigation of Bugh's theoretical insights and find confirma-
tory evidence in chapter 12. Formal civic education is a boon to civic literacy
but does not contribute to, and may even be a detriment to, other civic attributes. This finding corroborates Galatas and Pressley's assessment of
issue-specific civic education. Similarly, they found that formal education on
the national debt and deficit yielded improved civic knowledge in that issue
area, but did not improve students higher-level cognitive processing of public
policy issues, that is, their deliberative capacity.

The case study of presidential framing conducted by Drury and Drury
examining the evolution of presidential rhetoric on mental health policy correlates with Rogers' episodic depiction of civic education. The episodes of
presidential rhetorical attention to mental health, which wax and wane over
the course of American presidential history, hearken back to Rogers' theoretical motif and, as Rogers argues in chapter 1, demonstrates the importance
of political actors and institutions in generating moments of improvement,
sustained or otherwise, in civic education and the overall civic ecology. In
exploring the presidential capacity to both serve as an educator (reducing
civic ignorance on a policy issue) and as a civic educator (activating citizens
to get personally involved in solving civic policy problems) Drury and Drury
make an original theoretical contribution, confirm theory developed earlier in
the volume, and undergird both with qualitative empirical evidence.

From the development of theoretical insights into civic education and
civic ecology to the empirical study of civic education in the twenty-first
century, contributors to this volume have recommended an assortment of
policy and pedagogical innovations to improve civic educational efforts,
to improve civic knowledge and literacy, and to revitalize American civic
ecology. Maranto closes the loop on the meta-examination of civic knowledge with his proposal of a uniform, consensus-based civic education curriculum developed by political scientists to establish national standards and
benchmarks for civic knowledge. Maranto argues that political scientists
are uniquely situated to develop a common curriculum to address civic
knowledge deficiencies. He shows that there are points of consensus among
the subset of civic education elites, and that through this consensus we can
overcome the apparent stalemate among competing interests in the civic
education debate. Conversely, Hilmer takes a radical, anarchical approach
to civic education, arguing formal civic education is inherently pro-state.

Thus, appropriate civic instruction is antithetical to formalized civic education. He sees a contradiction in state-sponsored civic education, which simultaneously celebrates "radical democratic politics" traced to the American Revolution at the same time promoting a state-centric civic education which is at odds with radical state-dissolving politics. While Maranto seeks to revitalize, expand, and further institutionalize formal civic education, Hilmer wishes to accelerate the decline of formal civic education in favor of the state-less civic education derived from anarchical and revolutionary politics. Though Hilmer and Maranto take orthogonal positions on how to advance civic education in America, both are important, innovative contributions to the necessary public dialogue on improving civic ecology.

In *Pragmatist Democracy*, Ansell argues that public institutions can serve as a "lynchpin" for democratic action by building on societal consent for policies through problem solving and institutional evolution at the local level. Public organizations working on solving public problems can create opportunities for "focused and organized civic engagement."[10] Consent-building is at the forefront of Drury and Drury's case study contrasting presidential "educators" from "civic educators" on mental health policy (chapter 7). Drury and Drury examine presidential framing as a potential contributor to civic education and engagement. In breaking with previous frames on health, President Obama encouraged civic engagement and promoted civic education on public policy in the health domain. Obama's focus on local community solutions and creation of mediums for involvement (i.e., an interactive web tool designed to encourage personal citizen involvement and action on mental health) moved beyond the traditional "communicator in chief" role to a much more proactive stimulator of civic involvement. Their theoretical framework for the "civic educator" is part and parcel with Ansell's description of pragmatic democratic action through institutional revision (the evolution of presidential mental health policy involvement) and the focus on using twenty-first-century civic educative innovations (web tools) to encourage and support local civic involvement and problem solving.

Consistent with the pragmatic democracy paradigm, the bulk of our contributors have explored a variety of institutional contexts at the national, state, and local levels where public officials have the capacity to contribute to civic engagement and encourage civic involvement. Drury and Drury examine pragmatic democratic opportunities for public officials to encourage civic involvement—that is, public officials as "civic entrepreneurs" in leading, shaping, and inspiring civic engagement. Friedman and Aubin point to the Putnam-inspired view that civic engagement has declined and suggest new avenues and mediums for promoting civic involvement through the leadership of public officials.

But while personal contact by political actors to motivate civic activity may be effective, there is a dearth of research on the role officials play as a stimulus for civic activity. Friedman and Aubin (chapter 5) seek to bridge that gap in their study of official websites for representatives in Congress. They argue that legislators can serve as civic entrepreneurs in encouraging participation by their constituents through their congressional websites. In the same vein, Evans (chapter 6) finds that legislators frequently "tweet" about civic engagement (43 percent encouraged followers to join a civic group or page) on the social media site, Twitter. Then, Brandon Toner (chapter 8) identifies an unlikely source of institutional civic education and engagement: the judiciary. Surprisingly, given the democratic insulation of the judiciary, Toner finds substantial evidence that courts peruse a civic engagement agenda. Taken together, these results suggest that federal and state public institutional actors have moved from a passive to active and assertive role in community outreach and education.

Several of our contributors echo Tocqueville and Ansell in arguing that civic education begins with local institutions and those local institutions are an essential force in promoting and encouraging civic engagement. Barbara Warner's study of county-level government and its online presence in Arkansas is part of a broader effort found within the volume to empirically assess local institutional capacities as civic educators encouraging civic participation and engagement. Armato and Friedman, noting per Putnam, that local election voting has declined in the late twentieth century, argue we should look to local officials as the front line for street-level civic engagement entrepreneurs. This is good news for civic involvement at the local level, but as with others like Gelbman, there is also a great deal of room for improvement in institutional efforts at civic engagement and education.

But perhaps the best exemplar of the Ansell paradigm is the citizen academy program Yawn describes in chapter 16. A methodologically orthogonal though theoretically compatible approach to that proposed by Rackaway and Campbell's civic education university at Fort Hays State University (chapter 15), Yawn's "Citizen Academy" is precisely the sort of local institutional interaction with the public with an orientation toward mediation and problem solving on public policy issues Ansell calls for. As Bugh noted in chapter 4, Yawn's model of civic education incorporates practitioners, local public officials, and students in an experiential learning environment ripe for Ansellian evolutionary learning through cross-hierarchical communication. Participants reported higher levels of social and political capital, in line with Ansell's and Bugh's theoretical expectations. Also, the citizen academy proved an effective treatment of political ignorance, with participants showing significant improvements on knowledge items on the posttest. While "old school" in its approach, Yawn's innovative, hands-on approach is yet another layer of civic education pedagogy that can contribute to civic ecology and the best illustration of a partnership between local political institutions and the communities they serve.

CIVIC EDUCATION: NEW MEDIUMS AND INNOVATIONS IN TRADITIONAL ONES

A point of emphasis for *Civic Education in the Twenty-first Century* is studying the new mediums and innovations in traditional mediums that twenty-first-century civic entrepreneurs use to educate, engage, and induce civic involvement. From Facebook to Twitter, from Instagram to Reddit, from LinkedIn to Google Circles, there has been an explosion in online communication mediums where citizens can interact on political and civic matters. Several of the chapters deal with the cutting edge Web 2.0 communication mediums. Evans (chapter 7) finds that significant numbers of legislators tweet about civic engagement (43 percent encouraged followers to join a civic group or page) but that such tweets make up a small portion of overall legislator use of Twitter. Thus social media is a new medium that public officials can use, and use more frequently, to improve civic engagement. Similarly, Gelbman's analysis of the Twitter activity of interest groups suggests that private civic actors use new mediums to encourage civic involvement and contribute to democratic vitality (chapter 11). Interest groups can fill the void left by the decline of political parties by serving as a countervailing, stimulative force for citizen participation in this Putnam-identified age of civic decline, but whether social media is an effective venue for such a role is debatable. Gelbman concludes that social media such as Twitter provide a fruitful but underutilized tool for promoting civic education and engagement. However, the Twitter 140-character limit limits the amount of information and degree of sophistication interest groups can bring to bear on policy problems in the medium. Gelbman's study thus highlights both the advantages and disadvantages of Web 2.0 communications as a medium for improving our civic ecology.

In chapter 15, Rackaway and Campbell take this discussion of twenty-first-century civic education mediums to a whole new level in their examination of the utility of Web 2.0 tools in encouraging civic engagement and improving America's civic ecology. Noting, as did Galston, that the decline in civic knowledge necessitates remedial citizenship training, Rackaway and Campbell argue that faculty must, in addition to traditional fact-based lecture, pursue multilayered co-curricular activities. These activities are designed to promote civic engagement by engaging students 'where they are,' which is across the gamut of social media. Web 2.0 tools lend themselves to multiple and overlapping approaches to civic education that can spur civic engagement, even among citizens (i.e., Fort Hayes students) who are not on campus. From student blogs on current political events and Twitter to summarizing important points in a political theory class, to using Wikipedia as a primary source and creating metadialogues on online discussion boards and social media, Rackaway and Campbell argue the benefit or detriment of the newest mediums for civic education are determined by how they are used. Blogging, for example, can be used to meet pedagogical goals such as critical thinking, collaboration, media literacy, and improved writing skills. Having students create their own content requires them to understand and synthesize political information and then provides a venue for them to share their analysis. Rackaway and Campbell side with the Web 2.0 optimists, seeing it as medium particularly situated to build community and reinforce civic values. They argue that Web 2.0 tools are a medium through which the battle to retain, revitalize, and re-create social capital can be fought (see Putnam for the contra argument of Web 2.0 skeptics). Web 2.0 civic engagement can draw reluctant and inactive citizens into politics for the first time. Further, Rackaway and Campbell argue that Web 2.0 tools are empowering—they allow students to create and disseminate civic knowledge.

Contrasting new mediums, Rackaway and Campbell assess the pros and cons of Web 1.0 mediums (one-way communication) and Web 2.0 tools (end-user/content provider metadialogue) for encouraging civic education. Twenty-first-century civic entrepreneurs can harness the capacity of Web 1.0 to enhance civic engagement and civic involvement, and civic researchers can utilize Web 1.0 civic activity to theory-build and analyze civic activity. Armato and Friedman used the web as a medium to conduct their content analysis of mayoral press release headlines. Warner (chapter 10) focused on a common Web 1.0 communication medium deployed by local governments—county government websites. The web simultaneously facilitates Warner's research and serves as an outreach tool for local governments to encourage community-building and civic involvement. Toner also used websites as his primary source for examining the role courts play in civic education and civic engagement. Likewise, Friedman and Aubin use the web to conduct their content analysis of House of Representative member websites. While congress members are self-interested and oriented toward reelection, this also motivates them to promote civic involvement and inform citizens about opportunities for civic engagement. Like Gelbman, they find both evidence of civic engagement and that this medium's potential for civic education is not being fully realized. They believe that this medium presents an opportunity for legislator-driven civic engagement. For Warner, Toner, and Friedman and Aubin, these Web 1.0 tools serve both as a primary source for research and as a method for community outreach by public officials and institutions.

While the new mediums of the Web represent exciting opportunities and significant challenges for civic education today, the traditional mediums of communication should not be ignored. Innovations in civic education through television, radio, and personal civic interactions are just as important to maintaining and improving America's civic ecology. Again, Yawn's citizen academy is an excellent example of the value of the latter—personal civic interactions.

Television and radio, legacy mediums of the twentieth century, are ripe for innovations in civic education. One such example is the award-winning NBC television sitcom *Parks and Recreation*. The program featured local politics and specifically focused on the relationship between a local agency and the community serviced by it. As noted earlier, Ansell argues public agencies can serve as the "lynchpin of democracy" through mediation, problem-solving, and consensus-building. The show featured a local parks department that regularly conducted public forums for community input; engaged in community-building projects, such as reviving a local festival; and conducted explicit civic educative activities, such as promoting a high school Model U.N. team. A regular character transforms from citizen activist, advocating an abandoned construction pit near her home be turned into a park, to a public official serving as a part-time health official in city government. The close relationship between the community and the local agency depicted in *Parks and Recreation* serves to illustrate for millions of citizens the potential for civic involvement and civic engagement to improve not only the immediate community but also the larger civic ecology.

In this volume, Elizabeth Bennion (chapter 17) uses television to promote civic knowledge, civic engagement, and civic education. Her political talk show, *Politically Speaking*, which airs on a local PBS station employs students as researchers, call screeners, episode critics, and videographers. By partnering with her local PBS station, Bennion gives her students invaluable experiential learning opportunities by bringing them into face-to-face contact with political figures and active roles in the production of the program. The program itself serves an educative role in the local community, as Bennion serves in the dual role of professor-moderator, bringing research-based expertise to the discussion of public policy issues. Bennion's program thus serves as a locus for community outreach and civic education well beyond the traditional college classroom environment.

TWENTY-FIRST CENTURY CIVIC EDUCATION:
MODELS, MEDIUMS, INNOVATIONS, AND CHALLENGES

Using the Bugh theoretical framework for civic education (chapter 4), I take up the challenge of putting the puzzle pieces together into a coherent picture of the multiple modalities of civic education in America today (table 18.1–table 18.4). For each of the four ideal types, I outline the theory building and empirical findings from the gamut of contributors to this volume. The tables lay out the strengths and weaknesses of each type along the civic spectrum. I evaluate the pedagogical mediums discussed throughout the book using the twenty-first-century innovations and challenges identified in the various chapters of this volume. I also use the trichotomy of civic dimensions identified in the model we provide in chapter 12. The first is the knowledge dimension, which encompasses pedagogies designed to expand the base of known civic facts among the citizenry and improve civic literacy. The second is the affective dimension, which is inclusive of teaching methods and strategies designed to sustain and build civic-minded motivations such as civic efficacy and political interest. The third is the participation dimension, which covers all civic activities such as voting, participating in a political rally, contacting a public official, displaying a bumper sticker, discussing politics with friends and colleagues in person or on social media, and so forth. I stratify the innovations and challenges to civic education according to a typology of pedagogical mediums: (1) traditional lecture, (2) experiential learning, (3) application and affective learning vehicles, (4) Web 1.0, and traditional broadcast mediums like radio and TV, and (5) social media and interactive Web 2.0 tools. While not exhaustive of all of the civic education innovations and challenges discussed, this is a representative cross section of the findings and recommendations of our contributors.

Formal Instruction

Bugh defines formal instruction as the teaching of basic and objective civic facts from a neutral perspective. While this definition may be more restrictive than that of other authors, it suffices to describe the instruction discussed in numerous chapters and in the empirical studies of Section III. The Gooch and Rogers (chapter 12) and Galatas and Pressley (chapter 13) studies, along with Yawn's citizen academy program (chapter 16), all suggest that formal civic education is a significant boon to civic knowledge of citizens. Their findings are consistent with and reinforce Bugh's theoretical expectation that formal instruction is superior to other types of civic education in communicating civic facts and improving civic literacy. However, formal education may not improve but rather hamper improvement in the affective and participation dimensions as Bugh (chapter 4) suggests and we (chapter 12) find.[11] While it may be possible to improve outcomes for the participatory and affective civic dimensions in formal education, as it is currently presented the weaknesses tend to outweigh the strengths for these types of civic attributes when traditional classroom lecture is used.

A number of innovations and challenges to implementing innovations in formal education are identified and discussed in the volume, and I highlight these in table 18.1. Many contributors called for increased coverage of civics in elementary, secondary, and higher education. Rogers, though more optimistic that scholarship on teaching and learning will best enhance America's civic ecology, calls for increased state-level statutory requirements for civic courses in colleges, universities, and institutions of higher learning. Maranto calls for a unified civic curriculum implemented across all levels of education in America. Galatas and Pressley note the need for focused units on important public policy issues (e.g., the federal budget). Issue-focused civic education goes to the heart of the political ignorance crisis identified by both our contributors and Somin. Contributors have made a diverse set of recommendations for innovations in civic experiential learning. Hilmer argues for an elimination of formal civic education in favor of radical participatory politics, while Yawn advocates for programs that bring public officials and citizens together for an interactive course on local politics. Furthermore, several contributors stress the need for formal instruction that explicitly engages students on public policy at higher cognitive levels than mere rote memorization. Lastly, contributors such as Rackaway and Campbell (chapter 15) and Bennion (chapter 17) argue for incorporating a diverse set of communication mediums in the classroom, that is, Web 1.0 and 2.0 tools. This may be a way to enhance civic learning and encourage civic participation and thus mitigate some of the affective and participatory problems inherent to formal instruction.

There are, of course, challenges to implementing these strategies. While Maranto is optimistic a nationwide consensus can coalesce around a uniform civic education curriculum, to the extent Hilmer's and Bugh's objections to state-centric civic education gain traction, consensus will prove difficult, if not impossible. Furthermore, the bulk of formal pedagogical recommendations made to date necessarily involve a great deal of time and commitment by civic educators. For example, incorporating more policy-oriented units in American government courses constitutes new preps for instructors and may mean giving short shrift to other important topics, such as institutional design and process. The transaction costs and commitment required for citizen academies are exponentially greater. And as Yawn acknowledges, the model's

Table 18.1. Formal Instruction Model—Pedagogical Mediums and Innovations for Twenty-first-Century Civic Challenges

Civic Dimensions			21st-Century Pedagogical Mediums	21st-Century Formal Instruction Civic Education Innovations	21st-Century Formal Instruction Implementation Challenges
Knowledge	Affective	Participation			
			Traditional Lecture	• More coverage of civics at all levels • More state-mandated civics requirements at all levels of education • Focused units on important public policy issues • Generalizable studies of civic knowledge deficiencies and motivators of civic engagement • A uniform civic education curriculum centered on consensus • A common core civics pedagogy with clear standards	• Convincing policy makers to adopt civics standards at all levels of education • Bringing diverse pedagogical strategies to the classroom • Improving civic knowledge • Boosting political interest and civic efficacy • Uncovering the consensus among civics teachers and political scientists on core civics pedagogy
			Experiential Learning	• Horizontal civic education: rejection of formal instruction in favor of de-schooling • Use of real-world experiences to teach students political access points and facilitate political activism • Courses, credits, and classroom activities married to real-world political roles and activities • Citizens academies that bring professionals and citizens together	• Convincing students that a non-state-oriented approach is viable • Using formal education to disassociate students from engrained, state-centered civic values • Convincing students to commit to necessary out-of-class political roles • Getting citizens and professionals to participate in citizen academies
+++	+/-	+/-	Application & Affective	• Assignments that ask students to apply civic learning to public policy problems • Activities that require higher levels of cognitive understanding of civic issues	• Fostering deeper understanding of public policy problems • Teaching requisite skills for applying civic knowledge and assessing civic problems
			Web | Radio | TV	• Using websites, blogs, radio, and TV to communicate civic lessons • Using blogs to enhance civics	• Overcoming high transaction costs for instructors incorporating web tools in classrooms
			Social Media Web 2.0	• Using social media (Twitter, Instagram, Facebook) as mediums for instruction, communication, and assignments within the classroom	• Engaging students through social media constructively • Overcoming the limitations of social media formats in classrooms

reliance on voluntary participation raises selection bias issues that may tend to oversell the benefits of the program. Generating commitment to intensive participatory civic programs is a tough task, and the students who choose such programs may not be those who would most benefit from them. As to the diverse set of communication tools discussed by the contributors, there are costs to implementing these tools in the classroom which may outweigh the benefits. Getting students to buy in to interactive participation on these mediums is difficult, and they may be more of a distraction than an enhancement to rigorous civic learning (table 18.1).

Minority Dissent

The minority dissent model is a form of civic education that focuses on "story-telling" rather than the communication of neutral facts. It is focused on using examples of resistance to political power, successful civic participatory activities, and individualized struggles for equality in America. While the bulk of contributors do not explicitly contemplate this pedagogy in their chapters, it is consistent with many of the goals and strategies they do discuss. Example-based modules in traditional lecture may serve as a counterbalance to the negative effects on the affective and participatory dimensions that fact-based instruction may have on student civic-mindedness. Furthermore, it can address, in some way, the concerns raised by Hilmer regarding the state-centric nature of traditional civic education in America. Minority dissent and political activism aimed at changing the status quo are certainly not as state-centric as patriotic fact-based civics. However, as Bugh notes, a focus on minority dissent necessarily means a lesser focus on civic facts and civic institutional learning. And while it is more likely to generate positive results on the affective and participatory dimensions, there are potential negative effects, that is, the 'narrative arc' bias where students view the struggle for civil rights and equality as a war that has already been 'won' and thus discourages them from a belief that participatory democracy is necessary or relevant to their lives (table 18.2).

A number of innovations across the pedagogical mediums to incorporate the minority dissent pedagogy are possible and may enhance the programs and tools explicitly discussed by our contributors. As already mentioned, focused modules using speak-truth-to-power stories and examples to underline the importance of dissent and resistance to power in the American experience is one such alternative, as is adopting texts that focus on stories of the struggle for equality. For example, an instructor could assign *Strength to Love*, by Martin Luther King Jr., a compilation of his speeches and sermons during the struggle for civil rights. Internships with civil rights organizations could give

Table 18.2. Minority Dissent Model—Pedagogical Mediums and Innovations for Twenty-first-Century Civic Challenges

Civic Dimensions			21st-Century Pedagogical Mediums	21st-Century Minority Dissent Civic Education Innovations	21st-Century Minority Dissent Implementation Challenges
Knowledge	Affective	Participation			
			Traditional Lecture	• Focusing modules and course sections on strategies resisting power and advocating equality • Featuring stories of civil rights and minority (or gender) rights struggles • Incorporating texts that relate civil rights and rights-suppression struggles	• Avoiding "narrative arc" bias • Helping students connect civil rights victories to democratically practicing dissent • Overcoming reluctance to instruction on rights-based challenges to government
			Experiential Learning	• Internships with civil rights organizations (NAACP, ACLU, etc.) • Civil rights simulations • Involving local civil rights leaders and officials in citizen academies	• Securing partnerships with civil rights organizations to facilitate student involvement • Student participation in experiential programs
		++/-	Application & Affective	• Highlighting minority rights struggles against power (e.g., visiting civil rights memorials) • Encourage students to put themselves in the 'shoes' of minority rights activists and asking them to devise strategies to challenge governmental power	• Devising pedagogical strategies to engage students on minority dissent on a deeper cognitive level • Avoiding "narrative arc" bias in exploring the history of civil rights
	+/-		Web Radio | TV	• Blogging about civil rights and current civil rights struggles by students and instructors • Using audio/visual tools to teach the history of civil rights and dissent struggles and current dissenter activities (e.g., Occupy Wall Street) • Using websites of civil rights organizations as class resources	• Students creating their own materials on minority dissent • Reducing disparities in technology experience & expertise • Fostering the use of web materials in defense of minority rights • Encouraging minority rights groups to increase/improve their online presence
+/-			Social Media Web 2.0	• Using social media to interact with civil rights organizations (e.g., 'follow' the NAACP Twitter account) • Participating in social media-based minority rights campaigns (e.g., #YesAllWomen)	• Fostering deeper appreciation of minority dissent through social media interactions • Discouraging slacktivism by hashtivism • Encouraging minority rights groups to increase their social media presence and its use as a means to activate citizens

students hands-on experience with the struggle for equality, as could civil rights protest classroom simulations. A focus on including civil rights leaders and officials in citizen academy or related program would be a significant innovation in civic education pedagogy that emphasized minority dissent. And as Gelbman makes apparent in her study of civic education and engagement activities by interest groups on Twitter, using social media and Web 2.0 tools to encourage engagement between students and civil rights leaders and organizations is yet another way that minority dissent can be implemented in civic education settings (chapter 11).

Despite the many successes and advancements in the struggle for equality, the challenges in adopting and implementing minority dissent pedagogies in civic education in America in the twenty-first century are not insignificant. Indeed, as Bugh argues, the minority dissent pedagogy may be the victim of its own success—the tendency of students to view the struggle for civil rights and equality as an historical event rather than a present-day *raison d'être* for participatory democracy may dilute the power of these examples to spur civic involvement and civic participation. Implementing the minority dissent pedagogy using the variety of communication mediums such as TV, radio, and Webs 1.0 and 2.0 suffer from many of the difficulties of incorporating these mediums in formal instruction. Slacktivism through "hashtivism," as Gelbman warns, is a real concern when it comes to social media as a medium for civic education and civic engagement. Getting interest groups to participate and engage in civic-oriented activities in live and online settings is a difficult task in its own right. It may be complicated by legitimate reluctance on the part of civil rights and minority dissent interest groups to engage and partner with state institutions such as colleges and universities (table 18.2).

Civic Engagement

A Bugh-defined intermediate pedagogy, civic engagement, is based in formal schooling and incorporates involvement of practitioners and active learning communicated through course assignments, classes, and activities. Civic engagement and formal instruction differ in that formal instruction is typified by passive acquisition of civic facts, while civic engagement takes a more applied approach through inquiry, collaboration, and discussion—all key components of the civic engagement "experiential" learning style. Civic engagement pedagogies are designed to promote a connection to community in addition to academic learning. Table 18.3 reports on innovations and challenges to implementing civic engagement pedagogies in the twenty-first century.

As noted previously, Ansell argues powerfully that local institutions are the best vehicle for civic engagement. Their capacity for mediation, consen-

Table 18.3. Civic Engagement Model—Pedagogical Mediums and Innovations for Twenty-first-Century Civic Challenges

Civic Dimensions			21st-Century Pedagogical Mediums	21st-Century Civic Engagement Civic Education Innovations	21st-Century Civic Engagement Implementation Challenges
Knowledge	Affective	Participation			
			Traditional Lecture	• Developing teaching strategies and materials emphasizing and encouraging civic engagement • Focus on local politics & citizen access points for community building & volunteering	• Developing civic engagement lectures challenging status quo • Avoid the rights/engagement dilemma without underselling rights in civic engagement
			Experiential Learning	• Community building activities incorporated as class assignments (e.g., devising changes to a city ordinance, planning and implementing a community service project, working with civic leaders and city planners)	• Reducing the learning transaction costs associated with experiential education • Providing students with activities that enhance civic efficacy, likely participation, and civic engagement
		++	Application & Affective	• Public officials across horizontal (branches) and vertical (federalism) institutional contexts enhancing civic information and civic activities • Problem-solving assignments and tasks which require students to apply public policy knowledge and tools to devise policy solution(s) • Collaborative projects requiring students to work together to solve community issues • Citizen academies that foster collaboration between citizens and officials	• Convincing public officials to enhance civic engagement through leadership and offering resources for such activities • Providing students requisite civic knowledge to engage in difficult cognitive processing—applied policy problem solving • Boosting citizen and official participation in citizen academies
	++		Web | Radio | TV	• Incorporating online resources for civic engagement into courses • Civic leaders and local officials using official websites to inform citizens and encourage civic engagement and civic participation	• Developing online & audio/visual components for civic education that encourages civic engagement • Increasing usage frequency of online civic engagement resources by civic leaders
++			Social Media & Web 2.0	• Use of social media by public officials, interest groups, and civic leaders to encourage civic engagement, action, and participation • Online community-building through social media • Facilitating community building and civic participation through informative links, direct info, interactive tools, and communications with issue leaders to generate community involvement	• Convincing groups, officials, and institutions that social media are an effective media for boosting civic engagement • Promoting real civic engagement rather than slacktivism or hashtivism • Developing civic engagement social media strategies that transcend medium limitations (e.g., Twitter's 140 character limit)

sus and community building, and flexibility in adapting their institutional structure based on evolutionary learning is unparalleled for American political institutions. A number of our contributors focus on the capacity of local governments and institutions to serve as vehicles for civic involvement and inducements for civic participation. Thus adopting modules, lectures, and activities that focus on the importance of local politics are important innovations in civic education that bring civic engagement to the fore. A local government simulation is one in-person method for implementing the civic engagement pedagogy. And, of course, Yawn's citizen academy is perhaps the most pure model for a civic engagement pedagogy that has been suggested by our contributors. As a number of our authors have argued, Web 1.0 and Web 2.0 tools are ripe for civic engagement activities for both students in the classroom setting and for citizens and officials to engage and participate, and problem-solve on policy issues. And civic educators can innovate with the traditional mediums as well. Showing an episode of *Parks and Recreation* which highlights community input, coordinated problem-solving, and community-sustaining activities through local government agencies partnering with community leaders would be an excellent way to incorporate civic engagement in the classroom. Facilitating online community-building may be a way to get citizens to buy in and for officials to invest time and resources, particularly in rural and sparsely populated communities where travel distance is a significant impediment to civic involvement. Warner's findings on e-government and the paucity of quality county websites in poorer and less populated counties suggests this is an area where significant improvements could be made that would yield substantial benefits.

As can be seen in table 18.3, there are a number of challenges to implementing the civic engagement pedagogy that are similar to those for implementing formal education and minority dissent pedagogies. I will focus here on the differing challenges presented by civic engagement exclusively. One of the biggest challenges that civic educators will have in implementing civic engagement pedagogies is generating interest among students in local government and local public problem solving. Furthermore, obtaining commitments from local officials and leaders to participate in experiential learning activities or in citizen academies is a significant hurdle to implementation. Since civic engagement emphasizes interactions and discussions, Web 2.0 tools represent a superior medium to that of Web 1.0 or the traditional mediums in that vein. However, the older communication mediums could certainly be used to supplement Web 2.0 tools. For example, a Twitter discussion on #Parks&Rec4Class about an episode of *Parks and Recreation* assigned and watched in class would be a good way to integrate the two technologies in a civic engagement curriculum.

Political Participation

Lastly, the most intuitive and commonsensical of the Bugh civic education pedagogies is political participation. Political participation is bottom-up civic education model: knowledge is acquired through the act of participating. Political participation as educative experience was emphasized by Tocqueville, and its primacy as civic involvement motivator finds great support in this volume's works.[12] It is essential to democratic theory, as evidenced by its prime location in the theory and arguments of Ansell, in promoting pragmatic democracy, and Somin, in diagnosing political ignorance. But political participation as civic education pedagogy is somewhat of a Catch 22. In order to receive the educative benefits of political participation and be spurred to future civic participation, one must first participate. To put it in baseball terms, if you cannot hit, it does not matter how fast you can run. You cannot steal first. Likewise, it does not matter how great the civic value of political participation is if those who would benefit from it the most cannot overcome the significant obstacles to first-time participation. These are the very obstacles which civic education is intended to ameliorate. Further, as Somin and Bugh aptly demonstrate, political participation presupposes citizens already have the necessary basic civic knowledge in order to effectively participate. Somin shows that even voting, the low-end of civic participation in terms of necessary civic skills prerequisites, requires a basic understanding of the issues, the facts that inform positions on those issues, and the position-taking on that issue by the candidates relevant to the vote decision. Political participation is thus an ad hoc transmission mechanism for civic skills, and, as Bugh notes, it has the potential to discourage further acquisition of civic knowledge and exacerbate societal fragmentation.

One significant political participation pedagogical innovation today would be to incorporate political participation into the course curriculum (table 18.4). For example, students could be credited with attending a political rally, a local city council meeting, or for writing a letter-to-the-editor on a public policy issue to a newspaper. In terms of application and affective activities, a party caucus simulation would educate students on how caucuses work, give them responsibilities for researching and presenting candidates and their resumes for office, and allow them to participate in faux nomination process. On the institutional side of things, local governments, local officials, and local political leaders can facilitate civic participation through web resources and social media. Through those portals, they can inspire citizens to participate in politics, to problem solve on local matters, and get involved in local politics as Warner (counties), Gelbman (interest groups), Armato and Friedman (mayors), Toner (courts), and Evans (legislators) argue for explicitly in their chapters.

Table 18.4. Political Participation Model—Pedagogical Mediums and Innovations for Twenty-first-Century Civic Challenges

Civic Dimensions			21st-Century Pedagogical Mediums	21st-Century Political Participation Civic Education Innovations	21st-Century Political Participation Implementation Challenges
Knowledge	Affective	Participation			
+/–	+/–	+++	Traditional Lecture	• Developing teaching strategies and materials that emphasize and encourage civic participation	• Inculcating requisite civic literacy • Minimizing negative messages about civic efficacy and participation sometimes accompanying civic education
			Experiential Learning	• Developing course credit activities that involve political participation (going to a rally, attending a local city council meeting, writing an op-ed, etc.) • Promoting sound political judgment by citizens through the de-state and de-school civic education of political participation	• Addressing contradictions between civic education and radical political participation that fosters citizen activism • Enhancing student political interest to overcome cognitive and transactional barriers to civic participation
			Application & Affective	• Civic educators, public officials, and interest groups encouraging bottom-up civic education through greater civic participation (e.g., voting, problem-solving, volunteering, organizing, etc.) • Incorporating political participation activities (e.g., party caucus simulation) in curriculum • Activities exploring the connection between political participation and political change • Citizen academies incorporating political action, civic education, and engagement into core mission	• High participation transaction costs • Addressing the gap between political participation and achieving policy goals • Developing course modules on applied politics to spur participation • Developing achievable policy goals in citizen academies • Civic leader and official buy-in to disseminate information about and encourage political participation
			Web Radio	TV	• Public officials and civic leaders facilitating civic participation through web resources that inspire citizens to develop public policy solutions and participate in politics • Using audio/visual mediums to encourage/inform citizens of political participation opportunities	• Developing accessible web resources for citizens that encourage and facilitate political participation • Partnerships to facilitate web, audio, and visual appeals for political participation
			Social Media Web 2.0	• Interactive web tools that foster opportunities for political participation • Interactive web tools that facilitate connections between public officials, civic leaders, and citizens	• Educating civic leaders and public officials (i.e., those in positions of authority) on the utility of web 2.0 tools and social media for encouraging political participation

The most difficult challenge that civic educators face in incorporating political participation pedagogies in their civic education curriculum is dealing with citizen apathy and overcoming the significant transaction costs associated with political participation (table 18.4). Basic ethics prohibit civic educators from directly incentivizing voting or specific political actions, thus overcoming the exponential increases in transaction costs as we move from voting to organized broad-scale political activities like rallies, and citizen action groups represent substantial barriers to implementing political participation in course curriculums (figure 18.1 below). Simulations can be used to moot the ethical concerns, but may not be 'real' enough to generate the kind of political interest and civic efficacy that actual political participation tends to instill. Furthermore, as we have seen, there is an apparent reluctance on the part of officials to engage in direct civic participation inducements with citizens—such as Evans (chapter 6), Armato and Friedman (chapter 9), and Gelbman (chapter 11). Concerted efforts and innovative strategies will be necessary to effectively implement political participation as part of civic education curriculums.

This is but a sampling of the innovations discussed throughout the contributors' chapters. Implementing those innovations, developing new innovations, and addressing the challenges of implementation are the task of civic educators nationwide. One way of sorting out the effective from the ineffective implementations of these innovations is improving on the generalizability of civic education research and thus better contributing to our understanding of how different civic education pedagogies affect civic attributes across the civic dimensions. The consortium discussed by Strachan and Bennion (chapter 14) is an important step toward developing research designs and implementing large-N studies across campus settings in order to achieve statistical generalizability. Such evolutions in the scholarship of teaching and learning (SoTL) are integral to achieving a better understanding of the mechanisms of civic engagement and the state of civic knowledge among the student populace. It will also allow for greater sophistication and depth of coverage in the analysis of civic education teaching and learning.

BUILDING ON THE CIVIC EDUCATION THEORIES AND FINDINGS IN THE TWENTY-FIRST CENTURY

While this volume has surveyed various and diverse theories, strategies, and pedagogies of civic education and advanced our understanding of civic education today through rigorous analysis, it is far from a capstone for civic education in the twenty-first century. Indeed, we hope the theory-building, analysis, and discussion of institutional innovations and practices of civic education here serve as a springboard for further analysis and theoretical developments in the field. Whether it be through adopting theoretical perspectives developed by our contributors, building on the findings of the several empirical studies we have presented, adopting similar strategies or programs to those outlined in the chapters, or using the important and innovative venues for civic education we have discussed, this volume is a first step down the path toward a sustained and focused civics curriculum in America that is capable of producing an improved civic ecology. In that vein, I provide a vignette of theory development and empirical analysis inspired by this volume.

The Calculus of Civic Virtue

In "A Theory of the Calculus of Voting," Riker and Ordeshook promulgate a simple model to describe the factors that go into a citizen's decision to vote that build on the traditional Downsian model of turnout in order to resolve the heretofore analytically intractable paradox of voting. The paradox of voting has long perplexed public choice theorists. It can be briefly described thusly: given voting is a costly behavior; voters must necessarily obtain a net benefit from voting. Otherwise, from a rational choice perspective, they should not vote. The problem, then, is that the small probability of casting a decisive vote dwarfs any benefit a voter could reasonably expect to redound to them as a function of their preferred candidate winning, no matter how polarized the candidates are on the salient issues for the voter. Since the benefit is conditioned by the probability of casting a decisive vote, and the probability of casting a decisive vote is very low in most elections, B, the benefit of the preferred candidate winning, must be a very large number—too large to achieve with most voters and most candidates. Thus the equilibrium point prediction of the traditional Downsian voting model is zero turnout.

Since this outcome flies in the face of reality, a number of scholars have attempted to revise the traditional model to account for the substantial amount of voting that does occur. Riker and Ordeshook developed a solution to the turnout paradox that adds another term to the model that is not based on the probability of casting a decisive vote. Like Downs, their model accounts for the perceived difference between the candidates, the probability the voter would cast the deciding vote, and the transaction costs associated with voting.[13] They added the variable of civic duty.[14] Given that factors such as "satisfaction with the ethic of voting," "affirming allegiance to the political system," and "affirming a partisan preference" are not dependent on casting a decisive vote, adding a term to the model to account for these factors allowed for rational voting under conditions where B has much lower values.

Civic duty, evidently, consists of many potential factors which may or may not be present for a given citizen making a decision to vote. Furthermore, Riker and Ordeshook's model was restricted to the decision to vote. They did not extrapolate their findings beyond that specific type of political participation. Civic education researchers thus have an opportunity to extend and build upon the Riker-Ordeshook model of voting. Civic duty, as described by Riker and Ordeshook, bears a close resemblance to the civic attributes discussed in this volume: civic efficacy, political interest, and civic ethic. Our contributors have developed theoretical and analytical insights that allow us to simultaneously generalize and extend the Riker-Ordeshook framework to other forms of political participation and permit the incorporation of additional vectors to the model, such as civic education. Civic education likely significantly influences both the right-hand side (RHS) factors and the R response variable. Thus we can theorize, and then empirically test, how the functional forms of these additional factors influence the model.

One useful finding from this volume, as illustrated in figure 18.1, is that different types of civic participation vary in their sensitivity to civic education. The likelihood of civic participation due to civic education is conditioned by

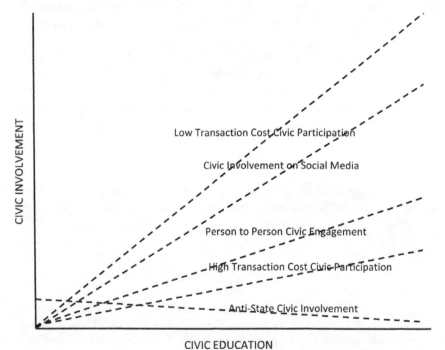

Figure 18.1.   Vectors of Civic Involvement as a Function of Civic Education
Don Gooch

factors such as the level of transaction costs associated with the activity. The probability of citizen participation in low-transaction-cost civic participation activities proving susceptible to civic education motivators is higher than for the high-transaction-cost civic participatory activities like person-to-person civic engagement (Gooch and Rogers, chapter 12). Thus a general model of civic participation must account for the differing impact that civic education has with respect to different types of civic involvement.

In this extension of the Riker-Ordeshook Civic Duty vote model, I will eschew describing the underlying mathematics of the model in favor of an informal depiction of the parameters and its dynamics. I generalize their model to many types of civic participation discussed in the volume. Factoring in what we have learned from *Civic Education in the Twenty-first Century* about the trials and tribulations of civic education, I sketch out a general theory of factors that influence civic activity, broadly classified, decomposing the 'civic duty' term into its constituent civic attributes. I discuss the benefits citizens receive from political participation, as well as consider the overall impact on civic efficacy in the body politic.

BASIC FORMAL MODEL OF CIVIC PARTICIPATION

$$if\ C_i < Pl_i + CE_i + CB_iP + SB_i + \log(CL_i) + CP_i$$

then ith citizen chooses to participate in civic activity

$$if\ C_i > PL_i + CE_i + B_iP + SB_i + \log(CL_i) + CP_i$$

then ith citizen chooses not to participate in civic activity

DETERMINISTIC MODEL OF CIVIC PARTICIPATION

$$CP = Pl_i + CE_i + CB_iP + SB_i + \log(CLi) + CP_i - C_i$$

where:

CP is the benefit the *ith* citizen receives from the act of participating in a civic activity

PL_i is the level of political interest the *ith* citizen has at the time of participation

CE_i is the level of civic efficacy the *ith* citizen has at the time of participation

CB_iP is the benefit the *ith* citizen receives from a successful civic activity
  conditioned by the probability the citizen's contribution will be decisive in
  the civic activity being successful
SB_i is the specific benefit the *ith* citizen received from the civic activity itself,
  independent of whether the civic activity is successful
$\log(CL_i)$ is the natural log of the *ith* citizen's level of civic literacy
CP_i is the level of past civic participation in this kind of civic activity
C_i is the transactional cost of participating in this civic activity

As can be seen from the deterministic model of civic participation, I have
generalized the response variable to any civic participatory activity, and thus
modified the benefit and cost terms in the model to account for the different
outcome variable. I have also unpacked the Riker-Ordeshook civic duty term
into individually defined terms as identified in the civic education studies in
this volume, such as civic efficacy (affective) and civic literacy (knowledge).
This allows us to assess each factor's relative impact on civic participation.
A comparative statics approach would allow for examining changes in civic
participatory outcomes as a function of changes in the parameters.

In the model I parse out as separate terms the specific benefit a citizen
receives from the activity itself from the collective action benefit the citizen
gets from the activity proving successful. This is because the benefit from
achieving the public good is conditioned by the probability the citizen's part
in the activity was decisive. Another dynamic is at play here. While some
civic involvement activities may be more costly in transactional terms,
these same activities may provide more particularized benefits independent
of the outcome of the civic involvement. In other words, participating in a
protest provides more psychic benefits than does the act of voting. Furthermore, those benefits are independent of the public good the citizens seek
to achieve through the civic activity. They are thus not conditioned by the
probability of a decisive action on the part of the citizen. For example, consider a citizen engaged at the local level in an Ansellian partnership with
local officials. Whether or not the policy problem is successfully resolved
is separate from the perceived benefit the citizen receives from the act of
participation itself and the relational benefits of interacting with others in
concert toward a common goal. Note I have already fixed the functional
form of civic literacy based on the findings presented in the Gooch and
Rogers as well as the Galatas and Pressley chapters (logarithmic). Further
empirical research and theory building could determine the functional
forms of the other terms as well as test the model with the gamut of civic
participatory activity types.

Analysis of Civic Engagement Pedagogical Medium Models

Having conducted some *post hoc* theory-building in developing a model of civic virtue, I now turn to a *post hoc* empirical analysis inspired by the research in this volume. A number of our contributors suggest that Web 2.0 tools and social media are useful twenty-first-century mediums through which citizens can participate in civic activities, engage in online community-building, and contact and interact with public officials and political leaders. They thus could potentially serve as a gateway to building the "strange loop" communication bridges Ansell anticipated as essential to deliberative democracy.[15] Of particular note, Rackaway and Campbell advocate that Web 2.0 tools can be used to create and retain social capital, to active apathetic citizens, to disseminate civic knowledge, and to empower citizens to engage in political and civic activities. They outline specifically how to use social media (e.g., the Tiger Talkback board and Twitter) to generate debate and conversation and to encourage civic activities such as voter registration and civic participation (chapter 15). In this way, social media may serve as a replacement for the interpersonal interactions that Putnam laments are on the wane in *Bowling Alone*.[16]

In table 18.5, I report an analysis that builds on the research in this volume's findings on the use of traditional, modern, and twenty-first-century pedagogical mediums of civic education. Specifically, I report models for three types of pedagogical mediums of civic education: (1) interpersonal communication (in-person discussions, the traditional source of social capital), (2) Web 1.0 tools (website visits), and (3) Web 2.0 tools (social media, e.g., Twitter). The table shows the results of OLS regressions from the pretest and posttest civic education data that Gooch and Rogers use in chapter 12.[17] The dependent variable is derived from the activity item on the citizenship survey which asks students to rate their frequency of engaging in the given activity over a given month.[18] Thus, higher levels for the "engage in a discussion about politics" item indicate that the respondent more frequently engaged in personal discussions about politics with a friend or acquaintance. Likewise, higher levels for "visiting a political website" and for "writing an online message"—for example, on Facebook, Twitter, and so on—indicate the respondent more frequently engaged in those activities. These models allow us to examine the change in the determinants for the use of these three mediums for civic engagement after having taken an American government course.

Setting the analysis of the control variables aside, the results indicate that, for interpersonal discussions of politics, likely participation was a factor both before and after the respondents took the course in American government. However, after the course in American government, civic literacy was

Table 18.5. Pretest and Posttest with Change Predictor Models of Engagement in Twenty-first-Century Mmediums

Variables	CIVIC ENGAGEMENT MODELS					
	Discussions Pretest	Discussions Posttest	Website Visits Pretest	Website Visits Posttest	Social Media Pretest	Social Media Posttest
	Parameter Estimate (Standard Error)	*Parameter Estimate (Standard Error)*	*Parameter Estimate (Standard Error)*	*Parameter Estimate (Standard Error)*	*Parameter Estimate (Standard Error)*	*Parameter Estimate (Standard Error)*
Intercept	1.536*** (0.523)	1.526*** (0.592)	0.881* (0.545)	1.471*** (0.590)	1.345*** (0.561)	2.495*** (0.614)
Ideology	-0.047 (0.045)	-0.093 (0.067)	-0.119*** (0.047)	-0.033 (0.067)	-0.111** (0.041)	-0.075 (0.070)
Party ID	0.041 (0.047)	0.139** (0.065)	0.109** (0.049)	0.096 (0.065)	0.076 (0.050)	0.106 (0.068)
White	0.337** (0.164)	-0.174 (0.248)	0.188 (0.171)	-0.221 (0.247)	-0.004 (0.177)	-0.485* (0.257)
Male	0.449*** (0.124)	0.684*** (0.173)	0.467*** (0.129)	0.134 (0.172)	0.417*** (0.133)	0.223 (0.179)
Family Income	-0.113*** (0.038)	-0.006 (0.054)	-0.064* (0.039)	-0.067 (0.054)	-0.076* (0.041)	0.072 (0.056)

College GPA	0.062 (0.083)	0.283*** (0.118)	-0.042 (0.087)	0.202* (0.117)	-0.034 (0.090)	-0.104 (0.122)
College Standing	0.042 (0.076)	-0.008 (0.103)	0.009 (0.079)	0.098 (0.102)	0.002 (0.081)	-0.022 (0.107)
Participation | P-DIF	0.152*** (0.059)	0.058 (0.080)	0.170*** (0.061)	0.010 (0.080)	0.160*** (0.063)	0.009 (0.083)
Likely Participation | LP-DIF	0.053*** (0.013)	0.054*** (0.016)	0.047*** (0.013)	0.027* (0.016)	0.044*** (0.014)	0.052*** (0.017)
Civic Literacy | CL-DIF	-0.002 (0.004)	0.022*** (0.005)	-0.001 (0.004)	0.019*** (0.005)	-0.001 (0.004)	0.016*** (0.005)
Political Interest | PI-DIF	-0.038 (0.052)	0.095 (0.085)	0.019 (0.054)	0.154* (0.085)	-0.176*** (0.056)	0.061 (0.088)
Civic Efficacy | CE-DIF	-0.123* (0.068)	0.046 (0.092)	-0.001 (0.004)	0.112 (0.091)	0.053 (0.073)	0.052 (0.094)
PID*IDEOLOGY	0.046*** (0.017)	0.034 (0.024)	0.041 (0.019)	0.021 (0.023)	0.035* (0.019)	0.023 (0.025)
R2	.244	.359	.233	.238	.184	.178
N	286	158	286	158	286	158

* P < .10, ** P < .05, *** P<.01

a statistically significant determinant of respondents having more frequent political discussions. This suggests that civic education did have an effect on the probability of students engaging in political discussions, and that it was conditioned by how much civic knowledge the students acquired in the course. Similar results are obtained for both Web 1.0 civic activities (website visits) and Web 2.0 civic activities (use of social media). This confirms findings presented in this volume suggesting that civic education can have a positive impact on civic engagement, and it is consistent with Rackaway and Campbell's argument that Web 1.0 and Web 2.0 tools can be useful alternative mediums for civic engagement.

THE PATH FORWARD

The Latin root of "education" is *educo* meaning to 'educe' or to draw out, or to 'bring forth from within.' Civic education focuses on bringing forth the virtuous citizen within us all. That is, a citizen capable of, and a willing participant in, participatory democracy and community involvement. Ilya Somin points to significant problems with this ideal model of the citizen that goes to the heart of the mission of civic education.[19] In order to effectively participate in civic life, a requisite level of civic knowledge and understanding is essential. Clearly acquiring sufficient levels of political knowledge and civic efficacy simultaneously is a collective action problem. The contributors to this volume have developed theories and reported on empirical findings from which they have identified a multiplicity of pedagogies, tools, mediums, and programs to help solve this problem. Collectively, these represent strategies for halting the decline in formal civic education, reducing civic illiteracy and ignorance and implementing effective treatments to reduce the generational gap in civic engagement and civic participation between Millennials and the older generations. Civic education can overcome the political knowledge collective action problem by supplementing the incentives that normally drive citizens to acquire political information and by driving civic efficacy. Per Ansell and various contributors, civic education need not be restricted to the schools: government and political institutions that span the horizontal and vertical divisions of government in this country can contribute to problem-solving, community-building, educational activities that contribute to evolutionary learning and civic efficacy. The authors here have demonstrated that multiple opportunities exist and multiple methods are necessary to achieve a sufficient saturation level of civic-mindedness to end the cycle of civics in America and to develop a self-sustaining civic ecology.

Inspired by Tocqueville's *Democracy in America*, the chapters in this volume collectively suggest there is a diversity of civic educative forces capable of promoting civic attributes essential to the body politic of America. While civic education certainly has changed in fundamental ways in today's technological and medium-driven world, *Civic Education in the Twenty-first Century* suggests that civic education is more vibrant, varied, and vital than most civic scholarship currently suggests. Across the dimensions of civic education, we have provided a representative cross-section of the essential innovations in twenty-first-century civic education. These innovations are simultaneously targeted and broad spectrum tonics to the civic ills that beset the body politic. We have also acknowledged the significant challenges civic educators face in implementing those innovations today. Work still needs to be done in theory building and application, empirical civic education research, and practical implementations that better our understanding across the levels of formal education. That new understanding needs to span the levels of government (national, state, and local) as well as carry in to our communities and in our interactions with one another as citizens. Improvements there will lead to a more involved citizenry, more effective and legitimate problem-solving, higher participation rates, and better public policy. And civic educators must be prepared to continually adapt and evolve their civic pedagogical strategies to prevent civic diseases like ignorance, apathy, and alienation to grow and metastasize across the body politics. Building on the work of this volume will put America on a path forward to a better, more informed, more efficacious, and more involved citizenry that will nurture and sustain the civic ecology of the country in the century to come.

NOTES

1. For a sampling of these works see Michael X. Delli Carpini and Scott Keeter, *What Americans Know about Politics and Why It Matters* (New Haven: Yale University Press, 1996); William A. Galston, "Civic Knowlege, Civic Education, and Civic Engagement: A Summary of Recent Research," *International Journal of Public Administration* 30, no. 6 (2007); "Civic Education and Political Participation," *PS: Political Science and Politics* 37, no. April (2004); Robert Putnam, "Bowling Alone: America's Declining Social Capital," *Journal of Democracy* 6, no. 1 (1995); John Dewey, *The Public and Its Problems* (New York: Henry Holt, 1927); Alexis de Tocqueville, *Democracy in America* (New York: George Dearborn & Co., 1835).

2. Ilya Somin, *Democracy and Political Ignorance: Why Smaller Government Is Smarter* (Stanford, CA: Stanford Law Books [Stanford University Press], 2013).

3. Ibid., pp. 23–25.

Ibid., pp. 65–68.

5. For an introduction to such inquiries, see the series of studies by the Intercollegiate Studies Institute (ISI). For example, see ISI, "The Coming Crisis in Citizenship" (Wilmington, DE: Intercollegiate Studies Institute's National Civic Literacy Board, 2006); "Failing Our Students, Failing America: Holding Colleges Accountable for Teaching America's History and Institutions" (Wilmington, DE: Intercollegiate Studies Institute's National Civic Literacy Board, 2007); "Our Fading Heritage: Americans Fail a Basic Test on Their History and Institutions," in *Intecollegiate Studies Institute's American Civic Literacy Program* (Intercollegiate Studies Institute, 2008–2009). Alternatively, see the more scholarly works of Henry Milner, *Civic Literacy: How Informed Citizens Make Democracy Work* (London: University Press of New England, 2002); Richard G. Niemi, "What Students Know about Civics and Government," in *Making Civics Count: Citizenship Education for a New Generation*, ed. David E. Campbell, Meira Levinson, and Frederick M. Hess (Cambridge: Harvard Education Press, 2012); Richard G. Niemi and Jane Junn, *Civic Education: What Makes Students Learn* (New Haven: Yale University Press, 1998); Delli Carpini and Keeter, *What Americans Know about Politics and Why It Matters*.

6. Christopher K. Ansell, *Pragmatist Democracy: Evolutionary Learning as Public Philosophy* (Oxford University Press, 2011).

7. Ibid., pp. 18.

8. Ibid., pp. 190–93.

9. Ibid., pp. 105–8.

10. Ibid., pp. 18.

11. The Gooch and Rogers study failed to find statistically significant positive effects for the affective civic attributes (civic efficacy and political interest) and civic participation, and in some models, they found a negative correlation between formal civic education and the affective and participation dimensions.

12. We find statistically significant and substantively large effects for past political participation on likely future political participation in chapter 12.

13. $R = PB - C$

where:

R is the benefit the voter receives from the act of voting
P is the probability that the citizen's vote will bring about the benefit (cast the decisive vote)
B is the differential benefit an individual voter receives from their preferred candidate winning over a less preferred one
C is the transactional cost of voting

14. $R = PB - C + D$

This model has the same terms as that presented in endnote 13 excepting term D, which is a term for an assortment of positive satisfactions that a voter obtains from the act of voting.

15. Ansell, *Pragmatist Democracy: Evolutionary Learning as Public Philosophy*.
16. Putnam, "Bowling Alone: America's Declining Social Capital."
17. For a description of the citizenship survey, and the data, methodology, variables of interest, control variables and statistical models reported on in table 18.5, see the coordinate discussions of the similar models using the same data in chapter 12.
18.

Political discussion medium question from the Gooch and Rogers Citizenship Survey: "Please indicate your frequency of engaging in any of the below activities in a given month with an "X" (how often would you expect to do the below over a 30 day period on average)"

TYPE OF ACTIVITY	Everyday	Few Days a Week	One Day a Week	Once in a While	Never
a) Watch a TV show on politics (world politics and/or American politics)					
b) Engage in a discussion about politics with a friend or acquaintance					
c) Write an online message about politics (includes blogs, discussion boards, Facebook status updates, tweets on Twitter, etc.)					
d) Visit online a political website (a website that predominantly covers political issues)					

19. Somin, *Democracy and Political Ignorance: Why Smaller Government Is Smarter*.

BIBLIOGRAPHY

Ansell, Christopher K. *Pragmatist Democracy: Evolutionary Learning as Public Philosophy.* Oxford University Press, 2011.

de Tocqueville, Alexis. *Democracy in America.* New York: George Dearborn & Co., 1835.

Delli Carpini, Michael, and Scott Keeter. *What Americans Know about Politics and Why It Matters.* New Haven: Yale University Press, 1996.

Dewey, John. *The Public and Its Problems.* New York: Henry Holt, 1927.

Galston, William A. "Civic Education and Political Participation." *PS: Political Science and Politics* 37, no. April (April, 2004 2004): 263–66.

———. "Civic Knowlege, Civic Education, and Civic Engagement: A Summary of Recent Research." *International Journal of Public Administration* 30, no. 6 (2007): 623–42.

ISI. "The Coming Crisis in Citizenship." Wilmington, DE: Intercollegiate Studies Institute's National Civic Literacy Board, 2006.

———. "Failing Our Students, Failing America: Holding Colleges Accountable for Teaching America's History and Institutions." Wilmington, DE: Intercollegiate Studies Institute's National Civic Literacy Board, 2007.

———. "Our Fading Heritage: Americans Fail a Basic Test on Their History and Institutions." In *Intecollegiate Studies Institute's American Civic Literacy Program*: Intercollegiate Studies Institute, 2008–2009.

Milner, Henry. *Civic Literacy: How Informed Citizens Make Democracy Work.* London: University Press of New England, 2002.

Niemi, Richard G. "What Students Know about Civics and Government." In *Making Civics Count: Citizenship Education for a New Generation,* edited by David E. Campbell, Meira Levinson, and Frederick M. Hess, 15–35. Cambridge: Harvard Education Press, 2012.

Niemi, Richard G., and Jane Junn. *Civic Education: What Makes Students Learn.* New Haven: Yale University Press, 1998.

Putnam, Robert. "Bowling Alone: America's Declining Social Capital." *Journal of Democracy* 6, no. 1 (Jan., 1995): 65–78.

Somin, Ilya. *Democracy and Political Ignorance: Why Smaller Government Is Smarter.* Stanford, CA: Stanford Law Books (Stanford University Press), 2013.

Index